Guide for New Weavers — Step-by-Step

Weaving for Beginners

An Illustrated Guide

Second Edition

by **Peggy Osterkamp**

Peggy

Dedicated to:

Elizabeth Austin, RN, CPCC, CEC
Life Coach for Visionaries and Social Artists

I cherish her support.

Also by Peggy Osterkamp:

Peggy Osterkamp's New Guide to Weaving series:
Winding a Warp & Using a Paddle
Warping Your Loom & Tying On New Warps
Weaving & Drafting Your Own Cloth

DVD: *Warping the Loom Back to Front*

Woven Work: *Retrospective of a Weaver*

Weaving for Beginners—An Illustrated Guide
First printing 2010
Second printing 2014

Peggy Osterkamp
501 Via Casitas, #813
Greenbrae, CA 94904

www.peggyosterkamp.com

ISBN: 978-0-9637793-8-0

Printed in China

Acknowledgements

My hope is to leave a legacy, which will keep handweaving alive for many more generations. I am presenting instructions and information that are essential for anyone to learn this craft. Without the basics, written clearly, one is likely to become frustrated and give up.

I am proud of my book, and I couldn't have done it without the team I assembled. This book is truly "our" baby.

Victoria Weill-Hagai edited the manuscript and illustrations. I chose her because of her competence and dedication to excellence. She contributed greatly to the high reputation my previous books enjoy. I am especially grateful for her patience and her consistent mindfulness that this book is for total beginners.

Diane Fitzgerald has designed my previous books. This book was a particularly challenging job because there are over 600 illustrations and over 400 pages—all of which had to suit the beginning weaver. I am grateful for her extraordinary design sense, and I'm extremely proud of the way the book looks.

Ron Hildebrand did the illustrations for my previous books, as well. People have raved about them consistently. He is a fantastically talented illustrator. I always trusted that he could convey what I had in mind in a way a beginning weaver might view it.

Joost Romeu is another person I trusted implicitly. He was the proofreader. What I especially trusted was his meticulous attention to all the details along the way. He also worked out a way for me to make the index, and his technical support was amazing.

Michaela McIntosh and Gail Ross are weavers who diligently read the manuscript. Martha A. Reitman, representing the beginning weaver, was also a committed manuscript reader.

I asked professionals to contribute to several chapters. Nancy Alegria and Deborah Holcomb worked on the chapter for computers. Patricia Townsend spearheaded the chapter on front-to-back warping. Angela Risser and Tracy Kaestner contributed to the rigid heddle loom and hand-manipulated weave sections.

Other contributors who gave expert advice were: Susan Bateman, Judie Eatough, Green, Tom Knisely, Linda LaBelle, Syne Mitchell, Rosalie Neilson, Jane Patrick, Patricia Stewart and Madelyn van der Hoogt.

My coach, Elizabeth Austin, was at my side and kept me going forward.

I owe a special thanks to the late Jim Ahrens for teaching the efficient European techniques that were so foreign to most other handweavers when I was a beginning student in the 1970's.

Illustrations and Covers

Ron Hildebrand, *All Things Illustrated*

Book Design

Diane Fitzgerald

Editor

Victoria Weill-Hagai

Technical Readers

Michaela McIntosh

Martha A. Reitman, MD

Gail Ross

Technical Advisors

Susan Bateman

Judie Eatough

Green

Tom Kniseley

Linda LaBelle

Syne Mitchell

Rosalie Neilson

Jane Patrick

Patricia Stewart

Madelyn van der Hoogt

Invited Authors

Nancy Alegria

Deborah Holcomb

Tracy Kaestner

Angela Risser

Patricia Townsend

Proofreader/Index/Special Technical Support

Joost Romeu

Extra Support

Jay Beatty

Shirlee Edwards

Jan Hudson

Flora Mangana-Trudeau

Penny Peters

Readers' Comments

Peggy's students say:

"I'm proud, lucky and relieved to be Peggy's student. There are so many important details in weaving, and Peggy's thoughtful attention to them made all the difference to me when I was first learning—and later. In person and on the page, she's an instinctive teacher."

—**Anne C. Wilson**, beginning weaving student

"Peggy explains all the steps and includes wonderful illustrations in an effort to make every student successful."

—**Judy Grady**, beginning weaving student

"This book is a must-read for the new weaver! Peggy gives easy-to-follow steps and a multitude of illustrations that are clear and precise."

—**Jan Marie Hudson**, beginning weaving student.

"Peggy Osterkamp's beginning weaving class was a transformative experience for me. It seems as though any technical question I have about weaving (and even those I never have thought of) can be answered in her books."

—**Bren Ahearn**, weaver/artist

"When I was an absolute beginner, I started using Peggy's books. The confusion of being a beginning weaver simply vanished."

—**Mimi Carruthers**, weaver and former student

Peggy's readers say:

"All of a sudden the light has come on for me and I love weaving! Thanks so much for putting this valuable information out there in an easy-to-read-and-learn format."

—**Deb Steinberg**, newbie weaver

"Your instructions are ideal: Well-organized, precise, and thorough without coming across as obsessive or dogmatic. . . .what a legacy for the weaving community."

—**JoAnne Cook**

"Since I'm more of a visual person, between your words and your illustrations, I'm able to get it."

—**Suzanne Woodhead**

"How your teaching brings a novice along more comfortably than other books I have is: Clarity and progression, from what to where."

—**Isabel Wilber**

"You really give solutions to the many possible needs or problems of the learning (aren't we all) weaver. Your cross-referencing is wonderful and the illustrations are so very clear."

—**Naeda B. Robinson**

"Your books by far exceed any of the weaving books out there . . .I find your books to be a wealth of information and I always turn to them for help."

—**Tina Watson**

"Peggy, you are so accessible—a true teacher. ... I feel like I can trust you take me through the process the whole way."

—**Martha A. Reitman**

Table of Contents

1 *Introduction*

As a beginning weaver

This is the book I wish I'd had when I was learning to weave. It's set up clearly, step-by-step, with over 600 illustrations to show exactly what the words say. The book builds on itself, with reinforcement, as new material is covered, making this mysterious thing, weaving, quite logical. And, you can learn to do all the steps entirely by yourself.

When I was a student, I thought I understood what the teacher was saying and demonstrating—then, when she was away or busy with someone else, I often realized I didn't know what she meant at all. How wonderful if I'd had this book at my side, to turn the pages with her and to refer to when I was ready.

There are many steps to the process of setting up the loom and weaving on it. When I was just learning, I was worried I would miss a step or wouldn't know what to do next. With this book, you don't have to worry about remembering the steps you've done previously—you can go back to read about them again when you need to. It will take several projects before you can remember what operation is to come next. Trying to hold it all in you head isn't possible and deters you from learning the task at hand.

After 12 years of teaching beginners, I am familiar with the things that are often misunderstood or need special explanations. I want to tell you all you need to know and not leave you in a lurch when something I know is sure to come up does, and you'll need help.

Along with a comprehensive index, I've cross-referenced copiously as to where previous information can be found.

As an experienced weaver

I wish I'd had this book as an experienced weaver because often, I forgot what I had been taught to do in a certain situation when I hadn't thought of it in a long while. I would have known where to look it up.

Most weavers learned "piece-meal" and feel there are gaps in their weaving knowledge. They will be relieved to have the process stated sequentially and in clear words—with no previous knowledge assumed. No other weaving book for beginners is this thorough and graphic.

This book is for people who, even though they've been weaving for a while, feel they missed out on the basics.

As a weaving teacher

This book would have been an enormous help to me as a teacher at any level.

A teacher can point to the illustrations when lecturing or demonstrating at the loom. The students can follow along with their own copies.

After a lesson, the teacher can be confident that the students can refer to the book on their own at their own looms. Often, the students don't "get" everything in a single lesson.

Re-explaining a lesson over and over to each student—or to ones absent, or to those not paying attention, or not yet at the step she is teaching is no longer a teacher's nightmare that impedes good teaching.

Often, teachers are weavers themselves and have forgotten what the beginner really needs to know. Teachers can pick up on the basics that they forgot, or never taught before, or found hard to explain.

This is a quotation that I really love by Louis Pasteur and is a guiding principle for me: "Chance favors the prepared mind." I think that if you know the techniques, you can be free to create your ideas.

My deepest motivation

I want to keep hand weaving alive. If it is a mystery and considered too difficult, it will die out. I am a teacher at heart and passionate about weaving, I want my books really to ***teach*** people to weave. I want people to enjoy the accomplishment of weaving things and to feel a sense of pride that they can do it. With my books, I tell clearly how to go about it.

What's important to me about the art and skill of weaving

I love that there are so many aspects of weaving that it can provide pleasure for many types of people and situations.

Weaving draws on many parts of the body and brain. It gives my mind, psyche, hands and body lots to do. My creative self is thoroughly connected to my being present in the world. I am inspired by things I see: someone's scarf, or coat, or a sky, or a mountain. Also, I love, having ideas dawn on me—and going "inside" to figure out what I might weave that resonates with the inspiration.

I think if you have weaving in your life, or another passion, you are happier for it for all your life.

Weaving gives a wonderful sense of making something. People love the inspiration and spontaneity. Some like getting an idea and then, the challenges—the doing or the planning. Some like to learn new things—there are so many techniques to know that you won't have to worry about being bored. Some like the computer for designing and for weaving—some hate the idea. Some want to weave art, some clothing and functional things. Some want to make a business, some want a hobby. Some like modern; some, ethnic. Some love to follow rules, and some love to break them. Some people like the loom to do the work, and some like to work the threads with their hands. Some like the colors and textures of the threads, others like the structures of the weaves more. Many like both equally. What you weave is what feels right to you. Many of my friends want only to weave useful things. I am a little bit of an oddball in that I don't want to weave anything useful. I want to explore yarns, weaves, colors, and ideas. That they aren't functional objects is just fine with me. That's one thing about weaving—you don't have to follow the norm, and you can if you want to.

How this book is different from my previous books

In this book, I start the new weaver out from the very, very beginning. The previous books take you deeper and deeper into the particulars of weaving. Each book covers one aspect of the weaving process.

Winding a Warp & Using a Paddle details how to make warps that make your weaving easier and without tangles. It covers in great detail sett, planning projects, and how to use a paddle.

Warping Your Loom & Tying On New Warps is devoted to putting the warp on the loom, adjusting looms, sectional beaming, knots and tying on new warps.

Weaving & Drafting Your Own Cloth explains efficient weaving techniques, end-delivery shuttles, drafting for multi-shafts, and analyzing fabrics. There are 48 pages devoted to troubleshooting—with both solutions to and causes of problems.

They are reference as well as "how-to" books that you'll have for the rest of your weaving life. One theme of all my books is independence. You will learn to perform every task in the books independently.

Many techniques in the books have never been in American weaving books. They are techniques that I learned from Jim Ahrens, who made a living building looms and weaving. He studied the European books to learn techniques that were used before weaving went to power looms. At that time, weaving had to be very efficient—it was a business, and time was money, even then.

I write in my first book, ***Winding a Warp & Using a Paddle,*** "Whether you want to weave for pleasure or profit or both, the techniques you'll learn here will help you weave more high quality cloth in less time, smoothly and pleasurably, with confidence in the result."

So, where do you go from the end of this book? Right on to my other three books (and DVD, ***Warping the Loom Back to Front***).

— *Peggy Osterkamp*

Available from:
Peggy Osterkamp
501 Via Casitas, #813
Greenbrae, CA 94904
www.peggyosterkamp.com

2 The Basics

What is weaving?

Weaving is making cloth from two sets of yarns or threads that interlace with each other. (See Figures 1 a and b) You might have made "cloth" out of paper strips as a child—weaving one set of strips over and under another set of strips that you had laid out parallel with each other. You might have had difficulty keeping the strips from sliding around, making it hard to weave them.

Perhaps you taped the first set of strips at one end to keep them in place and to make weaving under and over easier.

Weaving on a loom is similar in that two sets of threads interlace over and under each other. However, the loom takes the difficulty out of the process.

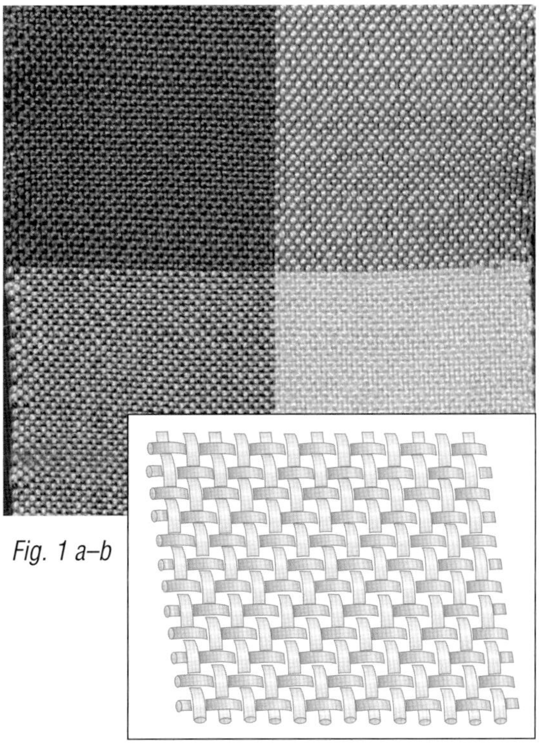

Fig. 1 a–b

What are warps and wefts?

Warps are the threads that are measured out and put on the loom first. Wefts are the threads that cross over and under the warp threads during weaving. See Figure 2.

Fig. 2

What are threads and yarns?

Generally, the two terms are used interchangeably, and I will do so in this book. Often, one thinks of yarns as being fat and threads as being thin. See Figure 3.

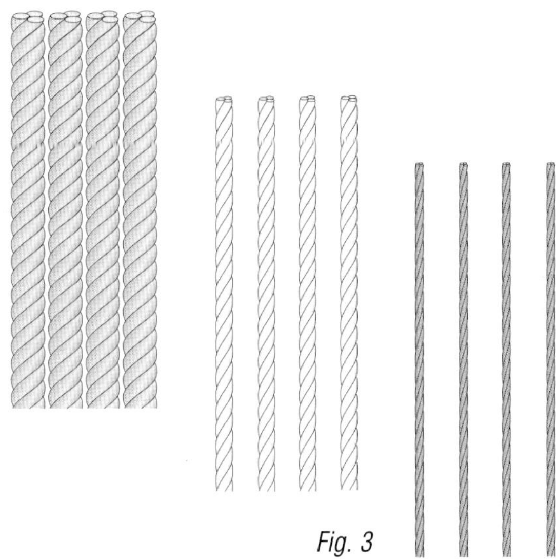

Fig. 3

What is a loom?

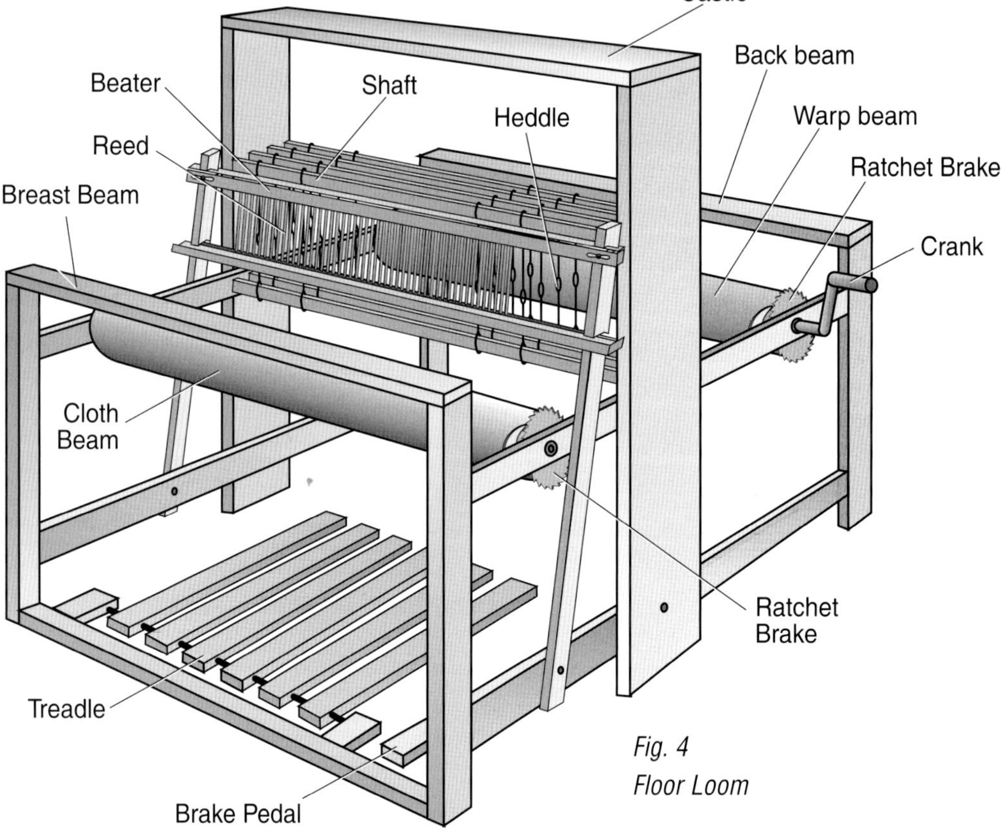

> *Note: Shafts are often called harnesses, but "shaft" is the correct term.*
>
> *How looms work is explained later on in the book.*

Figures 4 and 5 show two views of floor looms. Floor looms vary greatly in their design, but the illustrations show the generic parts. Figure 4 shows the pedals, called treadles, that are in the front of floor looms. Having treadles is the big distinction between floor looms and table looms. They are approximately 34" to the height of breast beam. Width can vary from 24" up to 60". Depth can be 36" for simple 4-shaft looms and deeper for complicated ones. Figure 6 shows a loom with threads on it.

Castle
Back beam
Beater
Shaft
Heddle
Warp beam
Reed
Ratchet Brake
Breast Beam
Crank
Cloth
Beam
Ratchet
Brake
Treadle
Brake Pedal

Fig. 4
Floor Loom

Fig. 5
Floor Loom

Castle
Shaft
Beater
Shaft Bar
Cloth
Beam
Reed
Warp
Beam
Heddle
Leg of
Beater

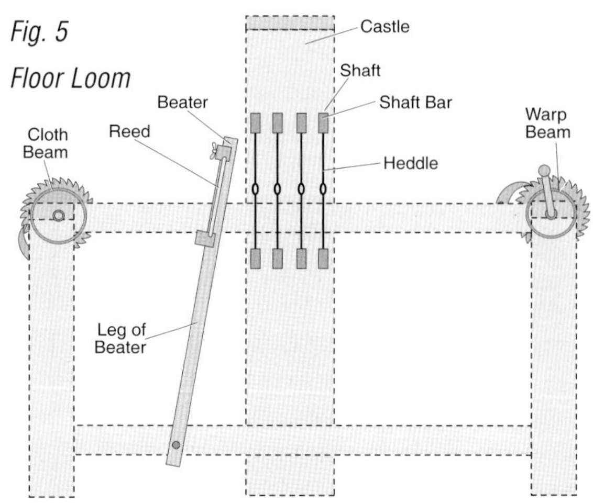

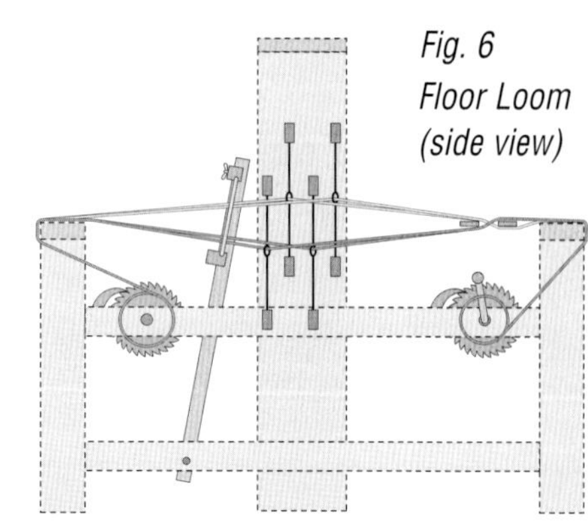

Fig. 6
Floor Loom
(side view)

Figures 7 and 8 show two types of table looms. They are used on table tops, and they have levers instead of treadles. There are many varieties of table looms, with the levers being at the front or on the side. The size of the loom in Figure 7 is: 19" wide, 23" deep, 25" high to the top of the levers.

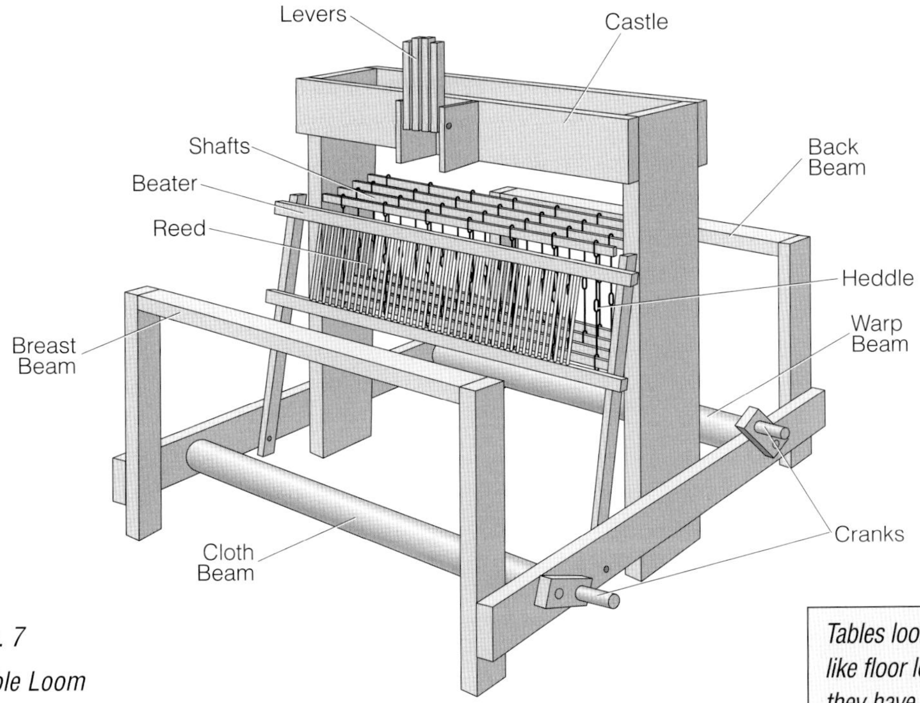

Levers
Castle
Shafts
Beater
Reed
Back Beam
Heddle
Warp Beam
Breast Beam
Cranks
Cloth Beam

Fig. 7
Table Loom

Tables looms work just like floor looms except they have levers instead of treadles.

Note: Shafts are often called harnesses, but "shaft" is the correct term.

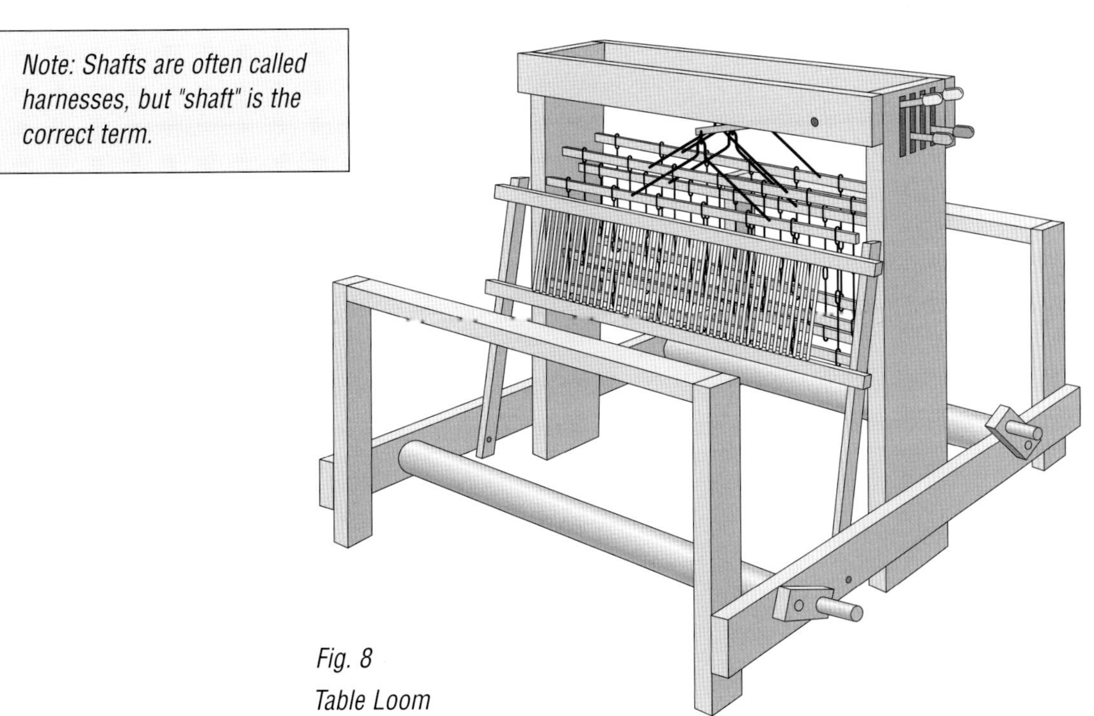

Fig. 8
Table Loom

Looms

You can tell the front of floor and table looms by locating the beater in the illustration. See Figures 4 and 9.

Figure 10 shows a rigid heddle loom. It is quite different from floor and table looms, and instructions for using it are given in Chapter 14, beginning on page 327. Rigid heddle looms are popular today because they are small, portable, and you can weave on vacations, etc. Sometimes, they are called looms for knitters. Using them is much simpler than using a regular loom, so it is especially good for children and those who aren't wanting too much of a commitment when they begin to learn to weave. Some people never stop weaving on them, and many "graduate" to floor or table looms.

Note: Shafts are often called harnesses, but "shaft" is the correct term.

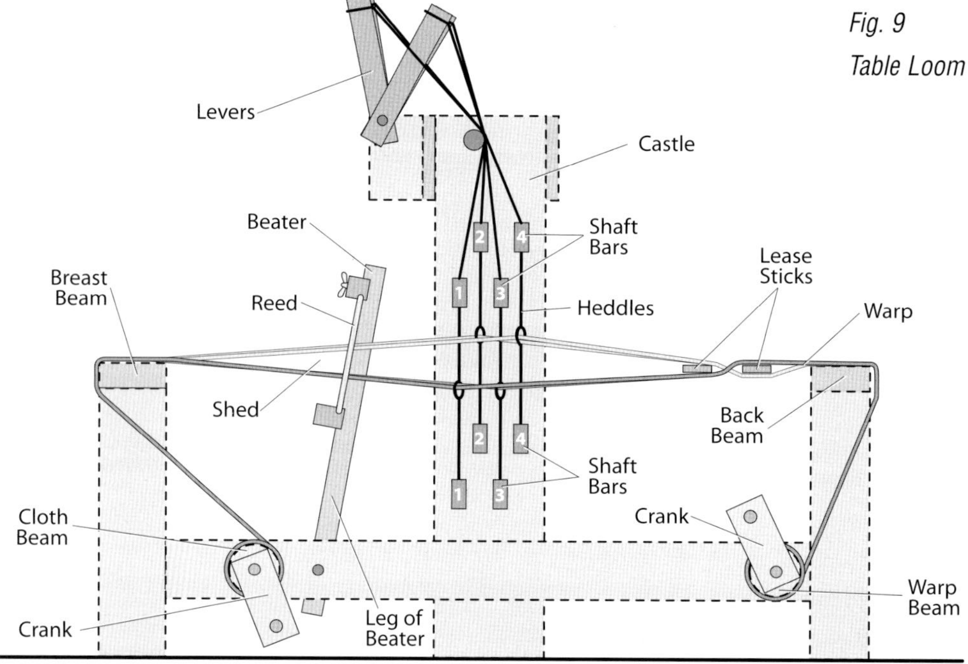

Fig. 9

Table Loom

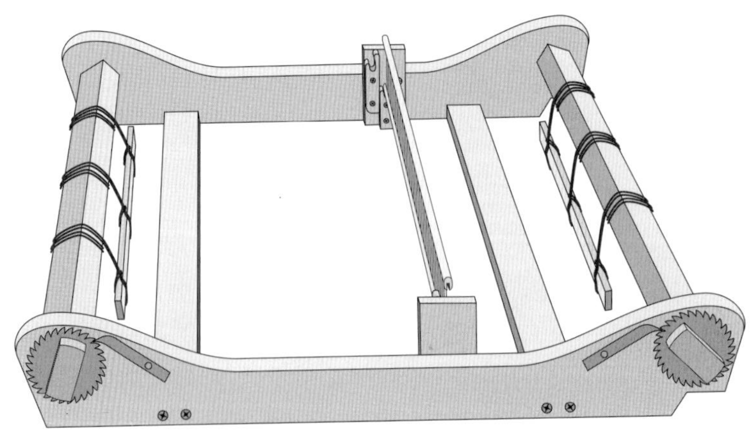

Fig. 10

Rigid Heddle Loom

See Chapter 14, Rigid Heddle Loom

Equipment and Tools

Here is a list (alphabetically) of the basic tools you'll need to start out. Keep on the lookout for things that other weavers use that you think would be handy. Some people love lots of gadgets and tools, and others prefer to get along with the minimum. I've included in the optional section things that I can't live without. (Sources for equipment are listed on page 382-384).

Adding machine tape: Figure 11. A couple of yards are enough to get started.

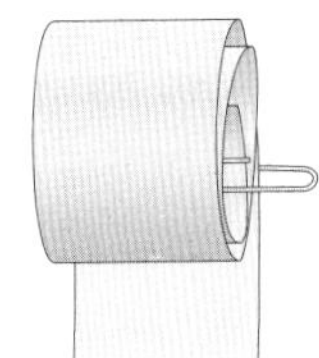

Fig. 11

Broom handle: Figure 12. This tool allows you to get comfortable to thread the loom without mistakes. A dowel or long stick is fine. Jim Ahrens, my teacher, used a broom handle so I've always called it that—whether it is really a broom handle or a stick. It only needs to be as long as the width of your loom.

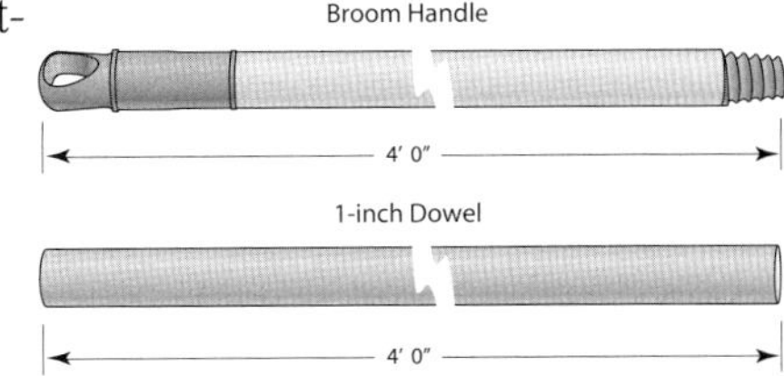

Fig. 12

Clamps: Figure 13. Nice ones from hardware stores are called "quick release bar clamps." Mine are 12½" long.

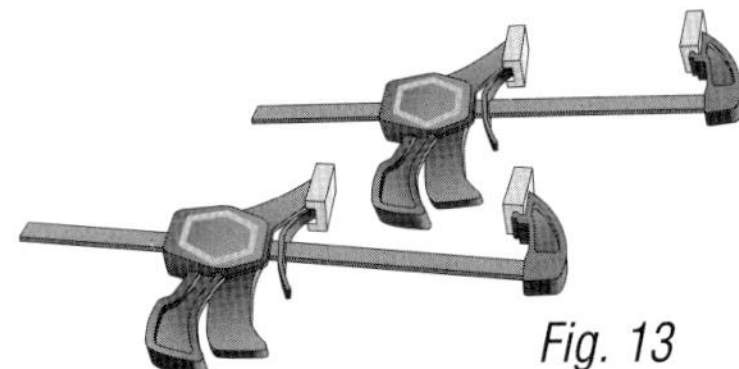

Fig. 13

Film canister: Figure 14. These are getting harder to find, so when you see them, pick up a few.

Fig. 14

Grocery bag: Figure 15. You'll use the paper when putting the warp onto the loom. Other similar paper will be just fine.

Fig. 15

Looms: See Pages 4-6.

Raddle: Figure 16. It can be commercially made or home-made. Ideally, the nails are ½" apart. If the spaces are 1" wide, it will work for projects in this book. Directions for making one are on page 31.

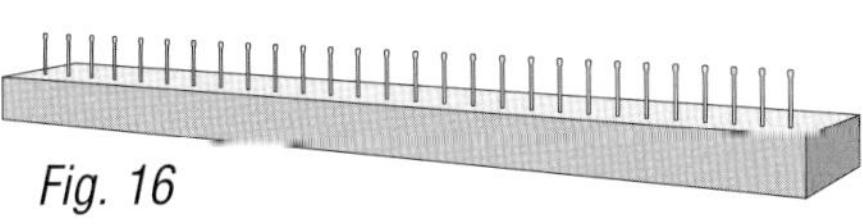

Fig. 16

Rags: Figure 17. Cut them into several long strips, one or two inches wide if they are cut from old sheets, or make them ½" wide if cut from bath towels. Cut them around 24" long or so.

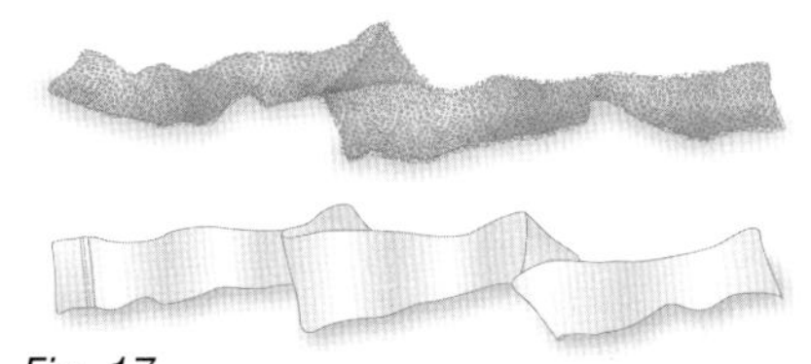

Fig. 17

Equipment

Reed: Figure 18. It needs to fit in the beater of the loom. 8 and 10 dent reeds are suggested for projects. See page 33 for alternate reeds that can be used.

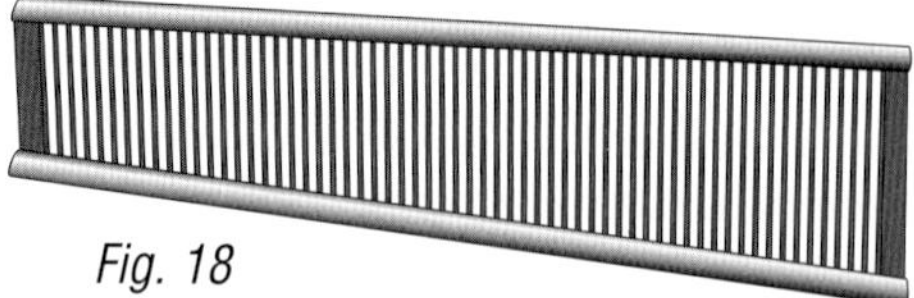

Fig. 18

Rubber bands: Figure 19. You need a few medium-sized ones, say, 6 or 8 of them.

Fig. 19

Scissors: Figure 20. These can be fairly inexpensive, but use better ones than those made for kindergarten children

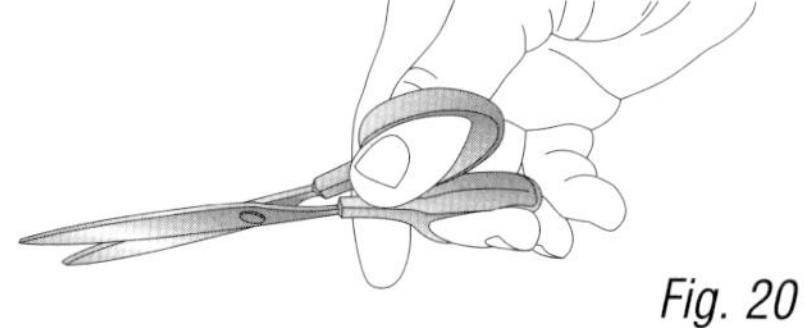

Fig. 20

Shuttles—stick and boat type.

Stick shuttles: Figure 21. You'll need two—about 6" in length. They are very important and make weaving immensely easier. You can make one out of very stiff card-board or foamcore board by cutting out the shape shown in Figure 21. Make it 6" long and around 1" wide. If cutting out the rounded shapes is difficult, you can cut straight lines instead to make large V-shapes at the ends of the shuttle.

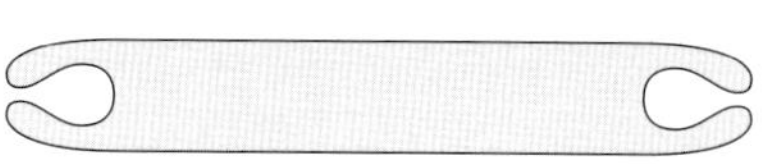

Fig. 21

Boat shuttles: Figure 22. Another type of shuttle you can use, but which is more expensive, is called a boat shuttle. (If you use boat shuttles, you should also have 2 or 3 bobbins that fit inside them, and a bobbin winder.) Boat shuttles are much superior to stick shuttles.

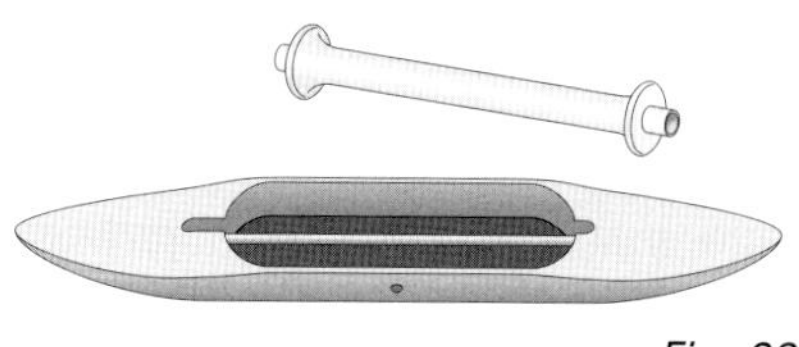

Fig. 22

Sley hook (also called reed hook): See Figure 23 for some varieties. I like plastic ones best.

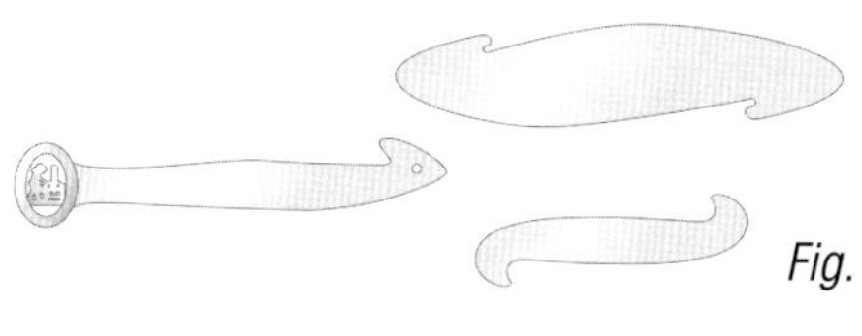

Fig. 23

Sticks as shown: Figures 24 a-d.

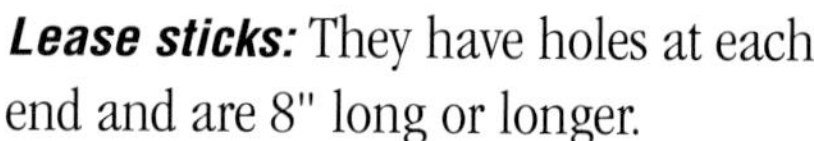

Lease sticks: They have holes at each end and are 8" long or longer.

Fig. 24a

End stick: It also has holes at the ends. It should be longer than 7", but not longer than the length of the warp beam (seen in Figure 4, on page 4).

Fig. 24b

A few packing sticks: They should be about 2" shorter than the length of the loom's warp beam. Buy thin sticks at a lumber store in the molding department.

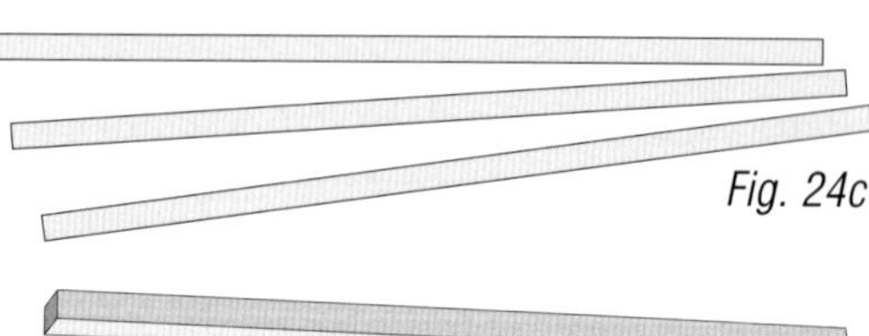

Fig. 24c

Kitestick: Approximately 1 ½" x ½" x 12" or longer. This is not a precise measurement. In a pinch, a ruler or a yard stick will do. See Figure 24d.

Fig. 24d

Straight pins: Figure 25. You should have a few–3-4.

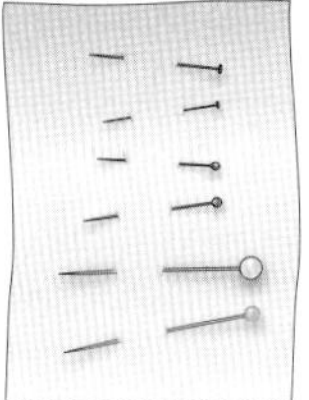

Fig. 25

String: Figure 26. It can be a ball or spool of inexpensive string like that used to wrap packages for mailing. It should be strong enough that it is difficult to break with your hands; but not heavy rope or fine string.

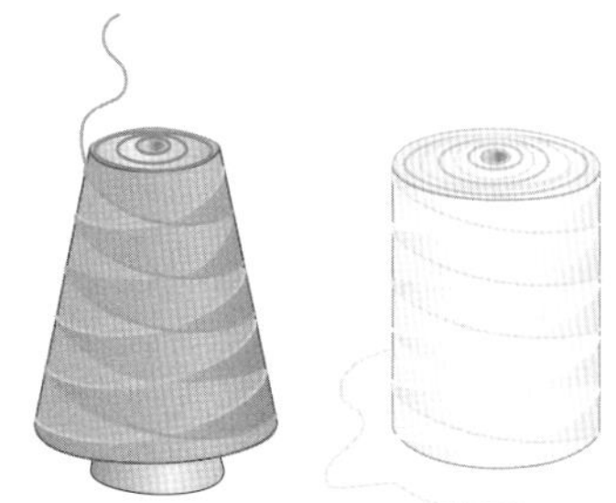

Fig. 26

Tape measure: Figure 27. I like the tape measures sold for sewing–the flexible paper or cloth ones rather than the metal ones used by carpenters.

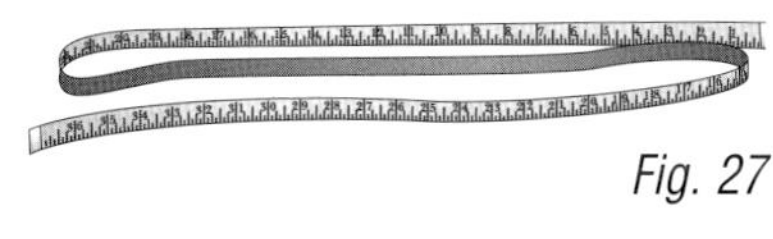

Fig. 27

Tapestry needle: Figure 28. This is a thick needle with a large eye and a blunt point.

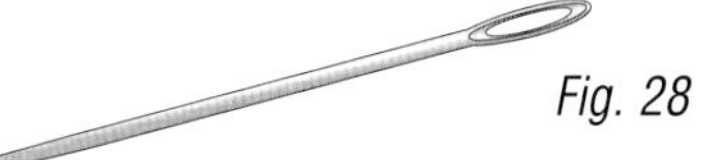

Fig. 28

Threading hook: Figure 29a. The shaft should be straight, as in the illustration. I much prefer this type to a hook with a bend in it. (Figure 29b).

Fig. 29a

Fig. 29b

Warping board: Figure 30. Its overall shape may be square or rectangular.

Warping pegs: An alternative for the warping board, are discussed on page 31.

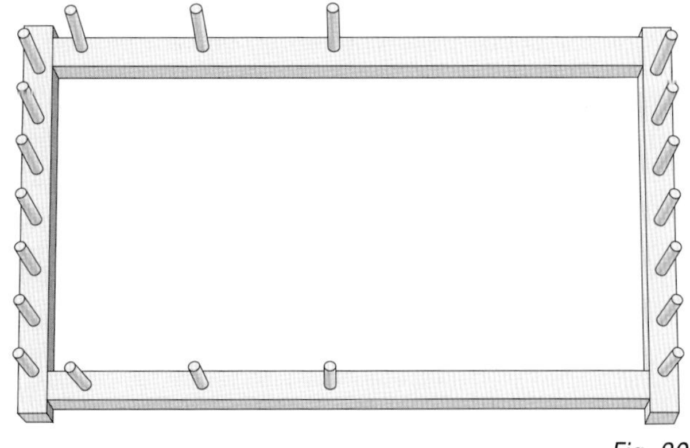

Fig. 30

Equipment

Yarns: For warp and weft, which are described with the instructions given for projects. Figure 31. Yarns come on cones or spools and in balls or skeins. Skeins must be wound into balls. Read about using a swift on the next page.

Fig. 31

Optional Equipment:

Apron: Figure 32 front and back. Directions for making my apron can be found on page 374. I can't work without it. It holds everything I need, and when I tie up the apron strings, it's a signal that I'm really getting to work. I wore out the first one, and this is the improved version.

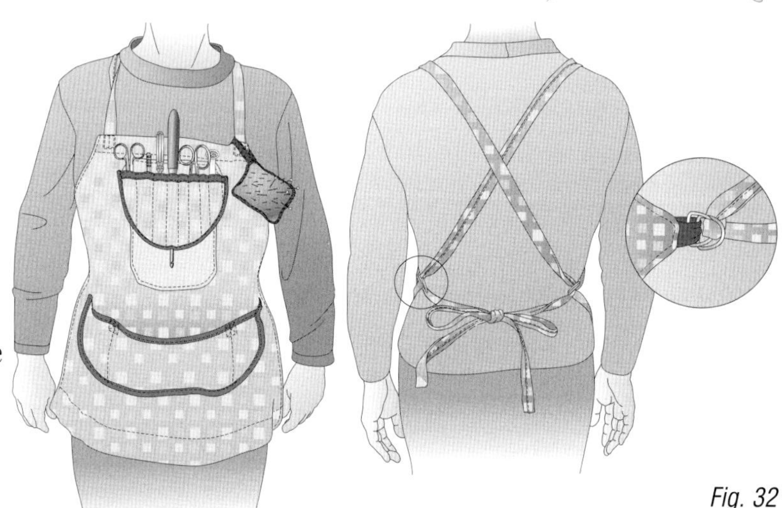

Fig. 32

Cart or side table: Figure 33. It's terribly handy to have a little table beside the loom while I'm weaving. One with wheels can be moved around to wherever I need it. Mine might have glasses, string, notes, shuttles, bobbins, a tea cup, etc. It's another thing I can't live without.

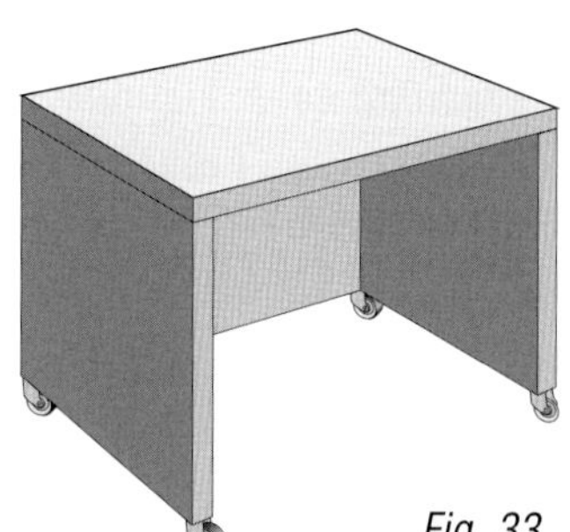

Fig. 33

Camera: It's nice to take pictures of the process as you set up the loom. These pictures will be quick references when you make future projects. It's also nice to have photos of the projects you make. And it's a great thing to use to take pictures of things that inspire you.

Journal or Idea Book: This is where I keep my ideas. They can be photos, or notes and sketches, or cut out from magazines or the newspaper. My teacher required us to get ones with the pages stitched in so you couldn't be tempted to tear out sheets for other purposes. I staple in notes I've written on scraps of paper, too. I never go anywhere without a pen and paper. It might even be a couple of sheets folded in my pocket if I don't want to take a tablet. I have 3" x 5" pads for these notes in the car, in the kitchen, at my bedside, and at my desk. Anything will do, but try to put down every idea. You certainly can't weave all of them, but one might lead to another idea that you will use.

Low Stool: This is helpful for threading the loom. Figure 34a.

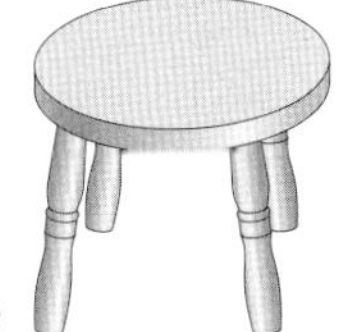

Fig. 34a

Needle Book: I made one of these in 4-H when I was 10. It's great for keeping track of your needles—especially the tapestry needles you need. It's made of a few layers of wool cloth stitched together like a little book. Directions for mine are on page 378 in the Appendix. Figure 34b.

Fig. 34b

Notebook: I started one in my first weaving class—for notes and observations and information I wanted to keep. It contained different sizes and types of yarns and their names, sources, etc. I kept a chart for sett (ends per inch) in it and a reed chart. Both are found in this book. Now, I put the pages of ideas and work sheets for projects I'm working on in separate notebooks. When the projects are finished, I staple the sheets together and put them in file folders. I often have referred to these old notes when I want to repeat something or use a yarn again.

Pincushion: I have one on my apron, and I couldn't manage without it. One hangs on the castle of one of my looms, another lives on my work table, and another one is in my regular sewing box. I don't keep my needles in it because they always get lost. I keep them in a needle book; see above. I have on my apron a wooden needle case, which a friend's husband made.

Swift: Figure 35. This is a handy tool to hold skeins while winding the yarns from the skein to a ball, spool, or cone.

Swift

Yarns must be on cones or spools, or in balls. If the yarn is in skeins, it must be wound into balls or onto spools. To keep the yarn on the skein from tangling, put it on the back of a chair or on a swift (Figure 35) to hold it while unwinding it. Of course, you could enlist a person to hold the skein between their hands while you unwind. How to open skeins without tangling is on page 373 in the Appendix..

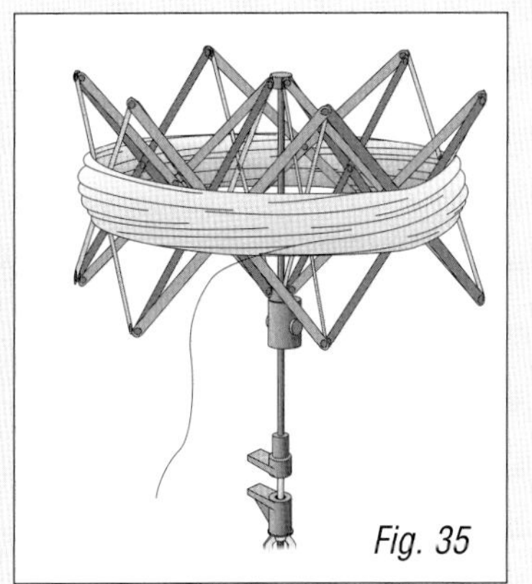

Fig. 35

Worksheets: These can be found in the planning projects sections. I use them for every project I begin.

Wrench: Or something similar in heaviness for a weight. Mine, illustrated here, weighs 3½ ounces. Figure 36.

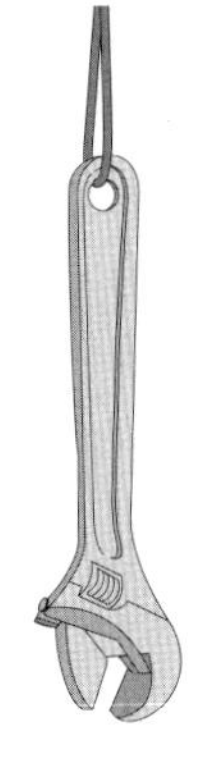

Fig. 36

Yarn Size Chart

This figure (Figure 37) shows different size yarns appropriate and not appropriate for the samplers. Check the size of your yarn by placing it on the pictures and matching your yarn to the one closest in size in the chart. If there are very few yards in a pound, it indicates that the yarn is rather fat. Conversely, if there are many, many yards per pound, the yarn is very fine. For example, 5/2 cotton has 2,100 yards per pound, and yarn with only 800 yards per pound is much thicker.

You can refer to this chart for future projects to compare yarn sizes when the yards per pound are given.

Fig. 37

Yarn Size Chart

5/2 Pearl Cotton - 2,100 yds. per lb.

Sport-weight Wool - 1,750 yds per lb.

2-ply Wool - 1,475 yds. per lb.

Worsted-weight Wool - 800 yds. per lb.

Rayon Chenille - 1,450 yds. per lb.

Rug Wool - 260 yds. per lb.

10/2 Pearl Cotton - 4,200 yds. per lb.

Mohair Bouclé - 1,175 yds per lb.

3 Back-to-Front Warping

What is a Sampler?

Fig. 38

My favorite way to learn something new in weaving is to try it out by weaving a sampler. Then, mistakes don't spoil anything, but are good for learning. Often, I provide extra length for experimenting—sometimes, breaking the rules I've just learned. After the sampler, I usually design a project using what I've learned. It is what I suggest for you, too.

I've designed a sampler for you so that you can learn to set up the loom and weave a variety of "patterns" (weavers call them structures). You'll make the different weave structures by learning how to read the draft notation used by weavers around the world. (Your "sampler" could be a scarf, table runner, head wrapper, or wall hanging.) Please allow yourself to make mistakes—sometimes, you like them so much you want to reproduce them again.

Projects you might try after your sampler are given on page 297. Future assignments are given in Chapter 9, page 233.

Part One: Measuring the Warp

Weave a Sampler: 5" wide and about 45" long. See Figures 38 and 39.

Use the back-to-front method of setting up the loom.

Yarn requirements for the sampler:

400 yards (3 ounces) of 5/2 pearl cotton thread in two contrasting colors: That is, 200 yards of each color. This is enough for the warp (see page 3) as well as the weft (see page 3). Figure 37 on page 12 shows yarns of various sizes. The size for the sampler is reproduced at the bottom of this page. Hold your yarn up to the photograph to see if it is about the same size as that for 5/2 cotton, at 2100 yards per pound.

I like pearl cotton because it comes in a lot of nice colors, is smooth, strong, and a good size for many projects. I like the look of the cloth made from it because the yarn has a bit of a shine to it. Sources for threads are listed on pages 382-384.

Note: See pages 31-33 for information about using other yarns for the sampler.

5/2 Pearl Cotton - 2,100 yds. per lb.

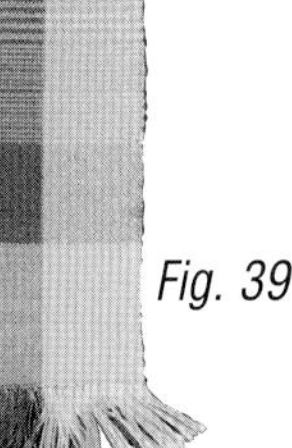

Fig. 39

Equipment List: See Chapter 2, Equipment.

Four-shaft loom: Either a floor loom or a table loom.

Clamps:

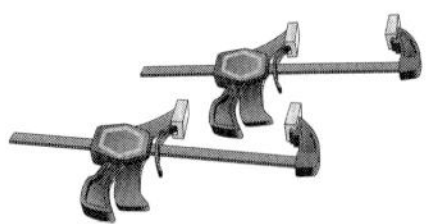

Kitestick:

Raddle: Ideally, the nails are ½" apart. If the spaces are 1" wide, it will work for this project.

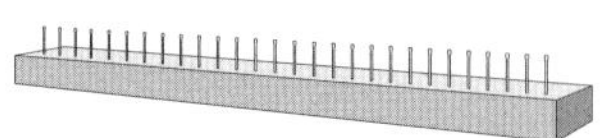

10-dent size reed: To fit in the beater of the loom. See page 33 for alternate reeds that can be used.

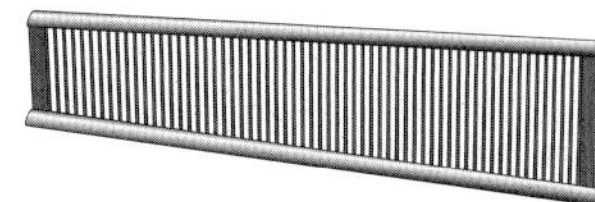

Sticks: Lease sticks, end stick, packing stick, etc.

String: A ball or spool of inexpensive string like that used to wrap packages for mailing. It should be strong enough that it is difficult to break with your hands; not heavy rope or fine string.

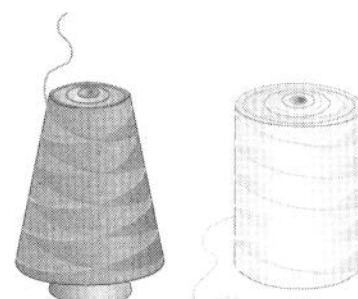

Rubber bands:

Scissors:

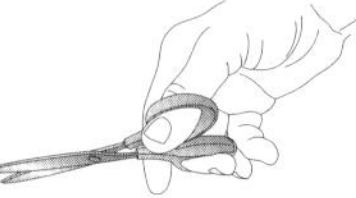

Tape measure:

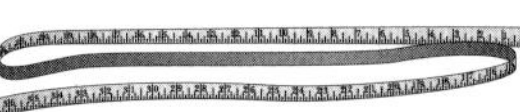

Warping board:

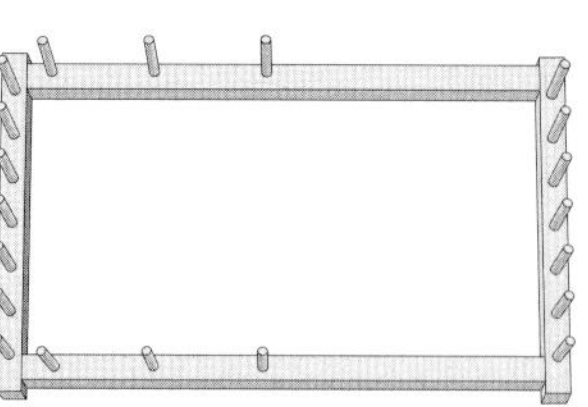

Optional

Notebook

Camera

Fig. 40 Fig. 41

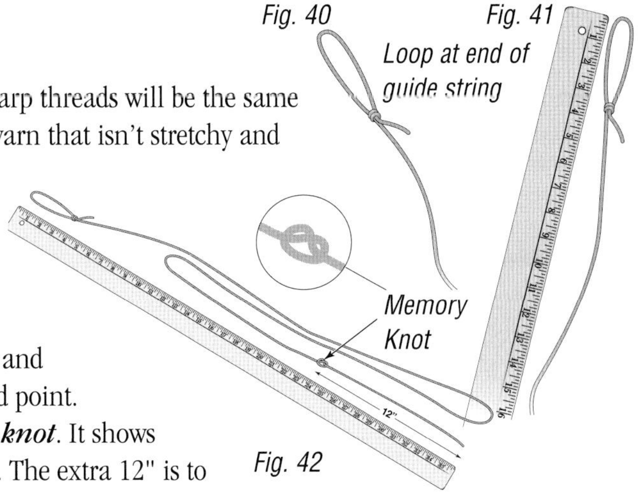

Loop at end of guide string

Memory Knot

12"

Fig. 42

Make a Guide String

This important string ensures that all the warp threads will be the same length. Use ordinary household string or a yarn that isn't stretchy and contrasts in color with the threads of your warp. Make a loop at the end of a string as shown in Figure 40. Measure out a length of the string in the following way: Begin to measure at the end of the loop, as shown in Figure 41. Measure out 2 yards and an additional 12". Tie a knot at the two-yard point. See Figure 42. I call this knot the ***memory knot***. It shows the actual length the warp is intended to be. The extra 12" is to accommodate the warping board.

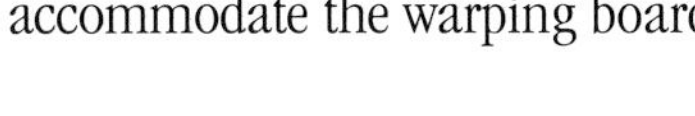

Position the Warping Board

You want to set up your warping board in a secure position and at a height that is comfortable for you. Ideally, it can hang on a wall, but many weavers and schools don't have the space to do this. I like to clamp the warping board to the edge of a table. See Figure 43. Wonderful clamps can be found at lumber and hardware stores–they are lightweight and handy to operate. Look for bar clamps with quick-release grips. Mine are 12½" long.

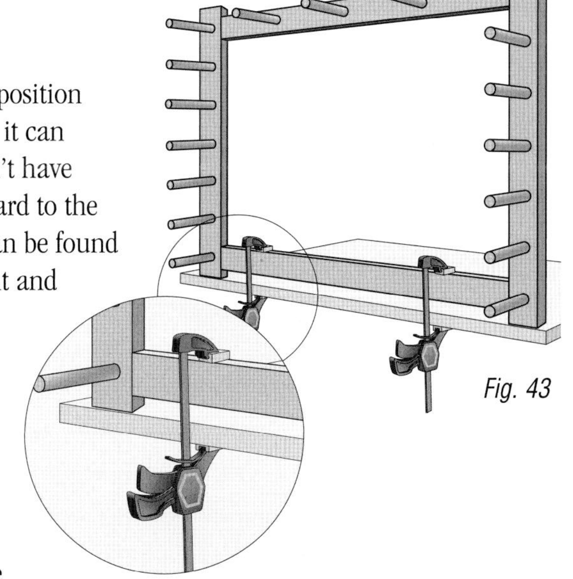

Fig. 43

Another strategy for anchoring the warping board is to tie it up to the front or the back of the loom. Figure 44 shows one tied to the front. Make sure it is tied sturdily to the loom.

Choose a comfortable height for you. When you are measuring out the warp threads on the warping board, you will carry the thread from peg-to-peg from beginning to end and back again. That's a lot of sideways movement for your arms and shoulders to make. Sometimes, I arrange my warping board vertically and move my arms up and down to avoid the side-to-side motion. Try moving your arms with the board at different heights or positions.

I don't recommend using a warping board flat on a table, but I've seen some of my students do it that way. See what is comfortable for you.

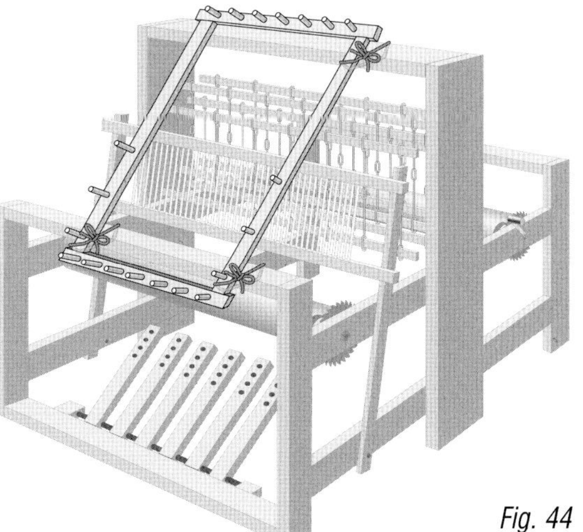

Fig. 44

③ Start the Path for the Guide String

To start laying out your guide string's path, hook the loop of the guide string around the top left peg of your warping board. I like to wrap a rubber band on the tip of that peg so the guide string won't slip off. See Figure 45.

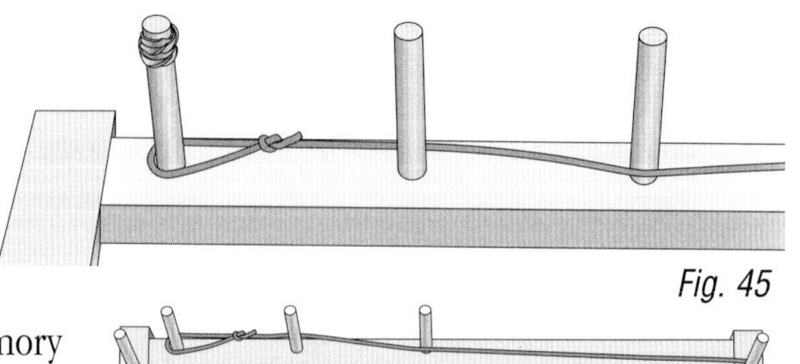

Fig. 45

Guide the string from peg-to-peg on the board until it is extended to its full length with your memory knot as close to a peg as possible. Some variations of paths you might take are shown in Figures 46, 47, and 48. Any arrangement can be made on the warping board as long as the length of the guide string extends from a peg at the beginning to a peg at the end. In each of the illustrations, the guide string is the same length, but there are three different paths that could be used. If the memory knot (see Figure 42) falls between two pegs, carry the string to the next further peg and tie it there ***temporarily.*** That extra 12 inches you allowed at the end of the guide string should give you plenty of leeway to get to the next available peg. You are tying the string temporarily onto that peg because in the next steps you will make adjustments to the path of the guide string.

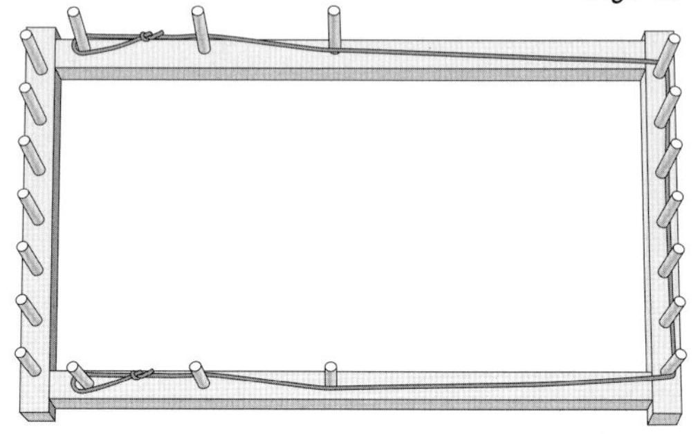

Fig. 46

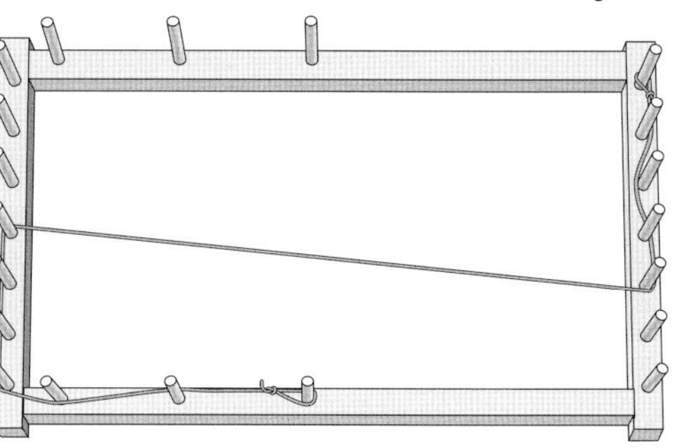

Fig. 47

Note: It is important that you keep the string going in one direction. In other words, the string cannot go back on itself. See Figure 49 in the warning box to see what you cannot do.

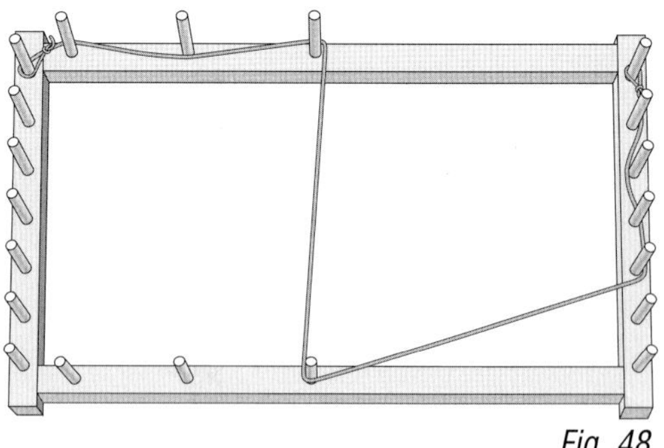

Fig. 48

Note: Sizes and shapes of warping boards vary greatly as well as where the pegs are situated.

Warning!

Do not take the guide string back on itself–it must always travel ahead, never backward where it has already been placed. See Figures 46, 47, and 48 for the correct way to direct your guide string–only going forward. Figure 49 at the right shows you what you cannot do.

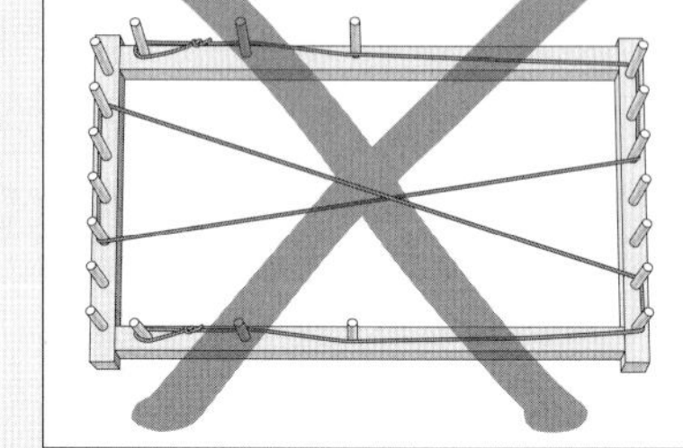

Fig. 49

④ Re-arrange the Path to Make 2 Crosses

Various arrangements of the guide string can be used if they also include the special pegs at the beginning and end. These pegs hold what we call the weaver's crosses. These X's (crosses) keep the threads in order and keep the warp threads from tangling. Figure 50 shows how to rearrange your guide string to make the crosses. First, position your guide string so there are 4 pegs in a straight line as shown in the illustration. Place the guide string over the second peg and under the third peg to form one half of an X. Do this placement at both ends of the guide string as shown in the illustration. At the bottom pegs, go under peg 7 and over peg 6. You want to make 2 crosses—one at each end.

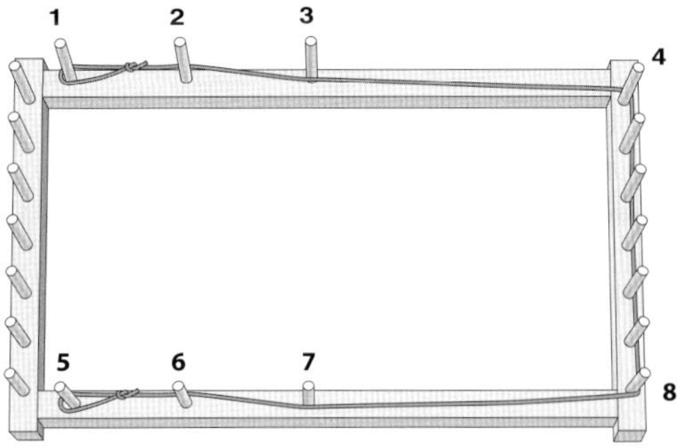

Fig. 50

When these two ½ crosses are accounted for, you can permanently tie the end of your guide string to its end-most peg.

Figure 51 shows why 3 pegs in a row won't allow all the threads to be measured the same length and that with 4 pegs, all the threads will be equal in length when measuring out the warp threads along the path of the guide string.

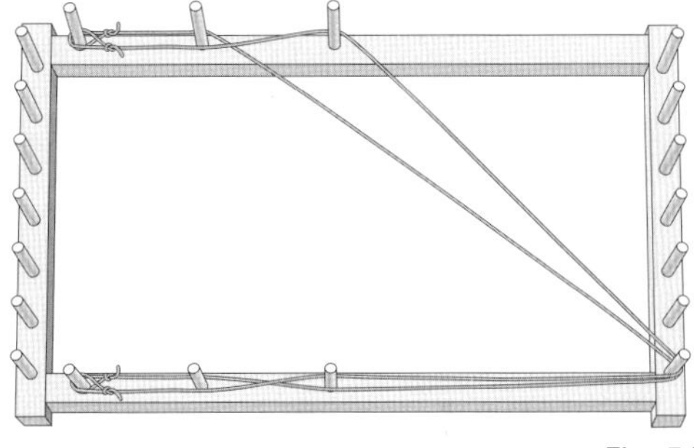

Fig. 51

Have 4 pegs in a straight line—never 3

The 4 pegs are:

Peg #1 = End peg
Pegs #2 and #3 = Cross pegs
Peg #4 = Peg to keep the warps aligned

And at the bottom:

Peg #5 = End peg
Pegs #6 and #7 = Cross pegs
Peg #8 = Peg to keep the warps aligned

> You'll be making two crosses simultaneously—at the thread-by-thread cross you'll *alternate the threads* that form the two halves of the cross (the X between the pegs). At the group cross, you will *alternate groups of threads* forming each half of the cross as shown in Figure 64 on page 20.

⑤ Make the Final Adjustment of the Guide String

Take another piece of string just like your guide string and tie it to the last peg (#5) on your warping board. Follow the return trip along your guide string's path except that at each cross you will form the other half of the X's between pegs 2 and 3 and 6 and 7 by going under and over pegs 2 and 3 and 6 and 7 instead of over and under them as you did at first. This path will complete the cross at the top and the bottom of the warping board. Some people say the crosses look like figure 8's—either way, X or figure 8, you are forming the weaver's crosses. Secure the string to the beginning peg (#1) as in Figures 52, 53, and 54.

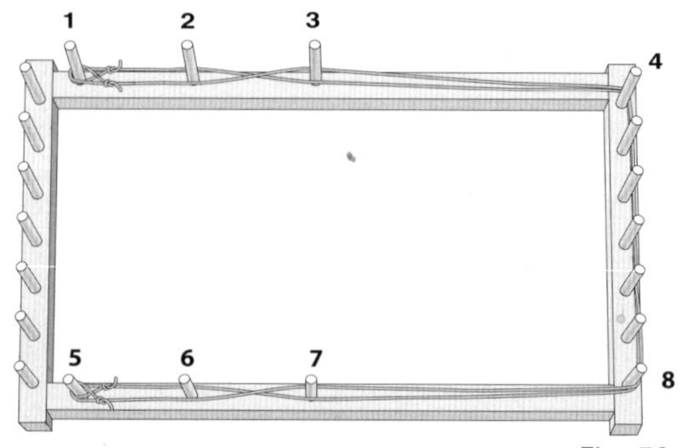

Fig. 52

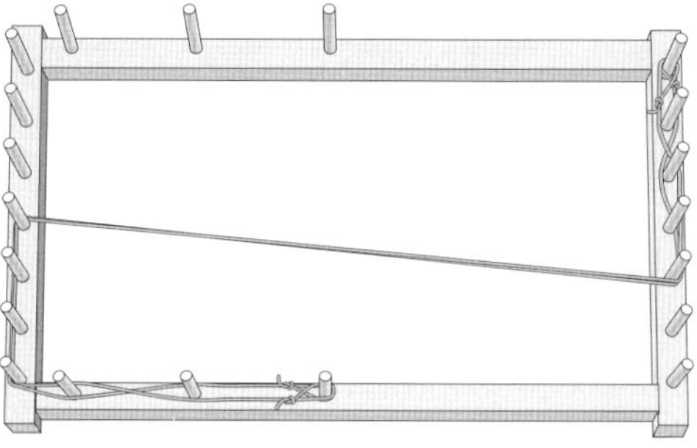

Fig. 53

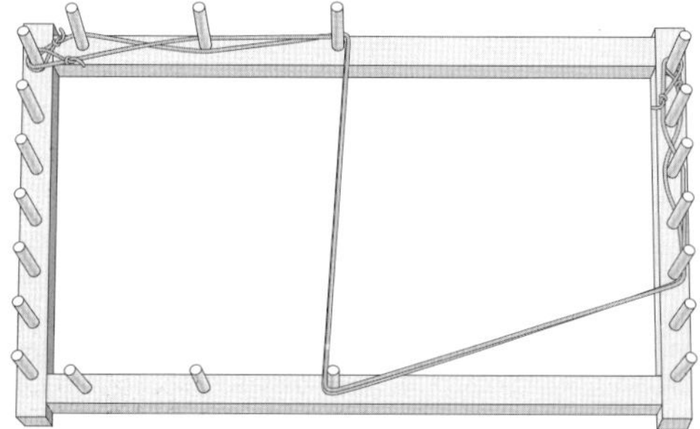

Fig. 54

Check to see if all the pegs you are using are secure and not the least bit wobbly. If any are, force the peg into the hole in the warping board's frame with a piece of thick yarn. See Figure 55. What you are doing is shimming the peg into the hole. This action should make the peg very stable. If it doesn't do the job, try using two pieces of yarn or a thicker one. If nothing works, use another path for your guide string so you can ***avoid using any pegs that are wobbly*** because eventually, they will bend, and your warp threads will fall off or be different lengths. See what to do on page 22.

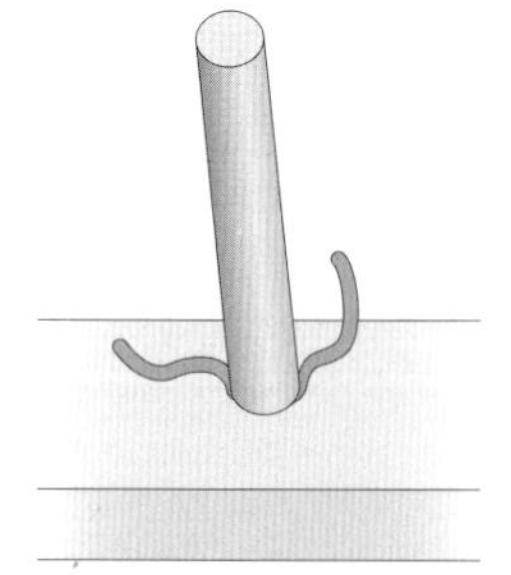

Fig. 55

(6) Measure Out the Warp Threads

Put one of your warp yarns on the floor below the warping board. (If the yarn is in a ball or small spool or cone, putting it inside a coffee can or small waste basket or large kitchen pot will keep it from rolling away from you). Make a loop in the end of the warp thread as shown in Figure 56 and place the loop on peg #1, which has the rubber band wrapped on it. See Figure 57. Read the next page before you begin to understand the differences between the two crosses.

Fig. 56

Take the thread along your guide string, over peg 2 and under peg 3, and follow along the remainder of the path until you reach peg 7 at the bottom of the warping board.

Take the thread under peg 7 and over peg 6, then around peg 5, which is the last peg at the end of the guide string. Now, you have measured out your first warp thread.

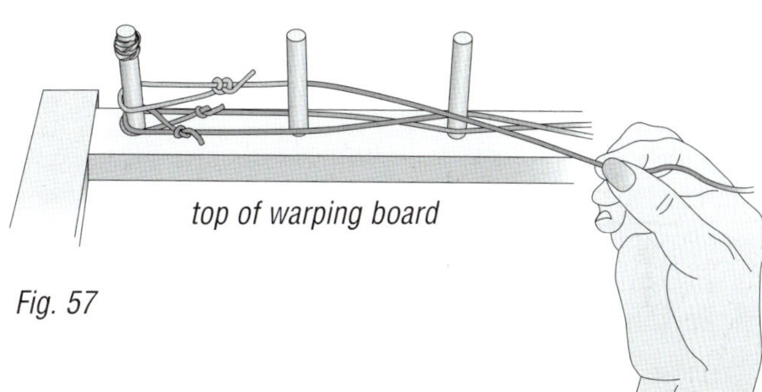

Fig. 57

Start to measure the second thread by going in the reverse direction following the path of your first thread ***exactly***, going over peg 6 and under peg 7. (Note that at the bottom, only ½ the cross is being made at this time—the full cross will be made later.) Figure 58 shows the path your warp thread will take at the end peg. (The guide string is not shown for clarity.)

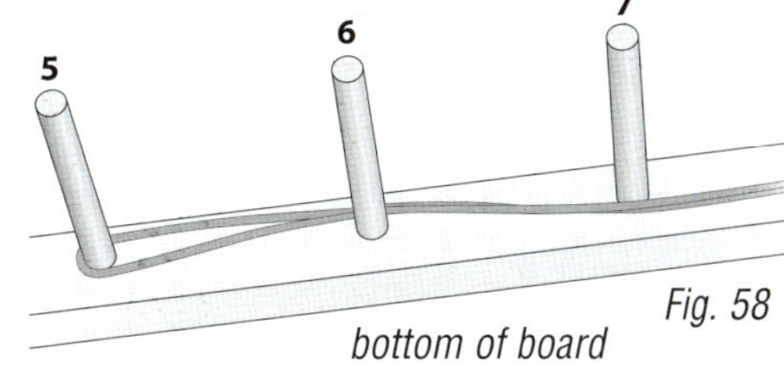

Fig. 58

Follow the guide string back along its path making a return trip toward the top peg where you began. When you get to peg 3 at the top of the warping board, you will take the thread over peg 3 and under peg 2 to complete the cross (an X or a Figure 8) between those two pegs. See Figures 59, 60, and 61.

For the third thread, follow the same path you made for the first thread. See Figures 59, 60, and 61.

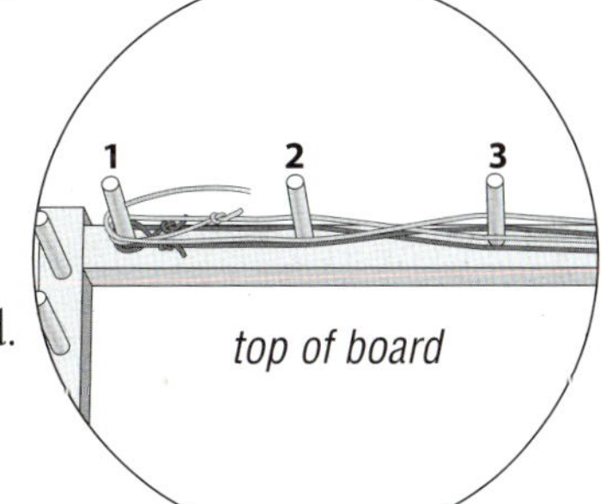

Fig. 60

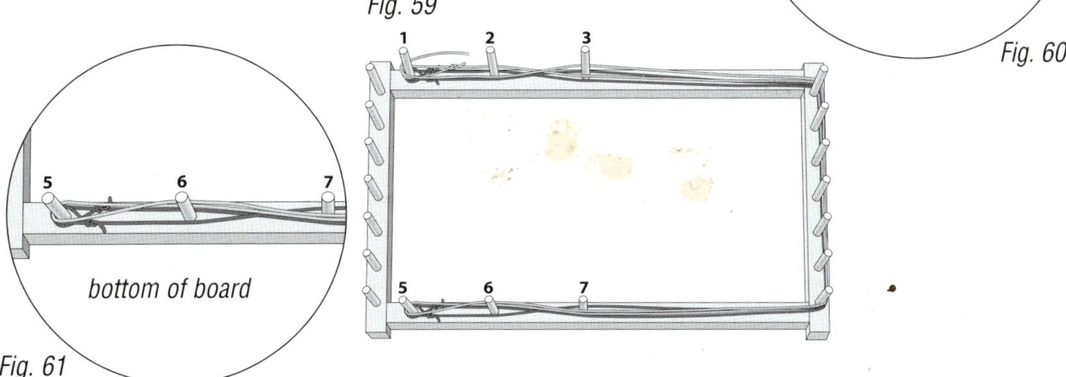

Fig. 59

Fig. 61

On all the roundtrips from now on, at the top of the warping board follow the same path at the cross that you did on trip number one. On the return trips, follow the same path you did on trip two. This makes a thread-by-thread cross at the top, and, for the present, a ½ cross at the bottom after each complete roundtrip. Figure 62 shows what the thread-by-thread cross will look like after 8 threads have been measured out.

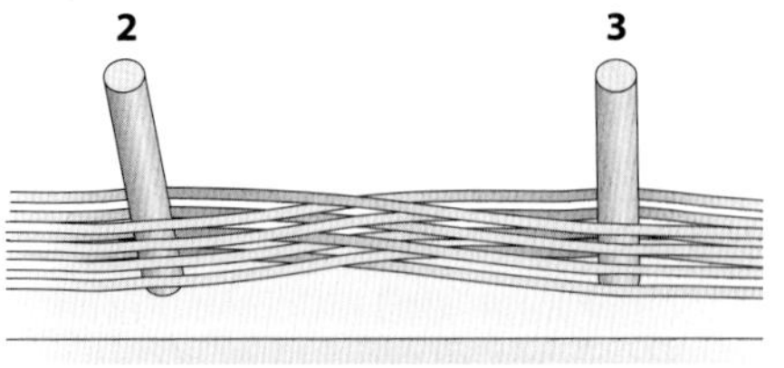

top of board Fig. 62

If you always go "over and under," at the thread-by-thread cross, the cross will form as you go. In other words, as you approach the first cross peg, always take the warp thread *over* that peg and under the next.

Continue measuring out your warp threads until you have 10 of them. On the eleventh thread you will make a change at the ***bottom*** of the warping board. Until now, the 10 threads have formed only ½ of the cross with all the threads following the same path between pegs 6 and 7 at the bottom of the warping board as in Figure 58 on page 19.

Make the other half of the group cross

When measuring out the 11th thread, make the cross as usual at the top of the warping board, but at the bottom, take the thread ***over*** peg 7 and ***under*** peg 6, which will be the start of the other half of the cross. The return trip takes you ***under*** peg 6 and ***over*** peg 7 again. Figure 63 shows the path that eventually the 11th and 12th threads at the group cross will take.

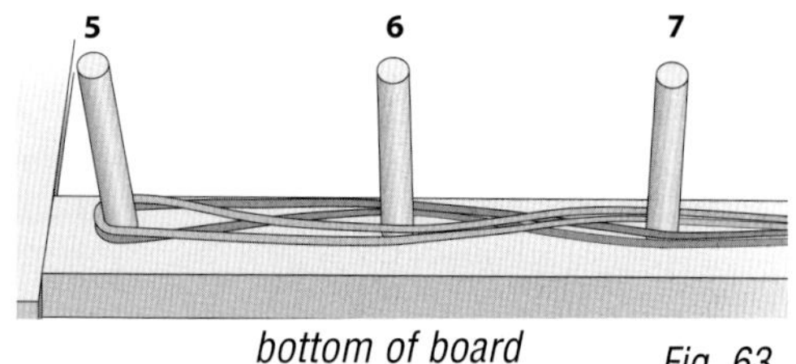

bottom of board Fig. 63

You will use this path for the next 10 threads. This cross is made of groups of threads as shown in Figure 64. For the sampler, there will be 10 threads in each half of the cross, which represents ½" worth of warp threads. It is the number of threads that will be placed in the ½" spaces between the nails in the raddle in Step Eleven on page 28. (Other projects are likely to have a different number of threads in ½".)

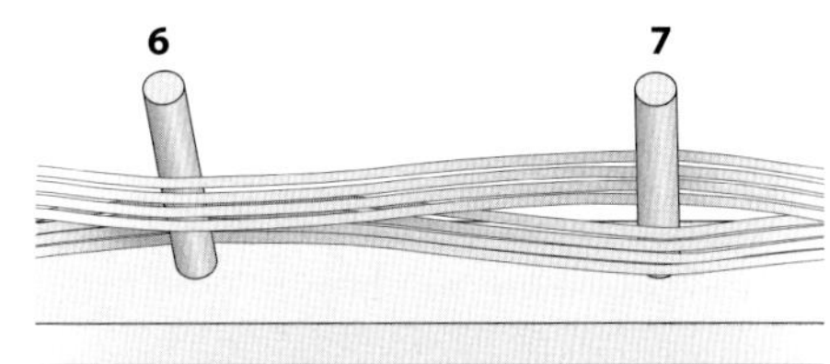

bottom of board Fig. 64

Figures 65 and 66 show what the warping board looks like after two groups of threads have been measured out. The configuration that appears automatically between pegs 5 and 6 at the group cross is called the false cross and is not usable, but cannot be avoided.

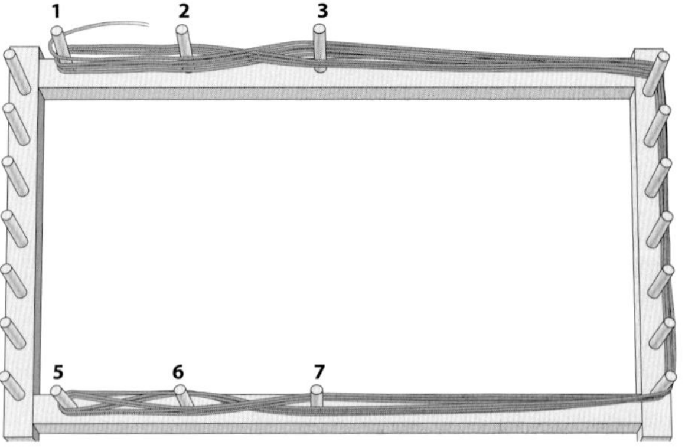

Fig. 65

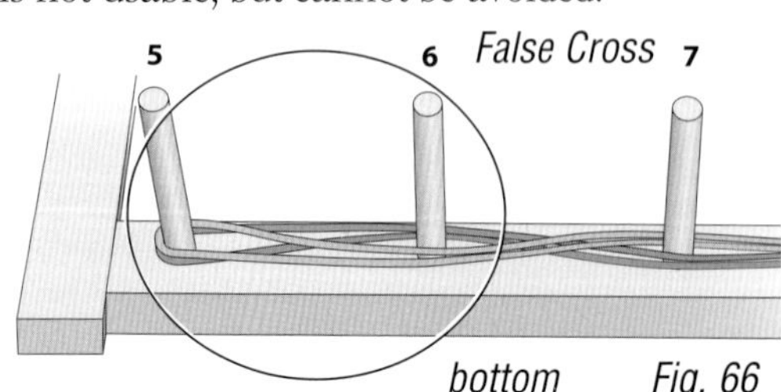

bottom Fig. 66

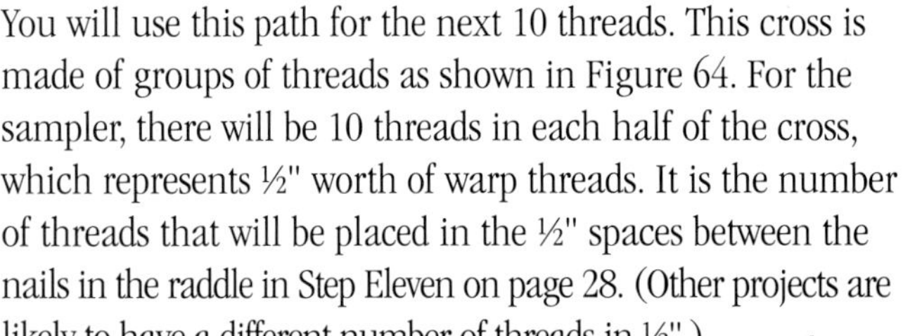

To summarize, at the group cross you'll follow the first path exactly until you have one-group's worth of threads (10 threads) as shown in Figure 58. Then, for the next series of trips, you'll follow the path that completes the other half of the cross. See Figure 63.

The thing to remember is that the number of threads in the group cross is the number that are in ½". Other projects with different threads will have a different number of threads in ½" if they have more or fewer threads ***in one inch*** (that is, are thicker or thinner than 5/2 pearl cotton). Read more about epi in the chapter on Sett.

> You'll be making two crosses simultaneously—at the thread-by-thread cross you'll *alternate the threads* that form the two halves of the cross (the X between the pegs). At the group cross, you will *alternate groups of threads* forming each half of the cross as shown in Figure 64 on page 20.

Measure out 50 warp threads in this manner. At the bottom, because the group cross is made of groups of 10 threads in each half of the cross, there will be 5 groups.

Change colors after measuring 50 threads: at peg #1 at the top of the warping board, tie the new color thread to the original one and continue warping (measuring). See Figure 67.

Measure out 50 threads of the second color making both crosses as usual.

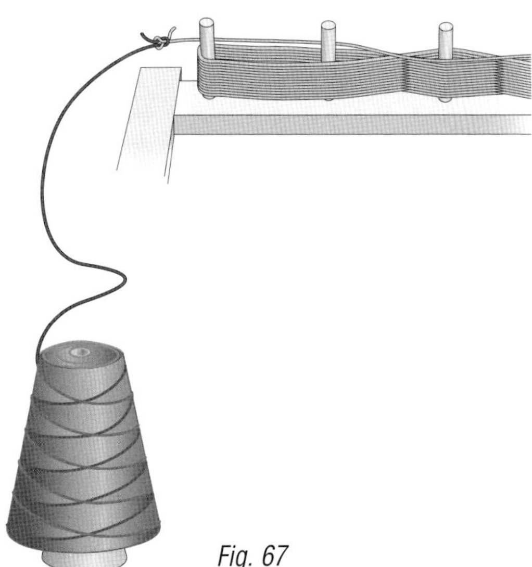

Fig. 67

When all 100 warps are measured, tie off the last warp thread just like the way you tied on the first thread—with a loop as shown in Figure 68. This tie off occurs at peg 1, at the top of the warping board where you started.

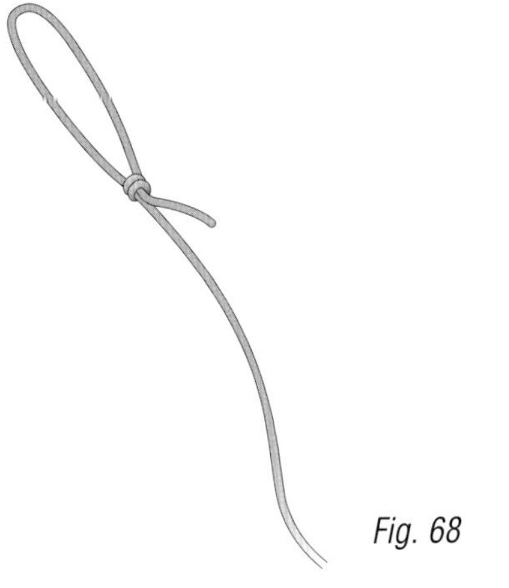

Fig. 68

Some important notes as you are warping:

- As you measure the threads, be conscious of their tension. Even tension, but not a lot of tension, is what you're after. Too much tension will bend the pegs.
- The crosses are there to guide you; a few mistakes won't spoil your warp and can be corrected later. If you discover a mistake a ways back, leave it alone, and don't undo your warp. If, however, you see a mistake you've just made, do go back and correct it.
- As you measure on a warping board, you must be careful to keep successive threads from overlapping. Overlapped ends will turn out to be of different lengths, so I always measure right on the wood of the peg and keep pushing the threads down on all the pegs as I go along. Figure 69 shows that the warp thread that is being measured is flat against the wood of the peg, and previous threads have been pushed down to the base of the peg. Pushing the accumulated threads down also prevents the threads from spreading outward on the pegs, which will cause the pegs to bend. If a peg bends, tie off the warp (page 23) and make a new path on the warping board (page 16). The warp will be in two sections. They will be joined together in the raddle.

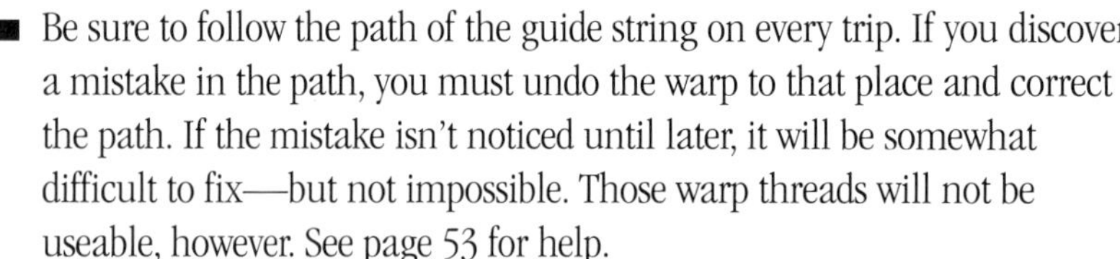

Fig. 69

- Be sure to follow the path of the guide string on every trip. If you discover a mistake in the path, you must undo the warp to that place and correct the path. If the mistake isn't noticed until later, it will be somewhat difficult to fix—but not impossible. Those warp threads will not be useable, however. See page 53 for help.
- If you want to pause while measuring at any time, temporarily wrap the warp thread you are working with around a peg a few times to keep the threads already on the board on tension. When you resume, remember to unwind the thread on the peg and continue measuring as usual. See Figure 70.

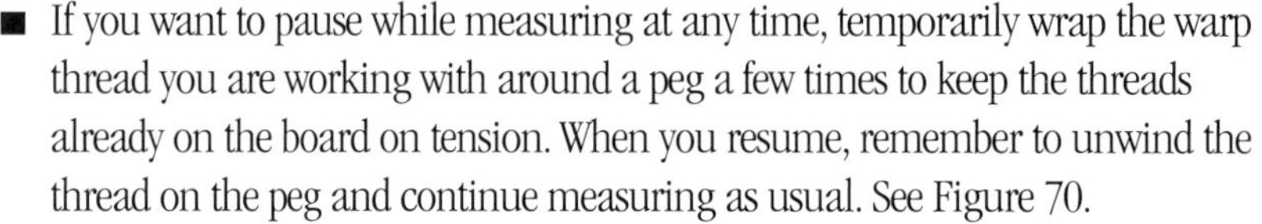

Fig. 70

- Be on the lookout for manufacturer's knots in the warp thread —they need to be eliminated. To do it, cut the warp thread at the knot and take the thread back to the beginning peg. Cut the thread leaving just enough to tie the old and new threads together just like when changing colors, and discard the portion of thread with the knot. See Figures 71 and 72.

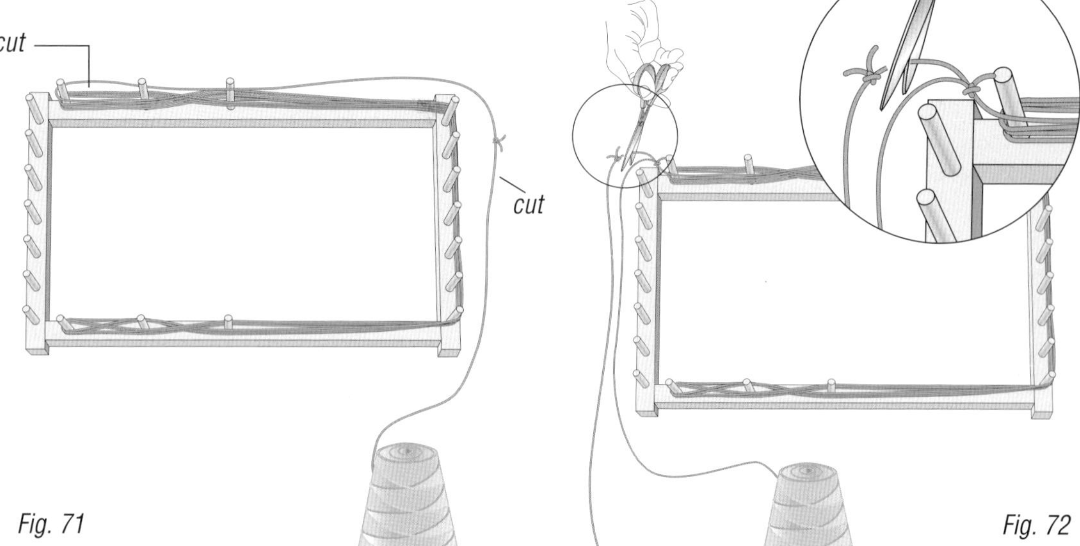

Fig. 71

Fig. 72

(7) Tie the Crosses

Cut 12 pieces of string about 8 inches long. If you have 2 colors of string, cut 6 pieces of each color. If possible, use colors that contrast with the warp color. (A third color string will be needed in Step 9.)

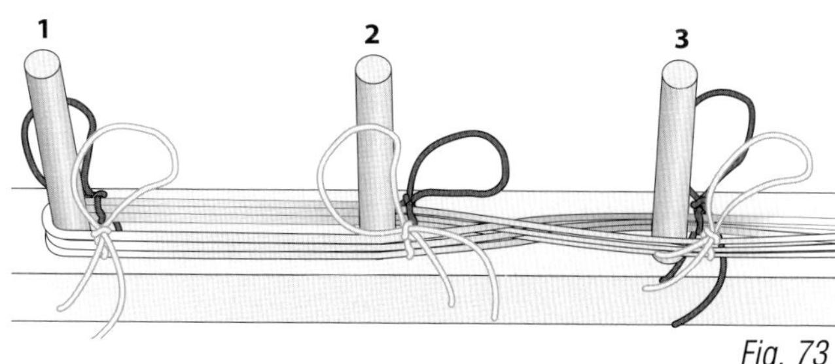

Fig. 73

The first ties to make are where the crosses are. You'll tie half-bows around the warp threads on ***the top and bottom*** of the #2 and #3 pegs and #6 and #7 pegs. There also will be ties at both ends of the warp for a total of 12 ties—4 at each of the cross locations and 2 at each of the end pegs. Try not to include the guide string in the half-bow knots (Regular bows are OK, too, but take more effort to undo later.) If you have two colors of strings, put one color around the warp threads that are on the tops of all the pegs and the other color around the warps that are at the bottom of the pegs. Figure 73 shows these ties and the ones to be tied next, those at the end pegs of the warp. Figure 74 shows how to tie the half bows.

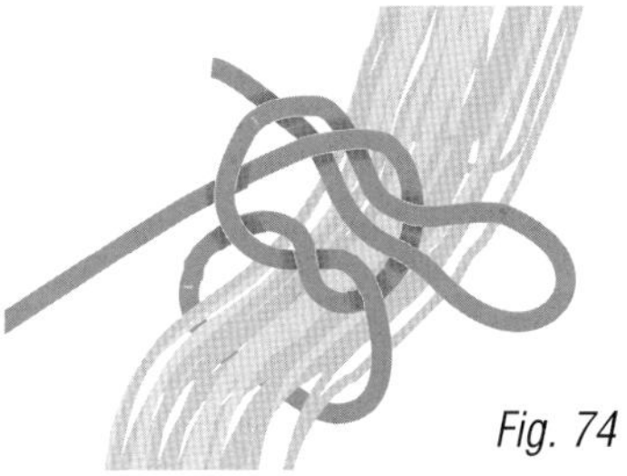

Fig. 74

(8) Tie the Ends of the Warp

The next sets of ties to make are at the end pegs at each end of the warp—pegs #1 and #5. At these pegs, tie half bows around the warps that are going above the pegs, and make another tie around the warps that are going under the pegs. Again, without including the guide string, color code the ties as before with the same color ties on the tops of the pegs and the other color on the bottoms of the pegs. Make the ties within the loops you made at the beginning and end of the warp. See Figure 75. Tying inside the loops as shown is very important.

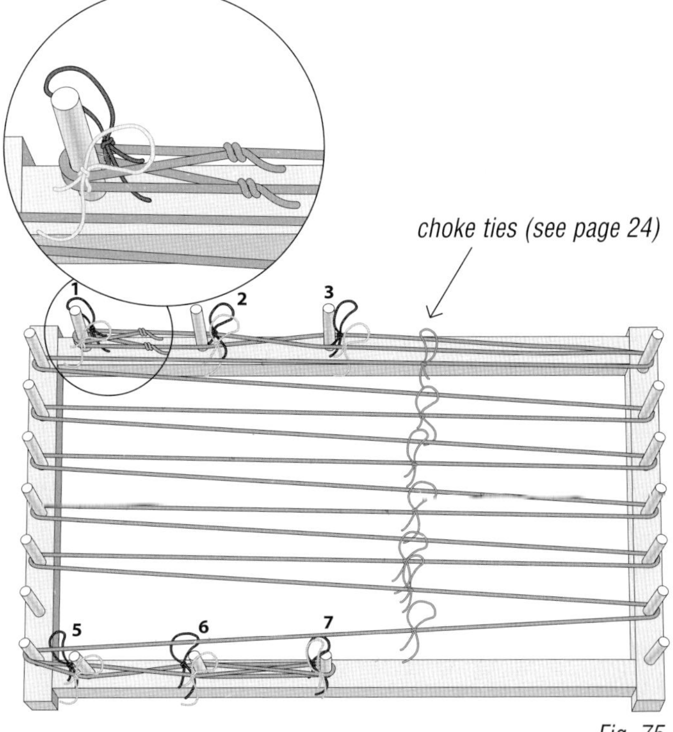

Fig. 75

Remember to tie both ends of the warp in this way. ***If you do not do this important step, you'll get the situation shown on page 34. A remedy to the problem is given on that page.***

> ***Remember*** *to tie two (2) ties at each end peg and 4 ties for each cross. There should be six (6) ties at each end of the warp for a total of 12 ties, not counting the choke ties.*

⑨ Tie the Choke Ties

Choke ties are ***very tight ties*** made every yard or so for the length of the warp. Figure 76 shows the choke ties that would be made for a long warp. If possible, use a different color thread from those used for the cross ties–that way there's no danger of untying the wrong ties later. Tie one choke tie about two feet from the group cross, then, tie another one about in the middle of the warp, between that tie and the end of the warp. For choke ties to do their job, they must be tied very tightly around the warp.

To make a choke tie tight, take a strong string around the warp twice and pull the ends taut. Then, tie a bow or a ½ bow on top of the warp at that spot. You can feel the string "bite" into the warps when you do that first step of going around the warp twice. See Figure 77, 78, and 79. The warps should be pinched tightly together at the point of the tie so that no single warp threads can slip past the tie.

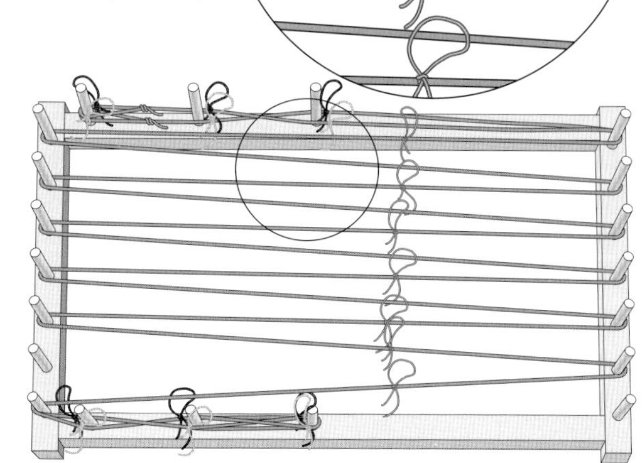

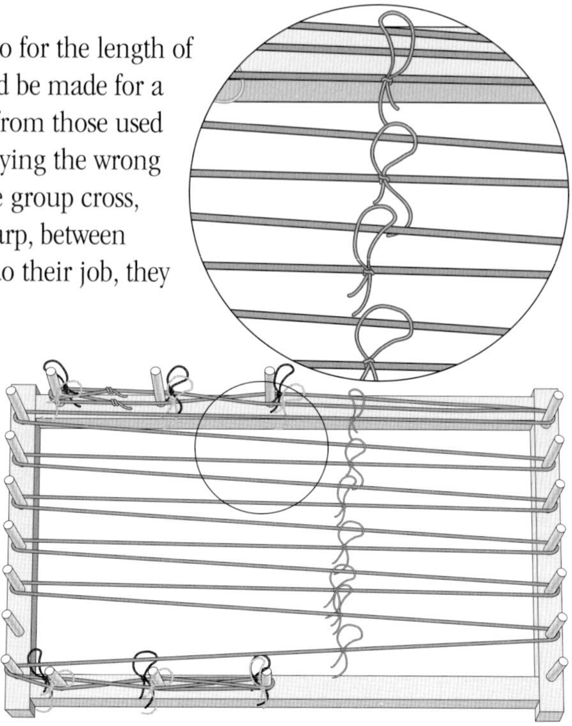

Fig. 76

Check all the ties

Check again to be sure you tied off everything.

- Tie both sides of the beginning and end loop pegs. (There will be 4 ties made.).
- Tie both sides of all the cross pegs. (There will be 8 ties.)
- Tie tight choke ties about every yard. (There will be a total of 2 ties.)
- Tie one of the choke ties about two feet from the group cross.

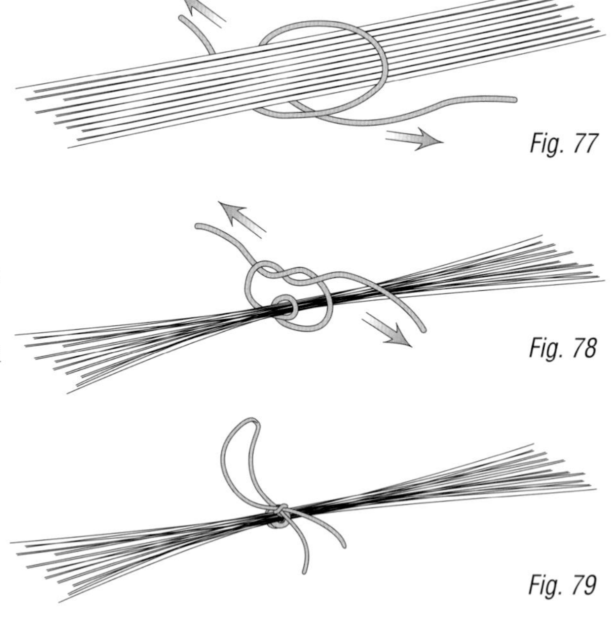

Fig. 77

Fig. 78

Fig. 79

> *For wide warps with many warp threads, I tie a counting string around every 5 raddle groups. I do this near the raddle cross and it helps to keep count. Read about the counting string in the Appendix on page 379.*

⑩ Remove the Warp

The warp will be wound on a stick in the same way a kitestick is wound. See Figure 80. Use your 1½"x ½" x 12" stick, or a ruler or a yardstick. This is the way I prefer to hold the warp at this point. It isn't necessary to wind the stick precisely. The instructions look harder to follow than they really are. Follow them any way you can at first, and master the technique another time. What's important is that the warp is wound up onto a stick so the threads can't tangle. Another way to take the warp off the warping board is given on page 34.

Before you begin, look at the points below, and read about the trick to winding the kitestick at the end of point 5.

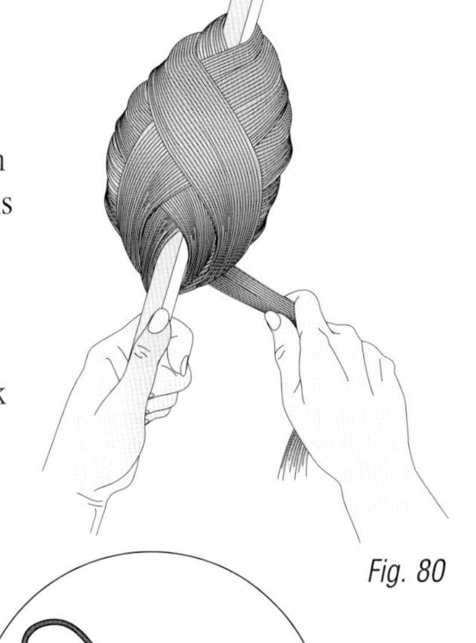

Fig. 80

Winding the kitestick

Begin by taking the warp off the warping board at the top end peg. See Figure 81. You just want to take off the beginning of the warp (at peg #1), say, about a foot of it. It may be that more of the warp comes off the board, and that's OK.

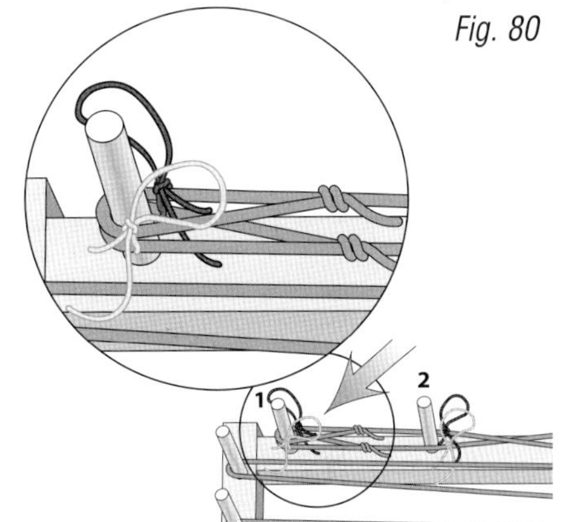

Fig. 81

1. With the loop at the end of the warp, form a lark's head knot over the stick. Be sure to include the loops of the first and last warp threads when you begin to form the lark's head knot. Look carefully where my forefinger and thumb are in Figure 82. To form the lark's head knot, reach with your finger and thumb through the loop and grasp a portion of the warp coming from the warping board. Make a new loop out of the warp itself by pulling some of the warp through the loop, and put the newly formed loop onto the stick. Pull up as big a loop as you need to go on to the stick. It's a little like crocheting. To see exactly how to make a lark's head knot, go to page 352. in the knots section. Figures 82, 83, and 84 show making the knot on the stick. Immediately pull the warp against the lark's head knot to make it firm.

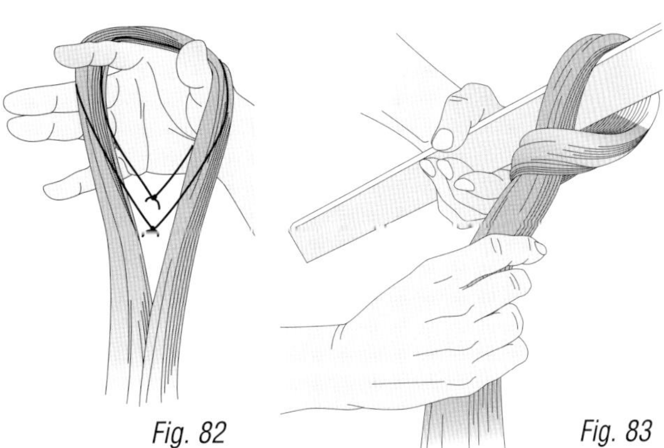

Fig. 82 *Fig. 83*

2. Begin to wind the kitestick with the warp going off to the left, and the loop of the knot behind the warps as in Figure 84. If the warp goes off toward the right, turn the stick upside down. If the loop of the knot is in front of the warps, turn the stick so that it's away from you and behind the warps. You'll be slowly and firmly winding the warp in the direction that tightens the lark's head knot against the stick. This ensures that the warp won't come loose on the stick.

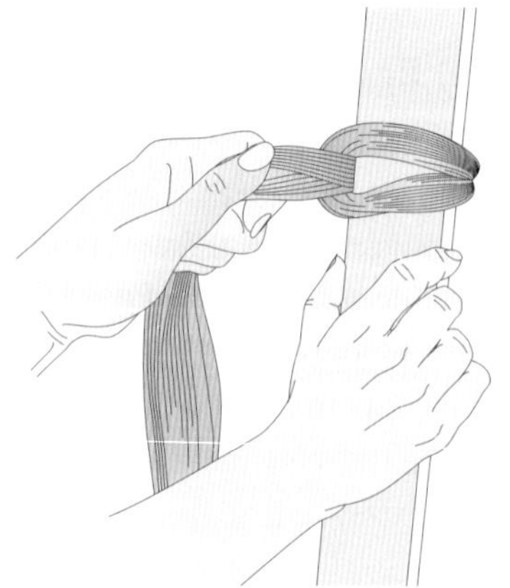

Fig. 84

3. Take the warp with your right hand around behind the stick, as in Figure 85. Then, take the yarn below the knot, and bring it up diagonally in front of the stick. See Figure 86. Then, go around behind the stick, above the knot. You've made the first half of an X.

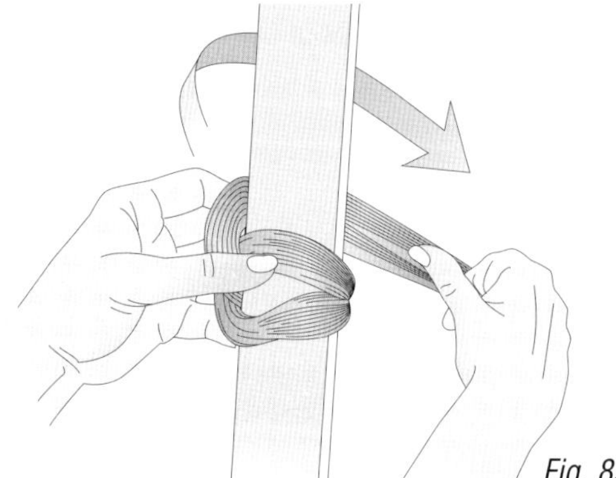

Fig. 85

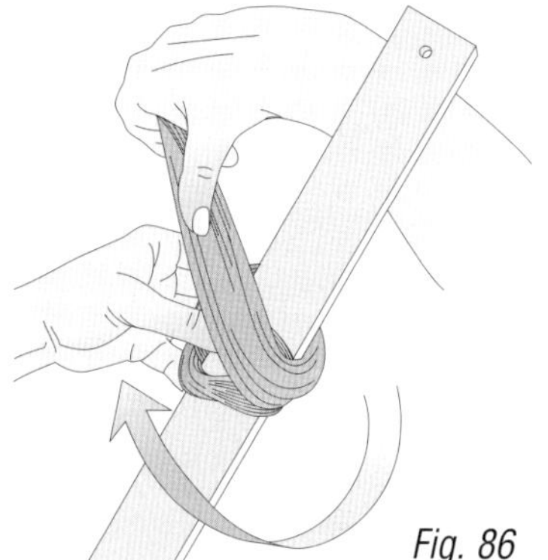

Fig. 86

4. Now, take the warp to the front, diagonally downward, toward the bottom of the knot, making the *other* half of the X. See Figure 87.

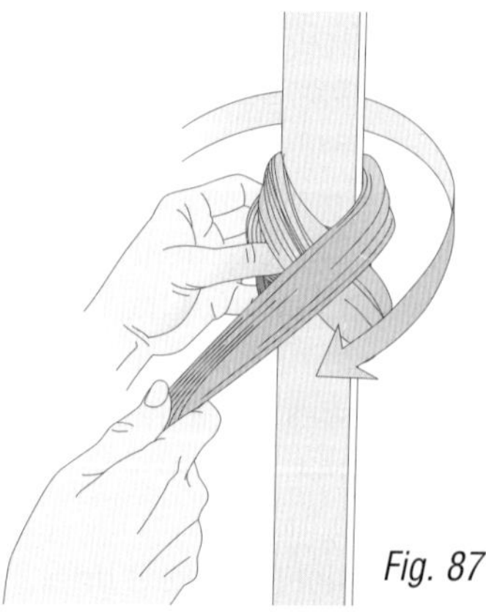

Fig. 87

5. With your left hand, rotate the stick a quarter turn to the left, to the next facet of the stick. This direction keeps the warps tight. You'll be turning your left hand until the palm faces you, as in Figure 88.

The trick is to hold the stick with your left hand, in the middle, where the warps are accumulating. Your left hand should rotate the stick so you can easily wind above and below the lark's head knot with your right hand in point 6.

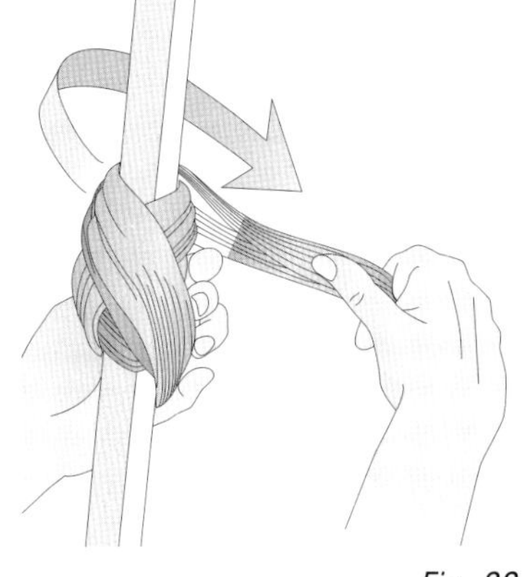

Fig. 88

6. Make an X on the new facet of the stick as in Figures 88 and 89.

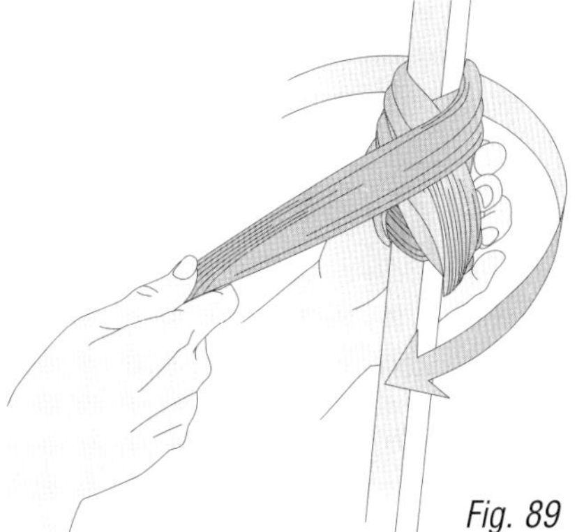

Fig. 89

7. After you have completed the X on that facet of the stick, take the warp behind the stick in preparation for turning the stick a quarter turn and beginning a new X on the third facet of the stick. See Figure 90.

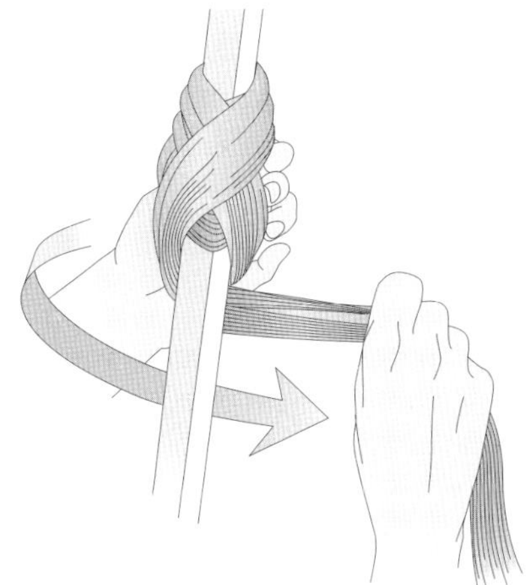

Fig. 90

8. Continue this process (points 3-7) of making an X on a facet of the stick, turning the stick a quarter turn to the next facet, making an X, and so on.

9. When the entire warp is wound, you can just lay the end of the warp on top of the bundle on the stick or tie it to the bundle if that seems more secure.

Put the Warp in the Raddle

Note: Your raddle should sit flat on a table without being tippy. Use clamps if necessary to hold it securely in place.

Undo some of the warp on the kitestick—say, about 2 feet.

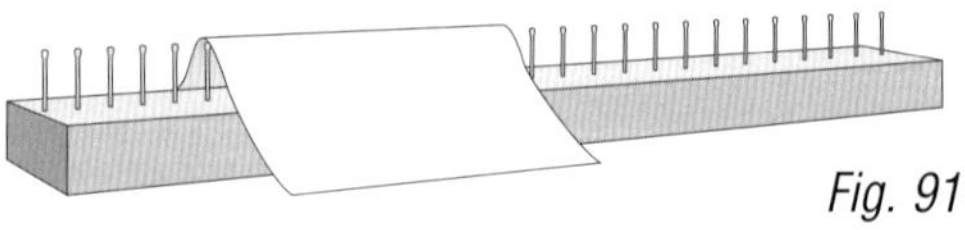

Fig. 91

Put a folded piece of paper over the teeth of the raddle as shown in Figure 91. The paper is there to prevent the teeth from snagging threads. Lay about one foot of the warp over the raddle, on top of the paper, with the group cross toward you. The bulk of the warp remains on the kitestick, and is behind the raddle, away from you.

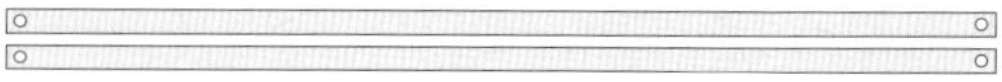

Insert a pair of lease sticks (Figure 92) in the places where the group cross pegs were on the warping board. It's easy to find the exact place by separating the warp where the cross ties are. If you pull the sets of ties apart from each other slightly, you will see the spaces to insert the two sticks. See Figures 93 and 94. Note in the illustrations that you want to separate only the ties on either side of the cross, not the space at the end of the loop where the false cross is located at this time. Be sure you're working with the group cross—the cross with groups of threads as shown in Figure 94a.

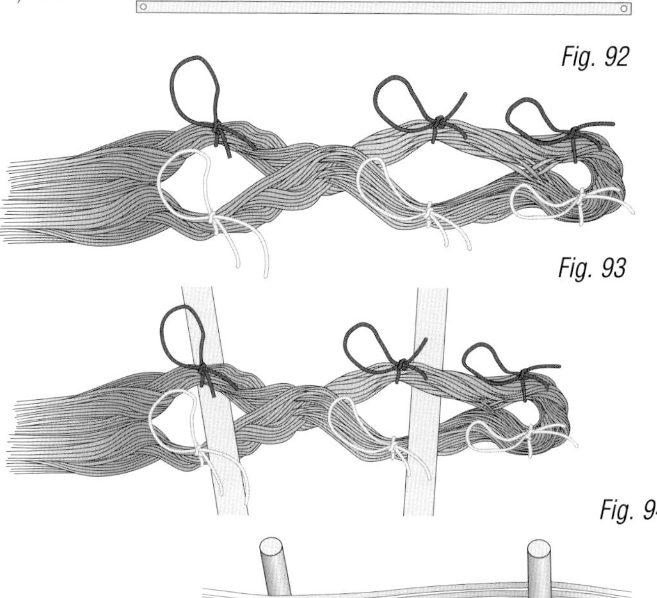

Fig. 92

Fig. 93

Fig. 94

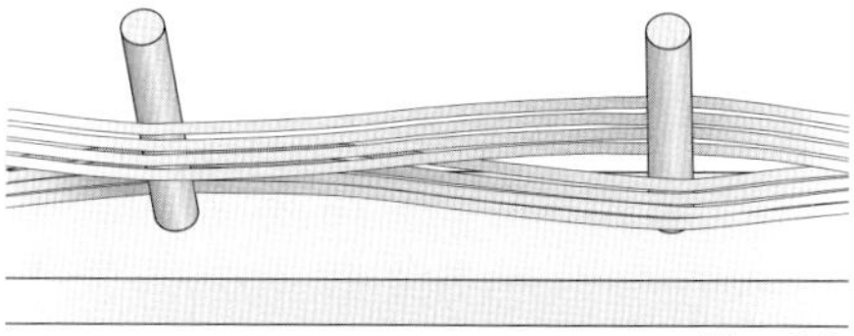

Fig. 94a

With the sticks in the group cross, tie the sticks together about an inch apart. I use half bows or bows to tie the sticks together. See Figure 95.

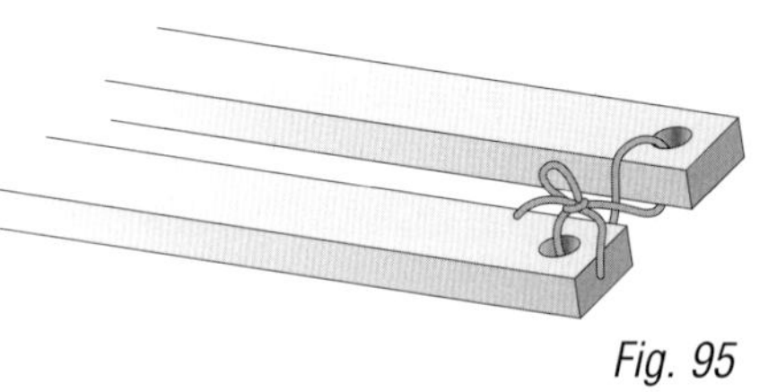

Fig. 95

Undo the 4 ties holding the group cross and spread out the warps on the lease sticks. See Figure 96.

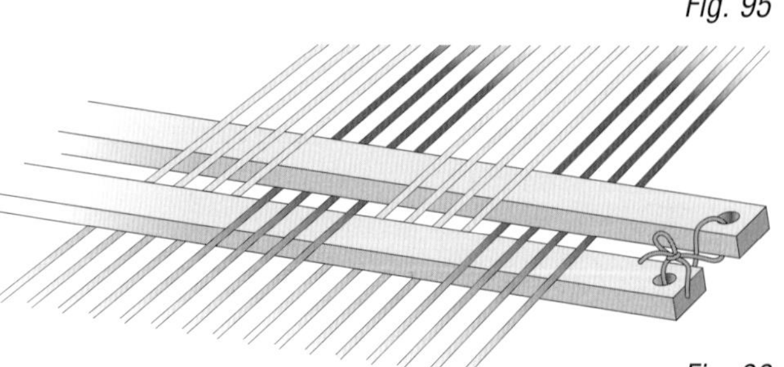

Fig. 96

Put the end stick in the warp's end loop as shown in Figure 97. Remember, be sure the stick is ***not*** longer than the warp beam on your loom—specifically; it must be short enough that it can lie on the beam without interfering with the brake or ratchet mechanism on the warp beam.

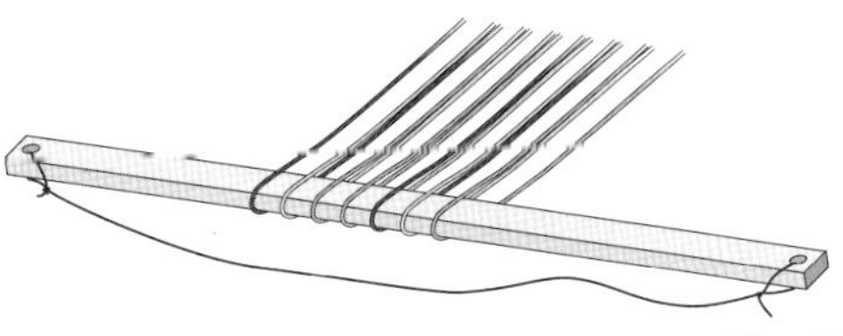

Fig. 97

Tie a string onto the end stick from one hole to the other, as in Figure 97, to hold the warp securely onto it. Some slack in the string is OK, but the knots at each end should be tight and not come undone. Untie the 2 ties at the warp's end loop.

If you don't have an end loop as shown to put on the end stick, go to page 34 and read what to do so you can put the warp onto the endstick. It is important that all the warp's end loops are placed onto the endstick.

Note: Test the ties on the end stick and on the lease sticks to be sure they are secure—they must not come undone.

Load the raddle

Here is how to put the warp groups into the spaces in the raddle. Working from the lease sticks makes it easy to find the groups and to put them in the spaces in their proper order. Figure 98 shows how to position the raddle, lease sticks, end stick and the bulk of the warp. Setting a heavy book or other weight on the bulk of the warp makes it easier to see the groups in the sticks. Spread out the warp slightly on the sticks, then, pick up the end stick and tug lightly against the weight. Almost magically, you'll see the groups of threads.

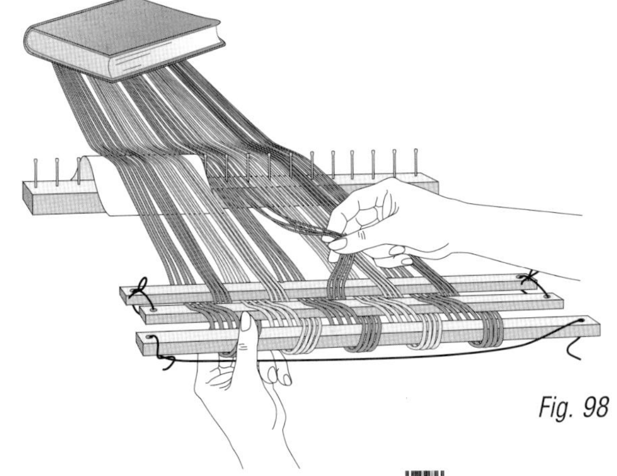

Fig. 98

It will be easier to load the raddle if you move the lease sticks close to the end stick as shown in Figure 98. To move the lease sticks you need to move the cross. Here's how to move the cross: Separate the threads behind the lease stick that is further away from you—since you'll be moving the cross toward you, away from the raddle. Open a space between the threads as if you were opening the long handles of a pair of hedge clippers; the threads will pivot at the point where they cross. See Figure 99. If you gently widen the gap, as if opening the clipper handles wider, you see that the cross moves. Move the cross gently, don't force it to move. Move it to the position shown in Figure 98.

If the cross is hard to move, divide the warp into sections and move each section separately.

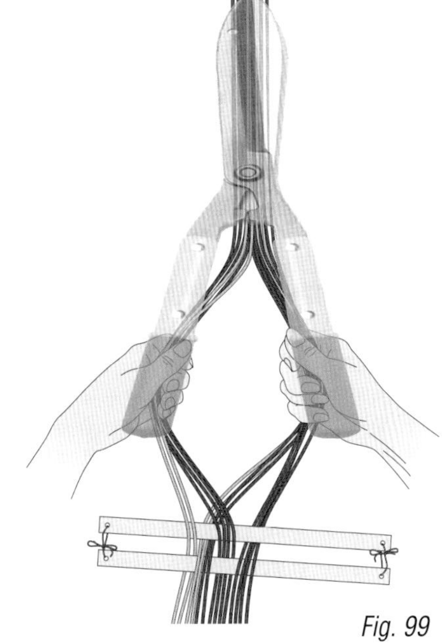

Fig. 99

Secure the Raddle

Center the warp in the raddle by finding the middle of the raddle and measuring 2 ½" out to each side. The 5" wide warp you are making then will be in the center of the raddle. Hold the end stick and both lease sticks in your left hand while you fill the raddle with your right hand. See Figure 98 on the previous page. Start at one edge and work across, dropping whole groups from the group cross, in order, between the teeth of the raddle. If you find a mistake in the group cross, with two groups together, never split up the group arbitrarily. Instead, leave an empty space beside the double group. In other words, there will be a double group in one raddle space and an empty space next to it, so the warps will still be spread out to the planned width of the warp.

Where is the false cross?

You may notice that now, after you've loaded the raddle, that the false cross no longer exists. It disappeared when you put the groups of threads into the raddle. You can see that the loops on the end stick now go in straight paths as in Figure 100.

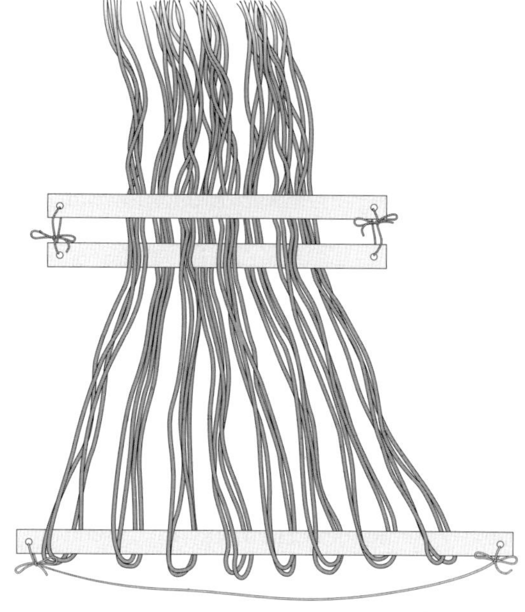

Fig. 100

Secure the threads in the raddle with rubber bands.

See Figure 101. Place the rubber bands across several pins and slightly above the warp threads, not touching them. If your raddle has a wooden cap, put rubber bands on as above. When it is completely loaded, remove the rubber bands and place the cap on the top of the pins. Then be sure to tie the cap onto the raddle. Make a tie in the center of the raddle first, then at 3" intervals, working out from the center. See Figure 101a.

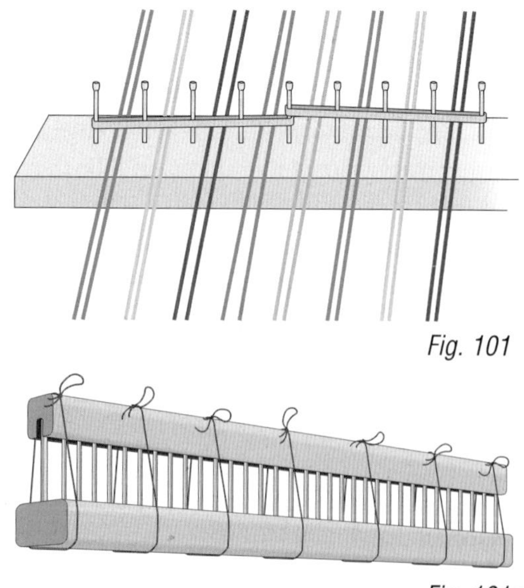

Fig. 101

Fig. 101a

Now you're ready to put the warp on the loom. Instructions start in Part Two.

More about measuring the warp

I. Using warping pegs instead of a warping board

You can use warping pegs to measure out your warp. They aren't ideal, but they are easy to store and inexpensive. You'll want two sets, and clamps to anchor them securely. Read where to find the pegs and clamps in the Sources section beginning on page 382. You'll need to clamp the pegs in four places. Clamp the first, single peg for the beginning of your warp and one of the pairs of pegs a few inches away from it, say, 6 or 8 (or fewer) inches away. Then, clamp the other single peg where the end of your warp should be–the length of your guide string. (You will need to make the guide string a little longer than where the memory knot is so you can tie it around the end peg.) Clamp the remaining pair of pegs several inches in from the end peg–say, about 6 or 8 inches from it. See Figure 102. The exact placement of the pairs of pegs isn't critical. I don't recommend investing much in warping pegs if you think you'll become a weaver because they can take up lots of real estate when measuring out longer warps, and a warping board is sturdier and much more satisfactory.

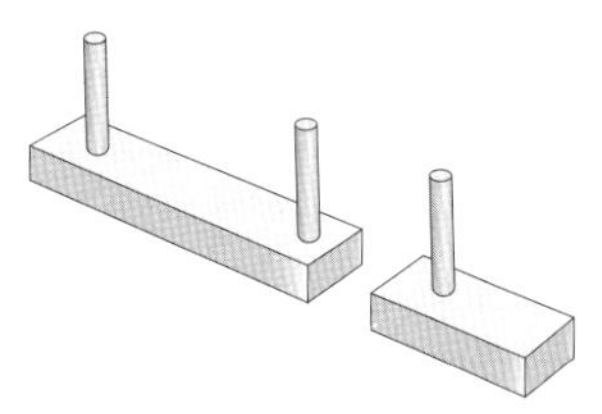

Fig. 102

II. Making a homemade raddle

Use a piece of scrap lumber (but use soft wood) as long as the width of your loom and about 2" wide. It should be about 1" thick. Mark ½" increments along the whole length on a line that is ¾" in from one long edge. This indentation offsets the nails to make room for clamps to clamp the raddle to the loom. Pound finishing nails or nails with small heads at every ½" mark. See Figure 103.

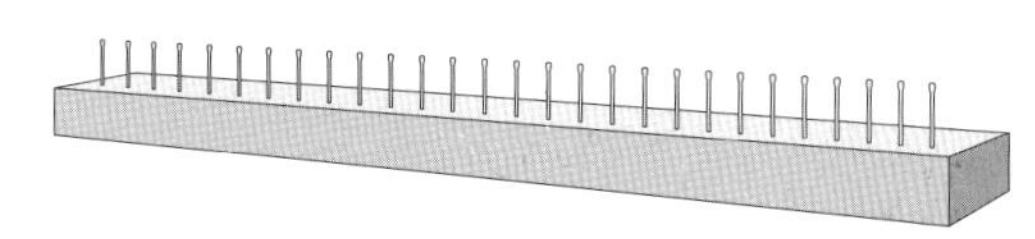

Fig. 103

III. Using other yarns for the sampler

Other yarns can be used for the sampler. They can be different sizes, but all warp yarns need the special consideration listed below. Read about the adjustments that need to be made for different yarns on the next page.

Suitable yarns for warp yarns

- Plied yarns—you should clearly see diagonal lines on the yarn. See Figure 104.
- Strong—cannot be broken easily with your hands
- Smooth—no lumps, loops, or fuzz
- Not stretchy, such as knitting yarns
- A suitable thickness for the project

Figure 106 on page 32 shows yarns suitable and not suitable for the sampler. Check the size of your yarn by placing it on the pictures and matching your yarn to the one closest in size in the chart.

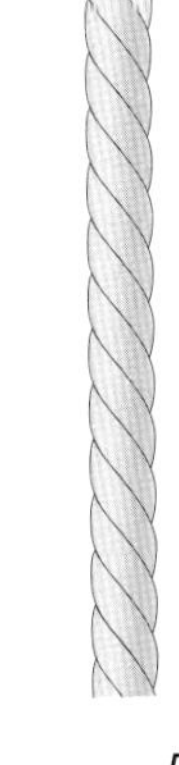

Fig. 104

Size of yarn and how many ends per inch

Adjustments need to be made for different size warp yarns

If you wrap your yarn around a ruler for one inch, you will easily see that fatter threads have fewer wraps per inch and thinner ones more, as seen in Figure 105. When weavers talk about the number of threads per inch, they use the word "ends" for warp threads and say, "ends per inch," abbreviated as epi. The chart in Figure 106 shows different size yarns appropriate for the sampler and the number of threads that will be needed per inch in the warp (epi). The chart also indicates the epi for both twill weave and for plain weave. Note that for 5/2 cotton, 20 threads per inch are called for in the Twill Weave Column and 16 epi in the Plain Weave Column. The twill weave needs to have more ends per inch because the wefts pack down more with this weave structure.

Fig. 105

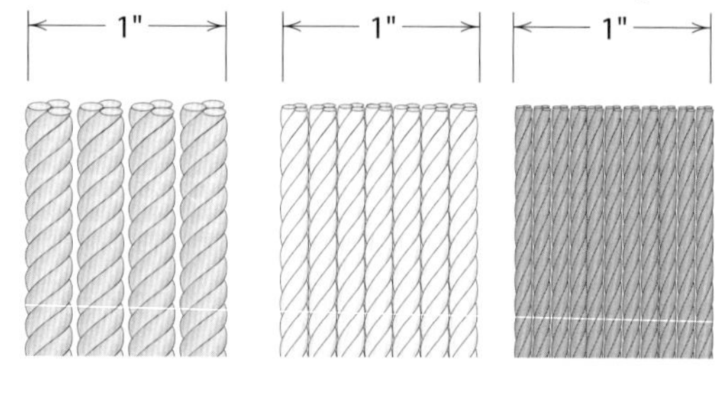

Place your yarn on top of the yarn in the chart that is the same or close to the size of your chosen yarn and note how many ends per inch you should use for that particular yarn. For the sampler, I recommend using the epi for twill weave because the sampler is mostly woven with twill weaves. Other projects (for exam-

Yarn & Sett Chart

Yarn	Yards per Pound	Ends per Inch (epi) Plain Weave (tabby)	Ends per Inch (epi) Twill Weave
5/2 Pearl Cotton	2,100	16 epi	20 epi
Sport-weight Wool	1,750	15 epi	18 epi
2-ply Wool	1,475	12 epi	16 epi
Worsted-weight Wool	800	10 epi	12 epi
Rayon Chenille	1,450	16 epi	N/A
Rug Wool	260	Too Fat for Sampler	
10/2 Pearl cotton	4,200	Too Thin for Sampler	
Mohair Bouclé	1,175	Not Smooth Enough	

Fig. 106

ple, on page 235) recommend that the epi for plain weave be used. You can refer to this chart for future projects, some of which require the epi for plain weave and some for twill. Often, directions in books or magazines give the epi for the yarn and the weave structure used in their projects.

Another way to know the size of a yarn is by the number of yards of it there are in one pound. This is indicated by yards per pound or ypp. The finer the thread, the more yards there will be in a pound, and the reverse, fewer ypp indicates a fatter yarn. You can see this in the chart.

IV. Size of yarn and the number of threads in the group cross

The number of threads or yarns in the group cross is determined by the number of threads in one inch (epi). If your raddle has spaces of ½" between nails or pegs, then ½ the number of epi is the number of threads to put in the groups in the group cross. If your raddle has larger, 1" spaces, then the number of threads per group will equal the number of threads in an inch—the epi. (For our project, using 5/2 pearl cotton, at 20 epi, and a raddle with ½" spaces, we have made groups of ten warp threads or ½ the epi.)

V. Substitute reeds

The ideal is to put two warp threads in each space in the reed. However, often, weavers do not have the size of reed that a project requires, and they need to substitute with a reed that they do have. This situation happens because reeds are expensive, so you may not have many different ones on hand. The substitute reed may not give the cloth the exact look that the ideal reed will give, but generally, if the guideline is followed, you can accept the slight variation in the look of the cloth. Often, but not always, the differences will not be visible after the cloth has been washed. How to use the chart is explained on page 73.

The guideline

The cloth will look distorted if you put a large number of threads, say, 4 threads, in one space in the reed. The threads will be grouped together in the spaces, and there will be vertical lines in the cloth between the groups. These vertical lines are called reed marks. This is an important concept. You cannot expect many threads grouped in the spaces in the reed to disperse evenly in the cloth after washing the cloth—the reed marks will remain.

Figure 107 shows a chart of reed substitutions for the yarns suitable for the sampler. More details on page 73.

Reed Substitution Chart

When you don't have the ideal reed to sley two warp ends per dent, use this substitution chart.

Sequence in dents = the number of empty spaces in the reed and the number of threads in each space.

Example: 0-1-1 = The sequence to sley the reed, repeated for the width of the warp:
1 empty dent
1 thread in a dent
1 thread in a dent
or "empty-1-1; empty-1-1", etc.

	Reed size (Dents per inch)					
Sequence of warps in the dents	8	10	12	15	18	20
	Warp Ends Per Inch (epi or sett)					
0-1	4	5	6	7½	9	10
0-1-1	5	7	8	10	12	13
0-1-1-1	6	7½	9	11½	13½	15
1	8	10	12	15	18	20
1-1-1-2	10	12½	15	19	22½	25
1-1-2	11	13	16	20	24	27
1-2	12	15	18	22½	27	30
1-2-2	13	17	20	25	30	33
1-2-2-2	14	17½	21	26	31½	35
2	16	20	24	30	36	40

Fig. 107

VI. Warps that are too big for the warping board

Read about this on page 190.

VII. Putting the end loops onto the end stick

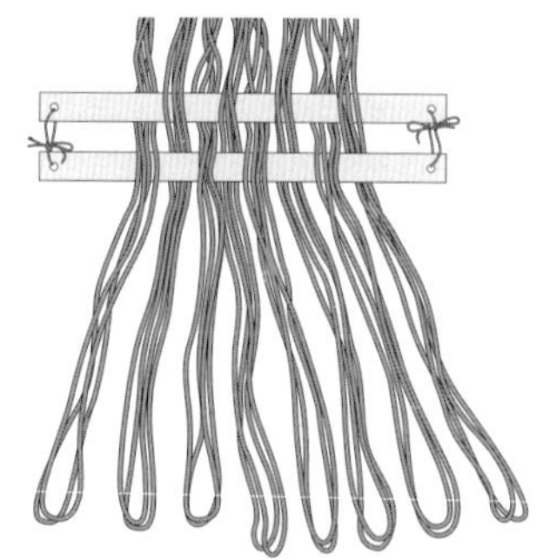
Fig. 108a

You may find that when you have put in the lease sticks for the group cross, you don't have the situation shown in Figure 98 on page 29 for loading the raddle. Instead, you have the situation shown in Figure 108a. This state of affairs happens when you don't tie the end loops at the end peg at the group cross end of the warping board. Some of my students have not realized how important it is to tie the end pegs ***at both ends of the warping board*** (pegs #1 and #7 in Figure 75 on page 23).

Because these ties were not made at the group cross position, the ends of the warp are loose, and you cannot put them onto the end stick easily. To remedy this situation, you will need to pick up the loops from each group, in order, and place them onto the end stick yourself. It is not too difficult unless you have a big warp with lots of warp threads.

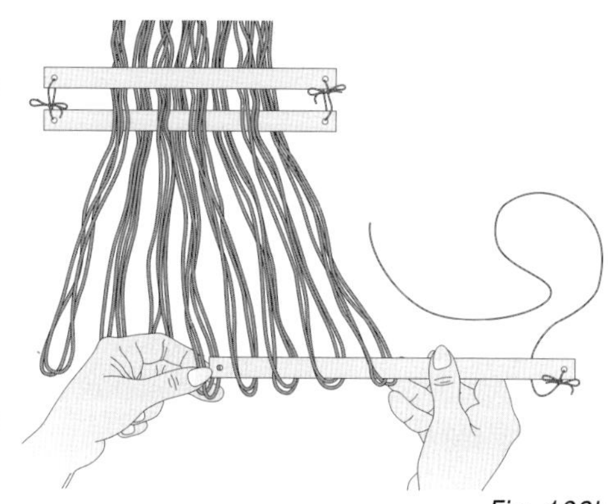
Fig. 108b

Figure 108b shows how to manually put the end loops onto the end stick. First, splay out the loops a bit so you can see them in order. Then, with your end stick (notice that it has its string attached to one end) pick up the loops one-at-a-time and put them on the end stick. In a sense, you are "threading" the loops onto the stick. Another way to think of it is that you are working the end stick through the loops. It's not necessary to separate out the individual loops within the groups—just place the group itself onto the stick. However, it's important that they are in order.

This problem will be avoided in the future if you make the ties at the end peg at the group cross end on the warping board before taking the warp off the board.

VIII. Chaining instead of the kitestick

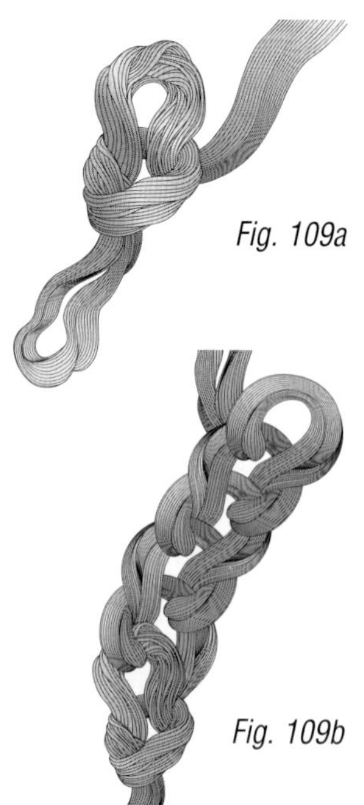
Fig. 109a

Fig. 109b

This is a method commonly used by weavers, but is not as desirable as the kitestick method because it doesn't keep the threads under tension as the kitestick does. However, since it is done so often, I am putting it here for you to try if you like. A completed chain is shown in Figure 109b.

Begin at the top of the warping board (the end with the thread-by-thread cross) as shown in Figure 81 on page 25. Take a portion of the warp off the warping board and make a slip knot, as shown in Figure 109a. How to make a slip knot is explained on page 349.

Reach your thumb and forefinger through the loop in the slip knot and grasp the warp, pulling it through the first loop just enough to make a new (second) loop. Continue with your forefinger and thumb through this second loop and grasp the warp, again pulling the warp through that second loop, forming another new loop—the third one. Continue pulling the warp through the just-made loops to form the new loops until all the warp is in the chain. You will stop when there isn't enough warp left to make another loop. Figure 109b shows the completed chain. More details are on page 162.

Back-to-Front Warping

Part Two: Putting the Warp on the Loom (Beaming)

Putting the warp onto the loom is called beaming the warp. It's not hard or fiddly to do, but it is extremely important and needs to be done with care. The whole weaving process depends on even tension of the warp threads on the loom. Following the steps in this section will give you the even tension you need. You have measured the warp carefully already. Winding the warp onto the loom's warp beam under even and tight tension will complete the processes needed for the weaving to be a pleasure—and that's the goal we are striving for.

The parts of the loom can be seen on page 56.

Equipment List: See Chapter 2, Equipment.

Broom handle, dowel, or long stick:

Clamps (2): If your loom doesn't have a back beam or the beam is on a slant and doesn't have an attachment device from the loom manufacturer, use clamps.

Packing sticks:

Packing Paper: For example, a paper grocery bag cut as per instructions in Step Two.

Rubber bands:

Scissors:

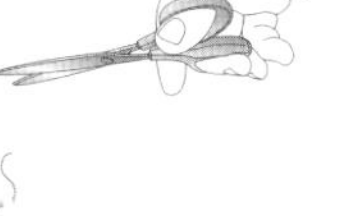

String:

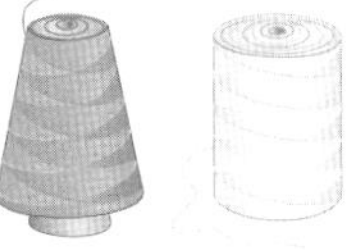

Tape Measure:

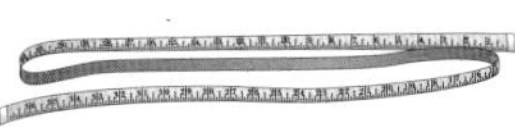

Warp loaded in the raddle:

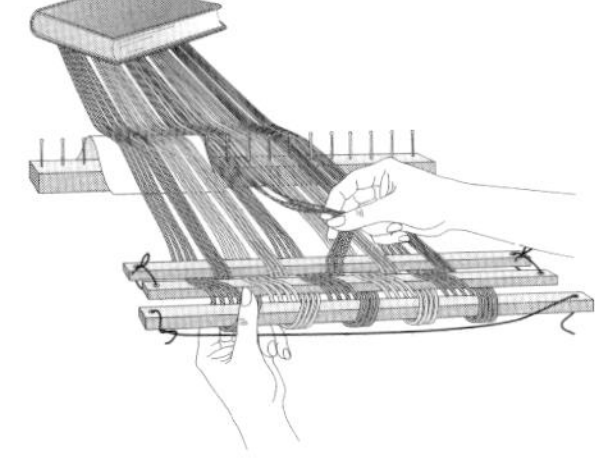

① Preliminary Work to Do

Be sure the warp is secure in the raddle: It's a good idea to have several rubber bands overlapping themselves. They should be about half way up on the nails, not touching the warp. See Figure 110a.

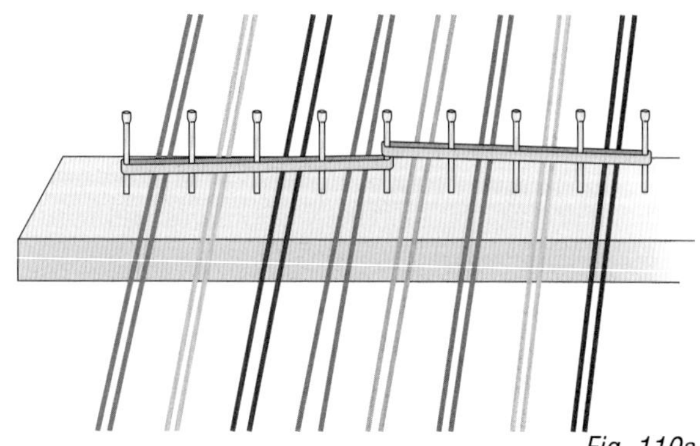

Fig. 110a

If your raddle has a wooden cap, be sure it is tied securely to the base of the raddle. Ties should be about 3" apart. See Figure 110b.

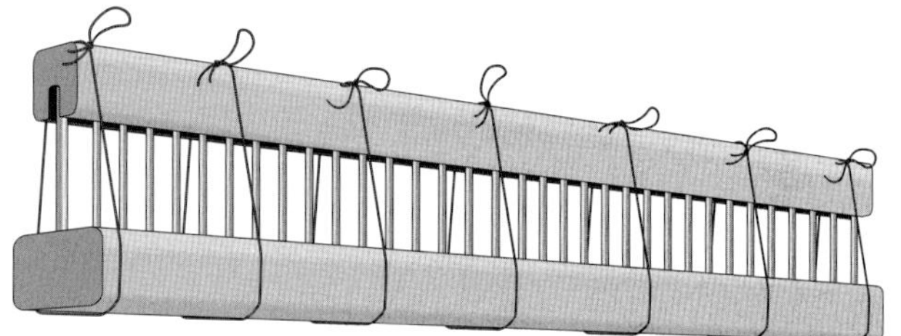

Fig. 110b

Check the raddle for mistakes: It's easy to spot mistakes made while loading the raddle if you push the lease sticks up close to the raddle. If you find threads or groups crossed, you need to correct them now. See Figure 111. Remember, if you doubled up two groups of threads in one raddle space, leave an empty space in the raddle next to that space. See page 30.

After you have checked that the raddle is loaded correctly, remove the lease sticks that hold the group cross.

Remove the raddle's lease sticks—***not the end stick.***

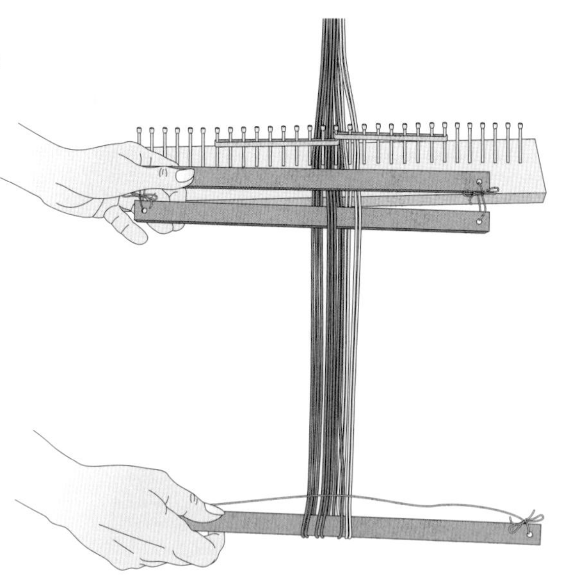

Be sure not to remove the end stick!

Fig. 111

② Prepare the Packing Paper

The principle is this: cut the paper 4" wider than your warp is intended to be and about 2" longer than the circumference of the loom's warp beam. For longer warps, you will need several sheets prepared—say, about one for every yard of warp length. ***The edges should be folded so they are double strength at the edges—these doubled areas will extend beyond the warp as described in Step Seven.*** See Figure 112.

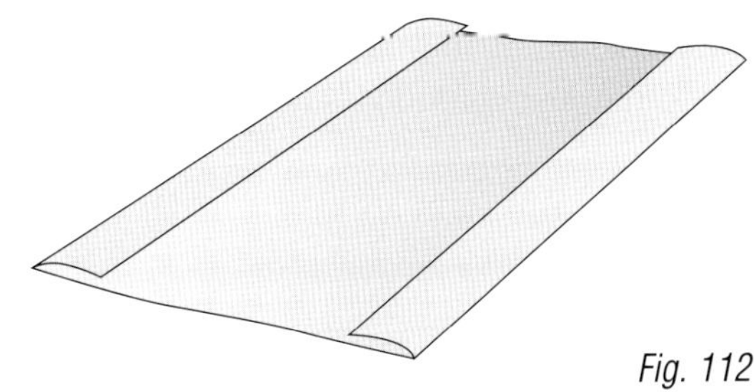

Fig. 112

Use heavy paper such as a grocery bag. Cut off the bottom, cut off any handles, and cut along the seam so it lies flat.

You want to cut two pieces that are 9" wide and as long as 2" more than the circumference of the loom's warp beam.

Fold each of the edges of the 9" length in 1", as shown in Figure 112a. The papers will now each be 7" wide.

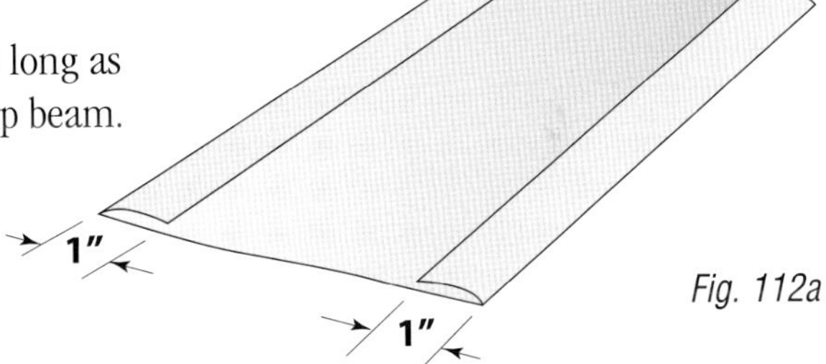

Fig. 112a

Your loom may not require packing paper

Look at the warp beam in the illustration that matches your loom on this page and on page 39. If your warp beam is like Figure 113, or the beam's circumference is very big, say, around 11" or more as in Figure 114, you don't need to use packing paper, so you can move on to Step Three. If your warp beam is like Figure 113, see page 52 for more instructions.

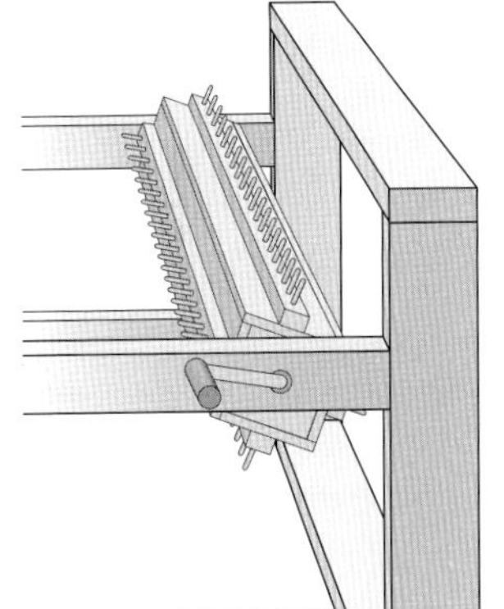

Fig. 113

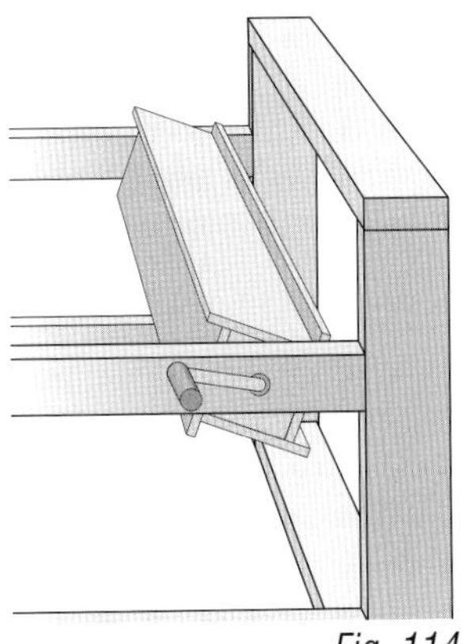

Fig. 114

③ Prepare the Apron (aprons are shown in Figures 119 and 120)

Note: Looms vary in which way the warp beams are wound. You must check that your apron rod is held securely by the brake on the warp beam—regardless of which type of brake you have. Figure 115 shows that some warp beams are wound in one direction and others in the opposite direction.

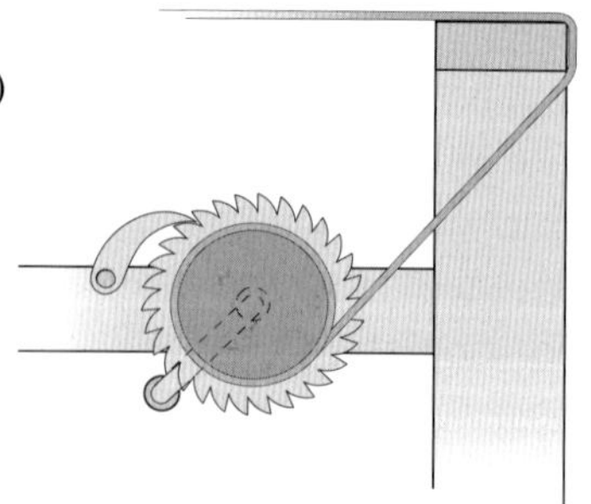

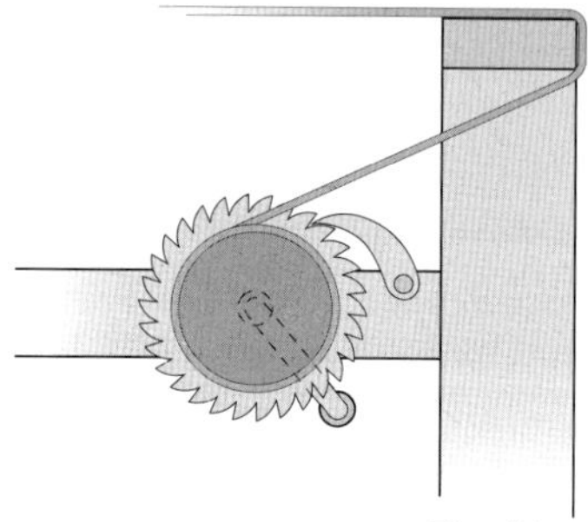

Fig. 115

Note: *Find out which way your loom's warp beam is wound.*

To wind up the apron, you must crank the warp beam in the right direction. If your warp beam has a ratchet at one end, you will know you are cranking in the right direction if you hear the pawl clicking in the ratchet teeth. A ratchet and pawl brake is shown in Figure 116. ***(The ratchet is the part of the brake with the teeth and the pawl is the lever which clicks into the teeth.)***

If your warp beam doesn't have a ratchet, it has a friction brake (also called the tension brake) as shown in Figure 117. In that case, you'll have to experiment to be sure you have wound the apron in the right direction. Pull on the apron rod (Figures 119 and 120)—if it doesn't move, then you have wound the apron in the right way. If it gives or moves, then rewind the apron in the opposite direction. Page 43 shows how this brake works.

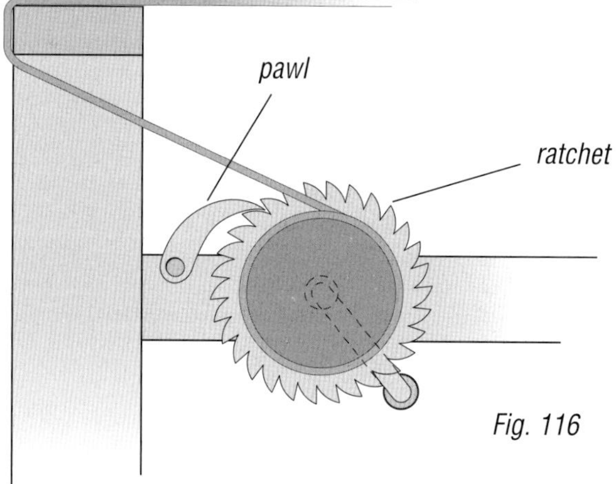

Fig. 116

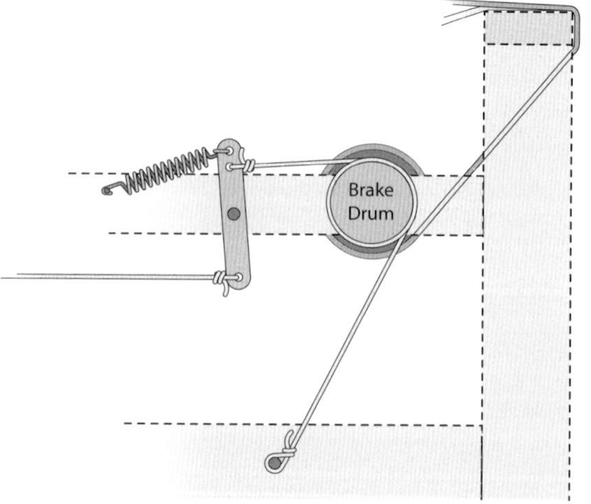

Fig. 117

Wind up the apron strings or cloth apron onto the warp beam so that the apron rod lies on the top of the warp beam as shown in Figure 118. Figure 119 shows an apron made from strings and Figure 120 shows a cloth apron. Eventually the apron rod will take the path shown in Figure 119.)

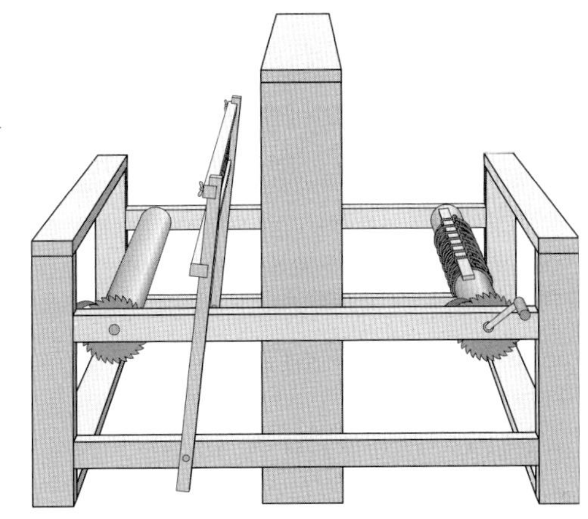

Fig. 118

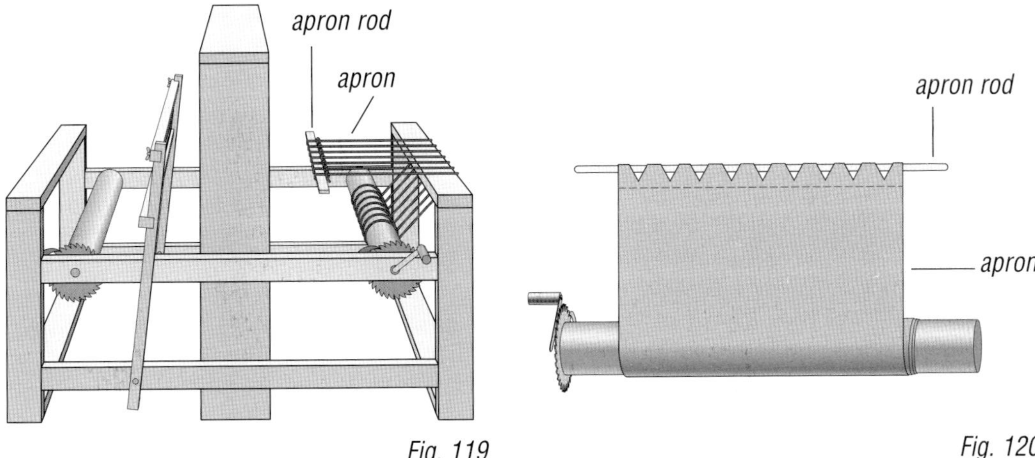

Fig. 119

Fig. 120

> **Note:**
> Be sure that your warp beam is wound in the right direction!!! Some looms have beams that are wound one way and other looms have beams that are to be wound in the opposite direction as shown in Figure 115.

④ Attach the Raddle to the Loom

Where you place the raddle depends upon the type of loom you have. ***Be sure the threads are secured in the raddle*** as seen in Figure 110a on page 36.

For looms with a back beam, you'll put the raddle on the back beam of the loom. The bulk of the warp will go off the back of the loom as shown in Figure 121. Center the warp carefully. Measure from the edges of the warp in the raddle to the outside framework of the loom on the back beam, as shown in Figure 122. Securely attach the raddle to the back beam with several rubber bands, or use clamps. Double up rubber bands or put the rubber bands on in more places, if necessary, to ensure that the raddle is very securely attached and can't wiggle. Figure 123 shows how to use rubber bands. Clamps are shown in Figure 124.

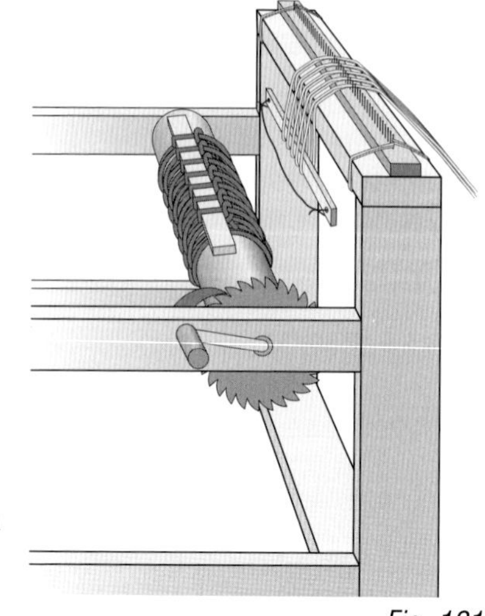

Fig. 121

If the back beam is on a slant, you'll need to clamp the raddle to the back beam. The bulk of the warp will hang off the back of the loom as shown in Figure 121. Center the warp as in Figure 122. The loom manufacturer may have an attachment device of its own, but clamps work very well. See Figure 124.

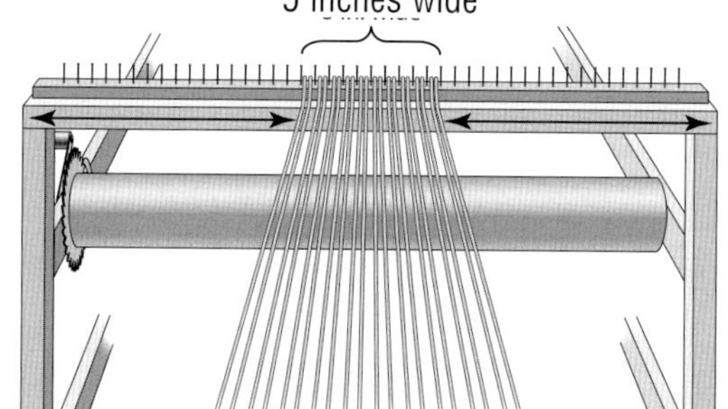

Fig. 122

If the loom has no back beam, attach the raddle on top of the castle with the bulk of the warp going off the front of the loom as shown in Figure 125. Center the warp as in Figure 122. Use clamps or rubber bands or string to secure the raddle tightly to the top of the castle.

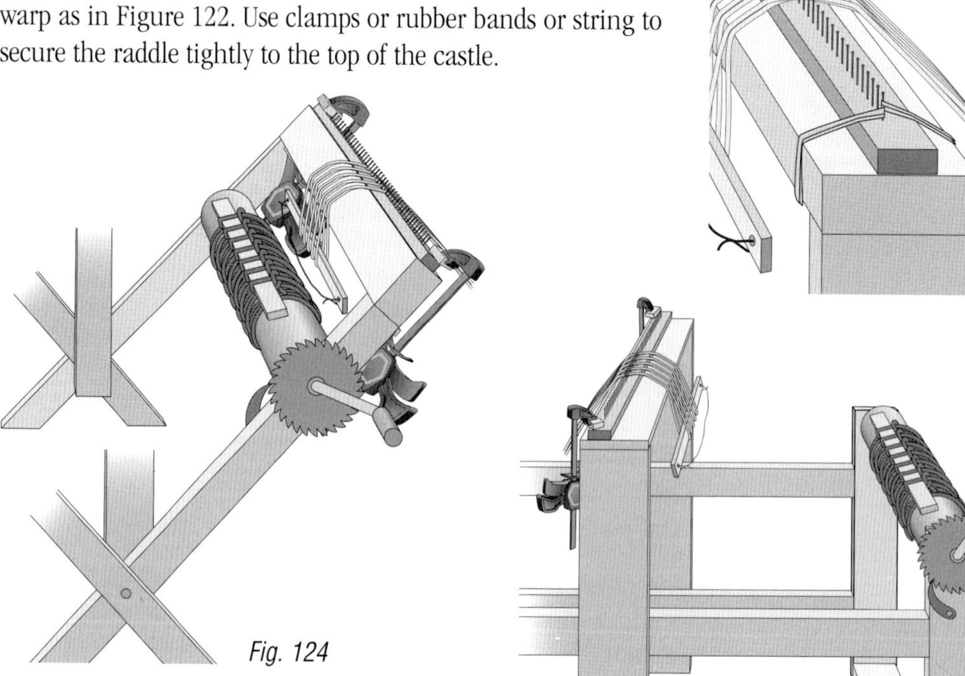

Fig. 123

Fig. 124

Fig. 125

⑤ Attach the End Stick to the Loom

Before beginning this step check once more that your end stick will fit on the loom's warp beam without interfering with the brake., If it is too long, change it *now* to a shorter stick, the longest that will still fit on the beam. Finding out the stick is too long mid-step will be another big frustration.

Hold the bulk of warp at a choke tie and snug up the warp so the end stick is next to the raddle. This action will spread out the warp threads on the end stick so that the warp is at its intended width (5" wide for the sampler). Let the threads be in approximate order—it's important not to try to arrange them or touch them very much at this stage. The main thing is that the threads are spread out on the end stick to the same width as they are in the raddle. See Figure 126. (Sometimes I leave in the lease sticks until this step. Then I take them out.) If the warp is wide, you may need to pull on sections of the warp instead of at the choke tie.

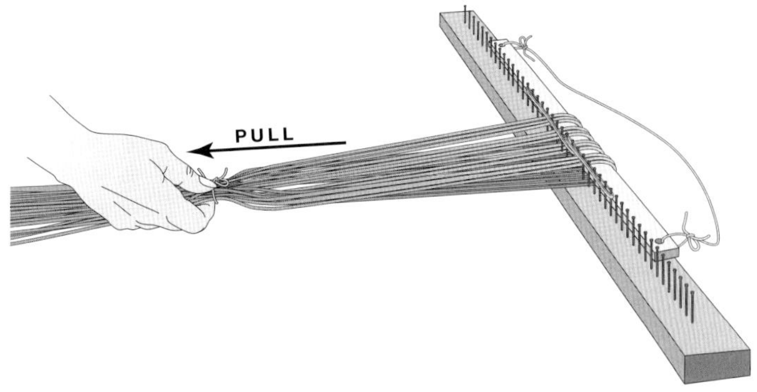

Fig. 126

It's important to center the warp on the end stick if it isn't already.

Now, you are about to connect your warp to the loom by attaching the end stick to the apron rod.

Take the end stick and place it beside or on top of the apron rod, which you have already positioned to lie on the top of the warp beam. (See Figure 118.)

Having the apron wound up on the warp beam makes attaching the end stick to it easier because it is stable on the warp beam and not flapping around while you are trying to attach the end stick to it.

Tie the end stick to the apron rod in this manner: Cut 3 lengths of string, each about 24" long, and double them to make them stronger. The first string will tie the end stick to the apron rod at its center and that of the end stick. Gently lift the apron rod a bit above the warp beam so you can get the string under it. Tie the two sticks together securely. I like to use a bow—it's strong and can be undone if needed later. ***Be sure you are only tying the two sticks together—your tie should not include the warp beam!*** Next, tie the remaining cords around the two sticks—one at each edge of the warp. See Figure 127a.

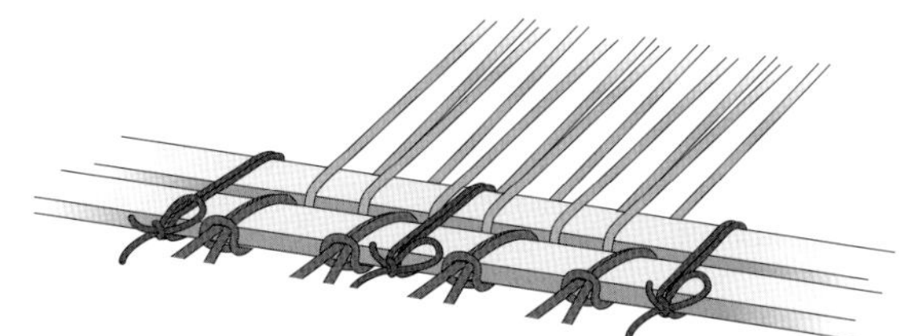

Fig. 127a

For wider warps, the principle for making the attachments is to tie the sticks together in the center and then about 3" apart for the width of the warp. Only make ties for the width of the warp. In other words, don't tie the sticks to each other where there is no warp on the end stick.

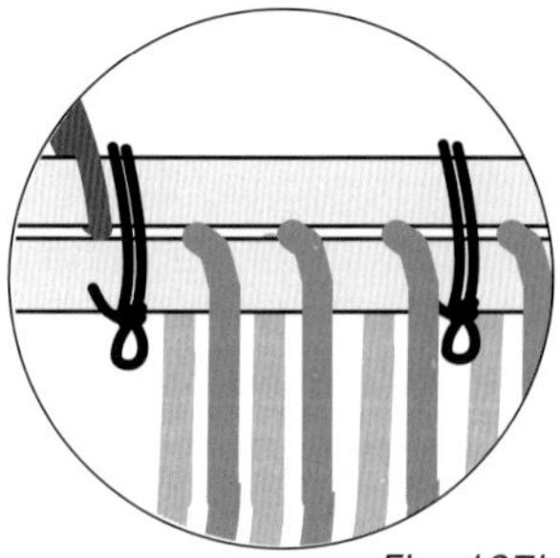

Position the knots on the edge of the end stick where the apron rod and end stick join as in Figure 127b. That position keeps the knots from forming bumps, so that you start winding the warp onto the warp beam with a very flat base. Figure 128 shows how lumpy knots can distort the flat layers of warp that are required as you wind the warp onto the beam in Step 7.

Fig. 127b

See page 50 if your loom has lumpy cords or straps.

Do this task gently and keep the loops spread on the end stick without disturbing them. If the threads are a bit crossed or out of order, that is ok—do not try to put them in perfect order. They are just as they should be the way they were after you spread out the loops above as shown in Figure 126. If you were to disturb the loops too much, you might pull on one side of loops, which would shorten the other sides of the loops. Then the warp threads would not be all the same length, which is what you accomplished so carefully at the warping board.

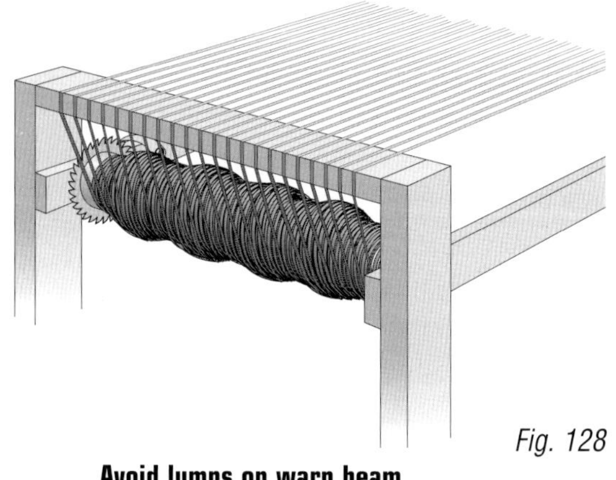

Fig. 128

Avoid lumps on warp beam

⑥ Adjust the End Loops

Now, crank the warp beam to wind one round of warp onto the beam. When you have one turn on the warp beam, the end loops of the warp are vulnerable. Since each warp is continuous with its neighbor on the other side of the end stick, a tug on one warp can shorten its neighbor. If that happens, the threads are no longer smooth and even all across the end stick; the tension of the first turn of the beam has pulled the top or bottom half of the warps over or under the end stick. To fix this situation, lift the end stick so the loops on it are free to re-settle. Gently jiggle or rotate the end stick. You're trying to re-position the end stick so that it is in the exact middle of the loops—exactly at the very end of the warp. You know it's right when the loops look smooth, even, and settled. See Figure 129. Sometimes, after a jiggle, I unwind and re-wind the first revolution of the warps to get the loops even.

Don't do a lot of smoothing and fussing at the first revolution of the warp beam, except at the loops. After the next layer of warps is wound on, the end loops are held fast and are no longer vulnerable to shifting.

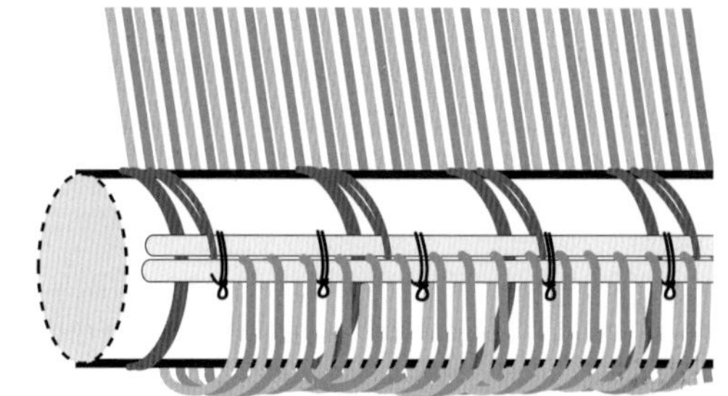

Fig. 129

7 Wind the Warp onto the Warp Beam

Winding the warp onto the warp beam is called "beaming the warp." It is one of the most important steps in the whole weaving process because the warp threads need to go onto the beam under even and tight tension. Care taken in this step will give great benefits during weaving. It is not a difficult or fiddly step—just important.

At this time, check to see if the loom's apron cords or straps are bulky or thick and will prevent the warp from being wound on without any lumps. The warp must go on in flat layers; and if the apron prevents it, read what to do on page 50. You want to avoid lumps on the warp beam while beaming, as seen in Figure 128.

Now, determine if your loom's brake should be on or off.

Ratchet Brake: See Figure 130. If your loom has a ratchet brake, engage it during beaming. You should hear the pawl clicking on the teeth as you wind on the warp. This ensures that you're winding in the correct direction. To review which direction to wind, see page 38 and Figure 115.

Ratchet brake

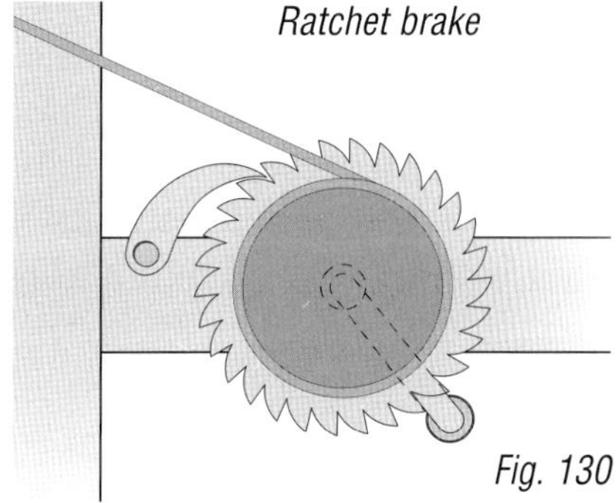

Fig. 130

Tension (Friction) Brake: See Figure 131. A metal cable wraps around a drum on one end of the warp beam. The friction of the cable when it's holding tight prevents the beam from moving. When the cable is released slightly, the beam can move. If your loom's warp beam has a tension (also called friction) brake, ***it should be disengaged during beaming***. Do it by pressing down on the brake pedal, which is at the side of the treadles at the front of the loom. Some looms have a wing nut on a leg of the loom, near the brake pedal, that turns to keep the brake pedal down, and the brake disengaged during beaming. Note that you will be engaging and disengaging the brake periodically during beaming. The brake should be disengaged while you are turning the warp beam and engaged when you are tensioning the warp as shown in Figure 132.

Tension (friction) brake

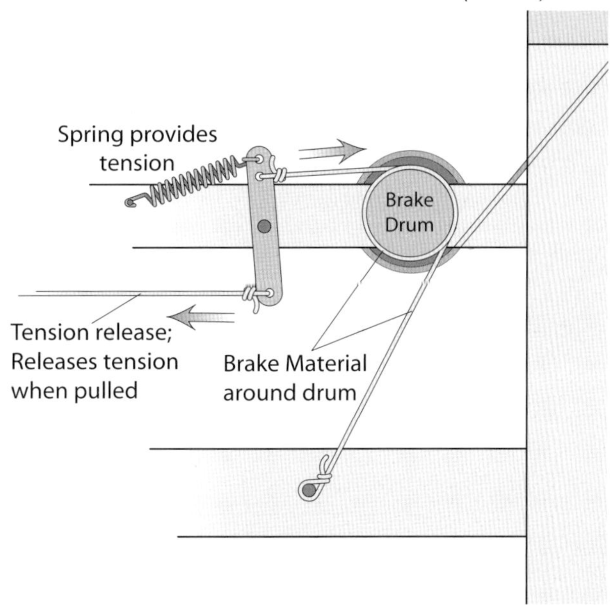

Fig. 131

Tension the Warp

Wind on the warp

Unwind the warp from the kitestick as you wind the warp onto the beam. I put the bulk of the warp on a chair or on the floor, if it is clean, and unwind a bit; then crank, and unwind some more when needed.

How to wind the warp tightly

Tensioning the warp so it is wound on tight is important. If you're working with a helper, see page 51 for directions.

If you're working on your own, use this "crank and yank" technique: Every time you crank the warp beam one full turn, stop, engage the brake, and then stand where the bulk of the warp is. Starting at one side of the warp, take a 1" or 2" section of the warp in each hand. Tension the sections by jerking hard, very hard. Drop those sections, and pick up the next two sections and jerk very hard again. (For wider warps than the sample, you'll continue jerking in 2" sections all the way across the warp.) See Figure 132. This procedure tightens the warp you just wound on the beam. Then, wind on another turn, and follow the same process again, starting from the other edge of the warp. Alternating right and left edges as the starting point helps prevent one side from receiving less tension than the other because you may have pulled harder on the first bundles every time.

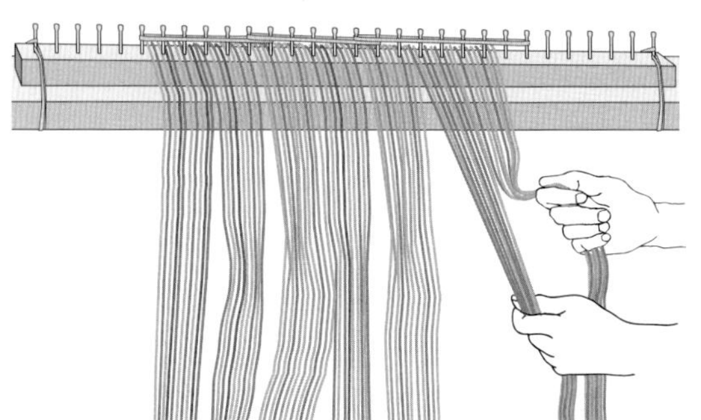

Fig. 132

To save a lot of stress on your hands, you can wind the sections around a short length of dowel and pull on the dowel. It is easy and quick once you get the rhythm of doing it. See Figure 133. The diameter of the dowel should be around ½".

Note that it is the turn of warp that you just wound onto the beam that is being tensioned. Warp that is not on the beam is slack as soon as you let go of it. If you must stop beaming and resume later, jerk all the sections of the last turn of the warp again before you start beaming.

Another way to achieve good, consistent tension is to use your body weight instead of jerking the warp. Grasp each 1" or 2" section at arm's length, lock your elbows, and lean back against the warp. Try this method if you feel you can't be sure of jerking with the same force all across the warp. Remember, the tension has to be not only tight, but even.

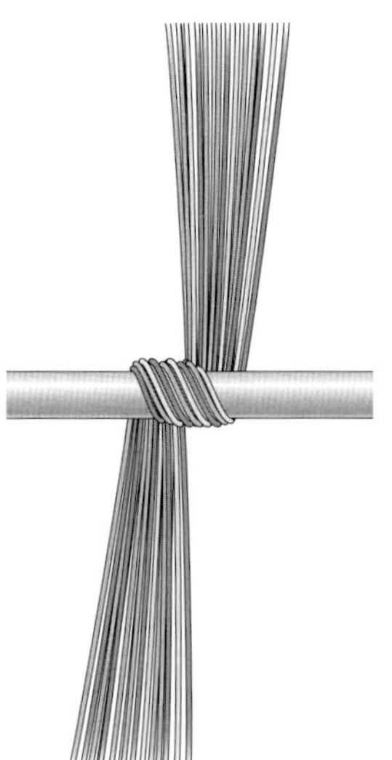

Fig. 133

Whether you're tensioning from the front or the back of the loom, make sure your body is lined up with the center of the loom.

Smoothing out the warp as you go

You might find it necessary to smooth out sections before tensioning to get the warp threads lined up. What ever you do, don't comb the threads! Combing can snag a thread or create tangles, often causing threads to break. If a thread does break, read what to do on page 51.

Often, it's enough just to shake the warp briskly, like a horse's reins, while pulling the warp toward you. You might also try holding a section of warp taut and slapping it with your palm or flicking it with your finger. See Figures 134a and 134b.

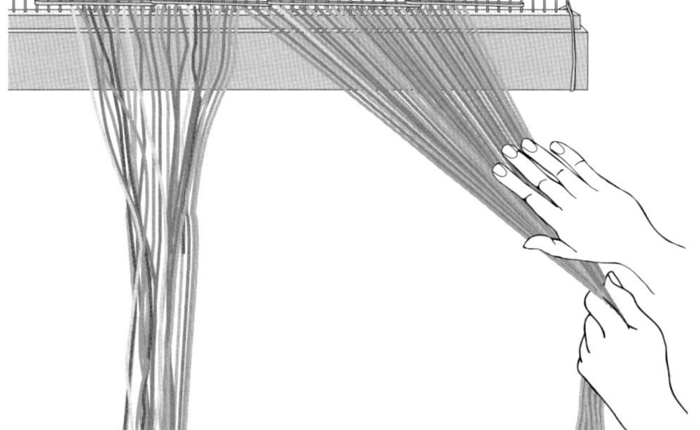

Fig. 134a

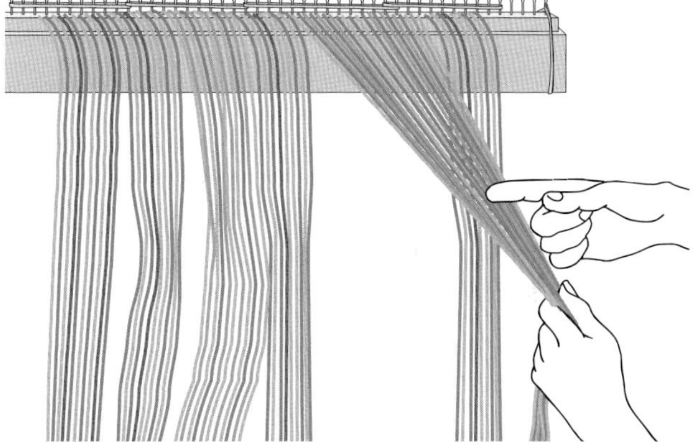

Fig. 134b

"Pinching" is another way to smooth the warp. Lay threads over the flats of your fingers, then, pinch them gently with the thumb and draw them toward you. By drawing the pinch along, the loose warps that have looped up are worked along the bulk of the warp. See Figure 135.

If threads don't line up nicely at the choke ties, say, some are looser than others, see page 51.

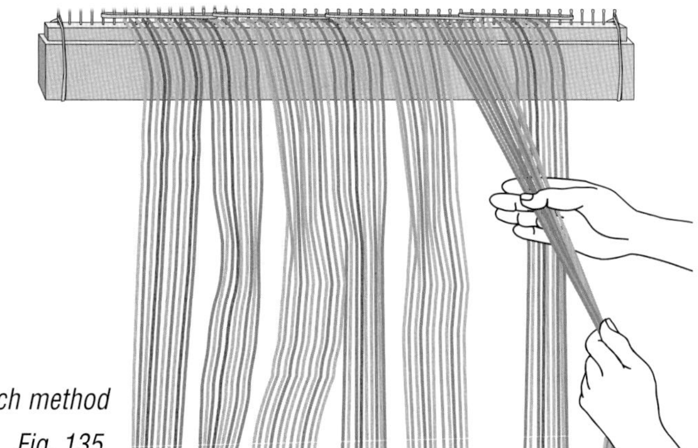

Pinch method

Fig. 135

Avoiding twists

Watch for twists between the raddle and the warp beam. If yarns are twisting around themselves in the groups, read what to do in the section about unbalanced yarns on pages 53 and 54. It won't happen with the 5/2 pearl cotton warp thread for the sampler, but can happen if a yarn is unbalanced. Most yarns available commercially are balanced and don't cause this twist problem.

Inserting packing paper

See how to prepare packing paper on page 37. You'll need to put packing paper in with the warp threads periodically as you wind the warp onto the warp beam. This is to keep the edges of the roll of warp in place as the as the warp accumulates during beaming. If the warp's edges on the beam are straight like sheer cliffs, you have edge threads that won't cause trouble later when weaving. See Figure 136.

Figure 137 shows a well wound warp on the warp beam, and Figure 138 shows a poorly shaped warp with threads sliding off at the edges.

Remember, some looms do not need packing paper as mentioned on page 37.

If your apron cords prevent the warp from going on flat, you need to insert packing sticks to create a flat base before you can use the pieces of paper. See page 50.

The longer the warp and the smaller the diameter of the warp beam, the faster the threads stack up as they accumulate, and the more vulnerable the edge threads are to slipping off. The principle is this: Insert a piece of paper when the threads on the edges of the warp on the warp beam look like they could slide off.

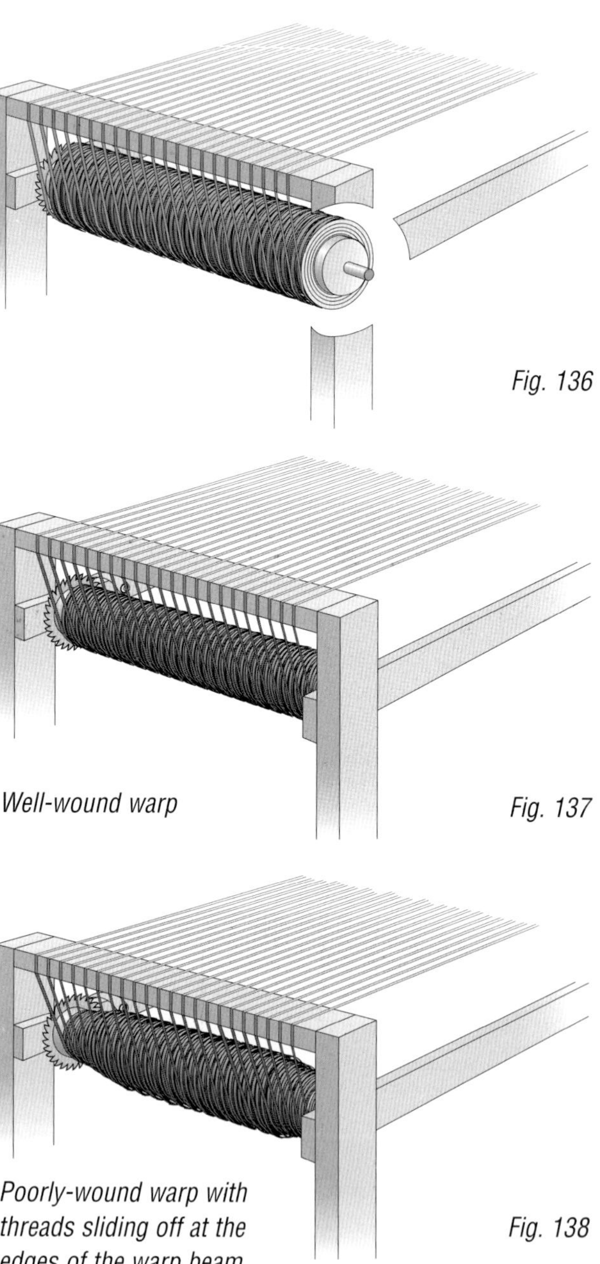

Fig. 136

Well-wound warp *Fig. 137*

Poorly-wound warp with threads sliding off at the edges of the warp beam *Fig. 138*

When winding in the packing paper, be careful that warp threads ***never travel over the paper folded double at the edges***. The warp itself only goes over the single-thickness paper with the folded extensions sticking out to strengthen the paper at the edges. You may put in the paper with the folded part on top or underneath--either way of inserting the paper is all right—just make sure no warp falls on the doubled edges. Also watch for paper that is crinkling or rolling in at an angle. A simple trick prevents this: Insert the paper so that it can be wound with the warp, then turn the beam a bit until the end of the paper catches in. With your thumb and forefinger, take hold at the center of the opposite end of the paper, as in Figure 139, right in the middle. Hold it taut there as you wind the paper in with the warp so the paper can't wrinkle.

Put the first piece of paper in after the first yard or so of warp is wound on in flat layers. Use one piece of folded paper for about every yard. See Figure 140.

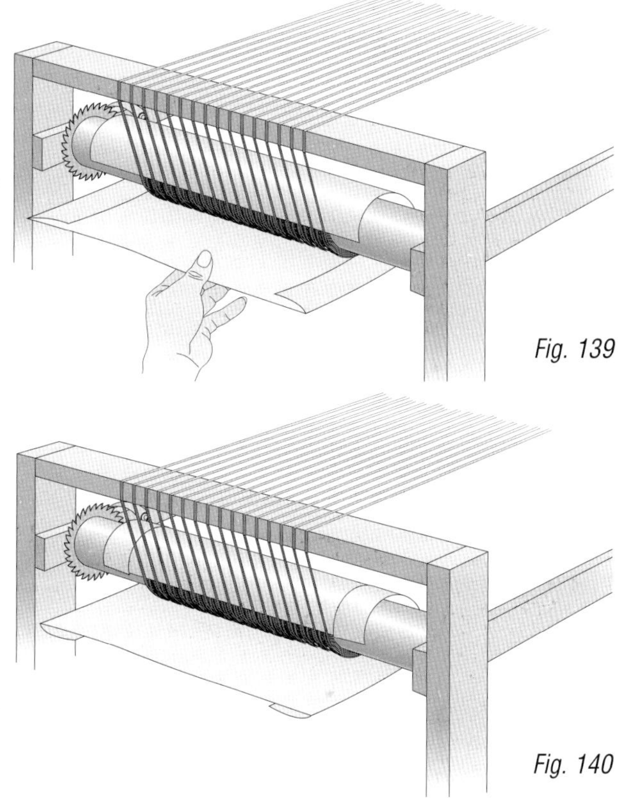

Fig. 139

Fig. 140

Note that some weavers use continuous packing paper as shown in Figure 141. I do not recommend this because it is very difficult to get it wound on without wrinkling, and it builds up the warp beam circumference faster than short pieces put in every yard or so.

Winding the warp tightly prevents the layers from biting down into one another so continuous packing paper isn't necessary.

Packing sticks can be used instead of paper and are discussed on page 52.

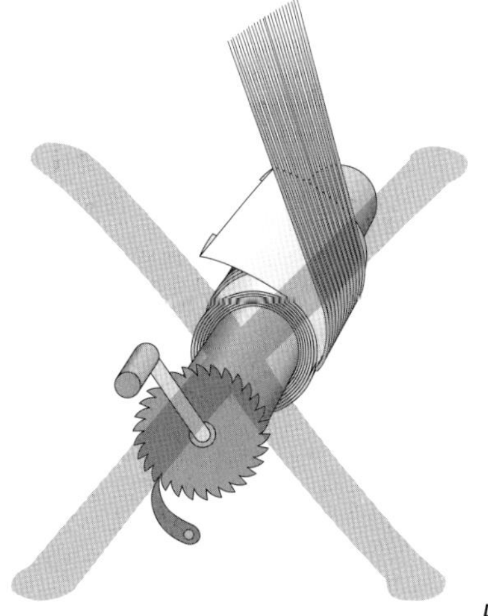

Fig. 141

Clearing tangles

As you wind on, keep an eye on the raddle. Threads normally do twist a bit and mingle within the raddle sections. They are not tangles, and they get sorted out later. However, if you notice a tangle starting at the raddle, clear it by drawing the tips of your fingers between groups of threads at the raddle while you hold the warp under some tension with the other hand. It's loose threads that usually cause trouble. A slap or shake or strum on the warp will clear any tangles that begin to appear as was discussed above in the section, "Smoothing out the warp as you go," on page 45.

A warp thread gets tight

As the warp moves through the raddle, a thread may become very tight and appear to be in the wrong raddle section; it is actually a loose thread that has wandered, and it may have traveled quite a distance before becoming noticeable. If it happens, unwind the warp until you can release the caught thread—you will be amazed to see that it is actually in its correct raddle space.

If a warp thread breaks, read what to do on page 51.

Loose threads at the choke ties

If you find some loose warp threads that don't align themselves at the choke ties read what to do on page 51.

Removing choke ties

Remove the choke ties encircling the warp as you reach them, well before they start to cause the warp to narrow into a steep V-shape as you beam. Be very careful not to remove the cross ties. You'll know easily which ties are in the cross if you used a different color for your choke ties than for your cross ties when you made them.

When to stop winding

You will leave a significant amount of warp not wound on the warp beam. This quantity will be needed to thread the loom. A general guide is to leave unwound the same length your loom is from the very front to the very back—plus a few inches more. It can be wound up later on and will not be wasted. Figure 142 shows the amount to leave unwound.

Leave in all the ties holding the cross and the end loop of the warp.

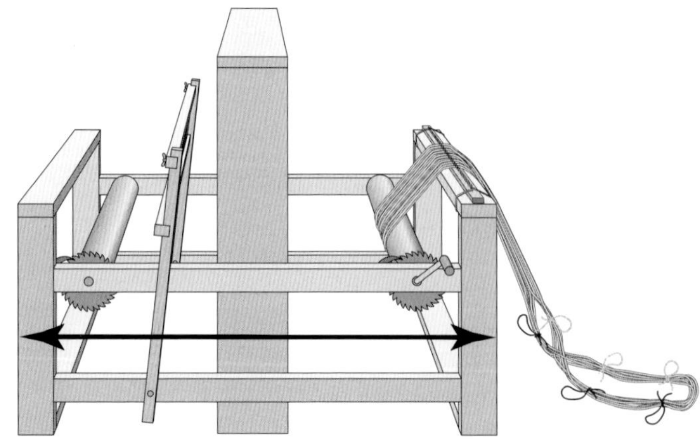

Fig. 142

8 Remove the Raddle

Now it's time to remove the raddle. First remove the cap or rubber bands on the nails, then, take the raddle off the warp beam or castle. Don't worry about the threads becoming tangled—they are safely wound tightly on the warp beam. The threads that remain unwound will become orderly and tidy when you do the next process, which is threading the heddles and the reed. The only precaution for this step is to watch as you remove the raddle that its teeth don't snag any warp threads. The raddle can be put away and won't be needed until you beam on the next warp.

Remember that the ties holding the cross and end of the warp should still remain in place.

 Re-position the Warp

This is a crucial step and ***must*** be done if your raddle was located on the back beam. What you'll do is rearrange the unwound warp so that it follows a path from the warp beam over the back beam to the castle. Grasp the warp and take it up over the back beam and then guide it so that it goes ***under*** the back beam and then over on top of the back beam. The unwound warp will now be pointing toward the castle of the loom. See Figure 143 a-e.

Note: On some looms the warp beam is wound in the opposite direction from the illustration. See Figure 115 on page 38.

Don't worry about threads becoming tangled or out of order because the cross ties and the ties at the end of the warp are still safely keeping the threads in order.

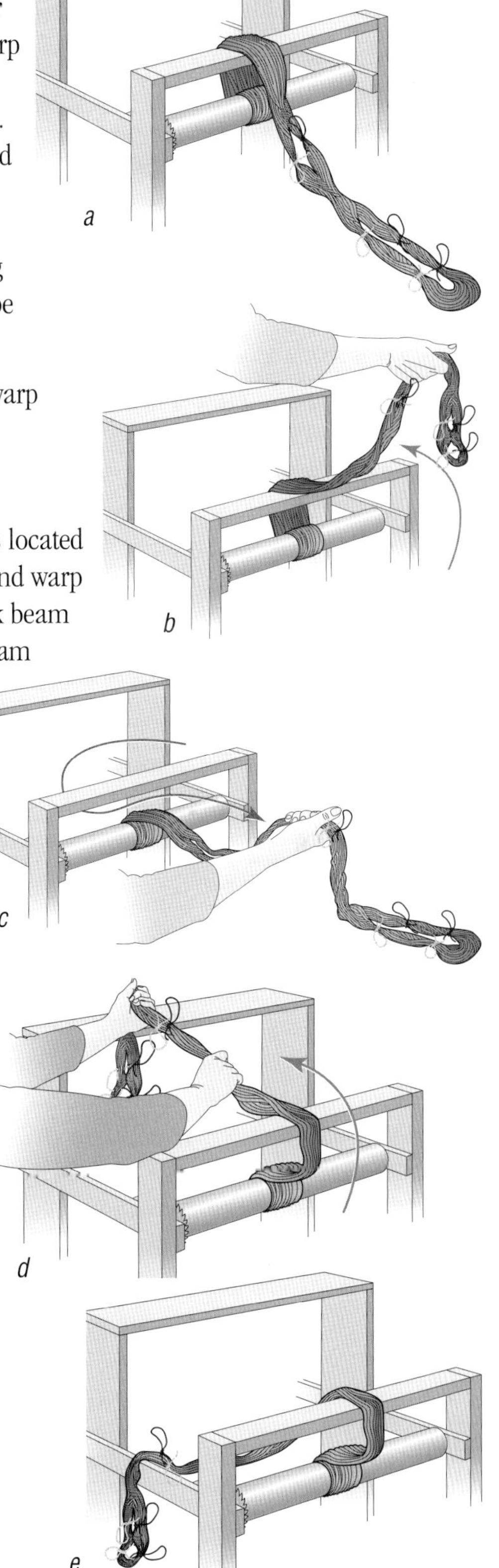

> Re-position the warp now: You won't be able to weave until you get the warp into its correct position. It will be very frustrating if you realize it needs to be done later on, when you are about to weave. So, make sure you reposition the warp now. You'll know if it's in the correct position if it is following a path ***over*** the back beam and the end of the warp is near the castle of the loom. See Figure 143e.

You're finished beaming.

Now you are ready to thread. Part III takes you through the process step-by-step.

More About Beaming

I. What if the loom has lumpy apron cords or straps?

You must take action on the first round of warp wound on the beam if the cords or straps are thick and will prevent the warp from winding on absolutely smoothly. The ideal solution is to place packing sticks (Figure 144) over the cords or straps. Find wood for packing sticks in the molding department of a lumber store—you want thin, narrow, flat sticks that are smooth. They should be about two inches shorter than the width of the warp beam of the loom. Five or six will do; a few more than that can always come in handy.

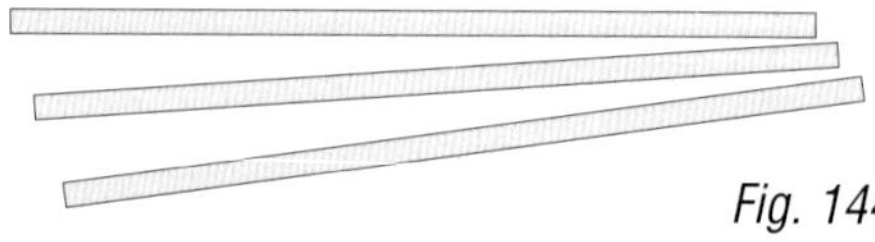

Fig. 144

If you do not have thin strips, you can use corrugated paper (from a carton or packing store) for this first project, and get sticks from the lumber store to have on hand for the next projects. Cut the corrugated paper so the width is 7" wide for the 5" wide sampler and the length is about 3-4" longer than the circumference of the warp beam.

Figure 145 shows packing sticks covering the apron cords. The sticks should be long enough to span all the cords that are on the beam to ensure a smooth base for winding on the warp.

You'll put in the sticks one-at-a-time while you wind the first round of warp onto the beam. Put in a stick each time the cords are about to touch the warp. Use as many sticks as needed to prevent the warp from touching the cords to make a flat base for winding on subsequent layers. Again, see Figure 145.

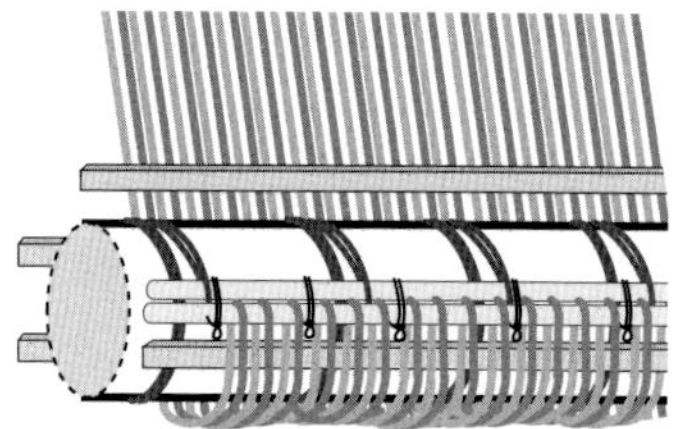

Fig. 145

II. Looms that don't require packing paper or sticks

Figure 146 shows a type of warp beam called a "sectional warp beam." Its pegs prevent the edges of the warp from slipping down so that paper or sticks aren't needed. You can wind the warp as the directions in this book show, or you can beam your warps on "sectionally," which is a topic in my book, *Warping Your Loom & Tying On New Warps*. The reason one might want to use a sectional beam that way is that it can save time with very long warps. However, for all weaving, the sectional beam can be used just like a regular warp beam. Be careful when beaming that no warps ride up on the pegs. Read how to use a sectional beam like a plain beam on page 52.

Figure 147 shows a warp beam with a very large diameter. Because of its size, paper or sticks aren't needed. The warp is beamed just like other warp beams.

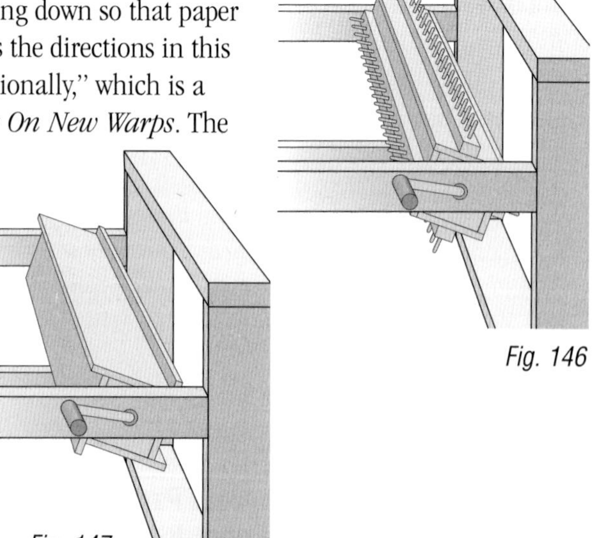

Fig. 146

Fig. 147

III. What if a thread breaks?

If you can find both ends of a broken thread, great; tie them together in a square knot (or any knot) if there's enough slack to do so. You want to make the knot as close to the ends of the threads as possible and with the tiniest knot. If you can't find both ends, the end you most likely will find is the one yet to be beamed on. When you find it, help it go onto the beam and continue beaming without a repair at this time. If you can't be certain of the thread's correct raddle group, run it over the top of the raddle's rubber bands rather than guessing which group it belongs in. You'll know its proper position later when you work with the cross. The repair can be done during weaving when the break reappears, as described on page 322.

IV. Loose warp threads appear at choke ties

If you find some threads are looser than others when you come to a choke tie, you'll have to undo the tie, and using the pinch method on page 45, work the loose threads back away from the warp beam as you go along. Eventually, a loose thread will work itself out at the end of the warp. The unevenness of the warp threads at this end doesn't matter—what matters is that the threads are even on the warp beam.

V. Beaming with a helper

If you have a good helper, beaming goes more quickly. You hold the warp on tension while your helper turns the warp beam, inserts packing paper, and watches for tangles at the raddle. Stand as far away from the loom as possible so that the outside threads of the warp don't angle in sharply. If you stand too close to the loom, the angle at the edges of the warp as it moves through the raddle becomes too steep as in Figure 148. If this happens, some threads will be tighter than others due to the steepness of the angle.

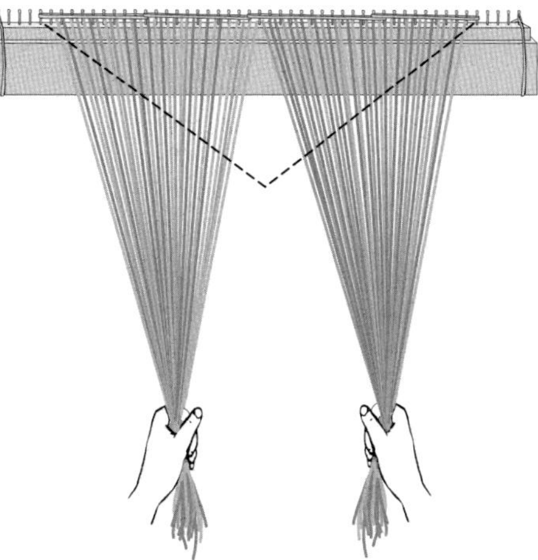

Fig. 148

Pull as your helper turns the warp beam. If the warp is too big to hold in one hand, you can divide it in half and hold it in two hands. Be sure to line up your body with the center of the loom and tension by leaning back and using your body weight, not the strength of your arms, because one arm is usually stronger than the other. Think about how taut the warp feels so you can keep the tension consistent throughout beaming. You know you're applying enough tension if your helper finds it difficult to turn the warp beam crank.

As the warp is wound on, slowly walk toward the loom, keeping the warp under tension. Don't let the warp slip through your hands. If you let it slip, you won't get as much tension as you do by holding tightly and pulling with your body weight.

If the warp is too thick for you to get a good grip, tension it by yourself with the "crank and yank" technique described on page 44.

VI. Using packing sticks

Figure 149a shows packing sticks (Figure 144 on page 50) instead of paper to wind in with the warp. Some people prefer them to paper, but I prefer paper because the warp beam builds up so much more if sticks are used. Some weavers prefer not to place the sticks on top of one another and stagger them in the layers. See Figure 149b.

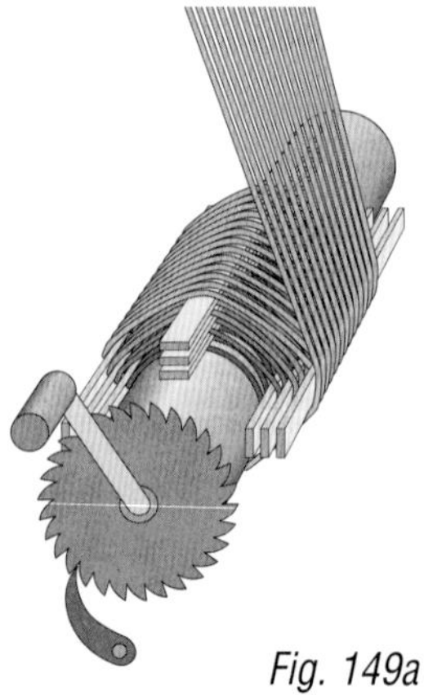

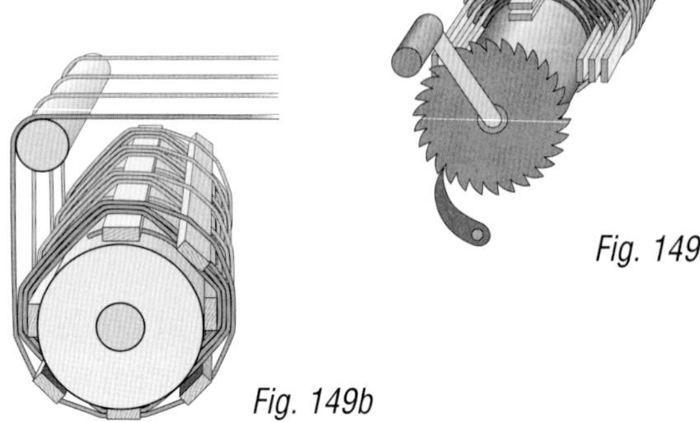

Fig. 149b

Fig. 149a

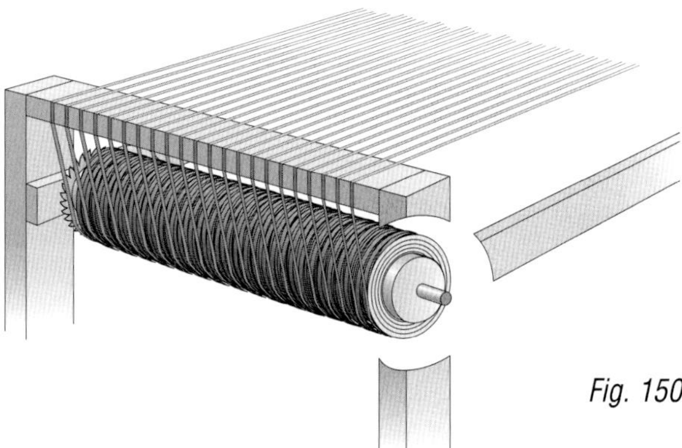

Fig. 150

Place them perfectly parallel to the warp beam. As you wind subsequent layers of warp, position the sticks as needed to prevent upper layers of warp from burying themselves in lower layers or toppling off the ends. You are striving for a firm roll of warp as the diameter increases. Sticks should extend at least about 2" out from each edge of the warp to keep the edges from toppling over. You want the edges of the warp to be absolutely straight, like sheer cliffs, as seen in Figure 150.

VII. Using a sectional beam like a plain beam

If the sectional beam doesn't have an apron rod, you'll have to make one. After that, follow the procedures given in this chapter.

Attach a smooth narrow stick or dowel (about ½" diameter) to the cords on the sectional beam with lark's head knots. See page 352.

If there are no cords, make some with strong string, not thick or bulky rope. Cut the cords twice the distance from around the beam to where the shafts are. See Figure 151. Fold each cord in half and knot the ends. Then, attach them to pegs at about 3-4" intervals to the sectional beam with lark's head knots. See page 352.

Attach the cords to the apron rod with lark's head knots as shown in Figure 151.

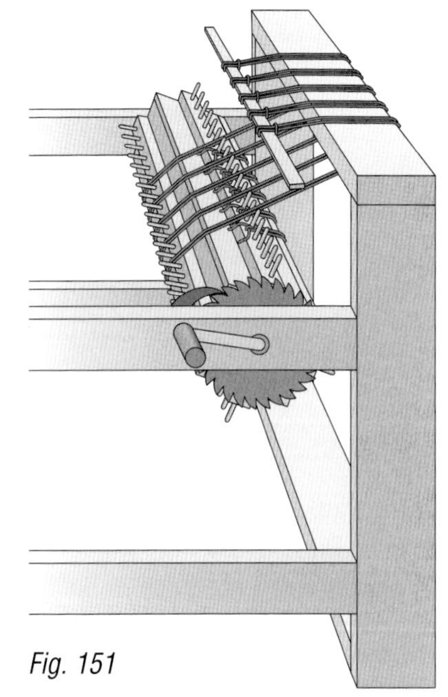

Fig. 151

VIII. What if you discover threads that are too short?

It means that you didn't follow the path exactly on the warping board for a round trip. The threads are too short and can't be used as is. I've never had this situation myself, or in a class or workshop—but it could happen.

There are some options. One is to ignore or eliminate them. If the threads have been wound on the beam, when you notice them, ignore them if they won't hurt the design of the warp. They won't hurt anything—will just be deleted. If, however, the loop of the short ends has not been wound on the beam yet, pull these short threads out of the raddle and eliminate them .

If you can't spare that thread (you might need that color thread and it can't be deleted), then try to attach new threads to the short ones. This is my suggestion if what you encounter is a loop and then a doubled thread: Cut the loop and tie a long new thread to the existing threads you just cut—one thread for each part of the loop. There are two threads because if you have a doubled thread at the loop—you have two threads to lengthen. Make the new threads longer than the warp just to be sure there is enough. Then continue beaming. If you don't know where in the raddle the threads should go, carry them over the top of the raddle. When you stop beaming, trim off the new extension threads to the length of the other warp threads. You'll know approximately where to put them by their color order in your warp design. Approximate is OK for a couple of threads in a short warp. I assume you won't do it ever again, and you can "get by" with this "fudging" for a short warp.

As a beginning weaver, you should avoid unbalanced yarns. How to identify balanced and unbalanced threads is shown on the next page.

IX. A little about unbalanced yarns

If you find severe twists in the groups of warps between the raddle and the warp beam, work your fingers through the threads to straighten them out so they are going onto the beam in flat, untwisted "ribbons." This problem is caused by yarns that are unbalanced.

Unbalanced yarns are not usually sold for weaving, but you might find some in someone's stash of yarns or try to use a yarn not meant for weaving.

To identify an unbalanced yarn, cut a piece of it about a yard long. Don't take the yarn sample straight off the cone or spool—cut off and discard the first yard and use the next yard of thread—not the one that has been hanging off the cone for years, because if there was any extra twist in it, it will have dissipated over time. Hold one end of your test sample in one hand and the other end in the other hand. Bring your hands closer to one another so the yarn drapes into a U shape. When you bring your hands very close to one another a balanced yarn retains the U-shape, but an unbalanced one will twist on itself forming one strand. See Figures 152 and 153.

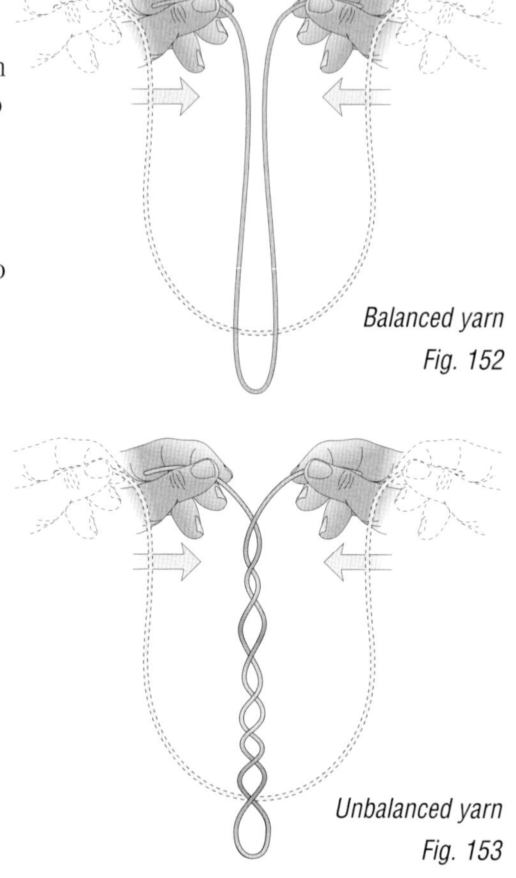

Balanced yarn
Fig. 152

Unbalanced yarn
Fig. 153

Another tell-tale sign of unbalanced yarns is that when they are left by themselves and not under tension, they will tend to roll together on themselves, automatically forming bunches of yarns twisted around each other, looking like ropes. See Figure 154.

More about dealing with these yarns is given in my book, *Warping Your Loom & Tying On New Warps*.

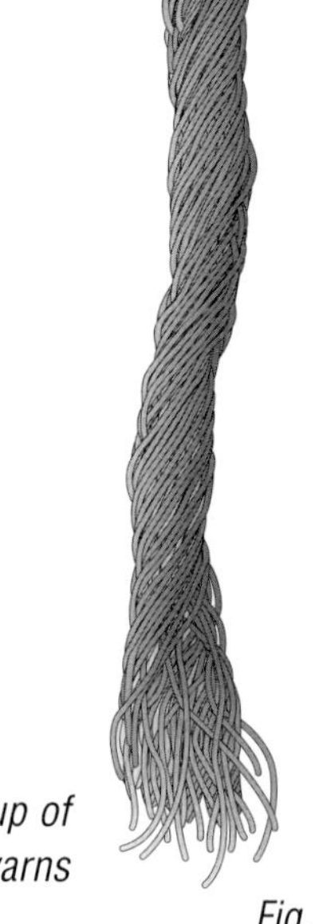

A group of unbalanced yarns
Fig. 154

Back-to-Front Warping

Part Three: Threading the Loom

In this section, you will thread all the warp threads through the eyes in the heddles and then through the spaces in the reed.

Once you set up the warp on the loom in a comfortable position, this threading will be easy to do—and without making mistakes. (However, there are directions for correcting mistakes, just in case, on pages 82 and 108-110.) Threading was one of the first weaving steps I learned to enjoy. Using the directions given here, threading is so repetitive and methodical that it becomes relaxing and therapeutic. I hope you will enjoy it, too.

It can be done in short periods, or in a few longer sessions—you can stop and start at any point that fits your life.

In my first book, I wrote that 98 percent of a person's time is spent working toward a goal. Only two percent is spent actually realizing and enjoying the goal. It has always made sense to me to learn to enjoy the 98 percent—in weaving, and in life. It did not take any effort for me to find threading part of the 98 percent and very satisfying.

Equipment List: See Chapter 2, Equipment

Broom handle or long dowel:

4' 0"

Lease sticks:

Low stool or chair:

Reed:

Sley hook (or reed hook):

Scissors:

Tape measure:

Threading hook: I prefer the one shown here.

String:

Wrench: or something similar in heaviness for a weight.
Mine weights 3 ½ ounces.

Optional: Two long sticks about a foot longer than the distance from the back beam to the breast beam—needed if you choose to sley the reed horizontally. See page 75.

An Introduction to Your Loom

Since you will be working on the loom now, you need to know something about its different parts and how they are involved with threading.

Look at the illustration(s) that show the loom you are working on to find the parts discussed in this section. Floor looms also are shown in Figures 4, 5, and 6 on page 4. Table looms are also shown in Figures 7, 8, and 9 on pages 5 and 6.

To review a bit: part of your warp should now be wound up on the ***warp beam***, and the remaining part of the warp should be over the ***back beam***. The end of your warp should be near the ***castle***. Within the castle are ***shafts***, which are frames that have ***heddles***, on them.

> *Remember, shafts are often called harnesses, but "shaft" is the correct term.*

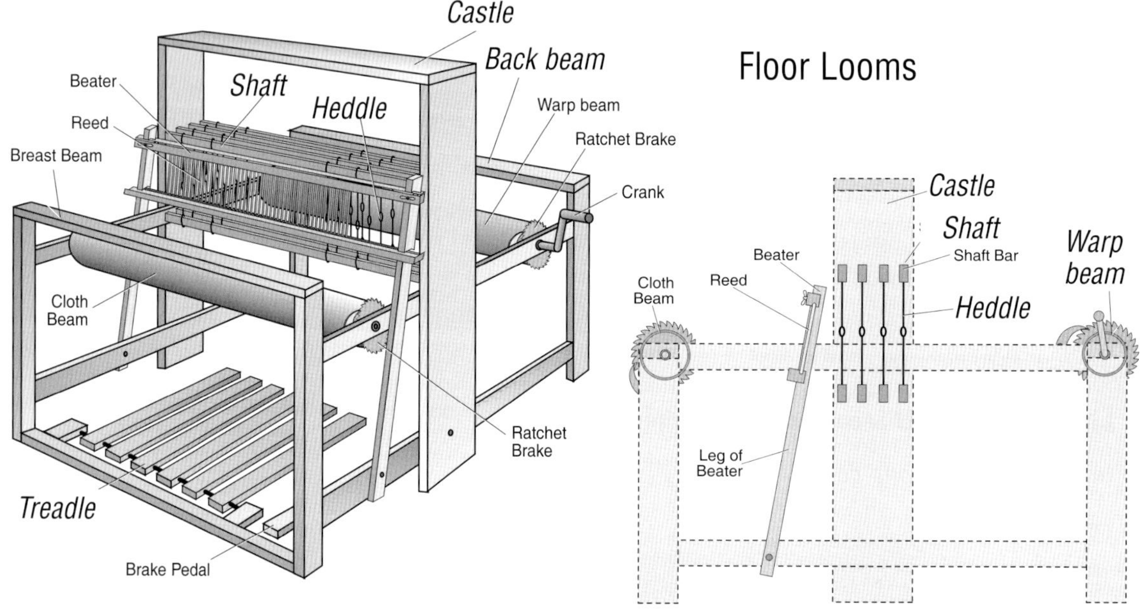

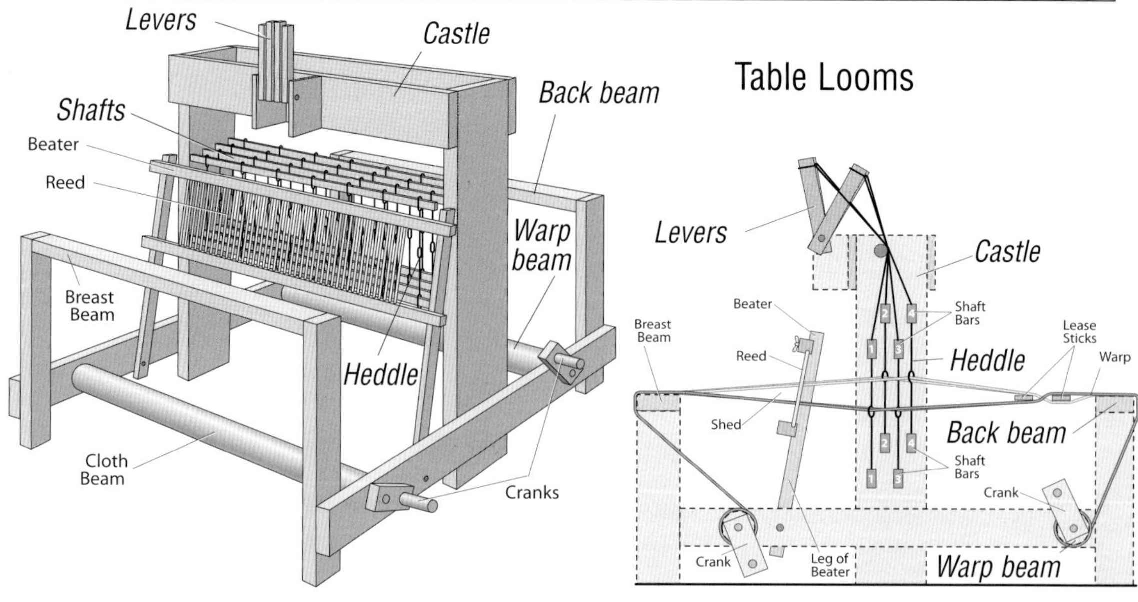

Heddles

Figure 155 shows what a shaft with heddles on it looks like. Count the shafts that are on your loom. There will be a minimum of four shafts, and there may be more than that. We will only use four shafts in this book. See how to use more than four in the Drafting and Computer chapters.

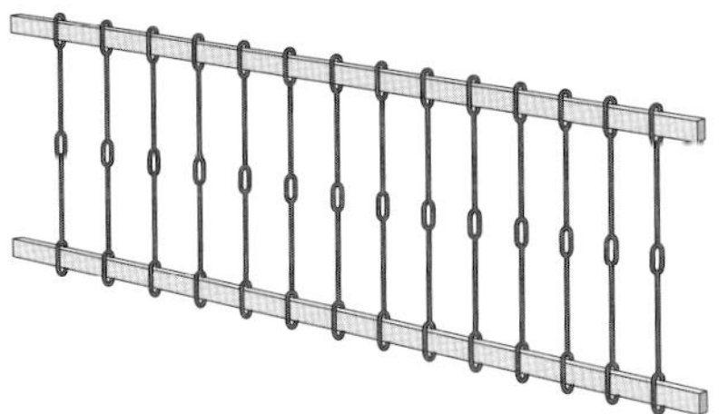

Fig. 155
A shaft, sometimes called a harness

The shaft nearest the front of the loom, where the weaver sits, is identified as shaft #1 in the American weaving books. Shaft #2 is behind #1, and so on, with the shaft farthest from the weaver, or at the back of the loom, being the shaft with the highest number. We will use shafts 1, 2, 3, and 4 for the sampler. Any extra shafts won't be in the way, but we just won't use them.

Heddles all have eyes, but there are several variations. See Figure 156. In this section the warp threads will be individually threaded through the eyes of the heddles in a specific way and on particular shafts according to the patterns the threads make in the cloth—called the weave structure. The sampler will be threaded so that many weave structures can be woven.

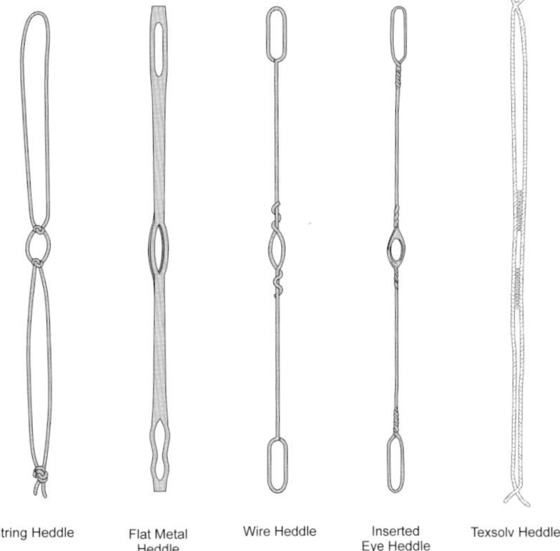

Fig. 156

When the shafts are lifted, so are the threads in their heddles. The shafts are lifted by the ***treadles*** on floor looms and by ***levers*** on table looms. Figure 157 shows that pressing a treadle raises a shaft with its heddles and warp threads on a floor loom. (In this case only 2 shafts are shown, and shaft #1 is being lifted by the treadle). Figure 158 shows how shafts are raised by levers on a table loom (in this illustration, shafts 2 and 4 are being lifted by two levers).

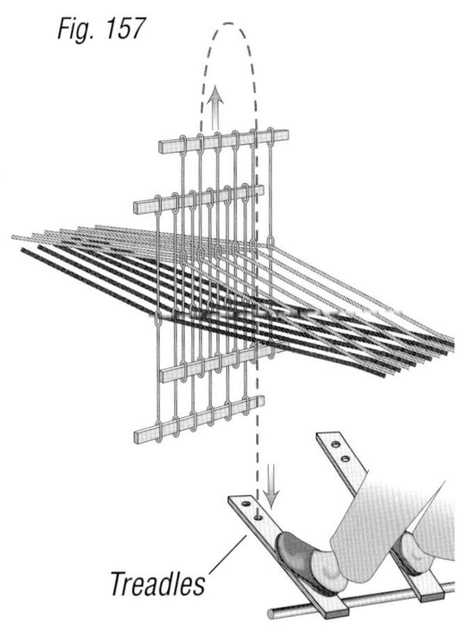

Fig. 157

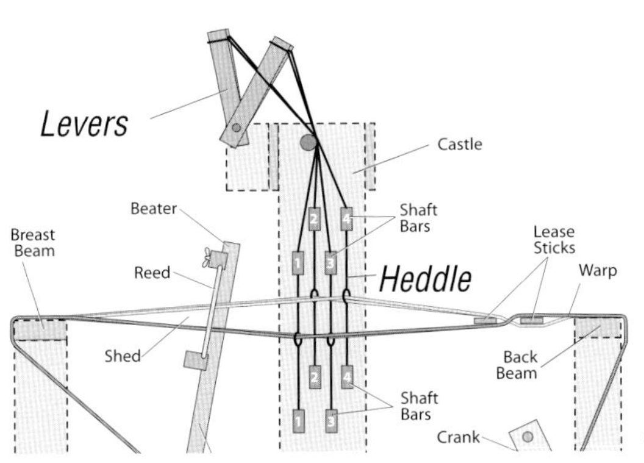

Fig. 158

Jacks

Figures 159 a–c show one way treadles can lift shafts by using *jacks*. A jack is a device for lifting heavy objects a short distance, like the jack used when changing a tire. The illustration shows three configurations for jacks on looms. Look at your loom (floor looms only) and see if you can find jacks in either of these locations: near the middle of the loom just below the shafts, or at either side of the loom above the shafts. If there are jacks at the top of the loom, check to see which illustration resembles your loom's jack arrangement.

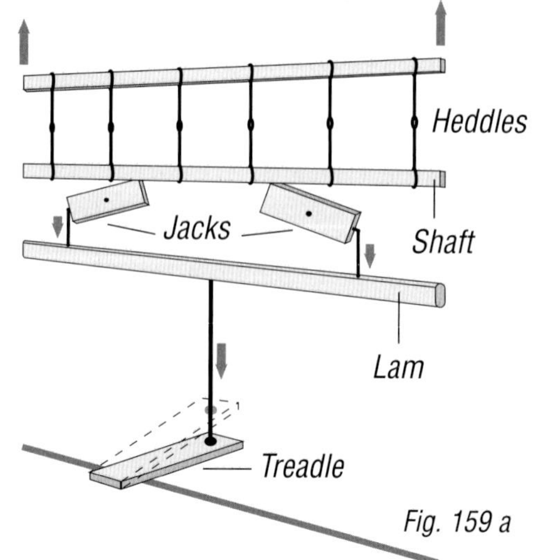

Fig. 159 a

Note that some looms do not use jacks, so if you don't find any, don't worry. And don't think about them too much, now—they won't be involved until you are actually weaving.

Notice in Figures 159 that there are horizontal bars between the shafts and the treadles. There is a bar for each shaft on the loom called a *lam*. Most, but not all looms have them. Lams are used as an intermediary so the pull on the shafts from the treadles is centered.

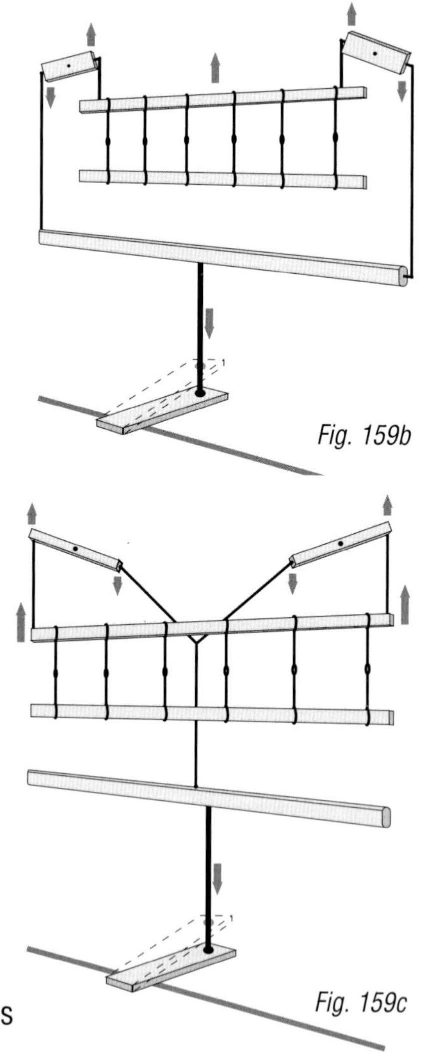
Fig. 159b

Fig. 159c

Jack Looms

Figure 160 shows one (of many) ways two treadles can be tied to the four lams on the loom and then, how the lams are connected to the shafts. It will be discussed in detail, beginning on page 95, when you begin weaving.

For the sampler you will thread the heddles in a specific way and lift the shafts in specific ways when you are weaving.

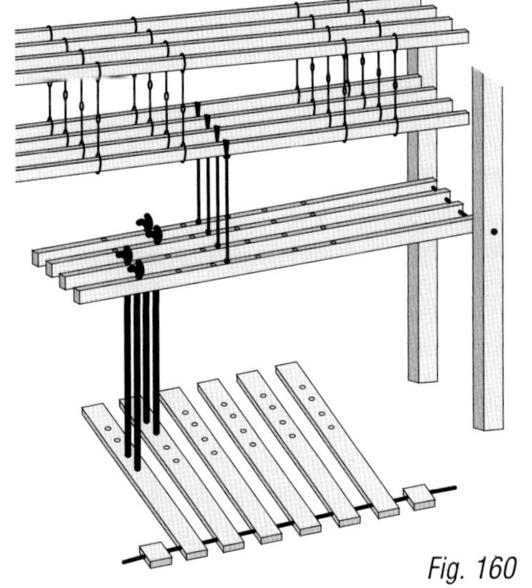

Fig. 160

After the threads are threaded in the heddles, you will put them through the spaces in the ***reed,*** which is located in the ***beater.*** A reed is shown in Figure 161. It will spread out the warp threads to the width the cloth is going to be (in the case of the sampler, 5"). Reeds come in different sizes and are discussed on page 33. The different sizes refer to how many spaces (called ***dents,*** there are in one inch. Besides being spread out to the desired width, the warps are spread out to be as close or far apart as is required by the type of yarn in the warp or what the finished cloth is to be like. If you don't have a 10-dent reed, as desired here, read how to substitute with another size reed that you do have on page 72. Your loom must have a reed, whatever the reed's size however.

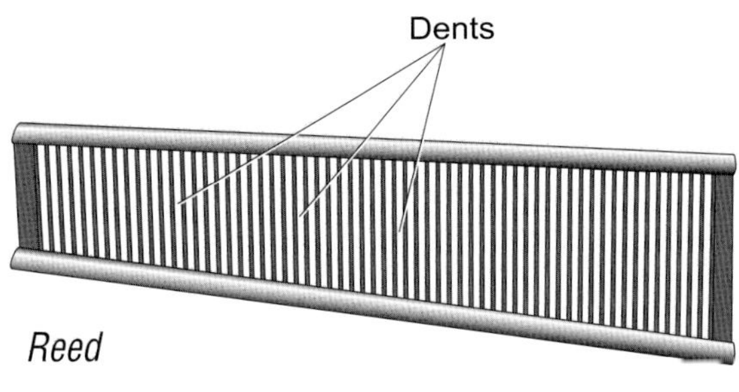

Fig. 161

Threading the Heddles

① Preliminaries

Check your warp

Make absolutely sure that your warp is on top of the loom's back beam with the free end of it near the castle. If this is not the case, you ***must*** reposition your warp as directed in Step 9 on page 49. See Figure 162.

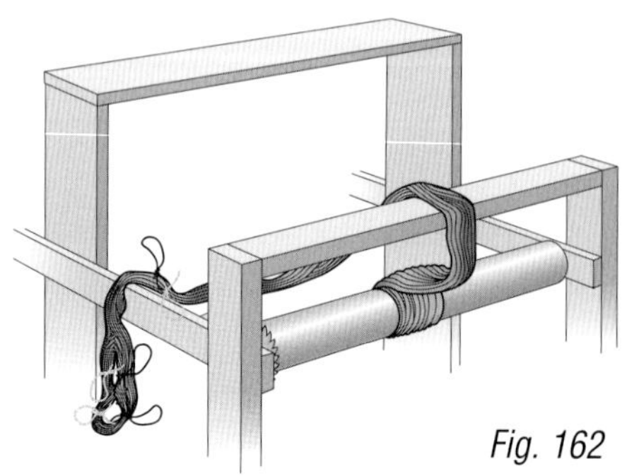

Fig. 162

Raise the shafts

Raise the shafts, if you can, on your loom so that you can see to thread the heddles more easily. On table looms raise the shafts by pulling down all the levers. On floor looms, do it by any means that works on your loom—weight down the treadles, tie all the shafts up to the top of the castle, or put shuttles under the jacks as shown in Figure 163. Read about jacks, above, on page 58.

My favorite way to raise the shafts is to prop something (for example, a shuttle) under one side of the jacks as seen in Figure 163. The next best option is to tie the shafts up to the castle. Weighting down the treadles to raise the shafts is my least favorite method because the weights get in the way while threading. If you do decide to weight down the treadles to raise the shafts, you must also have the shafts tied to one or more treadles. Read how to tie-up the treadles on page 95.

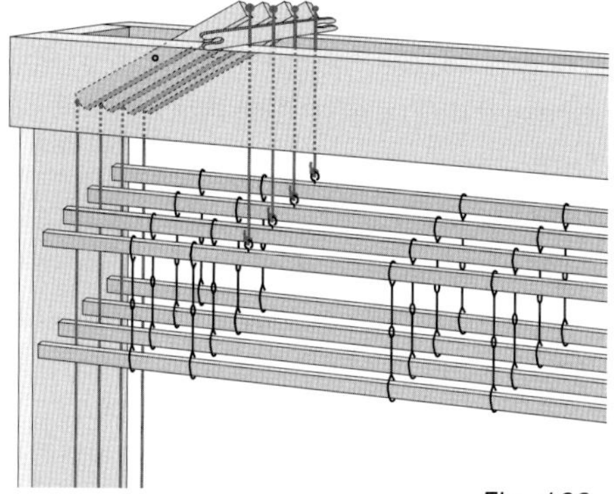

Fig. 163

Propping up the jacks uses the same principle for any configuration or location of jacks found on your loom. Remember the jacks can be located on top of the castle as in Figure 163, or directly underneath the shafts as seen in Figure 159a. Something other than a shuttle can be used—use what ever is around that can prop them up as high as they can go.

Note that not all looms have jacks, so you can tie the shafts up to the castle or weight the treadles as mentioned above.

Arrange the heddles needed

For the sampler you'll have 100 warp threads, with 25 heddles on each shaft. Count out the center 25 heddles on each of four shafts. Many looms have clips on the bars holding the heddles; read below how to deal with them to center your 25 heddles.

Push the excess heddles equally to each side of your 25 counted-out heddles centered on the shafts. Tie strings around the excess heddles on the sides of each shaft as shown in Figure 164. If you don't have enough heddles on each shaft, read how to move heddles on page 77. If you have too many (not likely), so there isn't a space of 5" on the shafts, between the pushed-away heddles, read about removing heddles on page 77.

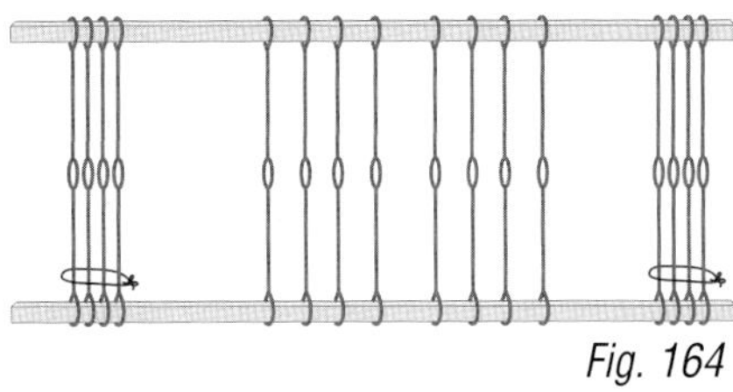

Fig. 164

If your loom has more than 4 shafts, push all the heddles to the sides on the extra shafts and tie them as in Figure 164. Divide the heddles approximately equally for each side of each extra shaft.

Clips on the heddle bars

The purpose of clips on heddle bars is to keep the heddle bars stiff and not flexed. See Figures 165a-c.

If there are clips on the bars that hold the heddles on the shafts, undo them, if possible. Read how to open the clips on page 79. Note that there are clips on both the upper and lower heddle bars, as seen in Figure 165c. The 25 counted-out heddles can be pushed to the left side (or right side) of the shaft and staggered, for threading. (See page 67.) You'll secure the clips in place on the heddle bars after threading the heddles. (A reminder to do this is in the section on sleying the reed.)

Fig. 165

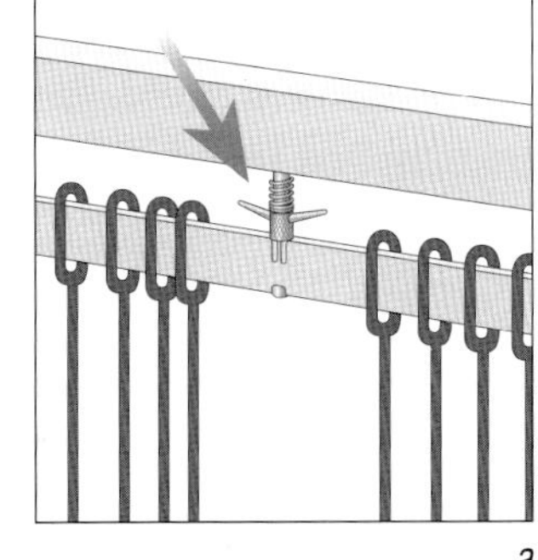

a

Note that on many looms the clips are not in the exact center of the shafts but to one side of the center. It is easy to see that they are not in the center if you look carefully. Figure 165d (on the next page) shows a screw on the bottom of the shaft in the exact center and a clip offset from the center. If you don't undo the clips and move all the 25 counted-out heddles to one side for threading, make sure you have the correct number of heddles for the left side of the warp to the left of the ***exact center*** and the correct number on the right side of the center. Since in the case of the sampler you need 25 on a shaft, give yourself 13 heddles on each side of the center. There will be one extra at the end of threading, which is perfectly okay.

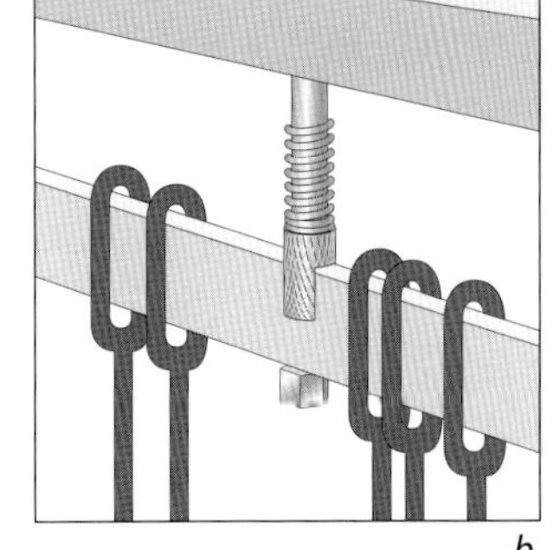

b

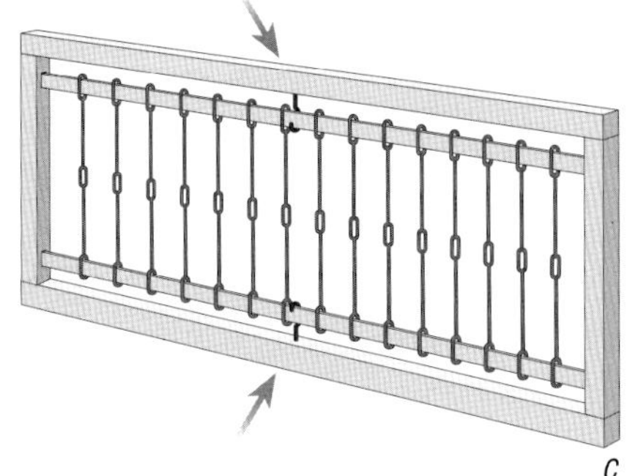

c

Arrange the Heddles

To find the center without centered clips, or clips at all—measure the shaft with a tape measure and divide the measurement in half. In real life, the exact center only matters when there are clips that can't be opened and prevent heddles from being moved to one side or the other. The threads themselves get centered when you sley the reed. If there are unmovable clips, you just need to be sure there are the heddles ***counted out*** as needed for each side of the center.

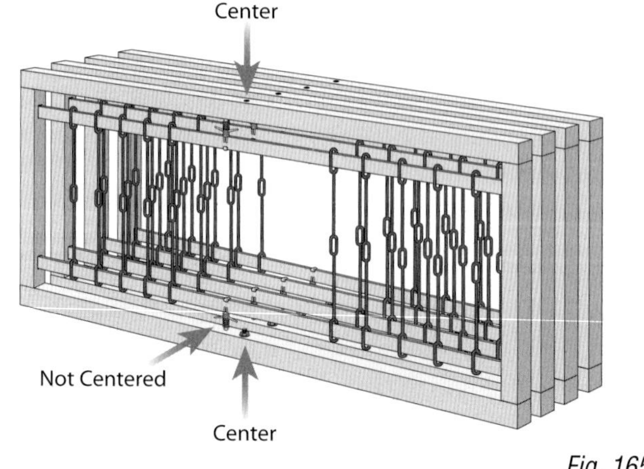

Fig. 165d

Be sure there is enough unbeamed warp

Figure 166 shows how much warp is the minimum you should leave unbeamed for threading. Measure the distance of your loom from the very front to the very back. It is the minimum amount needed.

Unwind some warp, now, if you don't have enough for threading. You need an ample amount to avoid threading errors.

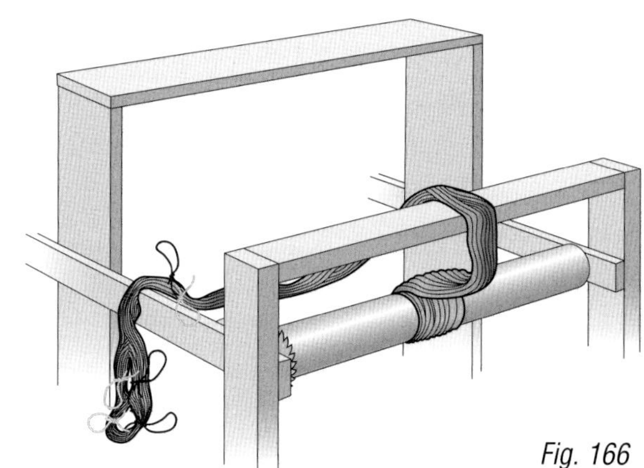

Fig. 166

Remove the beater

Remove the beater and the reed, and/or the breast beam if you can, so you can get closer to the heddles while threading. Perhaps, all you can remove is the reed, not the entire beater—that will still help you to see what you are doing.

② Put Lease Sticks into the Cross

Put the two lease sticks into the cross in the same manner as you put them into the group cross before you loaded the raddle see Figure 167. Tie them securely at each end about an inch apart as shown in Figure 168. Make sure the knots hold—it's important that the sticks don't come apart. Test to be sure the ties are secure by tugging and pulling the sticks apart. When the ties on the lease sticks are secure, remove the ties at the cross that you made at the warping board.

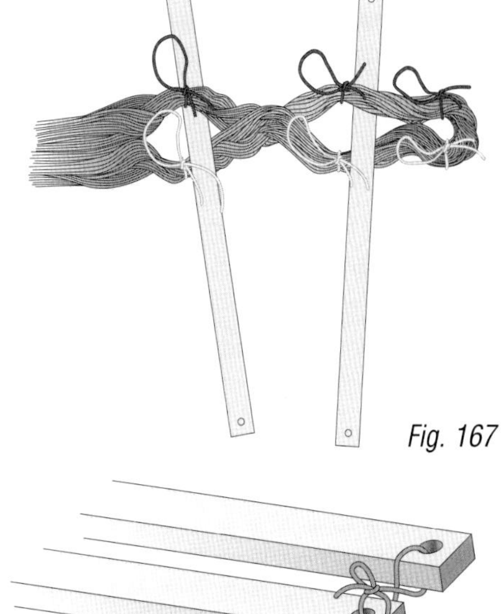

Fig. 167

Fig. 168

Don't remove the ties at the end loop at the end of the warp. Your cross will be held in place now by the lease sticks as seen in Figure 169. This is to keep the threads in order so they can be threaded into the heddles in order. Your warp should look like Figure 170 at this point.

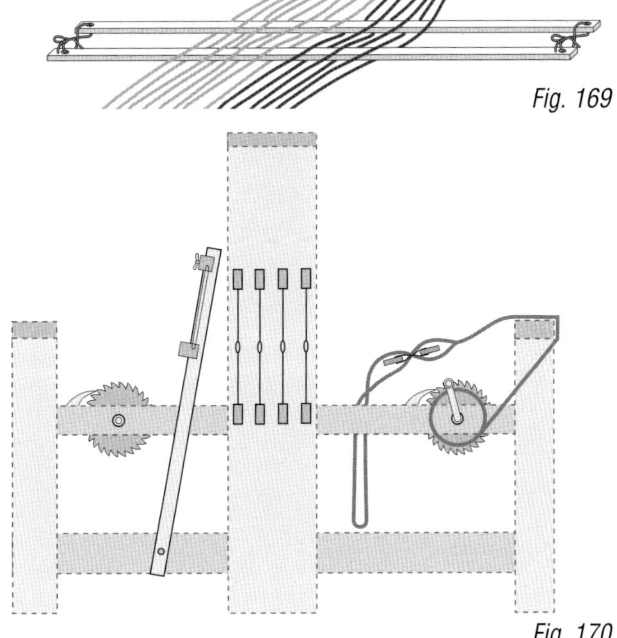

Fig. 169

Fig. 170

③ Suspend the Cross

You'll tie the broom handle (or long dowel) to the back of the castle. If your loom has a low castle, tie the broom handle to the back-most shaft and suspend the warp with its lease sticks over the broom handle, as seen in Figure 171. I do this job by tying loops that dangle from the top of the castle—one at each side of the loom. The finished loops hang down about 8-10", but I make the strings longer so I can lengthen them later when I adjust the height of the lease sticks. I tie bows in the loops so it will be easy to make them longer or shorter as needed. I put the broom handle into the loops and then, take the warp—lease sticks and all—over the broom handle as shown.

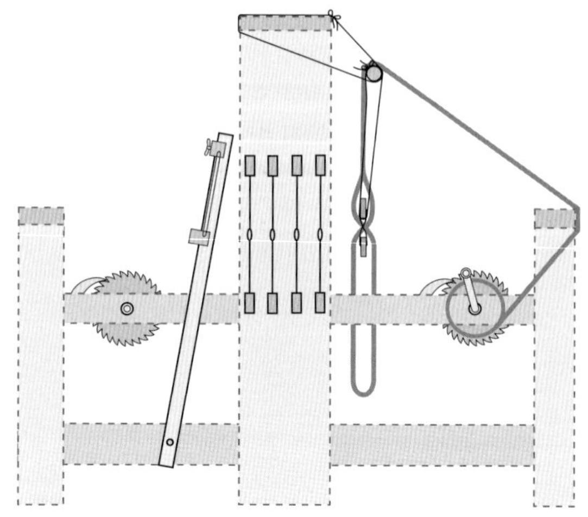

Fig. 171

④ Move the Lease Sticks if Needed

What you want to strive for is to have the cross itself (the area between the lease sticks) at the same level as the heddle eyes. You also want most of the warp hanging below the lease sticks for threading as in Figure 171, above.

Whether you need to move the cross or not depends upon where the cross itself was made on the warping board. It may be in the ideal position already. If it is not, move it now. It is important for it to be level with the heddles eyes so you can comfortably thread them accurately. (Threading accurately isn't difficult if you can see what you are doing.)

Move the cross as you did before when you moved the group cross before loading the raddle. See page 29 and Figure 99 also shown here.

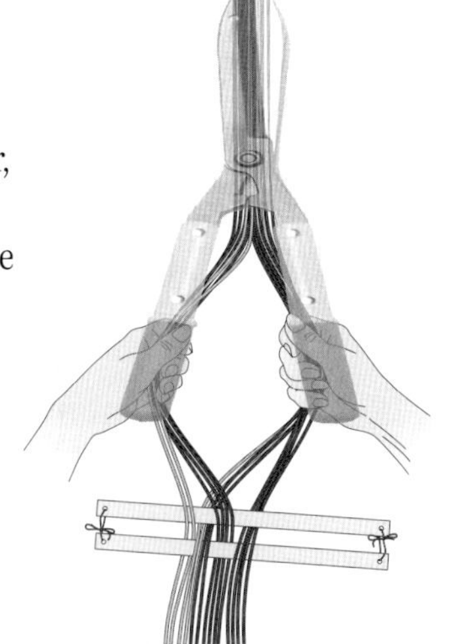

If the cross can't move because all the warp threads are too close together, put an end stick in the loop at the end of the warp and tie it with a string as shown in Figure 111 on page 36. Then remove the ties at the end of the warp and spread out the warps on the end stick and lease sticks a bit.

5 Stabilize the Lease Sticks

Tie the top lease stick to the broom handle with 2 loops of string—one on each side of the warp. Make the strings long, and use bows for ties so you can adjust the height of the cross later. Figures 171 and 172 show both sets of ties used to stabilize the assembly of the broom handle and the lease sticks. The upper ties hold the broom handle suspended from the castle of the loom, and the lower ties hold the top lease stick to the broom handle. When everything is stable, you can thread without mistakes and stop threading whenever you choose and resume later. (Remember, there is information on correcting mistakes, just in case, on pages 82 and 108.)

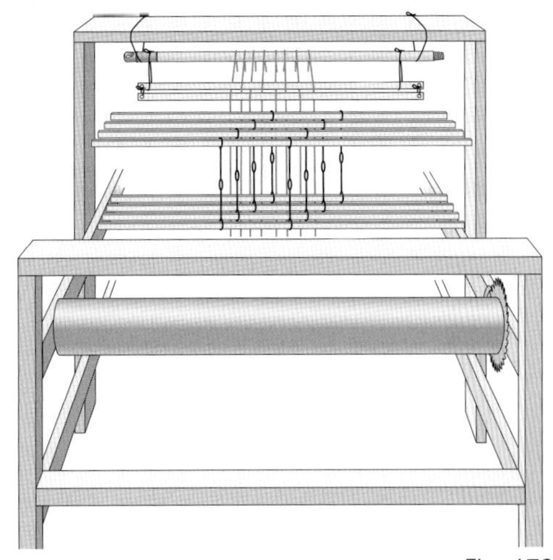

Fig. 172

Cut the Warp Loop

Before threading the individual warp threads into the heddles you need to cut the loop at the end of the warp. See Figure 173.

Then, I often tie the warp threads in rather large bundles in overhand knots as shown in Figure 174. This keeps things orderly and also reassures me that the lease sticks can't fall out, which would lose the cross. Since the lease sticks are tied together and also to the broom handle, this disaster really can't happen, but in case I forgot to tie the top lease stick to the broom handle, it is a little added insurance against losing the cross. That would be a situation you do ***not*** want to happen at any cost. (See page 77 if you do lose the lease sticks—and the cross).

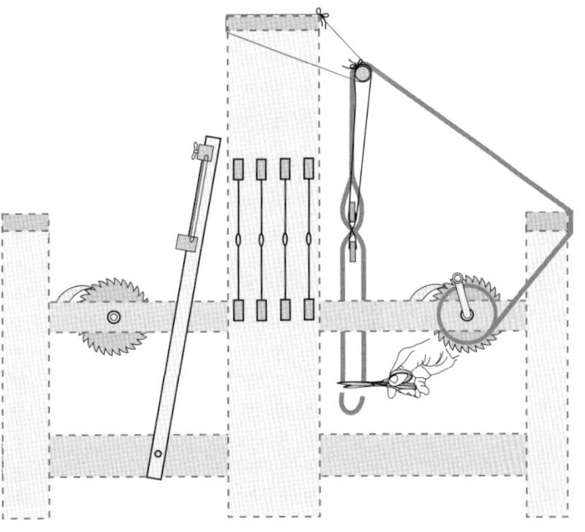

Fig. 173

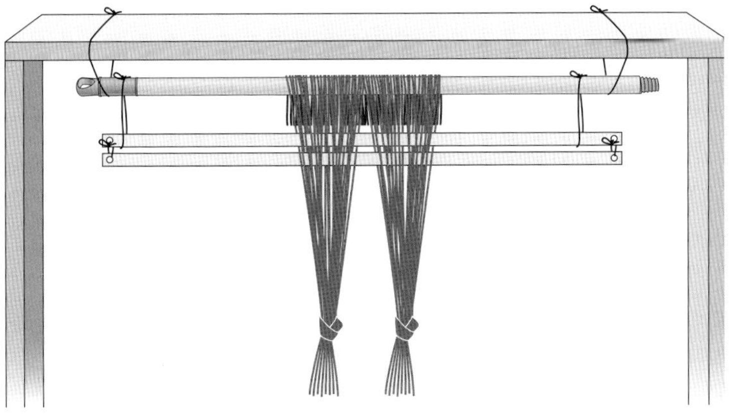

Fig. 174

⑦ Bring in a Stool or Chair

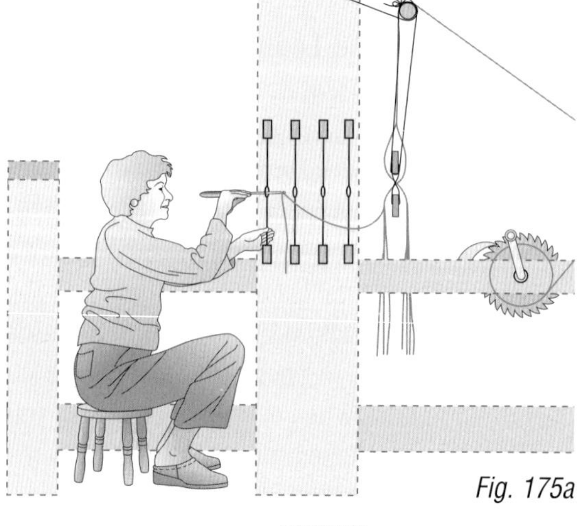
Fig. 175a

If you are using a table loom, find a chair and table that puts the loom at a comfortable height for you while threading the heddles. You want the eyes of the heddles to be at your eye level, so you can see better and so your arms, neck, and shoulders are comfortable. It might mean putting it on the kitchen counter, coffee table, card table, or other type of table.

If you are using a floor loom, bring in a low stool as close as you can to the heddles. The stool I use has legs that fit between the treadles so I can sit close to the shafts and heddles and is just the right height for my size and my loom: when I use it, the heddle eyes are at my eye level. It makes it easy to see the cross and the heddles and is comfortable for my arms, neck, and shoulders. See Figure 175a.

Hard to see what you're threading. Good light is invaluable when you're threading. Threads may be hard to see because they are back-lit or because they blend with the rest of the warp coming from the warp beam. Rig a cloth to help the threads stand out clearly. Put it just behind the lease sticks wherever you can on your loom. See Figure 175b.

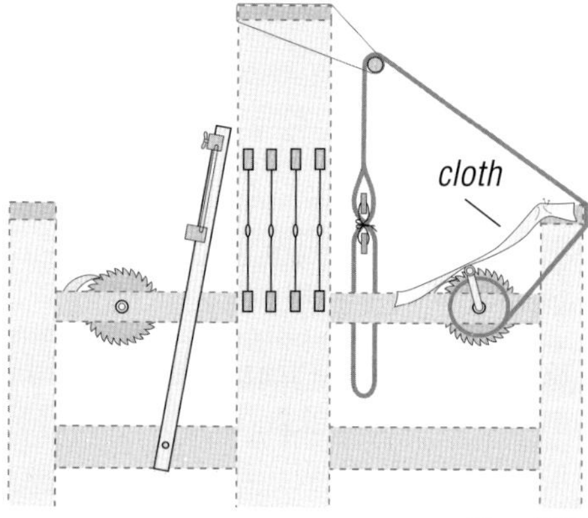

Fig. 175b

⑧ Learning How the Heddles Will Be Threaded

Your goal in threading is to thread each and every warp thread through a heddle on its correct shaft and in its correct sequence. For the sampler, I will tell you the order to thread the heddles. For future projects you will transpose a written shorthand called a threading draft from paper to the correct heddles and shafts. It is explained in the chapter on drafting and designing, beginning on page 195. Read all the way through page 71. Then start threading your own heddles.

Figure 176a shows how the shafts are numbered as well as the draft (which I will get to later) that will be used for the sampler. Note that the shaft closest to you is shaft #1 and the furthest one is shaft #4.

Thread the first thread of your warp into the first heddle on shaft #4, (the shaft furthest away from you). The next thread will go into a heddle on shaft #3, the third thread onto shaft #2, and the fourth warp thread will be threaded into the first heddle on shaft #1. This will be the threading plan for all the threads in the sampler. I say, "four, three, two, one," as I thread the heddles. Read on to know how the heddles are actually threaded.

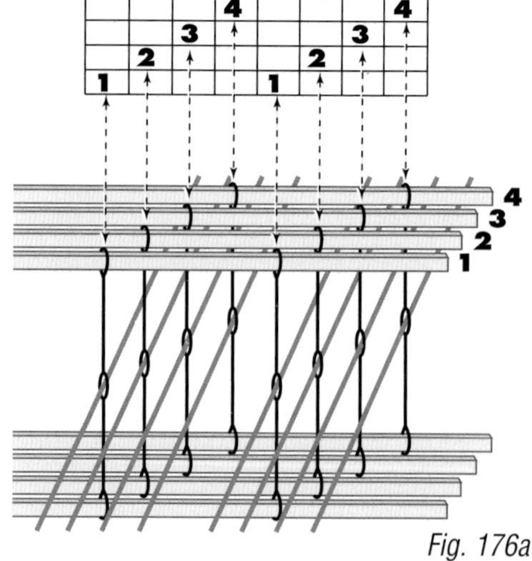

Fig. 176a

Left-handers will begin at the left side of the warp and thread 1,2,3,4—thus giving the same result as right-handers get. You would say, "one, two, three, four," because you are beginning where the right handers will end up.

For the sampler's threading plan (draft), I (a right-hander) like to start with shaft #4 because I think it's more efficient, and I can see what I'm doing better. If you are left handed you would use the same threading plan, but you would start at the left end of it, work toward the right, and begin with the front-most shaft. By the way, this is a threading that is often used because it can weave so many different structures.

However, when directions are given in a publication, you ***must*** thread in the sequence given. Most are meant to be read right to left with left-handers reading left to right.

For the sampler, the threads need to be in the heddles in the sequence shown in Figure 176b whether you start from the right side or the left. You will thread each thread as it comes from the lease sticks.

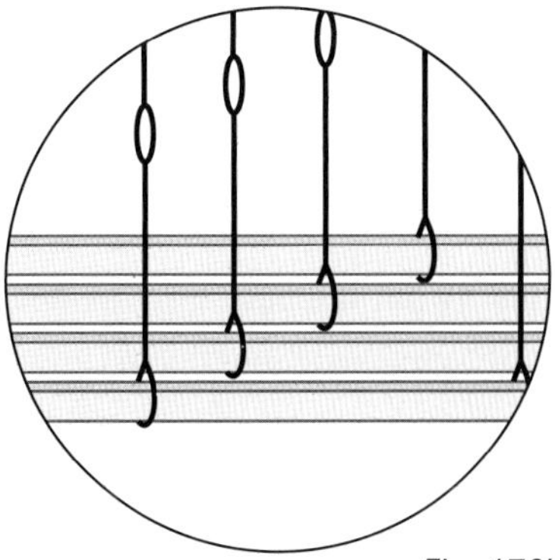

Fig. 176b

First you need to know how to tell which thread comes first, second, third, fourth, and so on. Here, the cross is incredibly valuable. Look at Figure 177 at the actual cross—the area between the lease sticks. Note that the threads cross over and under the lease sticks so you can tell their order at the area in between the sticks. Can you see that the first thread (from the right, remember) on the lease sticks goes over the front stick, then under the back stick and the next thread does the reverse? The second thread goes under the front stick and over the back one. The threads can easily be identified in order because of the way they cross one another between the lease sticks.

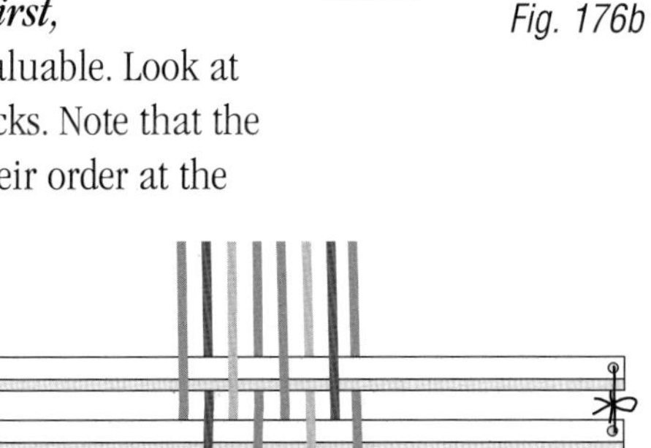

Fig. 177

In the illustration, the first thread is to be threaded into the first heddle on shaft 4. It means that you'll be looking in two places—first, to find the next thread in the sequence on the lease sticks, and second, which shaft and heddle to thread it in. (Starting on shaft 4 makes threading easier because you can see the shafts better.)

How to know which shaft a heddle is on

It's easier to see what shaft a heddle is on if you look at the bottoms of the shafts. See the closeup in Figure 176a.

Stagger the heddles

Push all your counted-out heddles to the left (for right-handers) and stagger the heddles on the shafts so you can find which one you need easily as shown in Figure 178. Left-handers would stagger them the same way, but have them over on the right side of the shafts. See Figure 189 on page 71 for clarity.

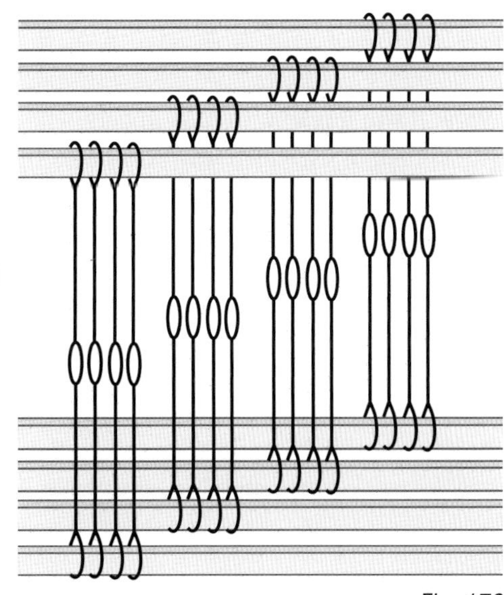

Fig. 178

⑨ Threading the Heddles

Use your long threading hook to thread the heddles. Get out the heddle needed and its thread and push the hook through the eye of the heddle from front to back, hook it onto the warp thread and bring it toward you through the eye. I like to use the hook upside down as in Figure 179a. (I prefer the hook in 179a rather than the shape in Figure 179b, which is a threading hook that is often sold.)

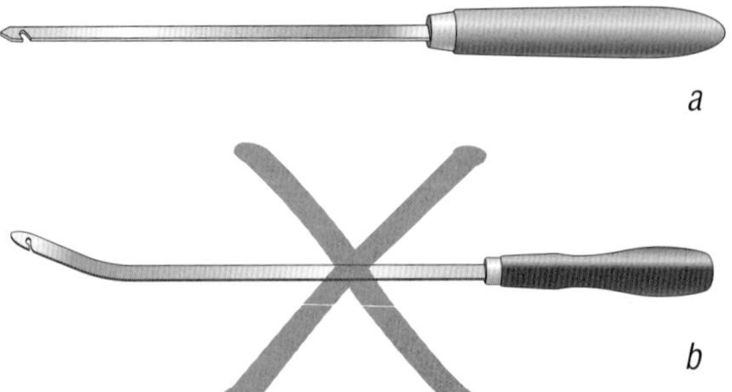

Fig. 179

How to put the hook into the heddle eye

With some heddles it doesn't matter how you enter the hook into the eye--heddles made of string or polyester, for instance, and "inserted eye" heddles. But wire and flat metal heddles open out to one side or the other. Flat metal and wire heddles can be turned so that the eyes are more "open" either to the right or to the left. Which angle is best depends on whether you enter the threading hook from the left or from the right. You want the threads to follow a perfectly straight path through the eye, with no drag or abrasion at the eyes. Figure 180 shows a warp thread that is ***not*** going straight through the heddle and shows what ***not*** to do. Figure 186 on page 70 shows the threads going straight through the heddles—what you need to do.

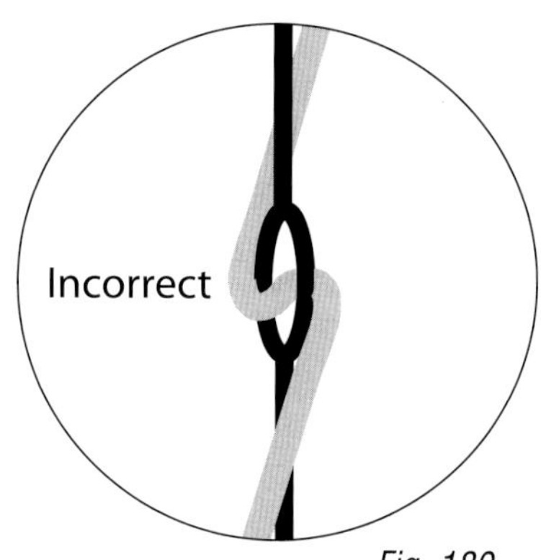

Fig. 180

If you thread with your right hand and your hook enters the eye on the right, then the heddle eye should open to the right. See Figure 181. If you thread with your left hand, then the eye should open to the left.

Note: If you thread with your fingers, without a hook, experiment to see which way works best for you.

In real life, your heddles may be mixed up on the shafts with some opening to the right and some, to the left. All you need to do is put the hook into the eye from the open side. In other words, if you come across a heddle that is open to the left, enter your threading hook into the left side of the heddle. Do the opposite if the heddle eye opens to the right. If all the heddles on a shaft are opening out on the same side, all the heddles will nest together like spoons. See Figure 182.

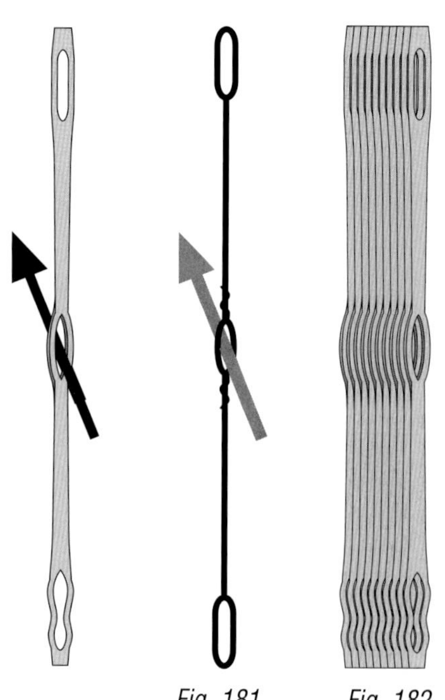
Fig. 181 Fig. 182

I do not recommend getting the heddles lined up on the shafts at this point—it's easy to enter the hook on the correct side, and moving heddles is a tricky business. Sometime, however, you may need to move heddles from shaft to shaft, add new ones, or remove excess ones. That is the time you will want to put them on properly so they all open to the side that you prefer, depending upon if you're right or left handed. There are instructions for how to align heddles on page 80.

If your heddles are staggered as in Figure 178 on page 67, and your cross is at eye level, threading should be pretty easy. You'll find that when you are looking at the cross you are actually checking if the thread you want should go over or under one of the lease sticks. You'll know which by observing the configuration of the previous thread on the sticks. This alternation, over and under, keeps the threads in order. If they weren't in order, they could get hopelessly tangled and weaving could be impossible.

After you have 4 threads threaded, tie them in a slipknot (see page 349) so they won't slip out of the heddles. Tie the knots close to the warp ends—so they can't get tangled in the heddles and shafts. See Figure 183.

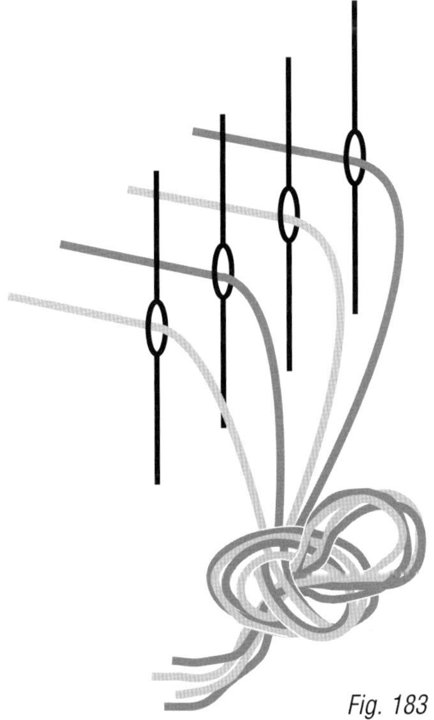

Fig. 183

A review of threading informatiion starts on the next page.

Remember:

- Work from right to left. (Left-handers work left to right .)
- Thread the heddles on the shafts in this order: four, three, two, one. (1, 2, 3, 4 for lefties) Shaft four is the one farthest from you, and shaft 1 is closest to you. *Do not remove the warp threads from the cross.* Figures 184 and 185 show that the cross should remain intact.
- *Be sure the threads go in straight lines*—in a straight path from the cross through the heddles. See Figure 186.
- *Do not let the threads cross over themselves* in the heddles as seen in Figure 187. If you discover this has happened, see what to do on pages 82 and

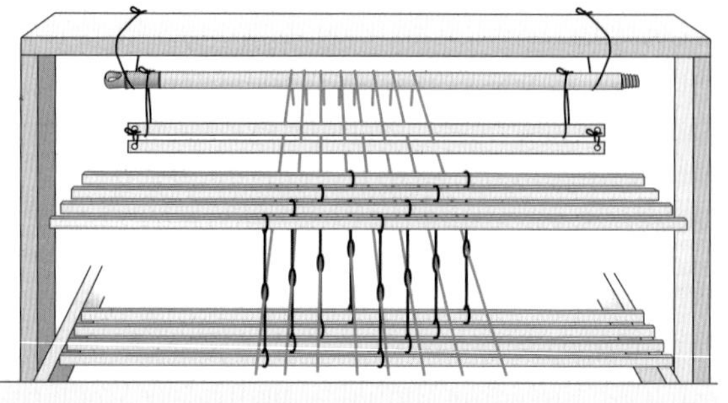

Fig. 184

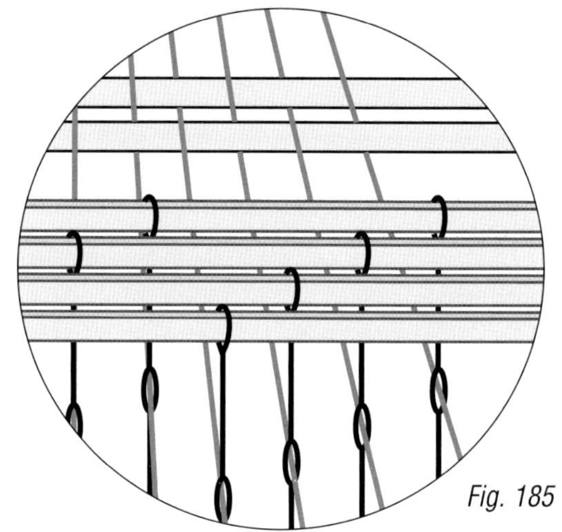

Fig. 185

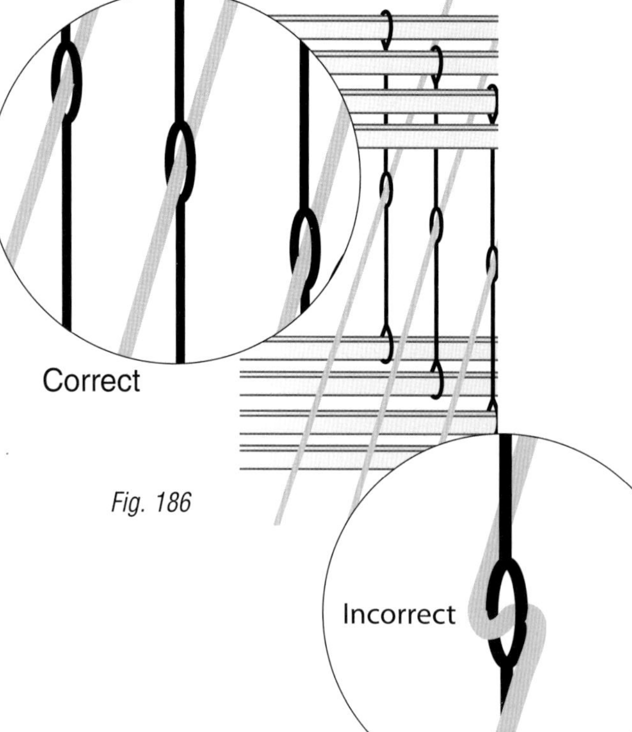

Fig. 186

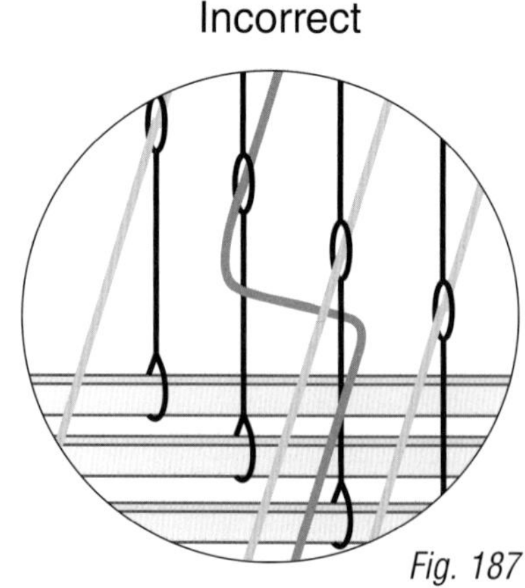

Fig. 187

Do not let the threads cross over themselves

What if there is a mistake in the cross?

When you were warping, I said a few mistakes in the cross wouldn't hurt. If you encounter any discrepancies in the cross, take the threads as they are on the lease sticks and don't try to correct them. The cross is there to guide you—not to rule you. If you find two threads in the same position just select one of them to thread first—it really won't make any difference which of the two are threaded first and second.

Thread the heddles according to what *should* be. The cross is there to help you, not to control you!

What if there is a mistake in the threading?

Mistakes in the threading must be corrected or else there will be a flaw running all the way through your cloth. Read what to do on pages 82 and 108.

Three tricks to try

You can try them or not; they are not required for threading.

One is to put some tension on the warp threads so they are taut when they are in the lease sticks making it easier to see which is the next thread. I use a wrench that lives in my apron pocket at all times. Anything of similar weight would work. My wrench weighs 3 ½ ounces. I almost never use it for any other purpose, but I did need it to escape a locked bathroom stall, once, at a workshop where I was teaching.

Put a loop of string on the weight and add a rubber band onto the loop with a lark's head knot (shown on page 352). Then, separate a bundle of cut warp threads about the thickness of a medium-sized carrot and with another lark's head, tie the rubber band onto the bundle near the end of the warp. The weight hangs straight down from the lease sticks, behind the shafts. Figure 188. When you select a strand to thread next, you pull it out of the weighted bundle.

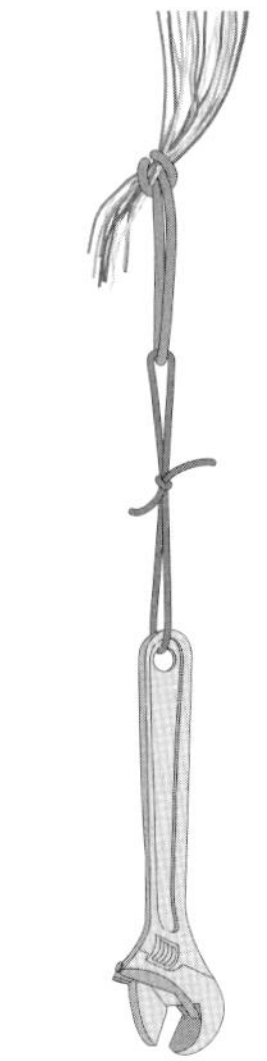

Fig. 188

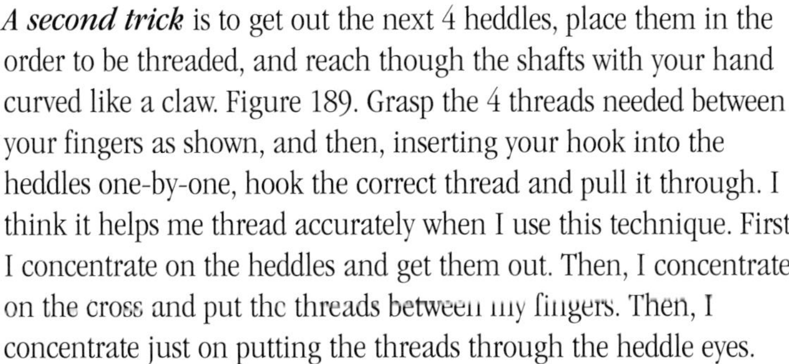

A second trick is to get out the next 4 heddles, place them in the order to be threaded, and reach though the shafts with your hand curved like a claw. Figure 189. Grasp the 4 threads needed between your fingers as shown, and then, inserting your hook into the heddles one-by-one, hook the correct thread and pull it through. I think it helps me thread accurately when I use this technique. First, I concentrate on the heddles and get them out. Then, I concentrate on the cross and put the threads between my fingers. Then, I concentrate just on putting the threads through the heddle eyes.

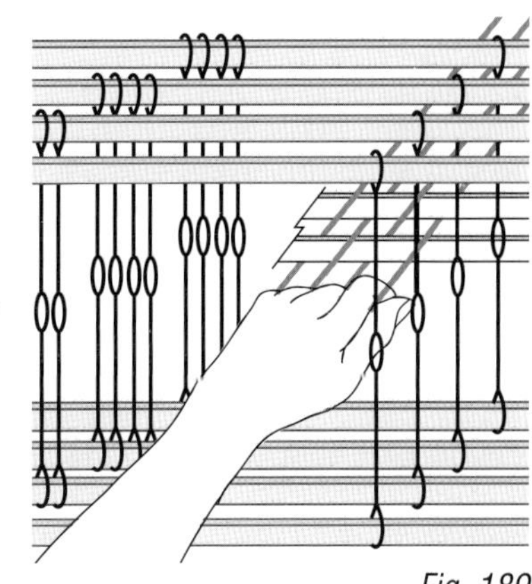

Fig. 189

The third trick is to watch for consistencies (and inconsistencies). For example, you might notice that when you thread the heddles on shaft four, the warp thread is always on the top of the lower lease stick. If that suddenly isn't the case, look to see if you made a mistake—either in selecting the correct warp thread or the correct heddle.

When you are finished threading the heddles, the next stage is to put the threads into the reed.

Sleying the Reed

Drawing the warp threads through the spaces (called dents) in your reed—"sleying" the reed—is one of your last steps in preparing the loom for weaving. Don't let your alertness flag! Even though the threading is finished, and it feels like sleying the reed is a snap, it's easy to make mistakes. Gather up some new energy and concentration. Being comfortable is just as important, now, as when threading the heddles.

(1) Preliminaries

Be sure that the length of the warp threads hanging in their knotted bundles from the heddles is long enough for both sleying and tying the threads onto the apron rod (which you do after sleying the reed). You should have around 12" in length. (A little more is better than a little less—you won't waste any warp because you can rewind any extra warp onto the warp beam later. If you have to unwind some warp from the warp beam to have about 12" worth to work with, do so carefully; the threads in the heddles are not under tension and can get tangled very easily. Release the brake and unwind no more than 2". Gently ease sections of the warp through the heddles one section at a time. If you need to un-wind more, do so in 2" lengths until you have all the warp you need. Watch out for slack threads that wind around the heddles and get out of sequence—tug on the knotted bundles of warps to be sure the threads are all in a straight path. Figure 190 shows the problem of a thread out of place in the heddles.

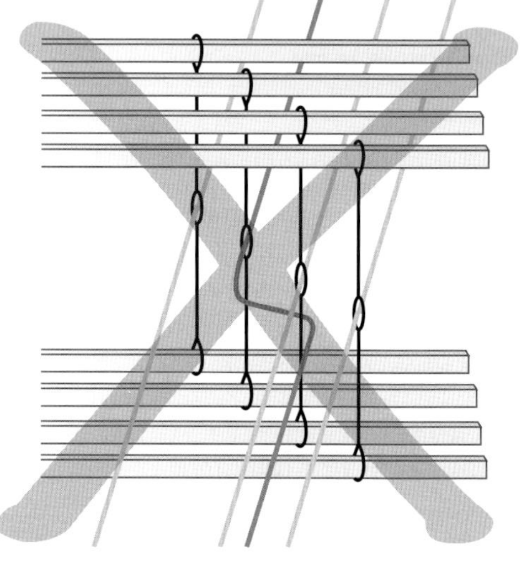

Fig. 190

Choose the reed

Sleying is an important step because it spreads out the warp in the reed to its exact weaving width and density. How many warp threads you draw through each space, or dent, in the reed depends on the sett (ends per inch or epi) you determined and the reeds you have available.

The ideal is to sley two threads per dent as shown in Figure 191. However, it isn't always possible to thread two threads per dent, and sometimes you may have to skip dents, sley more than two threads per dent, or even alternate the number of threads per dent. If you don't have the ideal reed on hand, see the Reed Substitution Chart in the sidebar.

The ideal reed for the sampler is a 10-dent reed with two threads per dent. Read how to use the chart in the sidebar.

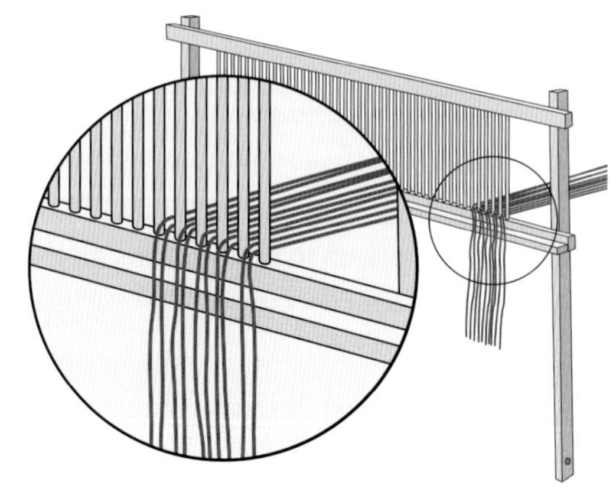

Fig. 191

Reed Substitution Chart

When you don't have the ideal reed to sley two warp ends per dent, use this substitution chart.

Sequence in dents = the number of empty spaces in the reed and the number of threads in each space.

Example: 0-1-1 = The sequence to sley the reed, repeated for the width of the warp:

1 empty dent
1 thread in a dent
1 thread in a dent
or "empty-1-1; empty-1-1", etc.

Sequence of warps in the dents	Reed size (Dents per inch)					
	8	**10**	**12**	**15**	**18**	**20**
	Warp Ends Per Inch (epi or sett)					
0-1	4	5	6	7½	9	10
0-1-1	5	7	8	10	12	13
0-1-1-1	6	7½	9	11½	13½	15
1	8	10	12	15	18	20
1-1-1-2	10	12½	15	19	22½	25
1-1-2	11	13	16	20	24	27
1-2	12	15	18	22½	27	30
1-2-2	13	17	20	25	30	33
1-2-2-2	14	17½	21	26	31½	35
2	16	20	24	30	36	40

Reed Substitiution Chart

When you don't have the ideal reed for the sett (ends per inch), you must substitute one that you do have. Reeds go by dents per inch—meaning the number of spaces in the reed in one inch. The ideal reed accommodates two warp ends per dent, so that knots can pass through, and to avoid reed marks. The main thing you want to do is retain the epi (ends per inch) required.

Say you want to have 10 threads in one inch, and you have a reed that will give you 8 threads in an inch, you need to change from the ideal of 2 threads per dent to something else.

So, look for the sett (epi) you require (here, 10) in the column headed by the reed that you want to use (here, 8).

Look over to the left column (next to 10) to see the sequence that you will need to sley the reed to attain the sett you need. I see that what is given for an 8-dent reed for 10 epi, is sequence: 1-1-1-2—that is, one thread in a dent, another single thread, and yet another, then, 2 threads in the next dent. Or, 3 single threads per dent, then, a double. Repeat these 4 dents for all the warp threads.

Another example, which isn't so pretty, is one where it doesn't quite work out for the exact sett you want, and you have to compromise. You have to pick the one that's close enough.

If your sett is 12 epi, and you only have a 10-dent reed, you would look in the column for 10 dent reeds and note that 12 ½ is close enough.

Then, look over to the left column to see the sequence (order) that the threads should be placed (sleyed) into the dents: one, one, one, two.

Replace the reed

Replace the reed and beater if you removed either or both of them to thread the heddles.

If you removed the beater for threading, put it back into position, taking care not to put it in backwards. The shuttle race (the ledge in front of and at the base of the reed) belongs on the side toward you as you weave. Also check that the wings of any wing nuts that hold the beater cap in place face toward you and away from the loom to prevent them from gouging the loom.

Position yourself and the reed

If you have trouble with your eyesight or if the warps are hard to see, experiment with the following suggestions until you find a way that lets you see the threads and the dents clearly.

Find a chair, stool, or bench that gives you the most comfortable position. I use a stool higher than my threading stool but a little lower than the loom bench. For one of my looms I use a dining room chair—don't think about using telephone books, they will slip and slide and cause frustration. If your chair/stool isn't exactly the best height, just remember to stretch periodically while sleying the reed to prevent aches in your shoulders, neck, and arms.

There are two basic positions for setting up the reed for sleying. In one, the reed sits vertically in the beater, in its most upright position. In the other, the reed is not in the beater but supported horizontally, lying flat, as if across your lap. Both methods work; choose the one that makes it easier to see.

In the vertical position, set the reed in the beater and be sure the reed itself is centered within the beater. Begin with the beater standing vertically about half way between the first shaft and the breast beam. You might adjust it to lean back or forward a bit so you can see what you are doing better. If your loom came with a beater-stop (a pin or a block of wood shaped to hold the beater upright by anchoring it to the loom frame), engage it. If your loom doesn't have one, use string to tie the beater upright—one cord tied to a front part of the loom and another tied to the castle will do it. See Figure 192. Use long strings and bow ties so that you can adjust the position of the beater, if needed, when you sit on your stool so that you can see clearly the threads and the dents in the reed.

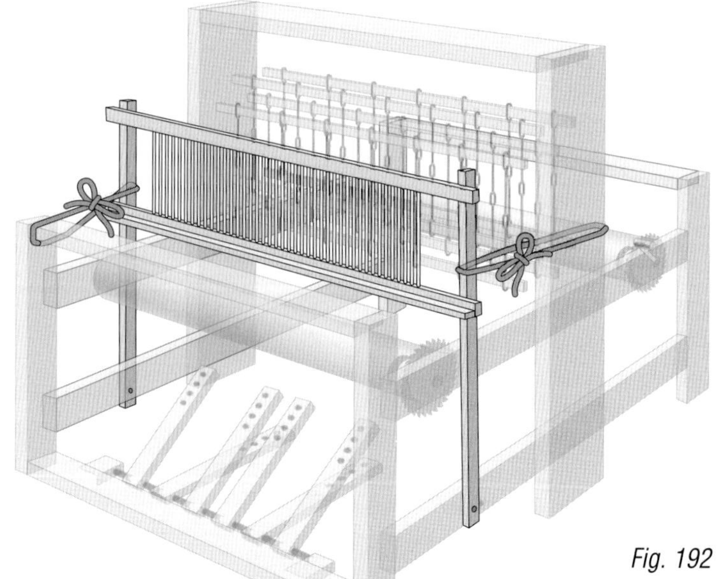

Fig. 192

In the horizontal position set the reed in front of you horizontally supported on 2 long sticks. The sticks are long enough to rest on the breast and back beams. See Figure 193. When the reed is set horizontally, you can either draw the threads ***up*** from underneath the reed or ***down*** from above the reed. A credit card can make a good tool to push threads down.

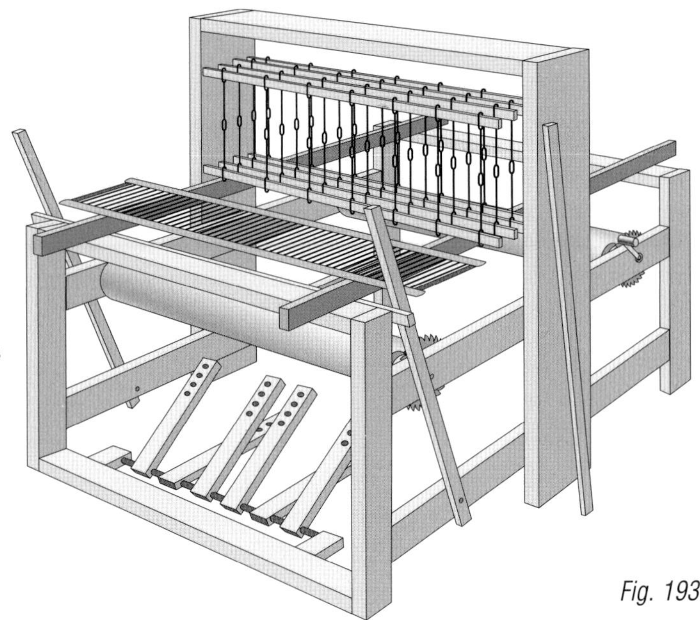

Fig. 193

For either position, I use a plastic sley hook, sometimes called a reed hook, as shown in Figure 194.

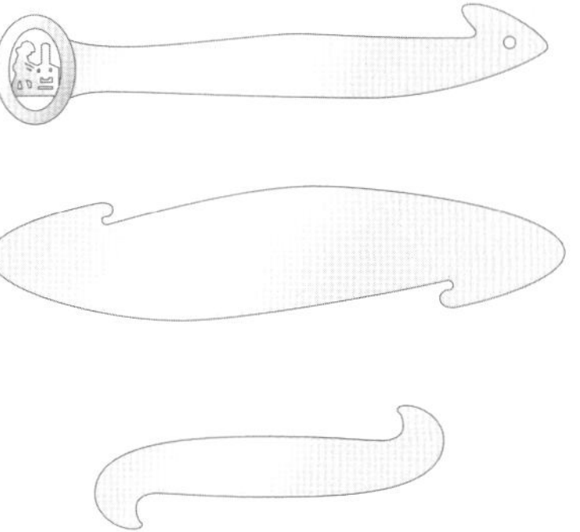

Fig. 194

When you put the reed back into the beater after sleying, be sure the threads are coming out toward the front of the loom as shown in Figure 196 on the next page.

② Sley the Reed

Find the center of your reed and measure one half of the warp width both to the left and right of the center. For the sampler, you'll measure 2 ½" to the right and left of center for its 5" width. I never count the dents themselves—just measuring with a tape measure is accurate enough. Mark the starting and ending points with pieces of string—I put them in the starting and ending dents. Start at one side—usually the same side you started threading. Using your sley (reed) hook, draw your chosen number of warp threads through each dent.

As I sley, I loosen the heddles from their bunches and align them with the reed's spacing. I take the handful of threads to be sleyed and position the heddles at approximately the place where they'll go in the reed, then, I put the threads in the dents. After the reed is sleyed, all the threads travel in a fairly straight path from the warp beam through the heddles and through the reed. If there are clips on the bars holding the heddles, secure the heddle bars in them now.

If there are clips on the bars holding the heddles, secure the heddle bars in them now.

As I said before, be alert so you don't make mistakes. The three most common errors in sleying the reed are doubling up threads in dents, skipping a dent, and getting the threads out of order. Skipping or doubling up the threads will cause vertical lines or flaws in the woven cloth. Getting threads out of order is more serious and must be corrected. Figure 195 shows you what to avoid. You probably won't notice this error until you begin weaving. How to detect this error and correct it are found on pages 82 and 108. If you notice doubled threads or skipped dents, correct them now. You may need to re-sley from the error to the nearest edge of the warp. See page 81 for an easy way to re-sley.

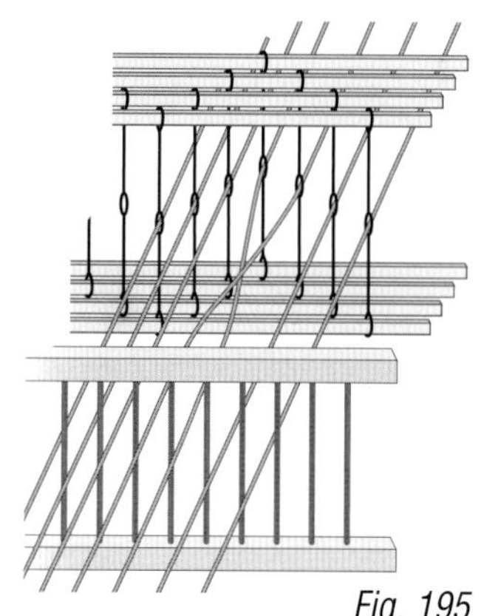

Fig. 195
Warning: Avoid crossed threads!!

While sleying the reed, check that you threaded the heddles correctly. Double checking now and catching any mistakes is a good idea because it is easier to correct them at this point than when you are ready to weave. Correcting mistakes information is found on pages 82 and 108.

Secure the threads as you go. To keep the threads from slipping out of their correct dents, tie them with slipknots, just as you did after threading the heddles. Now, you can tie larger bundles of an inch or so worth of threads. See Figure 196.

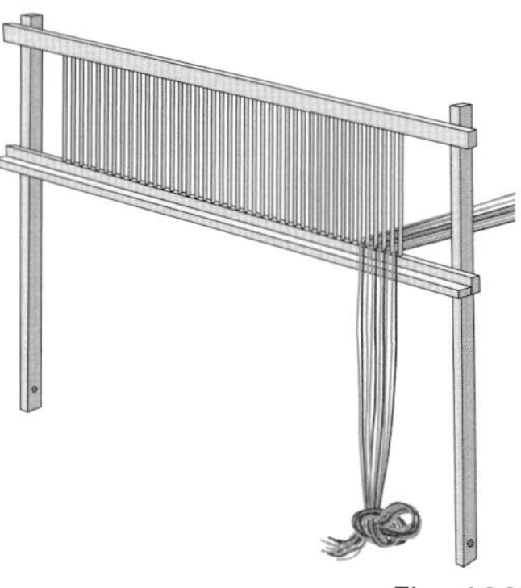

Fig. 196

Check that the heddles are spaced out. As I said, I space out the heddles as I'm sleying the reed. Now, there shouldn't be any bunches of heddles, and the threads should be pretty straight. The warp threads become very straight when they are tied onto the apron and under tension—the next steps. All heddle bars (upper and lower) should be secured in their clips at this time.

Now you have threaded the heddles and sleyed the reed. You are ready to tie the warp threads onto the apron rod. That process is called "tying on" and begins on page 83.

More About Threading the Heddles

I. What if you did not re-position the warp over the back beam?

If you notice that you did not re-position the warp over the back beam, finish threading the heddles and the reed and do the job then, if possible. It may be that you cannot do it until the warp has been tied onto the cloth apron rod as described on page 318.

There are two options: If possible, remove the back beam and replace it with the warp going ***over*** it by putting the back beam itself ***under*** the warp.

If the back beam is not removable, you need to reposition the warp after it is tied on to the front apron, as described on page 318 in the Troubleshooting chapter.

II. What if you lose the cross?

This is something you don't want to happen, but I've seen it often with my beginning students because they didn't realize they were untying the ties holding the cross. Usually, a person only does this once, and the lesson has been learned. The time it happened to me was when I was a student. I took the warp off the warping board before lunch. The lesson learned was: "Do not do an important task when you are hungry!!"

Since this usually happens with beginning weavers making small projects, you can get away with threading the heddles the best you can. You can ***never*** find the exact order of the warp threads; so don't even try. Just pick threads that are in the vicinity of where your heddles are and thread them. Perhaps, there are stripes in the warp, which can give you clues as to where a thread's neighborhood is. There will be some crossed threads behind the heddles, which you may need to work back as you weave along. It very likely could be that you don't have any trouble at all.

If the warp were large and the threads fine it would be a terrible thing if you lost the cross because the threads would get tangled, and you would have to unsnarl them constantly throughout weaving.

III. Moving heddles

There are three things to know about moving heddles on, off, or from shaft-to-shaft: How to get the heddles on and off the shafts, how to align them, and how to keep them tied securely for moving. Do this before threading.

1. How to get heddles on and off the shafts.

This is a tedious, I would say fiddly, process, which needs concentration and patience. Do not attempt this job unless you are prepared with both of these requirements. Be fresh and allow yourself plenty of time.

Sometimes, the shafts themselves must be removed from the loom before any heddles can be added or removed, and you'll work on a table or other flat surface, and you may prefer to lift out the shafts. Often, you can do the job with the shafts in place. When you look at your own shafts, you can clearly see whether or not you must remove the entire shaft. It's easy to remove the shafts on some looms—they simply lift out of the castle. Various looms are built differently, so you'll have to look at your own shafts and notice what holds them in place to see how to remove them.

The heddles on some looms are mounted on the top and bottom of the shafts themselves, as in Figure 197. Getting the heddles on and off of them is a process you can figure out by looking at the loom. Again, remember, patience, concentration, and time are important. Read how to carefully move heddles, below.

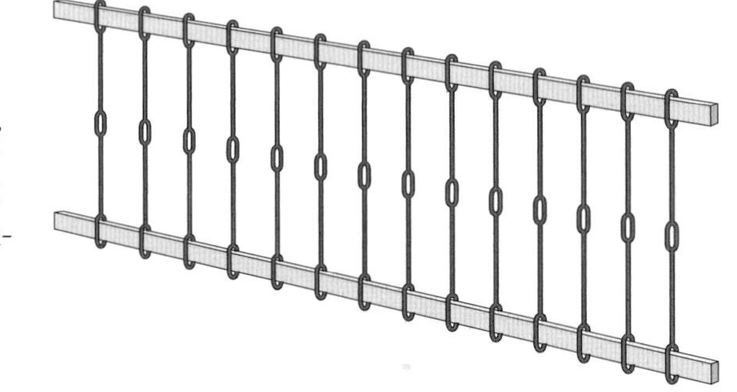

Fig. 197

Most shafts have flat metal bars on them, which hold the heddles. There is a top bar and a bottom bar on each shaft, and they are held in place in slots at each side of the shaft. See Figures 198 and 199. The bars are flexible, but can flex only when the heddles are pushed to the sides of the shafts. This configuration leaves room for "play" so the bars can be bent and then, removed from the holding slots. ***Be very careful when removing a heddle bar from its holding slots. Be careful that the heddles on the bar don't come off.*** Note that if there are clips on the middle of the heddle bars, they must be undone and the heddle bars released from the clips before you can flex the heddle bars. Read how to open the clips on page 79.

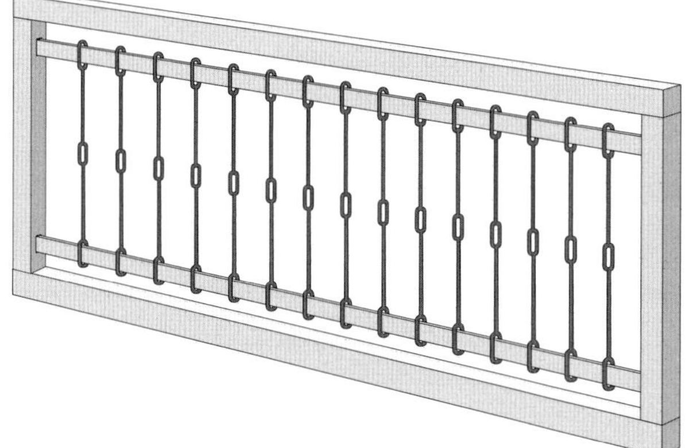

Fig. 198

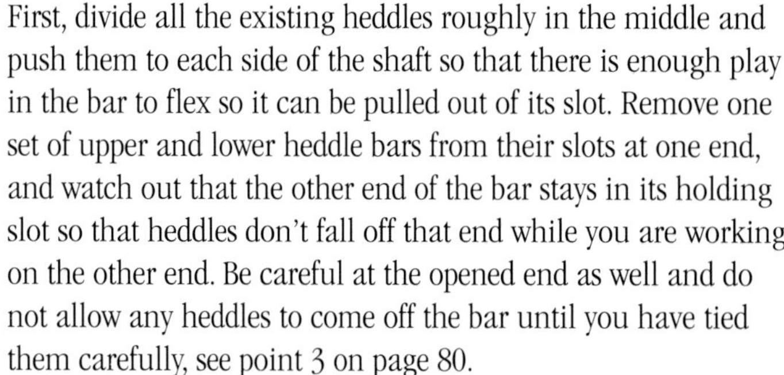

First, divide all the existing heddles roughly in the middle and push them to each side of the shaft so that there is enough play in the bar to flex so it can be pulled out of its slot. Remove one set of upper and lower heddle bars from their slots at one end, and watch out that the other end of the bar stays in its holding slot so that heddles don't fall off that end while you are working on the other end. Be careful at the opened end as well and do not allow any heddles to come off the bar until you have tied them carefully, see point 3 on page 80.

You'll work at one end of a shaft at a time. If you can add or remove all you need to at one end and distribute the remaining heddles across the shaft, fine. If, however, you can't move

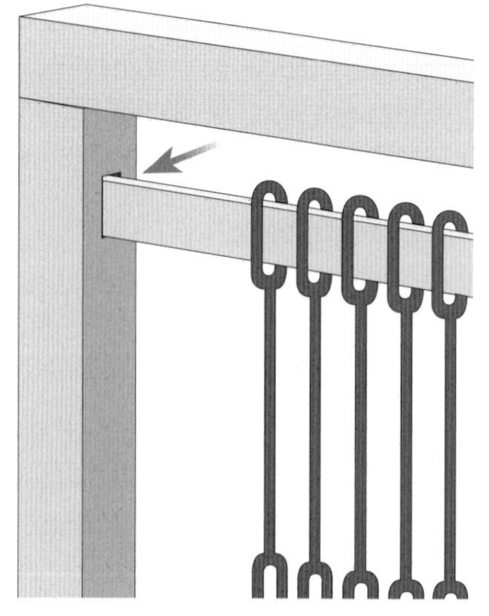

Fig. 199

the heddles past the clips in the center, you'll have to work on one side for its needed heddles and then work on the other side of the shaft to put on or take off the heddles needed on that side of center. Secure the bars in their slots before going to the other side to work. The larger the loom, the more cumbersome this job is. Smaller table looms are easier because you can get close to the shafts to see what you are doing and to work. Sometimes it's easier if you lift out a shaft and work on a table.

Opening clips on heddle bars

Floor looms and some wider table looms have clips or hooks in the centers of the bars that hold the heddle bars to the shafts, and to keep these very long, flexible bars from bending. If there is just a simple clip, flex the bar as explained above and take it out of the clip. However, clips vary—they may have tiny springs in them. For clips with springs, pinch the clip to squeeze the spring to open the clip, and then, release the heddle bar by flexing it out of the clip. See Figures 200a, b, and c. Remember, there are clips on both the upper and lower heddle bars. You'll need to undo the clips and release the heddle bars before you can take them out of their holding slots.

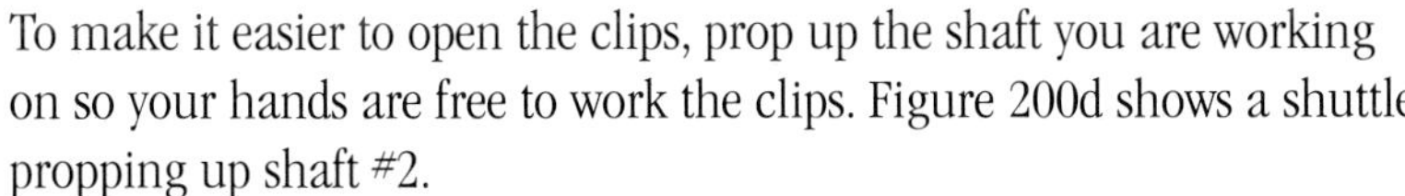

To make it easier to open the clips, prop up the shaft you are working on so your hands are free to work the clips. Figure 200d shows a shuttle propping up shaft #2.

To secure the heddle bars back into the clips after threading the heddles, push the heddles out toward the sides of the shafts just enough so you can flex the bars. Pinch the springs in the clips and slip the heddle bars back into them Remember, there are clips on both the upper and lower heddle bars.

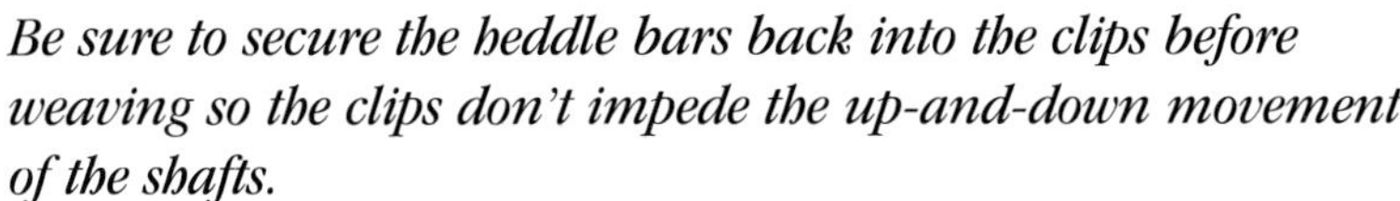

Be sure to secure the heddle bars back into the clips before weaving so the clips don't impede the up-and-down movement of the shafts.

Fig. 200

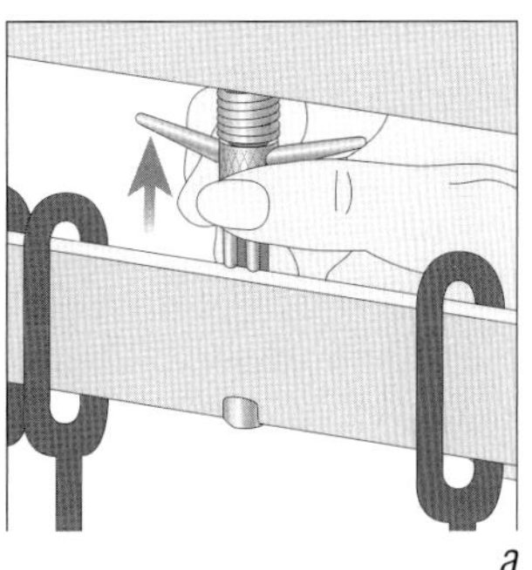

a

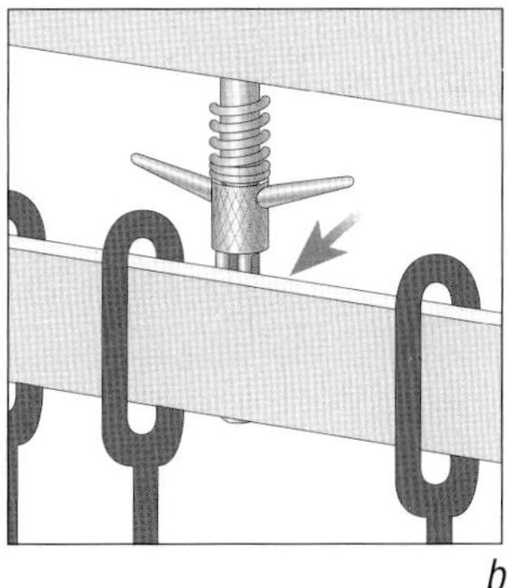

b

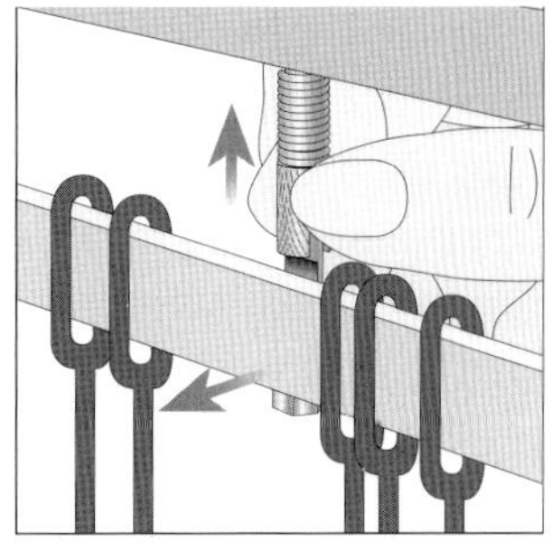

c

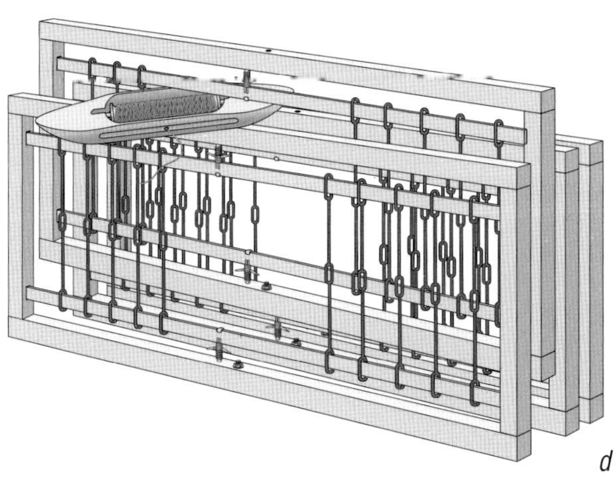

d

2. How to align heddles

Align heddles when you want to add or move them to other shafts. Your goal is to have all your heddles lined up alike on the shafts according to whether you are right-handed or left-handed. They will nest like spoons if they are all opening in the same direction. See Figure 182 on page 68 and repeated here.

With the loose heddles in your hand, look to see if a heddle is opening in the wrong direction for you; turn it upside down if it is, and you will see that it opens to the opposite side. If you look closely, the two ends of the heddle are sometimes slightly different—an aid to getting them all lined up and right-side-up. Look again at Figure 181 repeated here.

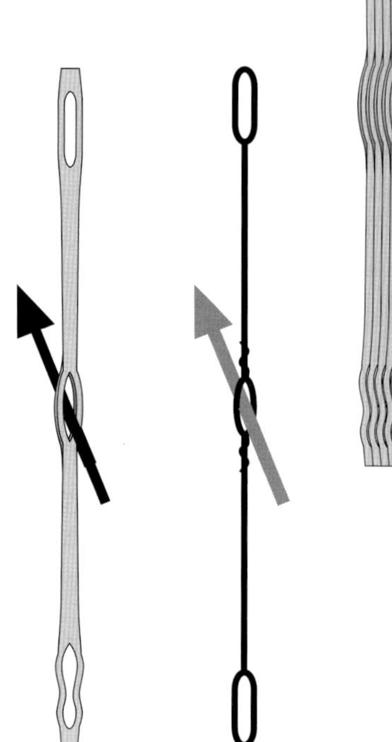

As you work aligning heddle-by-heddle, keep them nested and together until you tie them to keep them from getting loose, because if they are loose, the heddles will be in a tangle—causing a huge frustration. Work with small groups of heddles, rather than trying to keep many of them lined up. Read #3, below, about how to keep them tied together.

3. How to carefully move heddles.

Figure 201 shows how to tie metal heddles together so you can move them from shaft to shaft or remove them if there are too many on the shafts. By tying them this way, you can put them onto the shafts in order. It's easier if you tie them in small groups, say of 15-20 heddles per group—whatever amount you can handle easily. If you let the heddles be loose, the job of putting them on the shafts will be extremely tedious and frustrating

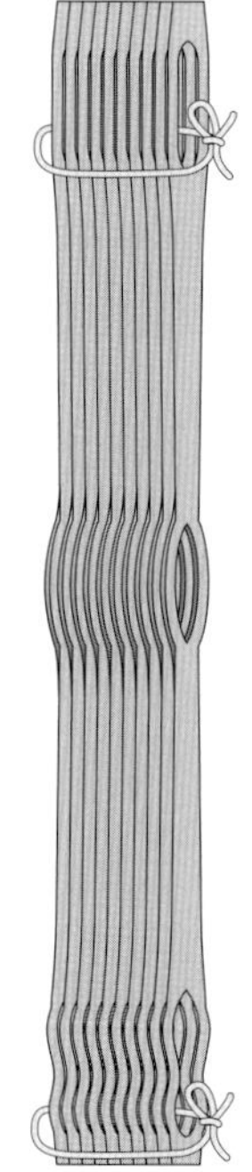

Fig. 201

String or polyester heddles are best handled by tying them together in bundles of 25 or 50 or so. Use a tapestry needle to run string through their tops and bottoms to tie the bundles. I like to tie four ties—one on each side of each opening—at the top and at the bottom, like I do when I tie the crosses at the warping board. This method keeps the openings for the heddle bars clearly open, making it easier to add the heddles to the shafts. Note in Figure 202 the ties are color-coded so the heddles don't become twisted.

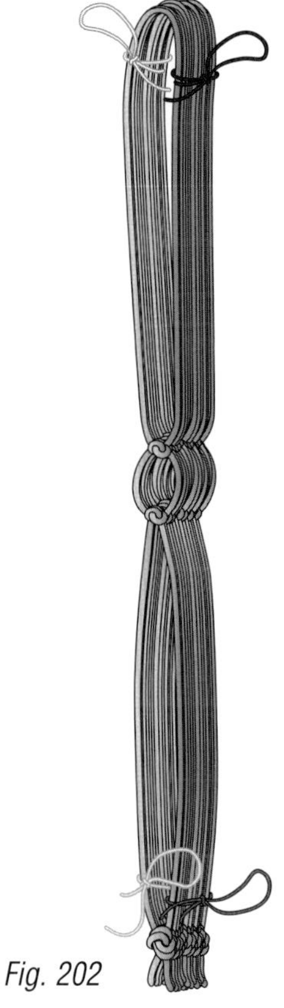

Fig. 202

IV. A fast way to re-sley errors in the reed

There's an easier way to re-sley the reed than unthreading all the threads that need to be moved at once. Instead, before un-threading anything, insert your sley hook into the new reed position for the incorrectly sleyed thread. Hook the thread to be moved behind the reed and draw it and the sley hook through the dent. In effect, you are "de-sleying" and "re-sleying" in one movement. See Figure 203.

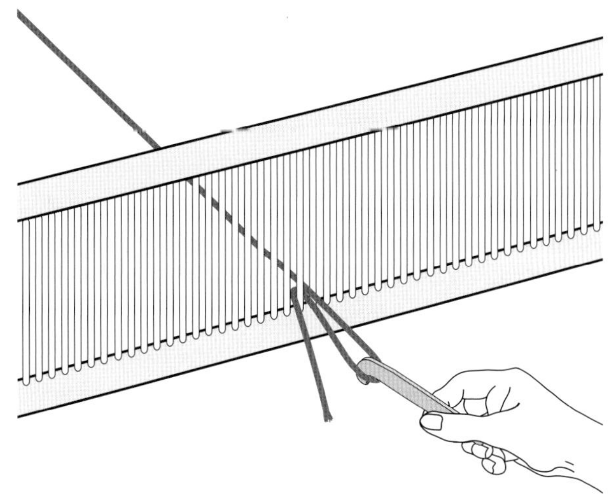

Fig. 203

V. How to correct mistakes in the heddles

Hopefully, you'll never have a threading error to correct, but that is highly unlikely in your weaving life. Errors often show up when you are sleying the reed and when you begin to weave. Read here how to correct errors found while sleying the reed. Errors found when you begin to weave are discussed beginning on page 108.

There are two common mistakes in the heddles. One is that threads are crossed among the heddles as shown in Figure 204a.

The other mistake is threads that are out of order in the heddles. Rearrange any mis-threaded heddles, now. You may have to re-thread from the place of the mistake to the nearest edge of the warp, but many mistakes can be corrected without all that work.

Look at the threads in the heddles carefully and see if one or more threads are not in the proper threading sequence. You may need to re-thread a few heddles to get the threads back in order. Check around the vicinity and see if you find an empty heddle nearby, if one is needed to get the threads in order.

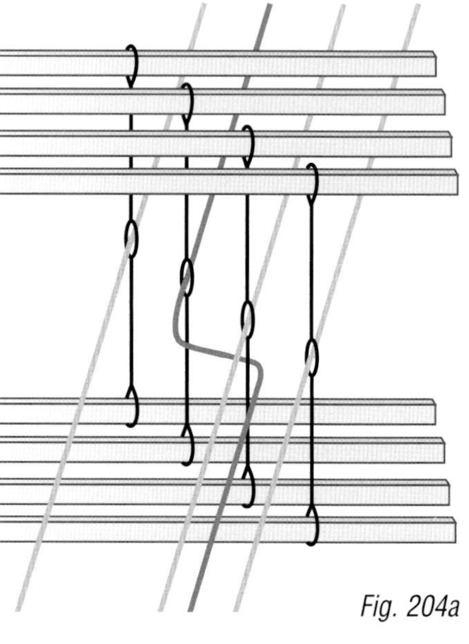

Fig. 204a

If you find two threads on the same shaft and all the other heddles nearby are correctly threaded, you can just pull out one of the threads and let it hang off the back beam. This action eliminates the thread altogether, and you can do it if a deleted thread doesn't harm the design of your project. It will not make a difference in your sampler. It's not a problem for empty heddles to be interspersed in with the threaded heddles.

It may be that a heddle is not in the place where you need it, and you will need to make your own heddle. Although commercially-made repair heddles are available, it's easy to make one. Loop a length of string around the bottom heddle bar of the shaft; tie a knot level with the base of the heddle eyes of the regular heddles on that shaft. To make the eye of your new heddle, tie another knot above the first one, even with the tops of the regular heddle eyes. Tie the top of the new heddle to the top heddle bar of the shaft. See Figure 204b. Be careful to tie the repair heddle onto the correct shaft on the top, as well as on the bottom. Be alert when making corrections—I can repeat the mistake instead of correcting it if I'm not careful. Be sure to make your string plenty long so it will be easier to tie all the knots.

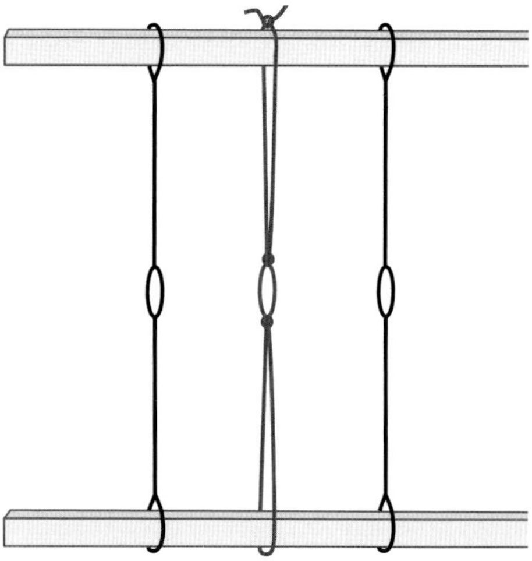

Fig. 204b

Back-to-Front Warping

Part Four: Tying On

In this section you will tie the warp threads onto a bar (called the apron rod) at the front of the loom, which will put the warp threads under tension—the last step before weaving. I find it thrilling when the warp threads are finally under tension—they are so orderly and ready for weaving. There is a saying from my mentor, Jim Ahrens. "The only thread that can't tangle is one under tension." I think that's the reason it's so satisfying to me to see the warp under tension.

How you tie the warp threads on to the front apron rod affects the tension of the warp throughout your weaving. The process is called "tying on" and goes very quickly, especially, if you find yourself a fresh supply of patience and concentration.

The goal is to have all the warp threads under equal tension.

Equipment List:

Packing Stick: to use for an apron rod, if needed

Scissors:

String:

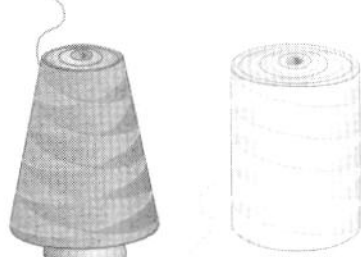

Step One: Preliminaries

Be sure the breast beam is in place if you removed it for threading.

Take down the broom handle. Now is the time to untie the strings tying the top lease stick to the broom handle and to carefully take down the broom handle, as well. I just slip it out of its string loops and leave the loops on the loom ready for the next warp I make.

Do not remove the lease sticks (Figure 205). If the lease sticks are very tipsy without the broom handle support, tie them temporarily to each side of the loom while you finish tying on. Attach long holding strings at each end of the lease sticks, where they are already tied together. Lash the lease sticks to the sides of the loom with the string. Now, the sticks are parallel to the floor, and are not likely to tip and fall down. Another way to stabilize the lease sticks would be in the same manner that they are tied in Figure 421 on page 191. However, if your loom has very little space behind the heddles, it's OK to remove the lease sticks.

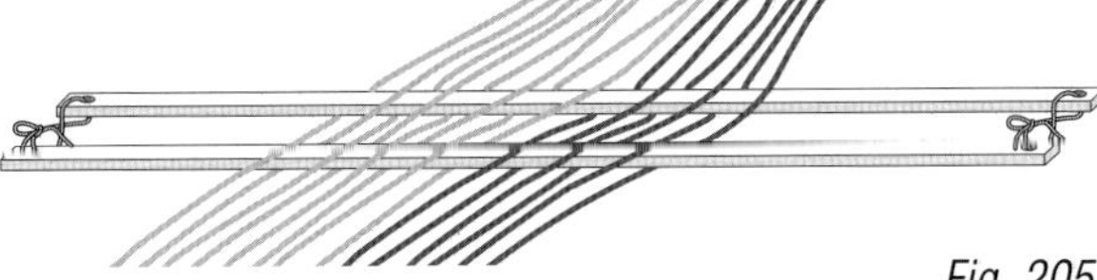

Fig. 205

Lower the shafts if you raised them for threading the heddles. (Remove the props or ties that held the shafts up for threading.)

Apron Rod

Prepare the apron rod if necessary.

Your loom has an apron at the front similar to the one attached to the warp beam. Just like the apron at the back of the loom, this one is made of either cords or cloth and has a bar attached. It is attached to the cloth beam, which you can see in the loom illustrations on this page. Figure 206 shows an apron made of cords and Figure 207 shows a cloth apron.

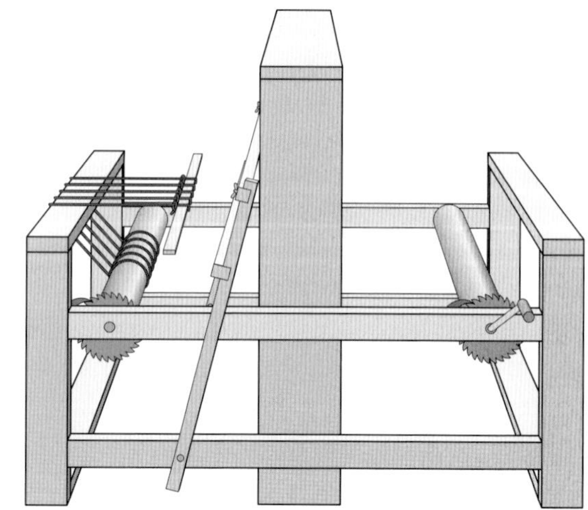

Fig. 206

If your loom has a cloth apron with a rod running through a pocket at the edge, you'll find it easier to tie on your warps if you lash another rod to the apron rod with sturdy cord. This way you don't have to jam many threads into the few, small, V-shaped spaces along the apron. See Figure 208. You can use a wooden dowel ½" diameter), or a metal rod (¼" diameter), or one of your packing sticks, for now. Get a proper apron rod (the dowel), so it will be ready for you for your next project. It should be about 3" shorter than the cloth beam, or short enough that it doesn't interfere with the ratchet brake on the cloth beam.

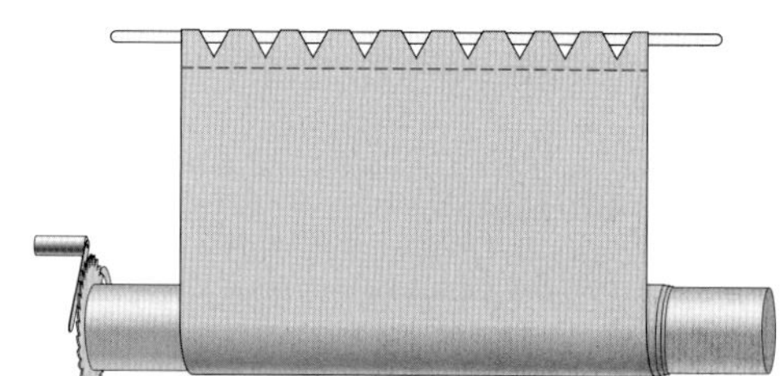

Fig. 207

Here is how to lash on the dowel: At one end of the dowel tie a strong string (double your string, if necessary) to the existing apron rod using a double half hitch knot (page 353). Zig-zag the string back and forth, as shown in the illustration, between the new rod and the existing apron rod at the V-shaped spaces. Tie the string at the other end of the rod, as shown, using another double half hitch knot. Don't worry if the lacing is even at this point. The two sticks should be approximately two inches apart. After the string is tied at each end, it is easy to make the two rods parallel by see-sawing the new stick back and forth a bit (pushing one end back and pulling the other end forward a few times).

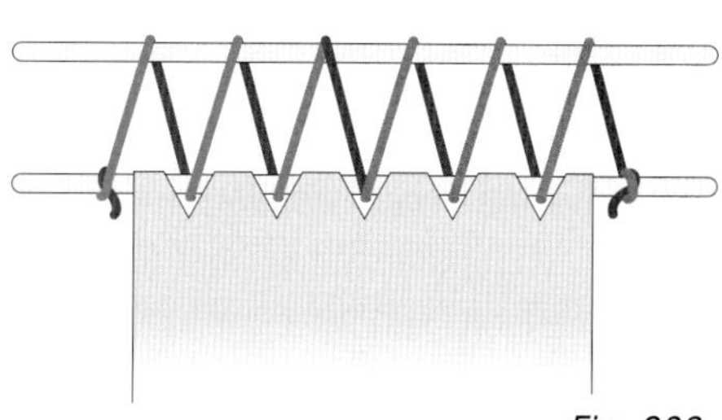

Fig. 208

The extra rod usually stays attached between projects—the string has enough purchase to keep it in place. There isn't much of a problem with it falling out because, between projects, you'll probably wind up the apron, including the new rod, onto the beam. When you start to use it again, you will see-saw it again to get it parallel to the original apron.

In real life, mine do fall out sometimes, but the string is there, so it is easy to put the stick back into the lacing.

Adjust the apron rod for a narrow warp

Since your sampler is only 5" wide, and the apron rod is significantly longer, you need to slip off any lashing that extends beyond the width of the warp. If you don't, the apron rod may bow under the tension of the warp. You can easily slip the lashing back on the apron rod for a wider warp at a later time. Figures 209 and 210 make this process clear.

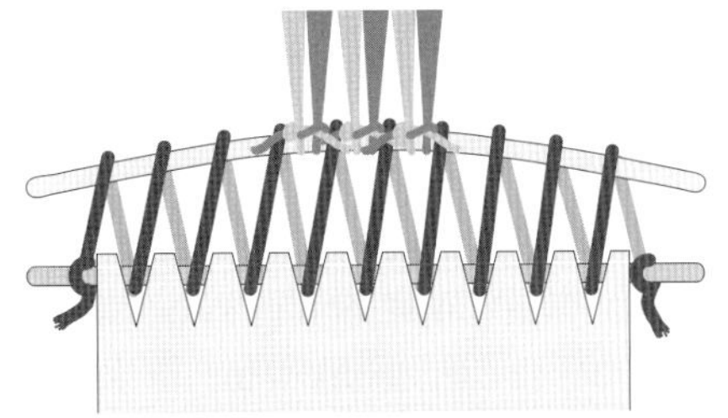

Fig. 209

If it is possible, do this adjustment even if your loom has apron cords, not a cloth apron. Just slip off any cords that extend beyond the 5" width of the warp. However, on your loom it may not be possible to slip the cords off at all.

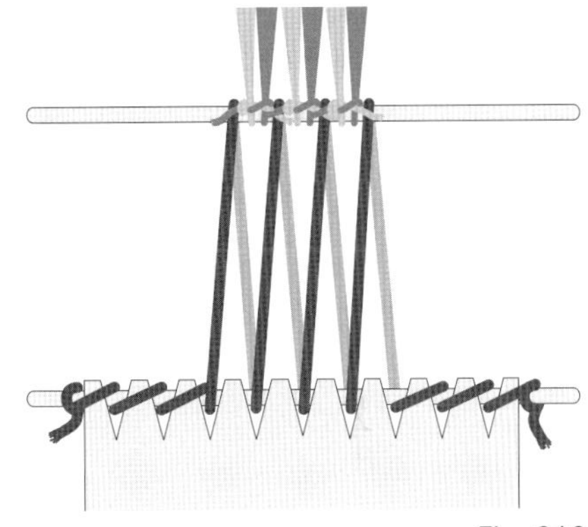

Fig. 210

Arrange the apron rod

Arrange the apron rod by winding up the cords smoothly, as described below, so that the apron goes on the ***top*** of the breast beam. This is very important. To weave, the warp needs to be level from the back beam to the breast beam, which means that the warp ***must*** be over both the front (breast) and back beams. See Figure 211 and Figures 6 and 9 on page 4 and 6. Some looms have a knee bar between the cloth beam and the breast beam to prevent your knees from bumping into the cloth while you're working. Be sure the apron goes ***over*** the knee bar and, then again, ***over*** the breast beam.

If the apron cords or straps are lumpy or thick, see page 50.

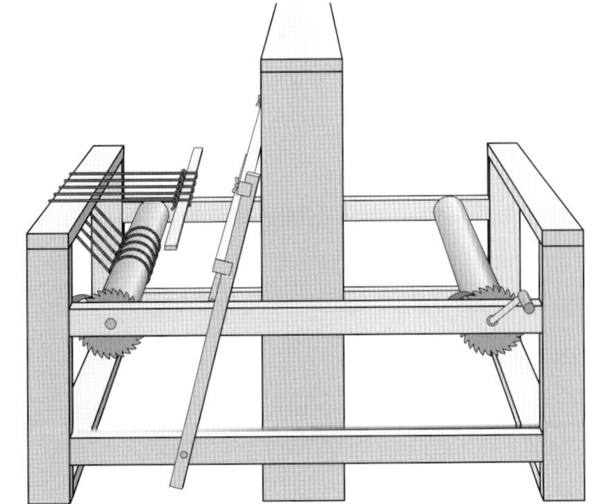

Fig. 211

When you wind up the apron rod be sure that the cords are as smooth and flat against the beam as possible. Smooth and flat are the operative words, so that the fabric will wind up without lumps on the cloth beam during weaving.

Place the apron rod ***midway between*** the heddles and the breast beam as shown in Figure 211. Engage the brake on the cloth beam.

Spread out the heddles

Be sure the heddles are spread out, so the warp threads match their general positions in the reed.

Wind up excess warp if there is more warp in front of the reed than is needed to tie on. You'll need enough warp to reach the apron rod, and then, about 8" more is needed to allow for the knots that tie the warp threads onto the apron rod. Wind the excess warp back onto the warp beam by turning the crank on the warp beam. If you have a tension (friction) brake, disengage the brake by stepping on the brake pedal while you turn the crank to wind up the excess warp. The brake pedal is on one side of the loom, beside the treadles.

Step Two: Tying On to the Front Apron Rod

Do this job with no shafts lifted. I'm going to give two methods. I recommend the surgeon's knot method for beginners and the lacing method for after you've made several warps. Lacing on takes less warp thread, and I use it for narrow warps. I like the surgeon's knot method for wider warps. The lacing method begins on page 90.

Method #1: The surgeon's knot

Make the bundles of warp about 1" wide

All the bundles will be about 1 inch worth of threads. You don't need to count out the warps, or the dents, but estimate an inch worth of threads as they come out of the reed.

For the bundles at the edges, I generally work with 1" of threads, and often, ¾". Don't make any bundles more than an inch—they can have fewer threads, but not more than one inch-worth.

Tie the middle bundle first

You'll tie the center 1" worth of warp threads first. Tying the center bundle first supports the apron rod, so it can't tip and makes it easy to tie the remaining warps to the apron rod.

Use the pinch technique

Smooth out and tension this first bundle by tugging it with the forefinger and thumb of one hand and passing it to the other hand. Don't comb the warp threads, but tug them while pinching with thumb and finger to even out any loose threads. Loose threads show up as being slack when the others are taut; work the slack towards you to the ends of the warps. Repeat this process a few times until all the warp threads in the bundle are evenly tensioned. See Figure 212.

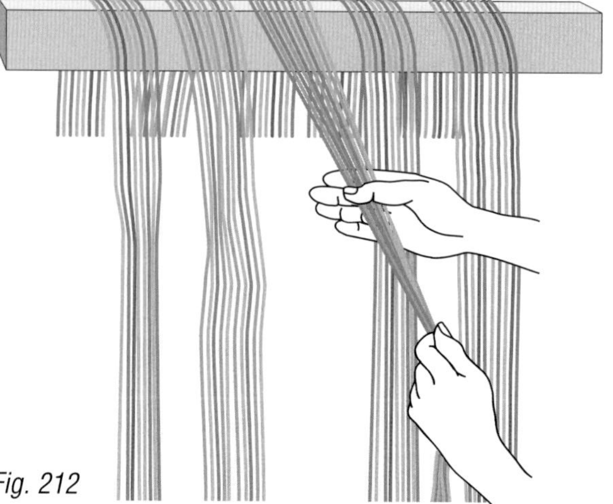

Fig. 212

Don't try to even up the cut ends of the warp threads. You want to even the tension on the threads coming from the warp beam. You may find that one side of the warp is longer than the other. This peculiarity doesn't affect the tension on the warp beam. Just be sure the tension is even through the heddles and to the front of the loom.

Tie bundles with surgeon's knots

Bring the first bundle toward you over the apron rod, then around under it. Divide the little bundle roughly in half and bring one half up on each side of the bundle. Use the ends to tie the beginning three steps of a surgeon's knot, which is just like the first tie you make in tying a shoelace knot except that you put the tail into the loop a second time before pulling the ends to tighten the knot. This gives the knot enough bite to hold while still being easy to loosen if you need to re-tension the bundle later. The last step in tying the knot is on page 89.

See Figures 213 a-c. Figure 214 shows the first bundle tied with a surgeon's knot.

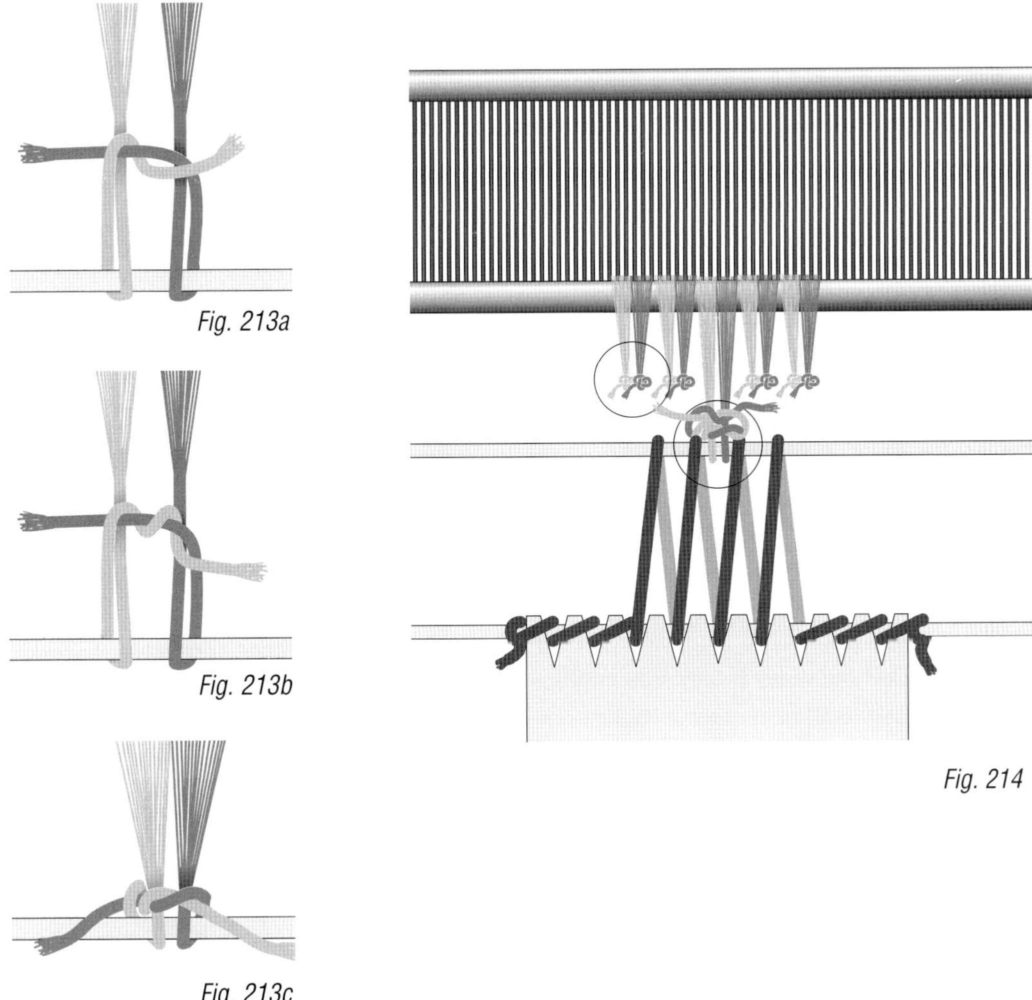

Fig. 213a

Fig. 213b

Fig. 213c

Fig. 214

Tying the Bundles

Continue tying 1" bundles

Choose the next bundle of thread from the reed—the 1" group to the right or to the left of the middle one—and tension the threads as before, pinching, tugging and smoothing to draw them all out to even tension. Take the bundle over the apron rod and divide it in half as before and tie the beginning of a surgeon's knot. Continue to tie the remaining 1" bundles, working out from the center and alternating a group on the left with one on the right.

It's important that the apron rod stays straight. If the rod begins to bow it may be that you couldn't slip off excess lashing on the rod, as shown in Figures 215 and 216. If you see the rod beginning to bow, undo the bundles you have tied until the rod is straight again. Then, tie the remaining bundles, working from the outside edges toward the middle—all the time watching that the apron rod remains straight and doesn't bow.

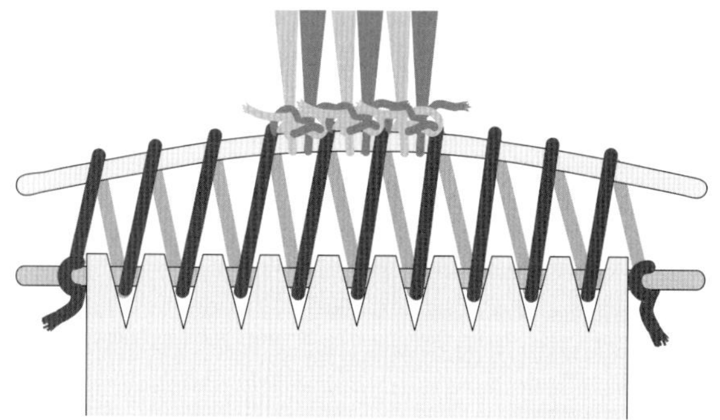

Fig. 215

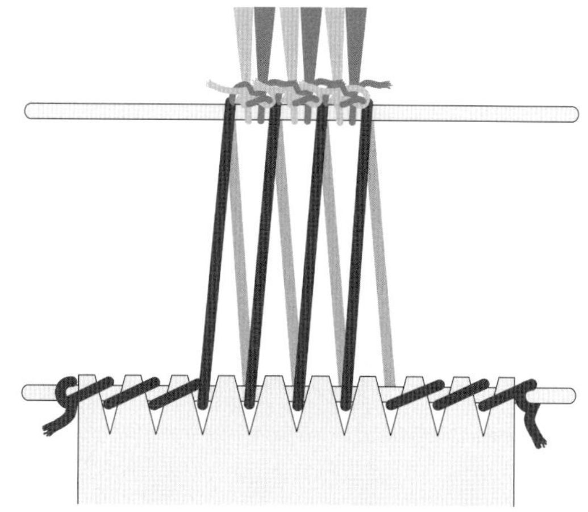

Fig. 216

Check that the tension is even

After all the bundles have been tied, check to see that all the groups are at an equal tension. Close your eyes (that's important; it helps you to concentrate), and use the flat part of your fingers to pat gently across the warp. See Figure 217. All the threads should feel the same. If they're too tight or too loose, they should be re-tensioned. Read how to do this on the next page.

Don't agonize. That's important, too. I've seen students insist on fiddling with the tie-on tension until their nerves were frayed, and it just isn't necessary. Unless a bundle of warps feels definitely softer or definitely tighter compared to the others, it is probably just right.

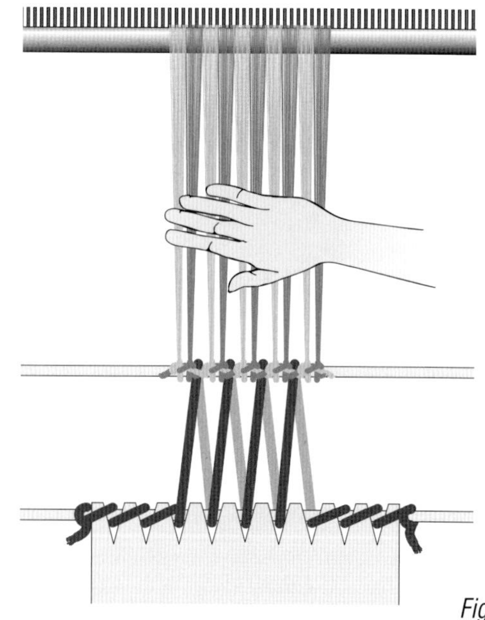

Fig. 217

If the distance between the heddles and the breast beam on your loom is short, and the threads are supported by the bottom of the beater, it may be deceiving you about the tension at the front of the loom. Go to the back of your loom and feel if the warp tension is even behind the heddles, between the heddles and the lease sticks or the back beam. The lease sticks should be pushed as far back toward the back beam as possible to give you more room.

Whether you check the tension at the front or the back of the loom, remember that a lot of tension isn't needed at this point, just even tension. The overall tightness can be regulated with the ratchet brake when you're ready to begin weaving.

Re-tensioning the surgeon's knots

If you need to adjust bundles, just tug one of the tails of the surgeon's knot to open or loosen it. There is no need to untie, then retie the knot. To tighten a warp bundle, brace the heels of both hands on the apron rod and pull the tails of the surgeon's knot to cinch the warps tighter.

Complete the surgeon's knot

When you're satisfied that the tension is even, take the tails of the knots and tie them together to complete the final part of the surgeon's knot. (See page 351.) In other words, each knot will consist of the beginning parts of a surgeon's knot (Figures 213a, b, c) with the final part of the knot on top of it. See Figure 217a.

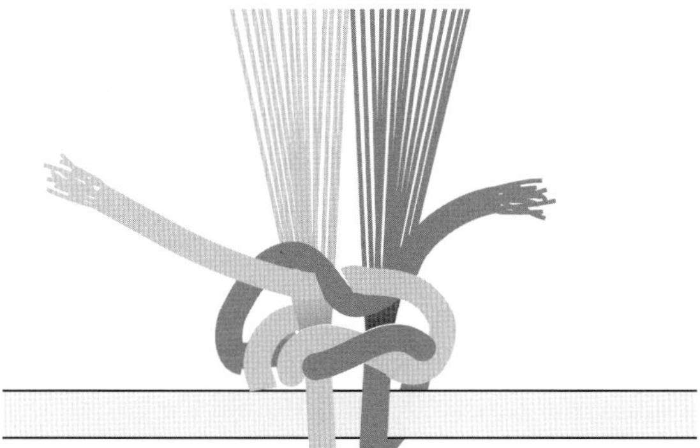

Fig. 217a

Now, you have the warp on the loom and are ready to weave. First, you'll weave a heading to get started. Then, begins the weaving of cloth—your sampler!

The last step of tying on. Weaving is next, beginning on page 93.

Method #2: Lacing

If your yarn is jumpy like linen,, or slippery like rayon, or so expensive you don't want to waste an inch, lacing on to the apron rod may be the choice for you. See Figure 218.

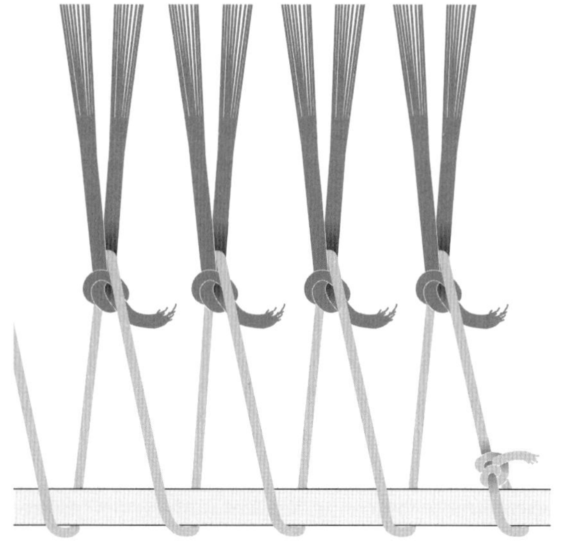

Fig. 218

How to lace the bundles

In succession, all across the warp, take 1" worth of warp at the reed and carefully tug and pinch the threads to get all the threads under the same tension, just as in tying on using surgeon's knots (page 86). Tie the warps in slip knots or overhand knots close to their cut ends. Usually, I tie overhand knots in the bundles as shown in Figure 218, but I might use slip knots (see page 349) at the end of the warp bundles if I worry that I might have made a threading error. Read how to correct threading errors when lacing on, on page 92. If your warp threads are very fine, you may want to tie the knots in ½" bundles. ***If the warps are at different lengths, trim the long ones, so the warps are about the same length before tying the knots.*** Remember, you've put the warps on under even tension on the warp beam, so any differences here do not effect your perfect tension.

Now, you are ready to lace the bundles onto the apron rod. Lace the bundles as they are, dangling from the reed. The warp should be slack.

Choose a sturdy, thin cord that is very smooth, even slippery, and about 10 times as wide as the warp. You can buy thin braided nylon, "chalk and mason line," at the hardware store; the size is around 600 yards per pound. Tie one end of this cord to the front apron rod at one edge of the warp, with a double half hitch knot, (page 353). Now, lace the cord down through the middle of the first bundle, then, take the cord under and around the apron rod, down through the next bundle you tied, under and around the apron rod, and so on. See Figure 218. Don't snug the bundle right up to the apron rod; leave about 2½" between the cut ends of the warp and the apron rod. Do you see the "V"'s being formed in the lacing cord? Always go through the middle of the bundles and be consistent about going down through the bundles and then under, and over around the apron rod. Fasten the cord by tying a double half hitch around the front apron rod at the edge of the warp.

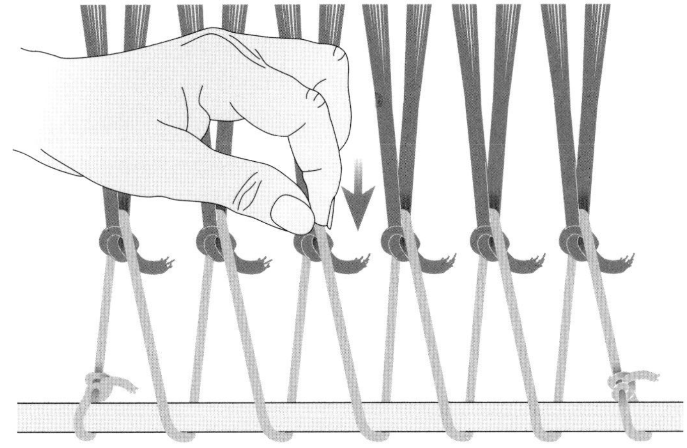

Fig. 219

Poke each bundle at the knot working across the warp from right to left. That is, put your finger into the space between the threads above the knot, and push down a little. See Figure 219. Then, tighten the tension by a click or two on the ratchet brake. Then, poke all the knots again, this time working across from left-to-right. Tension again a click or two.

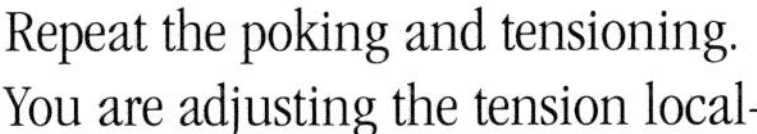

Repeat the poking and tensioning. You are adjusting the tension locally—not transferring tension from very slack sections to tighter areas. By the time the warp is under tension, all the bundles will be under equal tension. You shouldn't have to adjust the tension of any individual bundles.

The tricks to lacing on

The tricks to lacing are: use a slippery cord, start with a slack warp, and tighten it gradually, a little at a time. Poke each bundle at the knot across the warp and back. Then, tighten the tension a little bit. Poke the knots again, across the warp and back. See Figure 219. Then tension some more, and repeat the poking and tightening.

Don't agonize. If you can feel a tight or loose bundle, adjust it, but if you can't tell, then the tension must be even.

If some bundles are really very slack and some very tight, undo all the lacing and do it again. This time, draw up the tension on the lacing cord rather evenly—not precisely, but not allowing some to be very slack and some tight. Remember to keep the bundles slack at this point—just sort-of under even tension. I do this fairly often. It's easier to redo the lacing than to try to even out the tension of the groups by tugging on a lacing cord and passing the slack in the cord on to adjacent bundles while trying to even out the tension on all the bundles.

Never let the lacing cords cross over one another or get out of order. If you do, the tension can't pass along from bundle to bundle.

Correcting errors when you've laced on

I like to use slip knots at the end of the warp bundles. That way, if I later find a threading error, I can easily untie the bundle to make a correction. Slip knots take more warp than overhand knots, though, so if warp is precious, you may want to use overhand knots. However, it's fairly difficult to untie the overhand knot to correct an error. You may be able to pick it open with a strong tapestry needle or a nail.

If worse comes to worst, and you can't undo the knot and must cut it off, re-knot the bundle and re-lace it. The "V" for that bundle's cord will be much longer than for the rest of the bundles, but that is okay as long as the tension is even. As I said, I prefer to use the slip knot, so the bundle can be untied rather than cut.

When some weavers find an error after they've laced on to the apron rod, they cut the offending thread and correct the error. Then, they tie an extension to the warp with a short length of thread and pin the corrected thread onto a lacing knot. In other words, when you cut the warp and fix it in the reed or heddles, it will be too short to put on tension. Make it longer (say 6") by trying on a 6" piece of warp or string and anchor the (now long-enough) thread with a pin (like a cleat. Figure 220) to the knot of its bundle.

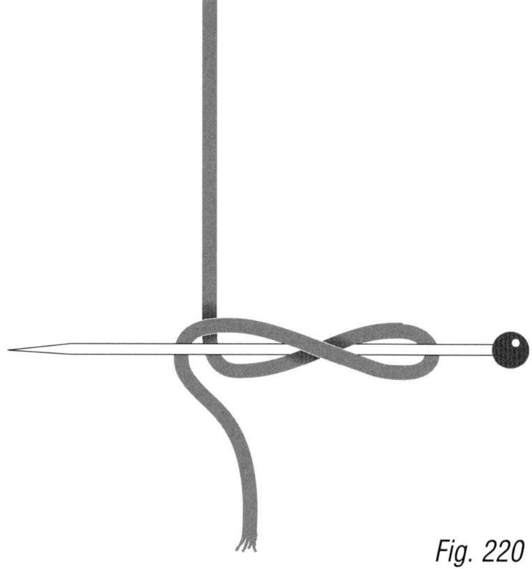

Fig. 220

4 Weaving the Sampler

Weaving the sampler

Now you are ready to weave the sampler! I think you will enjoy seeing the different types of cloth you will make. It is thrilling that so many different weaves can be made using the same set-up of the loom. Here, you will learn how to weave as well as how a variety of weaves are created. Just as soon as you get the rhythm and understand one weave, it will be time to try another one. Any of the weaves can make a wonderful project later.

How to weave

This chapter shows the process of weaving using the sampler as an example. You will use this information for almost every project you weave from now on.

Why make a sampler?

This is the way many weavers try out new things. A sampler is a cloth with several ideas woven into it. Some ideas to try out are using different colors, threads, weaves, or your own designs. (See Figure 221.)

You can try out more than one idea at a time by dividing the warp into sections. For example, if you were sampling different colors, you might make your warp have portions two to three inches wide, each with a different color you are considering. Notice that the sampler described in this chapter has two sections in the warp—each one a different color.

When weaving a sampler, you would try out those warp colors using the same ones as wefts, or perhaps, using other colors.

It is a good idea to try out different weaves as well. Say, you have four colors in the warp, and you try each color in the weft in plain weave–that would give you 16 different squares woven, or samples—useful information for designing a project. Weaving the colors again in twill weave would give you 16 more samples. Weaving the colors in herringbone, another 16 samples, and in a broken twill, 16 more.

You are weaving a plaid, so to speak, with the colors and threadings in the warp repeated in the weft. You also can see how colors look when crossed with other colors and how expected structures look when they are woven with other threadings.

Sampling is fun because you aren't under pressure to make a masterpiece. This is the place to try out lots of ideas. Then you can put the best ideas into a project, knowing that it is likely to please you.

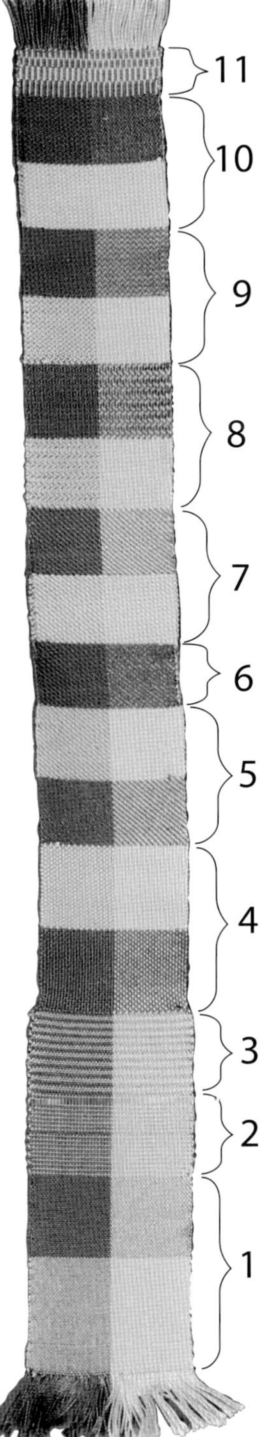

Fig. 221

Equipment List

Adding Machine tape (optional):

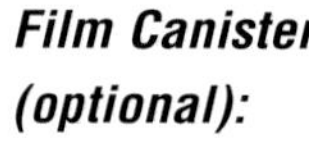

Film Canister (optional):

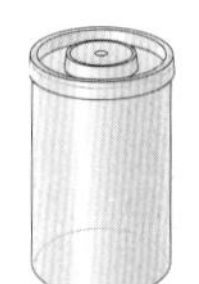

Scissors:

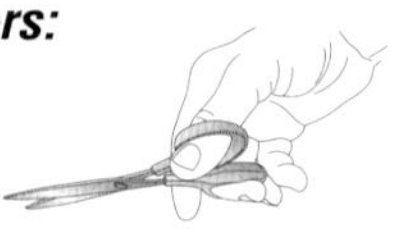

Straight pins:

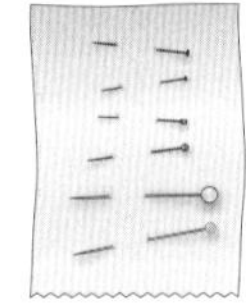

Tape measure:

Tapestry Needle:

Yarns for the weft:

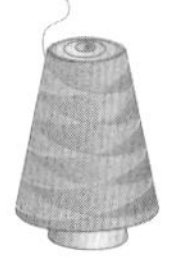

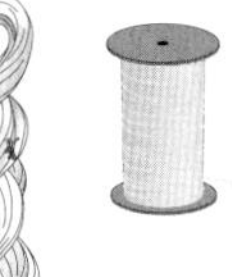

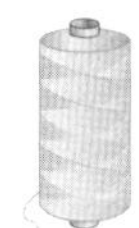

Shuttles: 2 stick shuttles or 2 boat shuttles with 2 bobbins that fit (or one boat shuttle with one bobbin and one stick shuttle). You will need two shuttles at once for parts of the sampler.

For wider warps you'll want longer stick shuttles or better yet, boat shuttles.

- ***Stick shuttles:*** You'll need two (Figure 222). You can buy them or make them out of very stiff cardboard or foamcore board by cutting out the shape shown here. Make them 6" long and 1" wide. If cutting out the rounded shapes is difficult, you can cut straight lines instead to make large V-shapes at the ends of the shuttles.

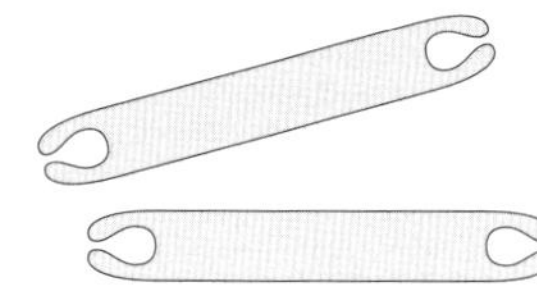

Fig. 222

- ***Boat shuttles:*** These are more expensive and easier to weave with, but not necessary for a beginning weaver. Perhaps you know a weaver who might lend you one. There are many variations, but what you want to look at is the cavity where the bobbin goes so you can be sure you have the type of bobbin that will work with that shuttle.

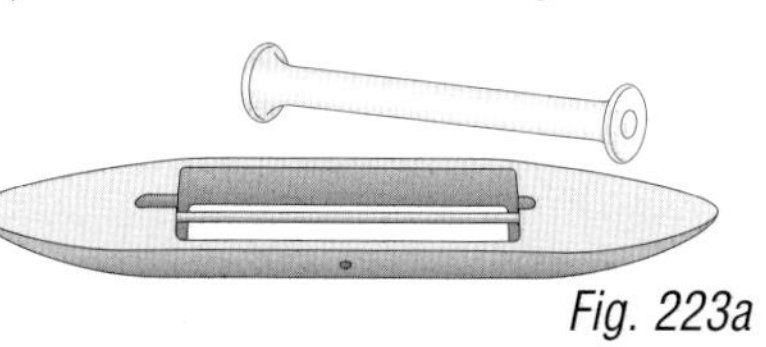

Fig. 223a

The cavity in the shuttle where the spindle is mounted has either squared-off corners or oval, rounded corners. You need to fit the bobbin to the cavity in your shuttle or the thread will jerk or jam as you are weaving. Squared-off corners of the cavity are for bobbins with flanges at the ends—similar to those on the ends of spools of sewing thread. See Figure 223a. In a round-cornered cavity, use bobbins with extensions sticking out from the flanges. See Figure 223b. Bobbins with extensions are readily available and can be used in either type of shuttle. You can put a small bead or a sewing machine bobbin on the spindle at each end of the bobbin if your bobbins don't have extensions, and your shuttle has rounded corners in the cavity. See Figure 223c.

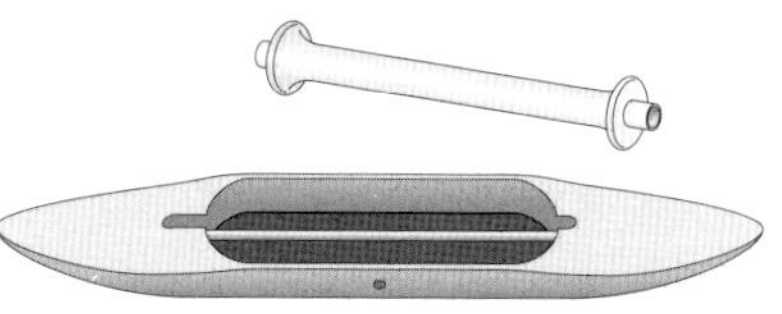

Fig. 223b

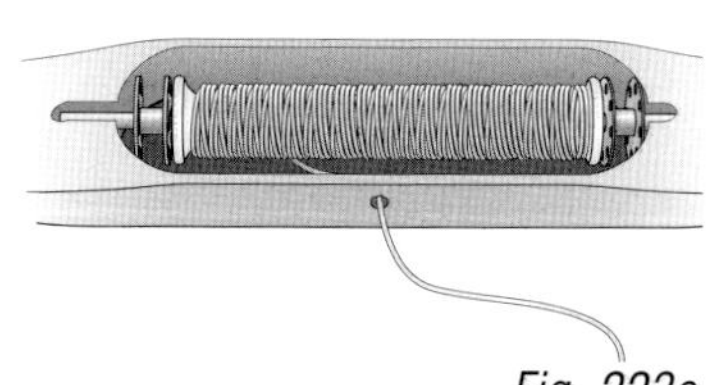

Fig. 223c

Preliminaries

If you are using a table loom, you can eliminate this step and proceed to "Load the Shuttle," on page 102, since table looms have no treadles.

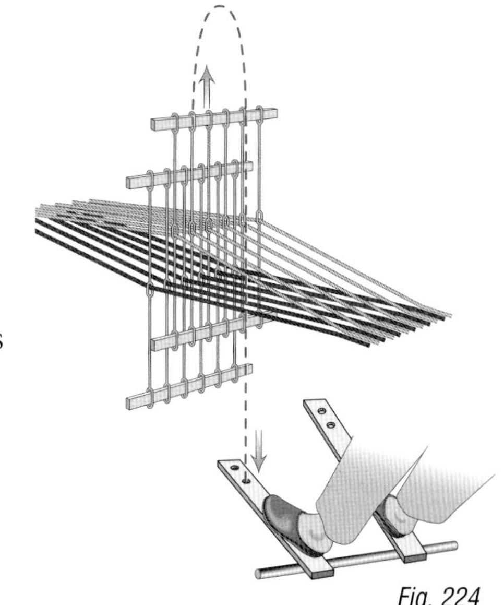
Fig. 224

Tie up the treadles

Tying up the treadles is the process of attaching the treadles to the shafts so that during weaving pressing the treadles makes the shafts move, which makes the threads in the heddles move as well. See Figure 224. (Remember, shafts are often called harnesses but "shafts"is the correct term.)

Look for lams on your loom

Many floor looms have lams (bars between the shafts and the treadles) that are connected to the shafts, and tying up the treadles is actually tying from the treadles to the lams. The illustrations at the right are repeated here from page 58. In Figure A you can see that by pressing the treadle, the lam is pulled down, which pulls down one end of the jacks, which raises the other end of the jacks, which eventually pushes up the shaft. Figures B and C show other arrangements of jacks and lams.

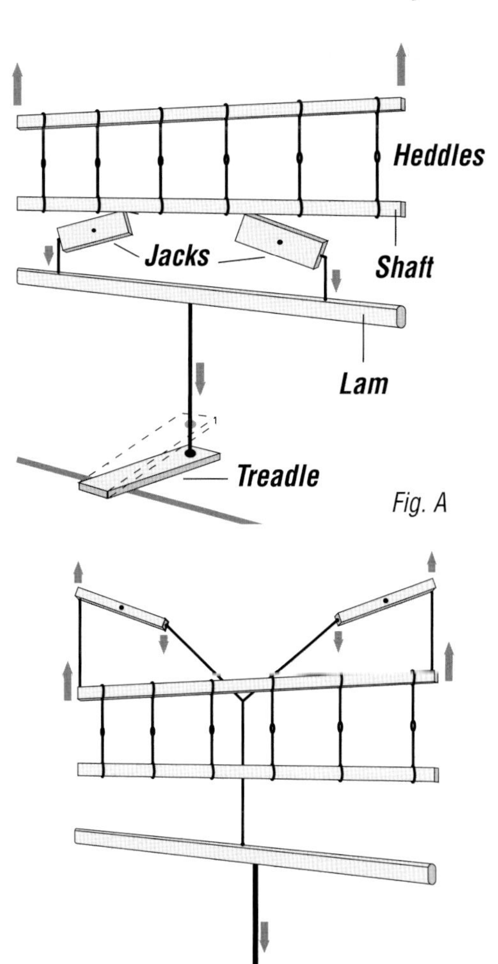

Fig. A

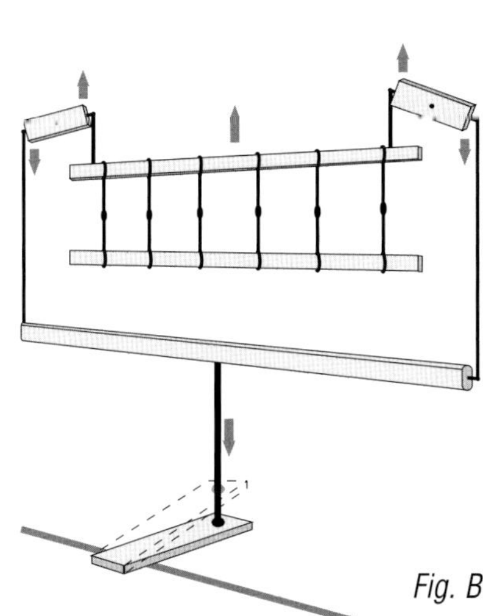
Fig. B

Fig.C

Tying Up the Treadles

The ties are actually made from the treadles to the lams because the lams are already attached to the shafts. See Figure 225.

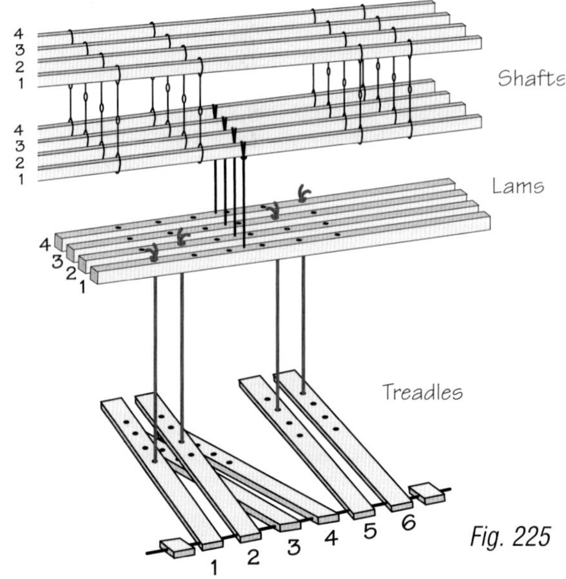

Fig. 225

How to tie treadles to lams

Cords, chains, or hooks may be used to tie up the treadles to the lams, and a variety of mechanisms are used in various looms. I cannot explain every method, but here are some common ones. You may be able to figure out your system by reading about them below; or consult your loom manufacturer. Figure 226 shows slots in the treadles and cord loops (Figure 227) attached with lark's head knots to the lams above them. Figure 228 shows cords tied with snitch knots.

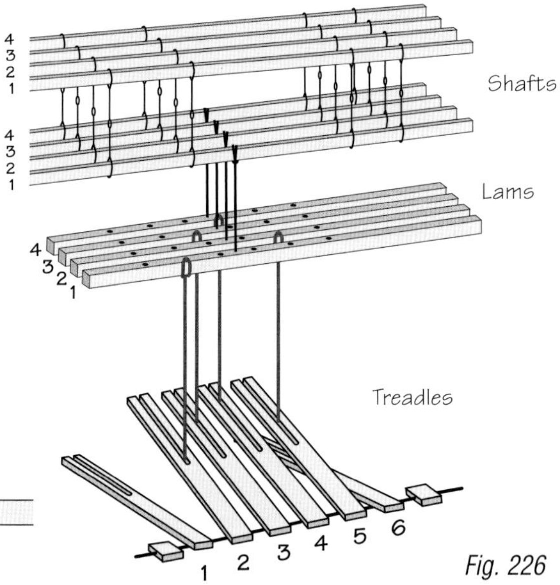

Fig. 226

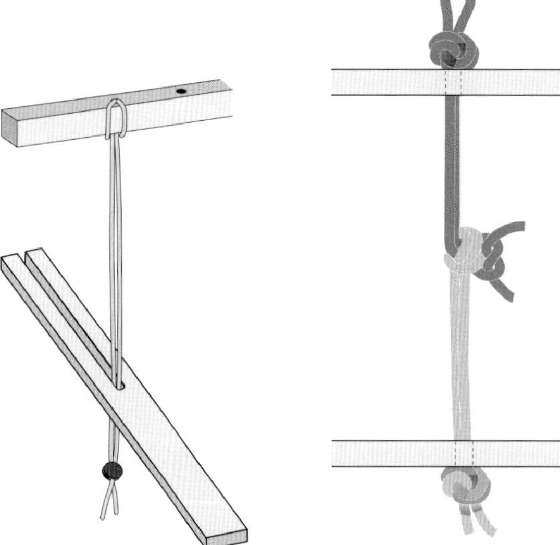

Fig. 227

Fig. 228

Figures 229 a, b, c and 230 show Texsolv cord used in a variety of ways. Figure 225 shows, schematically, how the ties relate to the lams and shafts. Read more about the cords and connectors in the sidebar on page 101. The number of connectors you'll use varies with the project's weave structure—sometimes, you might use only 4 cords, hooks, or chains and sometimes, many more.

Note: There is a lam for each shaft. When you want to operate a particular shaft, you must tie the treadle to the lam for that shaft.

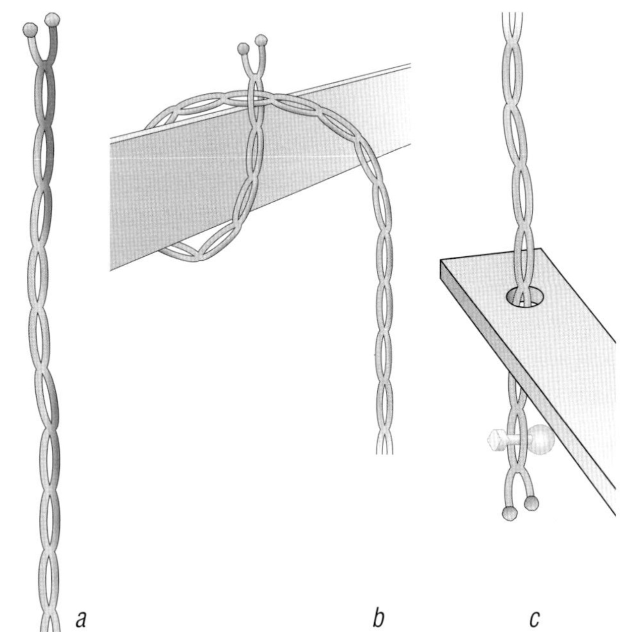

Fig. 229

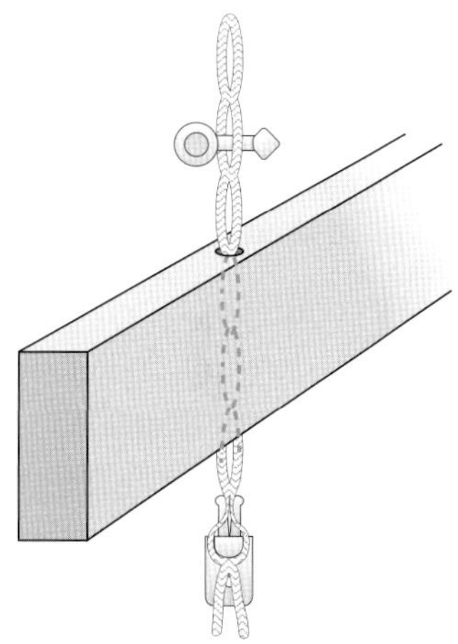
Fig. 230

The basic principle, no matter what mechanism is used on a particular loom, is as follows:

Cords attaching treadles to lams must be straight—not slanted in any way. That means that the position of a connector on a treadle must be ***directly*** under the corresponding position on the lam above it. See Figures 225 and 231.

On many looms there are holes on each lam which are directly above the treadles below them. For example, if there are 6 treadles on the loom, there will be 6 holes on each lam, directly centered over the six treadles.

In looms that have no holes, the connectors can slide on the lams, but must be placed directly over the treadle that is to be attached.

The locations ***on the treadles*** for the connections to the lams are often slots or holes. Notice that the treadles have several holes, going from close to you to further back so that the cords can be tied perpendicular to the floor whether the lam is for a shaft in the front of the loom or more toward the back beam. In tying up treadles there are two places to watch for—the correct place on the treadle and the correct place on the lam. One end of the connector must be on a lam directly over its treadle—and on the treadle, the other end of the connector must be directly under its position on the lam above for the shaft needed.

Figure 225 shows each of the ***4 lams (and their shafts)*** tied to their 4 treadles. Two treadles are not needed so they aren't tied to anything. (See page 99 for which treadles to use.) In the illustration, see:

- The left treadle is tied to lam #1 by a cord coming out of a hole in the treadle which is directly under lam #1.
- Treadle #2 is tied to the lam for shaft #2 with its cord connecting the second hole in the treadle to the hole in lam #2 which is directly over treadle #2.
- Treadle 5's cord is coming out of the hole directly under the lam for shaft #3.
- Treadle #6's cord is tying it to the lam for shaft #4, with the cord going to the hole in lam #4, which is directly over the fourth hole in the treadle.

Figure 226 shows ***treadles with slots instead of holes***. The connectors coming down from the lams must follow the rule and be straight. (In this case, the extra treadles not being used are the outside treadles. Which treadles to use is explained on page 99.)

- The connections from treadles to lams and shafts are straight.
- Treadle 2's cord is in the slot under lam #1 and in the hole on lam #1 which is directly over treadle #2.
- In this configuration, treadle 3 is to be tied to the lam for shaft #3, and treadle 4 to the lam for shaft #4 and treadle 5 is tied to the lam for shaft 2.

Many configurations or "tie-ups" can be used, but the cords or connectors are always straight from lam down to treadle.

If there are no holes in the lams and/or treadles, the connectors can slide into their positions on the lams and/or treadles, and the same principle applies. The connector should be for the shaft desired and positioned on the lam directly over the treadle to be used.

If there are cords both on the lams and on the treadles, they are meant to be tied with snitch knots. It is important to make these knots properly to avoid much frustration and broken fingernails. When properly made, the knots are adjustable, and more importantly, they are untied easily. See Figure 228 and page 352 in the Knots chapter. Cords are only used as they are needed for a particular project, so you will be undoing them and re-tying them periodically in your weaving life.

Figure 231 shows a treadle tied to a lam incorrectly. Note that the cord in the treadle is in the 4th hole—the one for lam #4 for that treadle. The tie is wrong on two accounts: it should go to the hole on lam #4 (not lam #1 as shown) and in the hole in lam #4 which is directly over the treadle. The illustration shows the cord going to a hole which is meant for treadle #2.

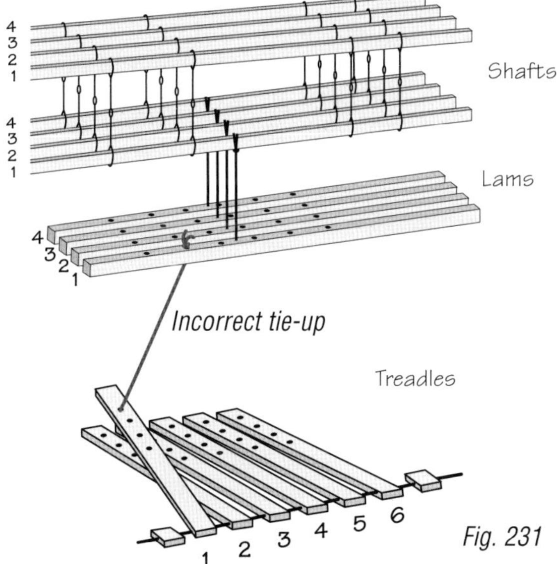

Fig. 231

Figure 232 shows schematically that more than one shaft can be attached to a single treadle. However, the rule must apply. All the connectors must be directly over the desired treadle: coming down from the lam(s) and coming up from the treadle to the correct shaft's lam(s). In this illustration, treadle #1 is tied with two ties—one to lam #1 for shaft #1 and one to lam #2 for shaft #2. The result will be that both shafts #1 and #2 will move when treadle #1 is pressed. Treadle #2 is tied to move shafts #3 and #4.

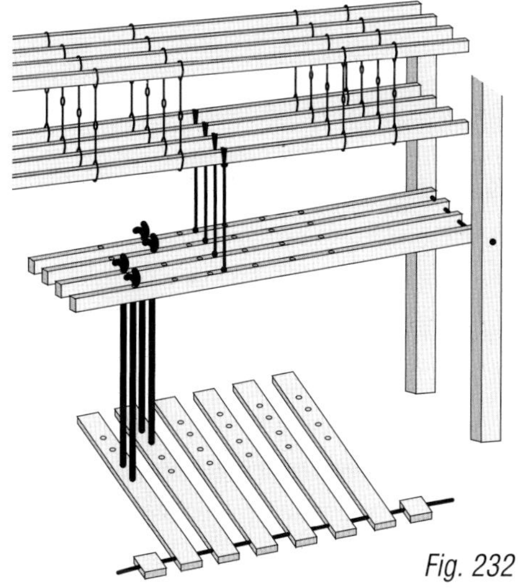
Fig. 232

Which treadles to use

You may not have a choice in which treadles to use because the treadles may be tied permanently to individual shafts. However, many looms have treadles that can be tied up to any shaft or shafts that your weave structure requires. On these looms, you can tie just one shaft to a treadle or more than one shaft to one treadle. Read below to know when to tie more than one shaft to treadle.

How you tie the treadles to the shafts can make a big difference every minute you spend at your loom weaving. The most efficient way to arrange the treadles is so you can alternate your feet, left, right, left, right, etc., as you weave your treadling sequences. It is called "walking the treadles." Walking the treadles makes it easier to get a good rhythm while weaving; it is faster, easier, and it is more beneficial to your back.

If your loom has six treadles, and you need only four for the sampler, two treadles won't be used and will lie flat on the floor because they aren't tied to any shaft. If your treadles are very narrow, you might leave out the center two treadles, giving your feet more room on the treadles as in Figure 225. If that is not the case, you might leave out the outside two treadles as shown in Figure 226. See which four treadles are easiest for you and your feet to use while alternating your feet.

Two configurations of tying up the treadles are given below for weaving the sampler, with my preference being the one where you can walk the treadles. I suggest using this special configuration for tying up the four treadles because, you can almost always walk the treadles and also weave all the weave structures possible with four shafts without changing the tie-ups to the treadles.

Tying more than one shaft to a treadle is often done while weaving projects that use just one weave structure or sequence for lifting the shafts. However, if you change the combinations of shafts to be lifted frequently, it is more efficient to tie just one shaft to a treadle. Changing the ties on the treadles is done on the floor, under the loom, so you don't want to do it often while weaving a project. In your weaving life, you'll usually tie up the treadles at the beginning of a project and use that configuration of treadles for the whole project. However, it's entirely possible that you could change the tie-up in the middle of a project. You might do this if you wanted to weave two different projects on the same warp.

Looms with no lams

Some floor looms have no lams, having each shaft permanently attached directly to each treadle. Table looms are generally of this type where the levers are permanently attached to the shafts and can't be adjusted. There are some table looms, however, where you can tie different shafts or combinations of shafts to the levers.

Looms with more lams

Some looms have two lams for each shaft, a long one and a short one immediately above it. This is a countermarch loom. See page 133.

Two configurations for tying up the treadles for the sampler

For the sampler you can tie the treadles in either of two configurations. Figure 225 shows the treadle on the left tied to shaft #1, the second from the left treadle is tied to shaft #2, and so on. When one treadle is tied to just one shaft it's called a direct tie-up. For the sampler we will use a direct tie-up in one of these two configurations.

Figure 226 shows another direct tie-up arrangement. This one is extremely useful and makes weaving go easier and more rhythmically, which is the goal of all weaving. See that the left treadle is tied to shaft #1, the second treadle, to shaft #3, the third treadle to shaft #4 and the far right treadle is tied to shaft #2. Try this arrangement first because it allows you to walk the treadles for most of the weave structures. With this arrangement it works out that you'll alternate your feet while weaving almost all of the sequences of the sheds for the sampler. In fact, this arrangement works so well that you can weave all the combinations of shafts possible with a four-shaft loom, and almost always be able to alternate your feet (that is, "walk the treadles"). If it becomes too hard to remember where the treadles and shafts are during weaving, change to the arrangement in Figure 225.

Tying up the treadles—Answers to questions you might have

What if you need to press three treadles at once?

You can press three treadles using two feet without a problem. In fact, during the sequence of sheds it might be that sometimes the left foot presses two treadles and the right foot one, and then vice versa with the right foot pressing two treadles at once.

Cords are usually sold by the loom's manufacturer. They are special because they need to be very strong and also small enough in diameter so that they can be doubled up in the holes in the lams and or treadles to make larks' head or snitch knots. Figure 227 on page 96 (and repeated here) shows a larks' head knot tying a treadle to a lam. Figure 228 shows snitch knots used for the connectors using loom cord. Often, these cords are attached to the lams with lark's head knots.

Treat them as precious objects—if you need cords, it will be almost impossible to find ones thin enough and strong enough. Guard them in the same way you guard your best scissors. Ask your weaving supply shop for "treadle cord." It may or may not be precut. You will use a few or many for a project, depending upon the weave structure you choose. You'll only put on the loom the ones that are needed for a particular project.

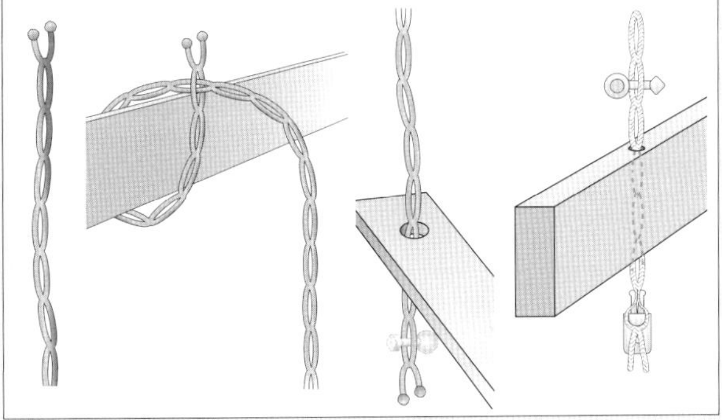

Figures 229 a,b, and c and 230 on page 97 (also repeated here) show a special cord called Texsolv cord, which can be purchased at weaving supply shops. The illustrations show examples of many ways it can be used to tie up treadles.

Special loops of cords are often used for treadles with slots. There are disks at the ends of the loops to prevent the cords from coming out of the treadle slots. The loops are attached to the holes in the lams with lark's head knots. See Figure 227 and repeated above.

Hooks of various configurations are sometimes used to connect the treadles to the lams, and sometimes, cord and hook-like attachments are made.

How long should the treadle cords be?

Usually, the cords or hooks are pre-cut, but if they aren't, you'll need to adjust the height of the treadles yourself. What you want is for the treadles to be high enough that when pressed down the shafts will go up. If they are too high you won't have room to raise your knees, and your knees will bump into the cloth. With most looms the treadles should not hit the floor. Counterbalance and countermarch looms have certain considerations for the height of the treadles and are discussed thoroughly in my second book, *Warping Your Loom & Tying On New Warps*, in the "Adjusting Looms" chapter.

Make all the treadles the same height after you've determined what is right

The distance between the shafts and the lams is predetermined. If not, consult my second book, as above.

Load the Shuttle

You are ready to begin weaving the heading on page 105 after the shuttles are wound (either stick or boat shuttles).

Stick shuttles

Wind two shuttles—one for each color used in the warp. Tie a slip knot (page 349) and hook the loop over one end of the shuttle as shown in Figures 233 and 234. Wind the thread (now called the weft) according to the illustrations, making figure-8's on the edges of the shuttle. By winding on the edges you can get more weft onto the shuttle.

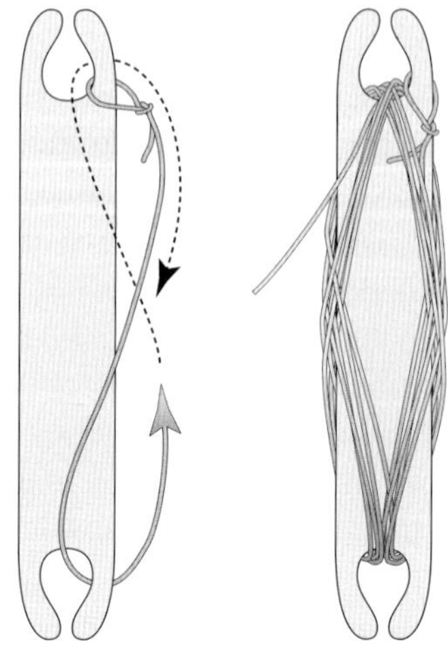

Fig. 233 *Fig. 234*

Boat shuttles

You'll wind 2 bobbins, one for each color in the warp. When the yarn or thread is on the bobbin, it is called the weft. Figure 235 shows a common type of bobbin winder, but there are many types. Electric ones are nice to have, but are expensive. Winding the weft onto the bobbins without a winder is slow and can be tedious. Put the cone of yarn directly below the bobbin on the winder. You could put it in a container such as a kitchen pot or wastebasket to keep it from rolling around. Wind the weft onto the bobbin back and forth in flat layers as shown in Figures 235 and 236. Put some tension on the thread as you wind so the bobbin feels firm (but not so much tension that you burn your fingers.)

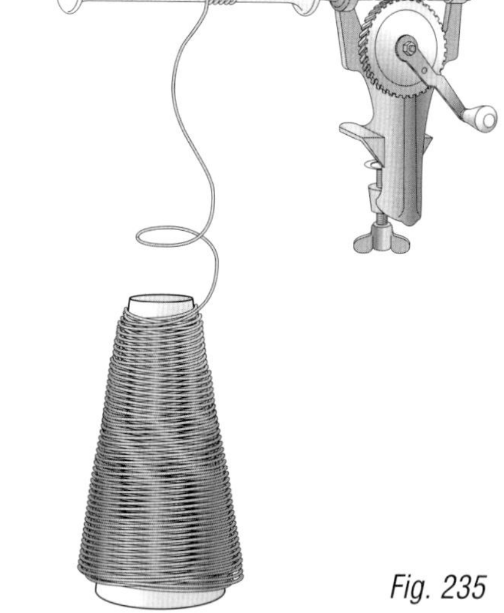

Fig. 235

Put your first color bobbin into the cavity of the shuttle with the thread coming off the bottom of the bobbin. Having the thread come off in this way is extremely important so that the weft comes off the bobbin smoothly during weaving. See Figure 237.

Fig. 236

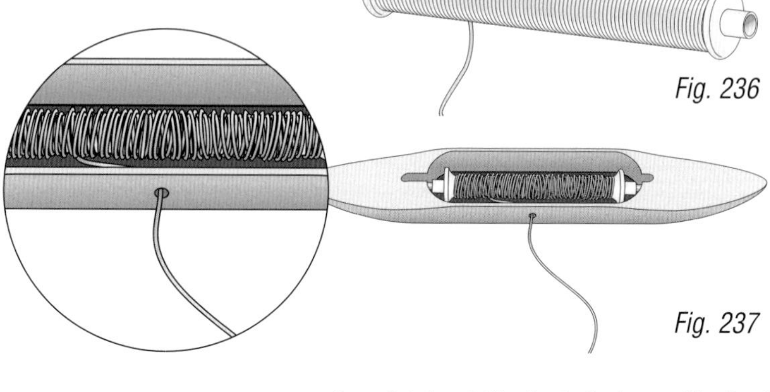

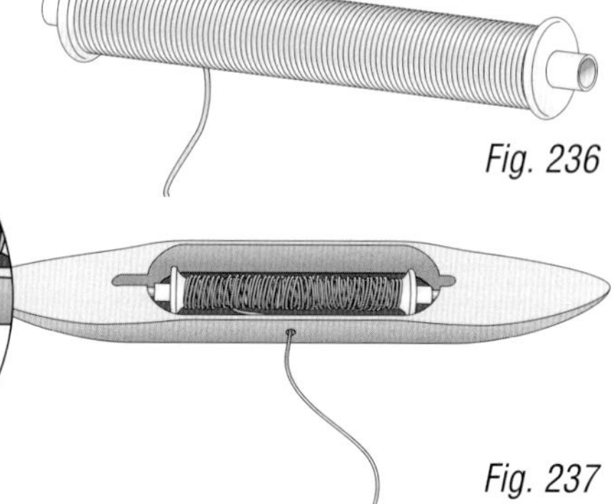

Fig. 237

A loom review

Review ***floor looms*** and ***table looms.*** Larger illustrations are on pages 4, 5, and 6.

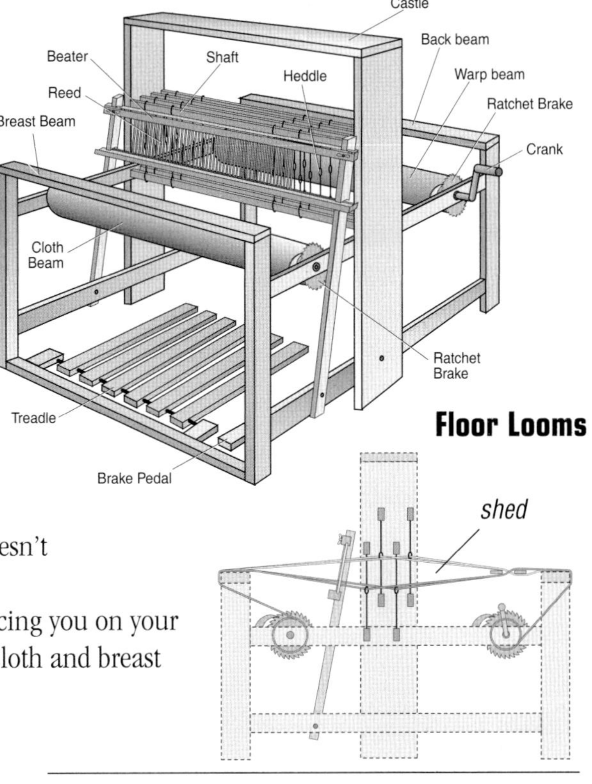

Now, you'll be mostly working at the front of the loom, and probably only going to the back when you release the warp beam. Find the warp beam (and its brake) and then look at the front of the loom for the levers on table looms or treadles and brake pedal on floor looms. Find the shafts and reed and beater. Remember, sometimes shafts are referred to as harnesses. There may (or may not) be a ledge on the beater at the bottom of the reed—this is called the shuttle race. That is where the shuttle will pass during weaving. If your loom doesn't have a shuttle race, that's ok—you will pass the shuttle near the reed. If it does, make sure it is facing you on your loom, or see pages 111 and 112. Also, locate the cloth and breast beams. Find the ratchet brake on the cloth beam.

Note that if the shuttle race is not facing you, it may be that the beater was put in the loom backwards. You can still weave now, but change the beater for your next project.

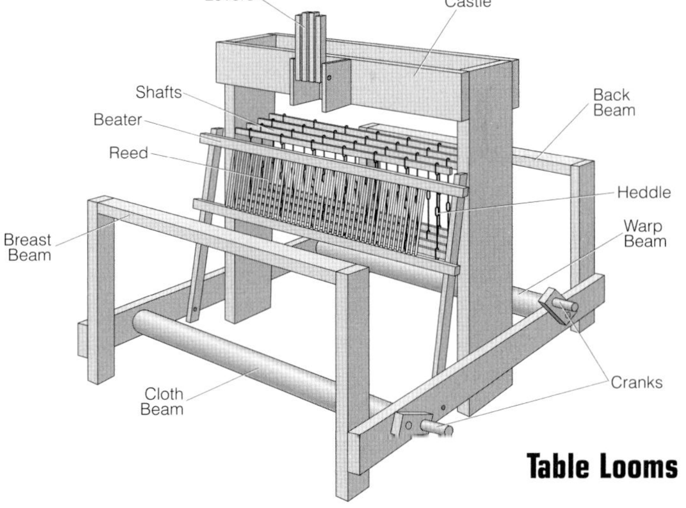

The small side-view figures show the ***shed***—the space between the warp threads that are up and those that are down. This is the space where the shuttle passes through during weaving. See page 111.

Table looms have levers instead of treadles. Notice in the figure at the right that when they are pulled, the shafts are lifted to form the sheds. During weaving you will be moving the levers a lot—either pulling them to lift shafts to open a shed, or pushing them back to close the shed in preparation for making a new shed.

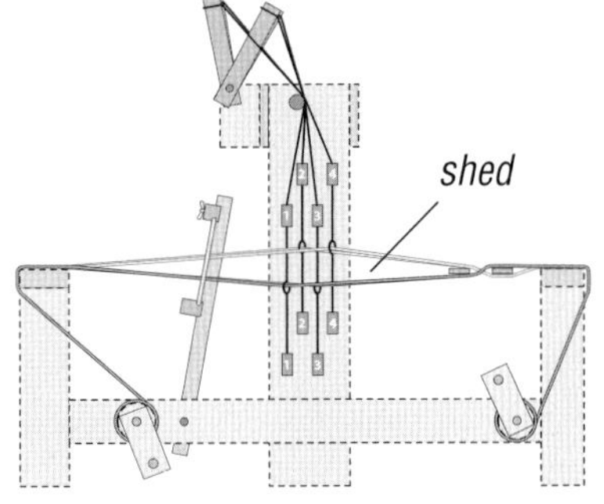

Tension the warp

Be sure the brakes and/or ratchets are engaged on both the warp beam and the cloth beam. There may be two pawls (levers that fall into the teeth of the ratchet) on the cloth beam's ratchet brake. Crank (wind up) the cloth beam and/or warp beam to tighten the warp so it is on tension. See Figure 238. The tension shouldn't be tight—it should give a little when you pat it. You need enough tension on the warp to get a shed, (the opening between the upper and lower threads where the shuttle passes through. See Figure 239.) Too tight warp tension causes lots of problems, and you don't want to start out with this bad habit. Remember, you made the tension even on all the bundles previously, on page 89.

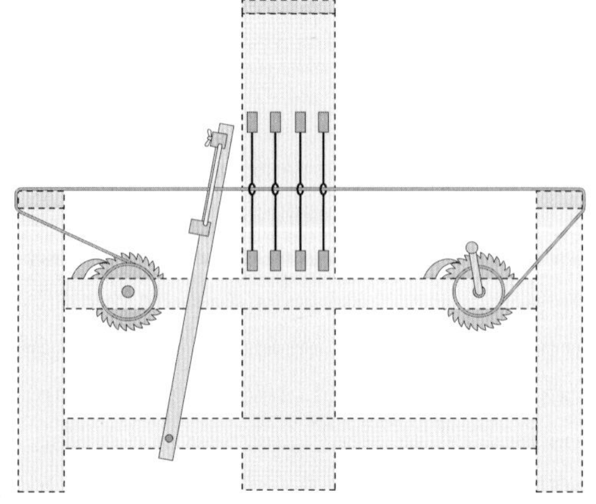

Fig. 238

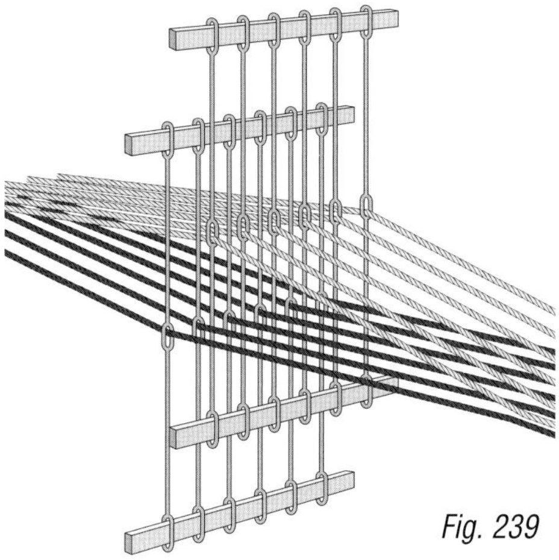

Fig. 239

Remove the lease sticks

I recommend removing the lease sticks, now. When you are no longer a beginning weaver, I would suggest leaving them in during weaving. Also leave them in when weaving fine or fragile warp threads—not what a beginning weaver will be using. More information is in my third book, *Weaving & Drafting Your Own Cloth*, on page 36. However, if you do decide to leave them in, tie the stick closer to the back beam, about 1 ½" away from the beam. Make a tie at each end of the stick so they won't move forward during weaving. (The two sticks should already be tied together as usual about 1" apart.) It may be that you need to remove them—that would be the situation if there was too little space behind the shafts and the sheds would be impeded by having the sticks in.

Weaving the Heading

Now you are ready to weave!

Raising the shafts: Making the sheds

Lift shafts #1 and #3. Press the treadles or pull the levers, depending upon whether you have a floor or a table loom. For looms with shafts permanently attached to the levers or treadles, you will need to locate which treadles or levers do this operation. What you want to see is that the shafts indicated are going up. Looms vary as to which levers or treadles are permanently tied to which shafts. Watch carefully that the specific shafts are going up. Do not count the levers or treadles as 1, 2, 3, or 4—it's the shafts to watch out for.

If you have tied up the loom for the second configuration given on page 100, you'll press the left 2 treadles at once with your left foot (for shafts #1 and #3). For the next shed, you'll press the right 2 treadles with your right foot (#2 and #4). When you are weaving, all you need to do is press left foot, right foot, etc.

There is a type of loom, called a counterbalance loom, where, when you press the treadles, the shafts go down instead of being lifted. When these shafts are being lowered by the treadles, the remaining shafts actually go up at the same time. The tie-up draft and the sequences of sheds given in this part of the sampler will remain as usual—what you are looking out for is to see that the correct shafts are going up. Follow the tie-up given or the sequence of sheds given: they tell you what is to be lifted. What you will actually be doing is pulling some shafts down to make this happen. Do what you need to with the treadles to make shafts #1 and #3 go up. Later in the sampler, you'll weave sequences of sheds where there are not 2 shafts up and 2 down, and some consideration will be needed to accommodate counterbalance looms. This will be explained when you come to Part Six of the sampler.

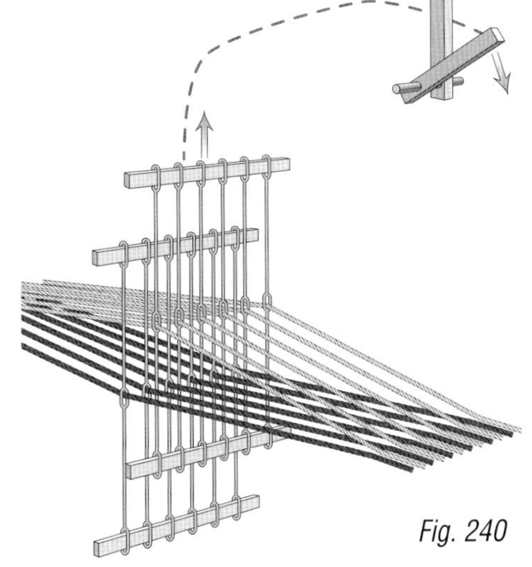

Fig. 240

If you have a countermarch loom, see page 133.

Notice that all the threads that are in the heddles on shafts #1 and #3 are raised. All the remaining warp threads are down—the space between these and the raised threads is the place you will put the shuttle. This space is called the ***shed***. See Figure 239. Figure 240 shows a shed made on a table loom with levers. Figure 241 shows a shed made using two treadles. A good picture of a shed is on the back cover of this book. You should clearly see the space between the upper and lower threads where the shuttle is to pass through. (If not, see page 318, "Can't get a shed.")

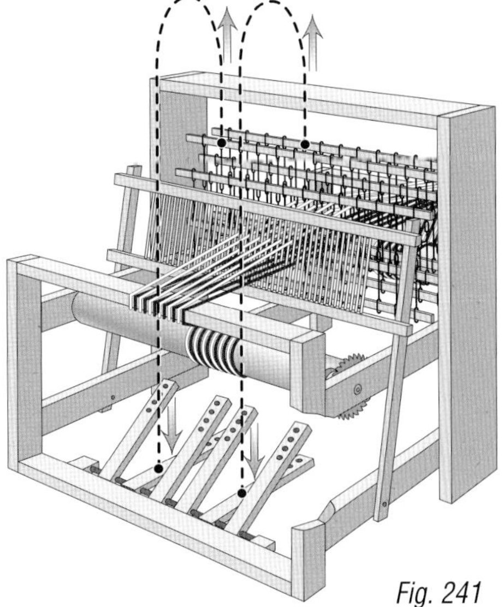

Fig. 241

Weaving the Heading

Now, lower shafts #1 and #3 by pushing the levers back into neutral or taking your feet off the treadles. The shed is closed—with all the threads on the same level. Open the other shed by lifting shafts #2 and #4. The #2 and #4 shed is shown in Figures 242 and 243. Notice that in Figure 243, one treadle raises both shafts #2 and #4. Tying 2 or more shafts to one treadle is often done in weaving. However, for the sampler, you will find it better to have only 1 shaft tied to a treadle. (You will be making a lot of different sheds in the sampler, and one shaft per treadle gives you the flexibility you need.)

If you cannot get these two sheds (#1 and #3 alternating with #2 and #4), see page 318. If the sheds aren't clear or large enough or seem to not be right, see page 318.

Using these two sheds you will weave about 3-4" for the heading for two reasons: (1) The warp threads that were tied on to the apron rod in bundles now need to be spread out. (2) This is the time to check for any errors in threading the heddles or sleying the reed, and to correct them. A few inches, say, 3 or 4, are all it takes, and then you are on your way to weaving Part One of the sampler. Often, I wait awhile to weave the heading, and I admire the warp under tension. I need to be ready to accept that there might be some errors to fix when I begin. My students often have none, or one or two, and corrections are not difficult. But in your weaving life, you probably will have some as you go along. See pages 108-110.

The heading isn't really part of the sampler, so mistakes and their corrections in this area won't appear in the "good" cloth of the sampler. It can be unwoven later and the warps used for fringe, or it can be used as a hem, or simply cut off.

Read about another useful heading on pages 134 and 135.

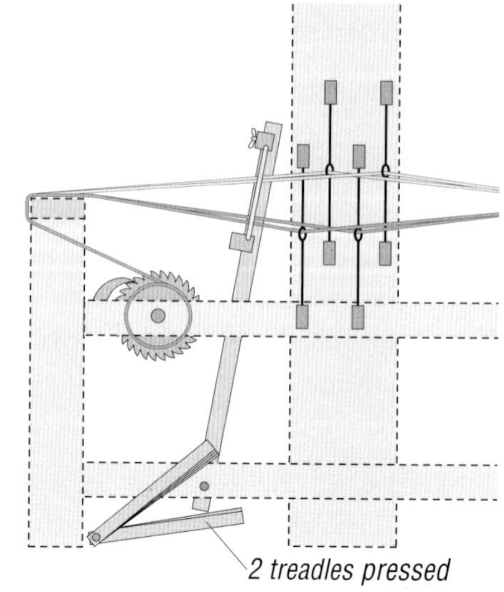

Fig. 242

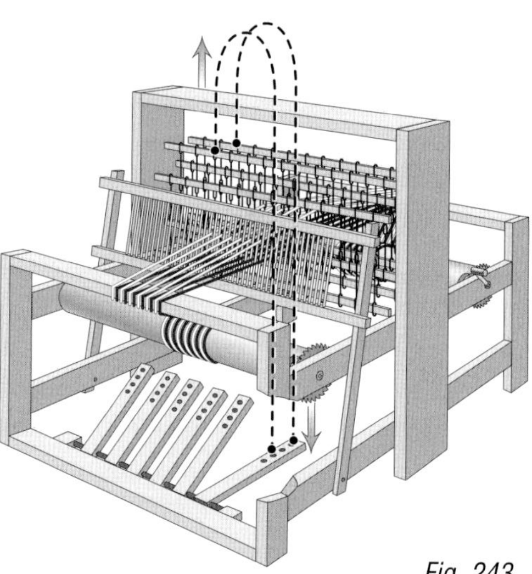

Fig. 243

Note that you will use two treadles or two levers at a time to weave the heading as well as for Part One of the sampler.

Spread out the warps

Read all the pages through 116 before you begin. Raise shafts #1 and #3 with either treadles or levers. Unwind about 10" of weft from the shuttle. Put the shuttle through the shed from right-to-left or vice-versa, leaving a tail of about 1" or so sticking out from the edge of the warp on the side where you entered the shuttle. Close the shed and lift shafts #2 and #4 and throw the shuttle through the shed. Lift #1 and #3 and throw the shuttle once more. Swing the beater forward towards you and beat in these 3 wefts at once. You are really not beating hard—more like gently putting the wefts in place. You will feel a bit of resistance as you beat in these 3 wefts. Beating in 3 wefts at once is how the warps are spread out from their groups in the bundles. See Figure 244. The wefts should now be close to or against the knots on the apron rod. If there are still separations in the warp between the warp bundles, repeat the process by weaving in 3 more wefts and then beating them in all at once. This time, you'll raise shafts #2 and #4 because the previous weft was in the shed with shafts #1 and #3 up. You will always alternate the sheds—shafts #1 and #3 followed by shafts #2 and #4. Notice in Figure 244 that the wefts extend out beyond the width of the warp. This prevents the warp threads from narrowing in when 3 wefts are to be beaten at once.

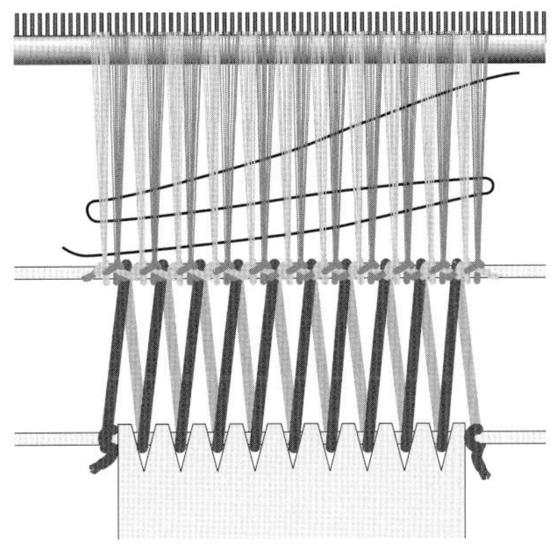

Fig. 244

Note: It was only to spread out the warps that you beat after 3 wefts were thrown. In regular weaving, you will beat after each weft is thrown.

Continue weaving the heading

Weave 1" of heading. From now on you'll be beating "normally" which is after each row instead of after 3 rows. If there is not enough room between the breast beam and the beater to weave, you'll need to advance the warp, which is described on page 114. The steps for weaving the body of the sampler begin on page 111.

Things to know before you throw a shuttle

Throw the shuttle into the correct open shed. Take out the shuttle so the weft is in the shed on a diagonal as shown in Figure 245. Holding onto the shuttle, snug up the weft to the outside warp thread—the side where the shuttle entered the shed—just so it touches and barely moves that outside thread. Then, swing the beater and gently place the weft next to the previously woven weft. You do not want to actually beat it as the name implies. You are simply placing the weft against the one woven before it. Now, while the beater is toward you after placing the weft, change the shed. Then, swing the beater back toward the heddles and begin the process again. ***The steps are: throw the shuttle, beat in the weft, and change the shed. I like the rhythm of saying: "Throw, beat, change the shed." That's 4 counts, with "the shed" as one beat. (On the fourth beat you're pushing the beater back toward the shafts.)***

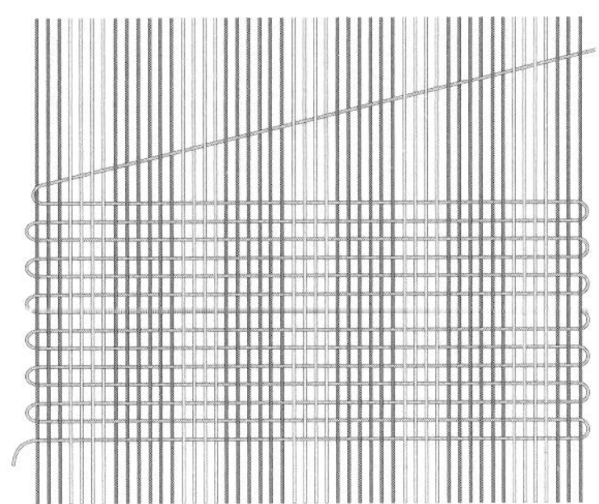

Fig. 245

Start now to check for errors while weaving the heading, which should end up about 3" long. When errors are fixed or if none are found, go to page 111.

Checking for Errors

Information about errors is on pages 109-110.

How to repair errors in the heading

Follow these steps to make corrections.

Several errors you might encounter while weaving the heading are given in this sidebar. Once you have discovered the offending threads, here is how to remove them from the heddles and/or reed and replace them after the error has been repaired. For example, if you have 2 threads out of order in some way, they will need to be cut and rearranged then put back onto tension. This job is a little easier if an inch or so has been woven, but the process can be done before anything is woven as well.

Isolate the error

Hold onto the offending threads. (At first you may find a single thread, but there will often be two of them next to one another.) While holding these threads, close the shed. Follow these threads back behind the reed to the heddles to determine what the problem is. Threads may be crossed or out of place as discussed below.

Now that you have the exact threads that need to be rearranged, hold on to them and follow them to the front of the reed. You will need to cut them to do the rearranging. See below and Figure 253 on page 110.

Cut the offending thread(s) in preparation for rearranging them

If there is a little bit of cloth woven already, follow the threads you are going to rearrange as far back (toward the knot) into the woven cloth as you can and cut them carefully at that point and pull the thread(s) out from the cloth. See Figures 246 and 247. Cutting as far back to the knot as possible will give you enough length in the thread so you can wind it onto a pin like a cleat to re-tension it after the rearranging has been done. See Figures 220 and 248.

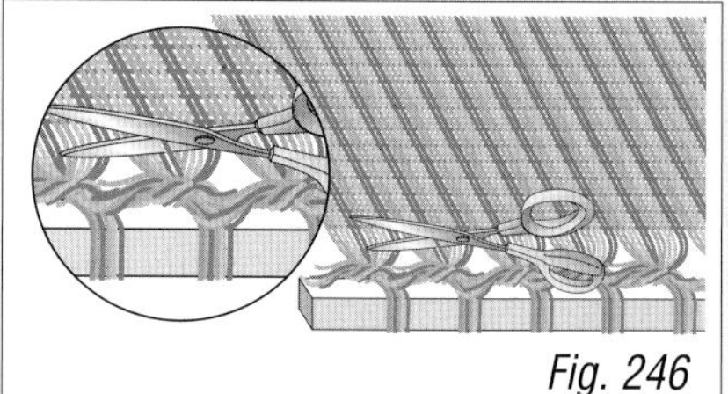

Fig. 246

If there is no cloth woven

Undo the bundle with the offending threads, pull the threads out from the bundle and rearrange them to correct the error. After the correction has been made, put the threads back into their bundle. Retie the bundle making sure that the tension of the threads is the same as the rest of the warp

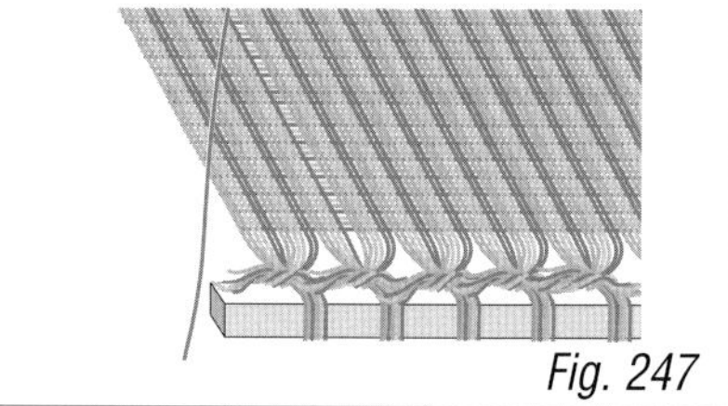

Fig. 247

Sometimes, I feel too lazy to untie a bundle, so I just cut the offending threads as close to the knot as possible and make the correction. After the correction is made, I tie a short piece of warp thread to each thread, making the threads long enough so I can pin the extended threads onto the bundle itself, like a cleat, shown in Figure 248. My extensions are about 6" long, giving plenty of length to work with.

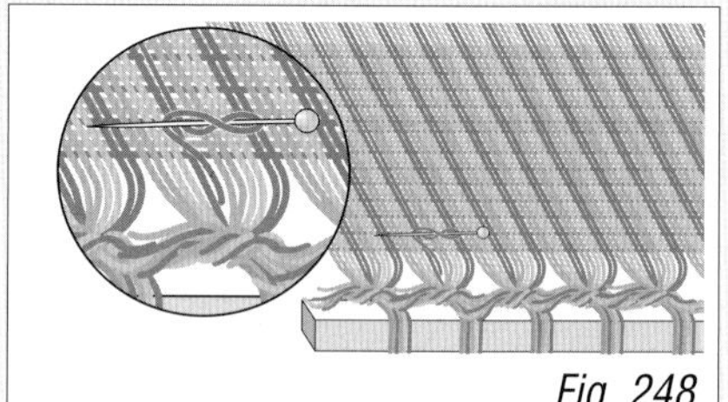

Fig. 248

A tight warp thread in a shed

Open each shed (1 & 3 and 2 & 4), one at a time, and reach into the sheds with your hand. Feel if there are any warp threads that are tighter than the others. If there are, look into the open shed, and you'll see the offending thread(s) in the middle of the shed—neither at the top of the shed or the bottom.

This is one of the most common errors—threads are crossed in between the heddles and the reed. See Figure 249. They must be

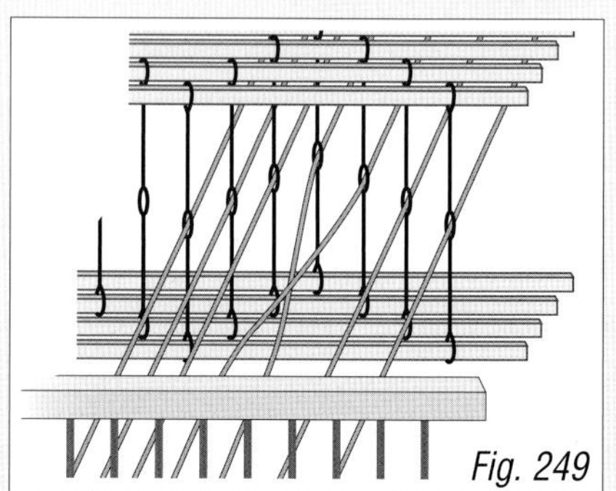

Fig. 249

corrected now, or they will never weave into the cloth, causing a glaring flaw. Sometimes, you don't notice them for quite awhile and then you discover that a thread isn't being woven in at all. See how to correct errors as you are weaving along, on page 321.

At first you may find that a single thread is tight, but there will probably be two of them next to one another that are crossed. See if the threads that came from the heddles are not in the exact dent of the reed where they should be—they are crossed. In other words, a thread that should be in a dent is in its neighbor's dent and vice-versa.

A thread isn't being woven in

Cause #1: Threads crossed in the heddles or behind the reed

Look on the cloth you've woven and see if there are any loose threads floating on the surface that are not woven in. Check the back of the cloth as well. A floating thread indicates that there might be some crossed threads in the heddles. See Figure 250. Follow the offending thread back into the heddles and check if it is crossed around its neighboring thread's heddle. If you find more than one or two of these situations, you may have misunderstood the directions for threading the heddles. See page 82.

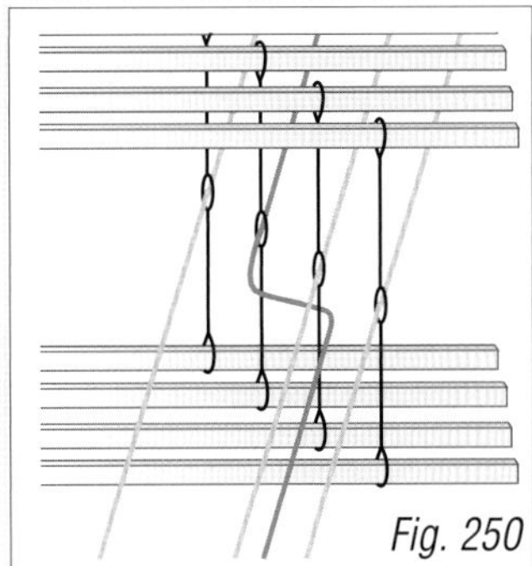

Fig. 250

Cause #2: Threads not in the heddles correctly

Another reason a thread might not weave in is that the thread wasn't entered into the heddle eye properly. See Figure 251. All the threads should travel in straight lines through the heddles.

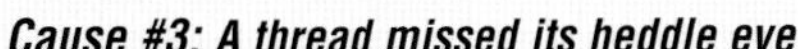

Cause #3: A thread missed its heddle eye

A thread may be above the heddle eye. You might have seen it when you looked into the shed as a thread hanging down in the shed.

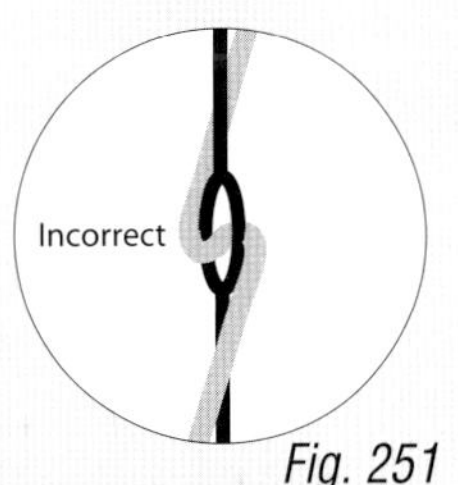

Fig. 251

Flaws in the cloth

You are weaving what is called "plain weave" or "tabby." The cloth should look like that in Figure 252.

There are several causes for flaws—they may happen in the reed, or in the heddles.

Flaws in the reed

For flaws in the reed, there's only one solution: re-sley the reed correctly from the point of the error to the nearest edge of the warp (called the selvedge). A quick and easy way to do this job is given on page 81.

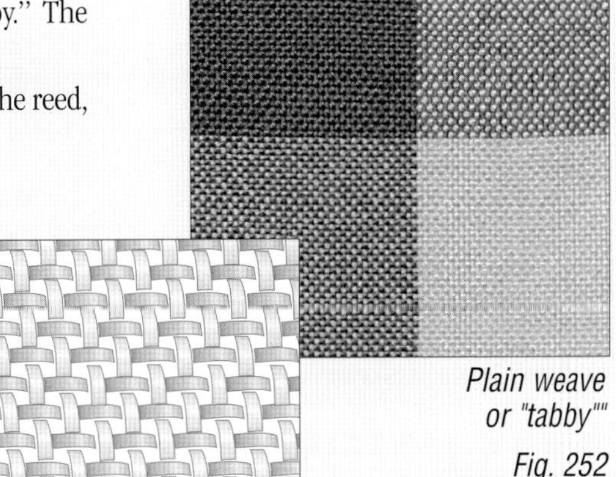

Plain weave or "tabby""

Fig. 252

Flaw #1: A thick or thin vertical line in the cloth

A thick line means too many threads were sleyed into a dent. Thin lines are from skipped dents or too few threads in a dent.

Flaw #2: A vertical space in the cloth

It could be that a dent has been skipped or it might be that a warp thread has broken, and that there is a corresponding heddle without a thread. Read how to repair broken warp threads on page 322.

Flaws in the heddles

Whenever you see a flaw that isn't in the reed, follow the offending thread(s) back into the heddles and check that the threads in that vicinity were threaded correctly. Figure 253 shows how you can hold the warps apart with a comb while making corrections in the heddles. Also, see pages 82 and 320.

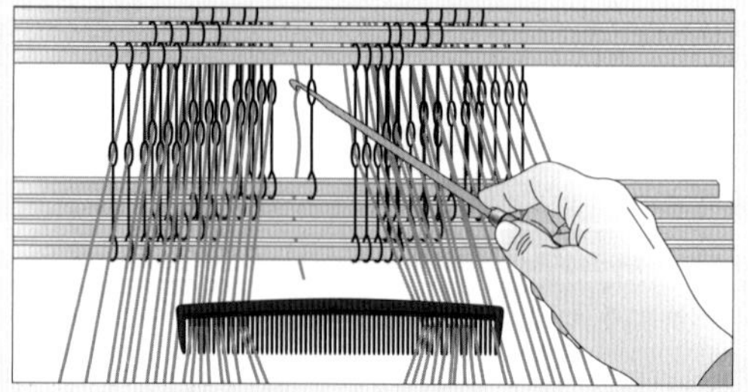

Fig. 253

Flaw #1: Two or Three threads weave together

If two or three threads weave next to each other, a thread has probably been threaded on the wrong shaft. Look at the threads in the heddles in the neighborhood of the flaw and check that each thread is threaded in the proper sequence. If you find a mistake, look around a little more and see if there is an empty heddle on the correct shaft nearby. Then, rethread them properly in the heddles.

If there is no heddle available, you'll need to make a repair heddle for the warp thread that needs a heddle. This is something you will make many times in your weaving life. It's not difficult. See Figure 254.

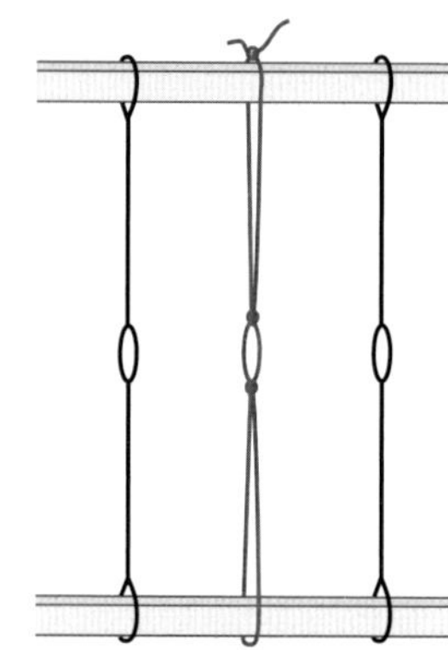

Fig. 254

Loop a length of string around the bottom heddle bar of the shaft. Tie a square knot (or any secure knot) level with the base of the heddle eyes of the regular heddles on that shaft. To make the eye of your new heddle, tie another knot above the first one, even with the tops of the regular heddle eyes. Tie the top of the new heddle to the top heddle bar of the shaft. Be careful to tie the repair heddle onto the correct shaft on the top, as well as on the bottom. Be alert when making corrections—I can repeat the mistake instead of correcting it if I'm not careful.

If two threads were threaded on the same shaft, you can eliminate one of them by pulling it out of the heddle and letting it dangle at the back of the loom, off the back beam. Then, re-sley the reed as needed. Read about flaws in the reed, above.

If two or more threads are weaving along next to each other, all weaving in the same way, it could be a crossed thread problem. See Cause #1 above.

Flaw #2: A thread is left out

If a thread is missing, you may find an empty heddle and dent space for it. The thread may have broken. Read how to repair broken warp threads on page 322.

Perhaps, a thread is completely missing. If this is the case, make a new warp thread and a repair heddle where it is needed. Re-sley the reed to accommodate this new addition. Anchor the new thread into the woven heading or onto a bundle with a pin used like a cleat. See Figure 248. Then, to put the thread on tension, wind up the supply of thread on the outside of a film canister. Place the unwound thread over the open end of the canister and hold it in place by snapping on the cap. See Figure 255. Put a few coins in the canister to tension the thread.

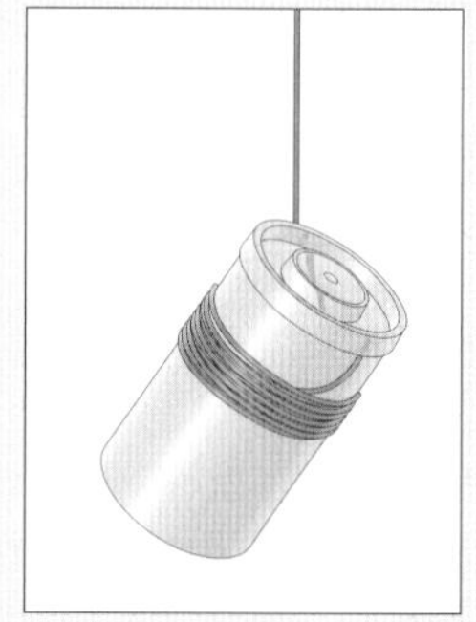

Fig. 255

Weaving the Sampler

Part One: Plain Weave (Tabby)

The whole sampler is shown on page 93 and on the back cover. Figure 256 shows the part to weave in this section. Tabby is another name often used for plain weave.

Start with your second color. Remember, for boat shuttles, the side of the shuttle facing you is the one where the weft thread exits the shuttle, and the thread should come out from under the bobbin.

Using the same two sheds as in the heading, (shafts #1 and #3 alternating with shafts #2 and #4), weave 2 ½".

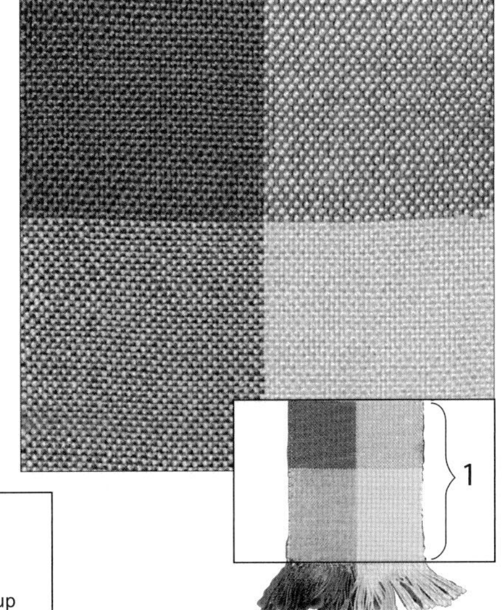

Fig. 256

Sequence of Sheds for Plain Weave

1. Shafts 1 & 3
2. Shafts 2 & 4
Repeat

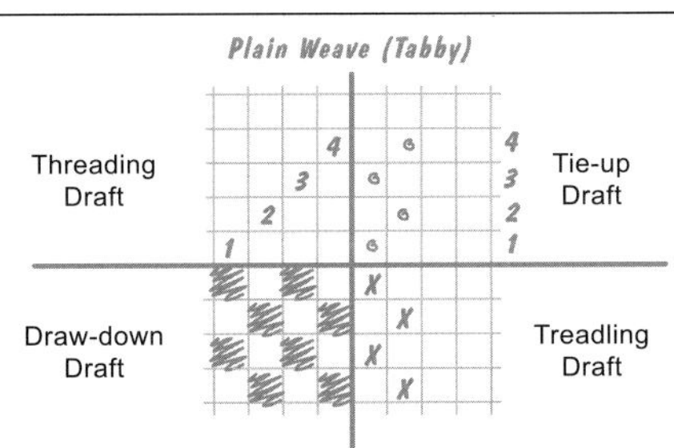

Learn how to read weaving drafts on page 195.

You can weave all the weaves in the sampler by following the sequence of sheds listed or by reading the weave drafts. After you know how to read drafts, however, you'll find that reading the drafts is the easiest way to see what to do.

① Throw the Shuttle

Figure 257 shows how to hold the shuttle (either stick or boat type shuttle) while weaving. Figures 258 and 259 show that this position remains when both entering the shuttle and taking it out of the shed.

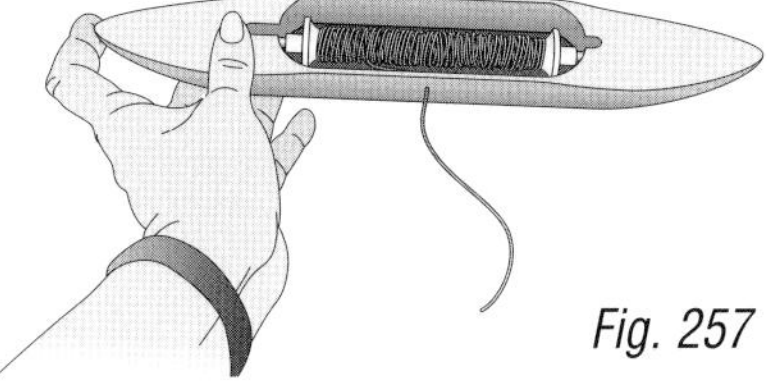

Fig. 257

Figure 260 shows how the shuttle glides along the shuttle race (the ledge on the beater at the base of the reed) of the beater. Note that some beaters don't have this ledge—in that case, you want to throw the shuttle close to the reed.

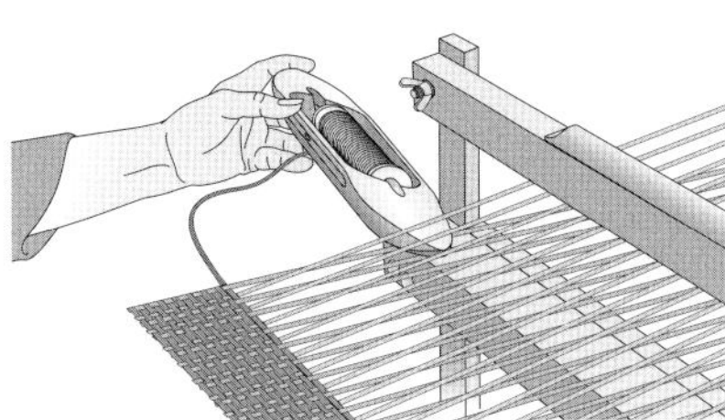

Fig. 258

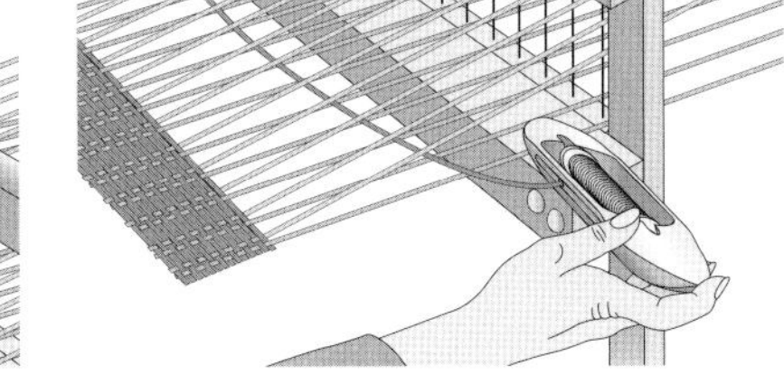

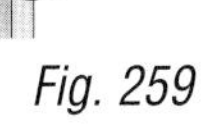

Fig. 259

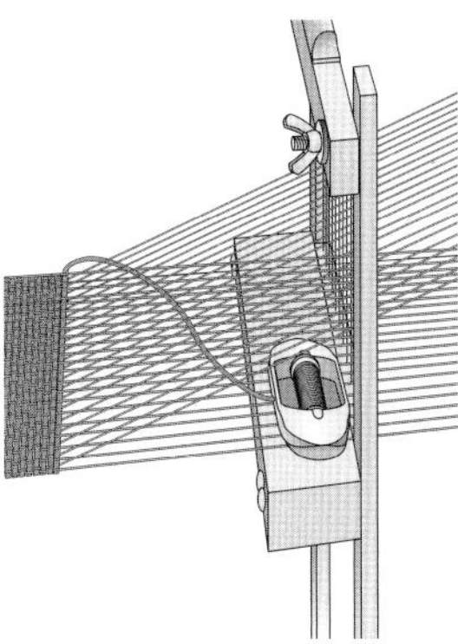

Fig. 260

Weaving

Place the weft in the shed on a diagonal as shown in Figure 261, below. A diagonal should form naturally from the edge of the woven cloth to the shuttle race. (The edge of the cloth where the last weft was woven is called the ***fell of the cloth***.) Figures 262 and 263 show this diagonal. Be sure to maintain the diagonal and always keep the shuttle on the shuttle race (or close to the reed). The natural movement might be to swing the arm back, pulling the weft in an arc down to the fell of the cloth. This shape doesn't allow enough slack in the weft and will cause the cloth to narrow in. Figure 264 shows the arc to be avoided.

What if the warp threads don't lie on the shuttle race?

If the warp threads on the bottom of your shed aren't resting on the shuttle race, check the tension on the warp. If the tension is too high, the warps will float above the shuttle race. If adjusting the warp tension doesn't put the threads on the shuttle race, adjust the height of the beater, if possible. Many looms have this adjustment on the legs of the beater. Sometimes, people put the beater on the loom backwards so the ledge faces the shafts and isn't available for weaving. If this is the case, don't change it now—you can still weave. However, do change it before you sley the reed for your next project. The shuttle race should face the weaver as shown in Figure 262. (Some looms do not have a shuttle race.).

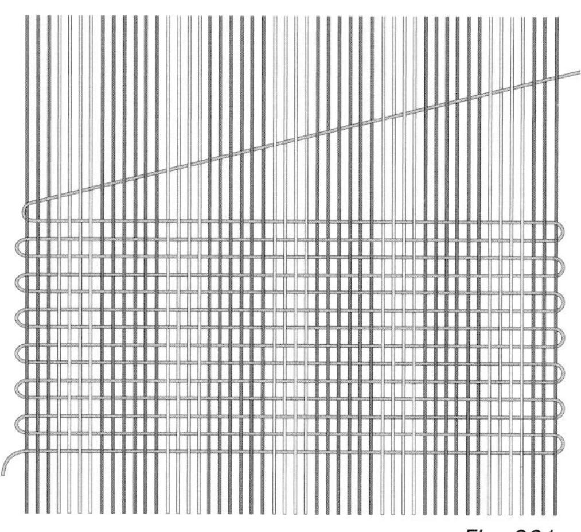

Fig. 261

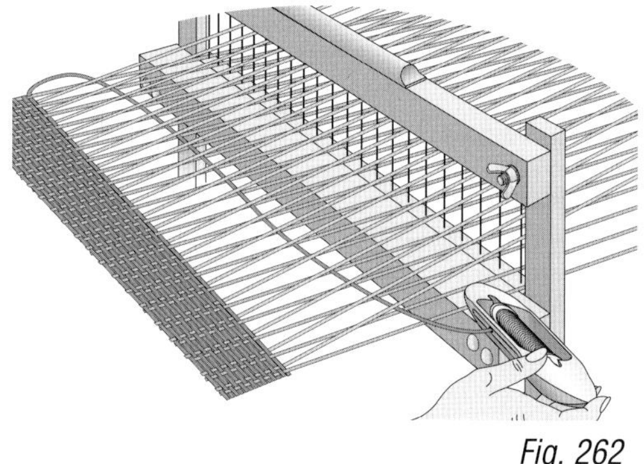

Fig. 262

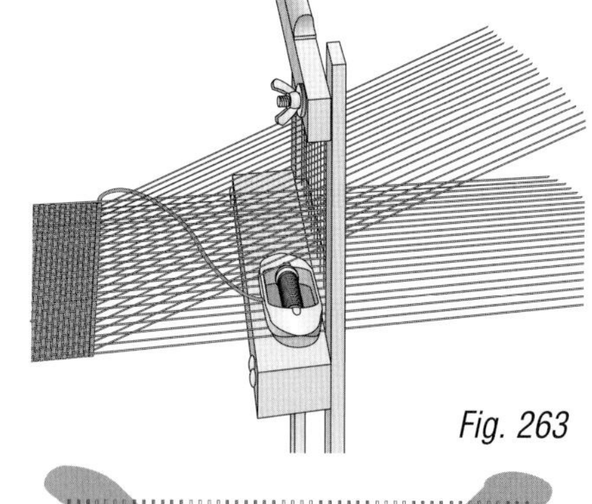

Fig. 263

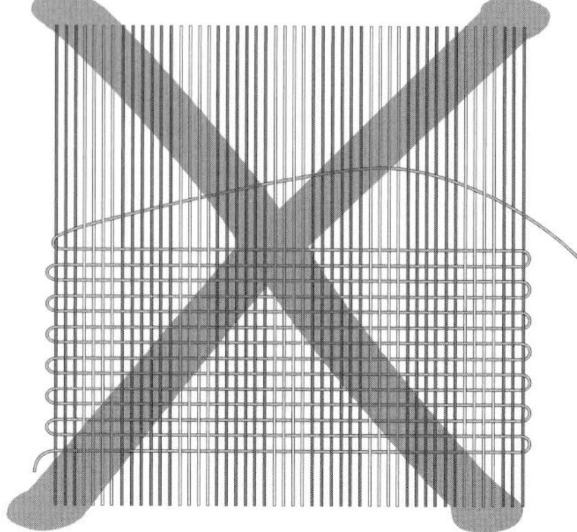

Fig. 264

Snug up the weft against the outside warp thread, (called a ***selvedge thread***)—neither pulling that thread in, nor leaving a loop on the outside of it. I like to snug the weft up until it barely moves that outside thread—just grazes it. This is how good looking selvedges are made. The selvedges are shown in Figure 265.

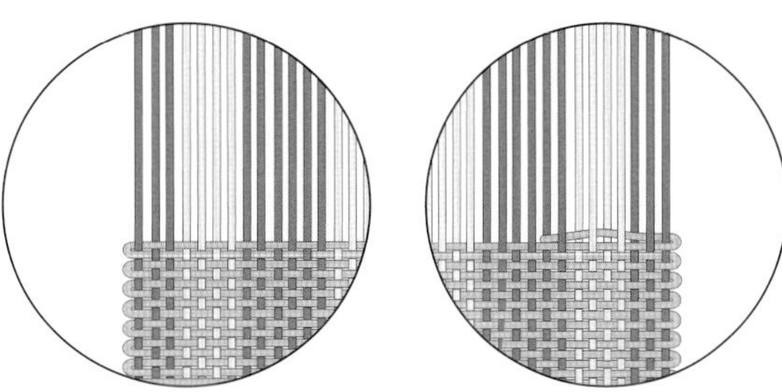

Fig. 265

Don't touch the selvedges. You can control the weft at the selvedges with your shuttle. As your shuttle comes out of the shed, press the weft thread onto the shuttle or bobbin and pull on the shuttle to snug the weft into place at the selvedge. For boat shuttles, if your shuttle cavity is open on the bottom of the shuttle you can use your ring finger to stop the bobbin to pull on the weft to snug it in place. See Figure 266. For shuttles that are closed on the bottom, use your thumb on the bobbin as shown in Figure 267.

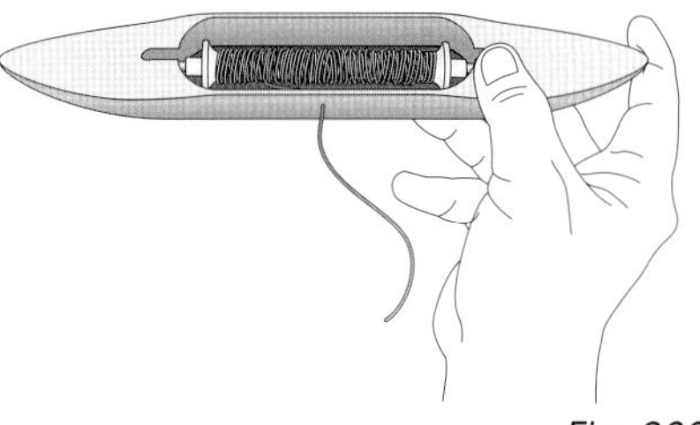

Fig. 266

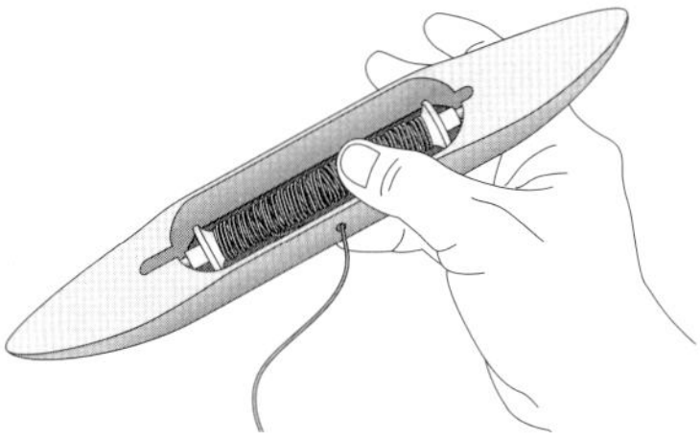

Fig. 267

 Beat in the Weft

Next, swing the beater with one arm; don't pull it. Tap the weft into place, do not press it in. All my teachers (me, too) say that "beat" is a misnomer. What you want to do, generally, is to place the weft with the beater, not beat it in.

When to beat is very important. Beat immediately after you've thrown the shuttle and adjusted the weft diagonal and snugged it up to the outside warp thread. ***The shed should still be open when you beat***.

Your hands on the beater don't need to be in the middle of the beater, provided the beater is rigid. In fact, when you're throwing the shuttle, the hand on the beater can change from side to side. However, if the beater on your loom is wobbly or flimsy you'll need to swing the beater with your hand in the center of it.

Figures 268 and 269 show the hand positions on the center of the beater and on the shuttle when beating and when the shuttle enters and exits the shed. (If your beater is not flimsy, your hands can be to the sides of the center—wherever it is comfortable as you reach your hands forward to beat.)

Beat evenly with the same gentle swinging of the beater and with the edge of the cloth (the fell) always about the same distance from it. You can picture it—if the fell is up close to the heddles, you can't get the same amount of "swing" with the beater as when it is near the breast beam.

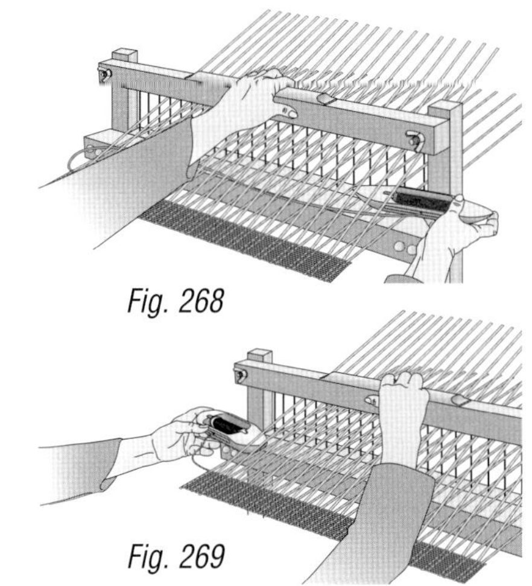

Fig. 268

Fig. 269

To keep the fell of the cloth about mid-way between the breast beam and the heddles, you will need to roll the cloth forward often. This is called "advancing the warp." You need to advance the warp after weaving about every 2". Read how to advance the warp in the sidebar.

③ Change the Shed

When to change the shed is important. Change the shed immediately after the beater has hit the fell of the cloth with the beater still against it. The fell locks in the weft as wide as the warp is in the reed—preventing the narrowing in of the cloth. If the cloth becomes too narrow, the outside warp threads will begin to break. See how to fix broken threads on page 322.

To change the sheds efficiently, try to tie up the treadles so you can "walk the treadles." That means you alternate your feet as you make the sheds—left, right, left, right, etc. This will be the case if you chose the second configuration for tying up your treadles described on pages 96 and 99. (You will press down both left treadles at once with your left foot. Do this by putting your foot in the crack between the treadles. Do the same with your right foot for the next shed.)

If your treadles are in numerical order you can still "walk" them. To lift shafts #1 & #3, first put one foot on the treadle for shaft #1 and then, put your opposite foot on the treadle for shaft #3—you will be using both feet and two treadles, but you'll be putting your left and right foot on the treadles one at a time. (It is not good for your back to move both feet at once.) For the next shed, put your first foot on the treadle for shaft #2 and then, your opposite foot on the treadle for shaft #4. Now, begin the process again by throwing the shuttle.

Advancing the Warp

After you weave a few inches, the edge of the cloth (called the fell) draws too near to the shafts, and the warp must be moved forward toward the cloth beam to make room for more cloth to be woven. This process also requires that the warp on the warp beam be released. It is called advancing the warp. Remember, do it often—about every 2-3 inches—for an even beat.

① Disengage the ratchet brake on the cloth beam. To do this, you'll need to crank the warp a tiny bit tighter so that you can remove the pawl from its space between the teeth of the brake. Flip the pawl(s) out of the way of the teeth so that the brake is disengaged, and the warp is not on tension.

② Disengage the brake on the warp beam. Now it will be easy to lift the pawl out of the ratchet. If you have a tension, or friction, brake, push down the brake pedal and hold it down to keep the brake disengaged as the warp beam unrolls while you are advancing the warp.

③ Place the pawl back into the teeth at the cloth beam and crank (wind) the woven cloth up on the cloth beam. You will hear the pawl clicking in the teeth if you are winding the cloth beam in the correct direction. Be careful not to wind up the cloth too much. You want the fell of the cloth to be midway between the breast beam and the heddles for when you resume weaving.

④ Engage the brake on the warp beam.

⑤ Adjust the tension on the warp. Do it by winding up either the cloth or the warp beam so the tension is not too tight, as discussed on page 89. I usually find that I'm winding up the warp beam at this point.

Change the weft Color

After you've woven 2 ½" of one color, switch to the other color and weave 2 ½" in the same manner. See Figure 252, repeated here.

Read how to change wefts on the next page.

Never knot the wefts together—never, never.

Knots form bumps that will be ugly and cannot be made pretty.

Checking Your Place (How to Tell which Shed Is Next)

Keep track of which shed to use

Enter your shuttle on the side of the warp where your lever or treadle is down for a particular shed. In other words, if your shuttle is on the right, then you'll know that the shed to open is the one using the right foot or the rightmost lever. Figure 270 shows an example of this arrangement with the shuttle being on the right side of the warp and the right treadle being pressed. Note that the illustration is showing one treadle lifting two shafts, shaft #2 and shaft #4. Tying up the treadles this way is often done, but it is not recommended for weaving the sampler, as I've said.

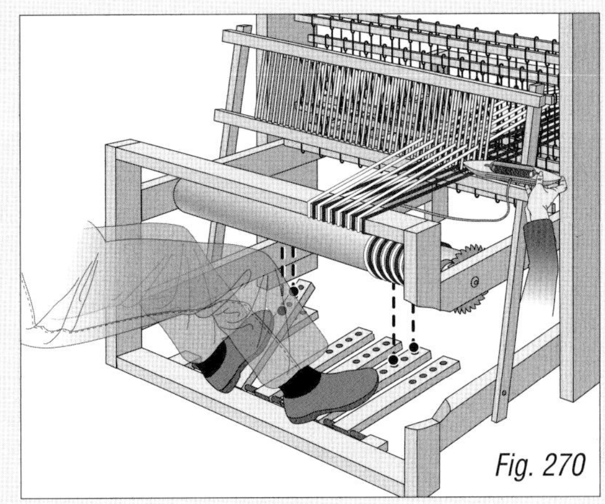

Fig. 270

Here's what to do if you're not sure which shed is the next one.

Open any shed

If the weft is loose, (it will form the diagonal as in Figure 271a), the weft has already been woven in that shed. Then beat, change to the new shed, and return the beater toward the heddles.

If the weft is tight (cannot be moved) as in Figure 271b, the shed is ready for the next weft. (The weft has not been woven in that shed.) Then, enter the shuttle and continue weaving.

If you make a mistake and put a weft into a shed that has just been woven, the weft will unweave—this is another way to check your place. In other words, if you put a weft into the same shed twice, the second one will unweave the first one.

Note: Until the sequence of weaving motions is complete (throw, beat, change the shed), the weft doesn't stay locked in place in the shed.

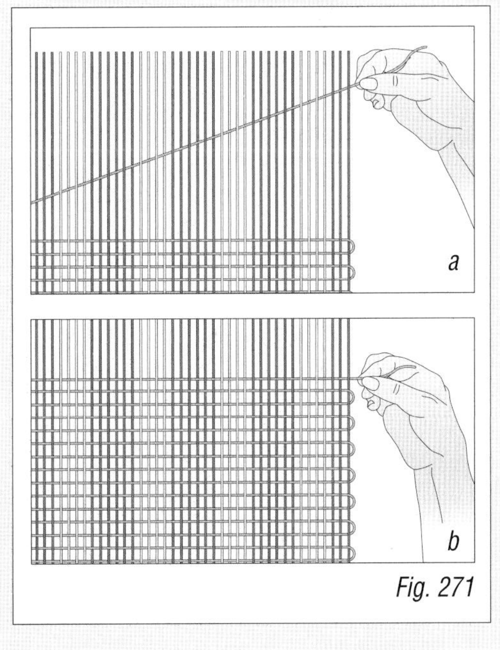

Fig. 271

How to change wefts

I like to tuck in the old weft about ½" into the next shed, snugging it up against the selvedge and pulling the tail out of the shed to let it lie on top of the cloth. The shed stays open, ready for the new weft. I leave the new weft's tail, which is about 1" long, dangling outside the selvedge and cut it off later. See Figure 272.

Other ways to change wefts for other yarns are given on page 131.

Remember to weave 2 ½" of each color before going to Part Two.

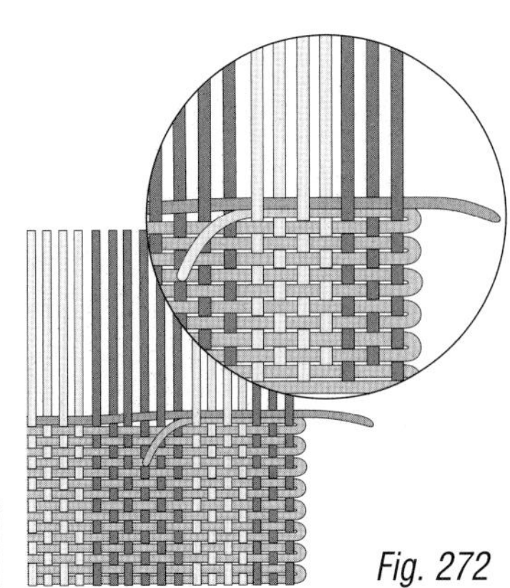

Fig. 272

Keep in mind while weaving:

1. With boat shuttles, the hole where the weft exits faces the weaver.
2. Always place the weft in the shed on a diagonal.
3. Glide your shuttle on the shuttle race—or close to the reed if there is no race on the loom.
4. Your hands should be in the same position for throwing and receiving the shuttle.
5. Don't touch the selvedges—see page 113.
6. Swing the beater gently.
7. Change the shed when the beater is at the fell of the cloth.
8. The motions for weaving are: throw, beat, change the shed.

Part Two: Using two shuttles

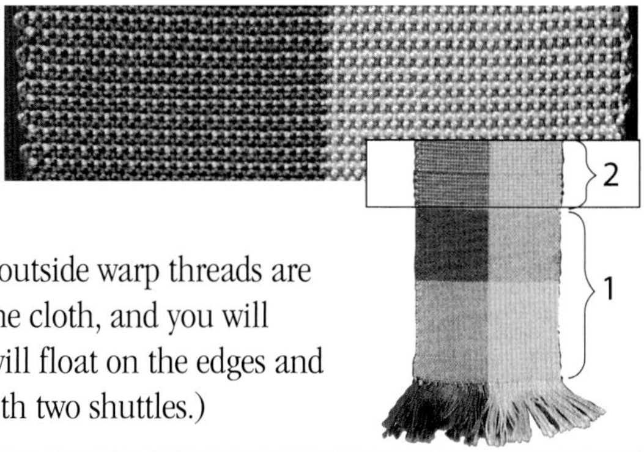

Weave 2 ½" using two colors at once. You'll use both shuttles, alternating them as you alternate the sheds. In other words, there will be a row of one color in one of the sheds followed by a row of the second color in the opposite shed. See Figure 273.

2
1

Fig. 273

See the sidebar below on how to use two shuttles so the outside warp threads are not left out. The outside threads should weave in with the cloth, and you will need to do something special to catch them in or they will float on the edges and not get woven in. (This effect happens when weaving with two shuttles.)

Using Two Shuttles

When using two shuttles, you'll need to do something special to catch in the outside warp threads. Here's what to do:

Check the area where the shuttle came out of the shed—(at one edge of the warp) and notice if it came out under or over the last warp thread.

If the shuttle comes out ***under the last warp thread***, place that shuttle on the woven cloth ***closer to the reed***. See Shuttle A in Figure 274.

If the shuttle comes out ***over the last warp thread***, place it on the woven cloth closer to you. See Shuttle B in the illustration.

I say to myself: "under, away from me" or "over, near me," to remember what to do.

Note: If the previous shuttle is in the position where you want to place your new shuttle, slide the previous shuttle out of the way a little bit so you can put this new shuttle where it should be:

away = closer to the reed

near you = nearer the breast beam.

This intertwines the two wefts at the edge and catches the outside warp threads into the cloth.

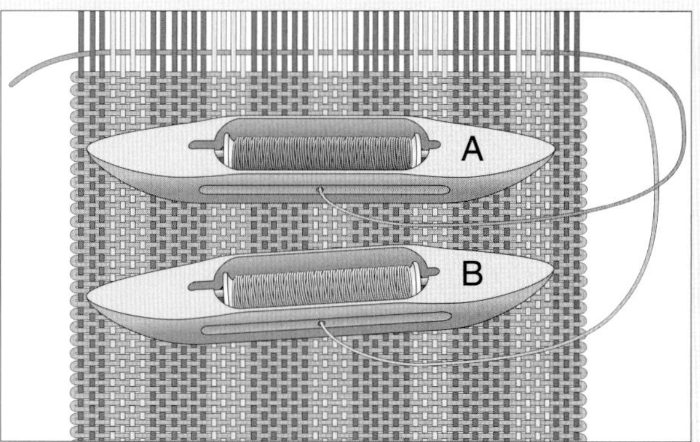

Fig. 274

Part Three: Weft Stripes

Weave 2 ½" alternating two wefts of one color with two wefts of the other color. (You'll be making 2 rows of each color in little stripes.) See Figure 275.

Note how to catch the outside warp threads when using two shuttles, in the sidebar on page 116.

Fig. 275

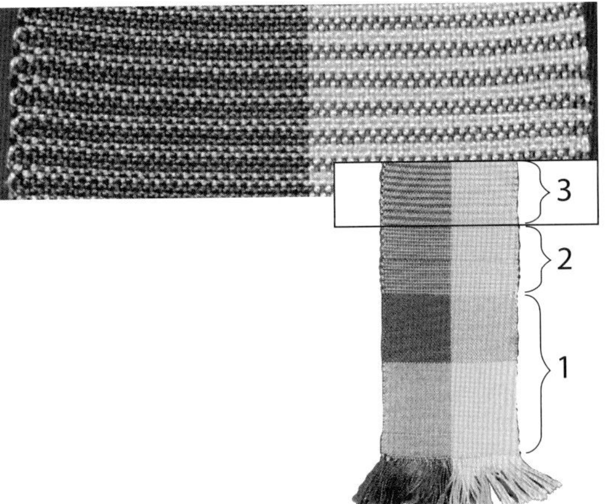

What If the Selvedges Splay Out?

If your outside selvedge threads begin to splay out as shown in Figure 276a, there is too much angle in the diagonal of the weft. You must stop this or the wefts will just continue to splay out more and more. To correct this problem, throw the next weft, and while it is still loose in the shed, tug the previous weft at the selvedge, pulling out the tiny bit of excess weft. See Figure 276b. Then, take up that extra weft in the new shed and beat it in as usual. Figure 276c. The tiny bit of slack that is taken out will straighten the warps.

When the selvedges are back in place, decrease the angle of the diagonal in your wefts. You should need to make this adjustment only a few times to get the selvedges back in place. The way to decrease the angle is to move the fell of the cloth a little closer to the reed

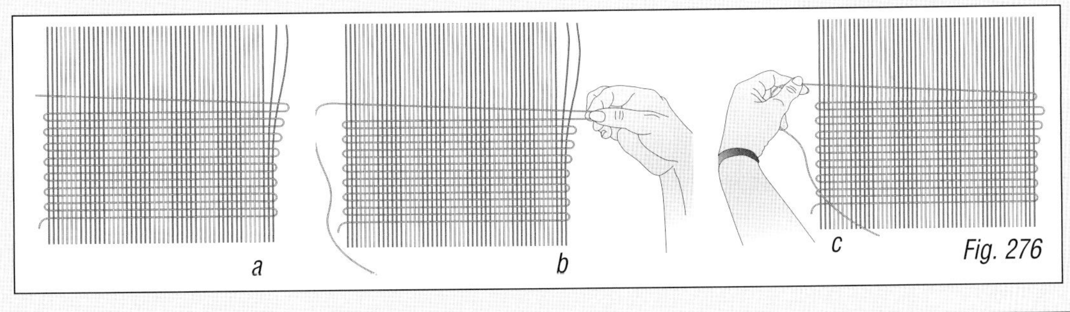

Fig. 276

Part Four: Basket Weave

Weave 2 ½" of each color for a total of 5" woven in basket weave. See Figure 277.

To weave basket weave, wind both shuttles with the same color. For this weave you need sheds that are different from those of plain weave. For the first shed, lift shafts #1 and #2. For the second shed, lift shafts #3 and #4.

Fig. 277

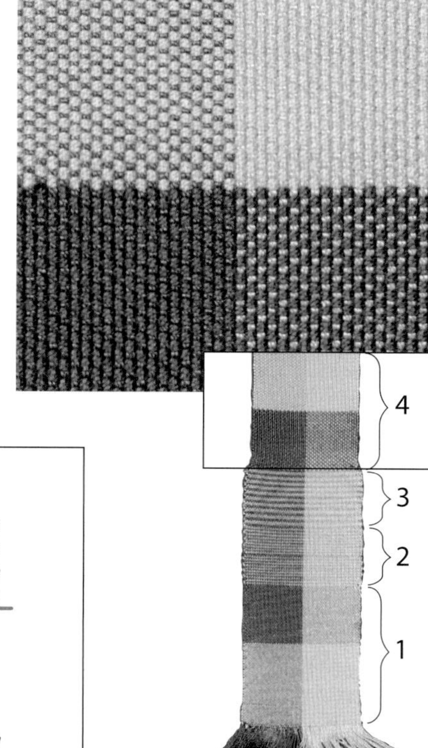

Sequence of Sheds for Basket Weave

1. ***Shafts 1 & 2 for 2 wefts***
2. ***Shafts 3 & 4 for 2 wefts***

Repeat

Basket Weave

Learn how to read weaving drafts on page 195.

To make the cloth look like a basket, you'll put both shuttles into each shed. Have one shuttle go through the shed from left-to-right and the other right-to-left so that the second weft in the same shed doesn't unweave the first one. Figure 278. In other words, there will be two rows (wefts) in each shed, and the two sheds will be made lifting shafts #1 and #2 alternating with lifting shafts #3 and #4.

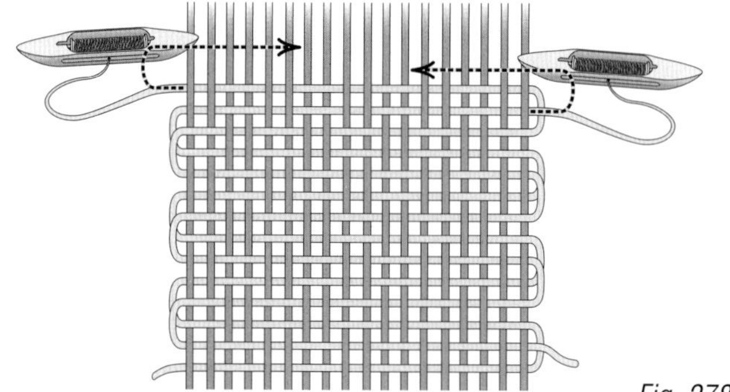

Fig. 278

You'll notice that the cloth is narrower now. See page 313 for why.

Part Five: Balanced Twill

Fig. 279

Now you'll go back to using just one shuttle to weave 2 ½" of each color. That is, with one color (1 shuttle), you'll weave 2 ½", then, another 2 ½" of the second color. You should see strong diagonal lines with this weave (Figure 279).

This is the mode now for the sampler until you get to the Rep Weave section. Specific instructions are given for what changes you'll make for that special weave structure.

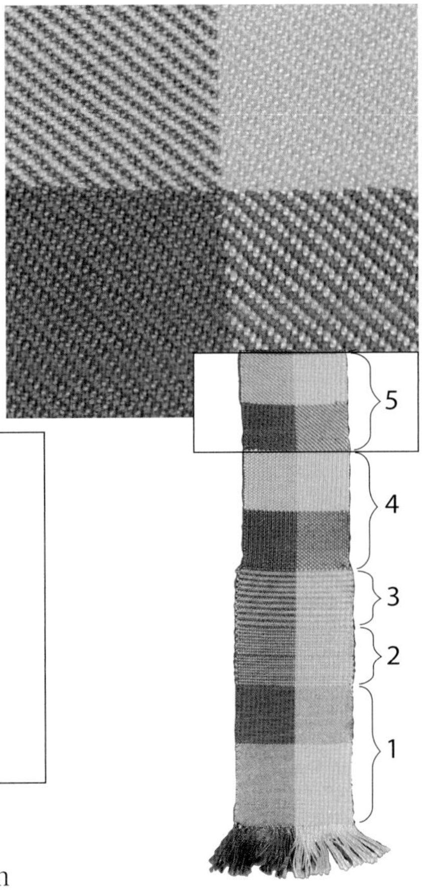

Sequence of Sheds for Balanced Twill

1. *Shafts 1 & 2*
2. *Shafts 2 & 3*
3. *Shafts 3 & 4*
4. *Shafts 4 & 1*

Repeat

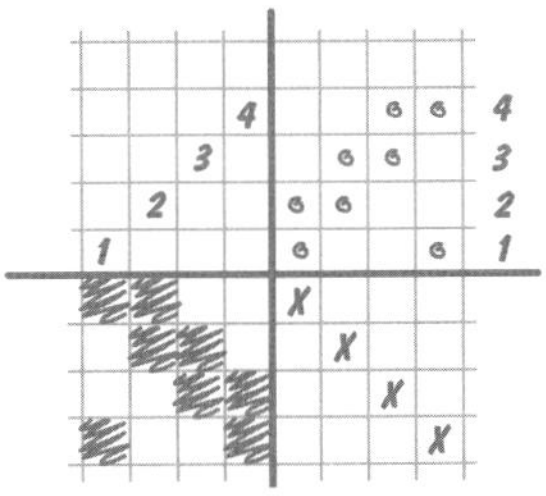

Balanced 2/2 Twill

Learn how to read weaving drafts on page 195.

A trick when weaving twills

Always start the twill weaving sequence by entering the shuttle on the even side of the warp. The "even side" refers to the side where the outside thread is threaded in a heddle on an even shaft, shaft #4 (or shaft #2). See Figure 280. If you threaded your sampler correctly, the other side of the warp will end with a thread on shaft #1—an odd number. Hence, the even side and the odd side. ***If you don't have an even side:*** It's possible that you may not have an even side because you corrected errors in the threading. See page 132 under "other ways to catch the outside thread."

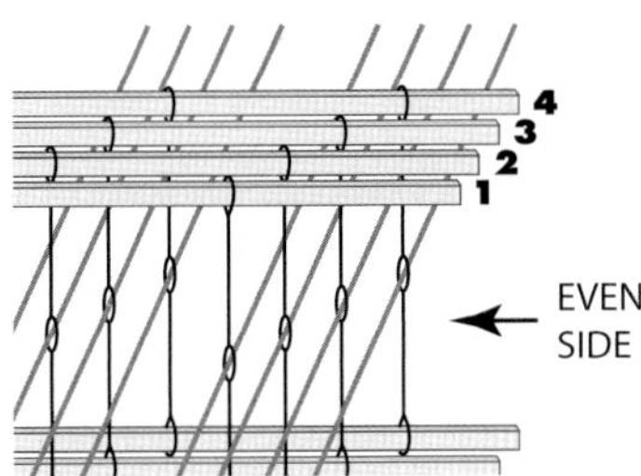

Start twill sequences on the even side of the warp.

Fig. 280

If you discover the outside warp thread not weaving in, you didn't use the trick given above. Figure 281 shows how the outside thread is skipped if the trick is not observed. If you are weaving along, and you notice the problem, you won't want to interrupt the sequence of the twill weave. In this situation, at the beginning of the next sequence, you can cut the weft thread (and put in the tail as usual) and enter the shuttle on the even side of the warp, leaving a tail as usual. Of course, you can take the shuttle around the outside warp by hand as you enter the shed for awhile. See method #3, page 132. Then, when you start the next section, begin the sequence by entering the shuttle on the even side. Another option is to use a floating selvedge. See page 304.

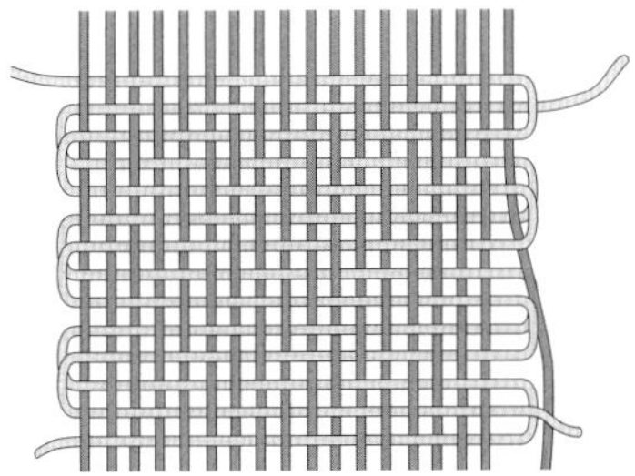

Fig. 281

Part Six: Weft-face Twill—also called 1/3 twill

See Figure 282. Even though the illustration shows only one color woven, weave 2 1/2" of each color as ususal.

Fig. 282

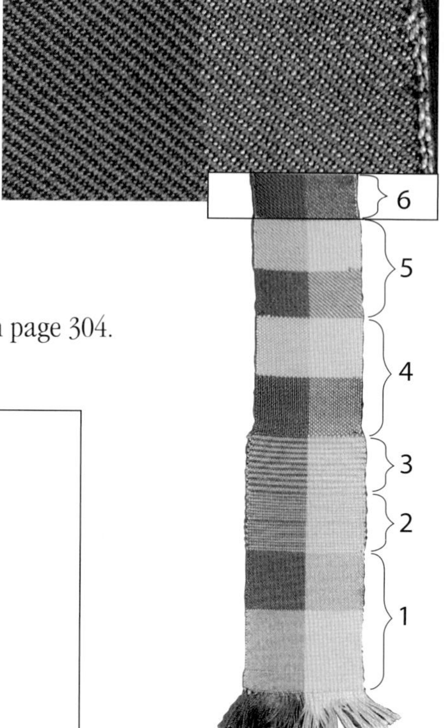

Note: the selvedges of this weave do not look very nice as you can see in the figure. Just ignore them for now. When you wash and iron the sampler later, they will look good enough. (If you choose to make a project in this weave, you would want to do something special at the selvedges to prevent this unsightly edge.—Read about floating selvedges on page 304.

Sequence of Sheds for Weft-face Twill:

1. Shafts 1
2. Shafts 2
3. Shafts 3
4. Shafts 4
Repeat

Weft Face 1/3 Twill

Learn how to read weaving drafts on page 195.

For counterbalance looms

For this weave and the next one, there will need to be an accommodation made for counterbalance looms. These looms operate differently from most of the looms available today. Most looms' shafts are lifted when you press a treadle. Figure 283 shows how the counterbalance mechanism works. When you press a treadle, a shaft is pulled down, and at the same time, another shaft goes up. Four-shaft counterbalance looms operate optimally when 2 shafts are lowered and therefore, two are lifted. You can see for this weave, just one shaft is to be lifted at a time. Read the sidebar on the next page for how to achieve this weave with a counterbalance loom.

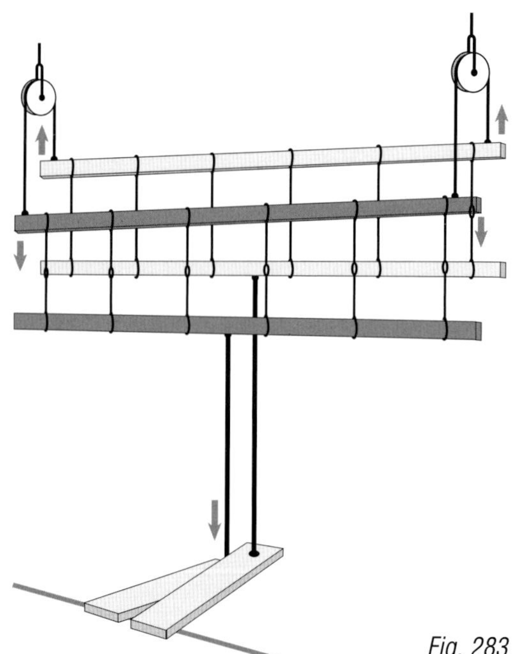

Fig. 283

Weaving on Counterbalance Looms

To achieve one shaft lifted, three shafts must be pulled down. Try different treadles until you almost accomplish this. I say "almost" because you might not recognize the shed. What often happens with counterbalance looms when an unbalanced shed is required (not 2 shafts up and 2 down) is that more than one shed can be seen instead of one nice, clear shed. You will want to put your shuttle into the little shed that will weave the structure you want. In the case of a 1/3 twill, one shaft should be up and three, down. Try the treadles until you see only one shaft raised (the first one is shaft #1). Look into the shed and see that a small shed is created near the upper warp threads. This is the shed where you enter your shuttle. I think of it this way. I only want one shaft's worth of threads above my shuttle, therefore I put the shuttle in where only a few threads are lifted, and most of the threads are at the bottom of the shed. This is very doable—you just need to realize which shed is the one you need.

For the 1/3 twill, the sequence of sheds lifted is: shaft #1, shaft #2, shaft #3, and shaft #4 repeated.

For the 3/1 twill (which is the next weave in the sampler), three shafts are to be lifted at a time. This time you'll put the shuttle nearer the lower warp threads—in the small shed where only a few threads are below the shuttle.

For weave drafts, look at the tie-up section of the draft. The spaces that do not have a bubble indicate which shafts you are to lower. In weave drafts for counterbalance looms, X's are put in all the blank squares in the tie-up draft, and the bubbles are ignored. They are ignored because they are telling the weaver what is to be lifted. Weaving on a counterbalance loom means you look for what shafts are to be lowered.

Figures 284 a and b show what the tie-ups would look like for counterbalance looms with the X's in place where there are no bubbles for 1/3 twill and 3/1 twill.

For the weaves already completed in the sampler—and those to follow where 2 shafts are up (meaning that two will be down) it doesn't matter which shafts you lower—you can concentrate as usual on which shafts are going up..

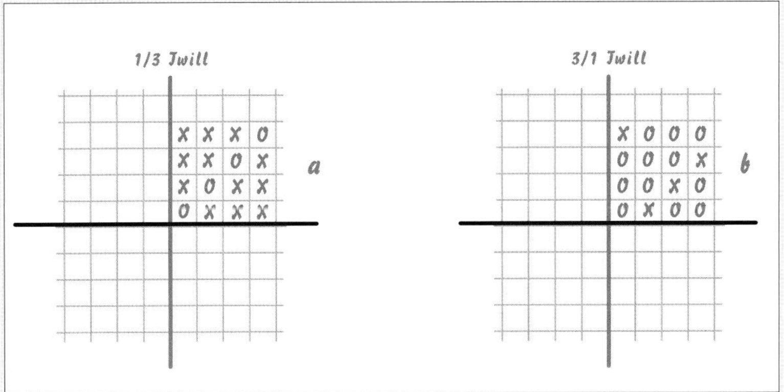

Fig. 284

Part Seven: Warp-face Twill—also called 3/1 twill

Fig. 285

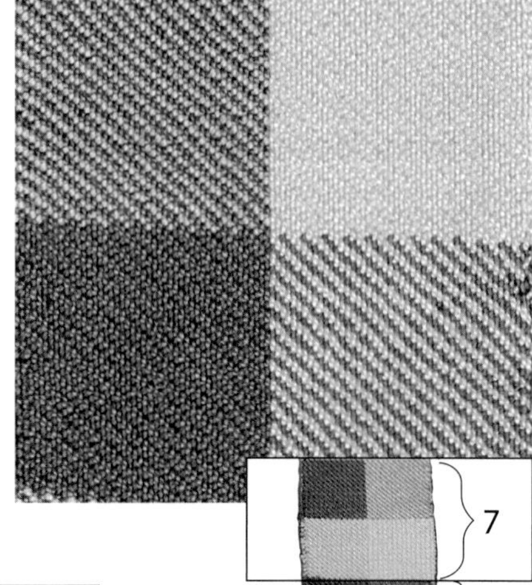

See Figure 285. Weave 2 ½" of each color as usual.

Note that 3 treadles will be used at a time. On floor looms, one foot will need to press 2 treadles and the other foot will press 1 treadle for each shed.

Sequence of Sheds for Weft-face Twill:

1. Shafts 1, 2, 3

2. Shafts 2, 3, 4

3. Shafts 3, 4, 1

4. Shafts 4, 1, 2

Repeat

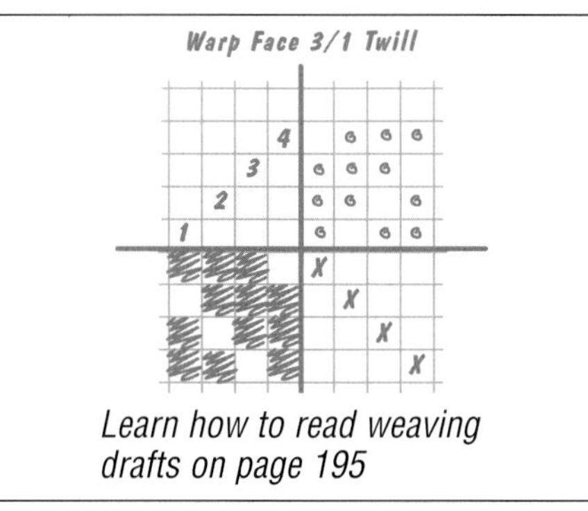

Learn how to read weaving drafts on page 195

Part Eight: Herringbone

Fig. 286

See Figure 286. Weave 2 ½" of each color as usual.

This is a weave many of my students really liked—after they got used to the longer sequence of wefts to weave it.

Watch carefully for which sheds to make to get the zig-zag diagonal lines.

The sequence for lifting the shafts for herringbone twill has 8 rows before it repeats.

Sequence of Sheds for Herringbone:

1. *Shafts 1, 2*
2. *Shafts 2, 3*
3. *Shafts 3, 4*
4. *Shafts 4, 1*
5. *Shafts 2, 3*
6. *Shafts 1, 2*
7. *Shafts 1, 4*
8. *Shafts 3, 4*

Repeat

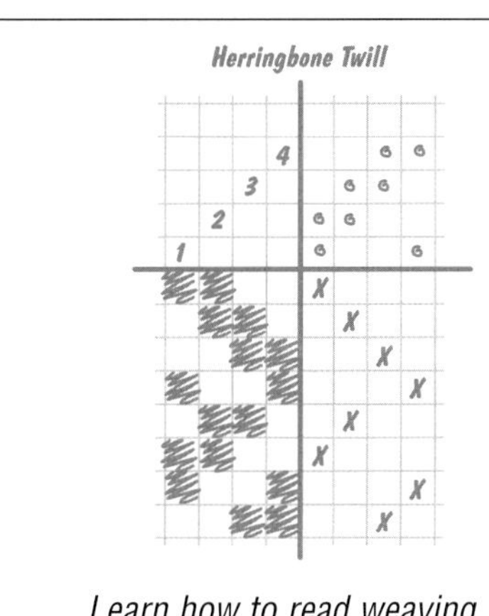

Learn how to read weaving drafts on page 195.

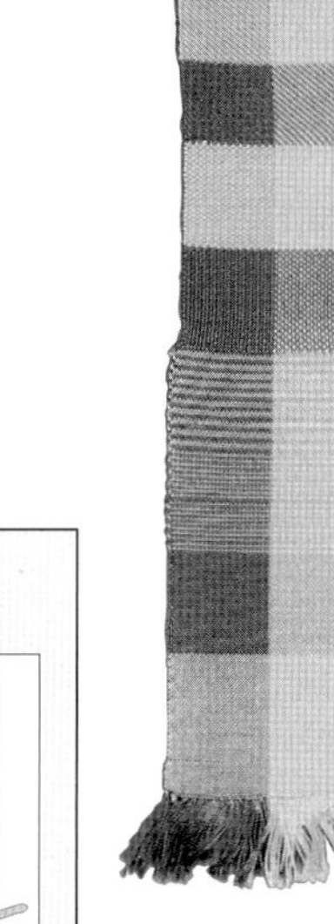

What if the wefts at the fell are wavy?

See Figure 287. The cause could be uneven tension on the warp threads. But the problem is probably caused by the knots you tied at the apron rod or lumpy straps on the rod.

The knots or lumps are underneath the cloth on the cloth beam, making obvious bumps in the cloth. Unroll the beam and put in packing sticks to span the cords, making a smooth roll for the cloth to wind up on. See Figure 288.The lumps make the tension on the warp uneven. The problem must be corrected or it will get worse and cause warp tension problems.

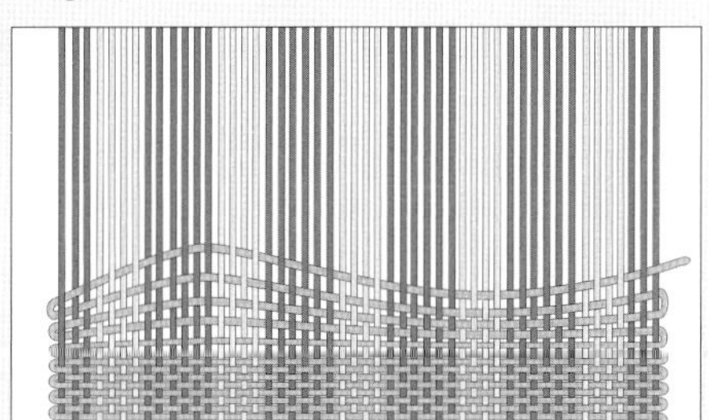

Fig. 287

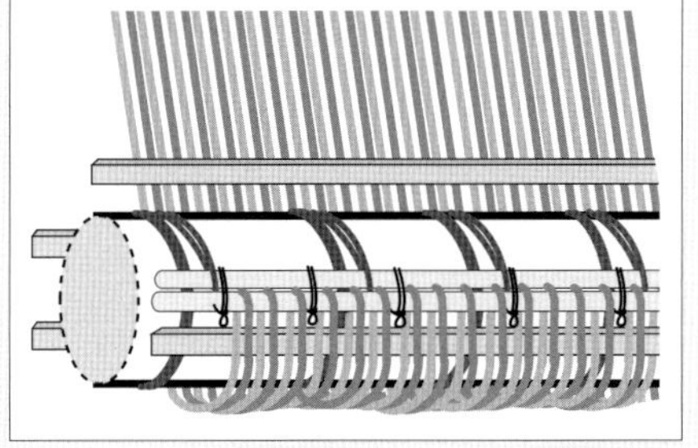

Fig. 288

Part Nine: Broken Twill

See Figure 289. Weave 2 ½" of each color as usual.

Watch the shed sequence carefully. In this weave the sheds break up the diagonal lines so there is no distinct diagonal.

Fig. 289

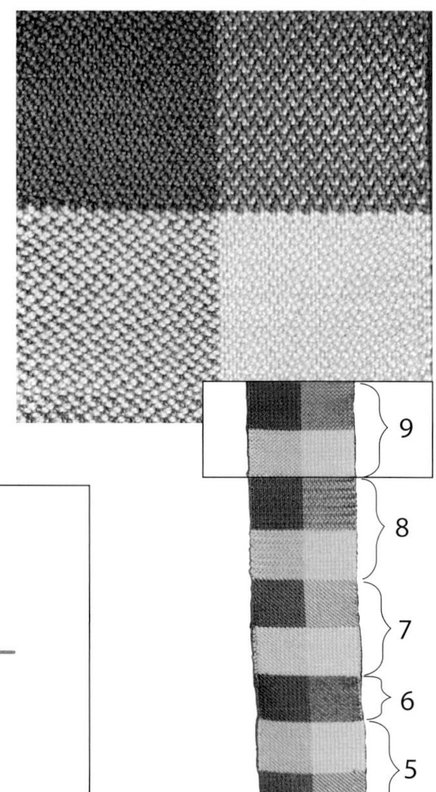

Sequence of Sheds for Broken Twill:

1. Shafts 1, 2
2. Shafts 2, 3
3. Shafts 4, 1
4. Shafts 3, 4
Repeat

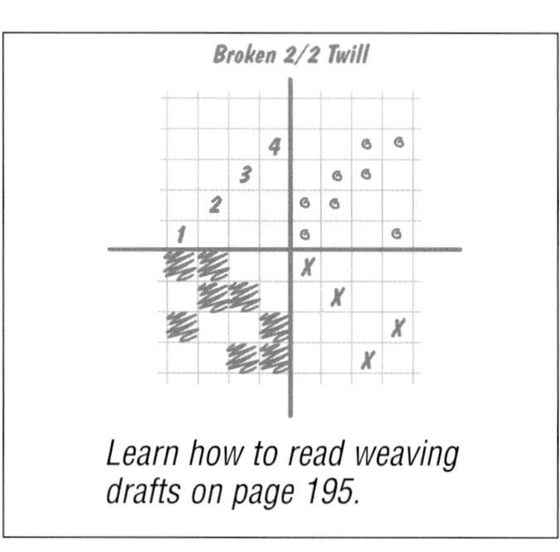

Learn how to read weaving drafts on page 195.

Part Ten: Weft-face Broken Twill (1/3)

See Figure 290. Weave 2 ½" of each color as usual.

The warp will dominate on one side of the cloth, and the weft will dominate on the reverse side. Again, the threads are scattered so there are no distinct diagonal lines. Watch the sequence carefully!

Fig. 290

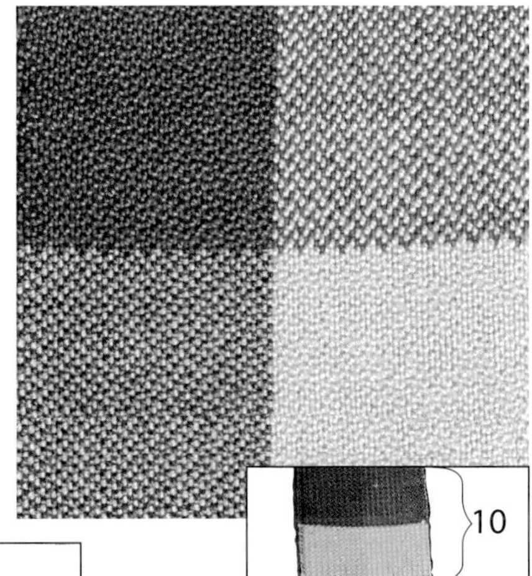

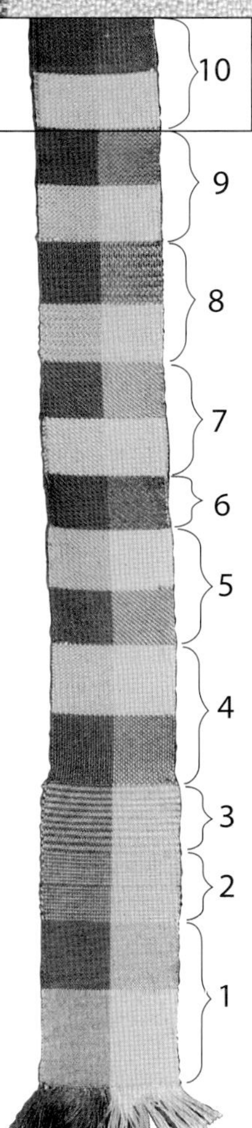

Sequence of Sheds for 1/3 Broken Twill:

1. Shaft 1
2. Shaft 2
3. Shaft 4
4. Shaft 3
Repeat

Broken 1/3 Twill

1 2 3 4

Learn how to read weaving drafts on page 195.

Part Eleven: Rep Weave

Fig. 291

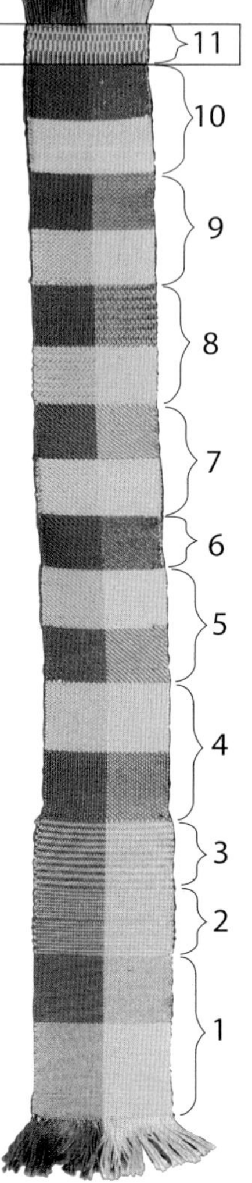

See Figure 291. This is a weave where only the wefts show. The warps are to be completely hidden.

Weave as many patterns/designs as you like. It will be slower to weave this section than the others—you may or may not like weaving slower. Weave as much or as little as you want. The warp wasn't really set up to weave completely weft face weaves, and maybe your loom doesn't weave this weave very well. If you weave a lot or little, it doesn't matter. Do what seems comfortable for you and your loom. Then, try other things in the next section of the sampler.

Now, you will use two shuttles for this weave.

Increase the warp tension

Increase the warp tension by cranking the cloth beam ratchet brake. Make it as tight as you can—when you can't crank the beam any more you'll know that the warp can't get any tighter. You might do this tensioning of the warp at the back of the loom at the warp beam, or in both places. Just note that when either beam won't move, you've tightened as much as you can. There should be no danger of breaking the warp if you stop tightening when you can't tighten it anymore using your ordinary strength. You don't want to call in a weight lifter to tighten it extremely, extremely tight for you.

Bubble the weft

This procedure is important so there is plenty of weft in the sheds to curve over and under the warp threads so the wefts completely cover the warp threads. See Figures 293a,b,c,d on page 128.

Beating in the wefts

For this weave you must beat the wefts in hard so they will cover the warp. You will also bubble the weft which is shown on page 128. Beat on the open shed as usual, then close the shed and beat again and you might even beat again on the next shed to get the wefts to completely cover the warp. Look carefully at the top of the sampler on the back cover.

Four things you need to do for this weft-faced weave:

1. Increase the tension on the warp.

2. Bubble the wefts—see page 128.

3. Beat the wefts in hard.

4. Alternate two colors. See the next page.

Sequence of Sheds for Rep Weave:

1. Shafts 1, 2
2. Shafts 3, 4
Repeat

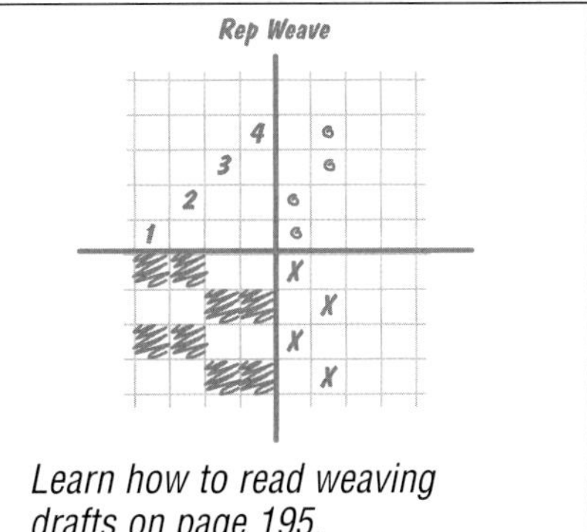

Learn how to read weaving drafts on page 195.

A variation of rep weave is described beginning on page 234.

Use Two Colors

By alternating your two contrasting colors, you can achieve the patterns in Figure 292. Use the sequence of sheds above, but in one of the sheds put the dark weft, and put the light weft in the other. Repeating this series will give you the top row in section A in the illustration. By putting the dark and light wefts into their opposite sheds, you begin to form a checkerboard pattern. Look at Part A of the illustration. In the top row, the lights are covering the threads on shafts #1 and #2 for a few rows; then, they switch position, and the lights are now covering the threads on shafts #3 and #4.

The patterns are made by where you placc thc dark and light wefts, Note in the illustration that you can have solid lines as well by putting the same color weft in both sheds.

Note that when using two shuttles, you might not catch in the outside warp threads. Read what to do to eliminate this problem on page 132.

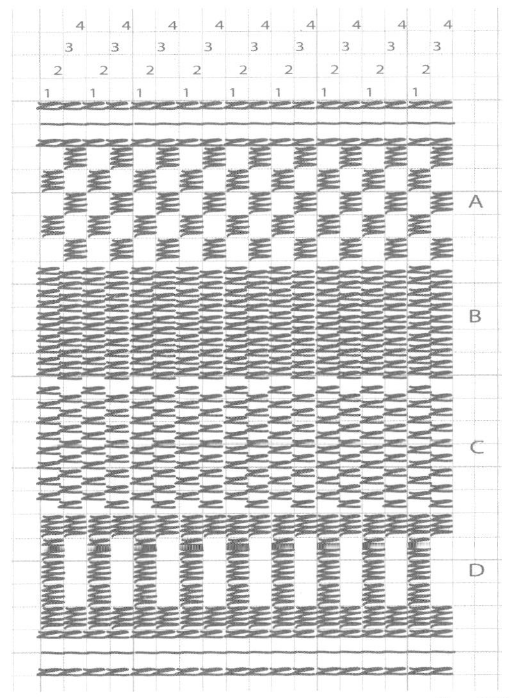

Fig. 292

How to Bubble the Weft

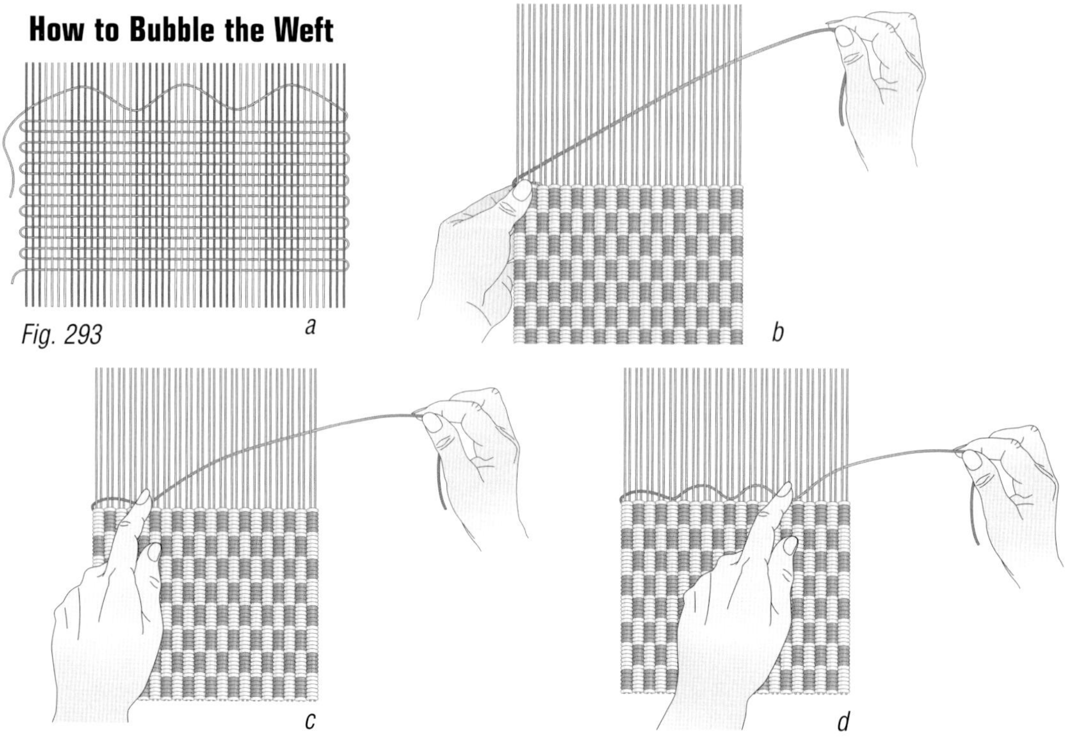

a

b

c

d

Fig. 293

How to change weft colors

You can change wefts colors for rep weaves so the change is not visible. (See Figure 294.) Wrap the old weft around the outside warp thread and tuck it back in on itself in order to put it back into the shed the weft just came out of. Tuck in the tail of the new weft by taking it around the outside warp thread and placing it in the new shed on itself just as you did when you put the tail of the old weft back into its own shed. Alternate sides where you make the weft changes so a buildup doesn't appear all on one edge.

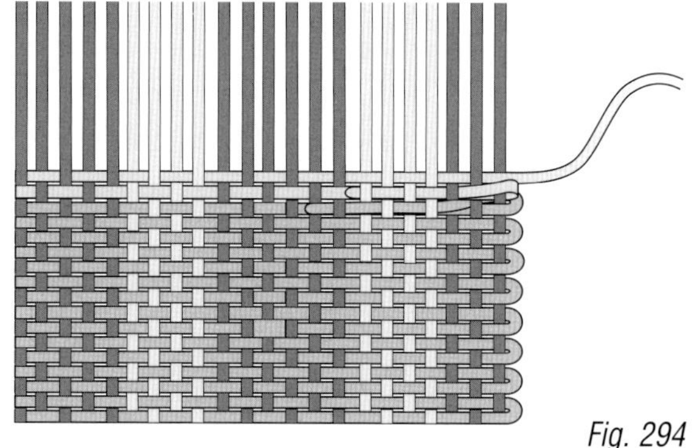

Fig. 294

Adding a new weft

When you have come to the end of your weft, and you need to add a new weft, taper the two ends of weft yarn and overlap them for about two inches in the shed and beat them down. Figure 295 shows the taper at the end of a yarn.

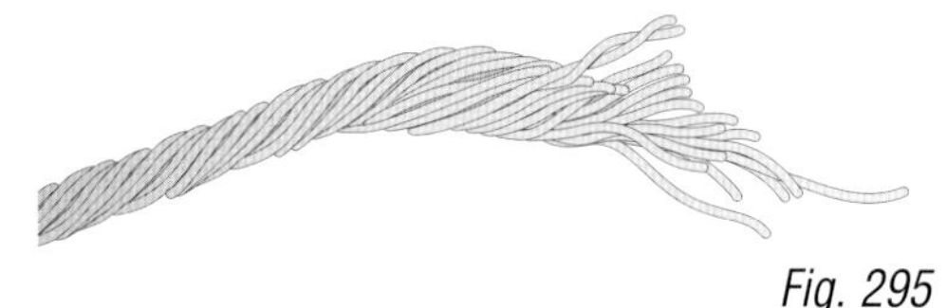

Fig. 295

Part Twelve: Hand-manipulated Weaves

Try some of the hand manipulated weaves starting on page 357.

Part Thirteen: Weave Your Ideas

You can weave your own ideas, now, for the remainder of the sampler. You might try other yarns—different colors, sizes, textures. You might invent your own weaves by making up your own ideas for the sequences of the sheds. Maybe, you'll weave more of some of the weaves you like—or had difficulty in weaving.

Ending the Sampler

When the end stick is close to the heddles on shaft #4, and you can't get a shed any longer, the warp is finished.

You may be surprised that you can't weave every inch of the warp you measured out. The amount that can't be woven is called "loom waste" and occurs with every warp you'll make. The amount of loom waste is calculated in the planning of the warp, so there will be enough warp for the project and for the loom waste, as well. See page 291.

Cutting off the warp

When the warp is woven as much as it can be, you'll cut off the threads at the back of the loom first, and then, untie the surgeon's knots at the front of the loom. This job is called "cutting off," and often, parties are given to celebrate the occasion.

First, reduce the tension on the warp a bit, not so it sags, but so it is not taut anymore. You can do it by releasing the tension at the cloth beam or at the warp beam.

At the back of the loom, as far back away from the shafts as you can, cut one-inch worth of warps at one edge of the warp. ***Make sure you do not cut the apron cords that belong to the loom***—just cut the warp threads at the apron rod. Cutting as far from the heddles as possible means you have flexibility when determining the fringe length. Later in your weaving life you may not plan on a very long fringe, but you never can tell what creative thoughts might come up when you see the cloth off the loom, so allow for any possibility by cutting the yarns as long as they can be. Fringe is shown in Figure 296. Making fringes is described on page 145.

Fig. 296

How to make fringe begins on page 145.

Ending the Sampler

Working now at the front of the loom, pull that inch-worth of threads towards the cloth—pulling the warp threads through the heddles and reed. Then tie the threads in a temporary knot at the fell, so that the last weft cannot come out. Use just the beginning part of a shoelace knot for this. See Figure 297.

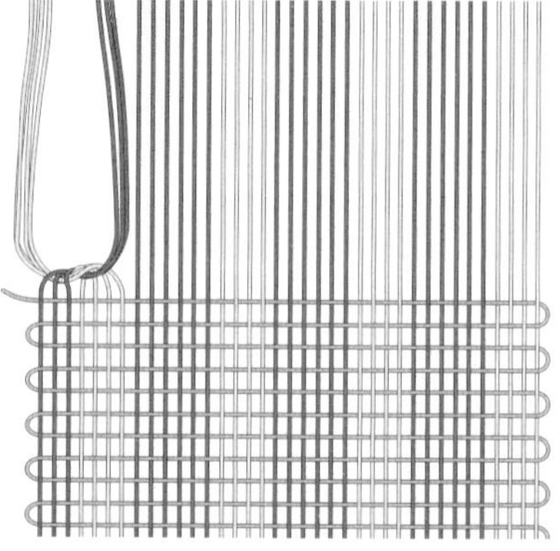

Fig. 297

Continue the process by cutting the next inch-worth at the opposite edge of the warp at the back of the loom. Work from the edges toward the middle in this way, alternating from side to side. The final group of threads should be the center warp threads. See Figure 298.

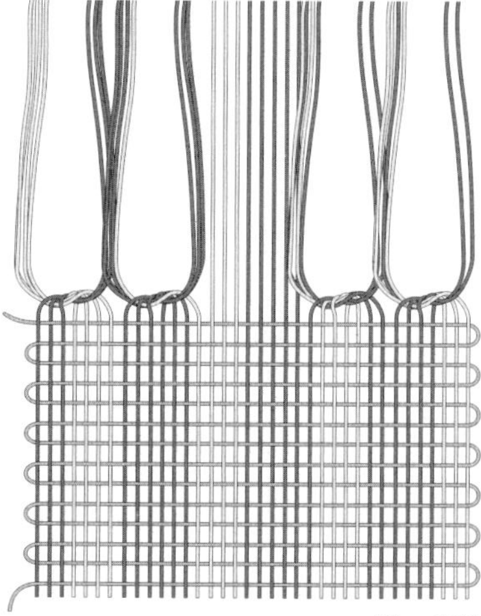

Fig. 298

Remove the cloth at the front of the loom.

Unroll the cloth and untie the surgeon's knots at the beginning of the warp so you can remove the cloth from the loom. If it looks like the first row of the heading will come out, tie temporary knots as above to hold the weft in place.

You're finished

Admire your work as soon as you take it off the loom. I'm sure you'll be amazed at all you've done.

Now the cloth is ready for "finishing"—for example: washing, fringing, and making the sampler look beautiful by trimming off extra threads, etc. See page 137.

More about weaving

I. Other ways to change wefts

For chenille yarn, leave the old thread end somewhere in the middle of the weaving, with the shed open. Leave it placed diagonally in the shed. Throw the new weft in the same direction you were going before, allowing the two tail ends to overlap each other by about 3 or more inches. You can later cut off the little ends, if they happen to stick up. See Figure 299.

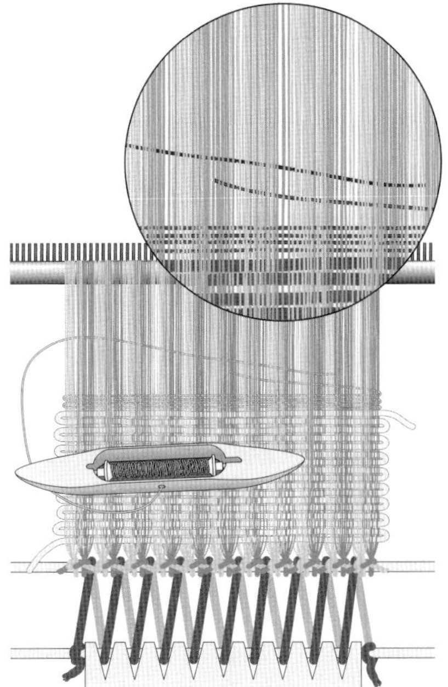

Fig. 299

For some wefts, the old weft might need to be put in the shed it just came out of so the change of wefts won't show. In that case, you must wrap it around the outside warp thread and tuck it back in on itself. Add the new thread with the new tail hanging outside the selvedge—to be cut off later, after the cloth has been washed. If you feel you should also tuck in the tail of the new weft, take it around the outside warp thread and place it in the new shed on itself just as you did when you put the tail of the old weft back into its own shed. You might need to alternate sides where you make the weft changes so a buildup doesn't appear all on one edge. If the threads are fine, though, it shouldn't make any difference which side you make the changes. See Figure 300.

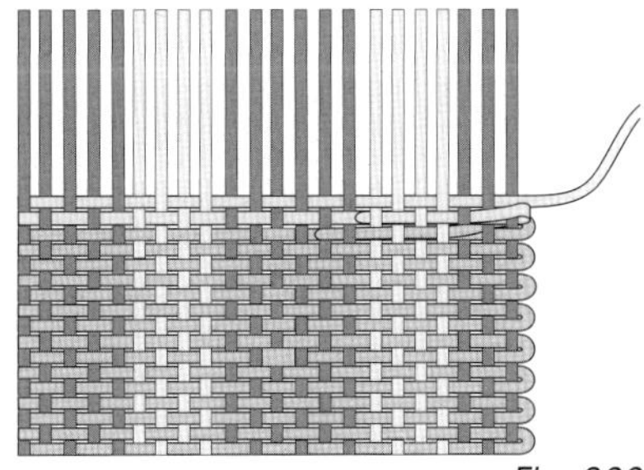

Fig. 300

For frequent color changes, the weft threads can be carried up the side, and not continually cut off and re-started. You can carry a weft up about ½ –1". Much more than that distance and the yarns show too much. See Figure 301.

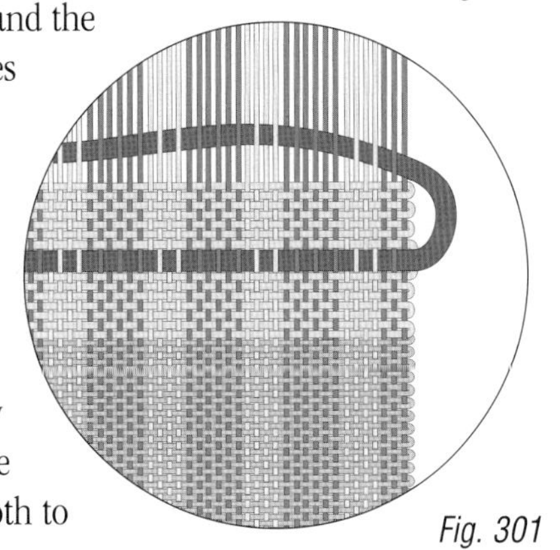

Fig. 301

For thick wefts, un-ply the last inch or two of both the old weft and the new weft. Working with the tail of the old weft, put one of the plies in the shed and bring that ply out to the surface of the cloth. Put the remaining ply into the shed for about 1 ½" further and then bring its tail out of the shed, so these plies are staggered in the shed. See Figure 302a. Un-ply the new weft yarn in the same way and put it into the shed so that the un-plied areas overlap those of the old weft. Bring the tails out of the shed at different places from the first tails. Where the two single plies overlap, they will add up to the size of one yarn and won't make a bump in the weft. See Figure 302b. Cut the tails that are sticking out of the cloth to about 1" long.

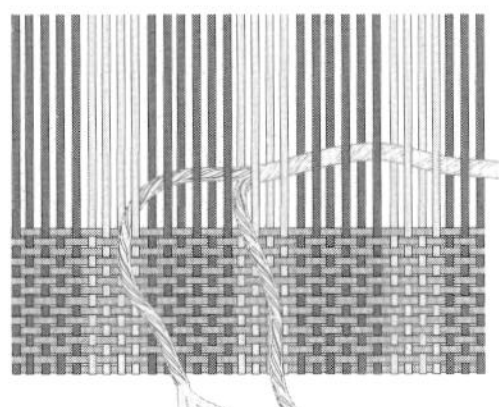

a

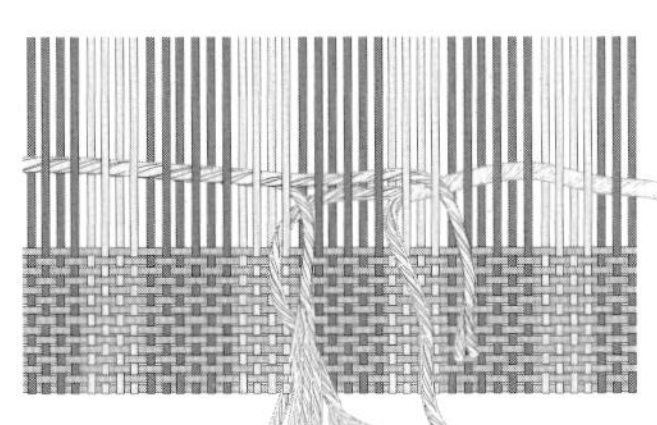

b

Fig. 302

II. Ways to catch in the outside warp thread

Method #1 – for twill weaves cut the weft and enter it on the other side

In other words, if the shuttle was on the right edge of the warp and normally would be entered from that side, Cut the weft and enter it from the left side. This procedure might need to be done a couple of times to get the right sequence and side of the warp to work out.

Method #2 – use floating selvedges

Read about floating selvedges on page 304. Use them for larger projects when the outside warp threads won't weave in.

Method #3 – hand manipulate the shuttle around the outside warp

To do this, you'll take the shuttle around the outside warp thread and place it into the new shed. You can do it every few wefts—just to keep the outside thread woven into the cloth.

III. How to measure your progress for future projects

Measure the cloth while the warp is under tension for accuracy.

I find it is the most accurate to mark my desired measurements on the edge of a long piece of adding machine tape. It may be just the final length or where any changes in the weft are to occur. Make small, fine marks. If you use a fat pen, the mark you make can be so fat that you won't be able to determine if you're exactly at the mark or if you need one more weft. See Figure 303.

Pin the strip of adding machine tape to the side of your cloth with 3 horizontally placed straight pins as shown in Figure 304. When you need to move the pin closest to you, "leap frog" it over the other pins and place it near the edge (fell) of the cloth. Using 3 pins keeps the tape from slipping and sliding so you can be accurate. The tape does not get rolled in with the cloth on the cloth beam.

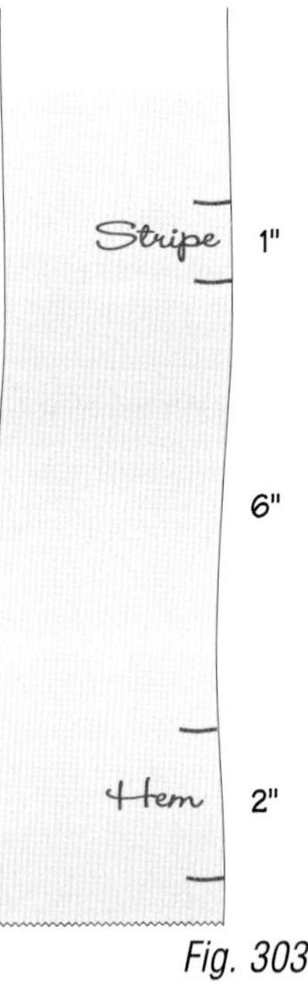

Fig. 303

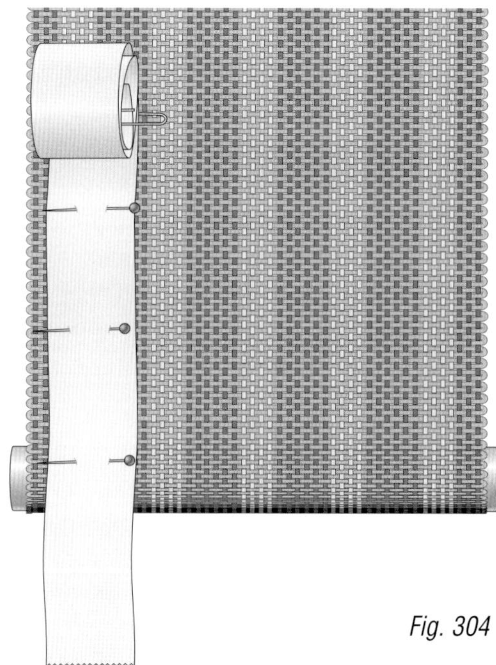
Fig. 304

IV. Tying up countermarch looms

Read about this interesting type of loom in my second book, *Warping Your Loom & Tying On New Warps*, in the chapter about Adjusting Looms. Basically, the way countermarch looms work is described in the sidebar. Read how to weave the sampler on the next page.

How Countermarch Looms Work

Countermarch systems vary, but all of them are designed so the shafts are both raised and lowered. The shafts work independently rather than being connected to each other as in counterbalance looms. Between the shafts and the treadles there are two sets of lams, which are levers or bars. The upper set of lams is usually shorter and the lower set of lams, longer. See Figure 305.

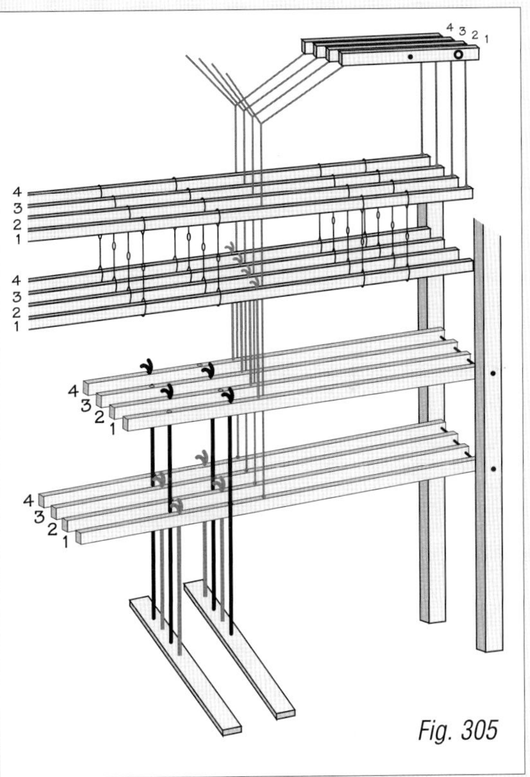

Fig. 305

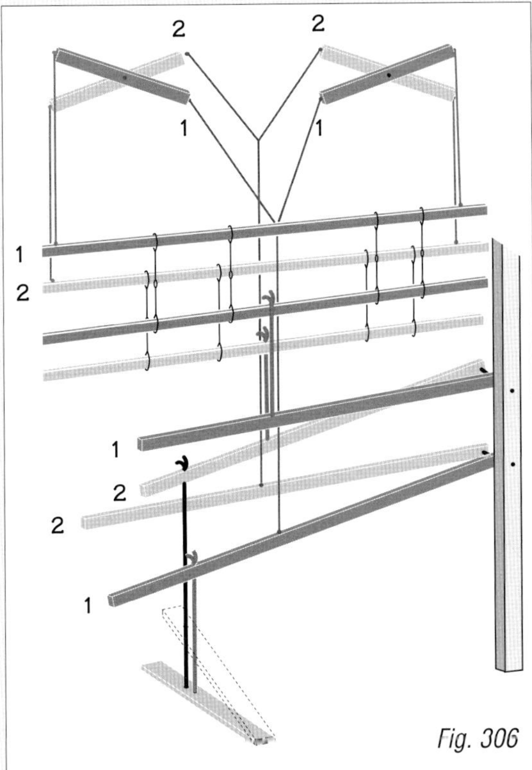

Fig. 306

Figure 306 shows schematically two shafts of a countermarch loom forming a shed with shaft #1 raised and shaft #2 lowered.

Most countermarch systems have a jack or a pair of jacks (levers with pivots in the middle) above each shaft. When one end of the jack is pulled down, the other end goes up. In the illustration shaft #1 is being lifted by its pair of jacks.

The lower set of lams is attached to the jacks overhead, and the upper set of lams is directly attached to the bottoms of the shafts. See that shaft #1 is being lifted in the illustration and shaft #2 is being lowered.

The sheds are made by tying up the treadles so all the shafts that are to be lifted are connected to the lower set of lams, and all the shafts that are to be lowered are tied to the upper set of lams. Note that both shafts #1 and #2 are tied to the single treadle. This is the situation for countermarch systems. Each treadle must have ties to all the loom's shafts—those that are to be lifted as well as those that are to be lowered. Remember: "lower lams to lift shafts and upper lams to lower them."

Note: Each treadle needed for a project for this type of loom needs to have ties made to each shaft on the loom.

How to weae the sampler on countermarch looms

Part One of the sampler

In the first part of the sampler, you'll need to make the tie-up on one treadle so shafts #1 and #3 go up (and shafts #2 and #4 go down). A second treadle will be tied so shafts #2 and #4 go up (and shafts #1 and #3 go down).

For the first treadle tie shafts #1 and #3 to the lower (longer) lams and shafts #2 and #4 to the upper (shorter) lams as shown in Figure 305 on page 133.

In Figure 305 note that the left treadle has shafts #1 and #3 going up. The ties from the treadle for these two shafts are made to the lower (long) lams. Also tied to the left treadle are two more ties—to pull shafts #2 and #4 down. These ties are made to the short lams for shafts #2 and #4.

The second treadle has its ties for shafts #2 and #4 going to the lower lams and the ties for shafts #1 and #3 to the upper lams. This will make shafts #2 and #4 go up and #1 and #3 go down.

For other parts of the sampler and other projects

You will need to re-tie the treadles for every change in the sampler. Use the same principle for other tie-ups required by other situations. The shafts indicated to go up are tied to the lower lams and all the remaining shafts are tied to the upper lams—Do this for each treadle (each shed) indicated in the draft.

You can have any number of shafts going up or down. For example, if you wanted three shafts to go up—on one treadle, all three shafts to go up would be tied to the lower lams. The shaft remaining, then, would be tied to go down (tied to the upper lam for that shaft).

This loom can be confusing, so if you own one I highly recommend my second book, *Warping Your Loom & Tying On New Warps* for detailed explanations and adjustments.

IV. The two-stick heading

This is a very useful heading. I have used it countless times. One reason is to eliminate the knots on the apron rod so that the cloth rolls up without lumps on the cloth beam. Another reason is so that you can cut off some of the cloth before the whole warp has been completely woven.

The lease sticks will stay in place because they are woven in the cloth.

You need a pair of sticks that fit on your cloth beam and won't interfere with the ratchet.

They can be lease sticks, dowels, or metal rods. I prefer thin and lightweight sticks rather than thick ones because they take up less warp and aren't so bulky.

- After you've woven the initial heading to spread out the warps (page 107) (or at least 1"), insert a stick in one plain weave shed; insert another stick in the next plain weave shed, and continue weaving for 1", or so. See Figure 307 on next page.

- Release the tension on the warp, and carefully cut between the knots and the first inch of the heading that you wove. Leave both plain weave sections and the sticks attached to the loom! Remember, you are cutting between the knots and the cloth which means only the knots are being cut off—the heading remains attached to the loom because it is part of the warp that is on the loom. ***Be careful not to cut the loom's apron cords!*** See Figure 308. (If you want fringe, see on the next page).

  The heading will be re-attached to the apron rod. See Figure 310. If the warp is sparse or slippery, put some white glue or tape on the cut edge to prevent the heading from unraveling or the warp threads from pulling the heading out when the warp is back on tension.

- Fold the first stick, with the first inch of the heading, under the second stick and the second inch of the heading. See Figure 309.
- Tie the two folded sticks across the front apron rod at 3" intervals. Make the ties strong by doubling a sturdy but not fat string. Use a tapestry needle to go through the cloth and around the rod. Make the first tie in the center of the warp to hold the sticks stable. You might find it easier if you wind up the cloth apron until the apron rod is resting on the breast beam. Then pull the heading sticks (and the warp) forward to the apron rod and tie them to it, while steadying them on the breast beam. Put the knots on the front edge of the apron rod so you won't make lumps with the ties. See Figure 310.
- Begin weaving again. The warp tension remains unchanged; since the heading sticks were woven in with the warp on tension before the knots were cut off, all the threads remain evenly tensioned as you resume.

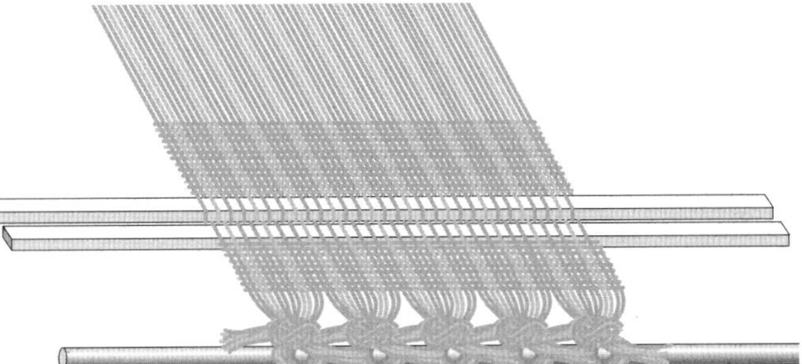

Fig. 307

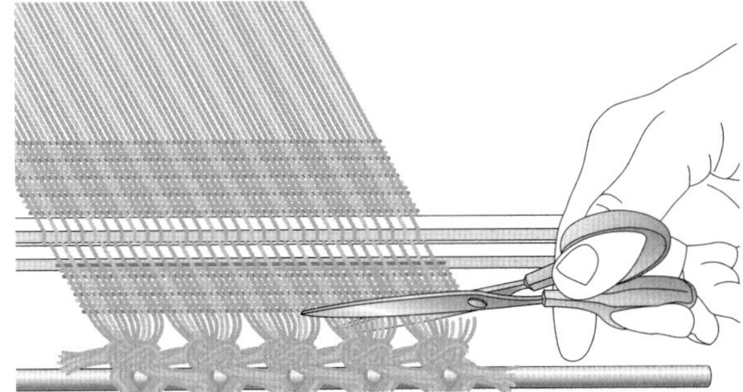

Fig. 308

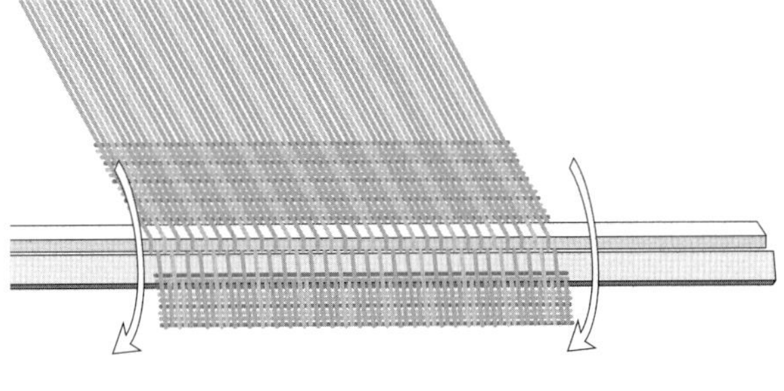

Fig. 309

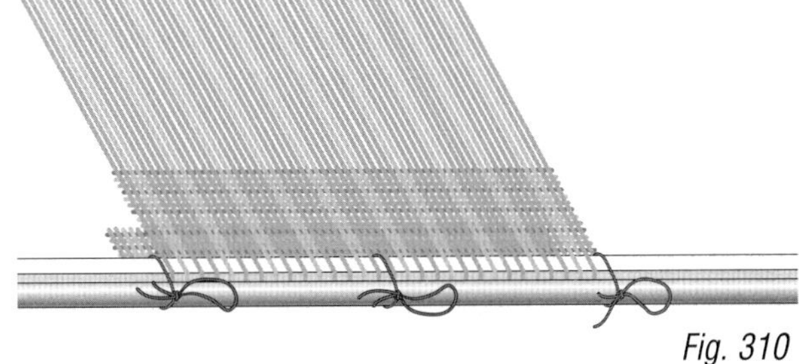

Fig. 310

Fringe

If you want fringe, untie the knots instead of cutting them off and fold the sticks as above. Then smoothly fold back the unknotted warp threads as well as the heading.

Another situation: Cutting off the cloth as you go

You can cut off pieces as you weave them; it's not necessary to wait until the entire warp is used up before cutting off the fabric. The headings and two sticks save precious warp because you don't need to tie the warps back on to the apron rod.

When you're ready to cut off a length of cloth, make the complete 2-stick heading just as above. (Weave 1" of plain weave, insert 2 sticks into the next two plain weave sheds, and weave one inch more. That's the complete heading. You do not leave any space between the cloth and the heading—you'll just cut the cloth and heading apart.

Cut between the cloth and the first inch of the heading you wove, leaving the complete heading attached to the loom. See Figure 311. Remove the cloth from the front apron rod. Fold the two sticks, and tie them to the apron rod, as above.

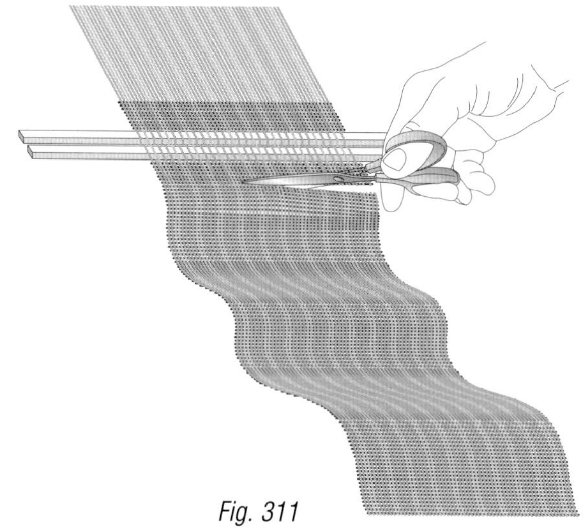

Fig. 311

Separations between projects without cutting

Often you don't want to cut between projects until later. In that case you will want to know where to cut when you go to cut them apart.

If you want fringe on the pieces you must leave enough warp unwoven for the fringes on both sides of your cut. I put soft cardboard strips about 1" wide in the sheds to make up for the space for the fringes. Cardboard from cereal boxes works well. Cut your pieces wider than the width of the warp so the selvedges won't slip off.

If you don't want fringe put a contrasting color thread in one of the sheds where the cut is to be. Don't give your marker string its own shed. You might change your mind and want to pull it out so you don't want to see an empty space or flaw where the thread was. Also, don't use red, black, navy or any color that might run when you wash the cloth.

For hems that aren't bulky you might weave the cloth for the hems with a thinner weft thread.

More weaving tips and solutions to problems that you may encounter are given in the chapter on troubleshooting.

5 *Finishing*

A cloth isn't finished until it's finished!

My teachers told me that when the cloth came off the loom, it was only half done! I could understand hems and fringes and any other sewing needing to be done, but I didn't realize that finishing the cloth was a process, as well. For our beginning projects, "finishing" meant washing the cloth in some way, not because it was dirty, but because it would relax the threads and make them curve around each other. The cloth off the loom looks flat and a little stiff, while finished cloth is soft and supple. Our teachers had warned us earlier not to beat our cloth too hard because after it is washed, it will shrink a bit and the threads will draw together, and if you start out with a very dense cloth, it will turn into cardboard after washing.

Finishing is anything done to a fabric after it's woven to change its appearance (what you see), its hand (what you feel), and its performance (what its purpose is). In industry, there are many ways cloth can be finished. In fact, unfinished cloth is said to be "greige" or "gray goods" or in the loom state.

Some familiar industrial finishes are dyeing, fireproofing, and stain resistance. Felting is an example of a finish that weavers and knitters might know. It is a process of washing the cloth so rigorously that it shrinks and becomes much thicker. Another example handweavers may use is brushing. It is sometimes used for blankets to give a lofty, fuzzy surface.

The change in the cloth can be very dramatic such as with chenille. In the loom state the cloth is stiff, but after finishing it is enormously soft and supple. Finishing chenille is on page 187.

This chapter, however, deals with just the basics—preparing the last weft, repairing errors or flaws, washing the cloth, hemming, and fringes.

A detailed chapter about finishing various fibers and types of cloth is in my third book, *Weaving & Drafting Your Own Cloth*, beginning on page 157.

Equipment List

Fringe Twister (optional):

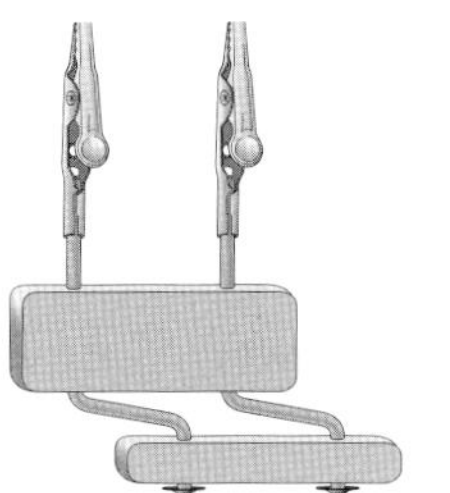

Scissors:

Tapestry Needle:

Sewing Machine or Needle and Thread

Iron

① Protect the Last Weft

Hand sew or machine stitch the first and last wefts on the cloth so that none of the wefts slip out during washing.

Hand sewing

I usually hand sew the cut edges of the cloth with overcast stitches immediately after removing it from the loom. See Figure 312. Later, I might machine stitch the edge if I want sturdier stitching. However, sometimes instead of hand sewing the edge, I take the cloth immediately from the loom to the sewing machine and stitch the first and last wefts as shown in Figure 313. What I do depends upon how vulnerable I feel the wefts at the ends of the cloth are to unraveling, and whether I plan to wash the cloth gently or vigorously.

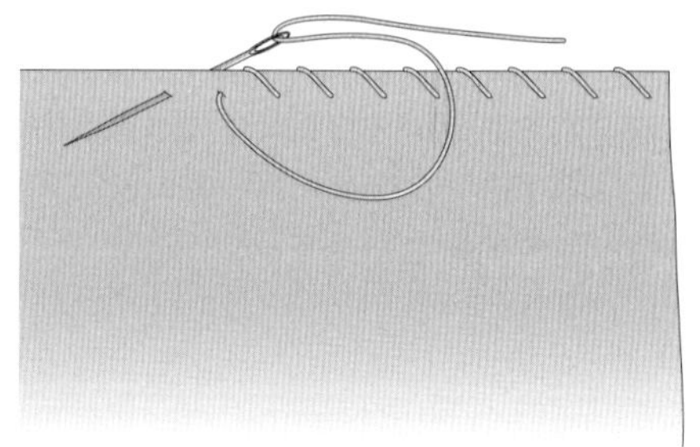

Fig. 312

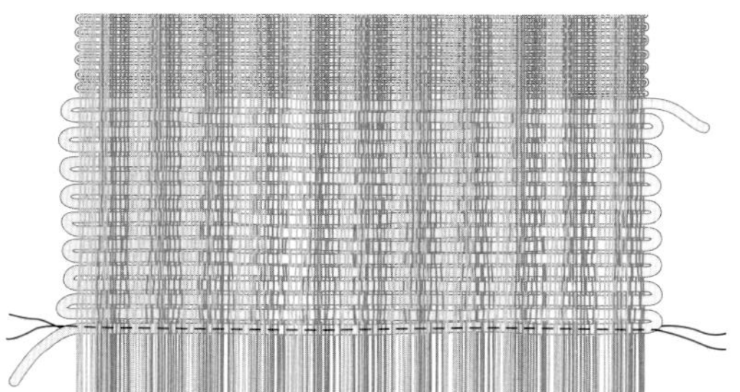

Fig. 313

Machine stitching

If I am going to cut apart pieces of the cloth, I machine stitch two rows of curving, straight stitches so that after cutting between them, each piece has stitching on its edges such that the wefts cannot come out during washing. See Figure 314. Use your judgment whether to hand or machine stitch the edges. If you plan to wash your cloth in the machine vigorously, hand sewing might not hold, so machine stitching would be better. See Step 4 on page 141 for the reasons to wash the cloth by hand or by machine.

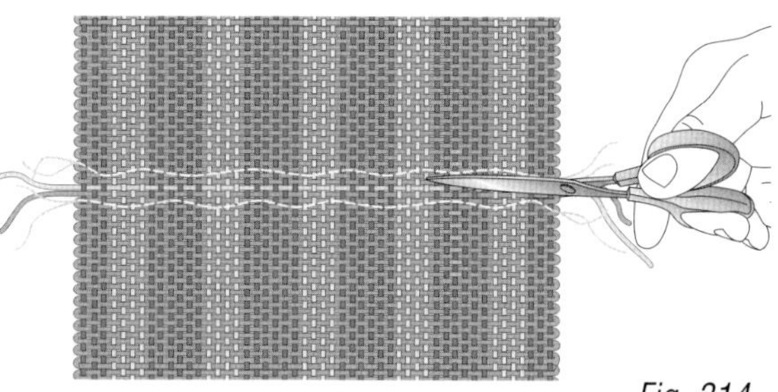

Fig. 314

Hemstitching

Hemstitching gives an attractive edge while protecting the wefts. See Figure 315. It can be done while the cloth is on the loom or after it has been cut off. Doing it on the loom is by far the most efficient way. The steps for creating this stitch are found on page 358.

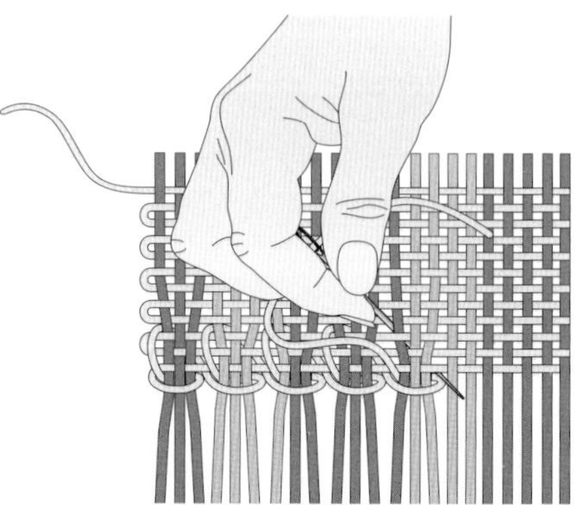

Fig. 315

 Cut the Warp and Weft Tails to 1" Long

Cut the tails of wefts sticking out from the selvedges and cloth to about 1" long. Cut the tails from any warp repairs as well. Tails that are too long get tangled during washing. They will shrink a bit during the process of washing, so you need to leave some length to them so they don't disappear into the cloth when they shrink. You will cut them flush with the cloth after washing.

 Repair Errors or Flaws

For the sampler, I recommend omitting this step. Any errors show what you have learned. And, besides, you might want to repeat an "error" in a project someday.

For later projects, however, you should repair errors or flaws before washing.

Look at your cloth carefully and closely—on both sides—checking for any flaws. Do it when you have a fresh supply of energy. Holding the cloth up to the light from a window or a lamp is a great way to discover flaws

Check for knots, bunched threads, thick or thin spots, warp or weft floating threads and any flaws in the weave. Look for any tails from repairs previously made and from changed wefts.

Remember, make all repairs before washing the cloth because you can see individual threads in the weave easier then, and the repairs will be less visible after washing.

To make repairs you will use a tapestry needle threaded with the warp or weft strand to weave, or darn, in threads the way they should be, and you will cut out the mistaken threads. Remember to leave tails (1" or so) on the repair threads as well as the cut-out threads for washing. Then, after washing, cut them flush as described on page 145.

How to weave in (darn) repair threads.

Basically, you'll weave by sewing your matching thread over a mistake, and at least 1/2" beyond it in both directions, so your darned-in thread overlaps the correct weaving a little bit. Figures 316 a, b, and c show repairing weft threads, and Figure 317 shows repairing a warp thread. Read how on the next page.

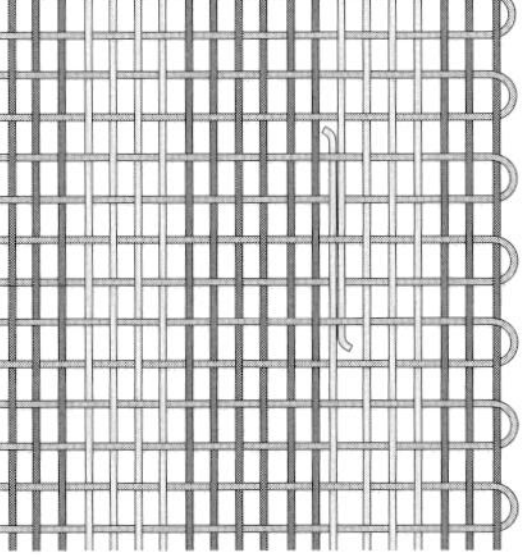

Fig. 317 Warp thread repair

Fig. 316

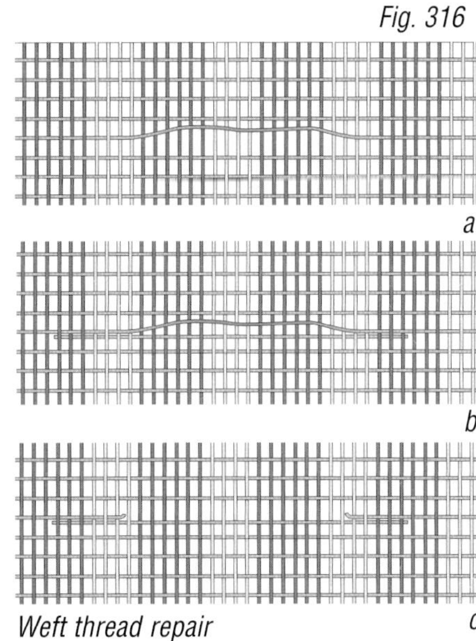

Weft thread repair

Examine the path the warp (or weft) travels in the cloth, and with your needle and thread, sew over and under the threads in the path that ought to have been taken, including the overlaps at each end of the mistake as shown in the illustrations. Then, cut out the incorrect yarn. When I'm repairing, I'm concentrating on the precise path my needle should be taking.

Be careful to put the right amount of tension on your darning or splicing thread. Usually, my thread is loose while I'm darning, then I tension it. If it is too tight or too loose, you are likely to see the repair after washing. To tension the thread after the darning is done I tug on the new yarn so it lies smoothly in with the rest of the cloth. Then, I tug the cloth on the diagonal in both directions to settle the mend into place.

Sometimes, I untie an offending knot in the yarn and use the short threads themselves for the darns. Untying the knot gives me enough thread to overlap them a bit at the cut. Because the ends of the yarns are so short, weave the tapestry needle into the cloth first and then thread it and pull the little short strand through the cloth. For thick yarns, taper, or rough cut, the yarns and pull just fibers into the cloth where the yarn overlaps the correct weaving at the ends of the repair for invisibility. See Figure 318.

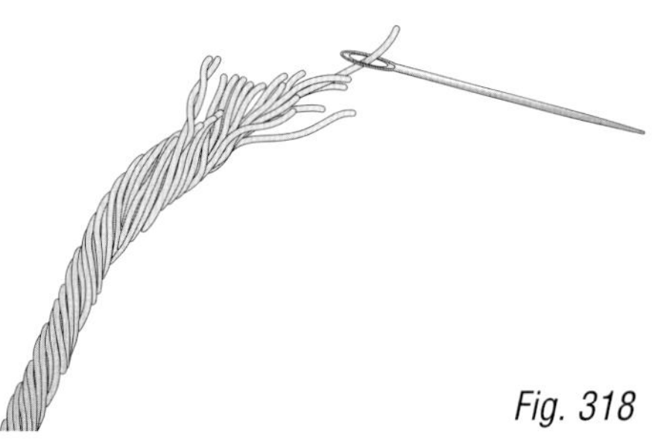

Fig. 318

Whether you darn in warp or weft threads depends on which seems easier. For example, if a warp is errant over several wefts, I fix the warp thread rather than all the wefts affected by it.

Warp repairs

If you previously made warp repairs in the cloth and wound the threads around a pin like a cleat, darn the tails in so they overlap at least ½", as shown in Figure 317 on page 139.

A loop in a weft

You might discover a kink or a loop in the weft. Work the excess yarn over to an edge with a tapestry needle, cut it on one side of the loop close to the edge and darn in the longer cut tail. If it is too far from the edge, cut the loop and darn the two threads into the cloth overlapping them a little.

A tight weft

Cut the weft at a selvedge and release the tightness, allowing it to slide into the cloth until it is smooth with the rest of the cloth. Darn in a new strand where the thread was released and pulled into the cloth.

Snags and worms

Any snags or loose threads hanging off the cloth must be mended, probably by darning. Chenille fabric, however, has a tendency to "worm"—its threads seem to work themselves out of the weave and look like snags. There's nothing you can do at this point except to poke the loops through to the back of the cloth.

The problem is that the cloth was woven too loosely or in a weave structure with too many floating threads. Weave chenille tightly, with both warps and wefts close together. Read more about weaving chenille beginning on page 184.

Variations in beat

Sometimes, variations of the beat can be disguised before washing by pushing wefts apart or closer with the tip of a tapestry needle. After washing, the variations will become more disguised.

A missing weft

You may find two wefts traveling together in the same path or shed. Either remove one, or weave in a new weft in between them in the correct shed. Decide which method will look the best and will be easy enough to do.

 Wash the Cloth

I recommend washing the sampler by hand. Read how on page 142.

For future projects, wash a sample

For woven projects, the way you wash the cloth may affect the shrinkage or the appearance or feel of the cloth. That's the reason you should try different methods of washing on a sample of the cloth before you weave the whole project. One student in a workshop brought in placemats that were so shrunken they were too small to use and so puckered that they looked terrible. When you know how much shrinkage there is likely to be, you can weave your piece longer to allow for it. Washing gently in lukewarm water will cause less shrinkage and distortion of a fabric than vigorous machine washing with very hot water. Drying in a drier may cause even more shrinkage and distortion. It may be that only dry cleaning will give the results you want—send a sample to make sure you like the cloth after dry cleaning.

It may be that you expect your finished project to be machine washable, but that after sampling different washing methods, you decide it must be gently washed by hand because you don't like the way the cloth looks or feels or that it shrinks too much when washed by machine. It makes sense to know what the fabric will do on a small sample rather than ending up with a complete disaster because you washed the entire project inappropriately.

Allow extra warp for your projects so you can make a sample. To make the sample, weave about 6-8" and cut it off. Figure 319 shows how to cut off a portion of cloth for a sample and then to reattach the warp to the loom to resume weaving using the two-stick heading. More details of this wonderfully useful "two-stick" heading are on page 134.

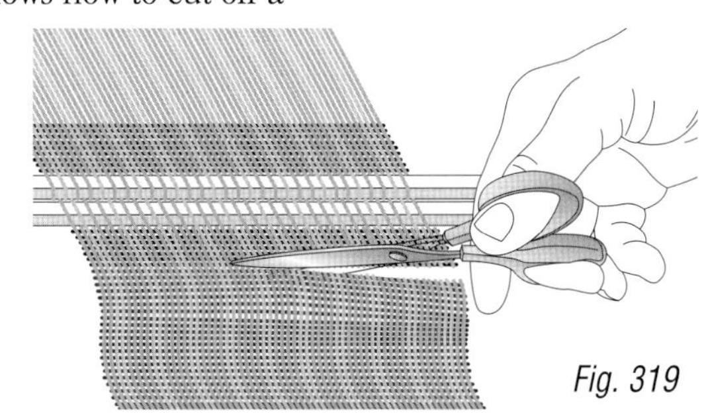

Fig. 319

After the sample is cut off, measure and write down the length (warp direction) and the width (weft direction) of the cloth. You can place the cloth on paper, and draw around it—what you want is to know the size the sample was before any washing.

Then, wash it in various ways to see how much shrinkage to allow for and to be sure the cloth can stand up to the method of washing you hope to use. Starting with gentle washing allows you to try more vigorous methods afterwards. If you start out with a hot, vigorous wash, you can't go backward and undo the shrinkage by then washing gently.

I recommend washing the cloth first by hand, gently, and in lukewarm water. Check the amount of shrinkage that has occurred and the look and feel of the cloth. Afterwards, you can wash it again with a little more heat and agitation (movement of the cloth in the water) or in the machine, perhaps, with hotter water and even more agitation. Read about agitation on page 143. If there is a lot of change in the cloth with the first washing, do not jump to a hot, vigorous machine washing next. Instead, try washing it in stages, getting more movement (agitation) and hotter water with each stage. If you want to wash a project by machine in its life, try it after gentler stages have been taken. In the later stages, you can try putting it in the dryer, gradually increasing the temperature and drying time if you hope to use a dryer for the final project. Don't squeeze or wring out the cloth or let it spin too much in the washer because permanent wrinkles can result. Check this effect with your sample.

Read about methods of drying the cloth on page 144. Try them on your sampler.

One way you can think of the stages is that you keep upping the ante until something horrible happens, and then you know not to go that far. However, it may be that the cloth can nicely withstand the amount of washing and drying that you hope for.

With the information from the sample, you can weave the project with confidence knowing how the cloth will look when finished.

Shrinkage

If shrinkage is an issue, figure out how much longer you need to weave your cloth so it will be your desired size after finishing. You would do the same thing if you wanted to know how much longer to weave a stripe so it would shrink to be the right length. Here is what to do:

How to Factor in Shrinkage

You want 30 inches. You have a 25" before washing and 20" after.

Divide 20 by 25 = 0.8 (shrinkage factor)

30 (desired length) ÷ 0.8 (shrinkage) = 37.5

You need to weave your cloth 37½" long.

1. Take the sample of your cloth and measure it before and again after washing. Remember to write down the "before" measurement.
2. Take the size after washing (finishing) and divide it by the size before finishing. That will give you a decimal number. (You will always get a decimal number because you are dividing the smaller number by the larger. I remember that from math class when we learned about decimals and percent.)
3. Take the final size you desire and divide that by your decimal number above. That will tell you how long you need to weave your piece or stripe.

Read about using a piece of adding machine tape to measure as you weave, on page 132.

For the completed woven project, use the same temperature and amount of agitation that you chose after sampling. Ideally, you would finish the cloth at a higher temperature and with more agitation than that you will employ after the cloth is in use. Then you would know for sure that the cloth will hold up during subsequent washings.

Dry cleaning

After experimenting, you may decide that dry cleaning is your only option—be sure to send a sample to make sure.

Colors that run

Check the colors if you are concerned they might run. Reds, black, and navy are colors to be wary of. To see if a color will run, put a wad of threads in a glass of hot, soapy water. Shake or stir the threads around and let them soak until the water is cold. If the water is colored, you'll know that color will run. Then you can try it with cold water and see if it will still run with cold water. "Color magnet sheets" are available where laundry detergents are sold and can be put in the water to keep the color from running into other parts of the cloth. Experiment before committing your project to a thorough washing. Synthrapol SP is a preparation that helps prevent excess dye from bleeding onto other yarns. It is available at weaving supply shops.

Chenille

Read how to finish chenille on pages 140 and 187.

Washing the sampler

Water temperature

Start with lukewarm water. If the cloth is fairly stiff, use a cooler temperature to prevent shrinkage and further tightening of the weave.

Soap or detergent?

Usually, a mild detergent is desired—one that you would use for washing dishes by hand. A little bit is plenty. Your cloth isn't dirty.

Soak or agitate?

Gently swish or soak the sampler in the water. Some agitation is ideal for the threads to move and bend around one another. Use the gentle or regular cycle in the machine if that is the way your project is to be maintained (after sampling first, of course). Soaking is more gentle than swishing, so if the cloth is already stiff, just let it soak to prevent more shrinkage and an even stiffer cloth. Never squeeze the cloth between your hands while agitating because that may cause permanent wrinkles. When swishing, gently push the cloth back and forth in the water.

Never squeeze or wring out the cloth—or allow it to spin very much in the machine. This can cause permanent wrinkles.

Rinse the cloth

Rinse the cloth in the same temperature water as was used for washing, or cooler. Rinse as many times as needed until the water is no longer soapy. Swish the cloth in the water gently. Remember not to squeeze or wring.

Drying

There are a few stages in drying the cloth.

- Remove excess water, by spreading out the cloth on a bath towel. Fold the towel around the cloth and gently press on the towel—just so the cloth is no longer soaking wet. You don't want to wring the cloth in the towel which would cause undesirable wrinkles.
- If the cloth was in the machine, don't let it spin very long and take it out of the machine immediately so that wrinkles won't permanently set in the cloth. Never wring or squeeze the cloth because that will cause permanent wrinkles to form.
- Iron the cloth. The sampler is cotton, so use the cotton setting on your iron. Push the iron back and forth on both sides of the cloth—pressing down on the iron fairly hard. You are "hard pressing" the cloth in this step—putting a nice gloss on the cloth. Iron it over and over, again and again, until it is dry or nearly dry. Use the setting on your iron for the yarns you are using. See below to complete the drying process.

  For wool, chose whether or not to press the iron directly on the cloth—if you want a fuzzy surface, hold the iron (with steam) over the cloth and go over the cloth without touching it with the iron. Hard pressing as described above will give a flatter surface.

  You can also get steam or a hard press by using a pressing cloth. Take a cloth similar to a pillow case or bed sheet and soak it in water until it is sopping wet. For steaming, lay the wet pressing cloth on your woven cloth and touch the iron to the cloth so there is a hissing sound. Don't press down on the cloth if you want a fuzzy surface—just go over the cloth area-by-area with the pressing cloth until your entire surface has been steamed. For a hard press with the pressing cloth, press down on the cloth while the hissing occurs—don't move the iron back and forth—only press on the iron, keeping it in one place. Work area-by-area until the whole cloth has been hard pressed. Try these methods first on your sample.

  More information on finishing various cloths is found in my third book, ***Weaving & Drafting Your Own Cloth***, in the chapter on finishing, beginning on page 157.
- Hang the cloth to finish drying in the air. Use a shower rod or pad a towel bar so a fold line won't form. (Often, I move the cloth a bit from time to time to avoid a fold line.) Do not manipulate or move it around until it is absolutely dry or wrinkles will form.

 The Final Cut of the Tails

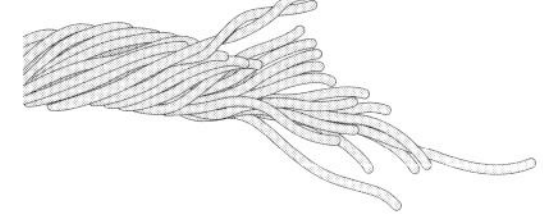

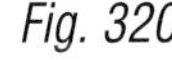

Fig. 320

After washing the cloth, you can cut all the tails flush with the cloth. Instead of cutting the tails straight across the threads, make rough cuts so the ends of the tails won't show in the cloth. See Figure 320. Do this job carefully, with good, sharp scissors and when you are alert and have good light.

 Make Hems or Fringes

On your sampler you might want to try different types of fringes or hems at the ends. See page 147 for information about hemming.

Knotted fringe

This is one of the simplest fringes and is also good looking. The twisted fringe method which follows is more elegant.

Fringe can be knotted with overhand knots up close to the edge of the cloth. Gradually undo the overcast or machine stitches as you work along so the last weft doesn't wander out before you get to the place where you're making the knots. Practice with different size bundles for the knots and with which side of the knot you want to be on the "right" side of the piece. See Figures 321 a and b. Trim the warp threads to the length you want the fringe to be.

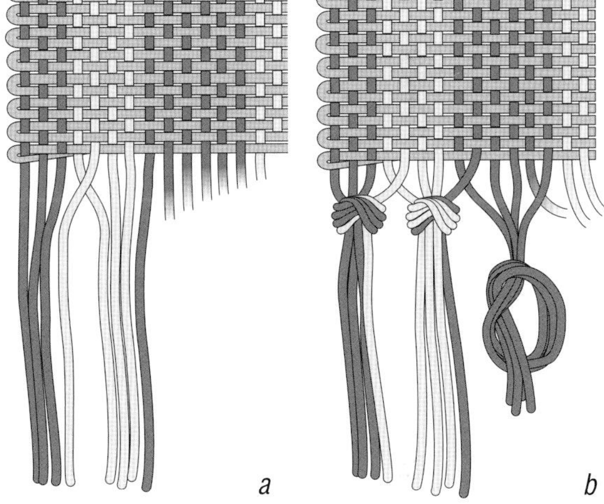

Fig. 321

Two tricks:

1. Put a weight (such as a big phone book) on the cloth and work with the fringe on a table, or hanging over the table's edge.
2. To get the knots up close to the last weft, keep them loose by putting a tapestry needle in the loop of the knot as you move it right up until it's snug against the weft. (Pull the warp threads with one hand, while holding the needle with the other, and push the needle up close to the last weft as you pull.) Then, remove the needle and tighten the knot in place.

Fringe

Twisted fringe

You can twist the fringe with your fingers as shown in Figures 322 a and b.

However, twisting tools are available from weaving supply shops. They can speed up the process a lot. See Figures 323 a and b.

Put a weight (such as a big phone book) on the cloth and work with the fringe on a table or with the fringe hanging over the edge of the table.

Experiment with the number of threads in each twisted fringe and with how many twists work best. A lot of variation can be discovered this way, and the twisted look can be loose or tight.

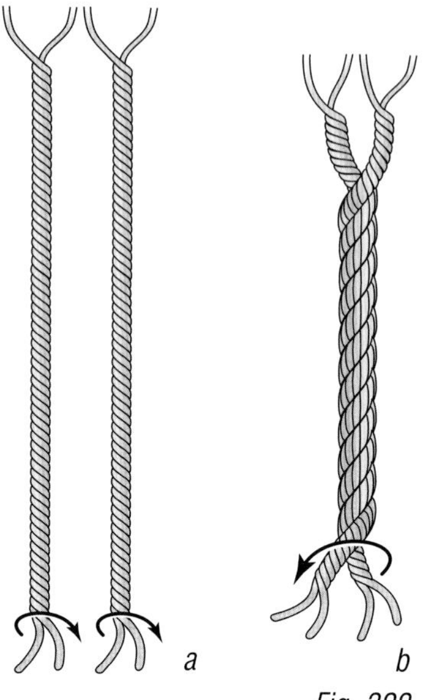

Fig. 322

Basically, you'll take two groups of warp threads and twist them separately in one direction. Keep twisting them until they begin to kink up on themselves. Then, put these two groups together by holding them next to each other and twisting them together in the opposite direction. You may not have to do very much twisting (or any at all); they'll tend to twist on themselves when you put them next to one another.

Tie overhand knots at the ends of each fringe and trim the ends evenly. To place the knots precisely, use a tapestry needle as described in the knotted fringe section, above. Make all the knots exactly match the length of the first bundle.

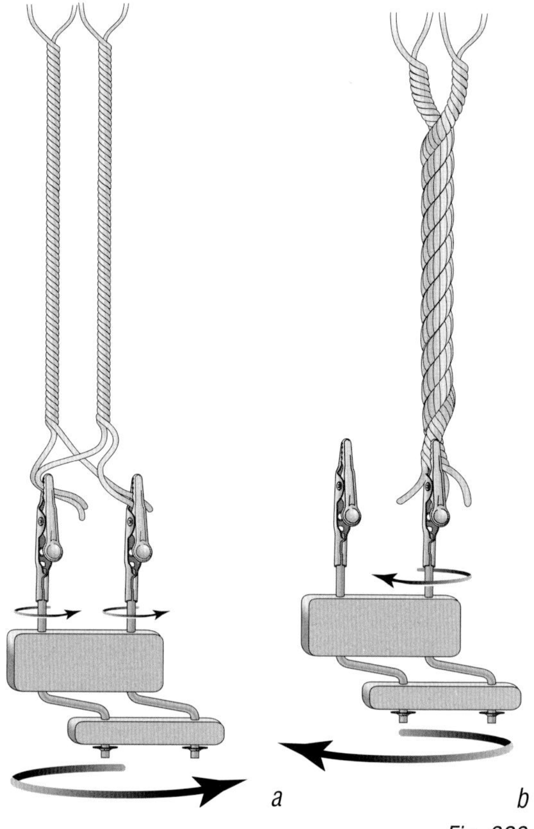

Fig. 323

Hems

Unsightly hems can be a tell-tale sign that you wove the cloth by hand. If you can't make hems that look beautiful on the right side of the cloth, ask a professional seamstress to make them for you. Practice on scraps of your handwoven cloth before working on the "real" project.

Very often, machine stitching that shows on a finished project is disfiguring. It might be sturdy, but it doesn't look good with the handmade cloth. Practice on a scrap to decide if you can make stitches that don't show. For machine stitching to be acceptable, it must be perfectly done. No matter how beautiful the cloth is, it will be ruined if the hem's stitches aren't done with absolute perfection. Practice on your sample cloth to see if you can find a stitch and color of thread that are beautiful. If in doubt, don't machine stitch, hand sew the hems in an invisible or decorative stitch.

The stitch I like to use for hems is a slipstitch because it is practically invisible. You slip the needle in the fold of the hem as you progress from stitch to stitch. See Figure 324.

Fig. 324

Another stitch is done inside the hem. I like it because the edge of the hem doesn't press into the body of the project, which can show as a ridge on the right side. It is especially good if the weight of the hem might tend to pull on the fabric. See Figure 325.

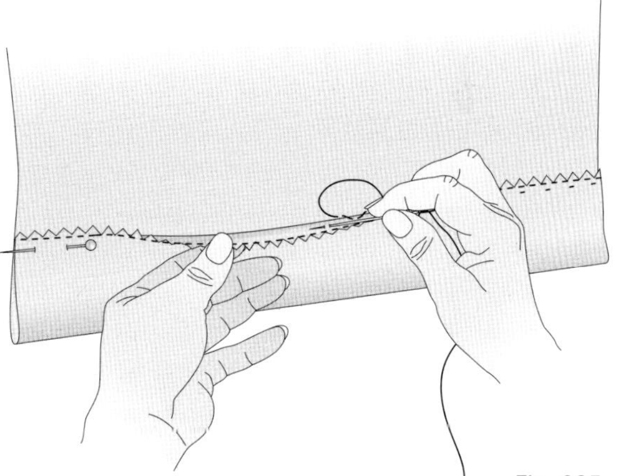

Fig. 325

Seams

Seams in handwoven cloth need extra consideration. Often, "regular" seams are too bulky, so the edges of the cloth are butted together or overlapped. Seams that are disfiguring ruin the entire garment—learn from sewing books or hire a seamstress.

To sew a seam where selvedges of the fabrics butt next to each other, without overlap, use a blunt (tapestry) needle and a thread that matches the weft and sew the edges by alternately picking up weft loops inside the first warp thread of each edge. See Figure 326.

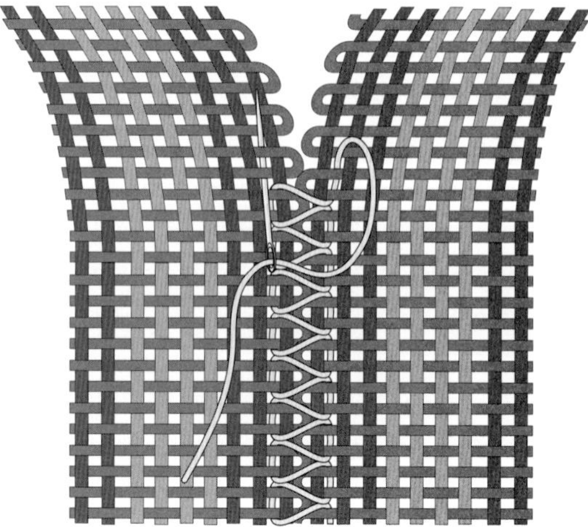

Fig. 326

6 *Front-to-Back Warping*

The author of this chapter, Patricia Townsend, has taught front-to-back warping the loom to hundreds of high school students for many years. She is an expert. Her students love weaving and make beautiful and beautifully woven chenille scarves for their beginning projects. In this chapter, she takes you step-by-step through the whole process, beginning on page 155.

Introduction: Back-to-Front or Front-to-Back?

By Peggy Osterkamp

These terms indicate two opposite methods of dressing (setting up) the loom. Figure 327a shows that in the Back-to-Front method, dressing the loom begins at the back of the loom. Figure 327b shows that the Front-to-Back method starts at the front. There are reasons to use both methods. A summary of the two methods is given on page 154.

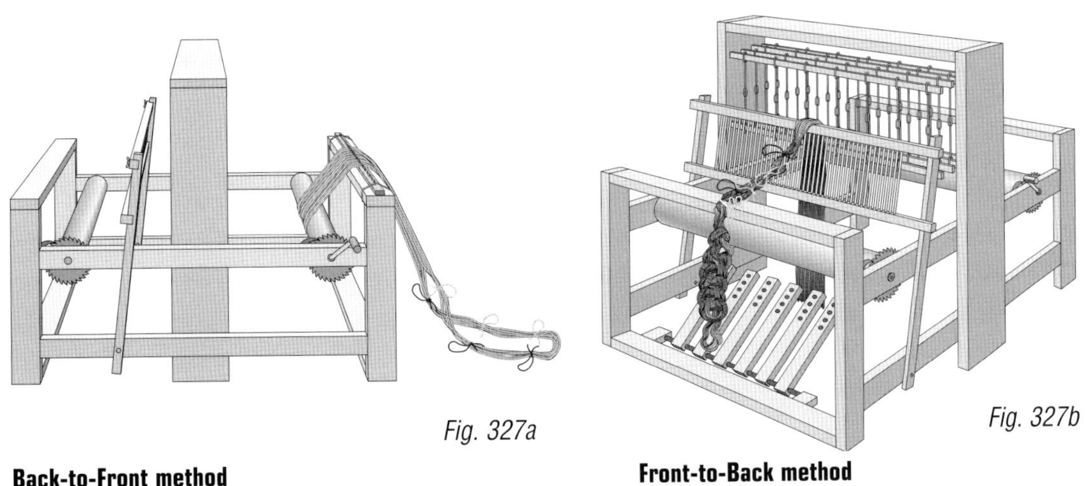

Fig. 327a

Back-to-Front method

Fig. 327b

Front-to-Back method

Why back-to-front

I think back-to-front is the ideal method for beginning weavers to learn because it is a method you can always depend on. I've also found that the first method you learn is usually the one you know best. Therefore, I think that a method that works for all kinds of projects is the best one for a beginner to learn first. When you want to weave fabric for a wedding dress, or a ceremonial cloth, or some very large project, probably using rather thin threads, you can do it because you know a method that can handle these complex projects efficiently without tangled and broken threads. Front-to-back is not suited for such projects.

Nevertheless, I believe that weavers or weavers-to-be should make their own choices about which method to use to set up the loom. For this reason, I am including the front-to-back method in my book. I encourage experienced weavers to learn front-to back, because, by then, they have a sense of what kind of weaving they want to do and can choose which method suits the types of projects they prefer to weave. Below is a list of the various advantages and disadvantages of each method.

Reason #1: Eliminates tangled threads

The only thread that can't tangle...is one under tension

Tangled threads cause frustration, waste valuable time and often break and must be repaired.

Compare the two illustrations above showing the beginning stages of both methods.

See that in back-to-front, the warp is all wound up onto the warp beam right at the beginning of the process. It means that all the threads are under tension except for the several inches required for threading the heddles and the reed. Thus, the warp threads are kept under tension and in order while setting up the loom and are prevented from tangling.

In front-to-back all the warp threads are in a chain and loose at the beginning of the threading process. Since they are not under tension, they can tangle at any stage of the process of dressing the loom—sleying the reed, threading the heddles, and beaming on—with the potential for breakage at every turn. Again, untangling takes valuable time from weaving.

However, this aspect of the front-to-back problem can be ameliorated somewhat by winding the warp onto a kitestick instead of a chain. See the sidebar.

Chain or Kitestick?

Generally, the chain keeps most warp threads organized enough so that they don't tangle.

However, some yarns (for example, linen) can be quite "jumpy" or springy and tangle easily as can a large number of fine, silky threads.

I recommend winding the warp on a kitestick instead of making it into a chain so that the threads are always on tension and thus, can't tangle.

Figure 328a shows winding the warp onto a kitestick, and the process is explained beginning on page 25. Figure 328b shows a chain, and how to make it is described on page 162.

In the case of a large warp made in sections, you would have each section on its own kitestick rather than in several chains.

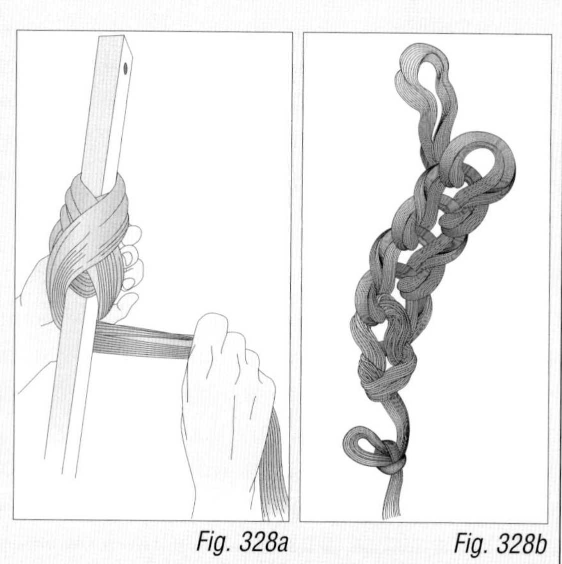

Fig. 328a Fig. 328b

Long or wide warps

Consider the chain in the front-to-back illustration and imagine what it would look like if the warp were quite long, say 15-25 yards or more. There would be a very long and perhaps, thick chain—a great potential for the threads to tangle.

Often, for wide warps, the warp needs to be made in sections so, in that case, there could be several chains dangling in front of the loom. Even if the warp was wound on kitesticks and not in chains, there could be quite a tangle while sleying the reed and threading the heddles, not to mention the struggle to get the threads untangled and through the reed during beaming.

Reason #2: Abrasion issues

Look at Figures 329a and 329b. In back-to-front warping, notice again that the warp threads are wound up (beamed) onto the warp beam first. Then, notice that in front-to-back the threads pass through both the reed and the heddles during beaming. It can put a lot of strain on fragile warps causing breakage. More important, however, is the abrasion of the threads, which can weaken them, making them vulnerable to breakage when the warp is on tension later during weaving. Also, remember that the warp threads must pass again through the heddles and reed during weaving. Forcing the warp threads twice through the reed and heddles can cause fragile threads to break.

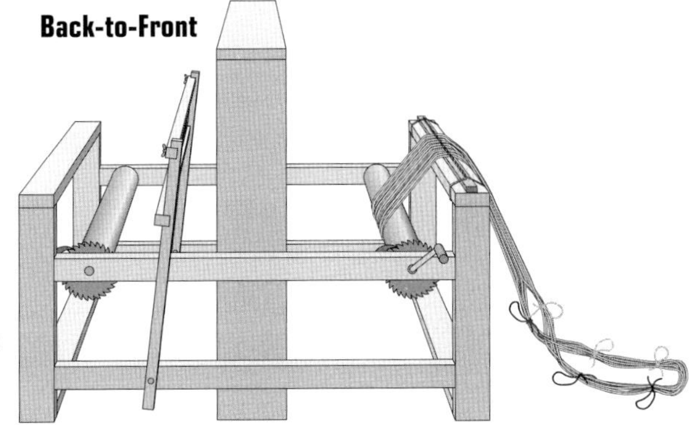

Fig. 329a

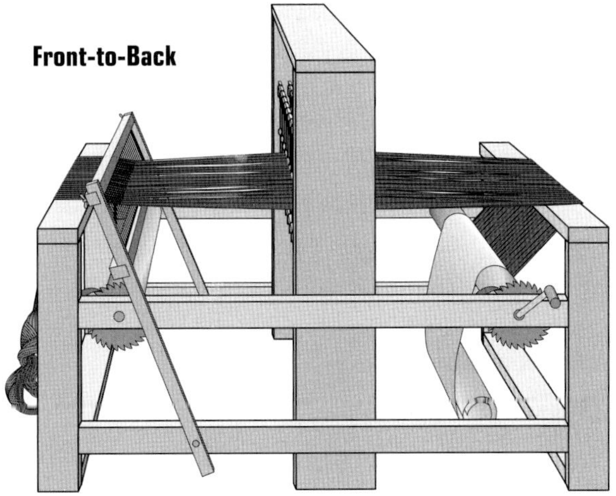

Fig. 329b

Admittedly, most yarns made for warp yarns are plied and don't abrade easily. However, very fine threads can be vulnerable. Abrasion can make some yarns fuzz up a bit and pill. These pills hook on to each other during weaving and actually knot themselves together forcing you to stop and undo the knots, or even cut them away and then repair the cut warp threads.

Other types of warp yarns that are especially vulnerable to abrasion are handspun yarns and other soft yarns. They can be put on the loom successfully without abrasion with the back-to-front way.

The beater can cause some abrasion during weaving regardless of the method for dressing the loom. Front-to-back adds its own abrasion.

Note that severe abrasion in the reed must be avoided or the warp threads will break. Wider dents with more threads per dent allow more threads to pass without abrading against the wires in the reed.

Reason #3: Ideal for fine and fragile threads

Many threads to handle

With fine threads, there are going to be many warp threads to handle—in the reed, while threading the heddles, and beaming. Keeping them under tension so they cannot tangle is essential or you will spend a lot of your time untangling them, especially, while forcing them through the reed when beaming them.

Consider that someday you might want to weave a fine, 60/2 silk scarf at 60 ends per inch (epi). If the scarf were to be 10" wide, there would be 600 threads in the chain Putting that many threads on the loom front-to-back would be a huge job—much more efficient with the back-to-front method—because the threads will be under tension and not vulnerable to tangling and breaking while beaming.

Future projects

So, you say, "I'll never weave anything that fine." Well, as a beginner, you can't know that for sure. If you learn back-to-front first, if you do ever want to make a project out of fine threads, you can, because you will know how to keep them all under tension so they won't tangle.

Many threads per dent

Another problem with fine threads is that there will need to be more in each dent making it more difficult to see them to thread them individually in the heddles.

I am now weaving with fine silk at 96 epi. My reed has 12 dents per inch, and I am sleying 8 threads per dent. With back-to-front, I can beam the threads easily and spread them apart enough on the lease sticks to see the individual threads for easy threading. It isn't until I put these dense warp threads into the reed that they will get jammed close together. Using the front-to-back way, there would be so many threads together in the dents in the reed, that I think it would be almost impossible to see the separate threads to put them in order into the heddles. One could consider transferring the cross to behind the reed (see page 194), but the threads would still be almost too close together to see them individually to thread the heddles.

Reason #4: Efficiency

Putting the warp onto the warp beam back-to-front is a smooth, efficient process.

The knots required in front-to-back allow discrepancies in the length of the warp threads, and a bulky connection to the loom. You must put in packing sticks so the knots do not cause lumps in the warp as it is beamed onto the warp beam.

Back-to-front is more efficient and practical if you are weaving with fragile yarns, fine threads at dense setts (epi), fuzzy or fragile handspun threads, and long and wide warps.

Some yarns, like singles wool and high twist yarns, kink up on themselves or twist into groups of yarns. It would be a great frustration to the weaver and the threads to force them through the reed and the heddles during beaming when they are not on tension. Getting them under tension on the warp beam first eliminates the struggle.

Reason #5: Tying on new warps

Tying on new warps to old ones is described in my second book, ***Warping Your Loom & Tying On New Warps***. Doing this job back-to-front is ideal for all the previous reasons. Many weavers do this operation front-to-back, which has all of the problems given above: threads tangling, abrasion issues, too many fine threads to handle efficiently.

Why front-to-back

Reason #1: Simplicity

It's quicker and easier.

Measuring the warp at the warping board is easier and faster because there is only one cross to make.

It is simpler in concept. You begin threading (sleying) the threads into the reed and see results immediately, rather then having to beam the warp first as in back-to-front.

It is a good method for teaching projects to get students started, to seduce them into loving to weave.

Many teachers prefer to teach their students to dress the loom front-to-back because of the classroom situation. It requires less "stuff" to have on hand—namely, raddles and lease sticks.

Reason #2: For short or narrow warps

It works especially well for short or narrow warps—say, up to 5-7 yards or so, but can work for wider, longer projects with medium or large size warp threads.

It is a quick method for making samples.

Reason #3: Design at the loom

This is a particularly popular reason to dress the loom front-to-back. Basically, it means that a separate warp chain can be made for each color or yarn that is to be used in the stripes. All the chains are attached to the breast beam and then each one's threads are distributed in the reed where they are desired to be in the cloth.

Often people make random stripes using this method. They take the warp threads from each chain and randomly distribute them visually into the reed.

Beaming on stripe chains

One of my mentors, Helen Pope, wove gorgeous afghans this way. She made two on each warp and gave them to family members and special friends for over thirty years. She had one loom devoted to them. She carefully chose and dyed her textured yarns. The weave structure was double weave in three blocks so the threading was very complicated and there were many warp threads per dent. She tied each new warp onto the end of old ones so she never had to thread the heddles again. I saw her beam on a warp one day—there must have been 6 or 8 warp chains. It was a tedious business untangling the yarns while beaming—but was worth the work. I realized that I would never have thought of designing such a project with my back-to-front mentality. It would be nearly impossible to wind the warp with all the yarn changes going back-to-front. Her afghans proved that even something that isn't very efficient, can be done and can be lovely—and the effect is worth the effort.

In Summary: Back-to-Front or Front-to-Back?

Reasons to Use Back-to-Front

1. Eliminates tangled threads
2. Abrasion issues
3. Ideal for fine and fragile threads
   - Many threads to handle
   - Future projects
   - Many threads per dent
4. Efficiency
5. Tying on new warps

Reasons to Use Front-to Back

1. Simplicity
2. Short or narrow warps
3. Design at the loom

Front-to-Back Warping

By Patricia Townsend

Setting up the loom front-to-back

For the process of setting up the loom from the front of the loom, here are instructions for making a rayon chenille scarf, 11" wide and 60" long, plus fringe. Figure 330 is a sketch of the scarf showing 4 warp color stripes: 1" of green, 2" of blue-green, 3" of blue, and 5" of blue-violet, for a total width of 11".

Terms and parts of the loom are explained in the Basics chapter beginning on page 3.

For suggestions for other projects, go to pages 297 and 233.

Projects can be warped either front-to-back or back-to-front. For a comparison of the the methods, see pages 149-154.

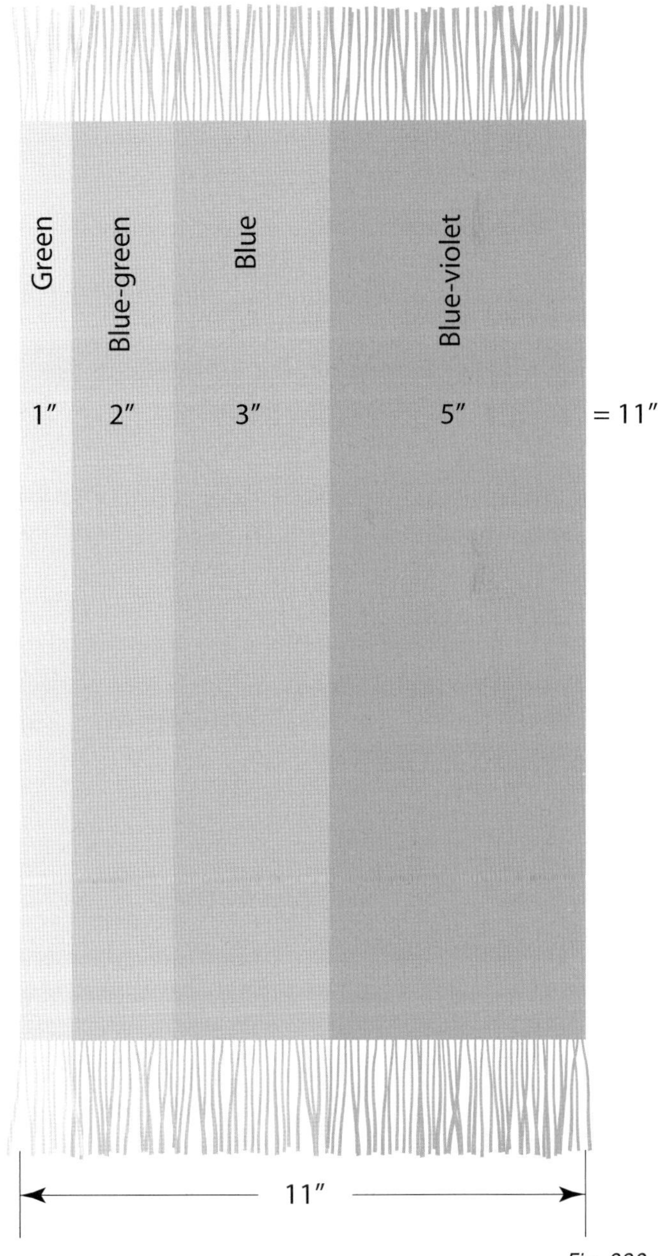

Fig. 330

Scarf Requirements

Equipment List: See Chapter 2, Equipment.

Adding machine tape, 60" long:

Corrugated paper in a roll (optional):

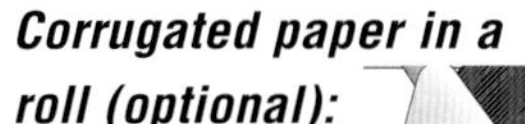

Grocery bag (optional):

Loom: See Pages 4-5

Lease sticks (optional):

Packing sticks: At least two are needed. They should be the length of the loom's warp beam (no longer).

Low stool:

Rags: (See page194 for an alternate to rags).

Reed: It should have 8 dents per inch. (See page 33 for alternate reeds that can be used.)

Reed holders (optional): See page 190

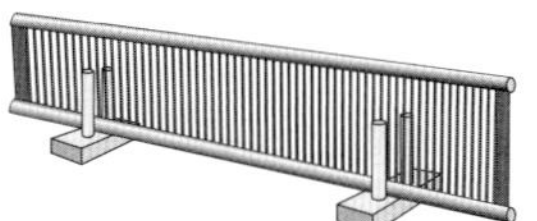

Scissors:

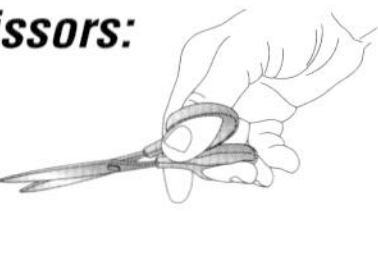

Shuttle: I prefer a boat shuttle (with its bobbin). A stick shuttle around 16" long could be used, see page 8.

Sley hook (also called reed hook):

String:

Tape Measure:

Tapestry Needle:

Threading hook:

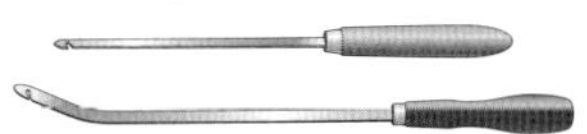

Warping board:

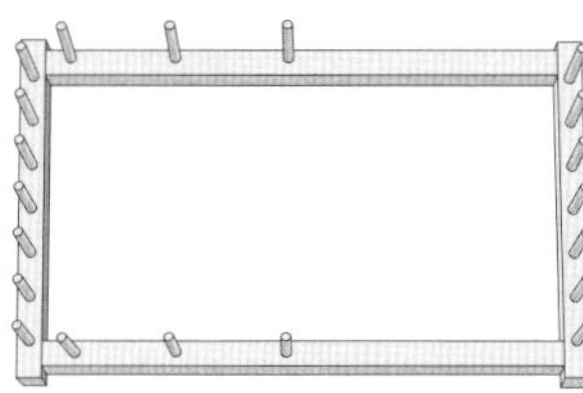

Yarn for Warp:

540 yards of rayon chenille divided into the colors given here.
(This type of yarn is sold as "rayon chenille at 1450 yards per pound")

54 yards of green

96 yards of blue-green

144 yards of blue

246 yards of blue-violet

Yarn for Weft:

540 yards of rayon chenille of the same kind as for the warp and in any color you like.

Here are a few suggestions that will look great: green, blue-green, blue, and blue-violet. To tone it down, try black or navy blue. Or choose other colors if you like.

Measure the warp threads

1. Mount a warping board at a comfortable height (see page 15) and place the cones of yarn on the floor below the board.
2. Make a guide string: Cut a colorful yarn or string 3 yards long (108"). This will be the length of one warp thread. More information is on page 15.
3. Figure 331 illustrates one way a guide string can be arranged. Tie a slip knot (see page 350) and put the loop of the knot over the top left peg (peg #1). Take the string over the peg to its right (peg #2), under the next peg to the right (peg #3), and across to the peg on the far right (peg #4) of the top row of pegs. From there, wind it across the warping board to create a 3-yard path for the guide string. Tie the end of the string to the last peg. (One arrangement of the guide string is shown here, but you can make your own path). Examples of other paths that could be used and that are all the same length are shown in Figures 332 and 333.
4. To start measuring the warp threads, tie on your first color—green—at peg #1, and follow the path of the guide string to the end. However, instead of cutting this first thread off, simply go around that last peg and guide it back up until you reach peg #3. Then guide the yarn over peg #3 and under peg #2, describing a figure-eight (or X) and continue on to the beginning peg #1. The figure-eight between pegs #2 and #3 creates the "weaver's cross." You have just measured two of your green threads. (See Figure 334) How did it get to be two threads, you ask? Remember point 2 above says that the length of the guide string equals the length of one warp thread. Here, you have taken the warp thread along the length two times—from peg #1 to the end and back to peg #1 again. You started to measure the second thread by following the path of the first thread—thus, you now have measured two threads
5. Repeat this same pattern to measure out 18 green threads. After counting to be sure you have measured a total of 18 green threads. Count the threads somewhere between peg 4 and the last peg to be sure you have 18. Cut and tie the end of the green thread you are holding at the beginning peg #1 to that peg. Here, you are tying off and cutting the green thread to end that section in preparation to start to measure the next stripe, which is the blue-green one.

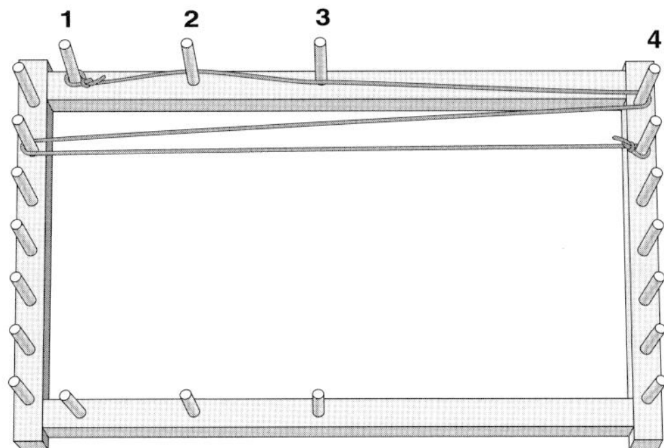

Fig. 331

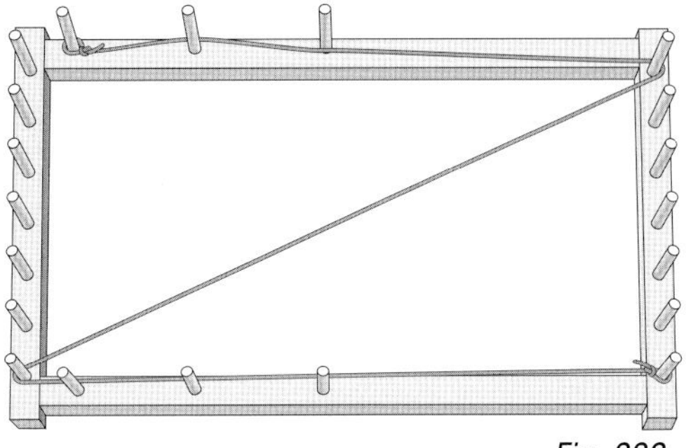
Fig. 332

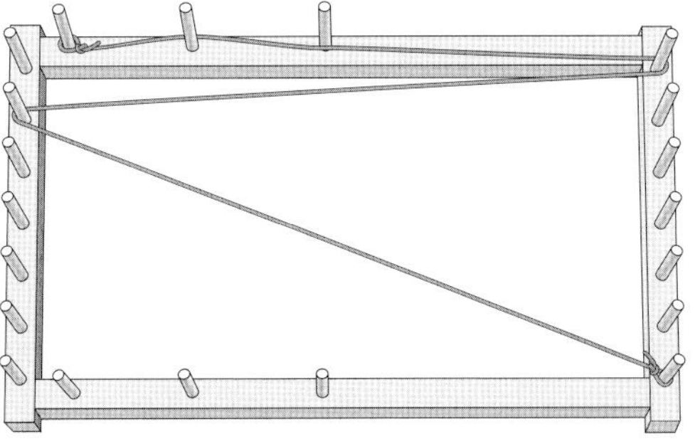
Fig. 333

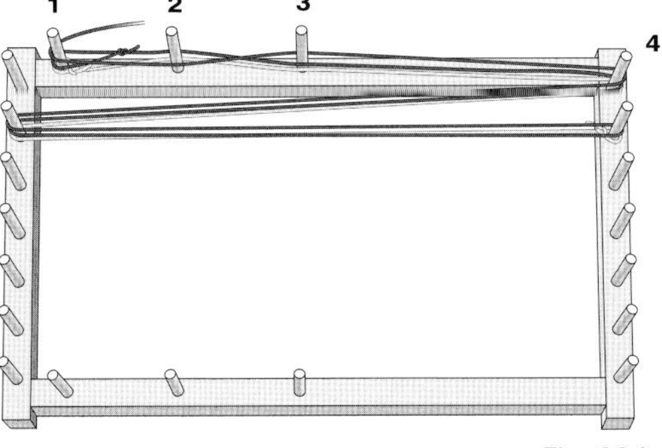

Fig. 334

Measuring Warp

Tie a blue-green thread onto peg # 1 and measure out 32 threads, as above, and cut and tie them off at peg # 1. In the same manner, measure out 48 blue threads, and 82 blue-violet threads. There should be a total of 180 threads. See Figure 335. Tie-off the last thread when you are finished. The build-up of colorful stripes on the warping board is an exciting preview of your scarf.

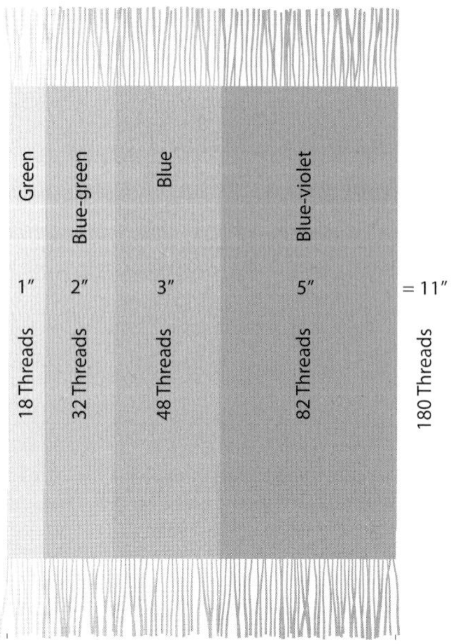

Green | Blue-green | Blue | Blue-violet
1" | 2" | 3" | 5" | = 11"
18 Threads | 32 Threads | 48 Threads | 82 Threads | 180 Threads

Fig. 335

Some important notes as you are measuring the warp

1. Assume a comfortable rhythm. Be mindful at the cross to keep the figure-eight motion. It's easy to remember what to do because you always go "over" the first peg of the cross, then "under" the second one, coming from either direction. The cross is an ingenious system to keep warp threads in order. A consistent, orderly cross will also keep the threads from tangling. Try to achieve a perfectly wound warp. Having said that, however, do not stress if a thread or two is out of place at the cross.
2. Wind the threads on the warping board with even tension, but loosely enough not to bend the pegs. If any pegs bend, see page 18.
3. Push the threads down to the base of the pegs as they begin to build up at each peg (see page 22). The 180 threads should be able to fit, when compressed, on the warping board. (See Figure 336.) For bigger warps that won't fit on the pegs, see page 190.

Fig. 336

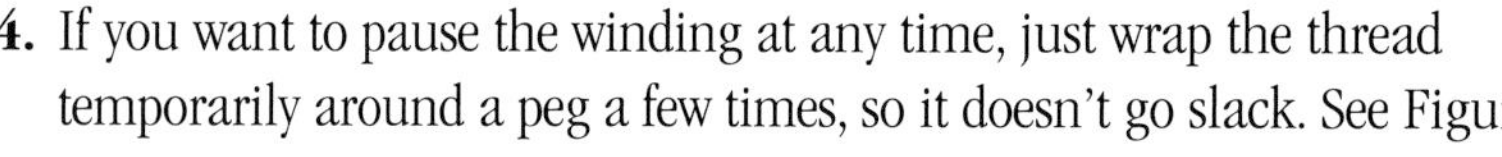

4. If you want to pause the winding at any time, just wrap the thread temporarily around a peg a few times, so it doesn't go slack. See Figure 337.
5. Be on the lookout for manufacturer's knots. They are common, and you don't want one of them showing up in the middle your warp. If you encounter a manufacturer's knot, simply tie your thread off at either the beginning or end peg. Dispose of the segment of thread containing the knot. Tie on again at that same exact end peg, and keep on winding. See Figures 338 and 339.

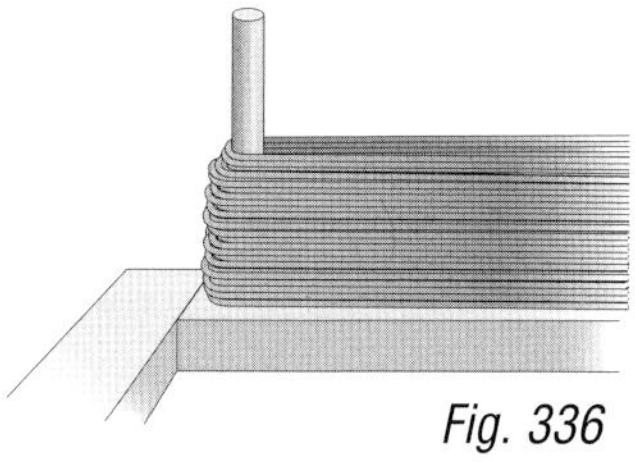

Fig. 337

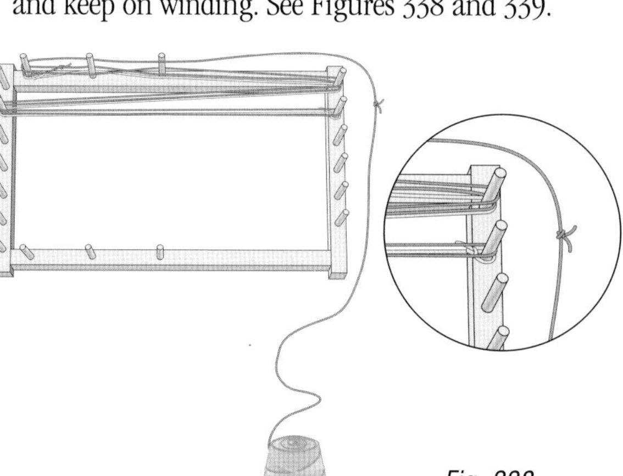

Fig. 338

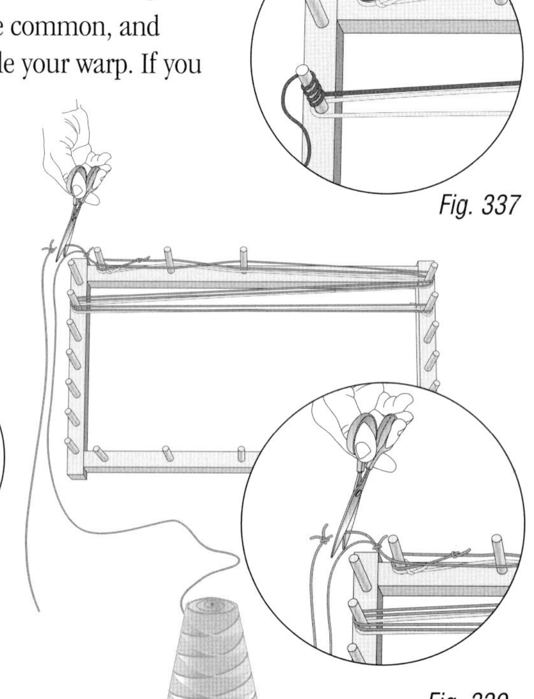

Fig. 339

Secure the warp threads

Be sure you have measured all 180 threads.

Go and measure your loom, from the breast beam to about 9" beyond the furthest rear shaft as shown in Figure 340.

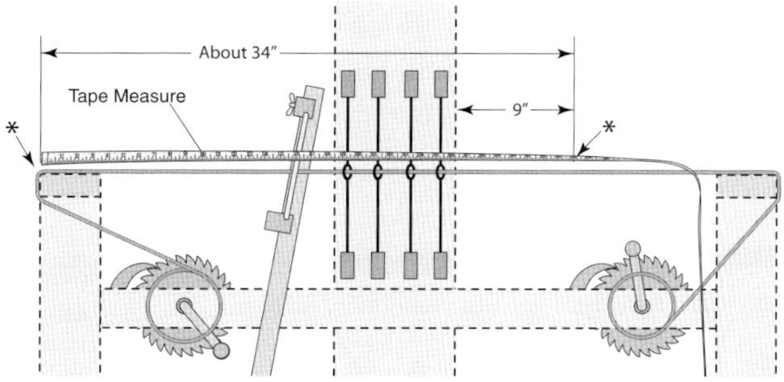

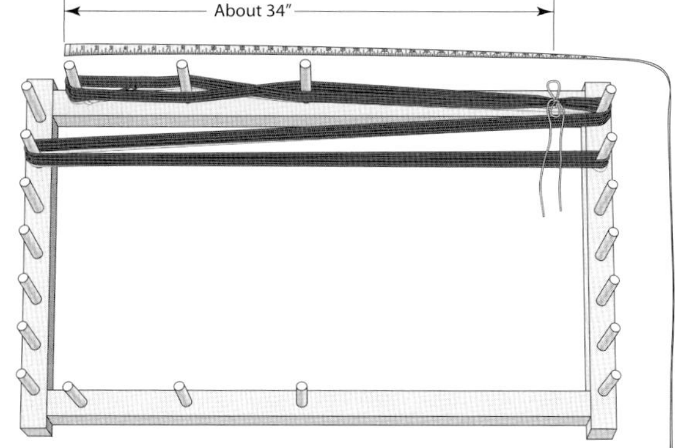

Fig. 340

Next, measure this same distance along your warp, starting at the beginning peg (#1) of the warping board—it will be the location of a special tie with long tails. See Figure 341. To make this "choke tie," cut a piece of string 30" long. Center the string on your measured spot and wrap the 2 long ends of the string twice around the bundle of warp threads from opposite directions, then pull very tightly and tie a bow. A choke tie prevents threads from slipping and sliding past one another. Take care not to include the guide string within it!

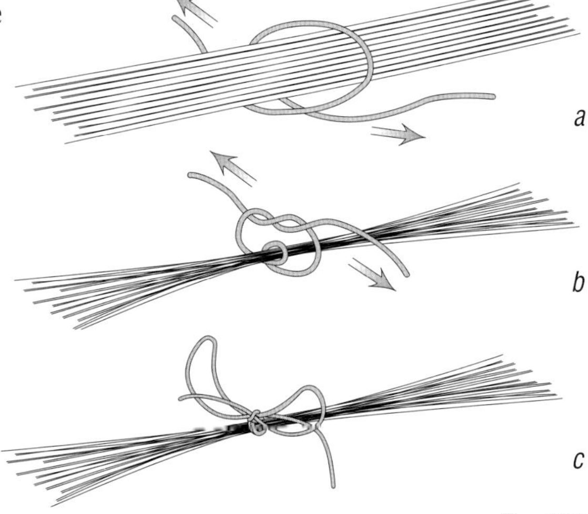

Fig. 341

Figures 342 a, b, and c show how to tie a choke tie wrapped tightly around the warps.

a

b

c

Fig. 342

Cut 2 two strings (about 24" long) to use as additional choke ties. Tie 1 choke tie about 1 yard from the choke tie you just tied, and another about 1 yard beyond that. Again, take care not to include the guide string. Figure 343 shows the warp with the three choke ties.

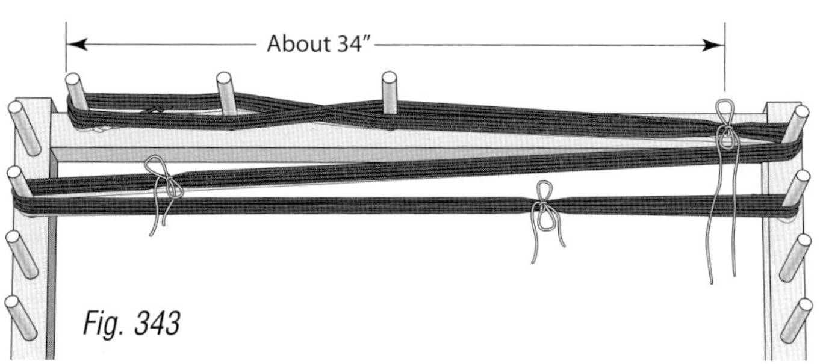

Fig. 343

Cut 5 strings about 15" long, but make 2 of them of brightly colored string or yarn. Use them for the following: Tie 2 simple, but snug, bows at each of the 2 cross pegs (a total of 4 ties), plus one tie threaded through the cross itself. See Figure 344. Note: it is helpful to use a particular color, for example red, to distinguish the two top ties around the cross pegs—it will help orient you later. You have now tied a total of 8 ties along your three-yard warp: 5 at the cross, and 3 choke ties along the warp threads. The warp is finished now. See Figure 345.

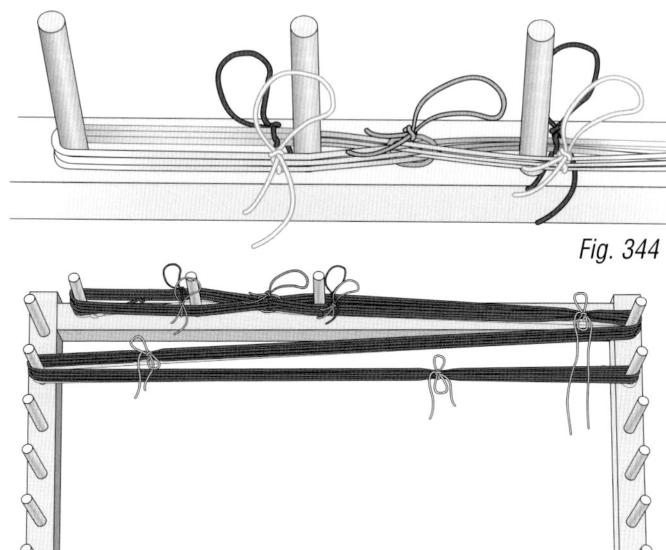

Fig. 344

Fig. 345

Before you take the warp off the warping board, however, make sure the loom is ready.

Prepare the loom

Prepare the reed

Insert an 8-dent reed into the beater, and make sure it is centered. (See page 33 if your reed does not have 8 dents per inch.) Next, you will mark the reed in three places with strings to indicate the center and the edges where the 11" wide scarf will be. Mark the center with a string tied around the reed and beater. Tie 2 more strings, 5 ½" to the right and left of center, where the edges of the warp for the scarf will be. See Figure 346.

Looms and their parts are shown on pages 4 and 5.

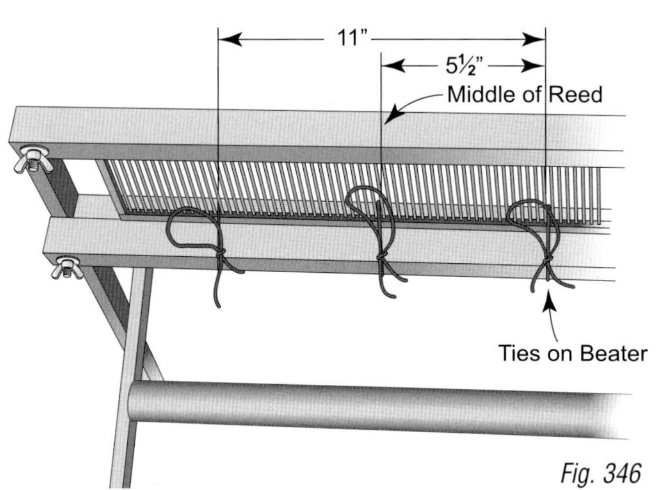

Fig. 346

If you are new to this process, you *must* read the pages referred to in the text.

Shafts are sometimes called harnesses, but "shaft" is the proper term.

Prepare the Heddles

For this project, there are 180 threads, each requiring a heddle. Count out 45 heddles on each of 4 shafts. These will end up distributed with roughly 22-23 heddles to the right and left of center. It is handy to unfasten the heddle bar clips at the center, if you have them, so that heddles can pass freely, back and forth as needed on the heddle bars, while you count them out. Read how to operate the clips, and find the centers of the shafts on pages 61-62 and on page 79. How to move heddles from shaft to shaft begins on page 77. Divide excess heddles on each shaft equally, pushing them out to the ends of the shafts. Slip strings around the excess heddles as shown in Figure 347. If your loom has more than 4 shafts, you should use the 4 shafts that are closest to the beater. Tie off the heddles on all the extra shafts, too, as shown in Figure 347.

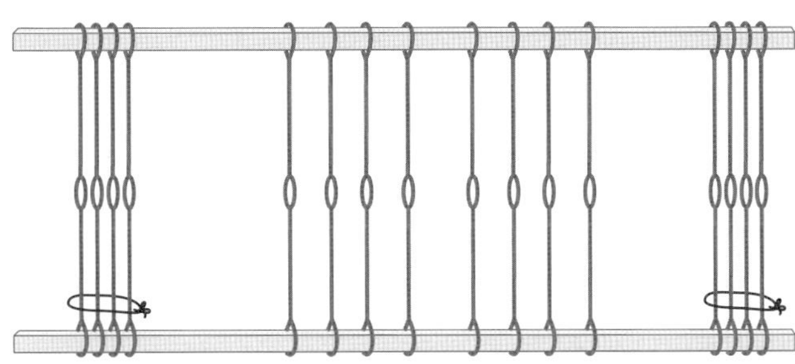

Fig. 347

Prepare the beater

Tie the beater into a standing upright position, so that it cannot swing. Tie 1 string around the end of the beater to the breast beam. Tie another string around the other end of the beater to the castle. See Figure 348. Some looms have a pin on a chain that fits through a leg of the beater to hold it in this position.

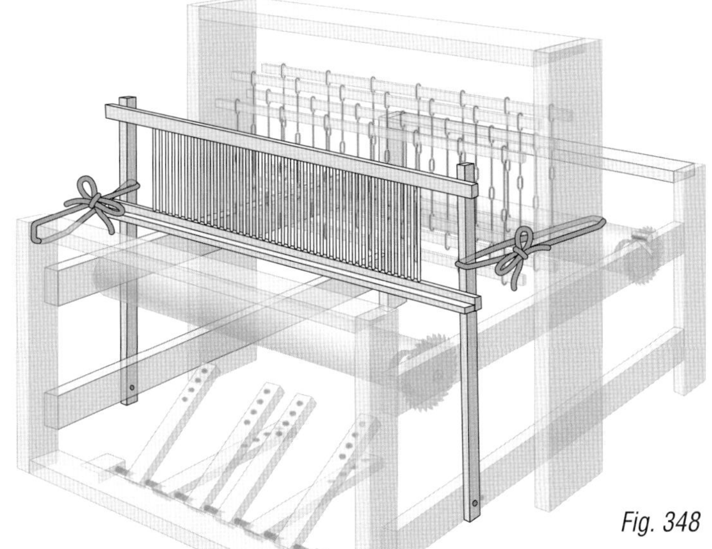

Fig. 348

Chain, cut, and carry the warp to the loom

Cut the threads at the bottom end peg, cutting through the loop, and immediately tie the bundle of warp threads in a slipknot. Remember not to include the guide string. See Figure 349. To make a slipknot, follow the directions on page 350, step-by-step.

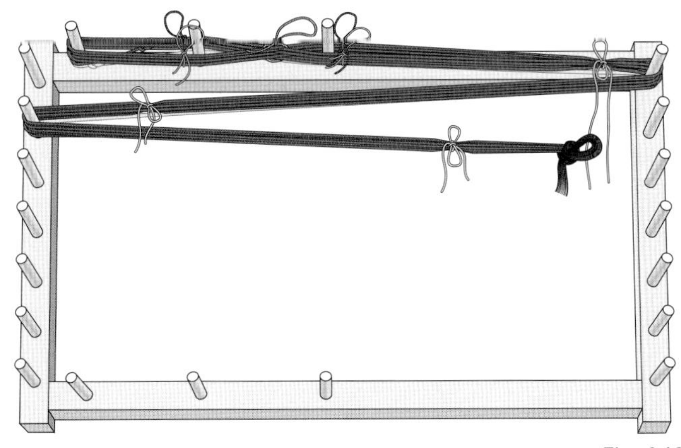

Fig. 349

Chain the warp

To chain the warp, make another slipknot as above (Figure 350). Then, take your forefinger and thumb through the loop of the slipknot and grasp the warp (Figure 351), pulling it through the first loop just enough to make a new loop (Figure 352). Continue with your forefinger and thumb through the new loop and grasp the warp, again pulling the warp through the new loop as in Figures 351 and 352. ***Take care not to let the unchained warp slip off of the side pegs of the warping board as you are chaining.***

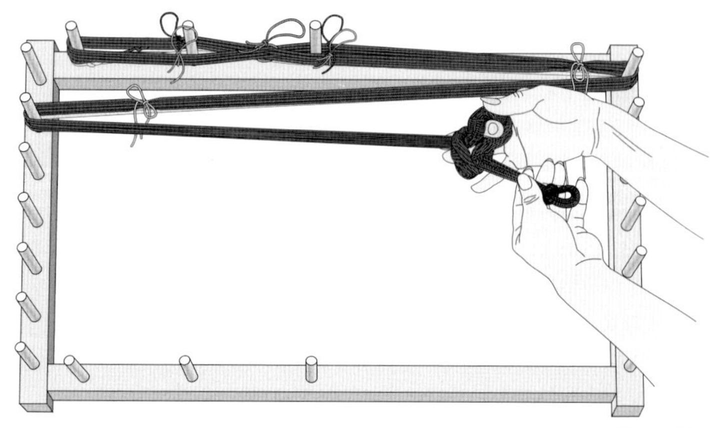

Fig. 350

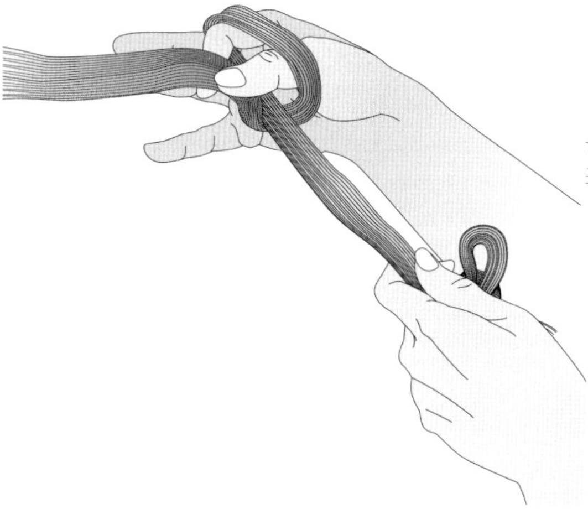

Fig. 351

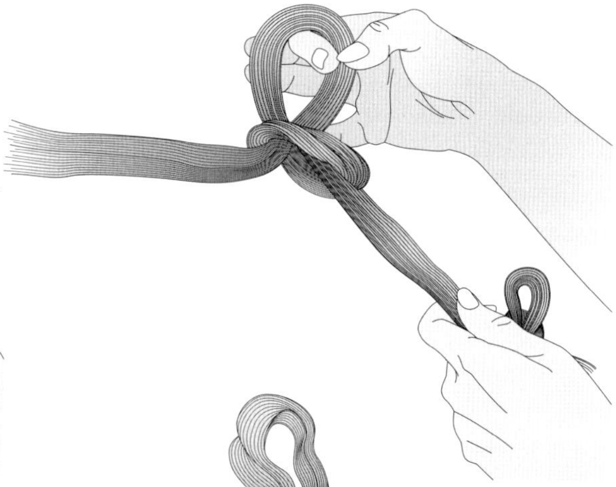

Fig. 352

Continue the steps of making the chain, following the illustrations:

1. Reach forefinger and thumb through the newest loop.
2. Grasp the warp and pull it through the loop, creating a new loop.
3. Continue looping in this way until the warp has been neatly chained up to the top choke tie (the tie with the long tails); then stop. Figure 353 shows a completed chain.

Fig. 353

Tie the warp and its special choke tie to the breast beam

Remove the remainder of the warp. Carry your chained warp to the loom. Secure the warp to the center of the breast beam of the loom with the cross-end of the warp lying on top of the beater. The chain will dangle at the front of the loom. To secure it well, untie just the bow portion of the long choke tie and use the ends to tie the choke tie securely to the breast beam. Check that the cross is right side up by turning it so that the 2 red top ties face up. The chain needs to remain securely tied to the breast beam at the choke tie, so double-check it by tugging against it. See Figure 354.

Note: Some weavers use another method to hold the warp to the breast beam. Instead of using a choke tie, they wrap the warp chain several times around the beam. Read about this on pages 191 and 193.

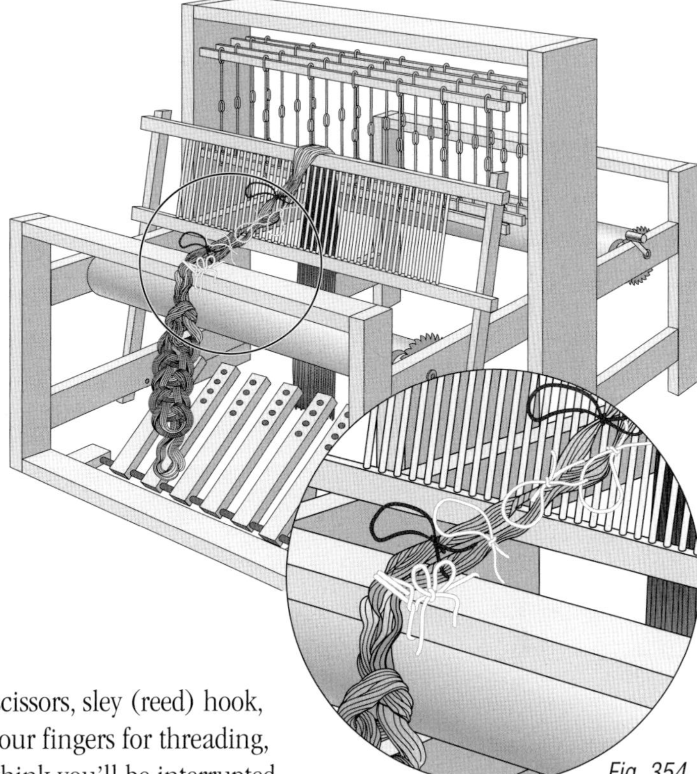

Fig. 354

Holding the cross

Gather the tools you will need: sharp scissors, sley (reed) hook, and threading hook (or you can use your fingers for threading, instead). Grab your cell phone if you think you'll be interrupted.

Note: Plan to thread the entire reed in one sitting. This step may take anywhere from 15 to 30 minutes, depending on how quickly you become adept. If you need to stop before finishing, see page 166.

I suggest that you read this section completely before you hold the cross in your hand and begin to sley the reed. It sounds more complicated than it really is. Visualize what you are to do, reading the text and looking at the illustrations.

Instead of holding the cross in your hand, you can use lease sticks to hold the cross. Read about this alternate method on page 191.

Hold the Cross

Hold the cross in your left hand by slipping your forefinger into the opening of the cross nearest the beater and slipping your ring and pinkie fingers through the other opening of the cross. See Figure 355a. (If you are left-handed, reverse the order so you are holding the cross in your right hand.) Close your hand by placing your last three fingers over the cross. Open and shut your three fingers a few times to get comfortable with this motion. (See Figures 355 a and b).

Hold the cross securely with your last three fingers keeping the cross in place while you untie the 4 snug bow ties at the cross. Use your right hand and forefinger and thumb of the left hand to untie these 4 ties.

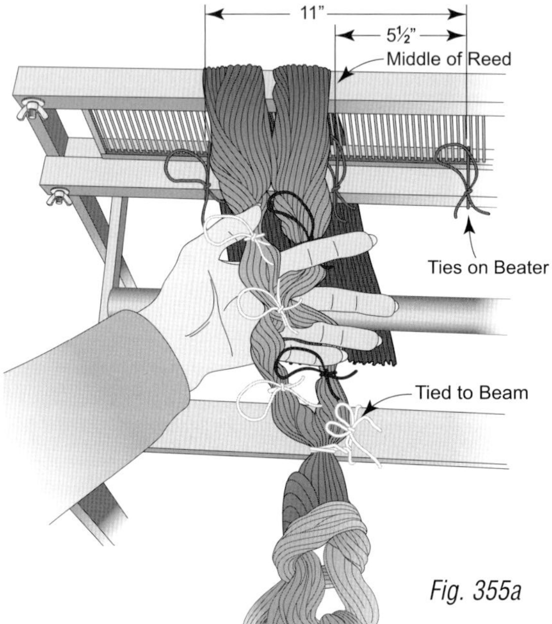

Fig. 355a

Fig. 355b

Keeping your hand in the cross, cut the end loops of the warp as shown in Figure 356. Finally, untie the tie you put through the cross itself. Now, only your left hand and fingers are holding the cross. See Figure 357.

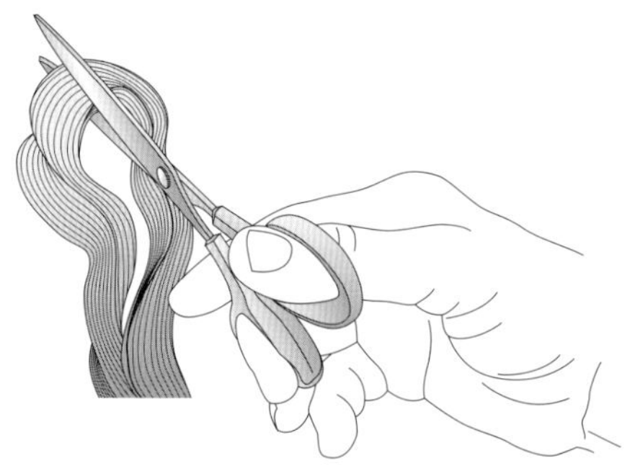
Fig. 356

Fig. 357

Thread (sley) the reed

The directions given are for using an 8-dent reed. Read what to do on page 33 if you have substituted a different size reed. If there are more than 2 threads per dent, read what to do on page 193.

The cross will allow you to remove the threads in the proper order needed for sleying the reed. The threads lie criss-crossed like little Lincoln Logs in your left hand. You'll take the top thread from the cross. To do it, lift up your last three fingers and take the topmost thread out of the cross with your right hand. (That's the first thread you are able to lift out of the cross.) Close your fingers back on top of the cross, to prevent other threads from escaping. Return the thread that you took from the cross to your left hand and hold it in a pinch with your thumb and forefinger. Be sure not to disturb the way the cross is being held while you're holding this new thread.

With the right hand, slip the reed hook over the beater, in back of the reed, and through the first "dent" (slot in the reed), on the right side that you previously marked with a tie. Use your left thumb, forefinger, and third finger to hand over the first thread. Catch the thread on the reed hook and slip it back out through the first dent of the reed. Pull back on the thread until there is no slack at the front, and let it fall straight down behind the reed. See Figure 358a. If you are left-handed, start the process on the left side.

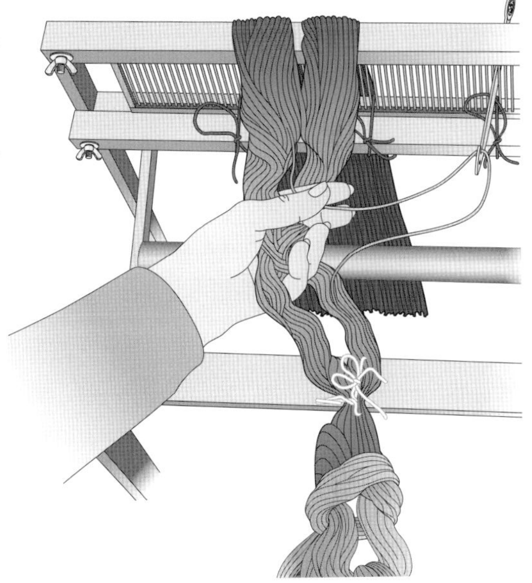

Fig. 358a

Lift up your last three fingers and with your right hand take the next waiting thread from the top of the cross. Close your fingers back over to protect the cross. Transfer the thread, from the right hand to the left hand's fingers. Reach the right hand in back of the reed, slipping the sley hook through the same first dent as before. Catch the thread, pulling it through to the backside of the reed, and let it fall. Repeat the same steps for the third thread waiting at the cross. You should now have three threads through the first marked dent on the right side of the reed. See Figure 358b.

Threading three threads in the two outside dents in the reed is recommended for this chenille scarf. Usually, the outside dents would have two ends per dent just like all the rest of the dents. See when more threads might be sleyed in the outside dents on page 308, in the chapter on selvedges.

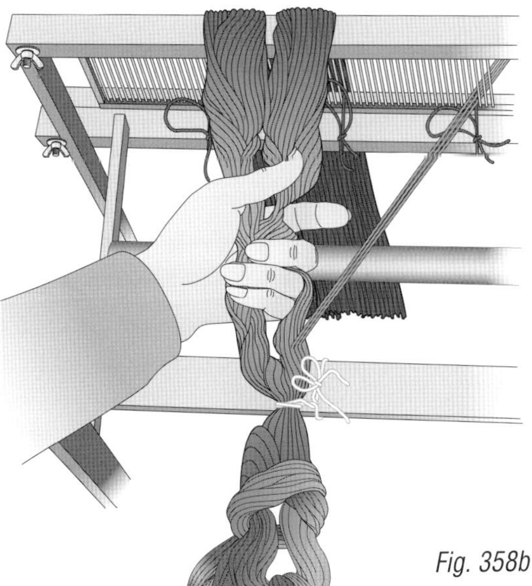

Fig. 358b

Continuing with the second dent, repeat the same process; threading three threads through it. From now on, however, thread only two threads per dent as you work your way from right to left across the reed. Make sure that the last two dents on the left hand side of the scarf also contain three threads each. With the extra threads sleyed at each edge of the scarf, you will have stronger edges (selvedges). Take care to be accurate and not to skip any dents as you thread the reed. If that does happen, however, simply thread the missed dent as soon as you realize the error, using the next threads available at the cross. A couple of threads that cross over each other, out of sequence from the cross, should not cause a problem with this short warp. For longer warps or with finer threads, mistakes should be avoided or corrected at this point to prevent the warp threads from tangling during beaming.

Remember, put two threads in each dent except for the two dents at each edge where there should be three threads per dent.

When you gain confidence in sleying the reed, feel free to begin lifting two threads at a time out of the cross. It will speed things up considerably. Finish sleying all 180 threads in the reed. See Figure 359.

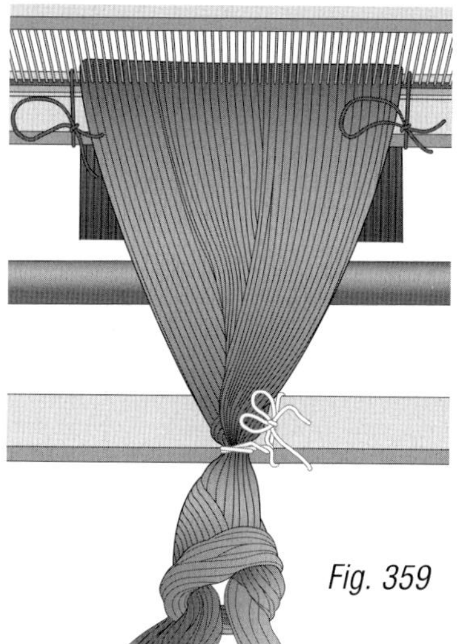
Fig. 359

If you need to stop before finishing this step, re-tie the 5 ties at the cross around the remaining threads and secure the cross by tying it to the breast beam to be continued later. Some weavers don't retie all the ties, but very carefully set the cross down and pick it up carefully when resuming. This is not a good idea if the warp threads are springy, however. Be extremely careful to pick up the cross so it will be in your hand exactly as it was before you laid it down—and do *not* lose the cross in the process. See what to do if you lose the cross on page 318 in the Troubleshooting chapter.

Thread the heddles

For this step, you will sit at the back of the loom, working at the right hand side, as you are looking toward the heddles. (Left-handers work at the left-hand side.) Good light is extremely important. It helps to sit on a low footstool so you can see the heddles easier. In addition, if your loom has a removable back beam, now is the time to remove it so that you can sit as close to the rear of the shafts as possible.

Remember, shafts are sometimes called harnesses, but "shaft" is the correct term.

Double check to be sure the warp threads reach to about 9" behind the heddles of the rearmost shaft. If not, stop and adjust the choke tie at the breast beam. Untie the choke tie, then pull the warp toward the back of the loom, and re-tie the choke tie tightly around the warp and the breast beam as shown in Figure 354 on page 163. Because you will need to pull at the warp while threading the heddles, the choke tie must tie the warp tightly to the breast beam to keep the threads from becoming tangled and uneven in length. An alternate way to hold the warps securely to the breast beam by wrapping the chain several times around the breast beam is described on pages 191 and 193.

Seat yourself at the rear of the loom, along with your threading hook. Everyone develops his or her own exact method of threading the heddles, depending on the type of loom and one's dexterity. Read the following paragraphs to grasp the overall procedure; then try threading in a way that makes your hands feel most comfortable. (Many weavers don't use a threading hook, preferring to thread the heddles with their fingers.)

All heddles have eyes, but there are several variations. See Figure 360. Read how to put the threading hook into the heddle eyes on page 68.

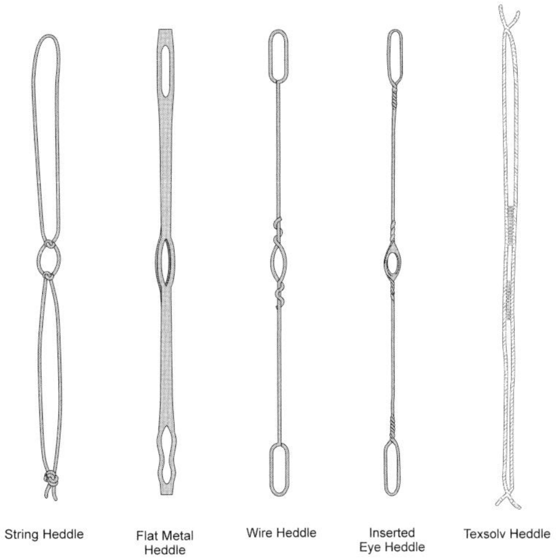

String Heddle

Flat Metal Heddle

Wire Heddle

Inserted Eye Heddle

Texsolv Heddle

Fig. 360

If you are new to this process, you *must* read the pages referred to in the text.

Notice that the heddle eyes can twist and turn slightly. Be sure, when you start threading, that each one remains straight. (See page 68.) Slide a group of 4 heddles, one from each of the four shafts, to the right of the center. See Figure 361. Start on the left side if you're left-handed.

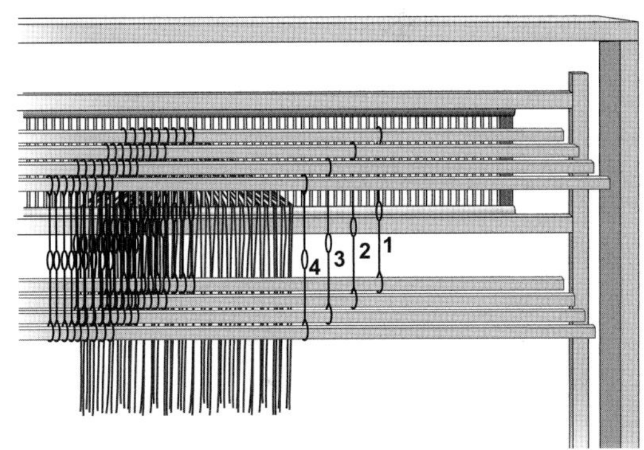

Fig. 361

Starting on the right, with the heddle on the furthest shaft from you (shaft #1), insert the threading hook into the heddle eye, using your right hand. Using your left fingers, lift up the three threads in dent #1 of the reed. Pull them forward, close to the threading hook, which is waiting. See Figure 362. Note: left-handers would do the reverse and start at the left edge of the warp.

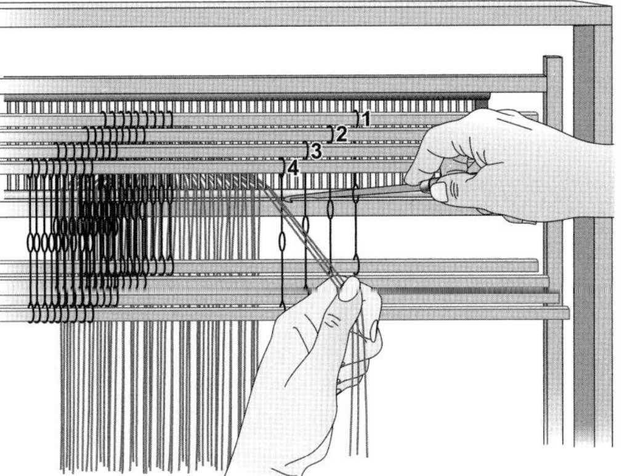

Fig. 362

Note that the three threads can slide easily past one another in this dent; therefore, it does not matter which one is threaded first through the heddles. Lifting up all the threads in the dent helps to see them and makes sure you won't miss one, so make this practice a good habit. Catch any one of the three threads with the threading hook (facing the hook up or down as you prefer). Draw the thread straight back toward you, through the heddle eye, and let it fall straight down in front of the heddle. Thread the second thread through the heddle waiting on shaft #2, and repeat with the third thread through the heddle on shaft #3.

You have now threaded one thread per heddle, in each of the first three heddles, and there are no threads remaining in dent #1. See Figure 363.

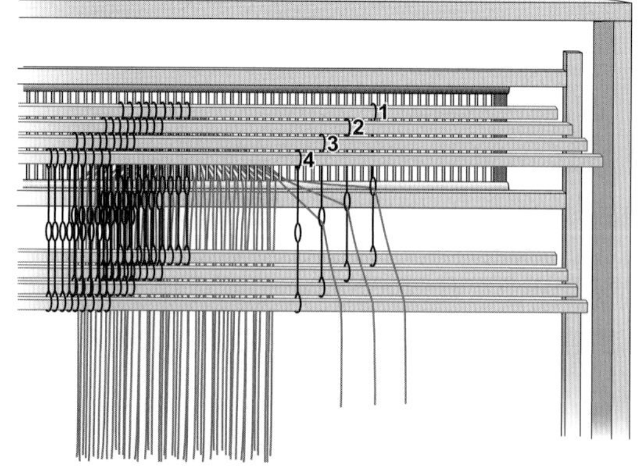

Fig. 363

Now move on to dent #2 in the reed. There are three threads there also. Lift them up and select one to thread through the heddle waiting on shaft #4. Slide a group of 4 more heddles, as before, to the right. Thread them in the same order, which you will repeat all the way across the warp: shaft 1, 2, 3, 4; 1, 2, 3, and 4. This pattern is known as "straight draw threading." Go ahead and thread a total of 16 threads (4 groups of 4 heddles).

Check for threading errors

After you have threaded a group of 16 threads, it is time to check your accuracy in threading. It is much easier to correct any errors now rather than later, mid-way through threading the heddles.

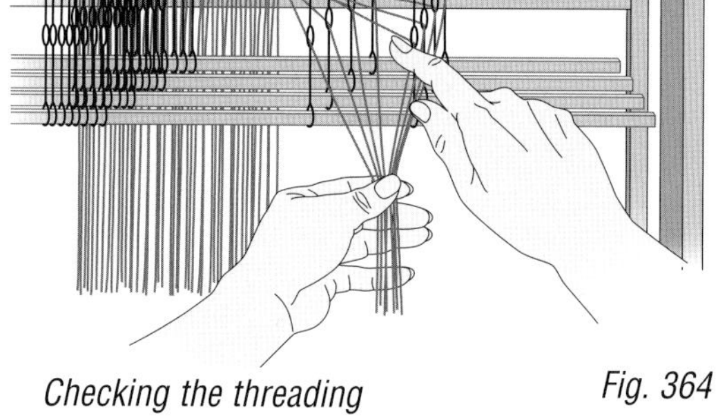

Checking the threading *Fig. 364*

To check for errors, pull the bundle of threads out straight with your left hand and slide each one to the right, in order, with your right hand, to determine threading accuracy. (See Figure 364). You quickly learn to discern the pattern of 4 sets of 4 heddles, in formation. Remember also to glance at the dents in the reed to check that the threads have been chosen in order there as well. Every thread must travel in a straight line, from the reed through the heddle, without crossing over another thread. If not, the loom won't weave properly! Correct any errors right away.

Here are a few types of threading errors to watch out for. More information is given on pages 108-110.

1. A thread may not come in exact order from the reed. See Figure 249.

2. A thread may get crossed within the heddles, instead of coming precisely straight, through the heddles. See Figure 250.

3. A thread may not go straight through a heddle. Figure 251 shows the incorrect way to thread the heddles.

4. Threading the heddles out of order, instead of the correct sequence of 1, 2, 3, 4.... Therefore, check for errors after every 16 threads (4 groups of 4). And stretch your back at the same time.

If you are new to this process, you *must* read the pages referred to in the text.

Tie the threads into bundles

After your have checked for errors and corrected them, pull the bundle of the 16 threads straight toward you, without twists, evening out the ends before tying them into a snug overhand knot. See Figures 365 a and b. Tie it so that the finished knot is about 3" from the end. Each subsequent bundle should also have its knot about the same distance from the cut ends so as not to waste threads. (There will be 3" of the bundle beyond each knot.) It is important that the knot be cinched tightly. (Tying an overhand knot is described on page 350.)

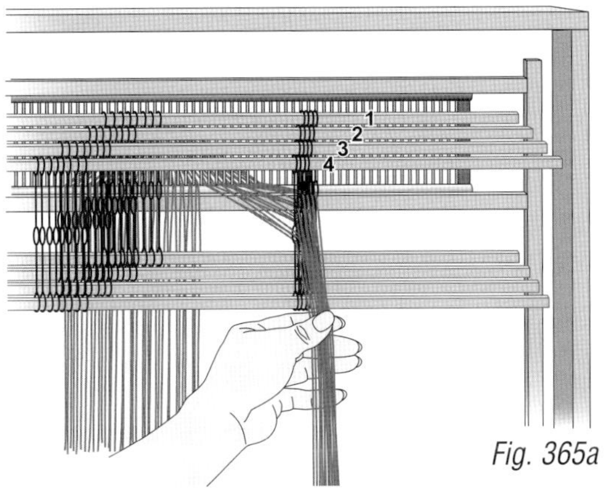

Fig. 365a

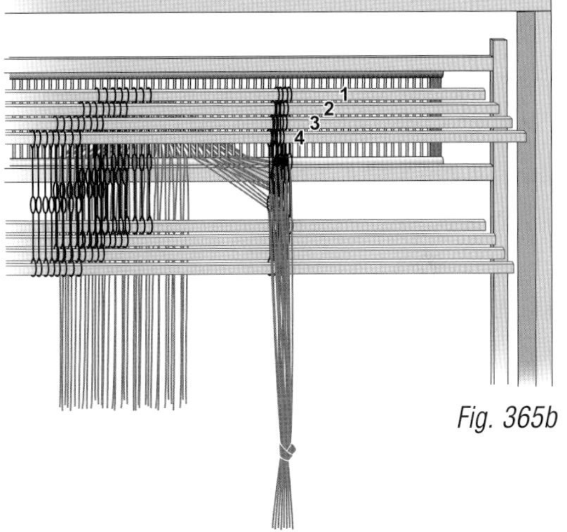

Fig. 365b

Repeat the same steps for threading the next 16 threads through the heddles and tie the bundle with a snug overhand knot. Work your way across the remaining warp threads, threading and checking each successive group of 16 threads. Work from right to left, (left to right for left-handers) taking care to tie each bundle evenly and consistently before proceeding to the next.

All the heddles have now been threaded in order, checked for accuracy, and tied into 11 bundles. See Figure 366. Note that the last bundle will actually contain 20 threads because 11 bundles of 16 threads equal 176 threads, and there are 180 in all.

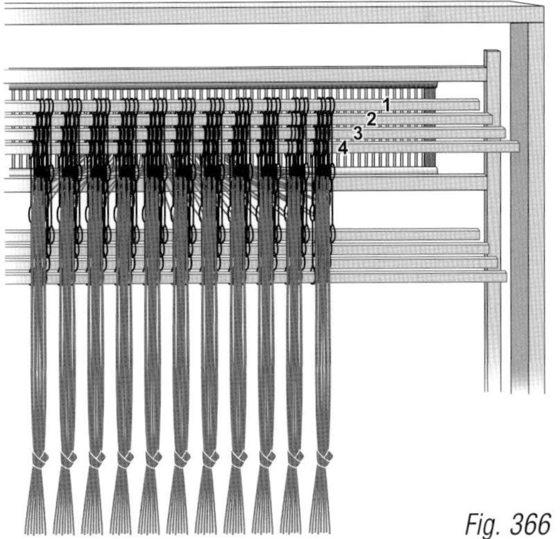

Fig. 366

Replace the back beam, if you removed it while threading the heddles.

Tie the bundles on to the back apron rod

For the next step, all the bundles will get tied to the back apron rod. They will be spaced out along on the rod, centered, for 11".

Bring the back apron rod up and over the back beam, ready for tying on the warp bundles. This step is vitally important in order for the loom to raise the shafts properly, so take a moment to be certain that the back apron rod has been brought up, behind and over the back beam. Bring it up close enough to the heddles to be able comfortably to tie the knotted bundles to the back apron rod. See Figure 367. Read on page 171 about different types of aprons and rods.

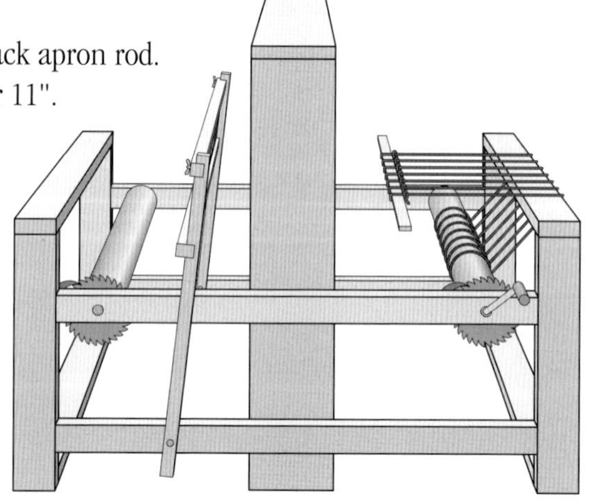

Fig. 367

Engage the brake

Engage the brake on the warp beam so that the apron cannot be pulled farther toward the heddles. Two types of brakes may be found on warp beams. Figure 368a shows a ratchet brake, and a friction (tension) brake is shown in Figure 368b. Read more about brakes on page 38.

Make sure the apron is wound on the warp beam in the correct direction so when the brake is engaged it will prevent the apron from unwinding.

Looms vary in which way the warp beams are wound. You must check that your apron rod is held securely by the brake on the warp beam—regardless of which type of brake you have. Figure 369 shows that some warp beams are wound in one direction and others in the opposite direction. See page 38 to determine the correct direction on your loom.

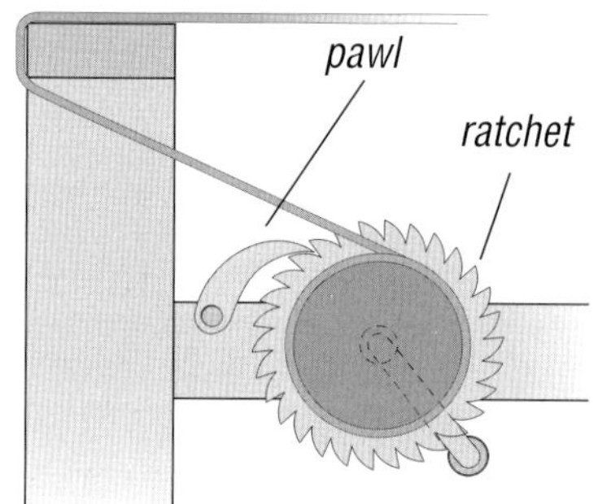

Ratchet brake *Fig. 368a*

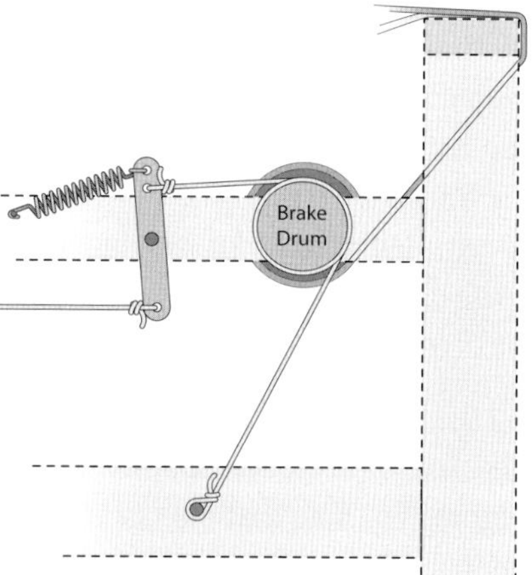

Friction (tension) brake *Fig. 368b*

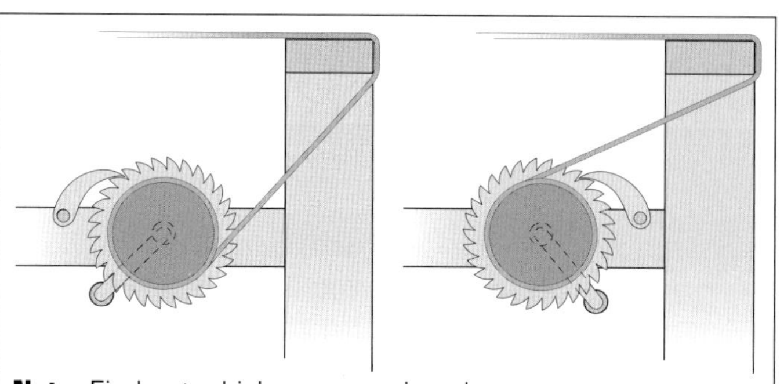

Note: Find out which way your loom's warp beam is wound. *Fig. 369*

Prepare the apron rods

Looms come with various types of back aprons and apron rods. Figure 367 shows an apron made of strings or cords with its apron rod in the position required for tying on the bundles. Figure 370 shows a cloth apron.

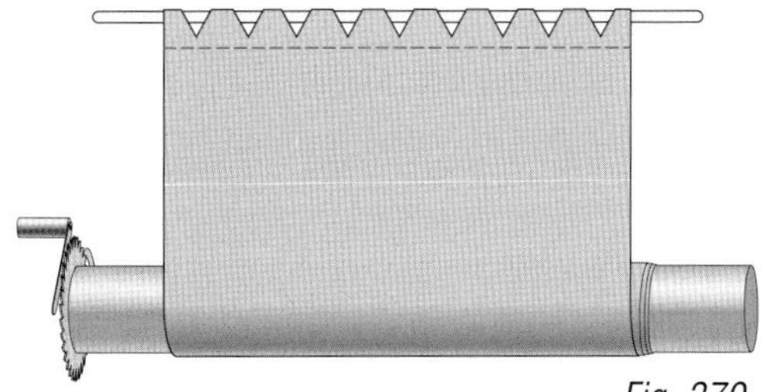

Fig. 370

Cloth aprons need a second rod attached to them so you are able to tie on anywhere along the rod, rather than being confined to where there are gaps in the fabric of the apron.

See Figure 371. Read how to create one on page 84.

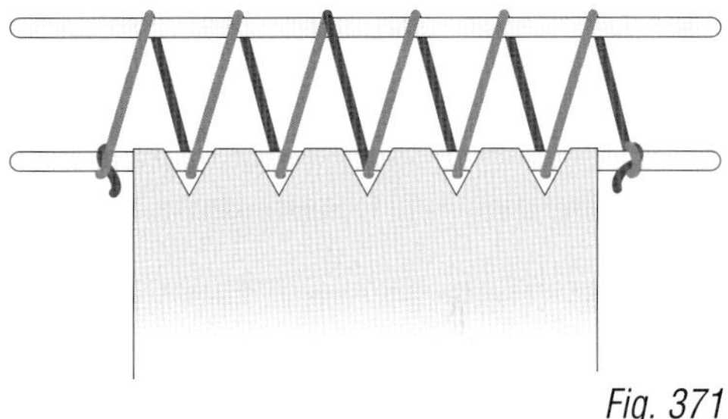

Fig. 371

To prevent the new rod from bending during weaving, always check your project's width beforehand (in this case, 11"). You want the rods to be laced together only for the width of the project. Read on page 85 how to slip the excess lacing off of each side of the rod to achieve the 11". See Figures 372 a and b.

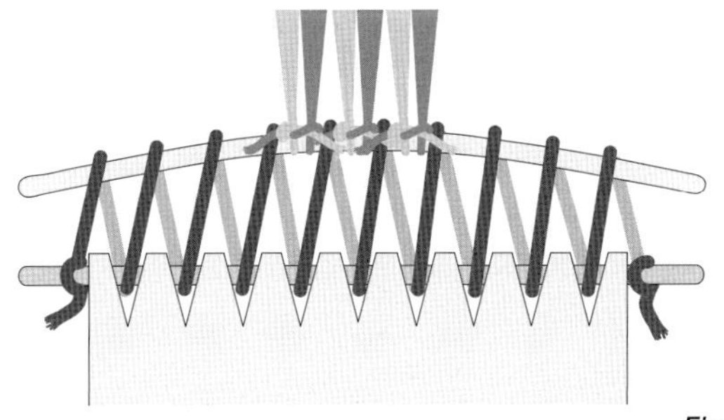

Fig. 372a

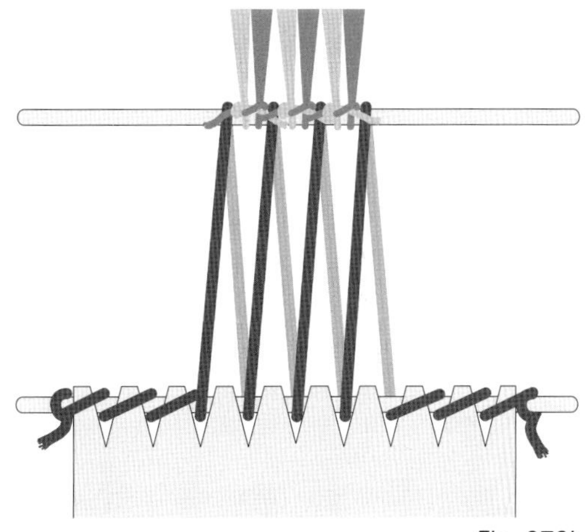

Fig. 372b

Tie the bundles on to the apron rod

Take a moment to straighten out the heddles and warp bundles. Stand at the back of the loom. Look at the full 11" width warp passing through from the reed. Tug on the bundles, from the back of the loom, sliding heddles and bundles as necessary to conform, approximately, in order of the threads passing through the reed. All threads must pass in a straight line, from the reed, through the heddles, to the back apron rod.

To tie the bundles to the apron rod, start with the bundle nearest the center. Pull it out straight, untwisted, and find the very center of the apron rod. Bring the bundle over the apron rod and up to the right of the bundle. Tie it in an overhand knot and be sure to cinch the overhand knot down snugly against the existing knot. The overhand knot and the knot tied at the end of the bundle work together, acting as a brake. The two knots should rest directly against the apron rod. See Figure 373. How to tie an overhand knot is on page 350.

Working from the center, out to each side, alternate tying the bundles to the apron rod (left side, right side, etc). Be certain to double-check for proper spacing as you go so that when you are finished, the width of bundles tied at the back rod should match the width of the threads passing through the reed and heddles—11". See Figure 374.

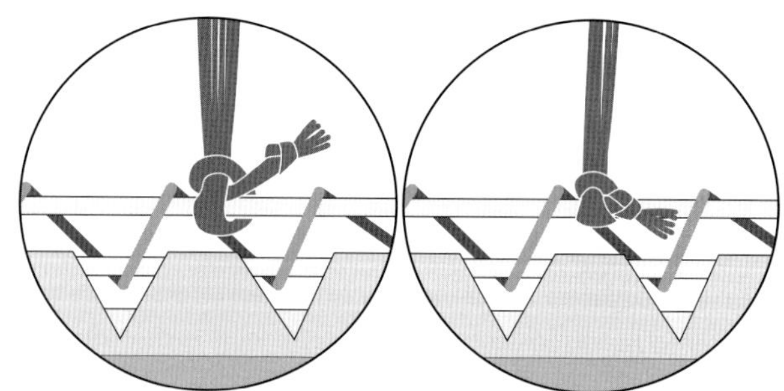

Fig. 373

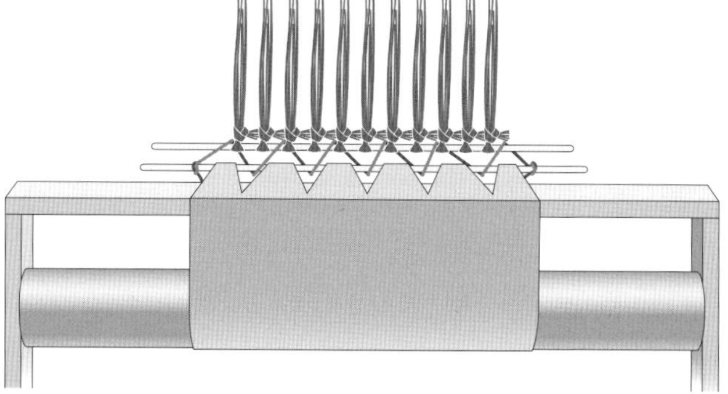

Fig. 374

Prepare to wind the warp on to the warp beam (beaming)

1. At this point, refasten all eight heddle bar clips at the centers of the shafts if you have them, so that the heddles are locked into position on their shafts. Figures 375 a and b and Figures 376 a and b show two types of the clips. Detailed information on operating the clips is found on pages 61-62 and on page 79.

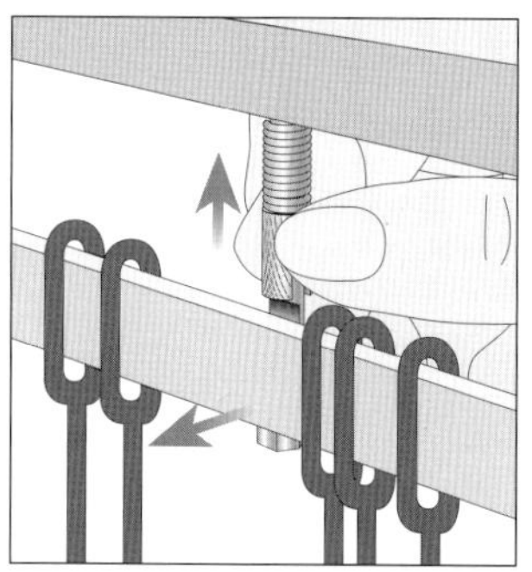

Fig. 375a

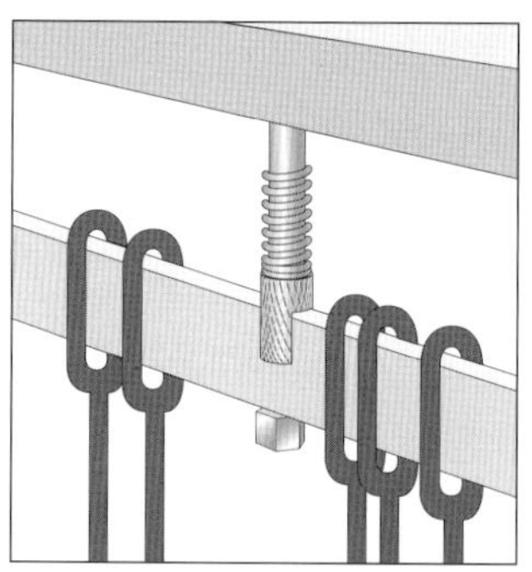

Fig. 375b

If you are new to this process, you *must* read the pages referred to in the text.

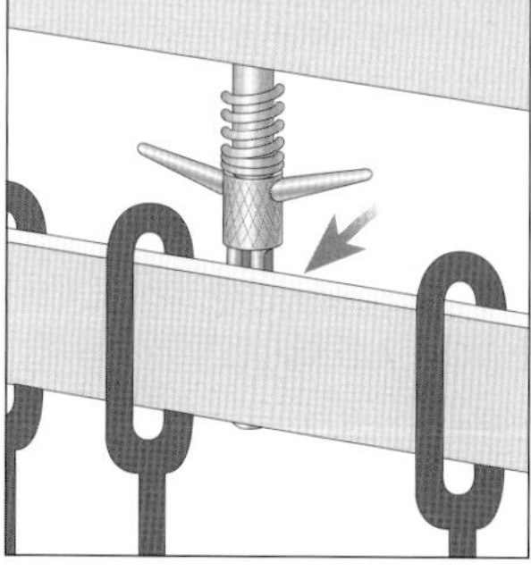

Fig. 376a

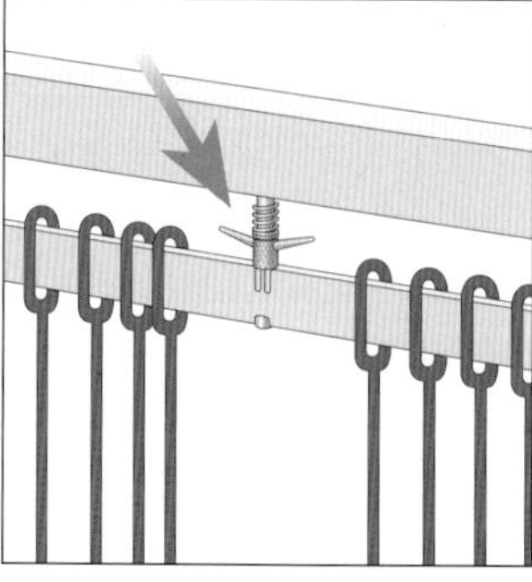

Fig. 376b

2. Remove the ties holding the beater upright. See Figure 377.
3. Go to the front of the loom. Be sure the brake is engaged on the cloth beam. The pawl (or pawls) should be in the teeth of the ratchet brake. To know that the brake is engaged, check that the cloth beam can only be wound in one direction, and you can hear the pawl(s) clicking in the teeth as the beam is wound. See Figure 367 on page 170.
4. Untie the choke tie holding the warp onto the breast beam (or unwrap the warp if it is wound on the breast beam).

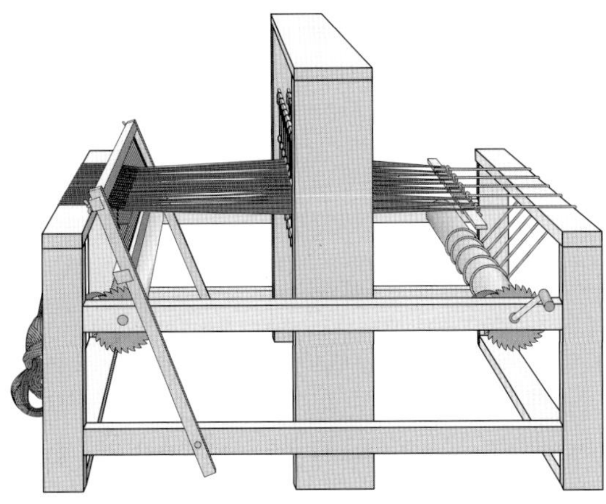

Fig. 377

Tension the warp at the front

Push the beater back to rest against the castle. Unchain a few loops of the warp chain. Spread out the warp and divide it into two halves. Take hold of the "reins" with both hands. Place one foot squarely on the floor, just in front of the treadles. Lean away from the loom and use your body weight to shake and snap the threads so that there is no slack behind the heddles. Tug particular areas if they seem slack in comparison with others, but never pull on a single thread—it may snap! When satisfied that tension seems even on all the threads, let go of the threads, and bring the beater forward to rest against the breast beam as shown in Figure 377.

Go to the back of the loom and turn the crank to wind up the apron, until the knotted ends of warp wrap once around the warp beam. This much cranking may cause the beater to move/fall backwards until it falls against the castle. This is normal, and it is also your cue that it is time to stop winding and return to the front of the loom.

Make the warp beam smooth

Before you return to the front, however, smooth the knots at the apron rod: take 2 packing sticks, inserting one on either side of the row of knots tied to the apron rod. See Figure 378. This action will help prevent lumps in the warp as shown in Figure 379. Lumps can cause the threads to become longer or shorter when the warp threads go over the knots as the warp is wound onto the warp beam. A well-beamed (well-wound) warp looks like Figure 380.

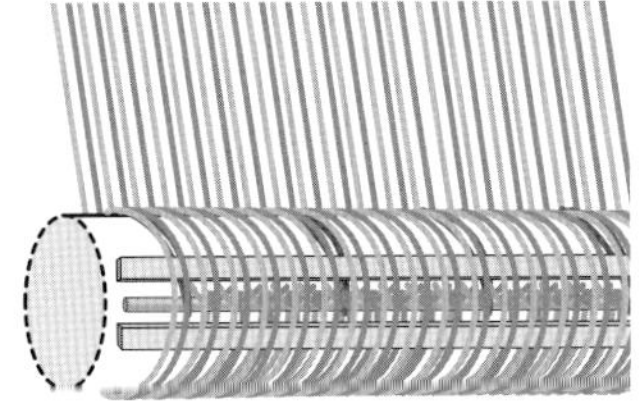

Fig. 378

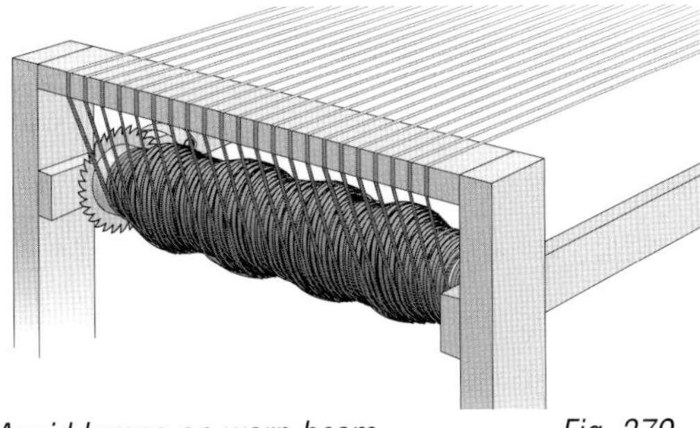

Avoid lumps on warp beam *Fig. 379*

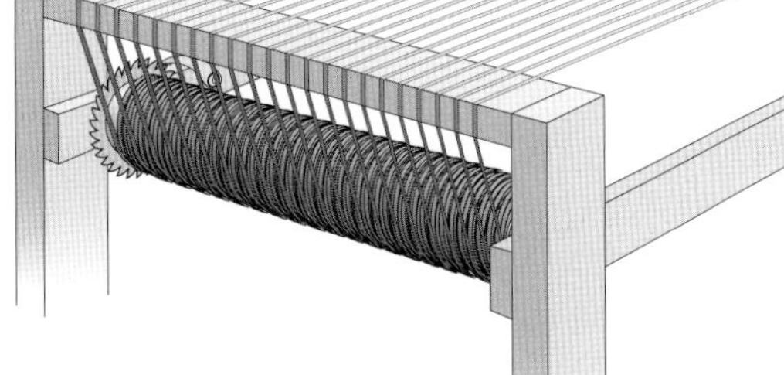

Well-beamed warp *Fig. 380*

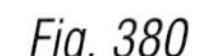

Now, choose something to insert between the layers of thread you will be winding on to the warp beam. Rolled, corrugated paper works well, as do thin, flat sticks, called packing sticks, or paper cut from grocery bags. Make sure whatever you choose is at least a few inches wider than your warp at each side. Center and insert the corrugated side of the roll facing down or add more packing sticks, as needed, to help smooth out the knotted edge at the beginning of the warp. If there are bulky cords or straps attached to the apron rod, you will need the corrugated paper or packing sticks now, when you are beginning to wind on the warp. See page 50 for more information. You must avoid lumps on the warp beam! Figure 381 shows packing sticks smoothing out the knots and any bulky straps that may be used for apron cords. Figure 382 shows continuous paper inserted in the layers. Figures 383 and 384 show two ways packing sticks can be inserted between the layers rather than continuous paper.

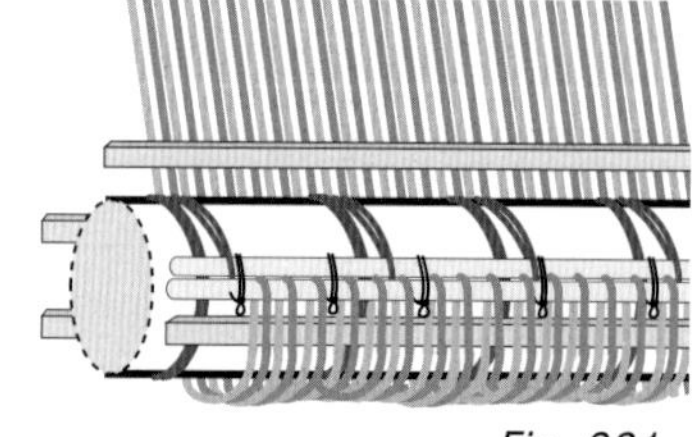

Fig. 381

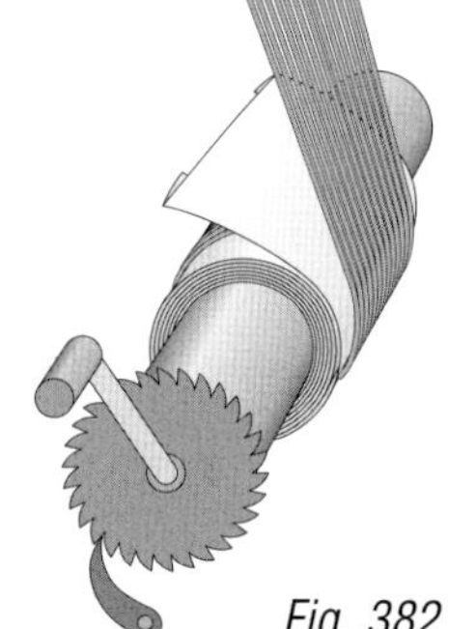

Fig. 382

Many weavers prefer to use short pieces of packing paper for this purpose as described on pages 37, 46, and 47. Check to see if your loom does not need any packing material, on page 37.

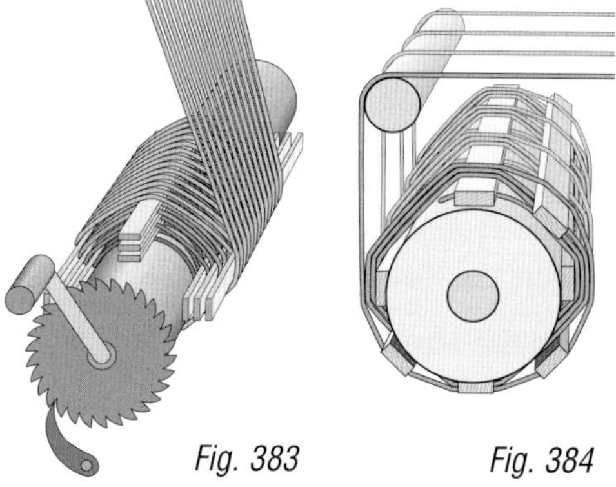

Fig. 383 *Fig. 384*

Warp Beam

Beam the warp

Winding the warp onto the warp beam is called beaming.

For beaming wider warps—too big to hold in your two hands—see the method described beginning on page 44.

Go back to the front of the loom, and un-chain more of the warp. Untie a choke tie, if necessary, to spread out and relax the warp. Then, repeat the motions, above, of leaning away from the loom, taking hold of the warp with two hands, and snapping the "reins" to tension the threads in the warp. Don't forget to rest the beater forward against the breast beam before you return each time to the back to turn the crank. See Figure 385.

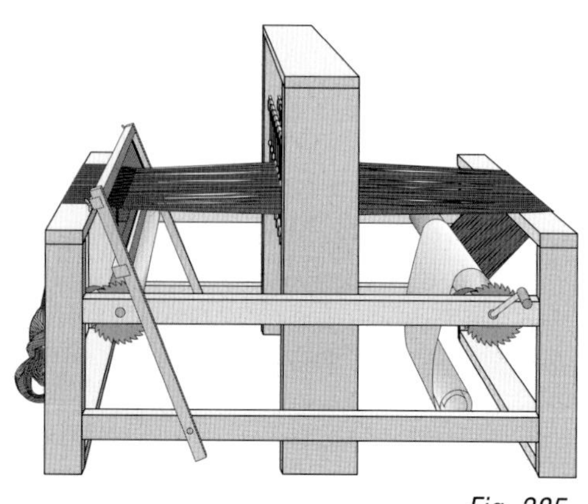

Fig. 385

Wind about one or two revolutions at a time, or until the beater swings backward to hit the castle; then, repeat the steps above each time. If you are using sticks, remember to add a few for every revolution. Don't handle the warp as it winds on, but do check the warp beam itself, often, to confirm that the threads wind on smoothly and tightly—similar to how sewing thread looks when wound on a spool. See Figure 386.

Untie the remaining choke ties when you reach them. Stop winding when the ends of the warp reach about 10-12" from the front of the reed. See Figure 387.

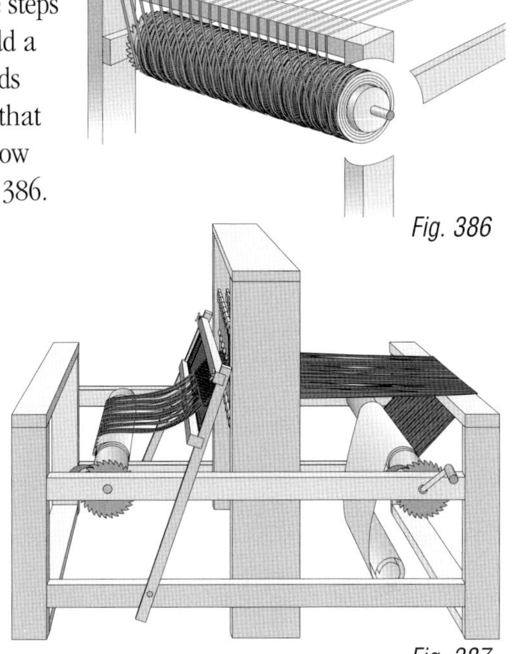

Fig. 386

Fig. 387

Tie the warps on to the front apron rod

Find the front apron rod and bring it up and over the breast beam as shown in Figure 388. If the front apron is made cloth, you may wish to lace on another apron rod as was discussed on page 84 for the warp beam's apron. See Figure 371 on page 171. Figure 389 shows an apron made of cords rather than cloth.

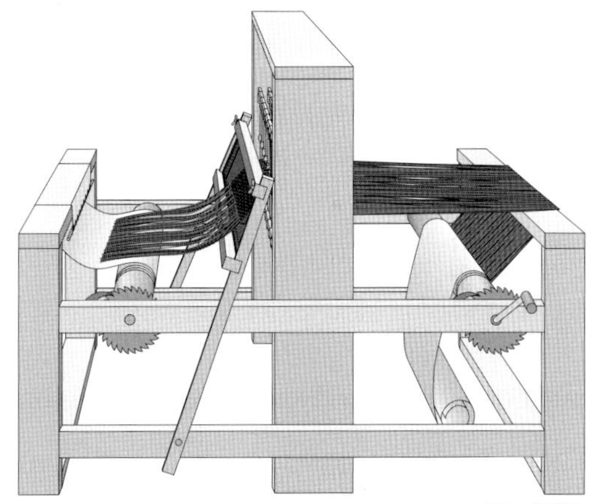

Fig. 388

If necessary, trim the warp threads to an even length.

Unwind some of the apron so that the apron rod is near enough to the heddles that the warp threads can be knotted onto it. Then, position the ends of the warp threads so they extend past the apron rod by about 5". (Do it by winding or unwinding the threads at the warp beam.) Figure 390 shows the first bundle of warp threads knotted onto the apron rod and shows the positions of the apron rod and the ends of the warp threads.

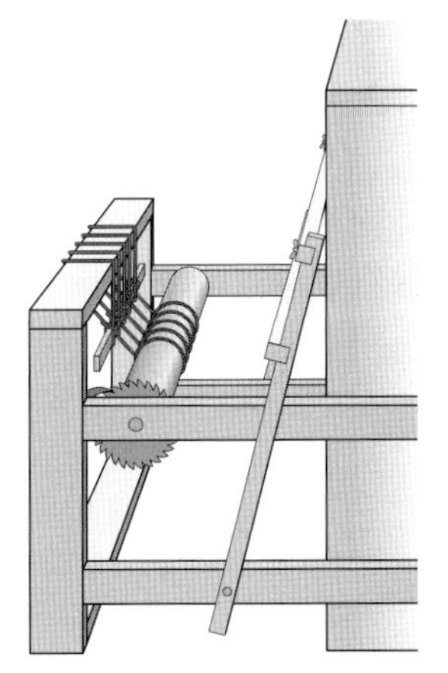

Fig. 389

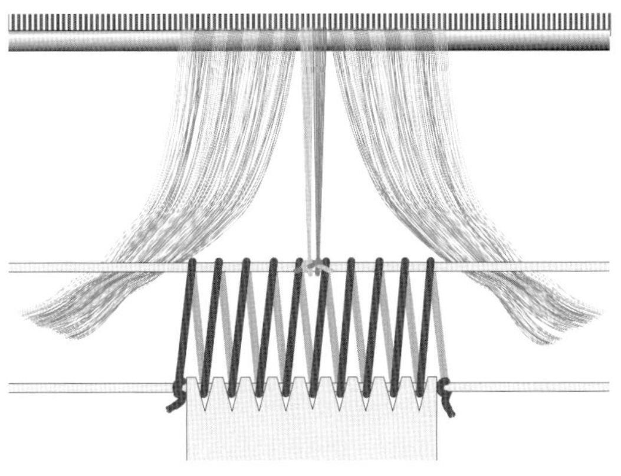

Fig. 390

Tie on the first group of warp threads

Starting at the center, find a group of threads that make up 1" of warp. Since there are 16 threads per inch, you'll gather 2 groups of 8 threads coming from 4 dents on each side of the center mark at the reed. Pull the threads towards you and comb out each half with your fingers to untwist the threads and to even out their tension. Tie them on to the apron rod with a surgeon's knot. Begin by bringing both halves over the rod and out under the rod to the sides, forming a "W." Then, tie half of a knot, but bring the ends through twice. Tighten your surgeon's knot. See Figure 390.

After you are satisfied that all the threads are equally tensioned, complete the last part of the surgeon's knot. Take the tails and tie another knot on top of the first part of the knot shown in Figures 391 a, b, and c. Figure 391 d shows the final step.

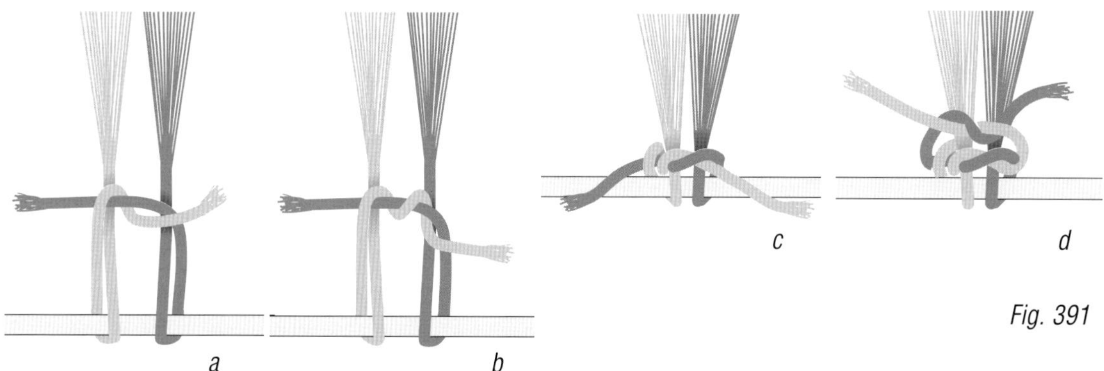

Fig. 391

The beauty of a surgeon's knot is that it holds well but is also easy to release. To release, lift both ends up and away from you—toward the loom. It is an ideal knot to use when fine-tensioning the threads later, before starting to weave. At that time you will tie the final knots on the tops of the knots to complete the surgeon's knots.

Work out from the center, alternating sides, until you have gathered and tied all of the threads into 1" groups. The groups at the edges may not contain exactly 16 threads, but that is ok. See Figure 392.

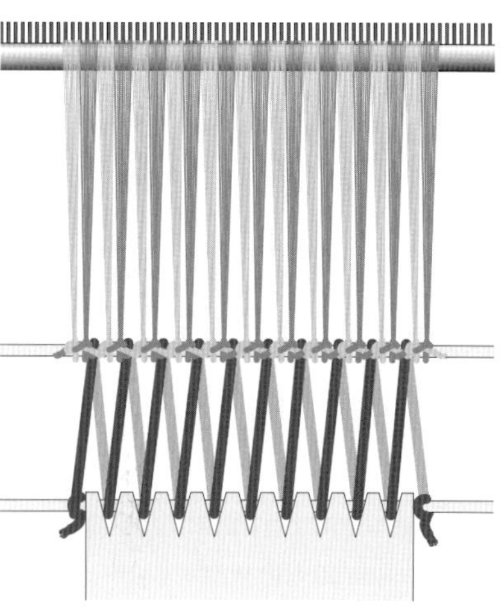

Fig. 392

Tie up the treadles

Cords, chains, or hooks may be used to tie up the treadles, and a variety of mechanisms are used in various looms. More comprehensive information on tying up the treadles and how they work is on pages 95-101. ***Read that section before continuing.***

When you finish tying the surgeon's knots, it is time to "tie up" the treadles below the loom. Then, you will check for threading errors in the reed or within the heddles, by stepping on each treadle in turn, before tightening each surgeon's knot one last time.

Since table looms have no treadles, you can eliminate this process and proceed to "Check for Threading Errors," beginning on page 179.

"Tying up the treadles" is the process of attaching the treadles to the shafts so that during weaving, pressing the treadles makes the shafts move, which makes the threads in the heddles move as well. See Figure 393. The space between the raised threads and those below is called the shed.

If you are new to this process, you *must* read the pages referred to in the text.

Read about tying up the treadles beginning on page 95.

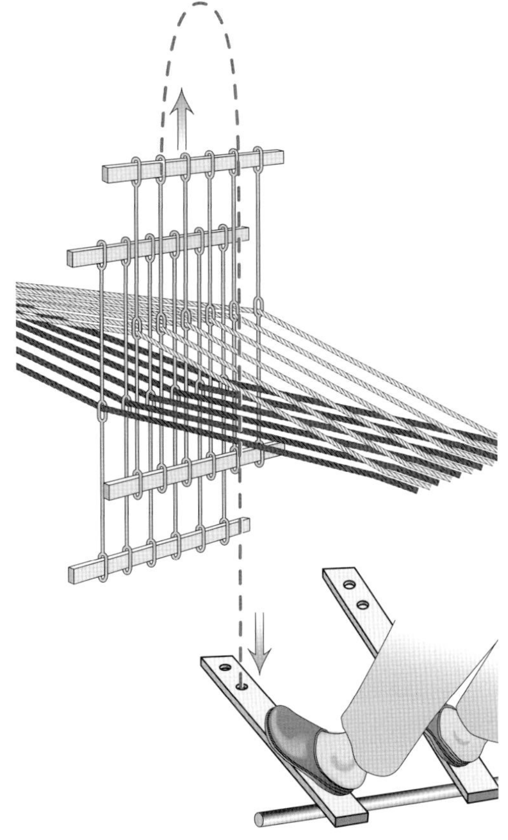

Fig. 393

Lams

Many floor looms have lams (bars between the shafts and the treadles) that are connected to the shafts, and tying up the treadles is actually tying the treadles to the lams. See Figure 394. In the illustration you can see that by pressing the treadle the lam is pulled down, which pulls down one end of the short bars (the jacks), which raises the other end of the jacks, which eventually pushes up the shaft. This is the situation found in many but not all looms. Lams and jacks are discussed on page 95. Some looms have no lams. See page 100. If your loom has two lams for each shaft, see page 133.

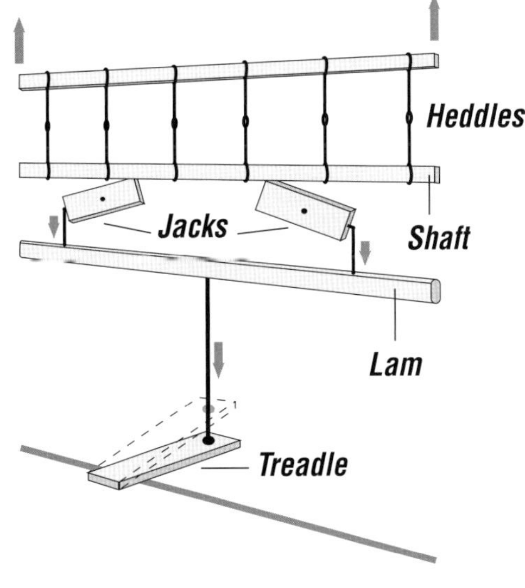

Fig. 394

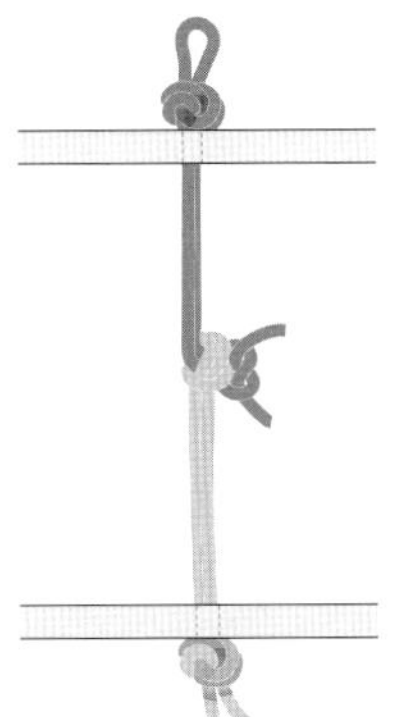

If there are cords both on the lams and on the treadles, they are meant to be tied with snitch knots. It is important to make these knots properly to avoid much frustration. See Figure 228, on page 96 and repeated here, and Figure 583, on page 352 in the Knots chapter.

Two ways to tie up the treadles

Direct Tie-up

Look beneath the front of your loom to determine how to tie up, or attach, the treadles to the shafts. If the treadles can only be tied up to one shaft each, it is called a "direct tie-up." See Figure 395. In this case, no further tie-up is necessary, and you can proceed to next section below to check for errors.

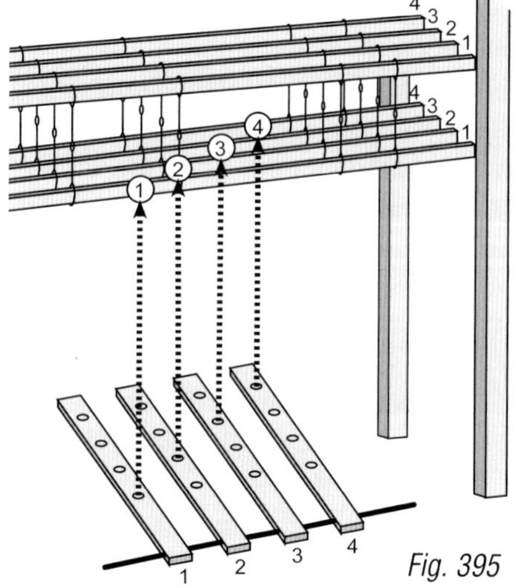

Fig. 395

Multiple tie-ups

Many looms, however, have a multiple-tie-up arrangement, allowing various possibilities of tying-up the treadles. For example, two shafts can be tied to a treadle as shown in Figure 396 where the left treadle is tied to move shafts #1 and #2.

For this project, select two treadles that are a comfortable distance apart for your feet. Tie up one treadle so that it can operate both shafts #1 and #3. Tie-up the other treadle so that it will operate shafts #2 and #4. See Figures 397 and 398. Be sure to test that each treadle is actually moving the shafts you intended by stepping on them in turn.

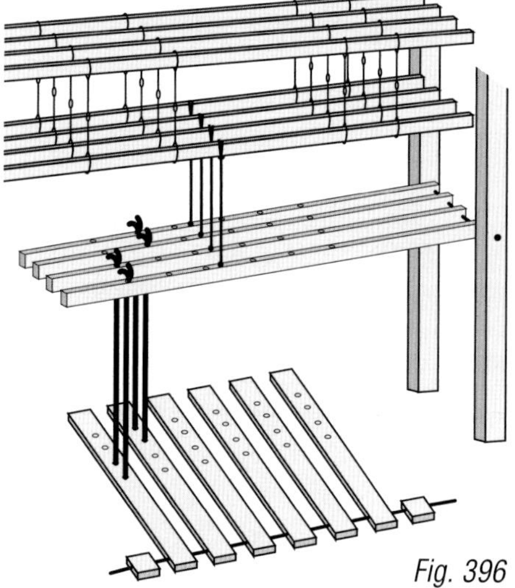
Fig. 396

More about how to tie up the treadles is found beginning on page 95.

Tying the treadles for other projects

Note that this arrangement of tying up the treadles to shafts is for this project only. Read about other combinations of shafts used to create other weaves in the chapter on weaving a sampler beginning on page 93. Also, see page 96 for other arrangements of tying up the treadles.

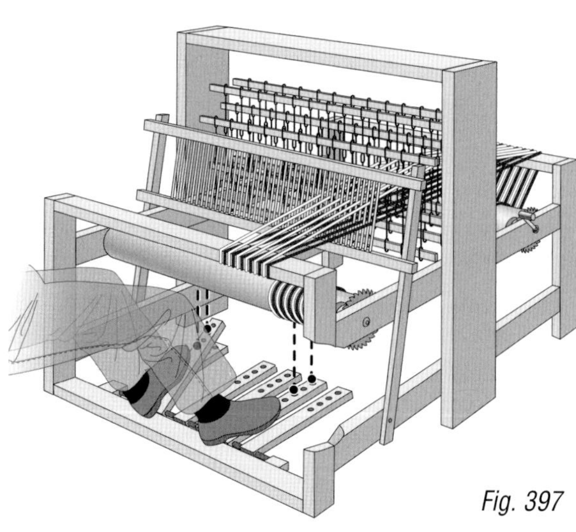
Fig. 397

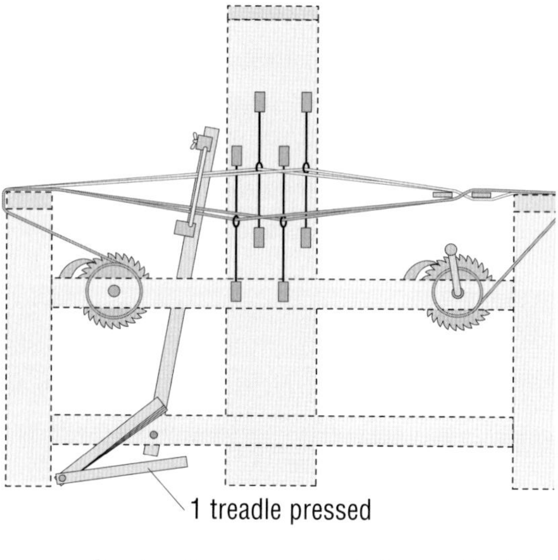

One treadle moves two shafts
Fig. 398

Check for Threading Errors

Read more about checking for errors and correcting them on pages 108 through 110.

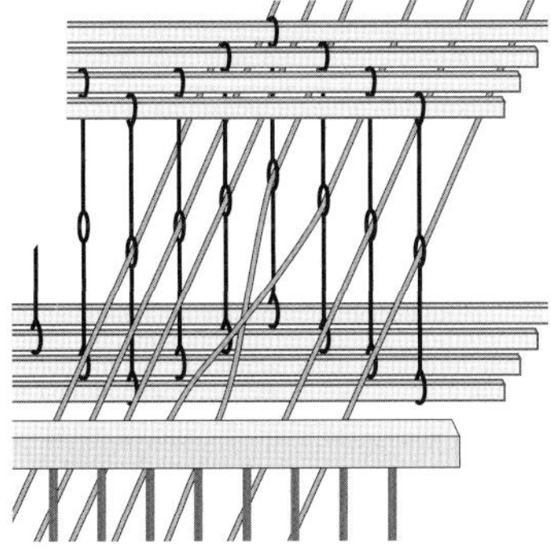

Crossed threads between the heddles and the reed

Step on each treadle, in turn, to raise the shafts to check for any errors, which might have occurred while threading the reed or heddles. Lean to one side of the loom, to carefully watch the threads raise and lower. If you see one or more threads sitting in the center of the shed, and you can't tell whether they belong in the top or bottom layer of warps, you probably have a crossed thread in these areas. (Crossed threads are discussed below.) Be sure that no threads appear twisted or crossed. Check the areas, both in front and behind the reed. Are all threads orderly? Identify any threads that may need to be untied and traced back to the reed or heddles for correction. Make any needed corrections now. Then, see below to re-tension the warp.

If you can't get the sheds to open, read what to do beginning on page 318.

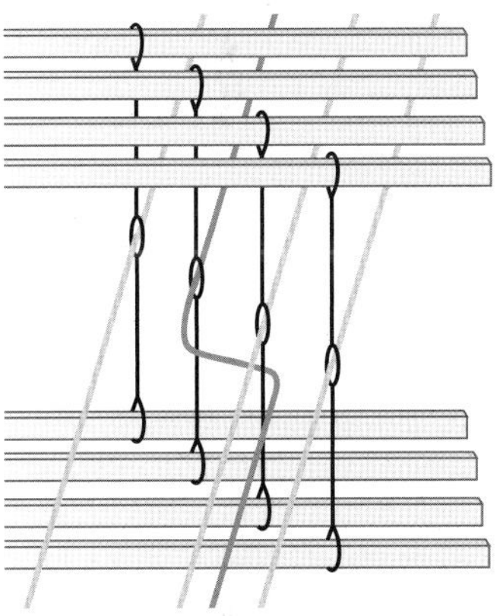

Crossed threads among the heddles

Crossed threads: A common error

You can quickly tell if a crossed thread is a problem by reaching into the open shed and feeling for any tight warp threads.

A tight warp thread in the space between the raised threads and those below (called the shed) is a common error. Threads might be crossed in either of two places. A crossed thread between the heddles and the reed is the most common error. See Figure 249 repeated here. Threads could also be crossed among the heddles as shown in Figure 250 repeated here. Read how to fix threading errors on page 320.

Re-tension the warp

When you are satisfied that any errors you found have been corrected, release and re-tighten each surgeon's knot, alternating from the center out to both sides—right, left, right, etc. Check the treadles and warps one last time.

Finally, close your eyes and strum or pat your fingers across the warp, ever so slightly (you can also do this behind the heddles). See Figure 399. Fine-tune your instrument, if needed, (re-tension any loose or tight groups of threads) until the tension on all threads feels even. You want the tension to be firm to taut but not tight. You only need to fine-tune a bundle if it is definitely looser or tighter than the others. Tie the final part of the surgeon's knots when you are satisfied. This is explained on page 89. You are now ready to make your loom sing!

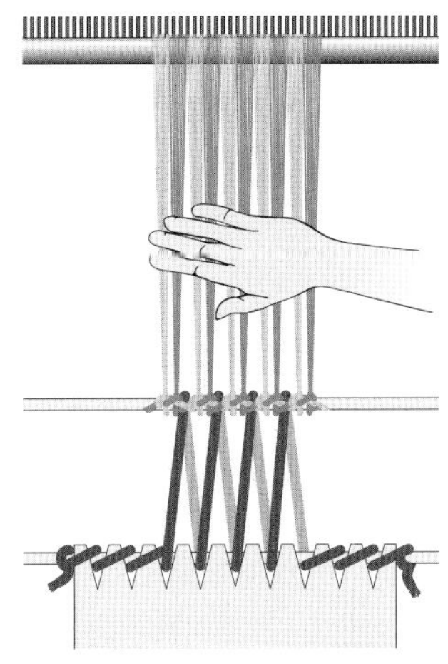

Fig. 399

Weave the heading using rags

Note: An alternate to using rags for the heading is to use your regular weft yarn. This method is described on page 107.

You will weave your scarf by lifting shafts #1 and #3 together, alternating with lifting shafts #2 and #4 together. On table looms, you will use two levers at one time. For floor looms with a direct tie-up, you will use two treadles at a time. For looms with multiple tie-ups, you will press one treadle at a time, with each treadle lifting two shafts. (See "Multiple tie-ups," above). This sequence of treadling, in combination with straight draw threading (threading the heddles 1, 2, 3, 4, etc.), will produce a plain weave structure (also called "tabby"). Plain weave is the most basic weave structure, with warp and weft threads intersecting in a simple "over, under, over under…" fashion. See Figure 400.

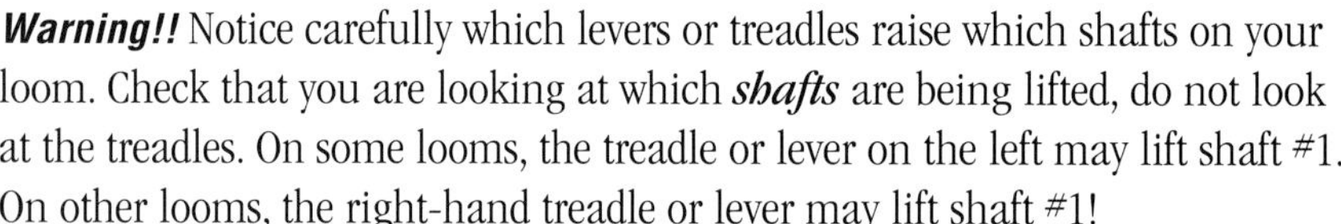

Fig. 400

Note: Other weave structures are described in the section on weaving a sampler beginning on page 111, in the Future Assignments chapter, and in the Drafting chapter.

Warning!! Notice carefully which levers or treadles raise which shafts on your loom. Check that you are looking at which ***shafts*** are being lifted, do not look at the treadles. On some looms, the treadle or lever on the left may lift shaft #1. On other looms, the right-hand treadle or lever may lift shaft #1!

Notice that the warp threads are still not evenly spread out in a parallel fashion at the front, because they remain tied into bundles. There are various ways to spread out the warp threads to get started weaving. Here is one. Assuming you would like fringe at both ends of your scarf, weave in a heading of about 8" of rag strips. Rags can be cut into long strips, one or two inches wide, or torn from old sheets or towels, if you like. Make your rags 1" or 2" wide if they are made from old sheets, or make them ½" wide if made from bath towels. These rag strips serve as a placeholder for the length of your fringe at the beginning of the scarf, and they also spread out the warp threads. Of course, you will remove the rag strips later on. (More rag strips will be woven in at the end for fringe at the other end of the scarf.) The strips can be anywhere from around 25" long to whatever is convenient for you to handle, say, about 6 times the width of the warp.

To weave in the rags, raise shafts #1 and #3. Insert a rag strip with your fingers, into the widest point of the shed, leaving the tail end at the edge. As you insert the rag strip, bring it across the warp in a diagonal, rather than a straight line. A diagonal line is longer than a straight line; therefore, it helps to insure that your weaving will not draw in too tightly (See Figure 401). Place your right hand centered on the beater. Swing the beater toward you and press the rag strip gently into place against the surgeon's knots.

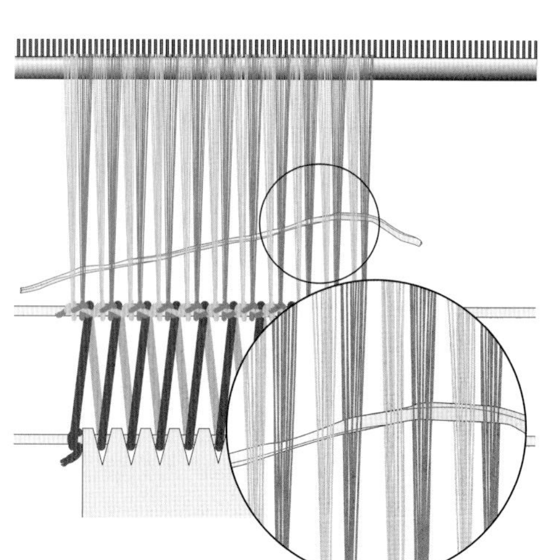

Fig. 401

Change the shed by lifting shafts #2 and #4. Then push the beater back towards the shafts. Take the end of the rag strip, and turn it around neatly at the selvedge (the edge of the warp). Insert it through the new shed—across in the opposite direction. It should not pull or draw in the sides of the weaving and should always go in on a diagonal. When you run out of one rag, simply add in the next one, by overlapping their ends in the middle of the shed by an inch or so, and beat. See Figure 402. Continue weaving, gradually acquainting yourself with the rhythm, until the heading is 8" long. The rhythm of the motions is: enter the rag strip, beat it in, change to the new shed and continue: "enter the strip, beat, change the shed." The shed is changed when the beater is against the fell (the last row of weaving).

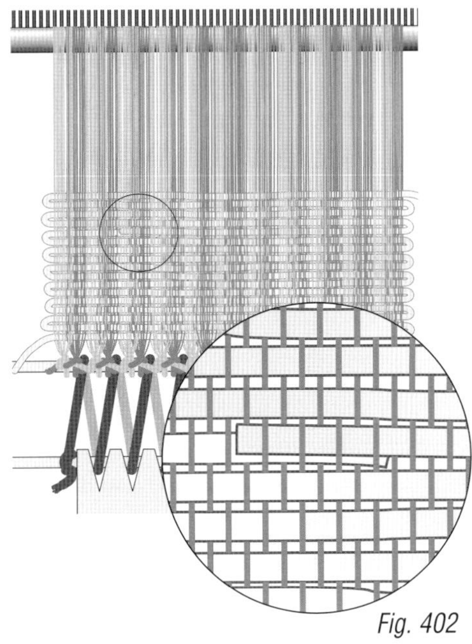

Fig. 402

More about checking for errors and how to correct them is found on pages 108-110.

Check again for errors and flaws

While weaving the heading, it's a good idea to check for flaws in the cloth, which usually indicate errors in threading the heddles or sleying the reed. Here is what to look for.

1. A tight warp thread in a shed usually means a crossed thread—see above and Figure 403.
2. A thread isn't being woven in—see page 109.
3. A thick or thin vertical line or vertical space in the cloth means there is an error in sleying the reed—see page 109.
4. Two or three threads weave together—see page 110.

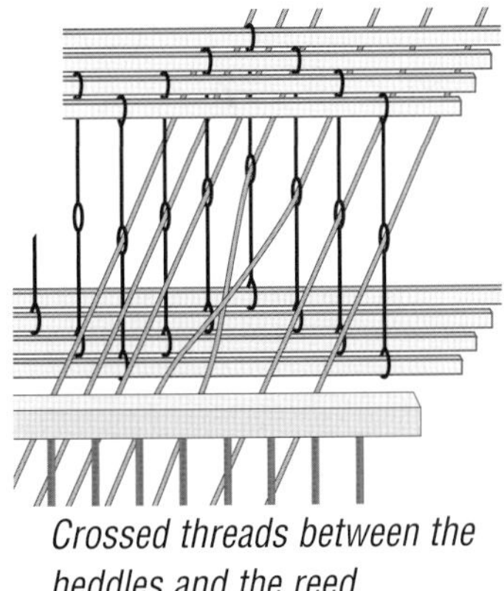

Crossed threads between the heddles and the reed

Fig. 403

Repair errors discovered in the heading

The heading is a good place to correct errors so they won't show up in the scarf because the heading will eventually be unwoven to make the fringe. Read how beginning on page 108 in the section on repairing errors in the heading and on page 320.

Weave the scarf

> **If you are new to this process, you *must* read the pages referred to in the text.**

Wind a shuttle or bobbin

For more information on how to load shuttles and wind bobbins, go to page 102.

For boat shuttles, wind your first color of weft thread onto a bobbin and load it into a shuttle. You are ready to start weaving your scarf. Figures 404 and 405 show how to wind a bobbin—make the layers of the weft thread lie in flat layers as you fill the bobbin. Put some tension on the weft as you wind so the thread is fairly tightly wound on the bobbin. However, don't use so much tension that you burn your fingers! Do not fill it above the flanges, which are at the ends of the bobbin. There are several types of bobbin winders—you can wind the bobbin without one, but you will soon want to own a winder. See the Sources section beginning on page 382.

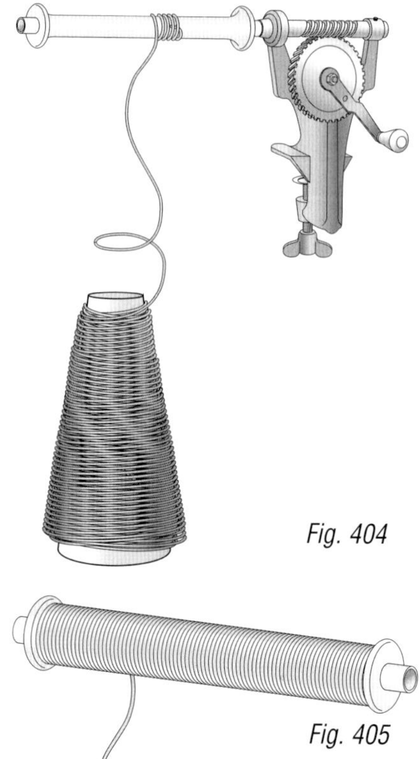

Fig. 404

Fig. 405

Important: *Wind bobbin in flat layers*

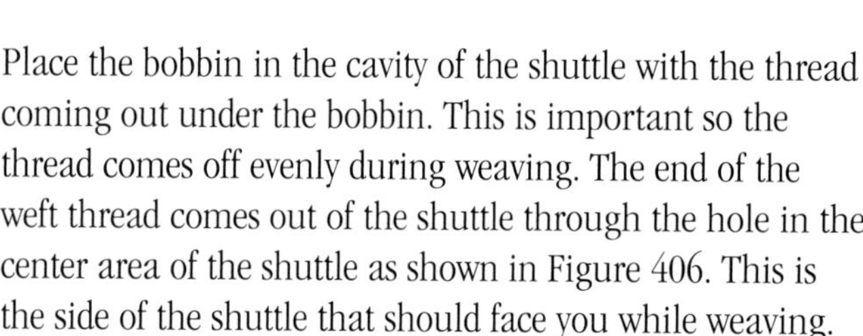

Place the bobbin in the cavity of the shuttle with the thread coming out under the bobbin. This is important so the thread comes off evenly during weaving. The end of the weft thread comes out of the shuttle through the hole in the center area of the shuttle as shown in Figure 406. This is the side of the shuttle that should face you while weaving.

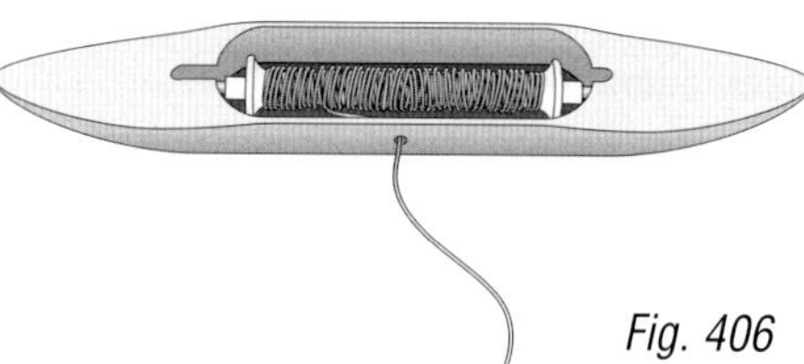

Fig. 406

Thread is to come out under the bobbin

Read about types of bobbins and the shuttles in which they are used on page 94 if your bobbin doesn't look exactly like the one in the illustration,.

To wind a stick shuttle, see Figures 407 a and b and page 102. How to make a stick shuttle is found on page 8.

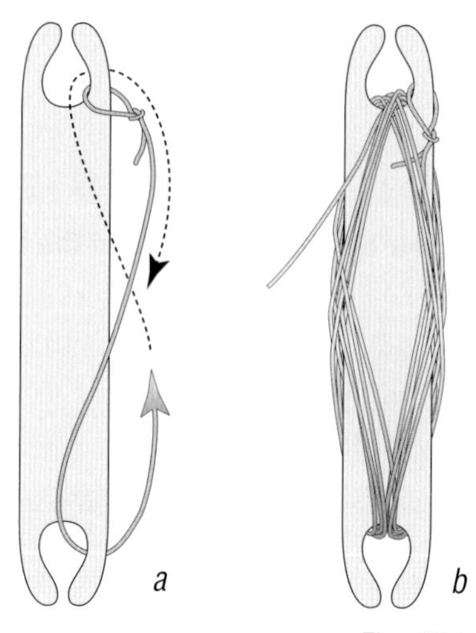

Fig. 407

Begin to weave

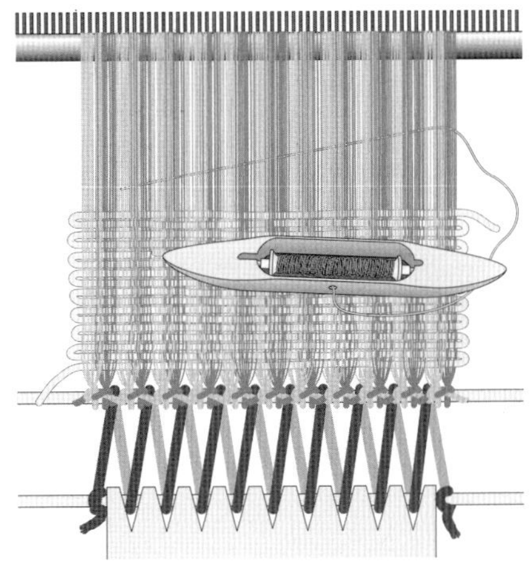

Fig. 408

Open a shed. Is it the correct shed to continue weaving? If it is, you will notice that the previous row of rag strip has been woven and is therefore locked into place. If it is not the correct shed, you will be able to lift up the last row of strip weaving. Find the correct shed and open it. See page 185.

Pass your shuttle through the shed, leaving the tail end of the weft thread somewhere in the middle of the weaving so the end will be hidden within the cloth. (See Figure 408.) Beat in the weft (the chenille thread). Change the shed. Pass the shuttle across in the opposite direction, making sure that the weft thread turns neatly against the selvedge (the outside edge of the warp). It should neither pull in nor look loopy. (See page 113.) As you "throw" (pass) the shuttle, draw the weft thread across the warp in a diagonal line, making sure to turn neatly at the selvedge, as above. Beat in the weft. Change the shed and continue weaving. The sequence is "throw, beat, change the shed"—for 4 counts. (On the fourth beat, the beater goes back toward the shafts.)

Tips to remember when starting to weave

Build good habits in the beginning and don't go too fast.
Be attentive to the following:

- Remember to make a diagonal line with the weft thread every time you throw the shuttle.
- Check to see if your loom has a shuttle race along the bottom front of the beater. This is a long wooden strip or ledge, which acts as a track to guide the shuttle while weaving. Be sure to use it to slide the shuttle on if you have one. If not, throw the shuttle close to the reed. Also, check that the wings of any wing nuts that hold the beater cap in place face toward you and away from the loom to prevent them from gouging the loom.
- Check the selvedge at each side, before and after beating, to be sure it is smooth and even, not loopy or drawn-in.
- Sometimes, when starting out weaving with chenille, the weft thread catches between the warp threads at the very edge. Check to see if it is bunching up there, causing a lump. If so, remember to pull the weft thread to straighten it before continuing on to weave the next row. See Figure 409.
- Check to see that your weaving width closely matches the width of the threads spaced in the reed. If your weaving draws in too much you risk breaking warp threads at the edges. If the weaving does begin to narrow in, ***do not*** try to correct this situation by making loops at the selvedges. Instead, make the diagonal of the weft steeper. Read what to do if a warp thread breaks, on page 322.

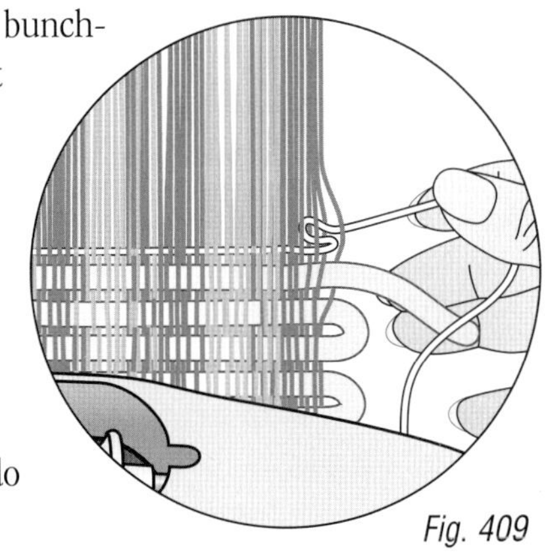

Fig. 409

- Chenille needs a firm, even beat, but do not beat forcefully or the weaving will become too dense and heavy to be a scarf. Aim for about 16 "picks" (rows) per inch, or "16 ppi." Check your weaving often for consistent beat. Learn to recognize when areas look compressed (beaten too hard) or spaced apart (not beaten hard enough). Read about "worming" in the box.
- Advance the warp often during weaving—about every 2". It will keep the quality of weaving more consistent. Read below.
- Watch out for inconsistent beating-in of the wefts and flaws that might appear. Consider going back and unweaving a few rows, if necessary. You may be glad you did so later on. Read how to unweave on page 321.

Worming

Chenille in French means caterpillar. Chenille fabric has a tendency to "worm," which means that its threads seem to work themselves out of the cloth and look like snags. There's nothing you can do if this happens except to poke the loops through to the back of the cloth. The problem is that the cloth was woven too loosely. To avoid worming, be sure always to beat in chenille wefts close enough (about 16 rows per inch).

Read about flaws you might encounter and how to correct them beginning on page 108.

Ending a weft thread and starting a new one

A good way to change chenille weft thread is to let the old thread end somewhere in the middle of the weaving because it eliminates any cut ends from showing at the edges and helps prevent them from worming out. Leave it placed diagonally in the shed and go wind the new bobbin or shuttle. Open up the same shed as before. Throw the shuttle in the same direction you were going before, allowing the two tail ends to overlap each other by about 3 or more inches. See Figure 410. Beat normally—this juncture is not likely to be noticeable. Later, you can cut off the little ends, if they happen to stick up.

Other ways to change wefts for other types of wefts are described on pages 115 and 131.

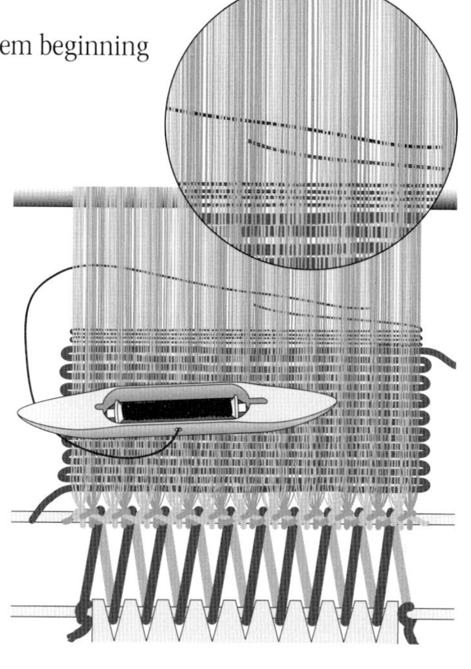

Fig. 410

Advance the weaving forward

When you have woven more than halfway between the breast beam and the beater, you will notice that the shed becomes smaller. The angle for throwing a diagonal line is also becoming flatter. It is time to stop and advance the weaving forward. Check your loom instructions, but in general, you must release tension slightly at the front brake, before releasing tension at the back brake. This action prevents the warp beam from jumping suddenly and starting to spin. After releasing the front brake, unwind a little bit of warp at the warp beam (at the back) and then, engage the ratchet brake at the front of the loom and advance the warp forward by winding up the cloth beam (at the front). Stop when the edge of the cloth (the fell) nears the breast beam. Test to see if you've brought the warp too far forward by swinging the beater towards you to make sure it makes contact with the fell. If you advanced too far, simply release the front break and wind backwards a bit by winding up the warp beam.

Fine-tune the tension by gently strumming the warp and tightening it by one increment at a time at the front with the ratchet brake on the cloth beam or at the back with the friction or ratchet brake on the warp beam. If you have a friction brake, simply turn the warp beam's brake crank until the tension is correct. You want the tension of the warp to be firm to taut, but not tight.

Further instructions are given in, "Advancing the Warp," on page 114.

Checking your place (How to tell which shed is next)

Often, you're not sure which shed is the next one—especially when you start up again.

First, open any shed.

If the weft is loose, (it will form the diagonal as in Figure 411), it has already been woven in that shed. Then, beat, return the beater toward the heddles, and change to the new shed.

If the weft is tight (cannot be moved as in Figure 412), the shed is ready for the next weft. (The weft has not yet been woven in that shed.) Then, enter the shuttle and continue weaving.

If you make a mistake and put a weft into a shed that has already been woven, the previous weft will unweave—it is another way to check your place.

Note: Until the sequence of weaving motions is complete (throw, beat, change the shed), the weft doesn't stay locked in place in the shed it was woven in.

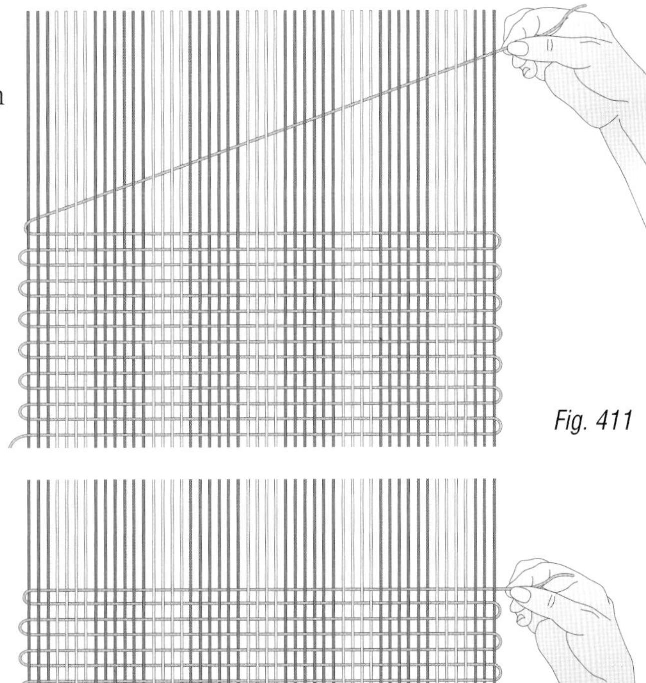

Fig. 411

Fig. 412

Measuring as you go

After a few inches of weaving with the chenille weft, pin the 60" strip of adding machine tape to the side of your scarf, with 3 horizontally placed straight pins, to keep track of your progress See Figure 413. When you need to move the pin closest to you, "leap frog" it over the other pins and place it near the edge (fell) of the cloth. Using 3 pins keeps the tape from slipping and sliding so you can be accurate. The tape does not get rolled in with the cloth on the cloth beam. Plan to weave the chenille for 60", and finish with 6" of rag strips, as in the beginning.

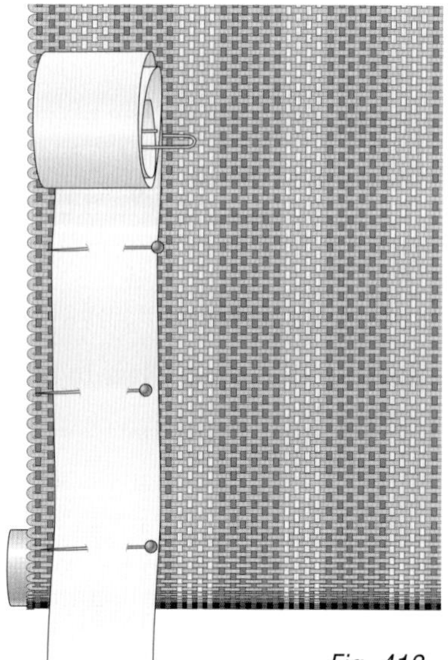

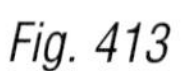

Fig. 413

What if a warp thread breaks?

In your weaving life, you are likely to encounter a broken warp thread now and then. Read what to do on page 322 in the Troubleshooting chapter.

Ending the scarf

Weave rags for fringe

Reminder: After you've woven 60" with the chenille weft thread, weave 8" of rag strips for fringe, just like at the beginning.

Cut off the warp

Reduce the tension on the warp a bit, not so it sags, but so it is not taut anymore. You can do it by releasing the tension at the cloth beam or at the warp beam. Then, ***at the back of the loom***, cut one-inch worth of warps at one edge of the warp ***as close to the apron rod as you can. Make sure you do not cut the apron cords that belong to the loom.*** Cutting as far from the heddles as possible means you have flexibility when determining the fringe length. Later in your weaving life, you may not plan on a very long fringe, but you never can tell what creative thoughts might come up when you see the cloth off the loom, so allow for any possibility by cutting the yarns as long as they can be.

Working now at the front of the loom, pull that inch-worth of threads towards the cloth—pulling them through the heddles and reed. Then, tie the threads in a temporary knot at the fell, so the last weft cannot come out. Use just the beginning part of a shoelace knot. See Figure 297 on page 130, and repeated here.

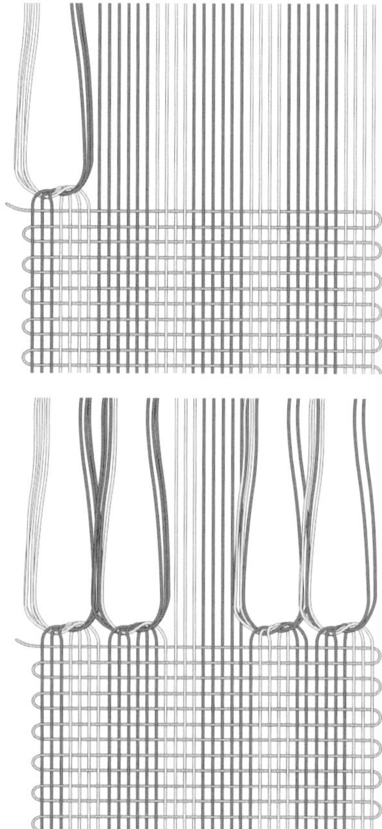

Continue the process by cutting the next inch worth at the ***opposite edge*** of the warp at the back of the loom. Work from the edges toward the middle in this way, alternating from side to side. The final group of threads should be the center warp threads. See Figure 298 repeated here.

Remove the cloth at the front

Unroll the cloth and untie the surgeon's knots at the beginning of the warp so you can remove the cloth from the loom. You can untie the knots working from one edge to the other because the warp is not under tension. If it looks like the first row of rags strips will come out, tie temporary knots as above to hold the rag weft in its place. Now, the cloth is ready for the next steps: "finishing."

Finishing a rayon chenille scarf

See the finishing chapter beginning on page 137 for how to finish cloth not made with chenille yarn.

A detailed chapter about finishing various fibers and types of cloth is in my third book, ***Weaving & Drafting Your Own Cloth***, beginning on page 157.

After it is cut off the loom, the chenille scarf is not usually instantly attractive—sorry! It will likely feel stiff, like cardboard, and may even appear crushed in places. Never fear—it is not yet "finished." To finish the scarf it must be washed so that the threads relax into place and shrink slightly. This is normal.

Repair any flaws you notice

Check the scarf to see if you notice any flaws that stand out and disfigure your cloth. Read about making repairs beginning on page 139. This job should be done before washing.

Prepare for washing

Be sure your rag strips will stay intact during washing and drying. It is to protect the fringe, which could otherwise get worn or tangled in the process. Sew across the rags by machine or by hand. Use a wide basting stitch, using a sewing machine, as shown in Figure 414, or sew the edge by hand with an overcast stitch as shown in Figure 415. Do it at each end of the scarf.

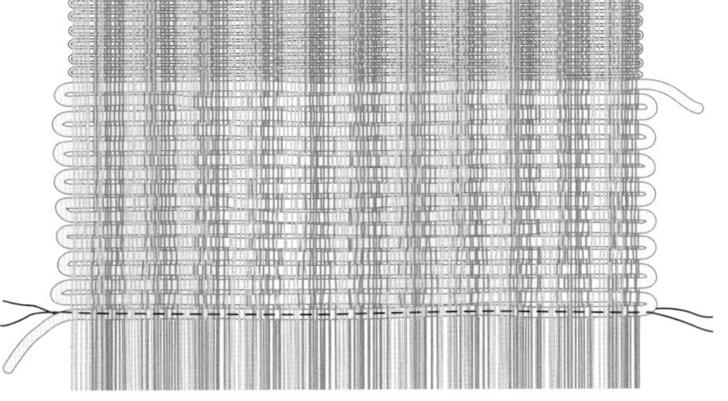

Fig. 414

Now, cut off and discard the excess warp threads next to the stitching on the rags at both ends of the scarf. There is a name for these short pieces of warp threads: ***thrums***.

Optional: at this point, you might also choose to sew a zigzag stitch across the fell (where the fabric meets the woven rags) with matching thread. Do this last step, especially, if you do not plan to tie, twist, or braid the fringe. However, note that, over time, with friction and wear, the fuzzy chenille is likely to disintegrate, leaving only the core threads—not very attractive for all of your hard work. Braiding or twisting the ends helps to protect and preserve them. Read about fringes next.

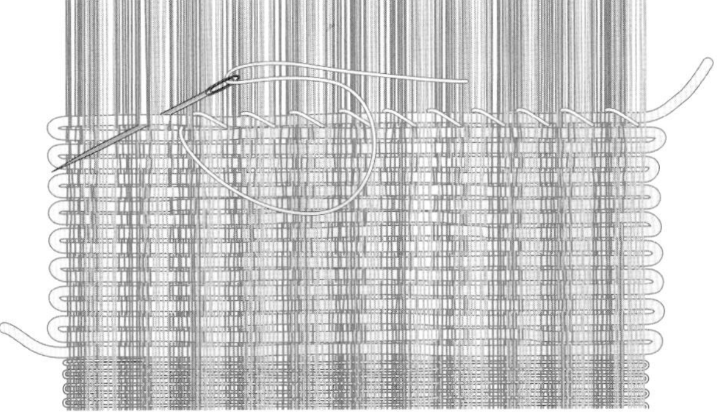

Fig. 415

Wash the scarf

Submerge the scarf in room temperature water, just to wet it through. It can be done in the sink or a dishpan, but is easily done in a washing machine. If you are using a washing machine, first, fill the tub. Then, without any agitating, simply set the machine for a short spin cycle. (Roll the scarf in bath towels gently to remove excess water if not using a machine.) Place the damp scarf into the dryer and tumble-dry for about 30 minutes on medium heat, checking halfway through to shake out and untwist the scarf. If the scarf is still damp, I always put it back in the dryer if I want it to be nice and soft. The heat helps to soften and fluff up the chenille. You can hang it up to dry, too, but the heat from the dryer makes it softer.

Afterwards, remove the rag strips. You can tie a row of overhand knots across the fringe to secure the first and last wefts in the cloth, or better yet, twist or braid the threads into bundles and then knot them. See below how to make knotted and twisted fringe.

Knotted fringe

Fringe can be knotted with overhand knots made up close to the last woven weft. Gradually undo the rags, protecting the last weft as you work along the edge so that the last chenille weft doesn't wander out before you get there. Practice with different size bundles for the knots.

Figures 416 a and b show how to make the knots. To get the knots up close to the last weft, keep them loose by putting a tapestry needle or something similar in the loop of the knot as you move the knot right up until it's snug against the weft. (Pull the tails of the warp threads with one hand, hold the needle with the other, and push the needle up close to the weft as you pull). Then, remove the needle and tighten the knot in place.

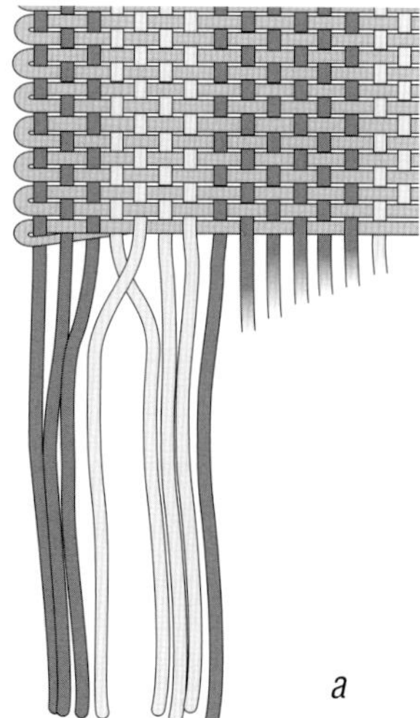

Fig. 416

Twisted fringe

Figures 417 a and b show how to make twisted fringe. Basically, you'll take two warp threads or two groups of threads and twist them separately in one direction. Keep twisting them until they begin to kink up on themselves. Then put these two groups together by holding them next to each other and twisting them together in the opposite direction. This time you may not have to do very much twisting—or none at all; they will tend to twist on themselves.

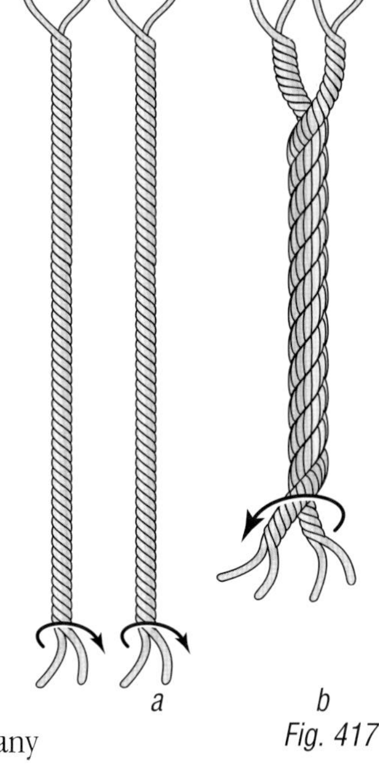

Fig. 417

To make this job much easier, put a heavy phone book or weight on the scarf while you work on the fringes.

Then, knot the ends with an overhand knot (see above) in the following manner. Before tightening the knot, put a tapestry needle in the loop and slide the loop up to where you want the knot to be at the end of the fringe. Remove the tapestry needle and tighten the knot. Then, tie all the remaining knots to match the length of the first fringe so your fringes will all be perfectly the same length. Trim off the excess threads beyond the knots.

Experiment with the number of threads in each group and with how many twists work best.

A fringe twister as shown in Figure 418 can speed up the process a lot. Figures 419 a and b show how it works. Another tool is a battery-operated device for twisting hair. They are available where hair supplies are sold. Fringe twisters are available from weaving supply shops listed in the Sources section, beginning on page 382.

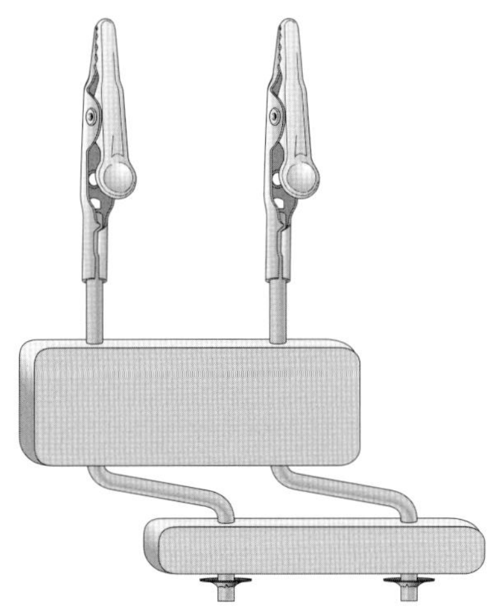
Fig. 418

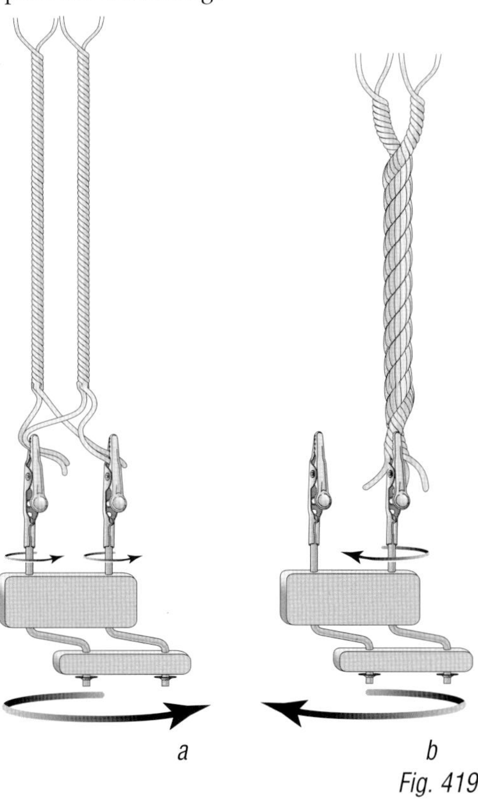

Fig. 419

More About the Front-to-Back Method

I. Measuring wider warps on the warping board

Ideally, never let the warp accumulate more than about 1 ½" from the base of the pegs on the warping board. If you do, the pegs are likely to bend, resulting in uneven lengths of warp. When you have 1 ½"of warp, it's time to tie the choke ties on the warp, and snug bow ties at the cross. Take the warp section off the warping board in a chain or on a kitestick. Then make another section of your warp, using the original guide string so it matches the first section. Make as many sections (called bouts) as you need to make the full width of the warp. Each bout will be in a separate chain or on a separate kitestick.

II. Sley the reed on a table instead of at the loom

You can use this method whether you hold the cross in your hand or use the alternative of putting the cross in lease sticks—see below.

Take the reed to a table and put the marker strings on the reed as described on page 160 and shown in Figure 346 repeated here.

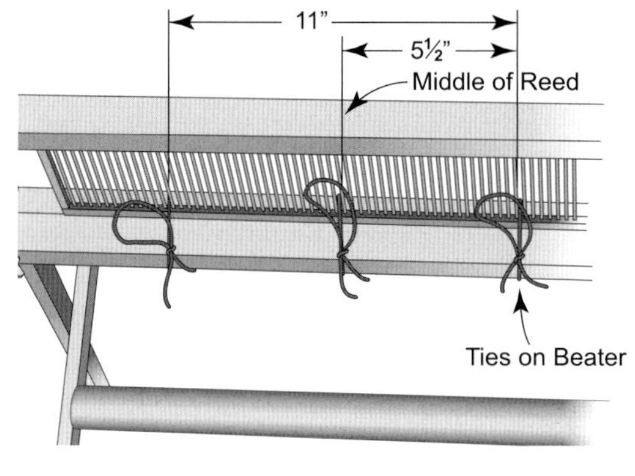

Prop up the reed securely by putting it in reed holders (Figures 420 a and b). (Homemade holders are described in the box.)

Sley the reed as described on page 165 doing the process at a table rather than at the loom.

After the sleying is finished, remove the lease sticks, if you used them, and put the reed into the beater and tie the special choke tie around the breast beam, or wrap the warp around it, as described on page 193. In some instances, you would not remove the lease sticks at this point—when more than two threads are in a dent—see page 193.

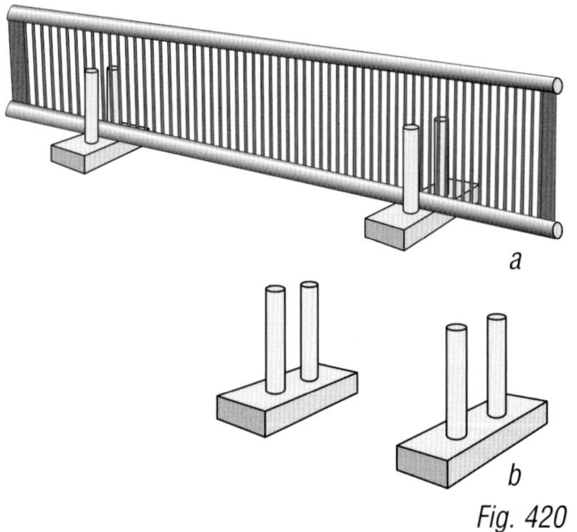

Fig. 420

Homemade reed holders are shown in Figures 420a and b. You can drill holes in soft wood and glue in short dowels (approximately ¼" diameter and 3-4" long). Space them apart so reeds fit in fairly snuggly.

III. Use lease sticks to hold the cross instead of your hand

If you use lease sticks rather than holding the cross in your hand, you'll have both hands to work with. You can do this job on a table (see page 190) or at the loom as described here. How to put in the lease sticks is on page 192

After putting the warp's cross onto the lease sticks, continue the process at "Thread the Reed," beginning on page 165.

Preliminaries

Cut 2 sturdy cords the length of the distance from the back beam to the breast beam plus about 15". This cord will need to handle a lot of stress so be sure it is very strong. Be sure that it is thin enough to go through the holes of the lease sticks.

Tie one end of each cord onto the back beam (one on each side) as shown in Figure 421. Push all the heddles to the center of the shafts and bring each cord through the shafts area between the heddles and the sides of the shafts.

Guide the cords through the beater by the outsides of the reed so that they can be supported by the shuttle race on the beater at the base of the reed as shown.

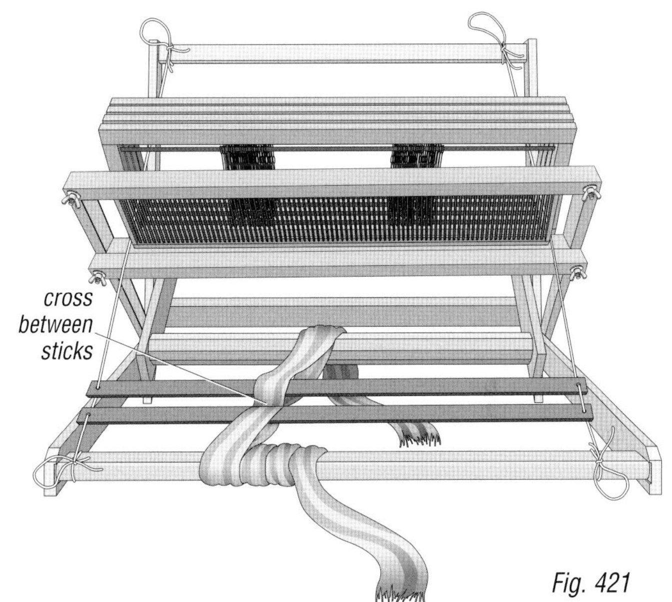

Fig. 421

Tie the lease sticks in place on one side

Thread the cord of one side through the holes in the ends of the lease sticks. Make it go up through the hole in one of the sticks and down in the hole of the other stick as seen in the illustration. Then, tie the cord onto the front beam using a slipknot so that the cord is taut. It should be really tight. Using a slip-knot to tie the cord makes it easy to untie and re-use the next time you warp.

Put the cross onto the lease sticks

You'll be inserting the lease sticks in the places where the cross pegs were on the warping board. It's easy to find the exact place by separating the warp where the cross ties are. If you pull the sets of ties apart from each other slightly, you will see the spaces to insert the two sticks. See Figures 422 a and b.

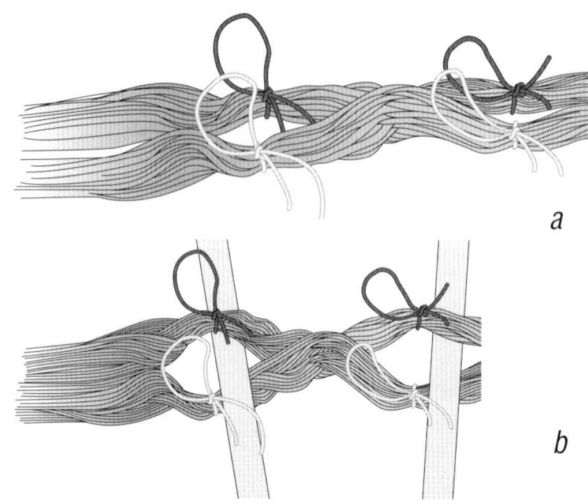

Fig. 422

Slide the cross onto the lease sticks.

Once the cross is on the sticks, turn them so at the tied end the sticks lie flat and butt up against one another. Hold the sticks in that position and thread the second cord through the holes in the other end of the lease sticks as shown in the illustration (Figure 421). If the first cord went down through the first hole and then up through the second stick's hole, make the second cord go up and then down through the holes. By threading the cords in the opposite way from one another, the sticks will be forced to stay flat. See the illustration.

Tie the second cord onto the breast beam

Make sure the cord is taut.

Note that the shorter end of the warp is on the side of the lease sticks near the reed, and the bulk of the warp is resting on the breast beam.

Untie the cross ties

Untie all the ties that you made on the warping board (see page 160) as seen in Figure 423. Figure 424 shows the cross on the lease sticks, now without the ties.

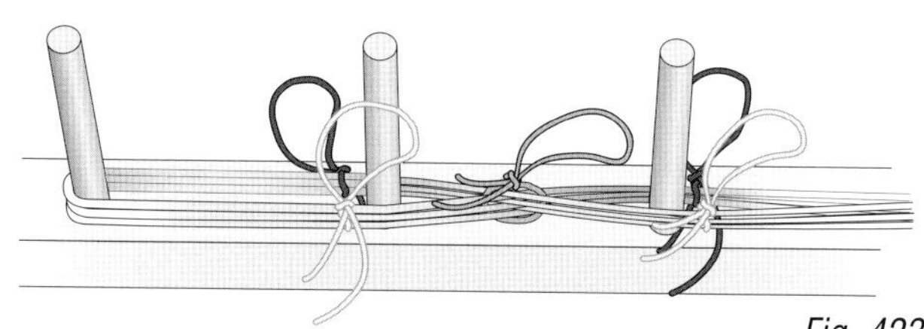
Fig. 423

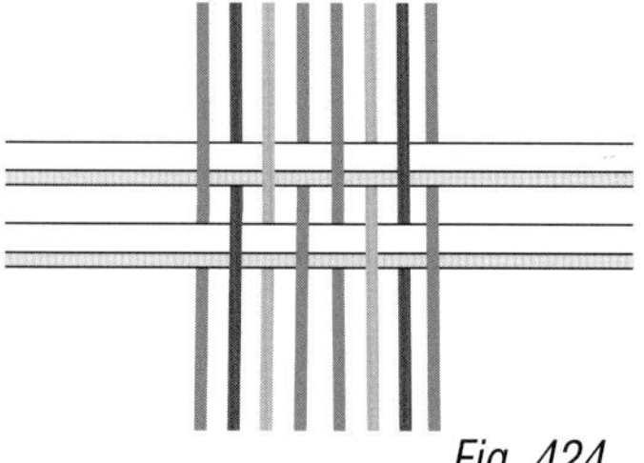
Fig. 424

Position the cross

There must be enough warp beyond the lease sticks to sley the reed, thread the heddles, and tie on to the warp beam apron. Figure 340 on page 159 shows this schematically. The lease sticks are to be at the point where the special choke tie was tied on the warping board, seen in Figure 341 on page 159. If the loop at the end of the warp is too close to the lease sticks, see how to move the cross on page 29.

Attach the warp chain to the breast beam

Either wrap the warp chain around the breast beam several times as seen in Figure 421 or tie the big choke tie around the breast beam as described on page 163.

Wrapping the warp instead is described next.

IV. Wrapping the chain on the breast beam

Wrap the warp chain several times around the breast beam as shown in Figure 421. This technique is another way to prevent you from pulling one thread more than another when threading the reed and heddles. Some weavers feel it is more secure than tying the warp to the breast beam with a choke tie as described on page 163.

Next, thread the reed, beginning on page 165.

V. When more than two threads are in a space (dent)

Ideally, no more than 2 threads should be in a space (dent) in the reed, but there are times when you need to substitute another reed for the one which allows you to put in 2 threads per dent. See the Reed Substitution Chart on page 33.

In that case, the optimum solution is to put lease sticks into the cross when threading the reed. This process is explained above. See Figure 421.
I recommend doing this job at the loom rather than at a table because of the next task to be done, which is to transfer the lease sticks (and thus the cross) to the other side of the reed for threading the heddles. Read on.

This method is needed because when 3 or more threads are together they will braid or knot up on themselves and cause unwanted tangles. Two threads can be together and will stay separate and unknotted. This braiding or tangling occurs as the threads come out of the chain and pass through the reed during beaming.

VI. Transferring the cross

Many weavers never need to do this procedure—because the threads don't tangle terribly in front of the reed while beaming on the warp. But, if you have more than two threads in a dent in the reed, it is ideal to transfer the cross to the other side of the reed so you can thread the heddles in the exact order as the reed was sleyed.

Transferring the lease sticks (and thus the cross) to the other side of the reed is easy—and I think is very satisfying to do.

Then, you can thread the heddles from the cross in the lease sticks.

You need an extra stick for this operation.

After the reed is threaded, to transfer the cross, start on the side of the reed where the lease sticks are in place. Untie any ties holding the lease sticks in place or together. Turn the stick that is closer to the reed on its side, (the stick then makes a little shed). Push this stick right up flat against the reed. See the shed that has opened on the other side of the reed? Insert an extra stick through that shed. In Figures 425 a and b, a round dowel is shown in the new shed on the other side of the reed so you can tell it from the original lease stick. Remove the lease stick that you stood on edge at the reed. In the same manner: put the second stick up flat against the reed to form the little shed on the other side of the reed and put a new stick into this shed.

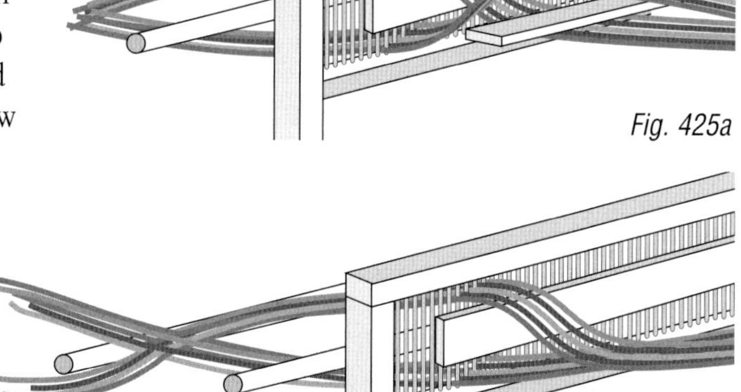

Fig. 425a

Fig. 425b

Remove the last original lease stick, and now, you should have a pair of sticks on the opposite side of the reed from where the original pair of sticks was.

For clarity, round dowels are shown being put in place on the other side of the reed. They would be replaced by the regular lease sticks after they have been removed from the original side of the reed. If you used the two holding cords as shown in Figure 421, tie the lease sticks (now behind the reed) to the holding cords so they will be in position for threading the heddles. If you didn't use the cords, tie the lease sticks together at the ends about 1" apart so that the warp won't fall out. Tie the sticks (now behind the reed) to the sides or legs of the loom in a position that keeps them stable and so you can easily see the cross when you thread the heddles.

VII. An alternative to using rags in the heading

Many weavers prefer not to use rags for the heading. Read about using regular weft thread under the section, "Spread out the Warps," on page 107.

7 *Drafting*

In this chapter, you will learn how to read drafts for the weaves in the sampler as well as in weaving books, magazines, and on line.

Comprehensive chapters on weave drafting, fabric analysis and the basics of multi-shaft weaving are in my third book, *Weaving & Drafting Your Own Cloth*. This chapter gives you the basics to get started.

Note: For beginning weavers only—the drafting information you need for now ends on page 204.

Knowing how to read weave drafts and write your own is enormously satisfying and is a tremendously important part of weaving and designing, but it is not the only part to know. What drafts don't tell is anything about the yarns, colors, ends per inch (epi), the beat or the wefts per inch (ppi), for instance. When you read directions for a project in a book or magazine, you must read every word that is written about the project. All that information is crucial to reproducing what the directions are for. Critical information might be given for washing or sewing or fringing the project—there are just too many givens to list them here. Just heed my words and read the text as well as the draft. Also, pay close attention to any photographs or graphics.

How drafts are written

Figure 426 shows the configuration for the four quadrants in weave drafts. Notice that there are thick, dark lines that divide the whole draft into its four parts.

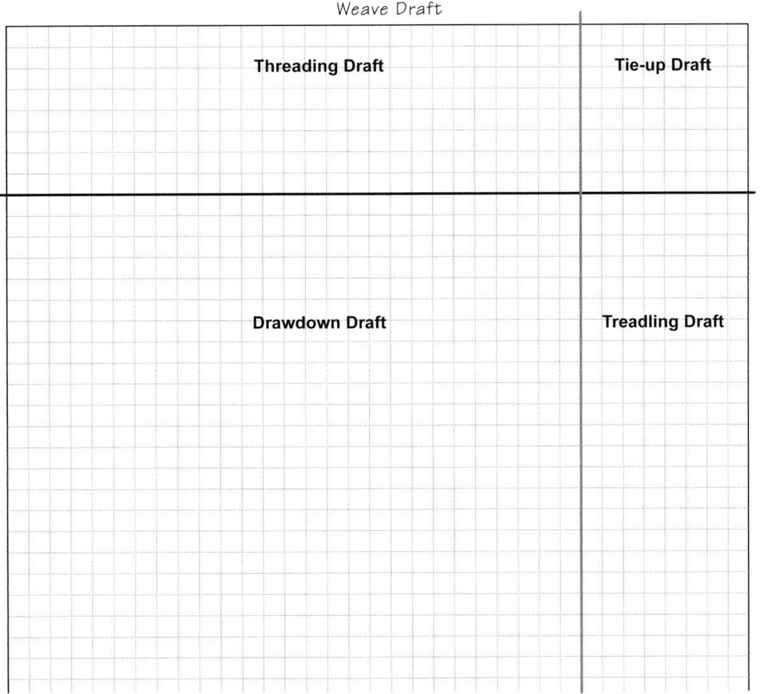

Fig. 426

Reading Drafts

Reading the drafts is easy once you learn how. See Figure 427 and notice all the arrows. Each section is read starting at the dark solid lines dividing the quadrants. It means that sometimes, you read right-to-left and sometimes, vice-versa. Sometimes, you read from the top down and other times from the bottom up. You can follow the arrows and see that they work outward from the dividing lines.

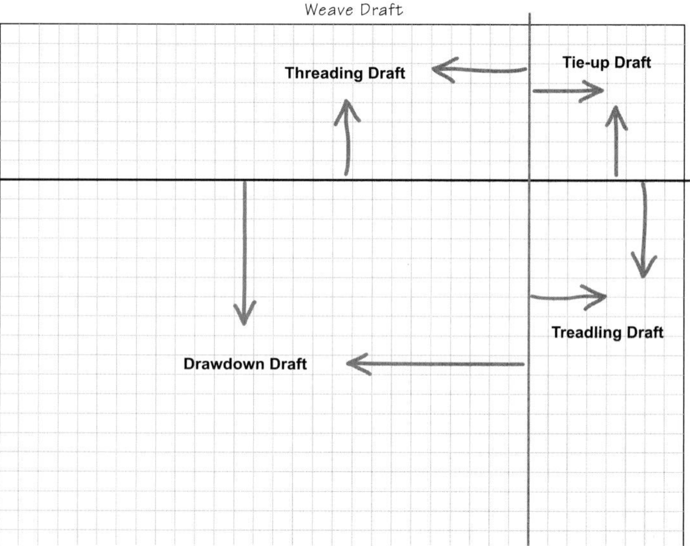

Fig. 427

For example, the Threading Draft begins on the right and ends on the left and also is read from the bottom of the quadrant to the top. Looking at the Treadling Draft, see that it begins at the top of that section and also on the left edge of it.

Look to see how the other parts are read now, to become familiar with the system. How is the Tie-up Draft read? (Left-to-right, bottom–to-top). How is the Drawdown Draft read? (Top-to-bottom and right-to-left).

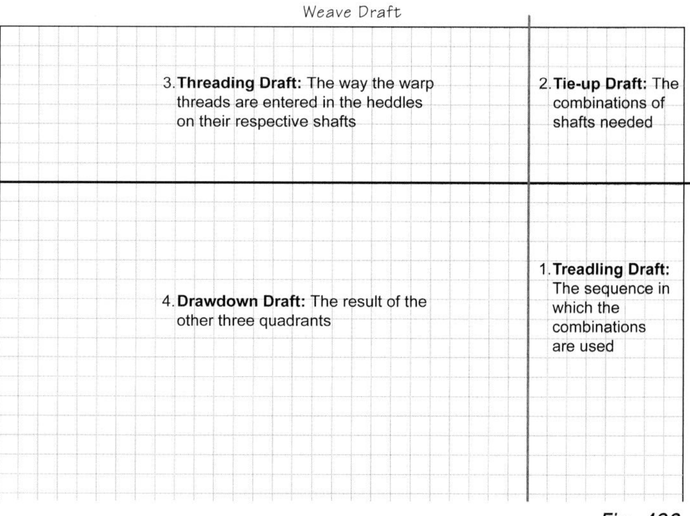

Fig. 428

I usually don't say to myself right-to-left, etc. I just picture the arrows and work my way outward from the lines. Once this simple concept is understood, you won't be confused by right-to-left, etc.

Figure 428 gives the definitions of what each quadrant's function is. You don't need to worry about remembering the definitions; you can always refer to the illustration. You'll learn them sooner than you might think.

Note: Shafts are often called harnesses, but "shaft" is the correct term.

How to read drafts

Figure 429 shows schematically how two parts of the draft—the threading draft and the drawdown draft—relate to one another.[1]

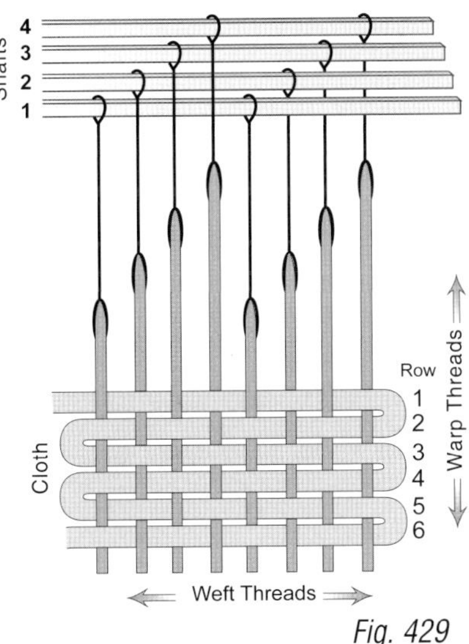

Fig. 429

The threading draft

The upper part of the illustration shows shafts with "heddles" threaded with warp threads. It is represented in the upper left quadrant of the weave draft chart, and is called the threading draft. Note that shaft 1 is on the bottom (this is always the case in American books) and shafts 2, 3, and 4 follow, going upward. Refer to the arrows in Figure 427 and see that the threading draft should be read from the bottom-to-the top and from right-to-left. In Figure 429, the first warp thread (on the right, remember) is threaded on shaft 4. The second thread is on shaft 3; the next on 2, and the fourth thread is on shaft 1. It is the same way the sampler was threaded as shown on page 66 in the threading chapter.

The drawdown draft

The drawdown in weave drafts represents (schematically) what the weave structure will look like in the cloth. In Figure 429 the "cloth" area represents the drawdown quadrant in weave drafts. In the illustration you can see that sometimes, a warp is on top of a weft and sometimes, the weft is on top. (Warp threads are shown as vertical lines and wefts are horizontal lines.)

Remember from the arrows in Figure 427 that the top row in drawdown drafts indicates the first row to be woven. Now look at Figure 429 at the first row of the cloth. See that all the warp threads on shafts 1 and 3 are on top of the weft thread and, therefore, were lifted by those shafts.

Now, look at the drawdown quadrant in the draft for plain weave, or tabby in Figure 430. The warps that are to be lifted are indicated as filled-in squares. In the first row, two squares are filled in. Look up above them and see that they are under shafts 1 and 3 in the threading draft. In the second row, see that shafts 2 and 4 are lifted.

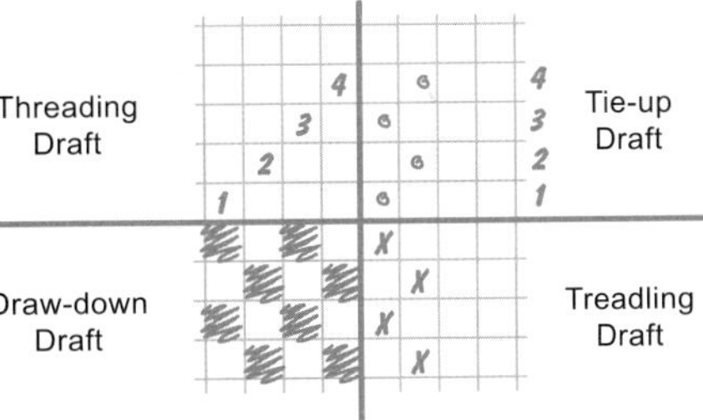

Fig. 430

You have seen that all the weaves in the sampler (pages 111-128) have the same threading, but the cloths look different. Look at the photographs at the beginning of each part of the sampler and see that the photographs show in real life what the weaves are to look like. Now look at the weave drafts next to the photos and see that the drawdown quadrant schematically represents the weaves. As I said above, when a warp thread is to be raised, it is shown as a filled-in square in the drawdown draft. Look on page 111 and see the photo for plain weave (also called tabby) and notice the drawdown draft beside the photograph which shows plain weave cloth schematically.

> *Remember, warp threads that are lifted are indicated on weave drafts as filled-in squares.*

[1] Adapted from: Sutton, Ann; Collingwood, Peter; St Aubyn Hubbard, Geraldine; *The Craft of the Weaver*, Lark Books, Asheville, NC, 1983, p. 89.

Drafts in the sampler

Look at the threading drafts for all the weaves for the sampler in Figure 431. Notice that they are all the same—reading outward from the vertical line separating the threading and tie-up drafts the threading is always "4, 3, 2, 1" (first warp is threaded on shaft 4, next on shaft 3, and so on. Now that you have threaded the heddles yourself, you can understand why all the threading drafts in the sampler are the same. To change the threading, you would have to cut the warp threads and re-thread—the sampler uses one threading to weave a variety of weave structures. Directions for weaving the sampler begin on page 111.

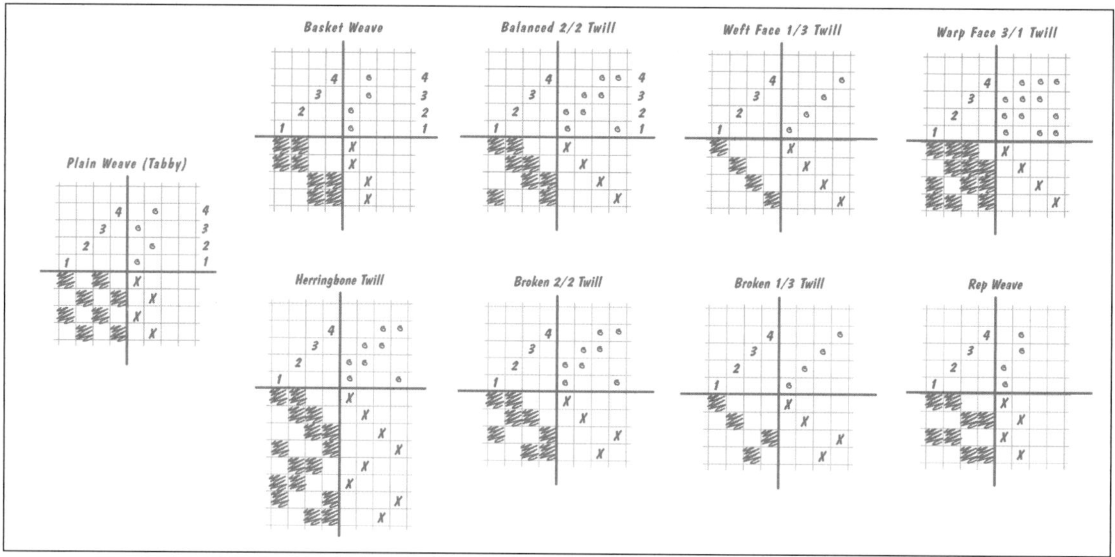

Fig. 431

How are different weaves shown?

So, how do you know what to do to get different weaves? This information is given in the remaining two quadrants of weave drafts. The tie-up draft quadrant shows all the combinations of shafts that will be used for a weave. The treadling draft quadrant shows the order these combinations are to be used.

> Some older books write the tie-up in the opposite way—what is indicated is for shafts to be lowered. A popular book written this way is: Davison, Marguerite Porter. *A Handweaver's Pattern Book*. Swarthmore, PA: Marguerite P. Davison Publisher, 1944.
>
> Read what to do on page 121.

Tie-up draft

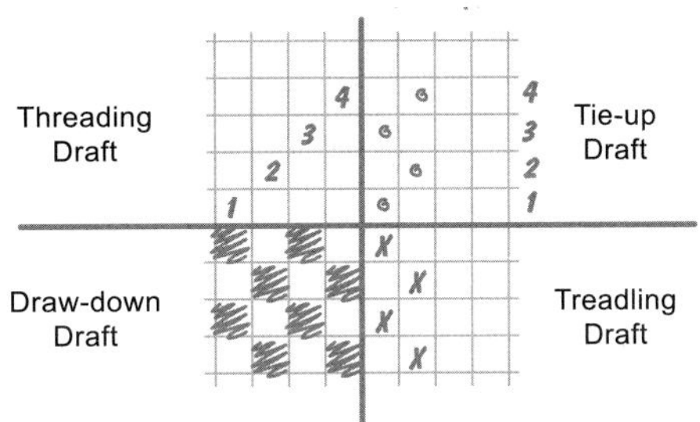

The tie-up draft for plain weave shown in Figure 430 (repeated here) is the quadrant in the upper right corner, and it shows the combinations of shafts that are to be lifted. For a different view of a tie-up draft, refer to the book listed in the box on the previous page. Remember when weaving plain weave in the sampler, you raised two shafts together—not one at a time? Shafts 1 and 3 were lifted together, and then the combination of shafts 2 and 4 was lifted.

You read the quadrant as per the arrows shown in Figure 427 on page 196—left-to-right and bottom-to-top. Notice that there are circles in the squares—these represent shafts that are to be lifted. I think of the circles as bubbles because bubbles rise, and they indicate shafts to be raised. The first column in the tie-up section has two bubbles in it: on the bottom row (shaft one), and on the third row (shaft 3).The first combination of shafts to be lifted, therefore, is shafts 1 and 3. Go to the next column to the right, and you can see that the second combination is shafts 2 and 4. The bottom row in tie-up drafts indicates shaft 1 just as it does in the threading draft. (Often, the shafts are not indicated in tie-up drafts—it is assumed that you know that the bottom row represents shaft 1.)

The treadling draft

The treadling draft shows the order to use the combinations given. Just knowing the combinations is not enough; you need to know the sequence in which they should be used in order to achieve the results shown in the drawdown draft.

To read treadling drafts, locate the X in the row of weaving you are about to weave, then look above that X in the tie-up draft and see the combination of shafts that is shown above the X. The combination of shafts to be lifted is indicated by the small circles (bubbles). Remember, the arrows in Figure 427 show that treadling drafts are to be read from the top down.

Looking at the draft (Figure 430) again, see the X for the first row of weaving. Look up above the X in the tie-up draft and see that the X is under the combination of shafts 1 and 3. Now look at the X in the next row in the sequence shown in the treadling draft and see above it in the tie-up draft that shafts 2 and 4 are to be lifted. See that the third and fourth rows in the treadling draft repeat the first two rows.

When reading a draft while weaving, begin reading in the treadling draft.

And that's how drafts are read. Begin in the treadling draft for the row (weft) you are ready to weave. Then, look up above the X to see what combination is to be used.

Notice that the tie-up and treadling drafts for plain weave indicate exactly the same as the words and numbers under "Sequence of Sheds for Plain Weave" (see page 111). Both ways indicate the same thing: lift shafts 1 and 3 alternately with shafts 2 and 4.

Reading the draft for basket weave

The draft for basket weave is shown in Figure 432. Look at the tie-up draft and see that the two combinations of shafts to be lifted to form this weave are 1 and 2, and 3 and 4. If you look on page 118, you'll see that the words under "Sequence of Sheds for Basket Weave" indicate that the combinations to be lifted are 1 and 2, and 3 and 4—exactly the same as those shown in the tie-up quadrant of the draft.

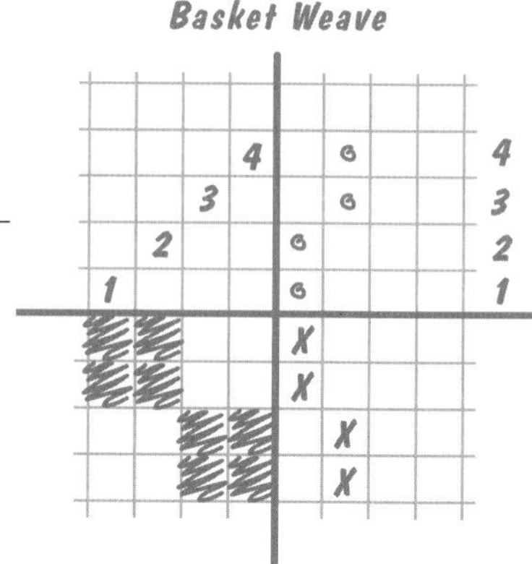

Fig. 432

The treadling draft for basket weave, shows the order to use those combinations. For the first two rows lift shafts 1 and 2, and then lift shafts 3 and 4 for two rows. See how to weave two rows in the same shed without unweaving them on page 118.

What makes basket weave look different from plain weave and like the photograph and drawdown on page 118 is that the tie-up and treadling drafts are different from those for plain weave.

Reading other drafts in the sampler

Balanced twill is shown in Figure 433 and also on page 119. Remember, the threading draft will continue the same as for the whole sampler. The drawdown draft shows some diagonals indicated by filled-in squares. The photograph on page 119 shows actual diagonal lines.

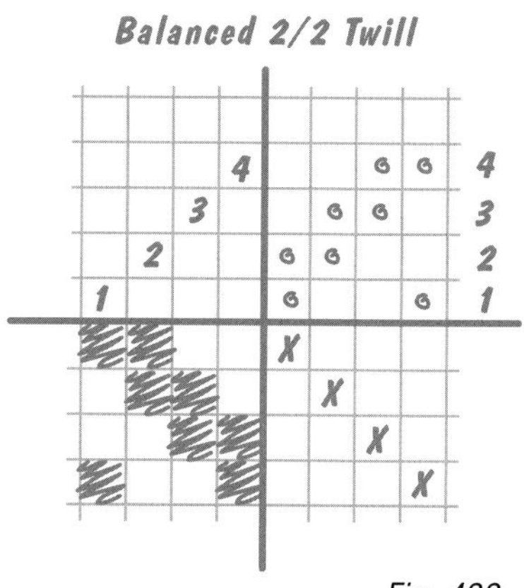

Fig. 433

Now, beginning in the treadling draft the top line indicates the first row of weaving. The X is under the combination in the tie-up draft of shafts 1 and 2. This tells you to lift shafts 1 and 2 and throw the shuttle for that row. Now, look down in the treadling draft for the next row to weave—see that the X is under the combination of shafts 2 and 3. The third row tells you to lift shafts 3 and 4 and the fourth row 1 and 4. See on page 119 that the draft compares exactly with the words given in the "Sequence of Sheds for Balanced Twill."

Weft-faced twill is shown in Figure 434 and on page 120. Beginning in the treadling draft as usual, see that the first row's X is under shaft 1 in the tie-up draft—not a combination at all, but a single shaft to be lifted alone. See that for this weave only one shaft is to be lifted at a time and the sequence seen in the treadling draft is to lift shaft 1, then shaft 2, then 3, then 4. This also makes a diagonal line which can be seen both in the photograph and in the drawdown draft on page 120.

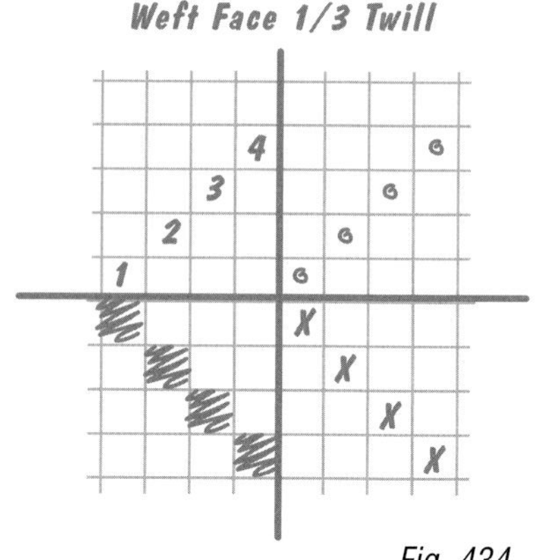

Fig. 434

Warp-face 3/1 twill is the next to weave in the sampler. See Figure 435 and page 122. Now 3 shafts will be lifted at one time for each weft. Shafts 1,2,3 then 2,3,4, then 3,4,1, and lastly, 4,1,2.

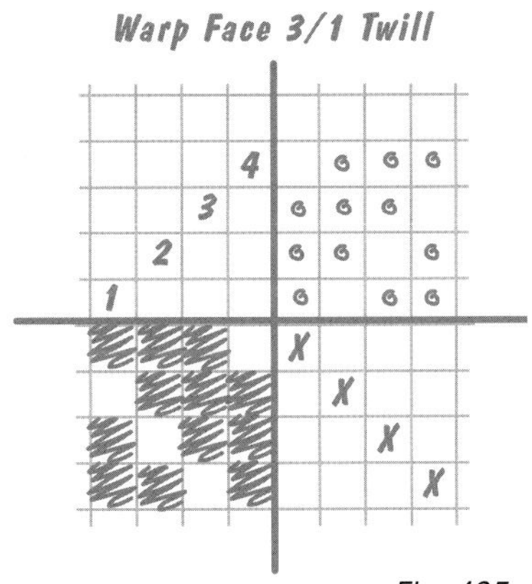

Fig. 435

Test yourself with herringbone

See Figure 436 and page 123. Notice that there are 8 rows in one repeat of the treadling sequence for herringbone. You must weave all 8 rows before beginning the sequence again. It's hard to see in the drawdown draft, but the diagonal lines in the cloth will zig zag as you might already know from weaving herringbone in the sampler. Watch the treadling draft carefully, especially beginning with row 5.

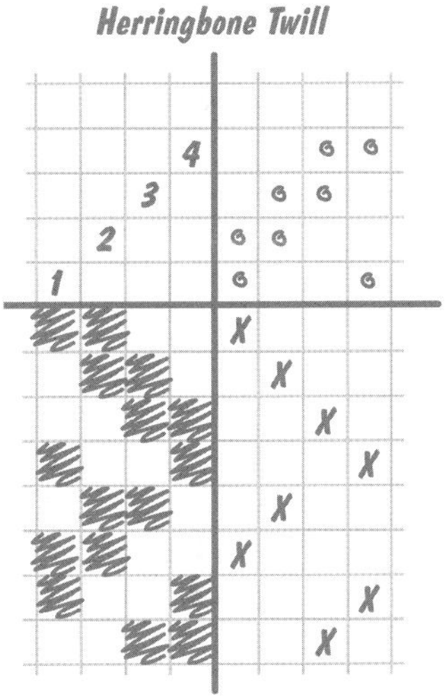

Herringbone Twill

Fig. 436

Reading the treadling sequence from the treadling draft:

Row 1: lift shafts 1, 2

Row 2: lift shafts 2, 3

Row 3: lift shafts 3, 4

Row 4: lift shafts 4, 1

Row 5: lift shafts 2, 3 — Did you watch the draft and see that 2 and 3 were next?

Row 6: lift shafts 1, 2

Row 7: lift shafts 1, 4 — Did you notice this combination was to be next?

Row 8: lift shafts 3, 4

Many of my students like this weave once they know the sequence. It proves that you understand the basics of weave drafting!!

Broken twills

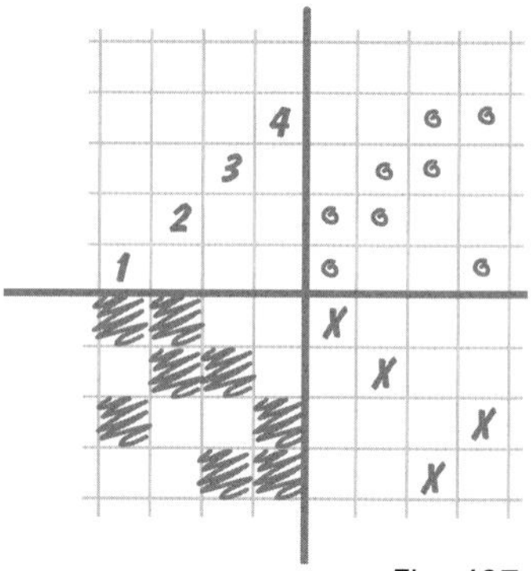

There are two broken twills to do in the sampler. They don't show the distinct diagonal lines like the other twills. It is a good weave for cloth because it is flexible just like twill weaves, but the diagonal is disguised.

Read the drafts carefully. For the ***broken 2/2 twill***, see Figure 437 and page 124. Read the treadling sequence of shafts to be lifted.

Broken 2/2 Twill

Fig. 437

Row 1: lift shafts 1, 2

Row 2: lift shafts 2, 3

Row 3: lift shafts 1, 4

Row 4: lift shafts 3, 4

Did you figure it out yourself? I hope so. If not, try to see what went wrong—many students forget that they should be following along in the ***treadling*** draft.

The ***broken 1/3 twill*** (shown in Figure 438 and on page 125) will give you another chance to check yourself that you are following the treadling draft in the correct sequence.

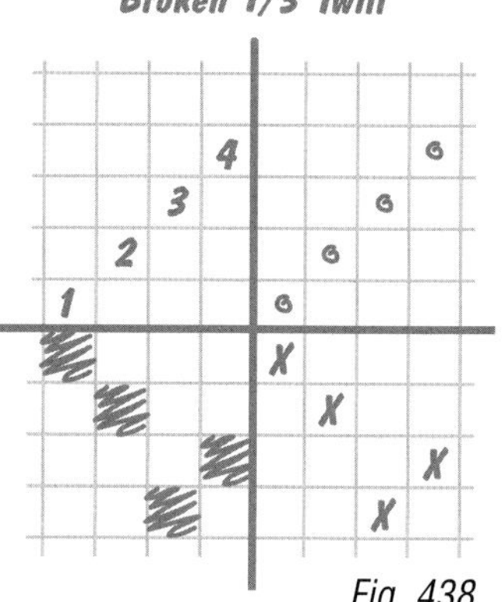

Fig. 438

Row 1: lift shaft 1

Row 2: lift shaft 2

Row 3: lift shaft 4

Row 4: lift shaft 3

I hope you have read this draft correctly.

How do the quadrants relate?

Perhaps you have already figured out the relationships between the different quadrants and the resulting weaves. Once you change any part (or parts) of a draft, the resulting cloth will change. For example, the three twills (balanced, weft-faced and warp-faced) all have the ***same treadling drafts***. What makes the weaves themselves distinct is that the ***tie-up drafts are not the same*** for each one. (The cloths differ in the amount of warp or weft that dominates the surface of the cloth. Balanced means there is an equal amount of warp and weft on the surface. Weft-faced means that the weft is predominant. Warp-faced means that the warp predominates.)

What makes herringbone and 2/2 broken twill different is that in each one, the ***treadling draft is different though the tie-ups are the same***. In other words, the same combinations of shafts are used, but the order or sequence for using them is different for each one.

Review with a completely different draft

So far, I have only used the threading called a "straight draw," which was used for the sampler. Here is a good way to look at drafting again, this time with a completely different threading.

Different weaves have different threadings, tie-ups, and treadlings and therefore, different results (drawdowns).

Figure 439 shows schematically a new threading draft and the resulting cloth.[2]

In the threading draft, instead of threading the shafts in the order 4,3,2,1, a different configuration is used. The first thread is threaded on shaft 2, the second, on shaft 1 and the third thread is threaded on shaft 2 again. To complete the threading draft the next three threads are threaded on shafts 4, 3, 4.

The resulting cloth is shown below. See the first row's weft: there are three warps on top of the weft. Look up above each of those three threads and see which shafts they are threaded on. See that the threads lifted (the threads that are on top of the weft) are on shafts 2 and 3. Two of the warps are threaded on shaft 2: when a shaft is lifted, all the threads on that shaft must go up.

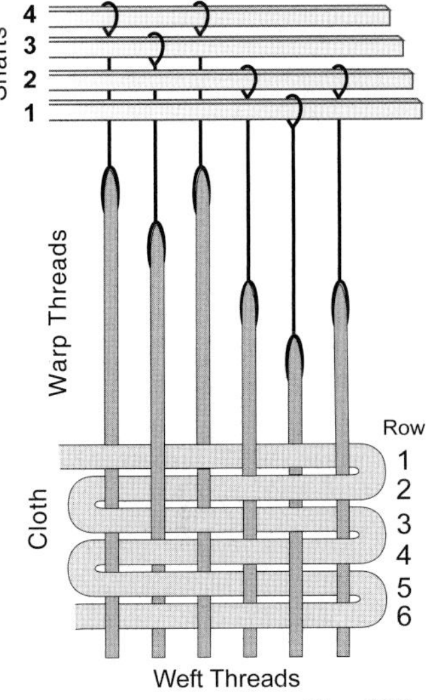

Fig. 439

Figure 440 tells us why the cloth looks as it does.

The treadling draft is the place to look first, as usual. The X in the top row represents the first row of weaving. Notice I put a tiny dot there to draw your attention to where to begin reading the draft.

Look up above the X and see what combination of shafts is indicated for that X—it is shafts 2 and 3. (We can see that shafts 2 and 3 are shown with bubbles.)

The second row in the treadling draft shows that shafts 3 and 4 should be lifted.

Looking again at the treadling draft we see that the X for the third row is under the combination of shaft 2 and 3 again.

Completing the treadling sequence from the fourth row onwards, see that 1 and 4 are lifted, then, 1 and 2 and then, 1 and 4 again.

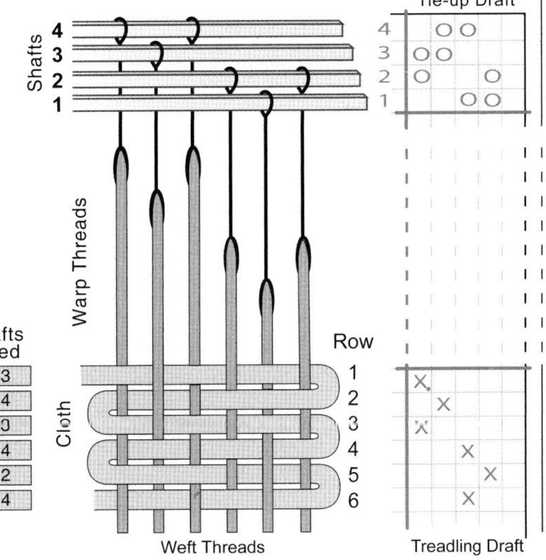

Fig. 440

If you like, you can follow the wefts in the schematic cloth and see that the warps that were lifted for each row are on top of the wefts. You can also see that the "cloth" looks completely different from any in the sampler. The reason is that all the parts of the draft are different—not just the threading, but also the treadling and tie-up.

2 Ibid.

Reading Drafts

Figure 441 shows the complete weave draft next to the schematic illustration. See what the threading draft would look like compared to the drawing. Read the draft and compare it with the "cloth" in the left part of the illustration. Can you see that in both the draft and in the "cloth" on the left, shafts 2 and 3 were lifted for the first row of weaving? Check yourself again. What is indicated for the last row in the sequence? Shafts 1 and 4 are indicated. In the cloth, look at the last row and follow the warps that are on top of the weft up to the shaft area. See that those threads in the cloth are threaded on shafts 1 and 4.

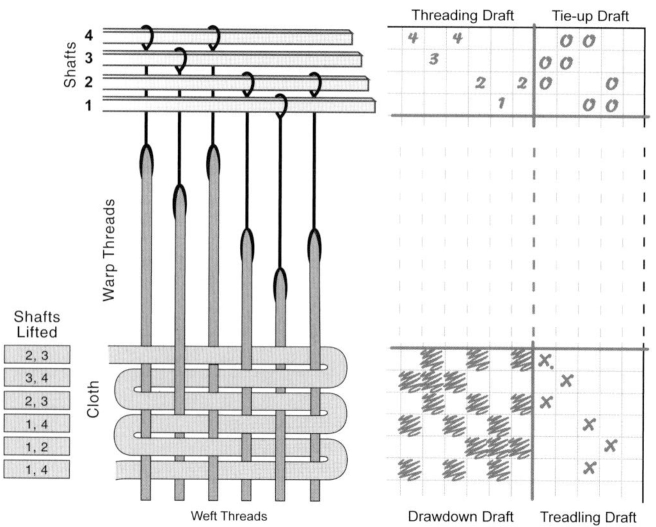

Fig. 441

See that the drawdown draft shows a little more clearly what the cloth might look like than the "cloth" drawing.

When reading a weave draft, begin in the treadling draft. Then, look above in the tie-up draft to see the combination of shafts that is to be lifted. The result is shown in the drawdown draft.

I usually don't pay much attention to the drawdown draft since it's hard to picture the squares as threads. What I pay attention to while weaving is: first the treadling, and then the tie-up drafts. (I use the threading draft to know how the heddles are to be threaded.)

There is a good reason that the tie-up draft has its name. See in Figure 442 how the treadles are used to do what the draft says to do. Look above the first X in the treadling draft, and see that the combination of shafts to be lifted is shafts 2 and 3. The treadle the left foot is on has cords tied up in the holes for that combination of shafts: 2 and 3. (The right treadle is tied up to shafts 1 and 2 which are the ones indicated above in the tie-up draft.)

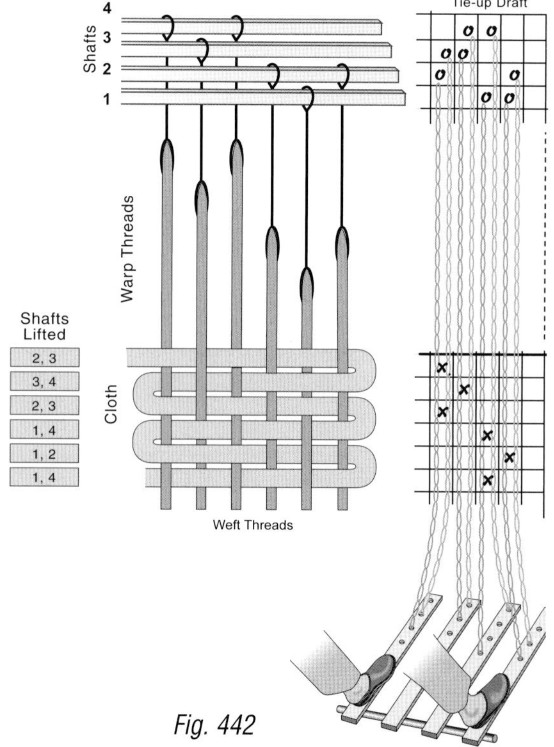

Fig. 442

Remember, to make weaves different, different threadings, treadlings, and tie-ups are used. Any or all of them can be changed and, with a computer, the resulting changes in the drawdown quickly seen. Read how to make your own original drafts below. Read the computer section on page 221 and "More about reading drafts" on page 207.

Making original drafts

The previous pages explain how to read drafts which is the basis that you need to know. The rest of this chapter covers the theory. You may or may not have an interest in this aspect of drafting. It isn't necessary. My first drafting exercises were so easy I could see the answer without having to work it out. For that reason, I'm going to suggest nonsense threads in the parts of the drafts. Do not try weaving this draft—it isn't one you would like.

Using a computer, this job would take a few minutes. You can learn a lot about how the results change by changing different parts of the drafts. Read the computer section, beginning on page 219.

By doing this exercise with the nonsense numbers in the parts of the draft, you can work out what the drawdown, or result, would be.

Using graph paper and a ***pencil*** for filling in the drawdown draft is described on page 206.

Create a threading draft; in this case, I arbitrarily chose numbers for the threading draft. See Figure 443. Remember, the numbers in the drafts represent one warp thread on a shaft. For example, the first thread is a "4" and is also on the 4th line up from the heavy solid line at the base of the threading draft. This indicates that the first thread should be threaded on shaft 4. The second warp thread would go on shaft 1, then 3, then 1, etc. with the final thread on shaft 4.

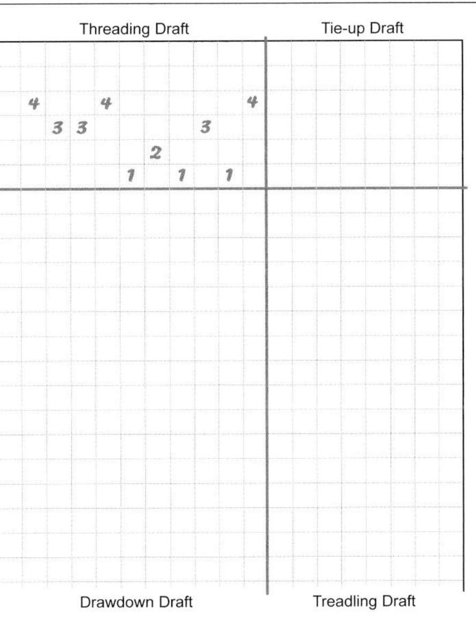

Fig. 443

Create a tie-up draft, again, with nonsensical combinations of shafts. Remember, that's what the tie-up shows—the combinations of shafts that are to be lifted. See Figure 444. Create a treadling draft in the same manner. See Figure 445.

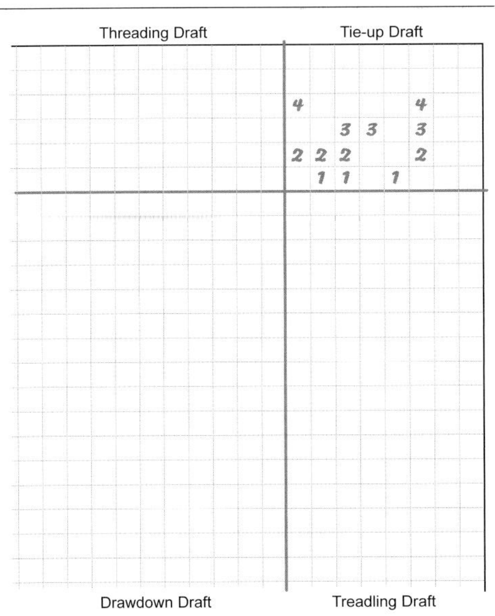

Fig. 444

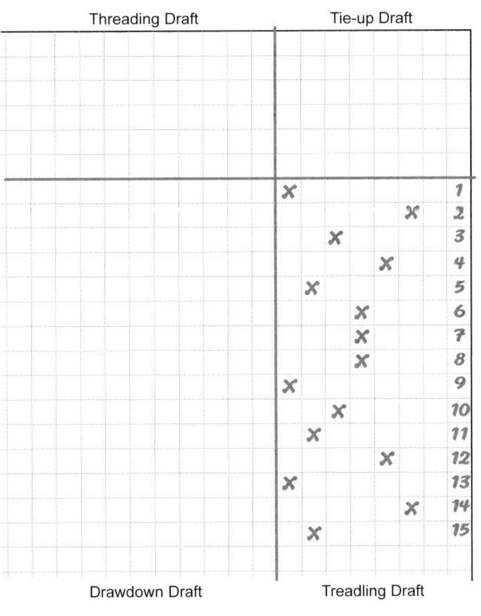

Fig. 445

Figure 446 shows X's under the combinations indicated for the rows. For example, the first row of weaving shows an X under the combination of shafts 2 and 4. Working down the draft, you'll see X's for 15 rows of weaving and the combinations each X indicates above in the tie-up draft.

Fill in the drawdown draft this way, following along in Figure 446.

1. First, look in the treadling draft and find the X for the first row of weaving.
2. Look up above for the combination of shafts that are to be lifted, in this case, shafts 2 and 4.
3. Then look over at the threading draft and find all the 2's and 4's shown.
4. Fill in the squares on the first line of the drawdown draft that are under all the 2's and 4's.

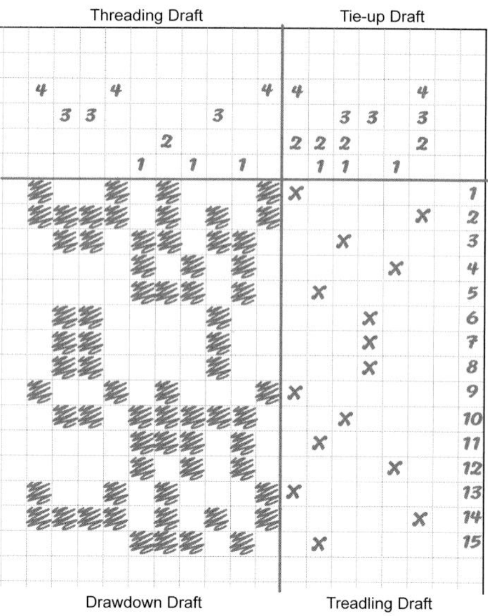

Fig. 446

Then, work out the 2nd row of weaving and fill in all the squares indicated by the tie-up and threading quadrants. See that for row 2, the combination in the tie-up draft is shafts 2, 3, 4. See that on that line in the drawdown quadrant all the squares that are filled in are under shafts 2, 3, and 4 in the threading draft.

This can be a very pleasant, but slow job. Probably, you won't have the patience to complete this draft by hand. The computer can fill in a drawdown instantly.

I hope you see by this exercise, how the resulting cloth depends upon the other 3 quadrants of the weave draft.

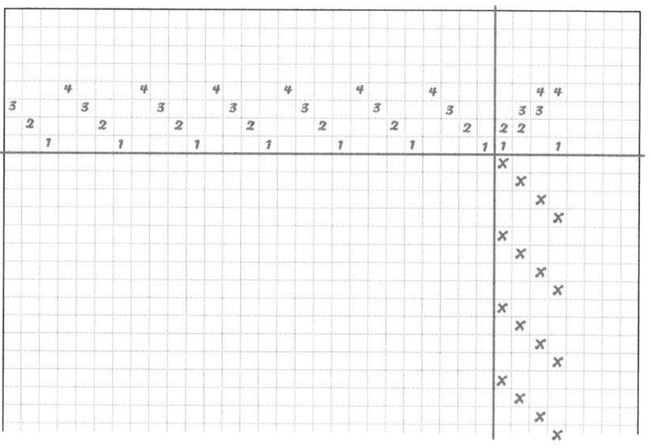
Fig. 447a

Satisfying drafts can be made if there is a sequence or pattern given, rather than random numbers. Figure 447a shows what is called a "straight" threading and also a "straight" treadling. The tie-up given is a very common one—for a 2/2 balanced twill. Figure 447b shows a "point" configuration in the threading and treadling. You can draft either one of these and find a design that might interest you. You also might exchange parts of the drafts, for example, use a straight threading and a point treadling. You can use any of the combinations given in the tie-ups for the sampler on page 198 and further change your results. This is fun, and there is much more to learn about different types of drafts. Read about things to try and experiment with in the computer chapter, beginning on page 219.

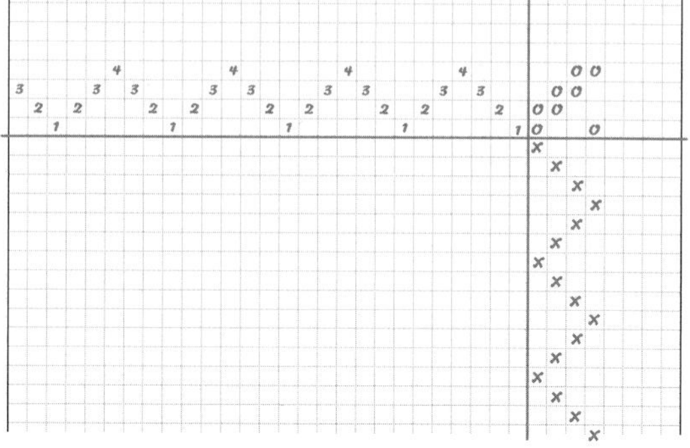
Fig. 447b

More about reading drafts

Use tabby

When "use tabby" (Figure 448) is given in the treadling draft or nearby, it means that in between every weft indicated in the treadling draft itself, you should put a tabby weft. Since there are two sheds needed to make a tabby (or plain weave), you must keep track of which tabby shed should be used as well as which row you are on in the treadling draft. It is much easier than you might think. (When the shuttle is on the left, use the left tabby treadle and vice-versa when the shuttle is on the right.)

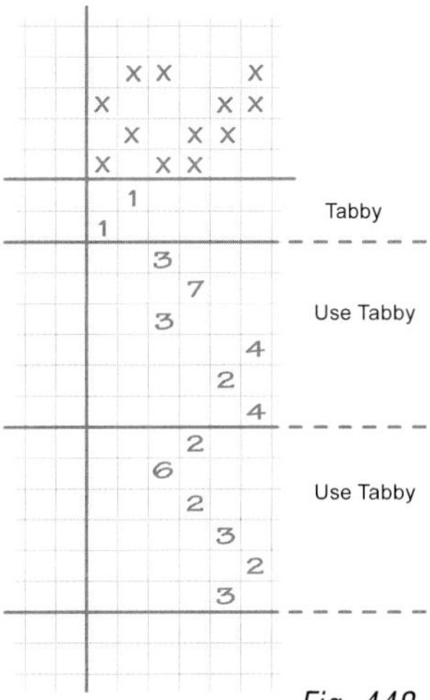

Tabby

Use Tabby

Use Tabby

Fig. 448

Numbers in the treadling draft

Figure 448 also shows numbers in the treadling draft. The numbers indicate that you should use that treadle (combination of shafts) that many times. For example, the first numbers given in Figure 448 are 3, then 7, then 3, etc. They mean the treadle indicated should be used 3 times before moving on to the next treadle, which is to be used 7 times, and so on. Since "use tabby" is also indicated in the draft, besides repeating the treadles as indicated, you will intersperse tabby wefts between each weft indicated in the treadling draft and so keep those repeated wefts from pulling themselves out.

Peg plan

A peg plan can be used instead of a treadling draft. It is a list of the shafts that are to be lifted for every shed. Peg plans are ideal for table looms and computer-driven looms. When a table loom is used, the levers are pulled for each shed, so a peg plan is easier to read than a treadling draft. In Figures 440, 441, and 442 the peg plans are shown to the left side of the cloth under the heading "shafts lifted."

Computers need to have the shafts for each shed entered, as well, so peg plans are used. My beginning students find it easier to treadle the weaves on their sampler by making peg plans from the regular treadling drafts I've given them, as seen in Figure 440 on page 203. In the illustration, see "shafts lifted" on the left.

A weave draft written with a peg plan would not have anything in the tie-up quadrant of the draft because no treadles would be tied up in combinations. Each set of shafts is lifted individually for each shed, or row of weaving.

Color order

Figure 449 shows drafts for the order to be used for the colors of warps and wefts. The color order for the threading may be above or near the threading draft, or somewhere in the text describing a project. The color order of the warp threads in the example is read this way (from right to left): 8 warp threads of green, 2 threads of black, 10 threads of brown, 2 black, 8 green, and 2 black, for a total of 32 warp threads.

The weft color sequence is usually given at the side of the treadling draft. The weft color order reads (from top to bottom): 8 wefts of green, 2 wefts black, 10 wefts brown, 2 wefts black, 8 wefts green and 2 wefts black.

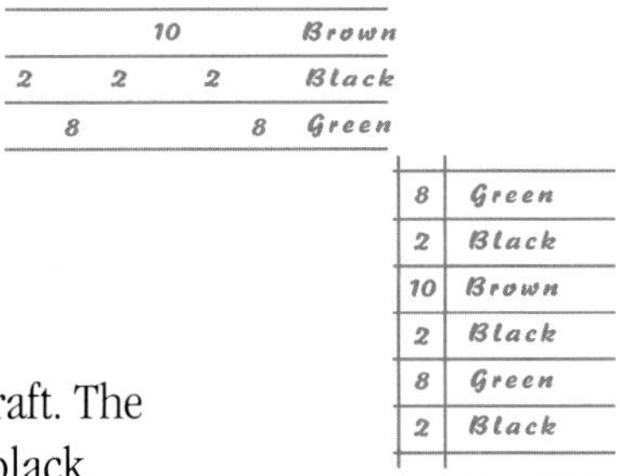

	10			Brown
2	2		2	Black
8			8	Green

8	Green
2	Black
10	Brown
2	Black
8	Green
2	Black

Fig. 449

Designing

All of these techniques can be done effortlessly on the computer. Here, I explain to you some of the possibilities and how useful they can be for designing. Two more ideas used in designing, "tromp as writ" and "turned drafts" are on pages 217 and 218.

Repeats

Usually, weave drafts show one repeat of the weave, and you can repeat it over and over as much as you like. A repeat can be given in the threading draft as well as in the treadling draft.

There are two ways to repeat a design or a draft: straight, and point (mirror image).

A ***straight repeat*** means that when you come to the end of a section, you start again at the beginning of the repeat. Figure 447a on page 206 shows a straight repeat both in the threading and in the treadling.

A ***point repeat*** reproduces a section in mirror image. That means, you begin again at the end of the section and work backwards to the beginning. See Figure 447b where there are point or mirror image repeats in the threading as well as in the treadling.

Drafting other weaves

There are 9 different weave structures, in the sampler. They are plain weave, basket weave, balanced twill, weft-faced twill, warp-faced twill, herringbone, two types of broken twill, and rep weave. Besides those, there are hand-manipulated weaves and your own invented weaves. This sampler is only the tip of the iceberg: there are many more weave structures.

There are other categories in the weaving books as well.

Just as the weaves in the sampler had specific directions to accomplish each one, every weave structure has its own rules for the threading, tie-up, and treadling. Some also have rules about the colors of threads and some about the size of threads. You can look them up on the web, too. Sometimes, only the weave draft is given, and it is assumed you know the weave's rules—so you should learn the rules to follow if you expect your project to look like a given structure.

These structures and rules are fun to learn and to weave. I have learned several, and some I like to weave more than others. There are many, many weaves that I've never explored. That is what I love about weaving so much—you can never run out of things to learn.

Many of the names given to specific weave structures are interesting and may or may not give any idea of what the cloth will look like.

A category of weaves called block weaves

One category of weave structures is Block Weaves. Some examples of block weaves are: Atwater-Bronson lace, damask, honeycomb, log cabin, overshot, rep, and summer and winter. Note: block weaves aren't just any weave structure. They are particular structures that can be woven in "blocks."

With block weaves, you have the option to vary different threadings across the warp to create patterns or designs in the cloth. Say, your idea for a design calls for a border that will show up differently from the main part of the cloth. In that case, the border areas will be threaded a certain way, and the body of the cloth will be threaded differently—all according to the rules for the particular weave. We name the sections "blocks" and we name the blocks A, B, C, D, etc. as explained below.

> ***Note:*** *Block weaves aren't just any weave structure; they are particular structures within the category called "block weaves."*

There is a convention for designing with blocks which is that first you plot out the design areas in the warp; the areas that are to be threaded in the different ways. This plotted–out design is just that—a sketch, so-to-speak. After you have your sketch, you plug in a weave structure according to its specific rules. In fact, the process of plugging a weave structure into your plotted-out draft has a name. It is called "Block Substitution."

> ***Block Substitiution*** *is a process for designing with blocks where you plot out the design areas in the warp and then plug in a weave structure according to its specific rules.*

We are talking about plotting out how the specific areas in the warp are to be threaded differently when you thread the warp into the heddles. We don't know what to do for the treadling until the threading design is determined, and we can't know what the actual warp and weft threads are supposed to do or what the tie-up draft will be until the weave structure itself has been chosen to substitute into the design. (Block substitution.)

Examples of block substitution follow.

Plotting out your design with a profile draft

The plotted-out design is called a profile draft, and it is placed in a weave draft in the threading quadrant. But, remember, the profile draft means only ***areas*** are shown (the blocks). Figure 450 shows an example of a profile threading draft—a cloth with borders on the sides. Note again, that we do not know what the threading, tie-up, or treadling drafts will be. All we know at this point is that there will be some variation in the warp so that borders can be woven on a cloth.

Notice in Figure 450 that the first area (reading from right-to-left as usual for threading drafts), the border area (block), is indicated on the bottom line of the draft and the main section (a different block) of the cloth is shown on the second line. Then, the other border is shown, also on the bottom line of the draft because it will be threaded exactly the same way as the first border. Since it is to be

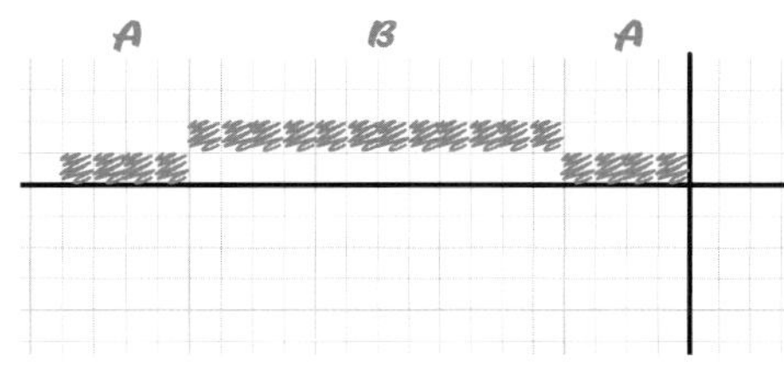

Fig. 450

threaded identically to the first block, it is considered to be the same block—or the same specific threading. The profile draft shows which blocks will be used, where they will be placed, and how wide they will be.

Naming the blocks

The blocks are named A, B, C, D, etc. starting on the bottom line of the threading draft—following the same convention as for an actual thread-by-thread draft where the bottom line is the first shaft, or shaft 1. In the example in Figure 450 (repeated here) with the borders, Block A is shown on the bottom line of the profile threading draft, Block B (the main part of the cloth) is shown on the second line and the remaining border is to be Block A indicating that it is to be threaded so it looks exactly like the first border on the other edge of the cloth. Read more about this on page 215, "How to count blocks."

Each block represents a unique threading.

Examples of block substitution

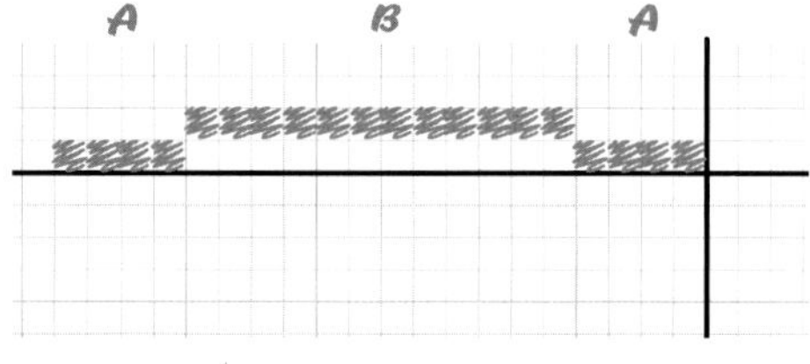

Here's an example for the profile draft shown in Figure 450 which shows Block A being the two borders and Block B being the center. Let's say you decided to use a variation of the rep weave structure. In this case, the border sections (Block A) will be threaded as follows on shafts 1 and 2 in this order: 1,2,1,2,1,2, and the body of the cloth (Block B) will be threaded on shafts 3 and 4 in this way: 3,4,3,4,3,4. Do you see that the two sections are threaded differently? In the weaving books the rules for a specific block weave will indicate the specific threadings for each block.

Note that other weave structures will require different threadings within the blocks—more examples are given below. The main point is that the different blocks will be threaded each in its own way according to the rules given for a particular weave structure that is chosen from the block weave category.

The weave structure itself makes it possible for the variations in the threading from one section to another.

Another example: Overshot

The threading rules for the overshot weave structure call for Block A to be threaded on shafts 1 and 2 in this way: 1,2,1,2,1,2, etc. Block B is threaded this way: 2,3,2,3,2,3, etc. Block C is threaded: 3,4,3,4,3,4, etc and Block D is threaded: 4,1,4,1,4,1, etc. Do you see now that different weave structures dictate that the threading of the blocks is accomplished in their own way? In the design in Figure 451 there are 4 blocks: A, B, C, and D. If overshot weave were to be chosen, then these threadings would be substituted in this profile draft. Note: the remaining rules for this structure are given in many weaving books and will be needed to construct a cloth in overshot.

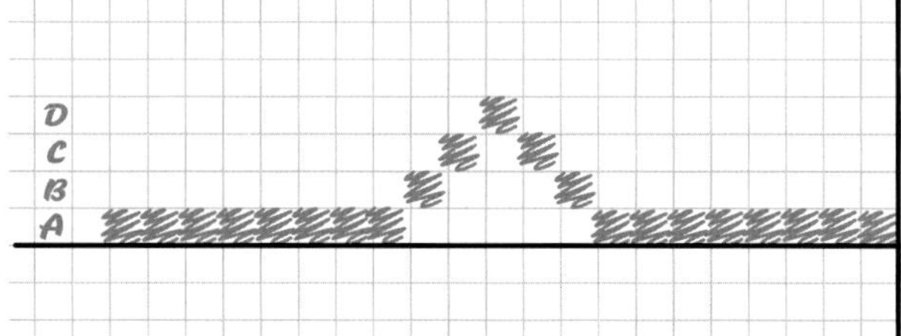

Fig. 451

Look at Figure 451 again to see the 4 blocks in this design. We can see that there are 4 lines used in the threading profile. The blocks are: A (on the bottom line), B (on the second line) and so on for Blocks C and D. Again, we see borders in the design, but there are 3 more unique blocks in the center section of the cloth. Reading this profile draft for the threading, we see that Block A is first on the bottom line and is wider than the small blocks forming the design in the center. See that next block is to be different so it is given the name B and is indicated on the second line. Then another small unique block is shown on the third line and its name should be C. There is one more unique threading which will be block D. From there the profile repeats itself in a mirror image with the blocks in this order: C, B, A, and Block A being a border which is not unique but identical to the first border.

Another example: Summer and winter

The rules for summer and winter are to thread Block A: 1,3,2,3. Block B: 1,4,2,4. Block C: 1,5,2,5. Block D: 1,6,2,6. Block E: 1,7,2,7. Block F: 1,8,2,8. This weave can be used for even more blocks, depending upon how many shafts there are on the loom. (Many looms have 8 shafts or more.) Read how to design and weave summer and winter in many weaving books.

Different block weaves dictate how to thread the blocks in their own, unique way. Read the rules for designing and weaving block designs in many books.

Summary

What block weaves have in common is that there are a number of variations you can make within the same weave structure. You could weave a border, and a tree, or a checkerboard all in one weave structure, but you would see variations in the weave so that these areas would show up differently. One way to think of it is to have a design that you want in the foreground with the remainder of the cloth as the background. In contrast, in the sampler, when you wove a structure, say herringbone, you wove herringbone from selvedge to selvedge—there was no way to alter the weave structure to make a border, for example.

How to work with block weaves

When working with block weaves the first thing you do is ***decide on a design***—then you ***select the weave structure***. You might have your weave structure in mind already, but you need to start working out the idea of the design first. This then becomes the profile draft.

After the design is chosen, you plug in the threads according to the rules for the weave structure you want. It is called Block Substitution because first you plot out the areas you want (called blocks) and then substitute in the weave structure. The computer can do this amazingly fast (see page 230).

Here's how it can work in real life. Let's say you want to weave baby blankets for twins. You'd like them to be similar, but you think it might be boring to weave them both exactly alike.

For the design of the blankets let's say you want to have borders on the sides and something else for the middle of each blanket. They both will be the same design: borders and a center part.

Let's say you wanted to weave one blanket in the rep weave variation and the other in log cabin. You would substitute the threadings, tie-ups, and treadlings according to the rules for each of the weaves into the areas you've designed—the borders and the main part. The profile shown in Figure 452.

Profile drafts and block substitution

So, you don't know anything about the threading or which treadles to use until you have substituted the weave structure's threading into the blocks you've designed. After you've done the "block substitution" you will have a weave draft that you can recognize—there will be threads on shafts in the threading draft, combinations of shafts in the tie-up draft, and a treadling order in the treadling draft. There may or may not be a drawdown shown because often it doesn't show what the cloth will actually look like—just what threads will be lifted.

Remember. Figures 452 and 453 are examples of some plotted-out block designs. We call this type of draft a profile draft because it is only the idea before any actual threads have been substituted in.

I will give two examples of weaves that are substituted into the profile draft in Figure 452—the profile draft of the threading for the baby blankets. Remember, the profile for the threading is located in the quadrant of the draft where the threading will go, because it is the idea for the threading. Also be reminded that profile drafts are read just like regular drafts, following the arrows working out from the thick lines . Block A is on the first line (the bottom line), Block B on the next line, and Blocks C, D, etc. would be above.

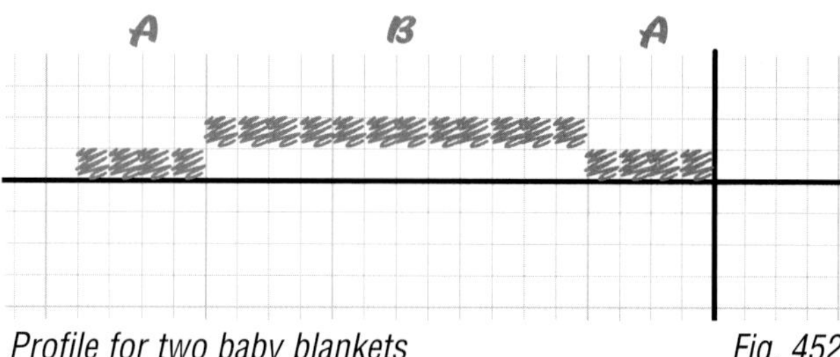

Profile for two baby blankets *Fig. 452*

Profile drafts can also be made for the ***treadling*** draft as seen in Figure 453. You can substitute a treadling that matches a threading (tromp as writ—see page 217) or you can substitute any other treadling you invent, or one that follows the rules for a completely different weave structure.

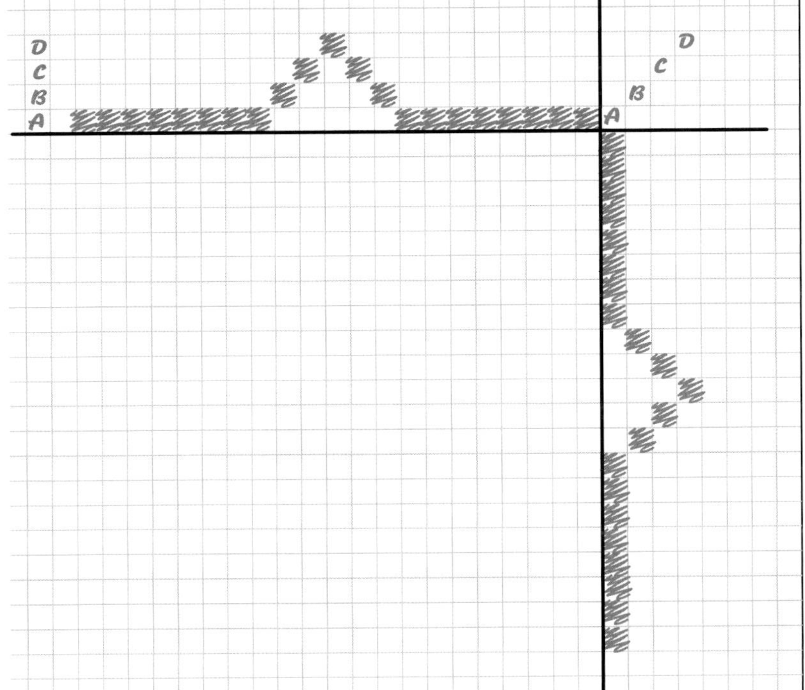

Fig. 453

How to make the substitution using variation of warp-faced rep weave

I have suggested two block weaves in the chapter on future assignments beginning on page 233. The rules are given there for two weaves: a variation of warp-faced rep weave (page 234) and the weave structure called "log cabin" (page 241).

Here, in this chapter, I show threadings, tie-ups, and treadlings that have been substituted for the blocks in the baby blanket profile draft in Figure 452. Read more about the weave structures in the future assignments chapter beginning on page 233.

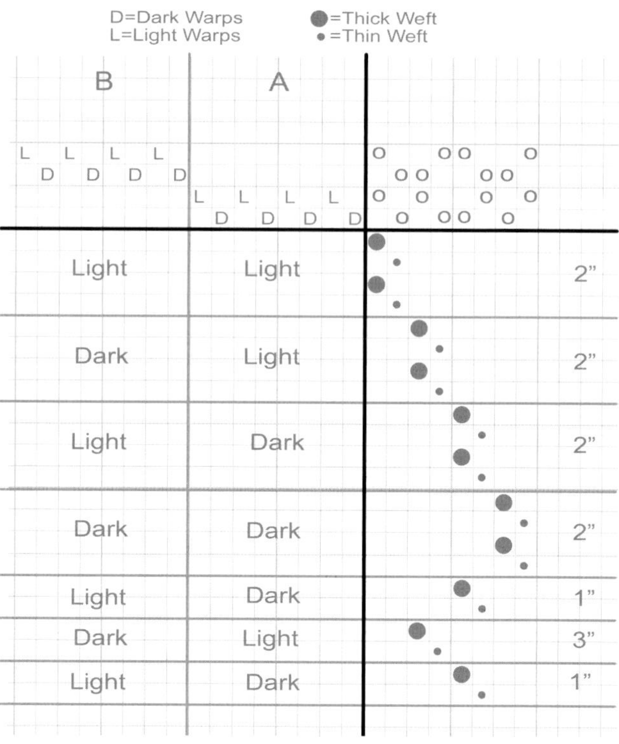

Fig. 454

First, examine the weave draft for the rep weave variation in Figure 454. In this weave, light and dark threads are needed in the threading draft. Also, thick and thin wefts are called for in the treadling draft.

The threading draft

The borders (Block A) are threaded on shafts 1 and 2 with alternating dark and light threads. The body of the blanket is to be threaded on shafts 3 and 4 with alternating dark and light threads as well. The threading was determined by the rules for this weave: Block A is threaded on shafts 1 and 2 and Block B is threaded on shafts 3 and 4 with alternating dark and light threads. I arbitrarily put the darks on shafts 1 and 3 (the odd numbered shafts) and the light threads on shafts 2 and 4. Rather than putting numbers for the shafts in the threading draft, the dark and light threads are indicated. It is assumed that you know that shaft 1 is on the bottom line of the draft as is the normal convention for weave drafts.

The tie-up draft

Look in the tie-up quadrant and see the bubbles indicating the combination of shafts that are to be lifted for this weave. See that the first combination given is for shafts 2 and 4. (Again, shaft one is always on the bottom line in tie-up drafts.) The second combination given is for shafts 1 and 3. There are two more combinations that will be used here: shafts 2 and 3 and shafts 1 and 4. The remainder of the tie-up shows the same combinations, but are conveniently repeated so the treadling draft will be easier to read.

The treadling draft

Thick wefts are indicated by fat circles and thin wefts, by small dots as per the rules for this variation of rep weave.

The first row of weaving calls for a thick weft—and the combination of shafts 2 and 4 should be lifted. The second weft is thin and the combination of shafts to use is 1 and 3. The treadling draft indicates that this should be repeated for 2". The next two inches are shown to be woven with the thick weft and shafts 2 and 3 lifted, and the thin wefts with shafts 1 and 4 lifted.

This is a sampler, and you can see that different variations will be woven each 2" worth. Remember, the weave is explained beginning on page 234. What you are to notice here is that threads and combinations of shafts are substituted for the profile draft.

The drawdown draft

As I've said, it's hard to see the weave structure in a draw down, and in Figure 454 it is shown only schematically which color will dominate in a block when a given treadling is used.

Block substitution for log cabin weave

Again, the profile draft is shown in Figure 452 (repeated here) for the second baby blanket with borders being Block A and the center area being Block B.

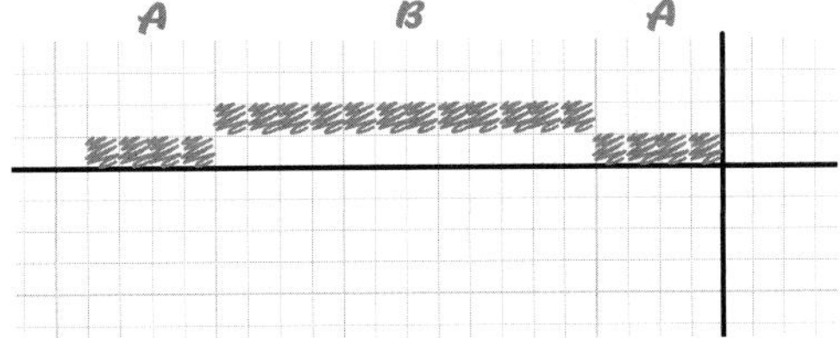

Profile for two baby blankets

Examining Figure 455, see that Block A and B are both threaded on shafts 4,3,2,1. What makes Block A different from Block B is where the light and dark threads are placed. Block A has the light threads threaded on the odd shafts (1 and 3) and the darks on the even shafts (2 and 4). Block B is just the reverse with lights on the even shafts and the dark threads on the odd shafts. This follows the guidelines or rules for log cabin which is explained in detail beginning on page 241.

The two combinations of shafts shown in the tie-up draft are 1 and 3 and shafts 2 and 4. Actually, the weave is plain weave, but will look very different because of the placement of the light and dark threads in both the warp and weft.

The treadling draft shows when dark and light wefts are used.

Again, this is to be a sampler with 2" sections of the different configurations for log cabin.

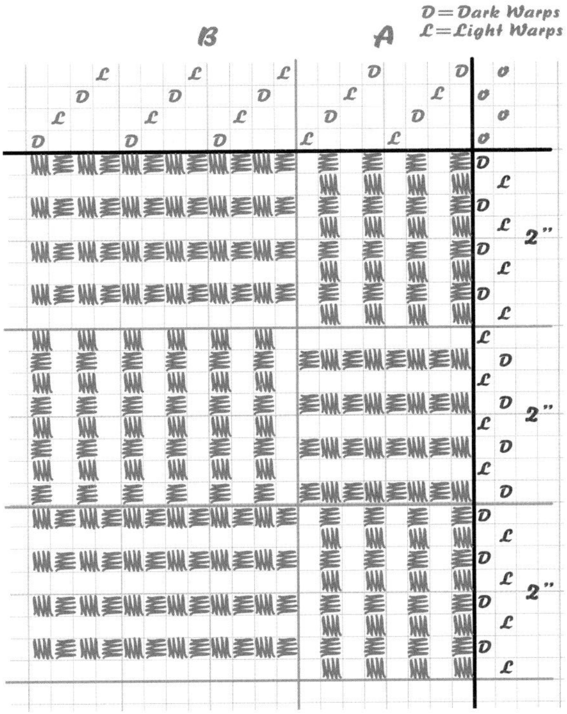

D=Dark Warps
L=Light Warps

Fig. 455

The drawdown draft shows schematically where there will be vertical and horizontal lines in the cloth

How to count blocks

As has been said, a group of warp threads that act alike equals one block. For example in the 2-block design in Figure 452, notice the border sections indicated in the profile draft. All the threads that act the same, regardless of where they are located (in this case, at both edges of the warp) are considered to be the same block, Block A. In the illustration, the middle section acts differently from the borders, so that means that the threads in that section are threaded differently so that they form another, different block, Block B.

Counting Blocks

When you begin to think about block substitution you want to know the number of blocks your design requires because it relates to the number of shafts you have on your loom. Blocks in some weaves require more shafts than other weaves; hence you may or may not be able to use a particular weave structure if it would need more shafts than you have on the loom. You will see this issue when you practice block substitution on the computer or as you read about the rules for particular weave structures.

Counting blocks in a design is easy if you follow a system. The rule is: Look for identical vertical columns. All vertical columns that act alike are the same block.

The vertical columns in a design (cloth or drawdown) represent the blocks, or groups, of ***warp*** threads. See Figure 456 and count the blocks. Starting at the right edge of the design, assign the first group of threads that act alike—in this case, the border—as Block A. The blank squares, you say? You're right—the blank squares count because cloth will be woven there—it's the background in your design. Then, as you move toward the left you see a column of 4 squares of graph paper. Since these are acting differently from those threads in the border, and they all are acting alike, we assign that column of threads Block B. Moving across there are 2 squares that are alike—that is Block C. The short column on the left is completely different from any block we have so far, and is Block D (identical vertical columns, remember?). The border on the left is the same as the border on the right so it is Block A again. Thus, this is a 4-block design.

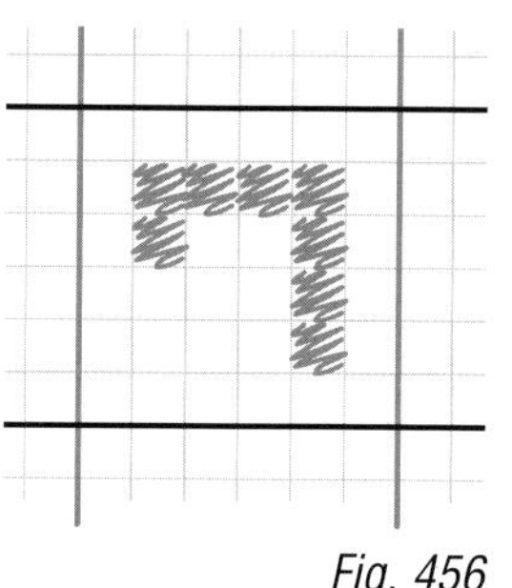

Fig. 456

Look at the illustration of the dog in Figure 457 and see if you can count all the blocks. Don't be fooled. Notice that the legs are different widths than the tail and ears. Counting from the right, assign the border Block A and work across the illustration. I'll give you a start. Block B is the tail and part of the hind leg. The remaining part of the leg that is wider than the tail is Block C. Block D is the body up to the point where the front leg starts. Now, see if you can count the remaining blocks. I see 6 blocks! A through F. There is a profile threading draft at the bottom of the illustration showing the placement of the different blocks and the width each is to be threaded.

You can use the computer to count the blocks for a design, and substitute the threads in the profile for a weave structure by using a wizard in the software. Read more about block substitution in the computer chapter beginning on page 219.

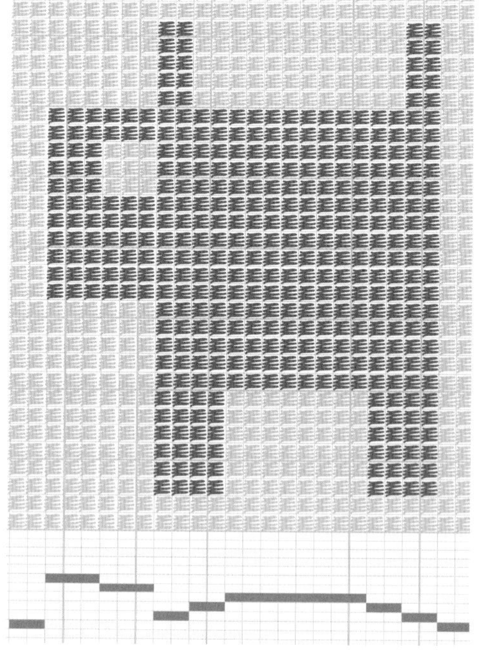

Fig. 457

> *Different weaves require different numbers of shafts for each block. The number of shafts on your loom will determine which weaves and how many blocks you can use.*

There are infinite ideas for two-block designs (and some for more than 2 blocks) that can be used on a four shaft loom. You can design many different profile drafts—either with pencil and paper or with a computer.

Two more design techniques

"Tromp as writ" and "turned drafts" are techniques used often in designing. They can be accomplished instantly on the computer. Here are the concepts for these useful tools.

Tromp as writ

When the treadling draft is exactly the same as the threading draft, we say the draft is treadled "tromp as writ." Sometimes, only the threading is given, and the words, "treadle as written" or "treadle as drawn in," tell you to tromp as writ. Figure 458 shows schematically a profile draft showing the treadling as the same pattern as the threading and thus is tromp as writ.

You can tromp as writ in other ways, too. For example, you can use the order the colors were used in the threading for the order of colors in the treadling. That sequence would make a plaid using the colors in the same order and proportion in the warp and weft.

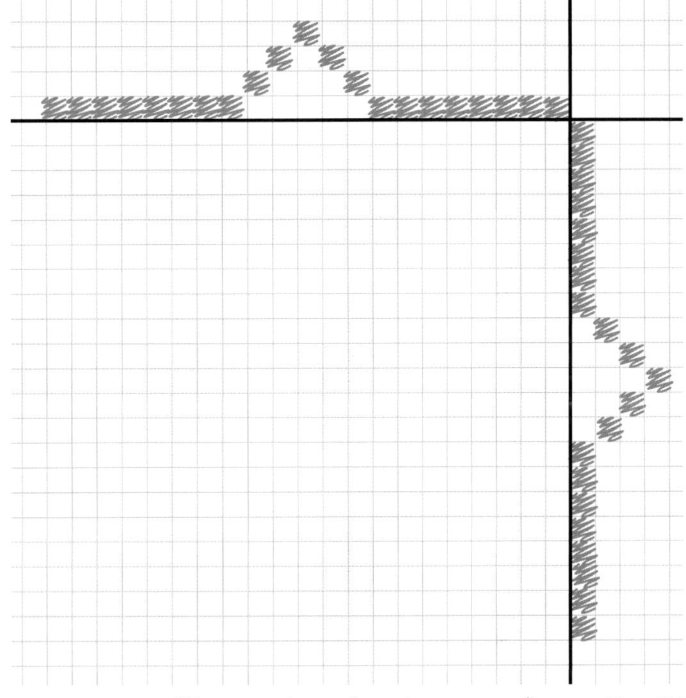

Weave as drawn in or tromp as writ *Fig. 458*

This design technique is often used and gives squared and symmetrical designs. Note that Figure 458 is a profile draft. Figures 459 and 460 show tromp as writ with thread-by-thread drafts. Tromp as writ is sometimes written as "TAW."

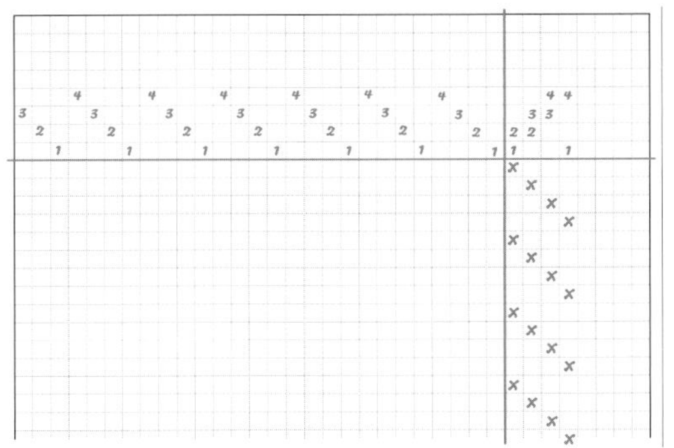

Fig. 459

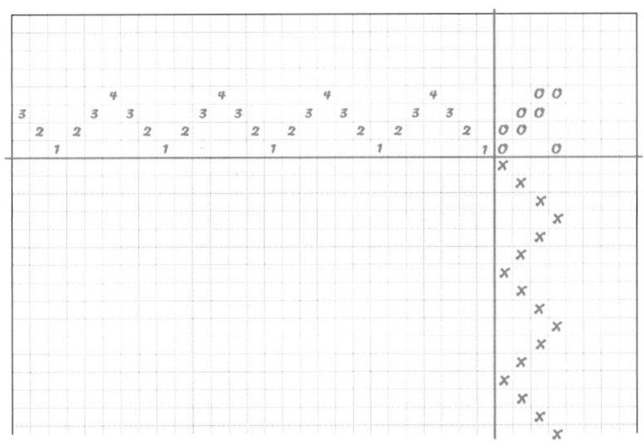

Fig. 460

Turned drafts

You can put the threading draft in the treadling area of a draft and the treadling into the threading area. It's called turning the draft. You literally copy one draft into the other position, and vice-versa. Figures 461 and 462 are profile drafts that show how the drawdown can change when you exchange the position of the treadling and threading drafts. You might want to do this exchange when the idea you have in mind requires too many shafts if threaded one way, and it might require fewer if you turned the draft.

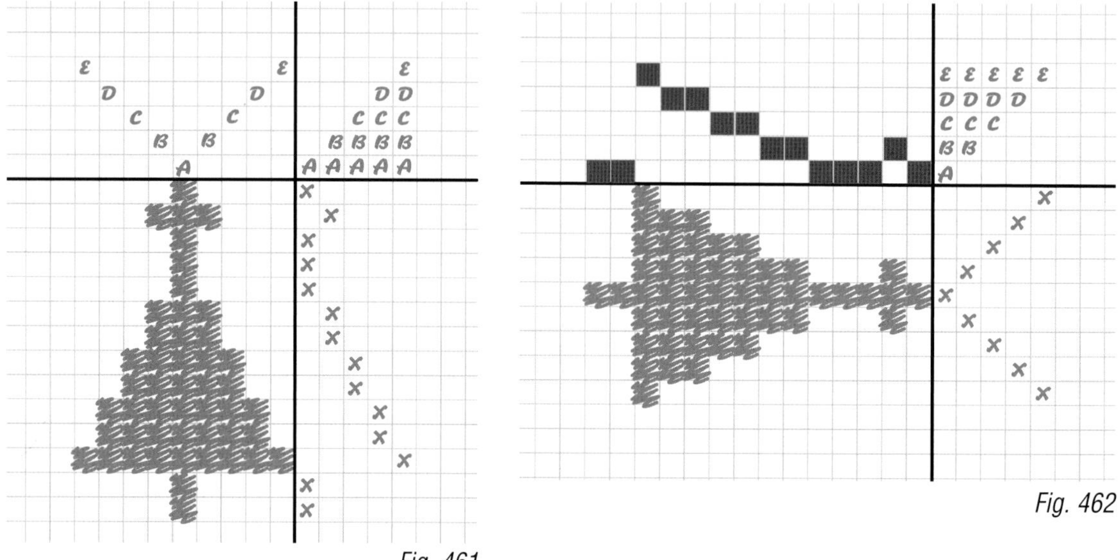

Fig. 461

Fig. 462

Some parting words of wisdom about drafting

Knowing how to read and make weave drafts is an important part of weaving and designing, but it is not the only part to know. When reading instructions in magazines and books, you must read all the words given. They tell you more information which you must know that the drafts don't indicate. Some examples are the colors, the sizes and types of yarns used, the number of warp threads per inch (epi or ends per inch) and the number of wefts per inch (ppi or picks per inch). Knowing how many ppi tells you how hard to beat. Knowing how many epi tells you the scale of the yarns and also how far apart they should be. Other information will be given for planning the project that is imperative to know. You cannot expect to weave a project like a picture in a magazine if you choose your own yarns, epi, ppi, method of finishing and ignore the very specific information for that particular project and only use the weave draft given.

Oh, yes, always look carefully at any photographs. If your weaving isn't like them, you might have missed some important piece of information.

I think it's a good idea to read the directions out loud to yourself. Another idea is to make a copy of the article and then use a highlighter pen to make sure you are aware of details. Sometimes, it's a good idea to magnify the article (or at least the draft) on a copy machine so it's easier to see while threading and weaving.

8 *Computers and Weaving*

In the drafting chapter I say that computers can easily make and manipulate drafts. You will learn how to do these jobs when you explore different software, which is what I strongly suggest you do. This exploration will help you understand drafting better and allow you to be very creative.

Modern technology for weavers may or may not appeal to you. In this chapter I give the bare bones—what software can do and where to find out about it. You can see what's involved and then decide how much you want to pursue the computer aspects.

To practice with the software, change the various parts of the drafts and see what you get. There will be plenty of drafts you don't like—consider it a game of curiosity. What if I do . . ., etc.? You can save the ones that you like.

Weavers as well as weaving software programs use the word "end" to mean a warp thread, and "pick" to mean a row of weft.

Some of the drafts shown in this chapter are very complicated—I just want you to know that very complex threadings and drafts are out there—and many people find them terribly creative. You might develop some yourself.

You should be familiar with weave drafting and the related terms, which are explained in the drafting chapter, beginning on page 195.

I asked several weavers to write or give advice for this chapter as they use the computer in their weaving lives. Since computer and software technology change almost daily, these authors' advice is to try out programs that are available to get familiar with how they work and what they can do for you. This chapter is to get you started, but there is nothing better than practice and playing around to learn. Some programs are listed here, but no attempt has been made to make a comprehensive list because any list is likely to become obsolete.

If you are not computer savvy, don't worry. Ask a friend or guild member to sit down with you and get you started with weaving software. Read about weaving groups on page 224. For computer basics, almost anyone (your neighbor, grandkids, etc) can tell you what you need to know, or very good free instruction is given at adult education classes.

Weaving is still a hands-on process. Even if a loom is connected to a computer, and the software generates the treadlings or lift-plans for each weft, the weaver still measures out the warp, threads the heddles, and pushes the treadles that lift the shafts. It is a physical proposition. Some people want to use all the technology they can while others eschew technology and want to do everything by hand. Of course, there are people in between. It is totally alright to find your own place in your weaving world.

The Experts

I am proud of the experts who have contributed to this chapter.

Nancy Alegria was a student in my beginning weaving class. It soon became apparent that she was weaving at home because nearly every week she had something new to show in class. It was also apparent that she was using the computer to design her assignments and gathering ideas for her own projects from the internet. I mentioned at our weaving guild that I was going to ask someone to write the chapter on computers and weaving. Nancy volunteered and also mentioned, casually, that she was a professional technical writer.

Deborah Holcomb worked full-time for 25 years in the software business while dabbling in the fiber arts in relatively rare leisure moments. Now, the tables are turned: weaving and teaching weaving are her primary occupations, and her computer is a favorite weaving tool.

While working on a project to develop interactive tutorials to teach programmers how to use the software products sold by her company, she got the idea of developing tutorials for the weaving software that she liked to use for designing textiles. It led to the development of an interactive tutorial, The Textile Design Studios, that shows you how to use software to approach the creative process in new ways.

Deborah Holcomb
www.riversidefiberarts.com

She is currently working on a new computer-based tutorial designed to teach block design and weave structure using animation and interactivity. You can visit her website to learn more.

Judie Eatough is well known for writing the weaving software section for the *Interweave Press* web site. Her own web site has up-to-date software listings and what programs have to offer. She loves weaving, computers, puzzles, and weave drafts. Creating drafts, whether for 4-shaft looms or drawlooms, is her passion. Weaving them is almost as much fun. Judie teaches weaving and the use of weaving software. Visit Judie at either of her two websites.

Judie Eatough
www.weavenotes.net

Patricia Stewart offered to show me what computers can do—she is a whiz and uses them while designing and weaving awesome fabrics for beautiful clothes that she designs, sews and wears. Her enthusiasm is contagious!

Penny Peters added advice and support all along the way.

Weaving Software

By Nancy Alegria

One of the great joys of weaving in the 21st century is the ability to create something beautiful and unique with tools that have been in use since the dawn of civilization. So what can today's technology add to this joyous experience?

Speed

So you've found a promising looking draft in a book, but the illustration is in black and white, and you're wondering what it will look like in color. You could pull out the graph paper and colored pencils and eraser, sit back in your favorite comfy chair with a cup of tea and work it out. We don't always have the luxury of time. With even the most rudimentary (and possibly even free) weaving program and a computer, you can visualize that draft in a matter of minutes.

Creativity

What if you add a color? Subtract a color? Move a warp thread to a different shaft? Make up something out of thin air? With graph paper and pencils, you better have lots of paper and pencils and a pretty big eraser on hand to check out several ideas for variations of the draft. With weaving software, you can make all the modifications you want, and if you don't like them, you can just click "Undo." If you love them, you can click "Save." Of course, the drawback to weaving software is that you may end up spending all day and night working out endless possibilities.

Resources

The Internet is a pretty big place—and it's full of information. Repositories like ***www.Handweaving.net*** (see page 226), and websites run by weaving guilds all over the world contain thousands of weaving drafts that you can download to your computer where you can customize them to your heart's content.

Sharing

With weaving software, you can create and share drafts with anybody else who has a computer, either via email, the internet, or on disc. You can send drafts to anyone with an email account just by attaching the file to an email message, the same way you would a photo or any other file. You can even contribute to online repositories of weaving drafts and share them with weavers all over the world.

Calculate

You can get that warp on the loom faster with weaving software. Many programs offer a feature that automatically counts heddles and warp threads for you. You can also use weaving software (or spreadsheet programs) to easily calculate yardage requirements.

Expand

Are you interested in weaving on more than 8 shafts? Wish for 24? Not even a centipede has enough feet to control that many shaft combinations. But a computer with a computer assisted loom can do it without even breaking a sweat. You will need to buy weaving software with a loom-control interface to accomplish this job. It is included in the basic software for some programs, but is an additional purchase for others. Read more in the Loom Control section, below.

Weaving Information Files

The thing that makes all this lovely information sharing possible is the Weaving Information File (or WIF) format. It was developed as part of a collaboration among programmers working on many commercial weaving software packages. Thanks to their generous efforts, weavers all over the world can share weaving drafts across platforms and across oceans as well.

Each program writes drafts in its own format. WIF files are used when sending or receiving drafts to different programs (e.g., Weaveit to Weavepoint, etc). When deciding on a weaving program, make sure that you choose one that both reads and writes files in WIF format, as it has become the *lingua franca* of high-tech weaving.

What's in a WIF File?

The reason that the WIF format is so portable across programs, platforms, and computer systems is that it's a very simple and straight-forward set of definitions. It's a text file, so it's readable by any computer, past or future. In fact, if you open a WIF file in a text editing program, you'll see a list of attributes as shown in Figure 463a.

But when you open it in a weaving program, you'll see a weaving draft. See Figure 463b.

Your weaving program takes all those definitions in the WIF file and translates them into a draft that you can view and manipulate. Not all features of the WIF format are supported in all weaving programs, and each program works a little differently, but if a program supports the WIF format, you can at the very least manipulate threading, tie-ups, treadling, and colors.

chocolatemint.wif - Notepad
File Edit Format View Help

```
[WIF]
Version=1.1
Date=1/3/2008
Developers=info@pixeLoom.com
Source Program=pixeLoom
Source Version=5.0.3
[CONTENTS]
COLOR PALETTE=true
WARP SYMBOL PALETTE=false
WEFT SYMBOL PALETTE=false
TEXT=true
WEAVING=true
WARP=true
WEFT=true
NOTES=false
TIEUP=true
COLOR TABLE=true
WARP SYMBOL TABLE=false
WEFT SYMBOL TABLE=false
THREADING=true
WARP THICKNESS=false
WARP THICKNESS ZOOM=false
WARP SPACING=false
WARP SPACING ZOOM=false
WARP COLORS=true
WARP SYMBOLS=false
TREADLING=true
LIFTPLAN=false
WEFT THICKNESS=false
WEFT THICKNESS ZOOM=false
WEFT SPACING=false
WEFT SPACING ZOOM=false
WEFT COLORS=true
WEFT SYMBOLS=false
PRIVATE PIXELOOM=true
[WEAVING]
Shafts=8
Treadles=8
Rising Shed=true
```

WIF attributes Fig. 463a

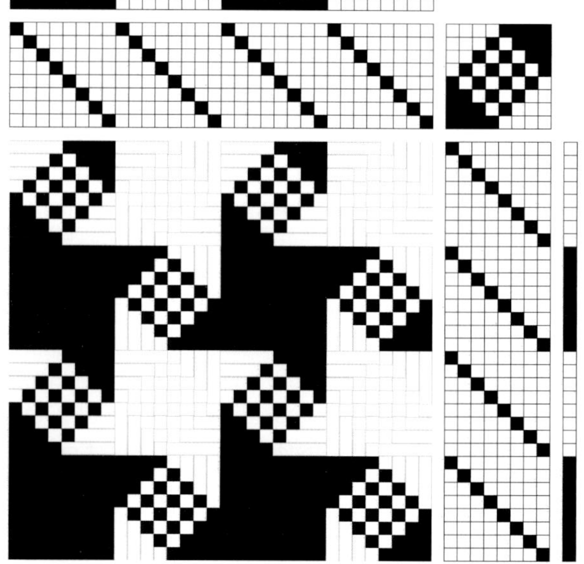

Weaving draft Fig. 463b

Deciding on a software package

There are several weaving programs available for computers that run Microsoft Windows. At the time of this writing, choices are fewer for Apple Macintosh or Linux users. With the growing popularity of both Mac and Linux systems, we can hope that there will be more weaving programs available for these platforms in the future. The new Mac with Intel chip can easily run Windows programs with appropriate software, such as Parallels, or VMware Fusion or Boot Camp, installed. See where to find weaving software on page 224.

What do you need?

Not all weaving software packages are the same. Each one has a unique set of features; consequently, a program that is perfect for one person may not be the best choice for another. The best way to determine what program will best suit your needs is to try it out. For this reason, most (if not all) weaving software packages are available on a demo basis, so that you can give them a try.

Probably the first thing you need to ask yourself is how much you want to spend. Weaving software packages cost anywhere from free to several hundred dollars, with most programs somewhere in between. If all you want to do is view and print WIF files, or just replace pencil, paper, and eraser, then a very basic program will likely be sufficient. If you're using a Windows PC, it's quite likely that a free program will meet your needs.

At the time of this writing, there aren't many free programs available for the Mac or for Linux. For the Mac, the free program—WinWeave will not read WIF files. The shareware program, WeaveDesign, will read many WIF files but not all. For Linux there is a demo version of ArahWeave that will read and write WIF files. You might start with the free/shareware programs if you are not sure you will use weaving software. With the growing popularity of tablets and smartphones, we're starting to see weaving software available on both iOS and Android platforms. Search for "weaving" in the app store to see what's available.

Design and manipulate

If you think you would like to take advantage of some more advanced features, you might want to look into spending a little money. Some of these features include the ability to manipulate or turn drafts, view a more accurate simulation of the finished fabric (warp- or weft-faced, doubleweave, thick and thin, etc.), calculate warp and weft requirements, or count heddles. Some programs will even let you design in the drawdown, automatically figuring out the threading and treadling. Others allow you to import a graphic file or photo, and will automatically translate it into a draft either minimizing the number of shafts or threading on a straight draw.

Loom control

If you have a multi-shaft loom that requires a computer to select the shafts, you may need to contact your loom manufacturer to find out if there is a recommended program for your specific loom. Many of the more popular weaving programs offer drivers for specific looms, at an additional cost.

Where to find weaving software

The easiest way to find weaving software packages is over the Internet. A quick Google search for "weaving software" will give you several places to look.

A good place to seek information is from the weaving groups and lists online and your local weaving guild. See below.

Judie Eatough has her own website with a lot of information.
www.weavenotes.net

Interweave Press

Interweave Press offers a wealth of information on their website.
www.weavingtoday.com

Handweaving.net

This is a valuable site. They have a huge number of drafts in their archive. Judie Eatough keeps the list current on her website. ***www.weavenotes.net***

Weaving groups and lists

There are several very active weaving groups and email lists on the Internet. Yahoo! Groups is a good place to find some very lively discussion groups for weavers. The two biggest groups are Weaving and WeaveTech. They are also good places to find recommendations for different software packages. You can join these online groups by visiting: groups.yahoo.com. If you do not already have a Yahoo! account, follow the instructions on-screen to sign up. All Yahoo! Groups allow you to view messages either on the Web or delivered to you in email messages. For more information, see Yahoo! Also, see Weavolution—***www.weavolution.com*** and Ravelry—***www.ravelry.com***, and Facebook.

Judie Eatough
www.weavenotes.net

Interweave Press
www.weavingtoday.com

Handweaving.net
www.weavenotes.net

Weavoution
www.weavolution.com

Ravelry
www.ravelry.com

Demo programs

Many weaving programs come in a demo version that you can download for free and try out. Some of these demo programs are limited by time—they will work for a relatively short period of time, say 30 days, after which they will no longer function unless you buy the program. Other demo programs have limited features, or will allow you to edit but not save, or save but not print. Nonetheless, a demo program will give you the ability to try out the software before spending any money, so you can decide if it meets your needs.

Safety of downloading software

The media is full of horror stories about destructive computer viruses lurking in the back alleys of the Internet, and many people are scared to do anything but the most innocuous of tasks online. If you are downloading a program from a reputable, known website that caters to weavers, there is little to no chance of "catching" a computer virus. If you are concerned about computer viruses in general, you should be running virus protection software. Most computer manufacturers these days pre-install virus prevention software on new computers, although you need to make sure that if it's on a subscription basis, you need to pay a renewal fee yearly to keep it up to date.

Basic computer resources

If you feel uncomfortable using a computer and/or the Internet, there are a variety of resources available to help you learn more about using today's computers and the Internet. If you are using a computer running Microsoft Windows, visit Microsoft's website. If you're using an Apple Macintosh computer, you can find help at Apple's website. See websites listed at the right. Other helpful web sites are also shown here.

If you need additional help, you can find many beginner-friendly computer and Internet books at your local library or bookstore.

Microsoft Windows website:
www.microsoft.com

Apple website:
www.apple.com

Other websites:
www.jegsworks.com/Lessons
www.comptechdoc.org/basic/basictut

Learning how to use weaving software

Most weaving software packages come with either a tutorial or a manual (or a link to documentation on the Internet). Take some time to learn how to use the software by opening sample drafts that come with the program or by creating your own basic drafts and playing with them. The controls in most weaving programs are quite similar – they typically have copy, cut, and paste options. Many programs allow you to ***turn*** a draft, in other words, swap the warp threading and the treadling to rotate the design 90°. If possible, try several programs before you buy, so that you can get an idea what features and controls best fit your needs.

The weave draft generated by your computer program is divided into four quadrants just as on printed drafts in American hand weaving journals and books and as described in the chapter on drafting, beginning on page 195. In that chapter you learned that threading drafts in most American publications are read from right-to-left and the treadling drafts are read from the top-to-bottom. However, some programs read the threading and treadling drafts in the opposite directions: from left-to-right and from bottom-to-top. You'll recognize all the parts of weaving drafts when you are exploring various software and should easily recognize how the threading and treadling drafts are oriented.

In addition, most programs have separate bars for warp and weft color—a bar above the threading quadrant to indicate the colors of the warp threads and another along the side of the treadling draft to indicate the weft colors. This can be seen in Figure 471 on page 232.

Downloading weaving drafts

Once you've installed a weaving program on your computer, and your computer is connected to the Internet, you can download weaving drafts in the form of WIF files. There are several places online where you can find weaving drafts.

Handweaving.net

The largest online repository of weaving drafts is Handweaving.net ***(www.handweaving.net)***. This site was created by Kris Bruland in 2004. Users all over the world can contribute drafts to the site; consequently, drafts are being added all the time.

Many of the drafts on the site are taken from out-of-print and out-of-copyright sources, including G. H. Oelsner's ***A Handbook of Weaves*** and the vast collection of drafts compiled by Ralph E. Griswold.

On the site, you can browse drafts by collection, or based on category, number of shafts, or source. Once you've found a draft you like, you can view it in several different ways—you can change the size, move the tie-up orientation, and even turn the draft. To download it, simply click on the link to the WIF file and save it on your computer the same way you would any other file. See Figure 463b (repeated here).

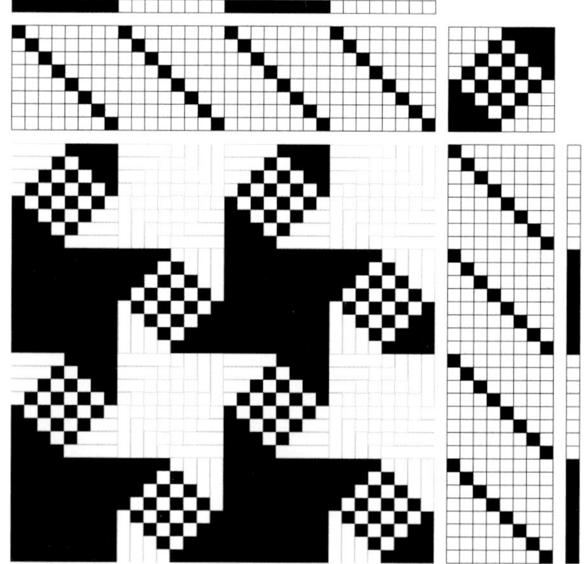

If you'd like to contribute drafts to the site, you need to register and follow the instructions for contributors.

Specialty software

If you are interested in other forms of weaving, such as tablet or card weaving, or kumihimo (traditional Japanese braiding), there are specialty programs available. For more information about tablet weaving or kumihimo software, see the Weavershand website at ***www.weavershand.com***, or ***www.weavenotes.net.***

The Place of Technology in the Hand-weaving World

By Deborah Holcomb

One of the reasons that weavers do what they do is because of the intimacy of the process and close connections it establishes between the weaver and the cloth. But we are living in the 21st century and in addition to beautiful yarns and well-made weaving equipment, we also have access to a whole world of technology that our weaving 'ancestors' could never have imagined.

Some people automatically assume that using today's high-tech tools somehow reduces that sense of intimacy and is incompatible with the very idea of hand-weaving. But in truth, these tools, far from 'contaminating' the process, simply expand our creative possibilities in ways that were unavailable to our predecessors. Scanners and digital cameras along with image editing software allow us to capture and interpret images that inspire us. And weaving programs allow us to generate creative ideas that we might not have thought of otherwise. After all, the best way to come up with a few great new designs is to generate lots and lots of them and throw the bad ones away.

Creativity is the outcome of an exploratory process. It is an act of experimentation and discovery. And herein lies both the beauty and the "problem" of weaving on a shaft loom, whether or not you decide to use software: The possibilities for combining threadings, tie-ups and treadlings are just about endless. And that, of course, leaves you with the question "Where in the world do I start?"

Weaving programs: Computer games for weavers

Often, a weaver will begin using a weaving program simply as a way to record project information and to check to make sure that the draft being used is accurate. The available programs all perform these basic functions perfectly.

But such functions are just the tip of the iceberg. The real beauty of weaving programs is in their creative, not their documenting possibilities. They can be computer games for weavers.

The beauty of any game, from Monopoly to the Super Bowl is this: Even though you use the same rules each time, the final outcome is unpredictable because of the things that happen along the way. Furthermore, if you don't like the rules for some reason, you can always change them to produce more interesting results.

The key is in the keyboard

One key to becoming a 'power user' of your weaving program is to replace all those carpal-tunnel-producing mouse clicks with key strokes whenever you can. Once you know where your favorite bits are in the software, go back to the menus and examine them to see if there are keyboard shortcuts, also called "hot keys," for the operations you perform most frequently.

For example, in most Windows-based applications, holding down the ***Ctrl*** key while pressing "N" will create a new document. In Mac applications, the ***Cmd*** key works the way ***Ctrl*** does in Windows.

It takes a little extra time to memorize those shortcuts, but it pays off down the road. Don't try to remember them all—just find the ones you are likely to use most.

Wizardry

One of the things that computers are especially good for is to automate repetitive mechanical tasks—especially those that are time-consuming and error-prone. For most of us, creating drawdowns is just such a task.

The weaving programs go much farther than just generating a drawdown automatically from a threading and treadling. They take complex, multi-step drafting techniques and package them up into handy little "wizards" that prompt for a few bits of information and then generate drafts that would take us forever to draw by hand.

Interesting iterations

The power of the weaving programs is in their ability to start with a basic design and iteratively process it to produce various refinements or completely new designs.

And you can produce these iterations so quickly that you will generate many, many more designs than you would ever generate by hand using pencil and paper. Furthermore, you will find in the mix some very beautiful little gems that would not have been discovered without the aid of the software, such as the ones below:

Figure 464: A "name draft" constructed using the palindromic phrase "a dog, a panic in a pagoda." In "name drafts," letters of the alphabet are assigned to shafts. The threading sequence is determined by the letters in a name (yours) or a phrase ("a dog, a panic in a pagoda").

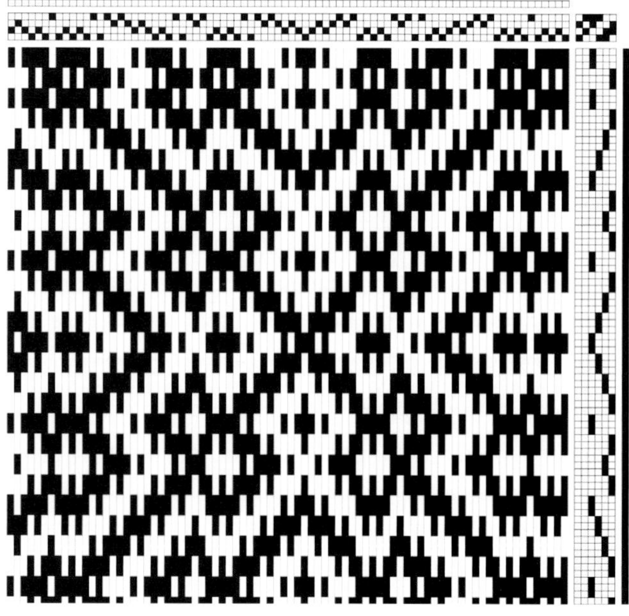

Fig. 464 A dog, a panic in a pagoda

Figure 465: 8-shaft twills developed by mixing and matching threadings and tie-up.

Fig. 465 Twill diamond

Figure 466: 8-shaft twills developed using a "network drafting" wizard.

Fig. 466 Twill net

A sample design game

The preceding drafts were all created just by playing around with the software, but playing around systematically--that is, by learning how different program features operate and then applying a set of 'game rules' over and over again.

Here is a sample: All of the major weaving programs have a block substitution wizard that allows you to take any block design and translate it into many different drafts each in a different weave structure. Block subsitituion is explained in detail beginning on page 209.

The weaving program does all the "heavy lifting" for you: replacing each block of the design with different interlacements and then doing the drawdowns. You supply the basic profile design, select a structure that can be woven on the number of shafts that you have on your loom, and the software does the rest. You just push a button and view the resulting draft. Keep the ones you like and discard the ones you don't.

If your loom has four shafts, begin by choosing an interesting two block profile design. Profile drafts are explained beginning on page 209. Some structures give you more possibilities than others when you are considering how to use a profile draft. Structures that allow you to repeat an individual threading unit indefinitely, like summer and winter or Atwater-Bronson lace give you more design options than a structure like overshot: overshot floats get impractically long if the block is too wide.

You begin this game by entering your block design in the threading area of the weaving program as shown below. Blocks are explained beginning on page 209. Figure 467 shows a two-block design constructed by making each block 1 unit wider than the preceding one

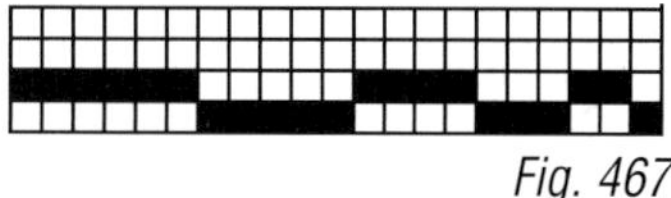

Fig. 467

Next, use the software to create a profile treadling. All of the programs have functions that allow you to "weave as drawn in" (sometimes called "tromp as writ"). It is one of the things to look for when you are exploring the user interface of your program. The specific details of the command vary from one program to another, but in all of them, once you have a threading, you can enter a treadling with just a couple of keystrokes or mouse-clicks. Figure 468 shows a profile threading with tromp as writ treadling. Tromp as writ is explained on page 217.

Fig. 468 "Tromp as writ" treadling

Now, you can simply enter the profile tie-up with two more mouse clicks and the software will instantly do the draw-down: Figure 469 shows the completed profile design.

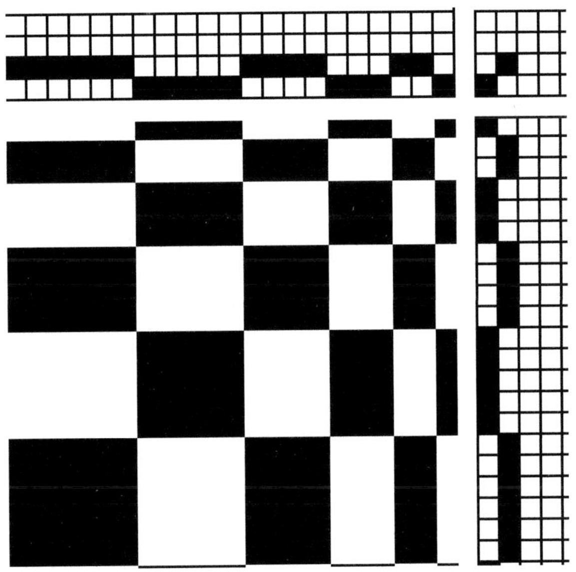

Fig. 469 Completed profile design

Endless possibilities

Now for the fun part: You get to try out this design in lots of different weave structures and color combinations. To do it, just locate the block substitution wizard in your weaving program. You can either explore the menus to locate this feature, or you can use your program's help function and search for "block substitution" or "profile drafts." This search will lead you to instructions for starting up a wizard that will give you a list of possible weave structures. The details vary from one program to another, but this capability exists in all of them. Once you choose the structure you want to try, the program will do all the work of translating your profile block design into a thread by thread draft. In the following illustrations, you can see just a few of the many possibilities. Figure 470 is an example of the design above woven in Bronson lace.

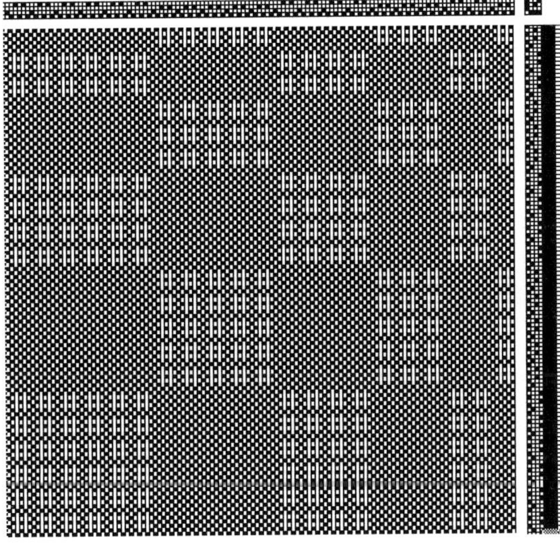

Fig. 470 Bronson lace

In the log cabin draft (Figure 471), there is something shown that we haven't seen before: the dark and light warp threads are indicated immediately above the threading draft—see the bar with the dark marks? Log cabin also requires darks and lights in the wefts—the dark and light wefts are shown in the draft immediately beside the treadling draft. In other structures the warp and weft colors (colors, instead of dark and light) would be indicated in these two areas. This drawdown is a schematic representation of what the cloth will look like. The vertical and horizontal lines are the result of using the dark and light threads in specific ways in the warp and in the weft. The actual weave is only plain weave. We call it "color and weave effect" when the look of the cloth is very different from the actual structure of the weave.

Fig. 471 Log cabin

Figure 472 shows a summer and winter version of the same design.

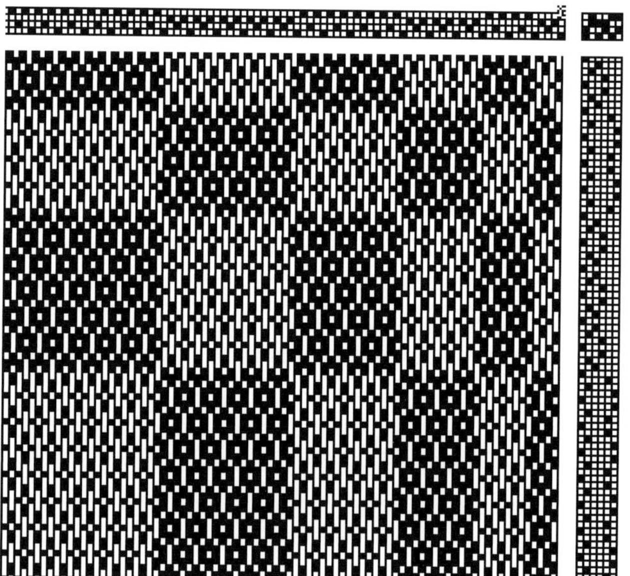

Fig. 472 Summer-winter

Once you settle on the structure you want to use, you can begin to play around with different color combinations.

There is only one real drawback to using weaving design software: It can be so much fun just to play with that you forget to weave.

9 Future Assignments

Introduction

In this chapter, I suggest some new weaves to learn after you've woven your first warp or two and how to proceed to make a sampler for each weave. Suggestions for projects you can make are given in the chapter on planning projects. Also in that chapter is the information you need for planning your own original projects—how much yarn you need, etc.

I assign my students to make a project of their own design using the information they have learned in their samplers. The drill goes like this: learn by making a sampler, design a project using what you have learned; then, learn something new with a sampler and make a project using that information, etc.

I highly recommend that these first real projects be small—not wide and not long. Then, you will not be intimidated by a large project with a big investment in time and money. See the chapter on planning projects, on page 285, for suggestions of projects to make.

Your first assignment

Two projects have been given in the chapters showing how to set the loom up either "back-to-front" or "front-to-back." Making an original project using the information gained would be your first assignment.

Your second assignment

Next, I suggest you try something new. It may be one of the weaves in this chapter. However, if you wove the sampler, beginning on page 93, you might decide to weave a chenille scarf as described on page 155. Or, if you made a chenille scarf, you might try the sampler. Use the method of setting up the loom that you have already learned at this point. I don't recommend learning the other warping method until you've made enough warps that you feel comfortable with the method you learned first.

Your next assignments: Three weaves to try

In this chapter, I explain three weave structures: a variation of warp-faced rep; log cabin; and double weave. Each structure has its rules to follow. The basics of the weaves will be explained. More information, complexities, and design ideas can be found in weaving books and magazines. After making a sampler for a new weave, design your own project putting into practice what you learned in the sampler.

What these three weaves have in common is that they are made with their warp threads alternating in color. Often, but not always, one color is dark and the other light. For the samplers for these weaves I suggest using two colors with high contrast. One student chose two colors that were only subtly different—the result was beautiful, but she was greatly disappointed because she couldn't see the patterns. In fact, she wove a sample for me to show future students so they wouldn't make the same mistake. In the directions, I will indicate dark and light threads as the contrasting colors.

What makes the weaves so different is that they differ greatly in their weave drafts, and in the rules that apply to each one.

Your next sampler(s)

You can make a separate warp for each of these weaves, and that is a very fine idea. If you follow each sampler with a project, you will have made six warps and set up the loom six times. You might feel quite familiar with weaving by then, and use the directions for setting up the loom in the book only as a reminder of what to do next.

Since my students had limited time in class, I had them make one sampler that was long enough to weave all three of the weaves. Then they chose one of them for their next project. I suggest if you use this idea that you follow up by making three other projects—one for each weave.

Directions for making all three weaves on one warp are given on page 258. Note that after weaving the first weave, a variation of warp-faced rep, you will cut the warp threads and re-thread them in the heddles in order to weave the remaining weave structures. This is quite doable, but you must be a little careful, so do read the information beginning on page 258.

A Variation of Warp-faced Rep Weave

Warp-faced rep and this variation are usually woven as a rather thick cloth—often used for placemats and table runners. See Figure 473. Another rep weave, weft-faced rep, was included in the sampler, on page 126.

In "regular" warp-faced rep, the warp threads are very close together—so close that they entirely cover up the weft threads as shown in the illustrations. It takes some extra knowledge and skill, so I prefer that my beginning students weave a variation where the warp threads are not that close together. Instead, in the variation, the threads are about as close together as they would be for weaving regular balanced plain weave—where the warp and weft both show.

In this variation, even though the warps will be spaced far enough apart that the warps and wefts both show, the warp threads will dominate the appearance of the cloth.

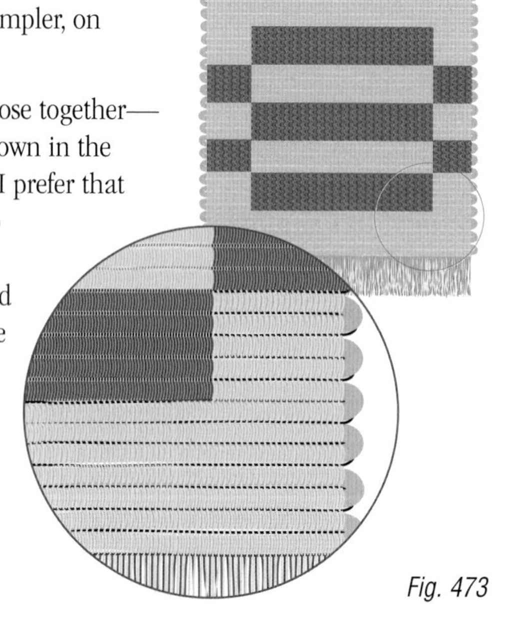

Fig. 473

A sampler for a variation of warp-faced rep

Here are the specifications to weave the whole warp in this variation of warp-faced rep: Remember that you need yarn for both the warp and the weft as shown below.

Warp length: 2 yards (length of guide string)

Warp width: 5 inches

Warp yarn: 5/2 pearl cotton, see below.

Weft yarns: one thick and one thin weft, see below

Warp threads per inch (also called ends per inch, or epi): 16 epi if 8-dent reed is used; 20 epi if 10 dent reed is used (Read below which to use.)

Total number of warp threads (ends): 80 threads at 16 epi; 100 threads at 20 epi.

Treadles: for floor looms, use one of the direct tie-ups as shown in Figures 225 and 226 on page 96 and repeated here.

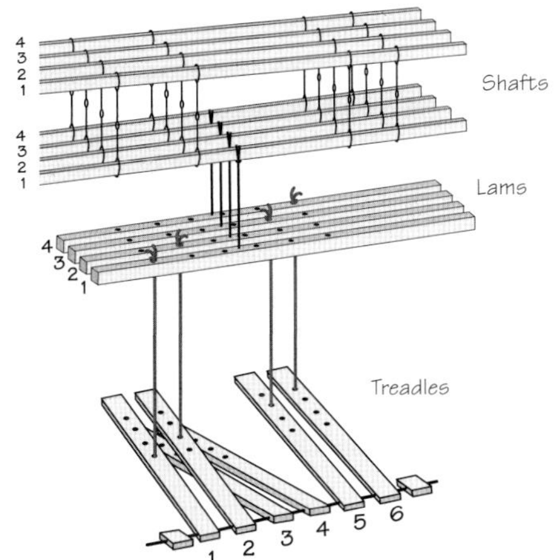

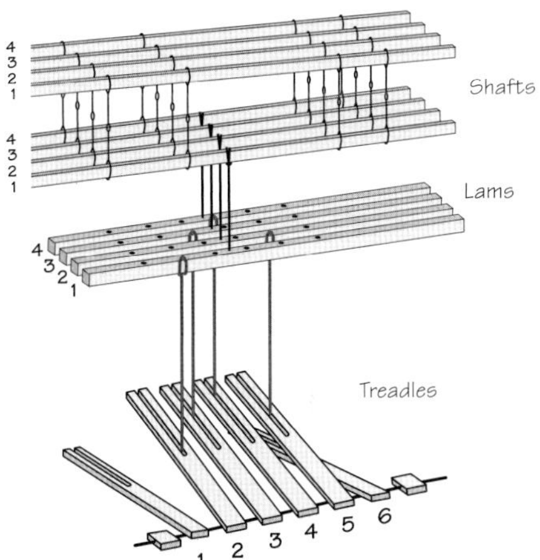

Supplies needed for the sampler

Regular weaving supplies—See pages 7-11 or page 156.

2 shuttles

Reed: 8 or 10 dents per inch. See below and read how to substitute another size reed on page 33.

Which reed to use

You can use either an 8 or 10 dent reed. The ideal number of warps per inch (ends per inch or epi) for two of the samplers in this chapter is that for plain weave. Looking at the chart on page 32 we see that the ideal for balanced plain weave is 16 epi for 5/2 cotton. Also, it is ideal to fill the reed (sley the reed) with two warp threads per dent. So, an 8-dent reed would make it easy to achieve both: the ideal of 16 epi, and the ideal of two-per dent.

In reality, for all of the weaves in this chapter, 20 epi will work just fine. So, if you already have a 10-dent reed you can sley two warp threads per dent to equal the 20 epi.

Rep Weave Variation

By using the Reed Substitution Chart on page 33, you can also choose to use 16 epi with your 10-dent reed. You can see in the chart how to achieve almost 16 epi (15 epi) with a 10-dent reed. The sequence of threads in the dents would be: 1 thread in a dent followed by 2 threads in a dent repeated for the width of the warp.

All it means is that you have a choice and can try either reed. As I said, the ideal is 16 epi, but if you prefer 20 epi because it will be simpler to sley a 10-dent reed that you already have on hand, that is ok, too.

Note that if you decide upon 20 epi you will have to measure out more threads than if you use 16 epi. The adjustments for each are given in the instructions that follow.

Warp yarn

5/2 pearl cotton—two contrasting colors. Read about pearl cotton on page 13 and substituting other yarns on pages 32 and 33.

If you plan to make just one warp for all 3 weaves, see page 258 for the amounts of each yarn that are needed.

With an 8-dent reed at 16 ends per inch (epi): You will need ¾ oz. or 100 yards of each color, for a total of 1½ oz. or 200 yards of both colors combined. A 5" width will need a total of 80 ends.

With a 10-dent reed at 20 ends per inch (epi): You will need 1 oz. or 130 yards of each color, for a total of 2 oz or 260 yards of both colors combined. A 5" width will need a total of 100 ends.

Weft Yarn

Two weft yarns: one thick and one thin—colors should be fairly similar to the warp colors.

The types of yarn you use for each weft (the thick yarn and the thin one) can vary greatly and still make good results. Examples of thick and thin yarns are shown on page 32.

Almost anything can be used as a thick yarn along with any thinner one. I suggest trying out what you have around, but if you have to buy the yarns, I've given suggested amounts that you'll need below.

Combinations of thick and thin yarns you might use.

For 4 strands held together of ***5/2 pearl cotton*** for the thick yarn and sewing thread for the thin, you'll need 260 yards or about 2 ounces of 5/2 cotton, and for the thin weft, a spool of ordinary sewing thread will be much more than you need.

For ***worsted weight*** (like knitting yarn—see page 32) for the thick yarn and 5/2 cotton for the thin, you'll need about 75 yards or 1½ ounces of the knitting yarn and about 100 yards or ¾ ounce of the 5/2 for the thin yarn.

 Measure the Warp Threads

Measure out a guide string for a 2-yard warp and arrange it on the warping board as described on pages 15-18 for back-to-front warping, or beginning on page 157 for front-to-back warping.

Measure out 80 threads for 16 epi or 100 threads for 20 epi

When measuring out the actual warp threads, this time, you will use 2 threads at once as you traverse the path on the warping board—one of each of your two colors. You can do this job with no more than two threads at once—any more than two will braid up on themselves and tangle badly. Warping with more threads at once can be done with a paddle, however, and is described in my first book, ***Winding a Warp & Using a Paddle.***

How to measure two threads at once

Refer to measuring out the warp threads on pages 19-22 for the back-to-front method and see page 157 for front-to-back warping.

Put both warp yarns on the floor below the warping board—but put each one in a separate container, such as small wastebaskets, or bowls.

Carry both threads together at the thread-by-thread cross at the top of the warping board (at pegs 2 and 3) so that the cross will be a 2-thread-by 2-thread cross.

Warning! It is extremely important to remember that you are measuring 2 threads at once each time you travel the length of the guide string. When you make the return trip back to the top of the warping board you are measuring out another 2 threads—the third and fourth warp threads.

To repeat: Remember that once along the length of the guide string with 2 threads counts as 2 threads. A complete round trip equals 4 threads.

The warping will go quickly because you are using 2 threads at once.

If you make a group cross in back-to-front warping, you will make groups of 8 threads for a project with 16 ends per inch. If you have chosen 20 epi, each part of the group cross should contain 10 threads. The group cross represents half the threads that will be per inch. Remember to count each thread—there will always be 2 threads to count.

Measure out 80 threads if you are using 16 epi (ends per inch). If you are using 20 epi, measure out 100 threads. Do you see that both will give you a 5-inch wide warp?

Tie the crosses and choke ties as usual as seen on pages 23 and 24 for warping the loom back-to-front, and on pages 159 and 160 for front-to-back warping.

Remove the warp from the warping board by putting it on a kitestick (see pages 25-27) or by making a chain (see page 34 or pages 161 and 162).

 Put the Warp on the Loom

If using the back-to-front method, first put the warp into the raddle (see pages 28-30) then, follow the directions for beaming the warp beginning on page 35. The warp is to be 5" wide.

If using the front-to-back method, follow the directions for entering the warp in the reed beginning on page 165. Put 2 warp threads in each dent of the reed unless you are following the Reed Substitution Chart on page 33. The warp is to be 5" wide. Read below how the heddles should be threaded for this weave.

(3) Thread the Heddles

There is a special way to thread the heddles. Use your preferred method for setting up the loom—either back-to-front (page 13) or front-to-back (page 149), but thread the heddles according to the rules for warp-faced rep, below.

The two different threadings

There will be two different threadings: one threading pattern for the borders (also called Block A) and another one for the center part (called Block B) of the sampler. The borders are to be 1" wide each, and the middle part is 3" wide. It means that if you are using 16 epi, each of the borders will have 16 threads, and the center section will have 48 for a total of 80 threads. For 20 epi, each border will have 20 threads and 60 threads in the middle section. Figure 474 shows this schematically. You may recognize this as a profile draft of two blocks as described beginning on page 209.

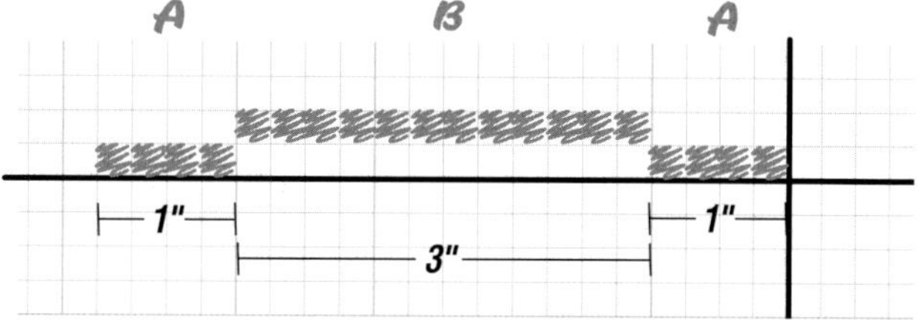

Fig. 474

Count out the heddles needed

For 16 epi you'll need:

16 heddles on shaft 1
16 heddles on shaft 2
24 heddles on shaft 3
24 heddles on shaft 4
That's a total of 80 heddles, one for each warp thread.

For 20 epi you'll need:

20 heddles on shaft 1
20 heddles on shaft 2
30 heddles on shaft3
30 heddles on shaft 4
That's a total of 100 heddles, one for each warp thread.

Arrange the heddles on the shafts

Push the excess heddles equally to each side of the shafts and tie them as shown in Figure 475. Put the heddles for the middle section (Block B) in the center of shafts 3 and 4 and place the heddles for each border on each side of the middle. In other words, ½ of the heddles for shafts 1 and 2 should be to the left of the middle heddles and ½ should be to the right of the middle heddles. See Figure 476.

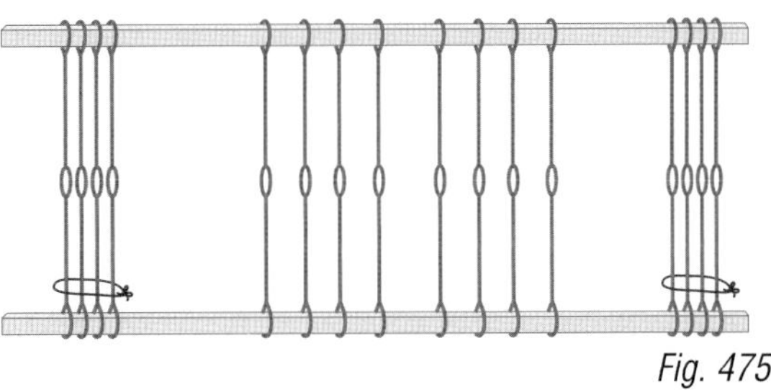

Fig. 475

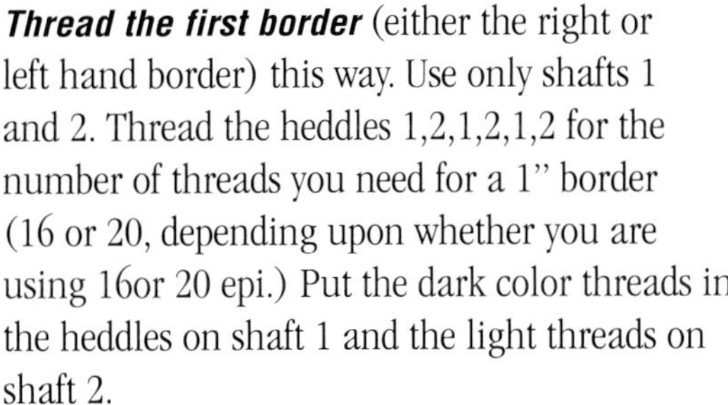

Thread the first border (either the right or left hand border) this way. Use only shafts 1 and 2. Thread the heddles 1,2,1,2,1,2 for the number of threads you need for a 1" border (16 or 20, depending upon whether you are using 16or 20 epi.) Put the dark color threads in the heddles on shaft 1 and the light threads on shaft 2.

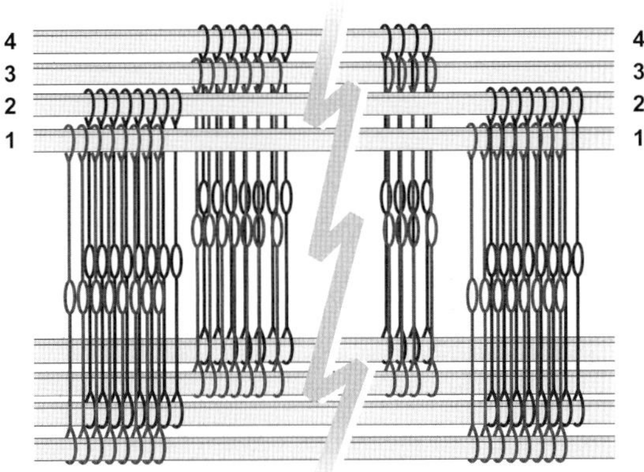

Fig. 476

Thread the middle section (Block B) using only shafts 3 and 4 this way: 3,4,3,4,3,4 for the number of threads you require for this section (48 or 60). Put the dark color threads in the heddles on shaft 3 and the light threads on shaft 4.

Thread the remaining border on shafts 1 and 2 just as you did for the first border—again, with the dark threads on shaft 1 and the light ones on shaft 2.

The draft for the threading is shown in Figure 477.

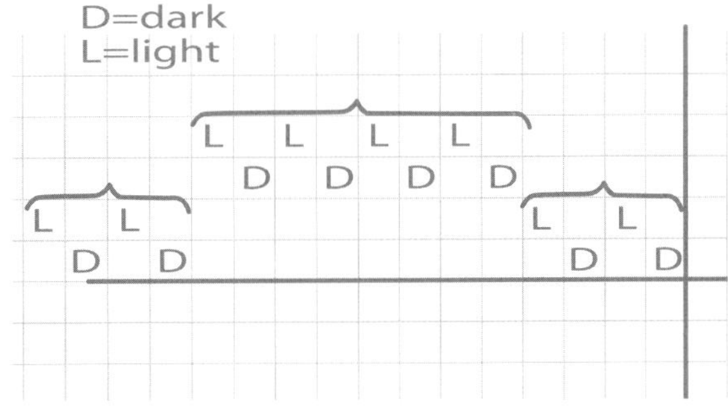

Fig. 477

④ Complete Setting Up the Loom

Using your preferred method, finish setting up the loom. For back-to-front, now put 2 warp threads in each dent unless you are following the Reed Substitution Chart on page 33. The warp is to be 5 inches wide. Weave the heading (described beginning on pages 105 and 180).

⑤ Weaving

The draft for weaving warp-faced rep and our variation is shown in Figure 478. What makes this weave work takes place in all the quadrants of the weave draft. You have seen the special threading required. Now look in the treadling draft and see that a thick weft and a thin weft are indicated by large and small dots.

The first row is to be woven using the thick weft with shafts 2 and 4 lifted. (How to read drafts begins on page 195, but words are given here in case you haven't learned to read drafts yet.)

The second row is to be woven with the thin weft and shafts 1 and 3 raised.

Continue weaving in this manner for 2": lift shafts 2 and 4 and throw the thick weft, change to shafts 1 and 3 and throw the thin weft.

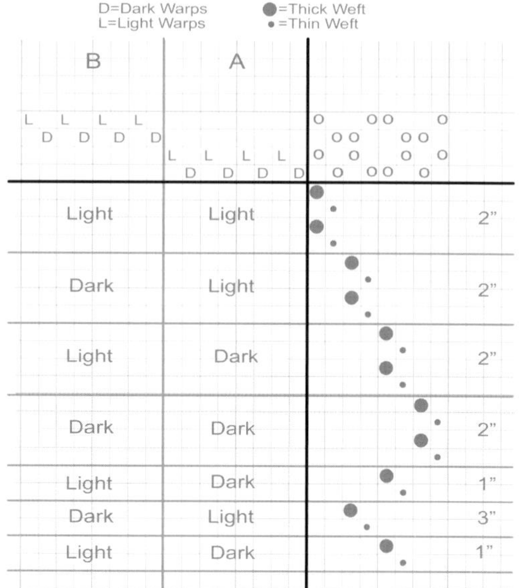

Fig. 478

The second section is woven with the thick weft used when shafts 2 and 3 are lifted and the thin weft is used with shafts 1 and 4 lifted. Weave this section for 2" also. Continue weaving as instructed below and shown in the draft. Always be sure to use the correct weft with the correct combination of shafts.

The third section calls for the thick weft to be thrown when shafts 1 and 4 are lifted, and the thin when shafts 2 and 3 are lifted. ***Notice in the draft that between the 2nd and 3rd sections 1 and 4 are lifted twice in a row.*** It means that to make the required change, you'll have both thick and thin wefts in the same shed. The fourth section calls for the thick weft to be thrown when shafts 1 and 3 are lifted and the thin when 2 and 4 are lifted.

How to change thick wefts is on page 131, Figure 302.

The last three sections are woven tromp as writ as described on page 217. Notice that you are to weave 1 inch, then 3 inches, then 1 inch. That is how tromp as writ works—by weaving the same dimensions that are indicated in the threading. In this case, both the threading and the weaving are in sections of 1 inch, then 3 inches, then 1 inch again.

The drawdown draft shows what colors should dominate in the A and B sections with the various treadling configurations. (This design is different from Figure 473 on page 234.)

Weave your own designs and ideas for the remainder of the warp. How much warp is left depends upon how fat your wefts were, so I can't tell you how much you will have for ideas and experimenting. You might make a mat or a table runner or try different wefts— sizes, colors, or textures.

This is the part of a sampler or project I love the most—where I am most creative. Often, the ideas I like to try are the ones that break the rules. (Let that be a hint.)

Log Cabin Weave

This is a weave with vertical and horizontal lines appearing in the cloth. It is actually plain weave, but looks like an entirely different structure. When the structure is disguised by the colors of the yarns, we call this phenomenon, "color and weave effect." These weave effects are based on dark and light threads in the warp and/or the weft.

Log cabin weave

A sampler for log cabin

Warp length: 2 yards (length of guide string)

Width: 5 inches

Warp yarn: 5/2 pearl cotton, see below

Weft yarn: 5/2 pearl cotton, see below

Warp threads per inch (also called ends per inch or epi): 16 if 8-dent reed is used; 20 epi if 10-dent reed is used. Read which to use on page 235.

Total warp threads (ends): 80 at 16 epi; 100 at 20 epi.

Supplies needed for the sampler

Regular weaving supplies—See pages 7-11 or page 156.

2 shuttles

Reed: 8 or 10 dents per inch. See which reed to use on page 235.

Warp and Weft Yarns

5/2 pearl cotton—two contrasting colors. The yarns for the warp and weft will be the same. Read about pearl cotton on page 13 and about substituting other yarns, see page 32.

With an 8-dent reed at 16 ends per inch (epi) you need 1 ½ oz. of each color or 200 yards of each color for a total of 3 ounces (400 yards) for the warp and weft combined.

With a 10-dent reed at 20 ends per inch (epi) you need 1 ¾ oz. of each color or 230 yards of each color for a total of 3 ½ oz. (460 yards) for the warp and weft combined.

1 Measure the Warp Threads

With a guide string for a 2-yard warp, measure out 80 threads for 16 epi or 100 threads for 20 epi using two threads at once as described on page 237.

 Put the Warp on the Loom

This step is described on page 238.

 Thread the Heddles

There will be the same arrangement of two different threadings as described on page 258. However, read below how to thread the heddles for this sampler.

Prepare the heddles

You will have ¼ of the warp threads on each shaft; therefore, there will be 20 heddles needed on each shaft for 16 epi (80 warp threads) and 25 per shaft if you have 20 epi (100 warp threads). Push the excess heddles equally to each side of the shafts and tie them as shown in Figure 475 on page 239 and repeated here.

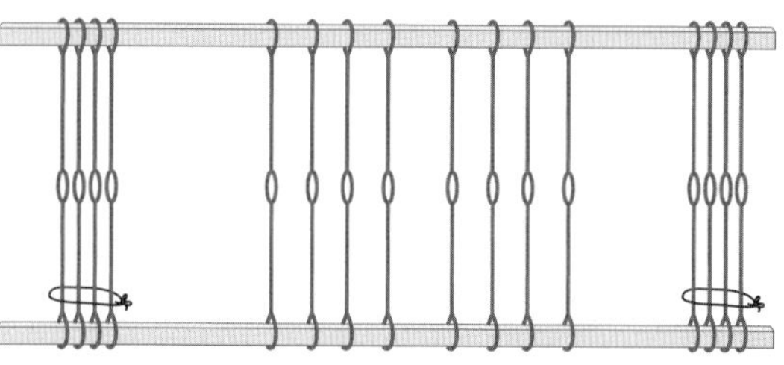

Thread the heddles

The threading will be 4,3,2,1 repeated across the warp. The difference between the borders and the middle section is in the placement of the dark and light threads.

For the borders, thread the light threads on shafts 1 and 3 and put the dark threads in the heddles on shafts 2 and 4, as shown in Figure 479. Remember, there are 16 or 20 threads in each border depending upon whether you are using 16 or 20 epi. You want one inch worth of threads threaded this way first. After one border is completed, thread the middle section as shown below. Then return to thread the second border just like the first one.

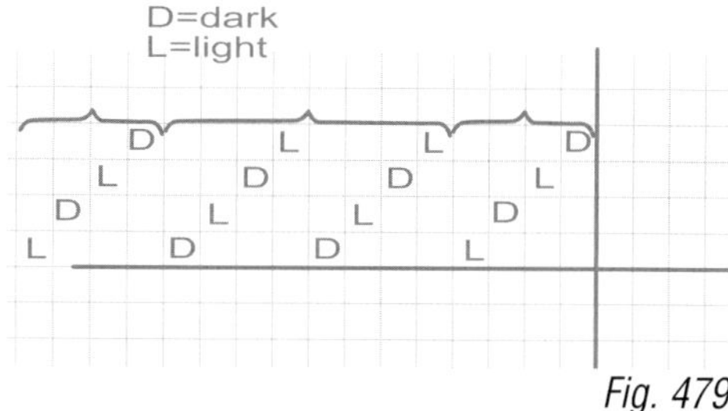

Fig. 479

For the middle section, thread the darks on shafts 1 and 3 and the lights on shafts 2 and 4. Remember how many threads go in this section. Since it is 3" wide, you'll either thread 48 warp threads (3 x 16) or 60 warp threads (3 x 20).

Thread the remaining threads in the way the first border was threaded.

 Complete Setting Up the Loom

Set up the loom and weave the heading as explained on page 239.

Weaving

Wind two shuttles: one shuttle of each color.

You will use the sequence of sheds for weaving plain weave, alternating lifting shafts 1 and 3 together with 2 and 4 together. Plain weave is described on pages 111 and 180.

Vertical and horizontal lines will appear as you weave along when you use the appropriate weft color with the appropriate lifted shafts. See below.

Weave the first part of the sampler for 2 inches.

Throw the shuttle with the dark thread when you lift shafts 1 and 3.

Throw the shuttle with the light thread when you lift shafts 2 and 4.

You should see vertical lines appearing in the borders and horizontal lines in the center. This is shown in Figure 480 in the form of a weaving draft. Drafts are explained in the drafting chapter beginning on page 195.

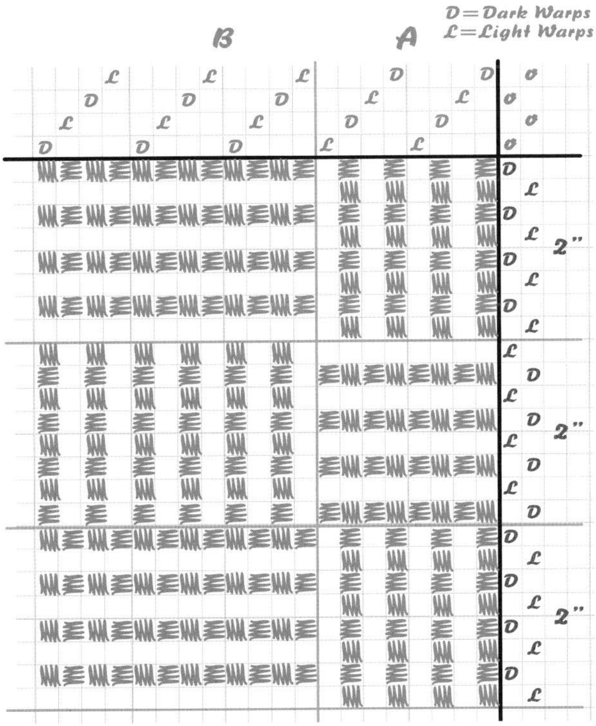

Weave the second part of the sampler for 2 inches.

Now weave the reverse of what you did in the first section: throw the light shuttle when shafts 1 and 3 are lifted, and the dark shuttle when shafts 2 and 4 are raised. You will get the opposite result with the vertical lines being in the middle and horizontals in the borders.

Fig. 480

Note that at the change of sections, according to the draft in the illustration, *you will throw 2 rows together with the light shuttle.* You get another "look" if you throw the dark shuttle twice when changing back and forth from horizontals and verticals. When you use two dark wefts together at the changes, the areas appear outlined and distinct. When you use two lights together, the blocks are not outlined and seem to float. If you look closely, you can see these effects in Figure 480. See the sidebar on the next page for more information.

Weave the third part of the sampler for 2 inches

Continue weaving as shown in the draft or described below, repeating part one for 2 inches.

Weave tromp as writ next

That is, weave 1 inch with horizontal lines in the borders and the verticals in the middle. (Just as you wove part two, above.)

Then weave 3 inches with vertical lines in the borders and horizontal lines in the middle. (Just like Parts 1 and 3.)

Then weave 1 inch with the horizontals in the borders again as above.

Can you see why this is called tromp as writ? It's that the design of the sections in the warp are repeated in the weft. Read more about tromp as writ on page 217.

Weave your own designs and ideas.

Instead of threads that match the warp colors, you might try other colors for the dark and light wefts. You might use colors that barely contrast, or just weave with one color. You might try contrasting textures, or decide to disobey all the rules completely and find pleasing (or at least interesting) effects. One student made a lovely sample weaving with rags. To see what is happening, weave at least 2 inches of each idea you try. Weaving twills gives interesting effects, too. You can use one weft color or two or more.

As I said at the end of the variation of warp-faced rep section, the end of the warp is the place where I am usually the most creative. Let yourself go—you have nothing to lose because you already have a sampler, which shows what log cabin is about.

Margins of the Blocks

See Figure 480 on the previous page and notice that the horizontal margins of the blocks are more distinct where two dark wefts are shown woven one after the other at the second 2" section change. You can make both the horizontal and vertical margins of the blocks solid colors (outlined) if you make both the warp and the weft changes with the dark threads together. In the threading, have two dark threads together at the edges of the blocks to make the vertical margins. Weave two dark wefts together at the section changes for the horizontal margins.

If you want the blocks to float, use two light colors as above, instead.

Double Weave

Double weave is one of my favorite weaves, and most of my students love it, too. It seems like magic that you can weave two layers of cloth simultaneously—but that is what happens.

The cloth will be double thickness with a pattern or design happening when the layers exchange places—going from top to bottom and vice versa.

I like to be the one to introduce weavers to this technique, because once they understand the concept, they feel so capable and proud.

There is a lot more to learn about double weave than the basics given here. Read more in weaving books. Some special techniques and considerations are given in my third book, *Weaving & Drafting Your Own Cloth,* beginning on page 153.

There are three basic variations of double weave

1. Weaving two separate layers at once: See Figure 481.

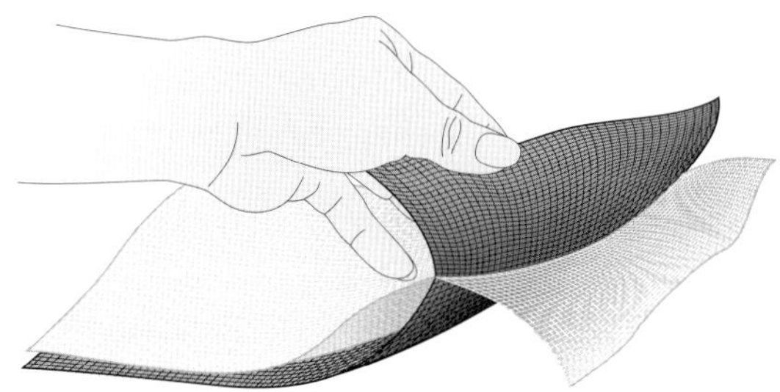

Two separate layers at once *Fig. 481*

2 Weaving a tube: See Figure 482.

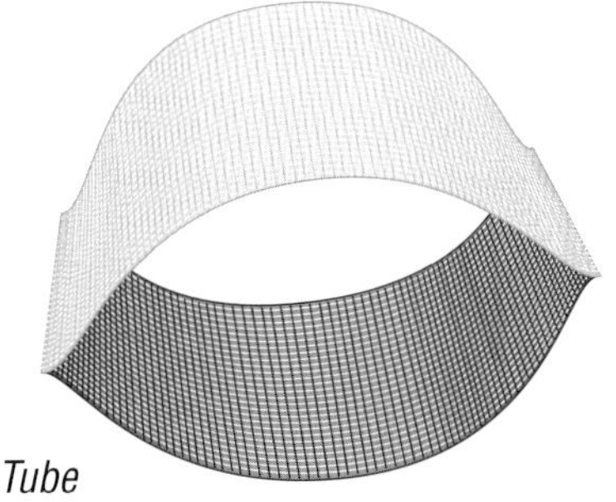

Tube *Fig. 482*

3. Weaving double width: (You can weave a cloth twice as wide as it is on your loom!) See Figure 483.

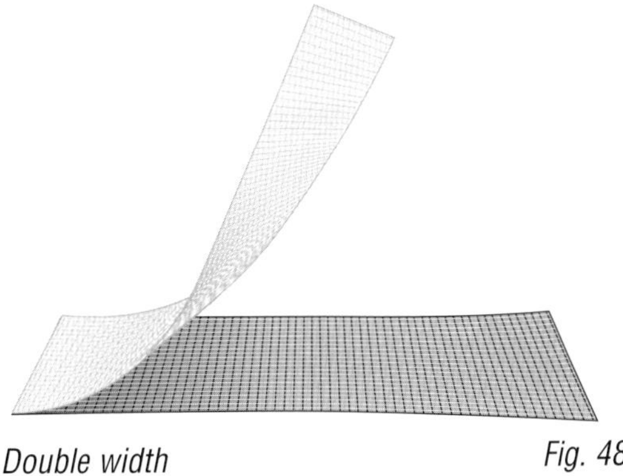

Double width *Fig. 483*

A Sampler for Double Weave

Warp length: 2 yards (length of guide string)

Warp width: 5 inches

Warp yarn: 5/2 pearl cotton, see below

Weft yarn: 5/2 pearl cotton, see below

Warp threads per inch (also called ends per inch or epi): 32 epi if 8-dent reed is used; or 40 epi if 10-dent reed is used. Read below which to use.

Total warp threads (ends): 160 or 200 depending upon reed used.

Treadles: for floor looms, use one of the direct tie-ups shown in Figures 225 and 226 on page 96.

Supplies needed for the sampler

Regular weaving supplies—See pages 7-11 or page 156.

2 shuttles

Reed: 8 dents per inch or 10 dents per inch. See which reed to use on page 235 at the beginning of the chapter. Note: for this sampler, you will put 4 warp threads in each dent of the reed.

It means you have a choice and can try either reed. As I said, the ideal is 32 epi, but if you prefer 40 epi because it will be simpler to sley a 10-dent reed that you already have on hand, that is ok, too.

Warp yarn and weft yarn

5/2 pearl cotton—two contrasting colors. Warp and weft will be the same. Read about pearl cotton on page 13 and substituting other yarns on page 32.

For an 8-dent reed, the ends per inch will be 32 epi, which will give you 16 epi per layer. (Remember, you'll be weaving two layers of cloth simultaneously.) You'll need 360 yards of each color or 2 ¾ oz. for a total of 720 yards (5 ½ oz.) for the warp and weft combined.

For a 10-dent reed, the ends per inch will be 40 epi, which will give you 20 epi per layer. (You'll be weaving two layers simultaneously, remember?) You'll need 430 yards of each color (3 ¼ oz) for a total of 860 yards (6 ½ oz) for the warp and weft combined.

① Measure the Warp Threads

With a guide string for a 2-yard warp, measure out 160 threads for 32 epi and 200 threads for 40 epi using two threads at once as described on page 237.

② Put the Warp on the Loom

Put the warp on the loom as described on page 238.

 Thread the Heddles

Thread the heddles according to the rules for double weave, below. This time the threading will be the same all across the warp. Read on.

Prepare the heddles

There will be ¼ of the total number of threads on each shaft. You need to count out 40 heddles per shaft for 32 epi or 50 heddles per shaft for 40 epi. Push the excess heddles equally to each side of the shafts and tie them as shown in Figure 475 as shown on page 239.

Thread the heddles

The warp will be threaded the same for the entire width of the warp: 4,3,2,1 repeated. One color should be on shafts 1 and 3 and the other color on shafts 2 and 4.

Complete Setting Up the Loom

Using your preferred method, complete the process. Remember to put 4 warp threads in each dent of the reed and that the warp is to be 5 inches wide. Weave the heading as described beginning on page 105 or 180.

The principles of double weave

Now begins the fun part—weaving the two layers. I like to teach double weave by using words to describe what to do instead of giving a weave draft because a draft doesn't really show what the cloth will be like. It does show both layers being intermingled, which is not useful at all for actual weaving. Drafts are shown in Figures 484 a-i (beginning on page 250), but here, the threading, tie-ups and treadlings are given in words.

The principles

1. The cloth to be on top at any given time is determined by you.
2. The cloth to be woven on the bottom at any given time is determined by you.
3. The two layers are woven simultaneously.
4. You determine which shafts will weave the cloth that is on the top and which shafts will form the bottom cloth.
5. The order, or sequence, that you use to lift the shafts to make the sheds is what makes the two cloths weave simultaneously and determines which variation of double weave as well.
6. Usually, in double weave cloth the layers exchange positions frequently to make the design or pattern—(what was on top at one time becomes the bottom and vice-versa).
7. If there were only one set of shafts used for all the top layer, you would end up with two completely separate cloths instead of one cloth double thick—it's the exchanging of the layers that holds the cloth together as one piece. If there were no exchanging of the layers, the two cloths would fall apart from one another.

Look at the illustration on the next page. See the two layers and notice where the layers exchange places: on the left side of the illustration, the dark layer is on the bottom and at the right side, the dark layer is on the top. Where the layers exchange places, the cloth is held together as one piece. You will learn how to do it when weaving the sampler.

Of course, you might want to weave two separate layers, but that might not be efficient. Weaving two layers at once is slower than weaving a single layer. You might think, why not weave a very long piece that is joined at one end and then opened out double length after the cloth is cut off the loom? Why not, indeed! It can be done—by joining the layers at the beginning (or end) of the cloth by exchanging the layers for a few picks. The join would not be invisible, however.

In the instructions that follow, the layers exchange when a new configuration is started in the sampler. You will see when you weave all the configurations in the sampler (and ones you invent) how you can design your cloth.

Planning the sequences of sheds

I like to have students practice writing the sequence of sheds on paper before weaving the sampler. I'll give you three examples to practice for each concept before suggesting that you go to the loom and begin to weave. That way you get plenty of practice and understand what to do. I write the sequence of sheds using T to indicate the top layer and B to indicate the bottom.

T *indicates the top layer*

B *indicates the bottom layer*

Make a key

Start with a key to plan the sequence of sheds for a particular variation of double weave (weaving two separate layers, a tube, or double width).

The key will indicate which shafts you have determined will be for each layer. I have given three keys to work with in this sampler. More keys could be made, but these three will give you a start to understanding the principles of double weave. In making a key, you may arbitrarily decide which shafts to use for the layers. On the other hand, the colors in the warp may make the determination, depending on which shafts each color is threaded.

Key #1: This key determines which shafts to use to form the top and bottom layers. For this key, let the top layer be woven with shafts 1 and 3, and the bottom layer with shafts 2 and 4.

Key #1

T *shafts 1 and 3*

B *shafts 2 and 4*

Key #2: This key indicates that shafts 2 and 4 are to be used to form the top layer, with shafts 1 and 3 forming the bottom layer.

Key #2

T *shafts 2 and 4*

B *shafts 1 and 3*

Key #3: In this key, shafts 1 and 2 are to be used to weave the top layer, and shafts 3 and 4 for the bottom layer.

Key #3

T *shafts 1 and 2*

B *shafts 3 and 4*

The sequence of sheds can be worked out once you know which shafts will be forming which layers. (The key) *The sequences change depending on which variation of double weave you want to weave (two separate layers, a tube, double width).*

It takes 2 shafts to weave plain weave, so with 4 shafts you can weave two layers. (With more shafts, you could weave more layers!)

Any two shafts can be combined to form one layer.

Two separate layers at once

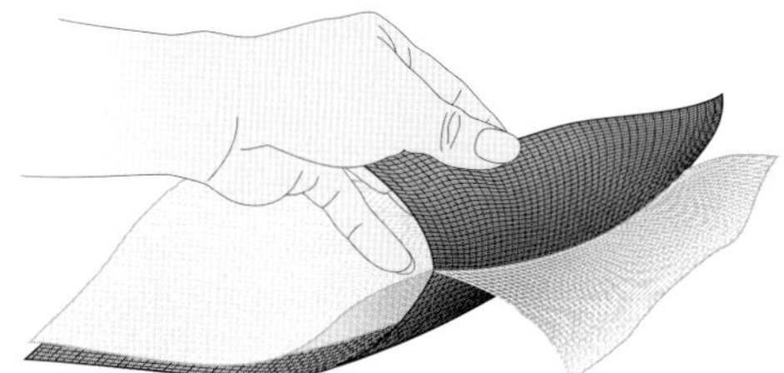

The sequence for weaving two separate layers is this:

1. Weave the two sheds for the top layer with one shuttle. See below.
2. Weave the two sheds for the bottom layer with the other shuttle. See below.

The sequence for weaving two separate layers can be written this way:

T
T
B
B

To weave the top layer

You will weave two sheds for the top layer with one of the shuttles.

1. Lift one of the shafts assigned to the top layer—in the case of Key #1, lift shaft 1. Throw the shuttle that matches the color of the warps lifted.
2. Change to the other shaft (shaft 3) designated for the top layer and throw the same shuttle in that shed.

To weave the bottom layer:

This is the principle of weaving all double weaves—you'll use this principle for all the double weave variations.

To weave the bottom layer, first lift the shafts for the top layer (shafts 1 and 3). Add to those shafts one of the shafts designated for the bottom layer (your choice, lift shaft 2 or 4)—a total of three shafts will be lifted to create the first shed for the bottom layer. Throw the second shuttle. The second shed for the bottom layer uses the same principle: Lift the shafts for the top layer and also lift the remaining shaft for the bottom layer (either 2 or 4—the one you didn't lift first.) Throw the second shuttle again.

Note that with a floor loom the shafts all fall down when you take your foot off the pedals, but with a table loom you have to raise and lower each shaft individually—and that means lowering shafts when you change to a new shed.

Sample One

Key #1

In this case, shafts 1 and 3 are to be used for the top layer. Weave the top layer: first lift shaft 1, then change to shaft 3. For the bottom layer 1 and 3 are lifted (top layer lifted out of the way) plus shaft 2. Throw the shuttle for the color that matches the color of the warps on the bottom layer.

The second shed for the bottom layer uses the same principle: Lift shafts 1 and 3 up out of the way and also lift the remaining shaft for the bottom layer—in this case: lift 1 and 3 plus 4.

The sequence of sheds is listed here along with the weave draft (Figure 484a).

Sequence of Sheds for
Two separate layers with Key #1:

T = lift shaft 1 (top layer cloth)
T = lift shaft 3 (top layer cloth)
B = lift shafts 1, 3 plus 2 (bottom layer cloth)
B = lift shafts 1, 3 plus 4 (bottom layer cloth)
Repeat

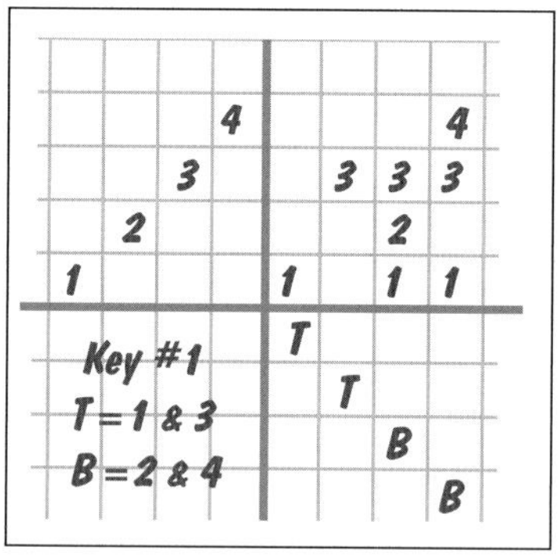

Key #1
T = 1 & 3
B = 2 & 4

Fig. 484a

Key #1
T *shafts 1 and 3*
B *shafts 2 and 4*

Practice with another key. Read the information for both Keys #2 and #3 and practice writing down the sequences of sheds for each of the keys for weaving separate layers before you attempt to weave. I recommend understanding all three variations of double weave before actually going to the loom and weaving them. I think it's a good idea because it gives you lots of practice with how double weave works. The sequences for Keys #2 and #3 are given here.

Sample Two

Key #2

Note that here the layers are exchanging places. What formed the top layer in Sample One is now on the bottom, and what was on the bottom becomes the top layer. See Figure 484b.

Sequence of Sheds for
Two separate layers with Key #2:

T = lift shaft 2 and throw the appropriate weft color

T = lift shaft 4 and throw the same weft color

B = lift shafts 2 and 4 plus 1 and throw the appropriate weft color

B = lift shafts 2 and 4 plus 3 and throw the appropriate weft color

Repeat

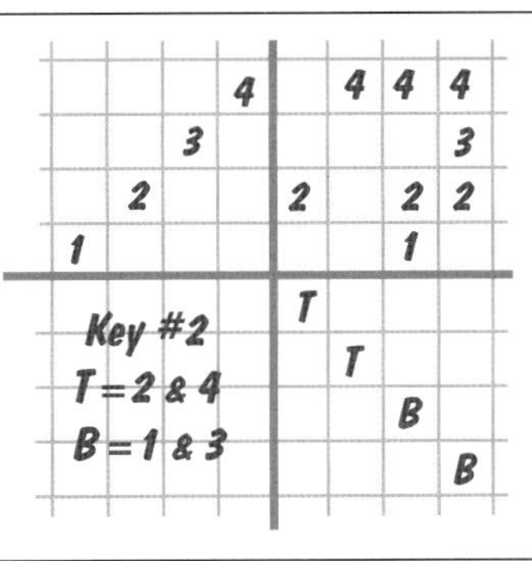

Fig. 484b

Key #2
T *shafts 2 and 4*
B *shafts 1 and 3*

Sample Three

Practice with a different key. Note that any two shafts can be used for the top layer. Figure 484c. Here the shafts 1 and 2 are designated for the top layer.

Key #3

Sequence of Sheds for
Two separate layers with Key #3:

T = lift shaft 1

T = lift shaft 2

B = lift shafts 1 and 2 plus 3

B = lift shafts 1 and 3 plus 4

Repeat

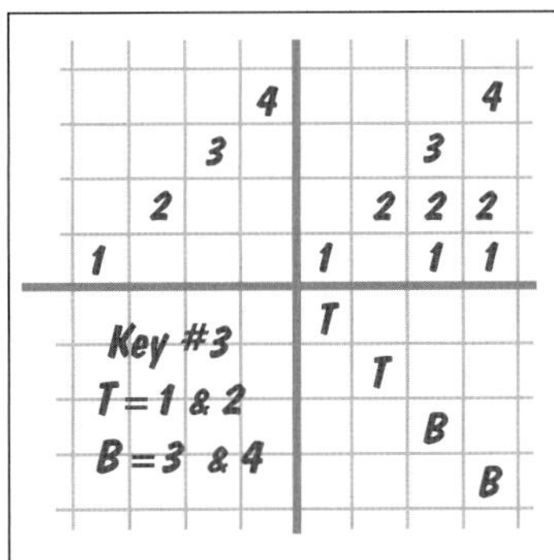

Fig. 484c

Key #3
T *shafts 1 and 2*
B *shafts 3 and 4*

More practice. You can try different shafts for the top and bottom layers and work out the sequence of sheds. Remember, any two shafts can form the top layer. Make a key for each new set of shafts for the top and bottom layers. See the box on page 249.

> ***Whether weaving a tube or separate layers, the principle always applies:***
> *To weave the bottom layer, lift the top layer's shafts up out of the way and also lift one of the shafts for the bottom layer for each bottom shed.*
>
> *Weaving the top layer is just like weaving a single cloth: Lift one of the shafts, throw the shuttle; and change to the other shaft and throw the shuttle.*

Tubes

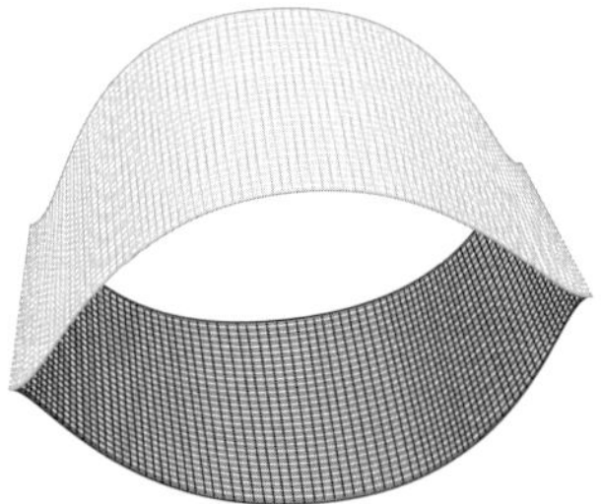

To weave a tube, you'll use only one shuttle, and it will go from the top layer to the bottom layer in a different sequence, which will close the layers at the edges of the warp, forming the tube. See Figures 484 d, e, and f.

Sample Four

Key #1

It's the sequence of sheds that makes the edges join as well as using only one shuttle. Figure 484d.

Sequence of sheds for a tube: Notice that the sequence is different from weaving two separate layers.

T
B
T
B

Visualize how the shuttle will go from the top layer to the bottom to the top again and to the bottom, which will form a tube as shown in the illustration.

Sequence of Sheds for A tube with Key #1:

T = lift shaft 1
B = lift shafts 1 and 3, plus 2
T = lift shaft 3
B = lift shafts 1 and 3, plus 4
Repeat

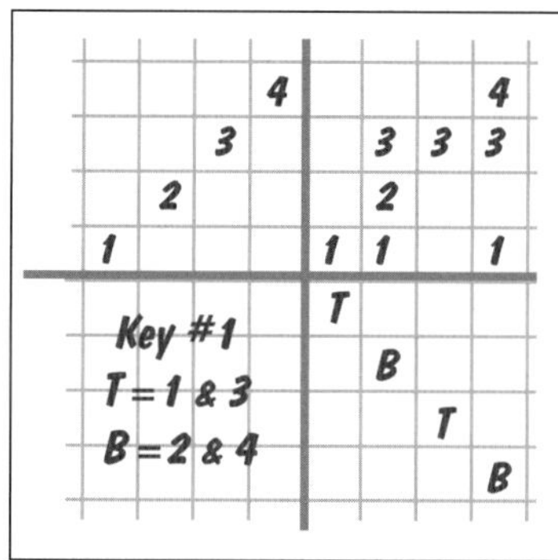

Fig. 484d

Key #1
T *shafts 1 and 3*
B *shafts 2 and 4*

Try figuring out the sequence of sheds for another key. Figure 484e

Sample Five

Key #2

Sequence of Sheds for A tube with Key #2:

T = lift shaft 2

B = lift shafts 2 and 4 plus 1

T = lift shaft 4

B = lift shafts 2 and 4 plus 3

Repeat

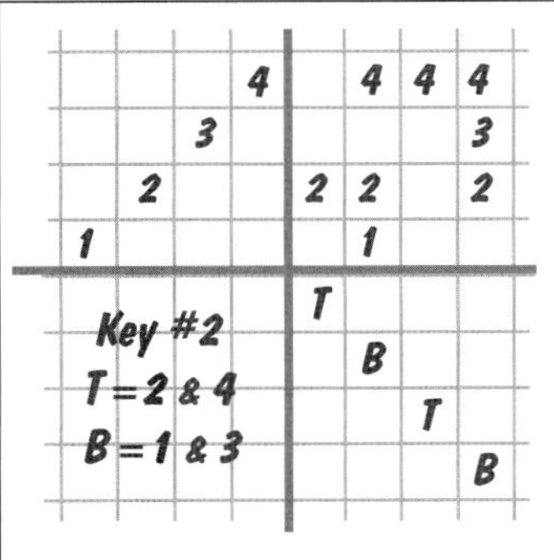

Fig. 484e

Key #2

T *shafts 2 and 4*

B *shafts 1 and 3*

Sample Six

Key #3

Figure 484f.

Sequence of Sheds for A tube with Key #3:

T = lift shaft 1

B = lift shafts 1 and 2 plus 3

T = lift shaft 2

B = lift shafts 1 and 2 plus 4.

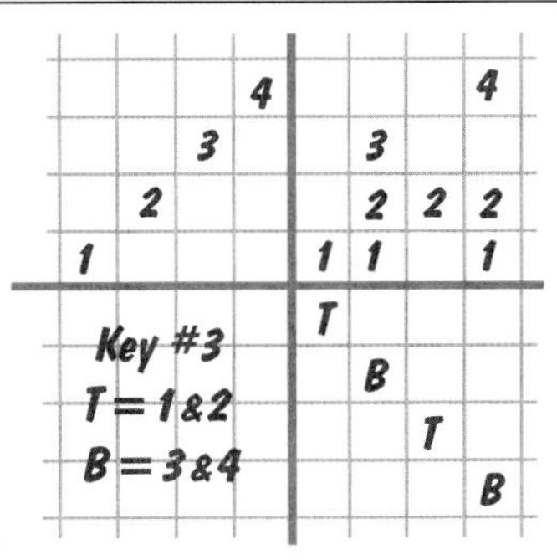

Fig. 484f

Key #3

T *shafts 1 and 2*

B *shafts 3 and 4*

Double Width

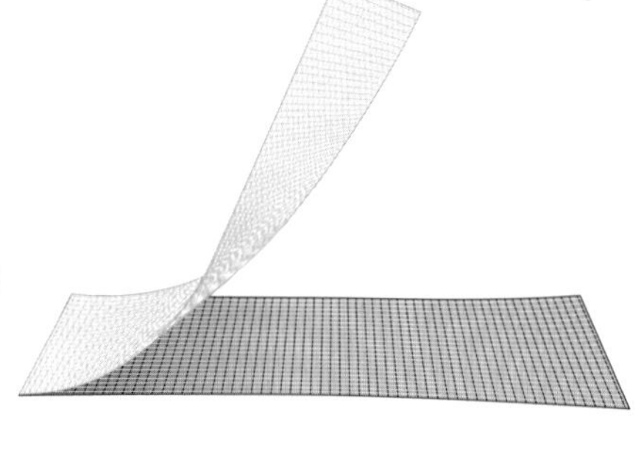

Again, the principle for weaving the top and bottom layers doesn't change. This time, it's the path the weft takes that joins one edge of the warp so that the cloth can be opened out to twice as wide as the warp. See Figures 484 g, h, and i.

Only one shuttle is used for double width.

Here's the path the weft will take:

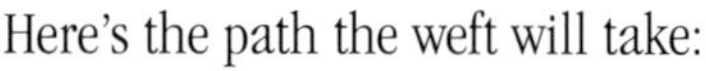

T
B
B
T

Try to visualize the path of the shuttle in the illustration. Use the principle that the shuttle weaves one top shed, then one bottom shed, then the other bottom shed and lastly, the remaining top shed. Figure 484g.

The fold will form on the edge opposite from where you entered your shuttle to begin the sequence. Read more about perfecting the fold in the sidebar on page 256.

Sample Seven

Key #1

Sequence of Sheds for Double width with Key #1:

T = lift shaft 1
B = lift shafts 1 and 3 plus 2
B = lift shafts 1 and 3 plus 4
T = lift shaft 3
Repeat

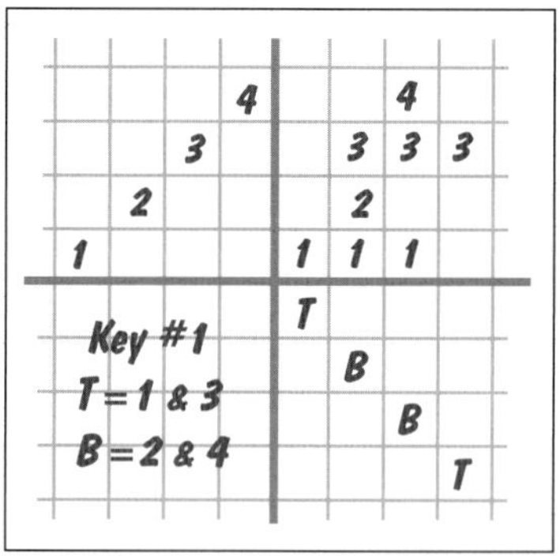

Fig. 484g

Key #1
T *shafts 1 and 3*
B *shafts 2 and 4*

Sample Eight

Key #2

Figure 484h.

Sequence of Sheds for Double width with Key #2:

T = lift 2
B = lift shafts 2 and 4 plus 1
B = lift shafts 2 and 4 plus 3
T = lift shaft 4
Repeat

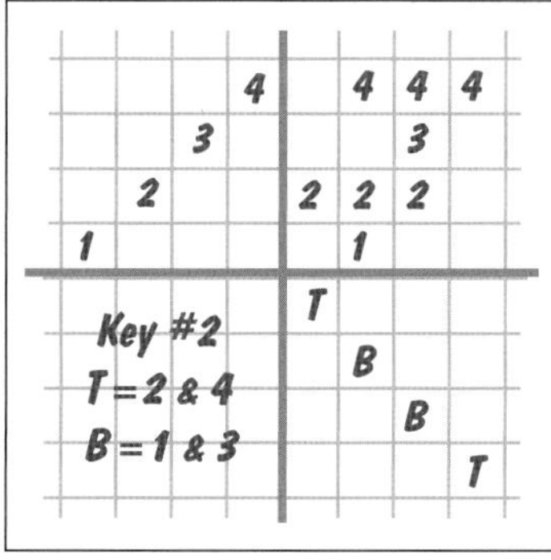

Fig. 484h

Key #2

T *shafts 2 and 4*

B *shafts 1 and 3*

Sample Nine

Key #3

Can you work out the sequence for Key #3? Figure 484i.

Sequence of Sheds for Double width with Key #3:

T = lift shaft 1
B = lift 1 and 2 plus 3
B = lift 1 and 2 plus 4
T = lift shaft 2
Repeat

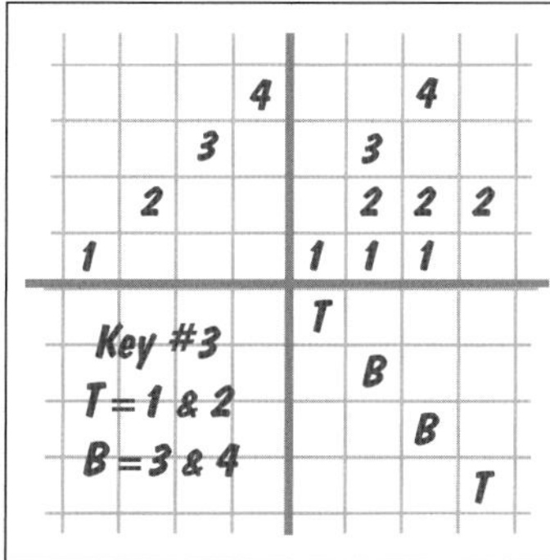

Fig. 484i

Key #3

T *shafts 1 and 2*

B *shafts 3 and 4*

Note: There are some techniques to use so that the fold doesn't show very much when the cloth is opened out. See the sidebar on the next page for some suggestions.

Some ways to make the fold less visible

It is easy to weave double width fabric, but the fold shows if you are not careful. What happens is that the warp threads at the fold tend to draw in or spread out making a line in the cloth of denser or looser threads. Some suggestions are given here. Read more in weaving books, magazines, and online.

If you decide on an important project using this technique, be sure to read about ways to avoid problems that make the fold show too much. Sample first before you weave the whole cloth to be sure you are satisfied with the appearance of the fold when the cloth is opened out double width.

Camouflage the fold

One good solution is to camouflage the fold by making a change in the warp color right at the edge where the fold is to be. It could be a narrow or a wide stripe of another color—just make sure the change (or the edge of the new color) occurs at the selvedge where the fold is going to be.

Using fishline at the fold

Thread fishline in with the selvedge threads at the fold. The fishline will be very, very taut. Then you snug up the wefts to it as you weave. Make the fold on the side where your better selvedge is. You might not know yet which is your better selvedge—often, it's the left one for right handers. The fishline will be pulled out when the cloth is off the loom. How to use the fishline follows.

Use two lengths of 25-pound-test fishline, each about 1 yard longer than the length of the warp.

Thread two fishlines in empty heddles immediately next to each of the outside 2 warp threads at the fold side—on the same shafts as the 2 threads. If empty heddles aren't available, make new heddles out of string as shown on page 110.

Put the fishlines in the reed in the same dent as the two outside threads.

Tie the fishlines to the front apron rod.

Hang the two fishlines over the back beam and weight them with about 2 pounds. That's a good bit of weight, and it will make them very taut. Fill bleach bottles with water or use whatever you find in the kitchen or around the house for weight. You can judge two pounds by thinking of a quart or 4 cups of water.

Weave with the fishline in place. Begin and end the weft threads at the open side of the warp (not the fold side). Take the wefts snuggly against the fishline, with no loops at the edge. As you weave along, you will have to let down the weights on the back and re-tie them. Pull out the fishlines after the cloth is off the loom.

Eliminating a double thread at the fold

A double thread at the fold can be eliminated no matter whether there is an even or an odd number of warp threads. You need to change the sequence of the sheds. If you're getting double threads, skip a shed and proceed weaving. It will change which shed follows which in relation to the shuttle movement and correct the problem, like getting back in step with a half-step in marching. Do it immediately when you begin, so the skip in the sequence doesn't mar the cloth.

Weaving the double weave sampler

After you've read how each variation is to be woven, begin weaving the sampler as given below. At first, you might make some mistakes so the layers won't separate as they should. More practice will make you confident that you know what you are doing.

To check for mistakes, lift the shafts for the top layer frequently to be sure the layers are not connected by mistakes in the shed sequences. You should be able to put your hand in between the layers if they are separate.

Variation: Weave two separate layers

Hint: A hand mirror can be useful in checking that the sheds are clearly open.

Weave 2" using Key #1 (page 254)

Weave 2" using Key #2 (page 255)

Weave 2" using Key #3 (page 255)

Variation: Weave tubes

Weave 2" using Key #1

Weave 2" using Key #2

Weave 2" using Key #3

Variation: Weave double width

Weave 2" using Key #1

Weave 2" using Key #2

Weave 2" using Key #3

Weave more configurations (keys) of different shafts for each layer if you like—or try different wefts.

In the sampler, all the configurations were equal in size. You can make different designs by making the layers change in different ways. For example, one layer could be on top only for narrow strips with the other layer being on top most of the time, making wider bands. Double weave is fun and you can be very creative. You might invent something you like on the sampler—it might not even be double weave—but something you like.

Practice perfecting the fold in double width cloth—see the sidebar on page 256.

At the end of the warp, you will need to cut out the section where the double width was woven so that you can open it out to its double width. (The whole sampler won't be intact.)

Two Threadings on One Warp: Cutting the Warp Threads and Re-threading

Here is a way you can cut the warp threads and re-thread the heddles for a different threading plan. It is useful when sampling because you make one long warp and can make several weaves from it. It can be time-consuming, but is efficient for weaving small amounts when you just want to try out a weave.

Here is a way that the three different weaves described in this chapter can be woven on just one warp.

The variation of warp-faced rep sampler is to be woven first. Then, before the warp is cut and re-threaded to weave log cabin and double weave. It is important to put in lease sticks behind the shafts so that you can thread the heddles in order from the cross. Read below how to do this.

A sampler for three weaves

Specifications:

Warp length: 3 yards (length of guide string)

Warp width: 5 inches

Warp yarn: 5/2 cotton, see below

Weft yarns: 5/2 cotton, a thick yarn, and a thin yarn, see below. Various sizes of yarns are shown on page 32.

Warp threads per inch (also called ends per inch or epi): 16 epi if 8-dent reed is used; 20 epi if 10-dent reed is used (Read below which to use.)

Total number of warp threads (ends): 80 threads at 16 epi; 100 threads at 20 epi

Treadles: for floor looms, use one of the direct tie-ups shown in Figures 225 and 226 on page 96.

Note: The sampler is to be woven at 16 or 20 epi. Double weave is usually threaded with double the amount given here, but you can learn how it works on this warp if you use a thick weft, such as knitting yarn, which is given in the supply list.

Supplies needed for the sampler

Regular weaving supplies—See pages 7-11 or page 156

Reed: 8 or 10 dents per inch. See which reed to use on page 235.

Lease sticks

Broom handle or stick longer than the width of the warp (optional)

Warp Yarn

5/2 pearl cotton—two contrasting colors. Read about pearl cotton on page 13 and substituting other yarns on pages 32 and 33.

If you use an 8-dent reed, you will have 16 warp threads (ends) per inch (epi) and if you use a 10-dent reed, you will have 20 threads (ends) per inch (epi). Note that if you have 20 epi rather than 16 epi, you will need a bit more yarn because you will have more threads in the warp: 100 vs 80.

With an 8-dent reed at 16 ends per inch (epi): You will need 1 1/4oz. or 165 yards of each color, for a total of 2 1/2 oz. or 330 yards of both colors combined.

With a 10-dent reed at 20 ends per inch (epi): You will need 1 1/2oz. or 200 yards of each color, for a total of 3 oz or 400 yards of both colors combined.

Weft Yarn

You'll need thick yarn similar to knitting yarn, and 5/2 cotton, and a bit of sewing thread (optional).

Knitting yarn—two contrasting colors, 2 oz. (100 yd) of one color and 1 oz. (50 yd) of a contrasting color. See examples on page 32.

5/2 pearl cotton—two contrasting colors. 1 oz. (130 yd) of one color and ¼ oz (35 yd) of a contrasting color

Sewing thread similar to one of the warp colors, or a neutral color

This amount of yarn allows you to weave all three of the weaves—using knitting yarn for the double weave section and also for the variation of warp-faced rep and 5/2 cotton for the variation of rep and log cabin. A bit of sewing thread is optional for the rep.

Measure the warp threads

Measure out a guide string for a 3-yard warp

Measure out 80 threads for 16 epi and 100 threads for 20 epi,using two threads at once as described on page 237.

Weave a variation of warp-faced rep

Follow the directions for setting up the loom and weaving the variation of warp-faced rep beginning on page 234. You will weave all the sections shown in the illustration only. That is, you will not weave any extra ideas. See Figure 478 on page 240 and repeated here.

Next, prepare to cut the warp and re-thread. Read on.

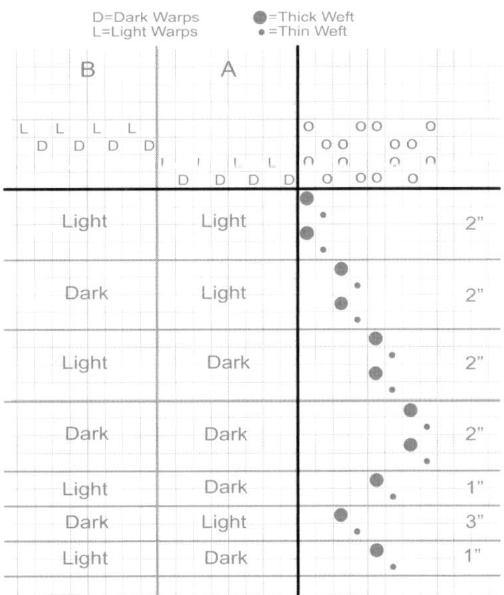

Cutting the warp threads and re-threading the heddles

1 Put lease sticks into the warp behind the heddles

Before you cut the warp you must put lease sticks into the warp behind the heddles!! This is very important so you can use the cross that forms between the sticks to re-thread the heddles. If you already have lease sticks in the warp behind the heddles, go on to Step Four on page 261.

To put in lease sticks lift shafts 1 and 3 and put a lease stick into the shed that forms behind the heddles. Close the shed, lift shafts 2 and 4, and put a second lease stick in that shed formed behind the heddles. Now you have made a cross between the sticks, and the warp threads are in order, ready for re-threading. Tie the lease sticks together about 1" apart as shown in Figure 169 on page 63 and repeated here.

2 Cut the Warp

About 1" away from the last woven weft cut an inch worth of warp threads at one edge of the warp. Take the warps out of the heddles, and tie an overhand knot in the cut ends behind the heddles to prevent the lease sticks from falling out of the warp. To protect the last weft woven, see page 138.

Cut another inch of warp at the other edge and tie the cut ends with an overhand knot.

Cut 1 ½" worth of warp next to the first 1" you cut and tie an overhand knot. Then, cut the remaining 1 ½" worth of threads and tie a knot.

Now the warp is in the lease sticks and dangling behind the heddles in 4 knotted sections.

3 Arrange the Heddles

For 16 epi, arrange the heddles so each shaft has 20 heddles grouped together. For 20 epi, put 25 heddles on each shaft grouped together in the center of the shafts. Push the excess heddles equally to each side of the shafts and tie them as shown in Figure 164 on page 61 and repeated here. (The total number of heddles will be 80 or 100, depending on your epi.)

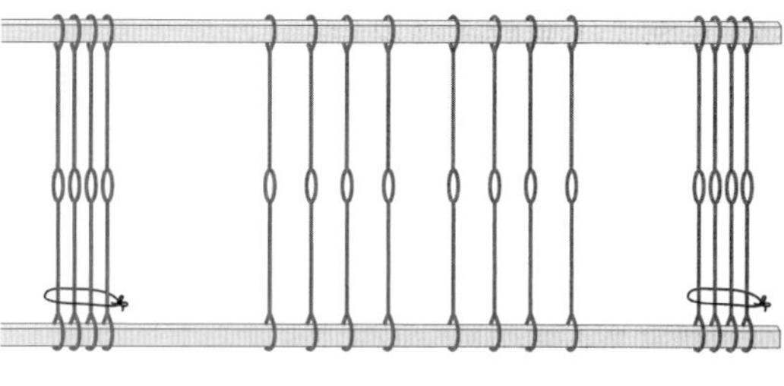

Stabilize the Lease Sticks for Threading

Figure 175 on page 66 and repeated here shows how you will position yourself and the lease sticks for re-threading the heddles. If your method of warping is back-to-front, this is the familiar way. If you warp the loom front-to-back, it will be new for you. (Refer to the threading instructions beginning on page 65.)

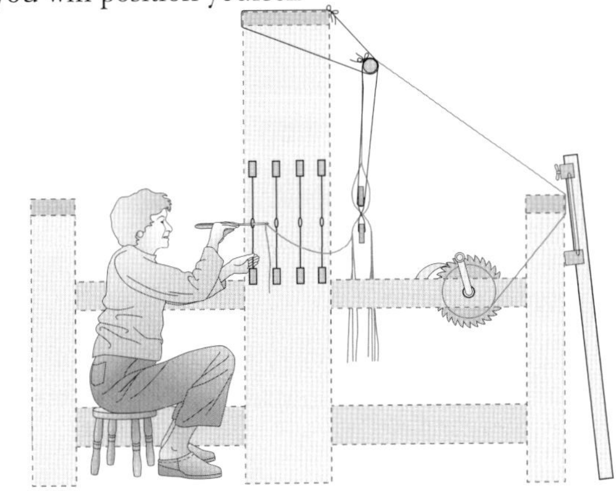

I recommend suspending a stick or a broom handle from the castle of the loom behind the heddles and hanging the warp, lease sticks-and-all, from it as shown in the illustration. Then, tie another string from the top lease stick to the broom handle. That way, the sticks are stable, and you can see the cross easily to thread the heddles.

If this arrangement won't work with your loom and the length of warp left, try tying the lease sticks to the sides of the loom to hold them stable. There aren't many threads to thread, so just try any arrangement you like so that you can see the cross, pull the threads from it, and thread the heddles.

Thread the Heddles

Thread the heddles the same as indicated for log cabin on page 242 and repeated here. The heddles will be threaded on shafts 4,3,2,1 repeated all across the warp. Besides the order of the shafts, the colors of warps must go on certain shafts: the one-inch borders will be threaded with the dark and light threads in heddles on certain shafts. In the center section, the dark and light threads will be threaded on different shafts. This is shown in the brackets in the illustration and is explained further below.

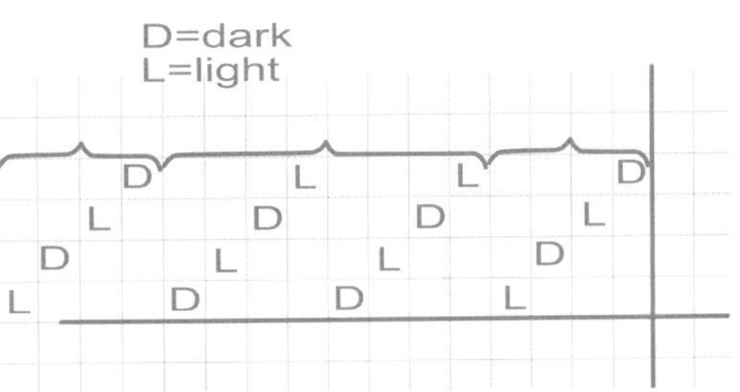

Thread one inch worth of threads (16 threads for 16 epi, or 20 threads for 20 epi) in the heddles on the shafts in this order: 4,3,2,1—putting the light threads on shafts 1 and 3 and the dark threads on shafts 2 and 4. Remember, only thread one inch-worth of threads with the dark and light threads in this manner.

For the center section continue threading the shafts in the same order, but put the dark threads on shafts 1 and 3 and the light threads on shafts 2 and 4. Thread 3-inches worth in this manner. (48 threads for 16 epi; 60 threads for 20 epi).

The remaining border is to be threaded just like the first border with the light threads on shafts 1 and 3, and the dark threads on shafts 2 and 4.

Sley the Reed

Fill the reed (sley the reed) putting 2 threads in each dent as described beginning on page 72.

 Tying On

Tie the warp onto the front apron rod as usual. Tying on is described beginning on page 83.

 Weave the Heading and Check for Errors

Read about weaving the heading and checking for errors in threading beginning on pages 105 and 108.

Weave log cabin

Using two shuttles, one for your dark color and the other for the light one, follow the instructions for weaving log cabin beginning on page 243. Weave 11". Then stop and leave a 2-inch space unwoven in the warp by weaving in a few rags or pieces of thin cardboard similar to that of cereal boxes, which can be easily pulled out after the cloth is cut off the loom

Weave double weave

There are three basic variations of double weave as discussed on page 245:

1. Weaving two separate layers at once

2. Weaving a tube

3. Weaving double width (you can weave a cloth twice as wide as it is on your loom!)

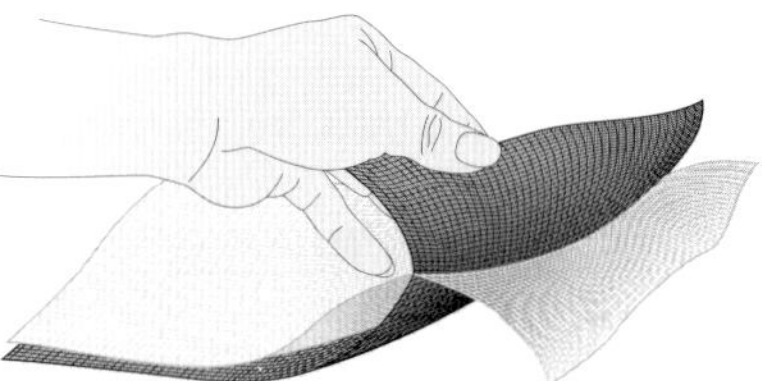

Two separate layers at once

Wind the shuttles

Wind two shuttles with two contrasting colors of knitting yarn-size yarns (for example, worsted weight wool, shown on page 12). To make the double weave sampler on this warp, you'll need to use thicker yarns. That is the reason that this warp isn't the ideal set-up for double weave. I use it because it is a way to sample three weaves on one warp. If you were to weave a whole warp of double weave, you would have many more threads in the warp—in fact, double the amount here or double the amount needed for regular plain weave. Read more about this beginning on page 245.

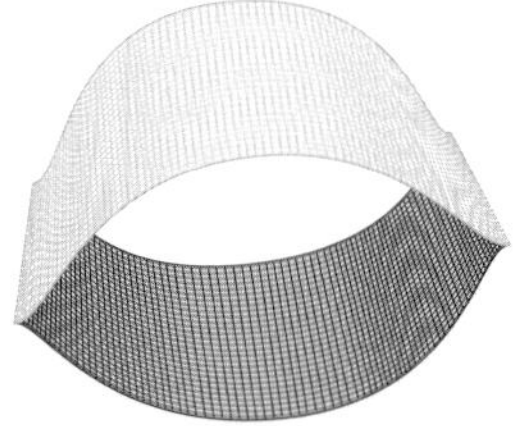

Tube

You can weave double weave on this warp and learn all the principles. The only difference between this way and the regular way is that, here, there are fewer warp threads per inch so that heavier weft threads are needed.

Weaving double weave

Follow the explanations and instructions for weaving double weave beginning on page 247. Weave 2" of each configuration for each variation as given. You may have some extra warp remaining to practice other ideas, or it may be the end of the warp, and time to cut it off.

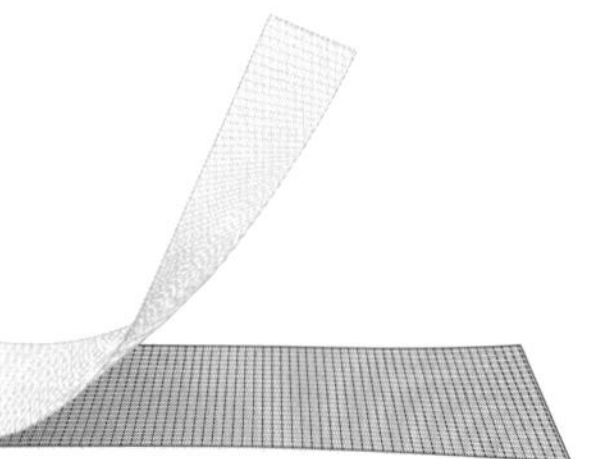

Double width

10 Sett (epi)

What does epi mean?

I can't remember when I first heard the term "epi," it's been so deeply enmeshed in my weaving life. It was a long time before I realized how very central it is to weaving. ***Epi means ends per inch***.

What is an end?

End is the word weavers use to mean a warp thread. They often talk about how many ends there are in a whole warp or how many ends there are in an inch of warp. Computer software uses the term, end, extensively.

The number of ends in one inch is involved, probably, with every single warp we make. The shorthand for that number is epi (ends per inch).

What does sett mean?

Sett refers to how many ends there are per inch—in other words, how close or far apart the warp threads are in the reed. Another way to say it—it is the density of the warp threads.

Weavers often say "epi" instead of sett when discussing this subject as in, "What is the epi of your warp?"

Why is sett (epi) important?

It is a crucial fact you need to know before you buy the yarn for a project. You need this information to know how much to buy, how many threads to measure out, and how many to put in the spaces of the raddle or the reed. Read the introduction to sett on page 264.

What are sett charts?

In this chapter, I'll explain different ways to find the sett for a chosen yarn and project. The charts you see on page 381 show what setts have been worked out already—for a variety of types of cloth—so you can rely on them or use them to compare with your own decisions. Many setts are given for each yarn, and you select the one that fits the type of cloth you want to make. The charts in this book not only allow for the yarn and the weave structure, but also for the purpose of the cloth. Read how to read them on page 266.

In other books and magazines, you'll see differences in suggested setts and sett charts, but they probably will be fairly similar. Sometimes, three numbers are given for three different epi for a yarn –wide for lace weaves, medium for plain weave, and close for twill. Sometimes, just two setts will be given with a range of numbers for plain weave and twill. Read more in the section, "An introduction to sett."

An example of a simple sett chart (Figure 106) is on page 32 and repeated here. More complete sett charts and information are in the Appendix on pages 380-381.

What does wpi mean?

You'll see below, that one way to determine the epi is to wrap the yarn on a ruler. Sometimes, you'll see wpi in weaving catalogs—it stands for the number of *wraps per inch*. Read more about this method beginning on page 267.

What does ppi mean?

The term often used by weavers for wefts is picks. When we talk about how many wefts are in a project we want to know *how many picks are in an inch, or ppi*.

More on ppi is in the chapter on planning projects. You'll need to know the ppi so you can know how much weft yarn you'll need.

What does ypp mean?

Yards per pound is abbreviated ypp. This information is used in determining how much yarn you need as well as the epi.

Yarn & Sett Chart

Yarn	Yards per Pound	Ends per Inch (epi) Plain Weave (tabby)	Twill Weave
5/2 Pearl Cotton	2,100	16 epi	20 epi
Sport-weight Wool	1,750	15 epi	18 epi
2-ply Wool	1,475	12 epi	16 epi
Worsted-weight Wool	800	10 epi	12 epi
Rayon Chenille	1,450	16 epi	N/A
Rug Wool	260	Too Fat for Sampler	
10/2 Pearl cotton	4,200	Too Thin for Sampler	
Mohair Bouclé	1,175	Not Smooth Enough	

Yarns suitable for warps

Before you can consider the sett, you need to choose a yarn that is suitable for the warp. In general, yarns for warps must be smooth and strong enough that they won't break under tension during weaving. They shouldn't be stretchy or vulnerable to abrasion, as well. To test a yarn for strength, take about a foot of the yarn, and with one end in each hand, pull hard on the yarn to see that it will not pull apart, or break. If it passes this simple test, it is probably OK Remember, it should be smooth and not stretchy, too.

An introduction to sett

To review, the sett is the density of the warp. It is the number of ends (warp threads) per inch (epi). The sett you choose depends on the yarns, the weave structure (e.g., plain or twill, etc.) and the intended purpose of the finished piece (e.g., a loosely woven shawl or upholstery in a tight, firm weave, or anything in between).

It is obvious that a thin thread like sewing thread would have more threads per inch than a fat, wool yarn. See Figure 485. But, how do you determine the sett considering all the factors that go into it? It is what you will learn in this chapter.

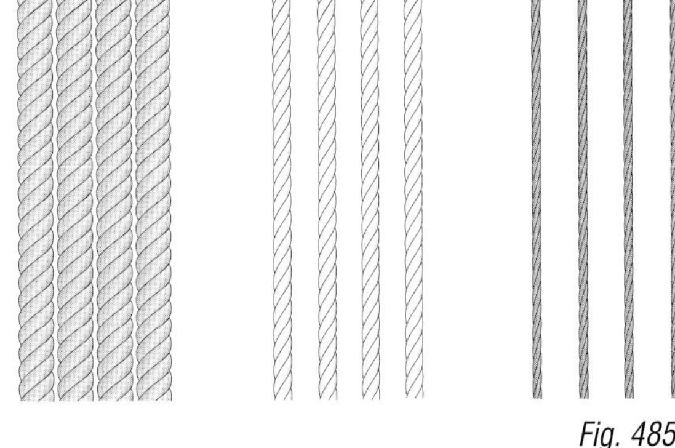

Fig. 485

You've read that sett is very important, but please don't agonize over it. There is a lot of leeway in the matter, and one sett might be just as satisfactory as another, similar one. For example, you might be considering 12 epi or 15 epi. In fact, either one might be okay. Read on for how I make my final determination.

I always sample at the beginning of a warp to see if I am happy with the results of my decisions. Read more about the sample on page 283 and in the many references to it throughout the book. You examine your sample after it is washed--either you like it or you don't. If you can't decide, probably, it is good enough. You might look at it at a distance as well as up close.

If you don't like the sample, now is the time to re-sley the reed to the sett that works for your purpose and vision.

How I finalize my sett decisions: Reeds and sett

Figure 486.

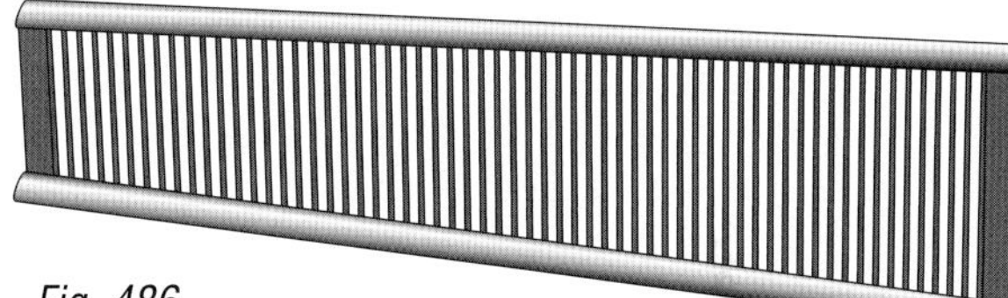

Fig. 486

When I am making my final decision regarding sett, I think about the reeds I have. I very much want to have two threads per space in the reed. That is, 2 ends per dent in most cases. Ideally, you need to have several reeds unless you only weave the same thing over and over. I have 8, 10, 12, and 15 dent reeds. If you don't have the size reed that will give 2 ends per dent, you can use the Reed Substitution Chart on page 73 to find out how to use the reed you have for the sett you want.

See the sidebar for why 2 ends per dent is ideal.

Why use two ends per dent

Two ends per dent allow manufacturers' knots that may occur in the warp to pass without getting hung up in the reed. It keeps you from having to interrupt your warping at the warping board and during weaving so you can keep your rhythm even. It's faster to weave the knots in and mend them later when the cloth is off the loom. I almost never stop and cut out manufacturer's knots at the warping board; I'd rather take care of them later. (This is the one time that I myself do something different from what I teach!) When you definitely would not stop to cut them out is the time when you are warping with a paddle and measuring many threads at once.

More threads per dent (say, 4) often make "reed marks," which are vertical spaces that appear in the cloth between the groups of threads spaced in the reed. Sometimes, but not always, these marks come out with washing.

A quick guide to determining sett: Charts, calculations, or wrapping

Charts are given with the setts worked out for various yarns, weave structures, and purposes. I refer to them almost always. See how to read them below.

Calculations are an excellent way to determine sett. If the yarn I want to use isn't on a sett chart, I calculate. The formula is given on page 270, and adjusting the sett for purpose is on page 279.

Wrapping on a ruler is a quick way to determine sett for yarns that are not too fine or slippery. This method works well enough, but for me, calculating takes all of the guesswork out.

How to read sett charts in this book

The sett charts are divided into two sectors: the first chart is for plain weave and the second is for twill. These 2 charts account for weave structure in determining the sett. Read about other weaves on page 278.

The difference between plain weave and twill setts is explained on page 275.

Look at Figures 487 a and b. In the illustrations, note the titles of the columns. Each heading is explained in more detail following on in the chapter. For now, you just need to see what information is given in the charts. You will need to know beforehand the yards per pound of your chosen yarn. How to get the yards per pound is explained on page 271. Diameters and taking into account plain and twill weaves are explained beginning on page 275.

The remaining columns show allowances for the purpose of the cloth—how to adjust the sett for upholstery or delicate shawls, for example. Read more about maximum sett and allowing for purpose on page 279.

Setts for Plain Weave (tabby) — Listed by Yarn Count

Plain Weave	yds/lb	m/kg	Diameters*	Maximum Plain Weave	90% of max (Upholstery)	80% of max (Production)	70% of max (Clothing)	65% of max (Woolen)	60% of max (Clothing)	50% of max (Delicate)

Fig. 487a

Setts for Twill — Listed by Yarn Count

Twill	yds/lb	m/kg	Diameters*	Maximum Twill	90% of max (Upholstery)	80% of max (Production)	70% of max (Clothing)	65% of max (Woolen)	60% of max (Clothing)	50% of max (Delicate)

Fig. 487b

How to find your own sett

Yarn size and diameters

The starting point is to evaluate the size of the yarn. It is done by laying out pieces of the yarn side-by-side, right next to one another in the space of an inch. (We don't actually cut the yarn-- what to do is explained below). Figure 488 shows different size yarns laid out in this way, all within one inch spaces. See that the fat yarn has 4-yarns to an inch, and the thinner one has many more to the inch.

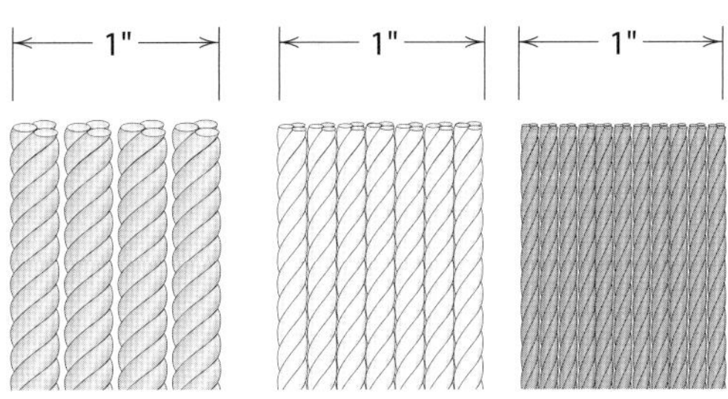

Fig. 488

So, we want, first of all, to know how many yarns fit into a 1-inch space. In weaving we call the cut ends of the yarn, diameters. To see the diameters, look at the cut ends of the yarns as though you were looking at the cut end of a log of wood. Figure 489 shows a row of circles, which represent the cut ends of yarns lying side-by-side. From this perspective, you can see that we are talking about how many diameters of the yarn fit in the one-inch space. See below for how to determine the number of diameters.

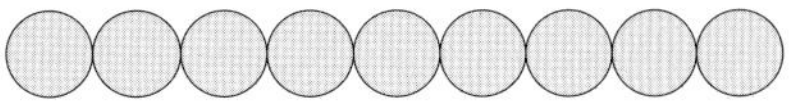

Fig. 489

Finding the diameters: Wrapping method

Weavers use two ways to determine the number of diameters of a given yarn in an inch: wrapping and calculating.

Wrap yarn on a ruler: A way to find the diameters without cutting the yarn is to wrap the given yarn around a ruler with the yarns side-by-side, closely touching. See Figure 490a. Notice that there are 15 yarns in the inch space, and we would say then that there are 15-diameters of that yarn in one inch.

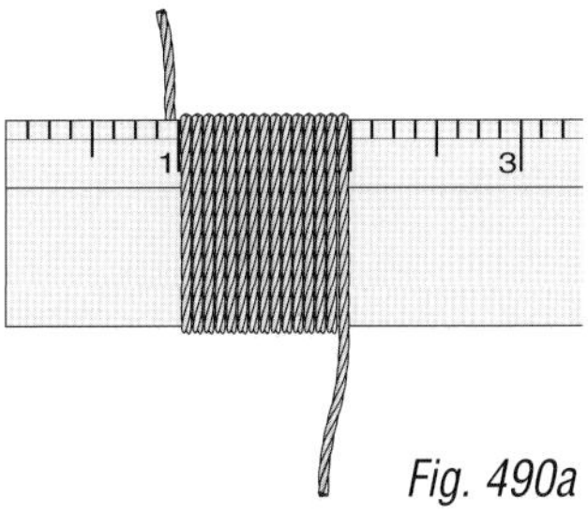

Fig. 490a

How close to wrap the yarns

You can wrap the yarns on a ruler fairly far apart so they just graze one another, or so the yarns are squashed together. I suggest wrapping the yarns somewhere between these two options; that is, touching one another very close-ly, but never overlapping.

How much to wrap on the ruler

Experience has shown me that the number of wraps in one inch on a ruler does not lead to the epi that is close enough for practical weaving of cloth. Rosalie Neilson[3] has a solution. That is, to have a good, usable number of "wraps per inch," wind the yarn for 1 ¼" and count the number you find in 1 ¼" instead of for only 1". Finally, I can now say that wrapping can give the realistic cloth I desire. See Figure 490b.

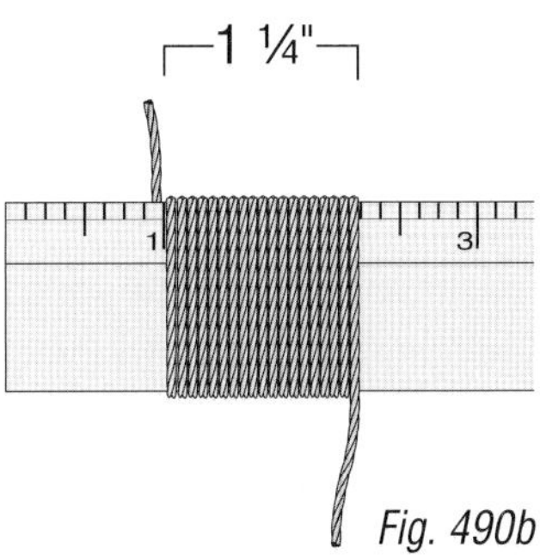

1 ¼"

Fig. 490b

Wrap 1 ¼" instead of only 1"

3 Rosalie Neilson, from a discussion in 2009. Rosalie's work can be seen at her website: www.rosalieneilson.com

To change a given wpi (wraps per inch) (say, from a magazine) to the number of wraps in 1 ¼", divide the wpi by 4 and add that number to the wpi. For example, if the wpi given is 28, divide that by 4 to get 7. Then add 7 to 28 for a practical "wraps per inch" of 35. (An easier way would be to multiply the given wpi times 1.25.)

Mixed warps

When different yarns are in the warp, find the diameters by wrapping the different yarns together on the ruler in the proportion they will be used. To get the number in 1 ¼", wrap a total of 2 ½" or 3 ¾" on the ruler. Then divide your number of wraps by 2 or 3 to get the average diameters per inch. Whether you wind 2 times or 3 times 1 ¼" depends on how many different yarns you have. What you want to accomplish is to get a reasonable average. Use your judgement as to how much should be wrapped to get it.

Wrapping gives a good-enough idea for a start. Whatever method you use, I recommend you weave a few inches to check that the sett suits you. If not, it is time to stop and re-sley the reed so the sett is exactly as you want it. (You check your sample after washing it to see how it looks and to check the shrinkage. See page 141.) I prefer to use the sett charts given in this book, if possible—the numbers are calculated and you don't have to worry about wrapping properly. However, you would still check your sett with an actual woven sample.

Why would you wrap and why would you use the calculations or charts? From my experience, some people just prefer one method over the other. Most weavers never learned the calculations given in this book and are comfortable wrapping. Weavers who use fine threads find wrapping is not practical, and they turn to the calculations. Having the charts (page 381 in the Appendix) is a big time saver to my way of thinking. Sometimes, I wrap if the yarn is very thick or my book is not at hand.

As I said at the beginning of this chapter, there is leeway, and I don't recommend splitting hairs over this. If you sample, you can always change the sett.

Calculation method to find diameters

Another way to determine diameters is by calculation with an inexpensive calculator as shown in Figure 491. It is the way that I prefer because it takes the guesswork out. The sett charts in the Appendix on page 381 use this method. After the diameters are calculated for a yarn, the sett, or epi, can easily be calculated for both the particular yarn and the particular weave structure of the cloth that is desired. (Subsequently, the purpose for the cloth can be considered by calculating one more time.)

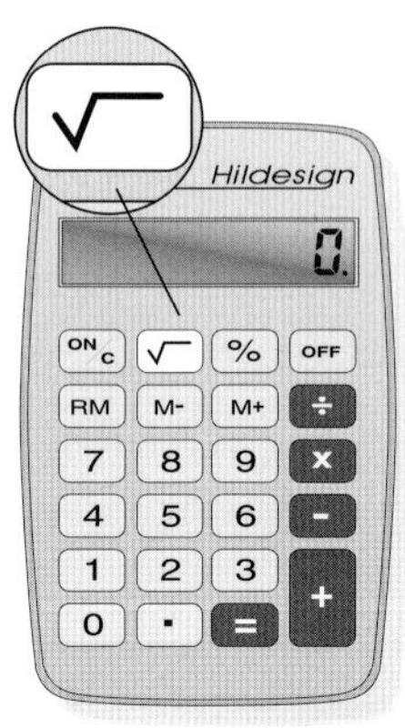

Fig. 491

Ashenhurst's Rule

Getting the diameters on a ruler is easy to do with a heavy yarn, but it would be terribly hard with a slippery, or nubbly, or fine thread. There's a way to find the diameters using a pencil, paper and an inexpensive calculator. For me, it makes finding the sett a piece of cake—no hassle or worry that the threads are touching too much or not enough. This method of calculating the diameters was worked out by Mr. Ashenhurst long ago for industry. I think the reason his number for diameters is higher than for wrapping is that it's a mathematical formula, which he found to work through his experimentation.

This calculation will give you the number of diameters, which will be used to determine the sett for a fabric. The reason you want to know the Ashenhurst number of diameters is that it's his number that is used to make allowances for yarns, weave, shrinkage, finishing, purpose (e.g. upholstery or sheer curtains, etc.). What you actually do is to calculate the maximum sett so that you can then take a percentage of it to allow for different purposes of the cloth or types of yarns. (Read about allowing for the purpose on page 279.)

Before I give you Ashenhurst's formula, you need to understand that you'll have to push a special key on your inexpensive calculator. It's the square root key and looks a lot like a check mark. See Figure 491. To find the square root of a number, enter the number on your calculator then push the square root key.

Fill in the worksheet (Figure 492) as you use the formula. I suggest that you make several copies of the worksheet so you can use a fresh one for each time you work out the formula. The formula is in the sidebar on the next page.

You can forgo Ashenhurst's formula and just use the sett charts in the Appendix on page 381 where some calculations are worked out for you. Then you can skip to, "Allowing for the Purpose" on page 279. To use the charts you'll need to know the yards per pound (ypp) for the warp yarn. See pages 271-273 for ways to get this number..

Worksheet for Ashenhurst's Rule

Project(s):____________________

Weave structure — Final sett ________

☐ Plain weave ☐ Twill — Reed ________

Diameters per inch

Yards per pound ________ ypp

$\sqrt{ypp}$ ________

X .9 ________ calculated diameters per inch

Maximum epi for Plain Weave

Diameters per inch ________ diameters

÷ 2 ________ maximum epi for plain weave

Maximum epi for Twill

Diameters per inch ________ diameters

X .67 (2/3 of diameters) ________ maximum epi for twill

Allowing for Purpose

☐ Plain weave ☐ Twill

Maximum epi ________ maximum sett

X ____ % ________ epi

☐ 90% for upholstery

☐ 80% for production

☐ 60-70% for clothing

☐ 65% for woolens

☐ 50-60% for delicate fabrics

Fig. 492

Now for the Formula

Ashenhurst's rule starts out with the yards per pound of the warp yarn. See ways to get this number on pages 271-273.

Number of diameters per inch = .9 times the square root of the yards per pound

That's it!! That gives you the number of diameters of the yarn in an inch (the *calculated* number).

On the calculator enter in the yards per pound, then, push the square root key.
Then, multiply that number by .9.

For example, take a yarn that has 1,000 yds per pound.

Ashenhurst's diameters per inch $= \sqrt{1{,}000} \times .9 = 31.6 \times .9 = 28$ diameters per inch

For Plain Weave

Take ½ the diameters for plain weave (see page 275 for why). Thus: ½ of 28 = 14 epi. However, in real life, this number is too close a sett for a balanced plain weave—it is too warp-faced. We call this stage in the calculation process the ***maximum sett*** for plain weave. From this number we make one more calculation for the plain weave that suits the purpose of the cloth. Read about allowing for purpose on page 279. Remember, the actual sett you use depends upon the purpose of the cloth. You are not likely ever to use the maximum sett for your actual sett.

Maximum sett for ***plain weave*** = Ashenhurst diameters = 28 x 1/2 = 14 epi (28 divided by 2).

Take another example: 5/2 cotton at 2100 yards/pound

Ashenhurst's diameters per inch $= \sqrt{2100} \times .9 = 45.83 \times .9 = 41.24$ diameters

For the maximum sett for plain weave, take ½ of the diameters as usual.

41.24 diameters x ½ = 20 epi, maximum sett

Remember, we need to know the maximum sett to determine what sett to use depending on the purpose of the cloth. It is explained on page 279.

Read, "Allowing for the purpose," on page 279 and, "Making your weaving easier," on page 280.

The reason for wanting to know a maximum sett is so that you can take percentages of it to allow for different yarns and types of fabrics. The percentages have been calculated and are in the charts in the Appendix on page 381.

For Twill

How the sett for twill for 5/2 cotton at 2100 ypp and 41 diameters per inch is determined

For 4-shaft twill (not plain weave)—instead of taking ½ the diameters, you'll take 2/3 of the diameters in the formula below for twill (see page 275 for why). How to take 2/3 is explained on page 278. Note that twill weaves have a closer sett than plain weave. The reason is explained on page 278 in the sidebar.

Maximum sett for ***twill***:=Ashenhurst diameters x 2/3 = 41 x 2/3 (or .67) = 27 epi

The reason I like this method is that it's so fast and reliable—no worrying whether the yarns are wrapped properly on the ruler. It's as simple as pushing a few keys on the calculator.

Warning: The maximum sett is probably too dense. Read, "Allowing for the purpose" on page 279 and, "Making your weaving easier," on page 280.

How to find the yards per pound

There are a number of ways to find the yards per pound. Read three ways to get this number below.

When you know how many yards are in a ball or skein

If you know the number of yards in a ball or skein or ounce, see the chart (Figure 493) to find the yards per pound (ypp) in your particular yarn. If your yarn isn't shown in the chart, use the worksheet on page 273 (Figure 496) to calculate the yards per pound

An easy way to find the yards per pound is to take the known yards in a 50 g ball or skein and multiply by 9.

From Yards in Balls and Skeins to Yards per Pound						
Type of Yarn	50g (1.75 oz) Ball or Skein		100g (3.5 oz) Ball or Skein		Yards Per Ounce	Yards Per Pound (YPP)
	Yards	Meters	Yards	Meters		
5/2 Pearl Cotton	231	210	462	420	131.25	2100
Sport-weight Wool	193	176	386	351	110	1750
2-ply Wool	162	147	325	296	92	1475
Worsted-weight Wool	88	81	176	160	50	800
Rayon Chenille	160	146	320	291	91	1450
Rug Wool	29	26	57	52	16	260
10/2 Pearl cotton	463	421	925	842	263	4200
Mohair Bouclé	130	118	258	235	73	1175

Fig. 493

Using a yarn balance (formerly McMorran yarn balance)

This balance scale is used to determine how many yards of a yarn are in one pound. See Figure 494.

It's great for letting you know how much yarn you have on an unmarked cone or skein. Place a length of yarn in the "V" on the balance arm, and cut off pieces until the arm balances. Measure the length of yarn in inches. Multiply the number of inches (and fractions) by 100 for the approximate number of yards in a pound. Measure carefully because you multiply your measurement and your error by 100.

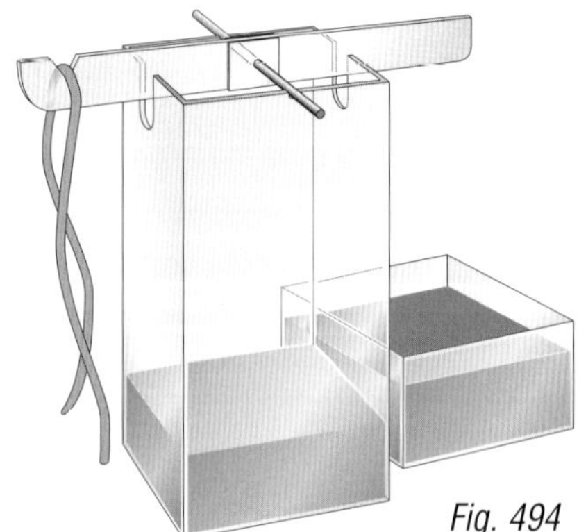

Fig. 494

Here's an example of how the balance works. Say the length of the yarn that balances on the scale is 21 ½". Multiply that number by 100 to get the number of yards there are in a pound. In this case, you get 2,150 yards per pound (21.5 x 100 = 2,150).

You can use the yarn balance to compare yarns too. If they are the same length when they balance on the scale, they are the same weight and therefore, have the same number of yards per pound and are generally equal in size, or thickness.

Another way to compare yarn sizes

You can compare two yarns quickly to see if they are the same size by hooking them together as if you linked your two index fingers together. Hold one set of yarns between your thumb and index finger. Twist the other two ends so that both sets twist. If they both feel the same, they are close to the same size. See Figure 495. ***Note:*** The term grist is sometimes used when talking about yarn size. For example, one might say, "I want a yarn of the same grist as this other yarn for my project."

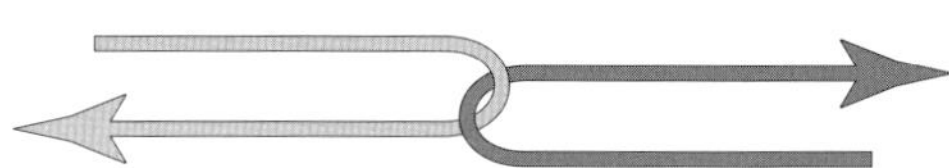

Comparing grist Fig. 495

Yarn count method

Another way to find the yards per pound is by knowing the yarn count, which indicates the size of the yarn and is explained in the sidebar. This method is enormously interesting to beginning weavers, but is also very complicated. What is so confusing is that this system was invented in the nineteenth century, and each fiber, such as cotton, linen, wool, or silk has its own specific method for determining the count. For some fibers, larger numbers mean finer yarns, and the opposite is true for others. It is almost impossible to remember how the counts are derived, so charts that give the yards per pound are used instead.

Labels on yarns often give a fraction next to the fiber of the yarn. This fraction tells the size of the yarn (the count) and the number of plies in the yarn. It's how you know one yarn from another.

Notice the fractions given for some of the types of yarns in the sett chart on page 264. The sidebar on page 274 explains how the yards per pound of a yarn are determined by the count (size) and the number of the plies.

Base Counts for Some Fibers	
Cotton, rayon, Tencel ™	1 hank = 840 yards per pound
Linen, hemp, jute, ramie	1 lea = 300 yards per pound
Wool	1 worsted count (wc) = 560 yards per pound
Spun silk	1 metric count (m.c.) = 496 yards per pound
Reeled silk microfibers*	1 denier = 4,500,000 yards per pound

Worksheet to Find Yards Per Pound

Project(s):____________________

☐ Warp yarn ____________________

☐ Weft yarn ____________________

Change meters to yards

Meters ________meters

X 1.09 ________yards

Change yards to meters

Yards ________yards

X .91 ________meters

Yards per Pound Worksheet

Method used ☐ **A** ☐ **B** ☐ **C**

A. Yards in a 100g ball or skein ________yards

÷ 3.5 (100g = 3.5 oz) ________yards/ounce

X 16 (ounces in a pound) ________yards/pound

B. Yards in a 50g ball or skein ________yards

X 2 (50g X 2 = 100g) ________yards/100g

÷ 3.5 (100g = 3.5 oz) ________yards/ounce

X 16 (ounces in a pound) ________yards/pound

C. Inches from yarn balance ________inches

X 100 ________yards/pound

Fig. 496

Yarn Count, Plies, and Yards Per Pound

Yarn count is a system of describing the size of yarns. Usually, the number of plies is given as well. Together, they denote the size of the yarn by indicating the number of yards per pound. (The more yards per pound, the finer the yarn is.) Typically, there are two numbers given in the form of a fraction. The size or count is given in the upper part of the fraction and (mostly) the ply portion is on the bottom. The ply portion of the fraction is explained below.

To explain how confusing the system is for identifying the size or the count, I will explain how the count (size) for cotton was determined in the nineteenth century. Each fiber has its own way of determining its count, however.

For cotton, number one is the size of one thread made from one pound of cotton with a length of 840 yards. This length came from measuring a cotton thread on a reel 1 ½ yards (54") in circumference. 80 threads wound around the reel made up a skein of 120 yards, and 7 skeins made up one hank, or 840 yards, and that amount of yarn weighed one pound. The "base count" for number one cotton (one strand) is 840 yards per pound. Other fibers used different size reels and arrived at different base amounts, and some are shown on the next page. (All fibers are considered to be number one at their base counts, like number one worsted for wool, number one lea for linen, etc.)

From number 1, other counts are derived. The count of 2 is the size of a thread if twice this yardage (2 x 840 or 1680 yards) weighed one pound. Number 3 would be three times the number of yards in one pound or 840 x 3 = 2,520 yards. It is obvious that a very thin yarn will take more yards to weigh a pound than a thick yarn would. Therefore, a higher number would indicate a thinner yarn. Labels tell you how your yarn relates to the base number (no. 1) for that fiber (here, the example being cotton). Next, the bottom number of the fraction or the number of plies in the yarn must be taken into account.

For example, 5/2 on a label for cotton yarn tells you that the size of the thread is no. 5 and that the yarn is composed of two plies. A plied yarn is a yarn that is made up of more than one strand. For example if you folded a one-ply yarn on itself, you would get a 2-ply yarn that would still weigh the same amount—in these examples, one pound—and would be half as long

For the example of 5/2 cotton, we can calculate that the "5" signifies a thread that is 5 x 840 (4,200) yards long in one pound. The number 2 below the line in the fraction signifies the number of plies. So, if there are two plies in this one pound instead of one, there must be half the yardage in the pound (2100). And that is the way the yardage is calculated. You know what one ply of your yarn is (the count), so divide the total of the yards by the number of plies.

Figure 497 shows what a plied yarn looks like where diagonal lines can clearly be seen on the yarn. If you look closely at the cut end in the illustration, you can see that there are 3 plies in the yarn, or 3 strands.

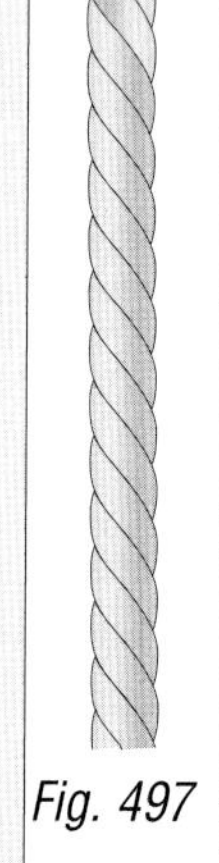
Fig. 497

Unfortunately, some yarn makers put their fractions upside-down. Usually, you can consider the smaller number to be the plies and the larger number to be the count or size. If after your calculations, you get a number that makes no sense, try flipping the fraction and recalculating. If you have the yarn in your hands, you can count the plies, so you can tell which part of the fraction refers to it.

Summary: The fraction given for a yarn tells if it is a thicker or thinner yarn by indicating the number of yards per pound. If cotton has a base count of 840 ypp for one strand, you can see that by looking at the counts only, 10/2 cotton (ten times the base count or 10 x 840, or 8400) has more yards per pound and, therefore, is finer than 5/2 cotton (5 x 840 or 4200). Finally, by dividing the count's yyp by the number of plies you get the yards per pound for 10/2 cotton as 4,200 ypp. The 5/2 cotton has only 2,100 yards in a pound (5 x 840 = 4,200 divided by 2 = 2,100 ypp).

Otherwise, look at the label for the yards per pound. Thinner yarns have more yards per pound than thicker ones. Look at the Yarn Size Chart on page 264.

In your weaving life, you'll become familiar with some types of yarns and will remember some fractions and what they mean. See the Base Counts chart on the previous page.

For more information, see my first book, ***Winding a Warp & Using a Paddle*** on pages 91 and 113-116.

From diameters or wraps per inch to epi

Whether the diameters are calculated or the warp threads wrapped on a ruler, it is just the starting point for determining epi.

Here is what the diameters of the warp threads and wraps per inch have to do with knowing the epi for a particular weave. Say, we want to weave plain weave (over one, under one, also called "tabby"). See Figure 498.

Fig. 498

The epi of the warp threads must accommodate the passage of the weft threads for any weave structure in some way or other. In plain weave, the wefts pass over one warp and under the next warp as the shuttle is thrown, hence we say, "over one, under one." To allow spaces between the warp threads to accommodate the wefts, the warps have to be spread apart a bit.

That space is the size of one weft thread if the warp and weft are the same size thread. In other words, we need to leave the space of one thread between every warp thread, so the weft has room to go between the warps. See Figure 499. This illustration shows the comparison of the warp diameters (or wpi) with the amount of space needed for the paths of the wefts. Since there are 2 wefts (one under and one over) interlacing 2 warps in one repeat of plain weave, we must leave 2 weft spaces for every two warps. So, to determine the sett (the number of warps needed for one inch) for plain weave, we divide our wraps per inch by 2 (the number of spaces needed for the weft).

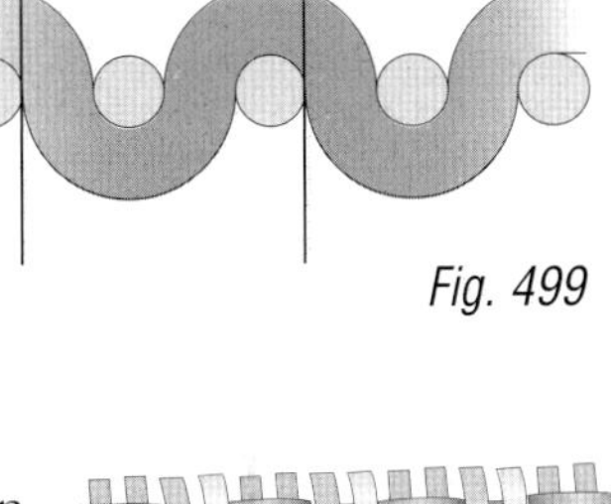

Fig. 499

For 4-shaft twill weave (See Figure 500), if we used the same spacing for the wefts, the wefts would pack down too much during weaving resulting in a cloth that was weft predominate rather than balanced. The reason is that the wefts don't intersect with every single warp as in plain weave. For this weave, the wefts pass over two and under two warps. So, for twill weaves, take 2/3 of the diameters or wpi (multiply by .67). See the sidebar on page 278 for how this fraction was derived for twill and how other weaves are accounted for. The reason the space to be left between warp threads varies for different weaves is that the over and under passage of the wefts varies with different weaves. The path of the weft only goes over one, under one for plain weave. This twill has the wefts going over two and under two. The sidebar explains how the epi for twill is determined.

Fig. 500

After reading the sidebar on page 278 about twill, here is a summary of the math.

Plain Weave: Two warps plus two spaces = 4.
Divide the number of diameters by the two spaces to find out how many warps per inch are needed (sett).

Twill: 4 warps plus two spaces = 6.
Two-thirds of the total space is occupied by the weft.
Multiply the wpi (diameters) by the weft spaces, or 2/3.

From wraps to epi

Many weavers discuss the wraps per inch (wpi) when determining the sett or epi rather than talking about diameters. Again, remember, this is only the starting place. Once the wraps (rather than diameters) are known, you make the adjustment for the weave structure to know the epi. For plain weave the wpi are divided by 2. For twill the wpi are multiplied by .67 (2/3). (The sidebar on page 278 explains the .67 (2/3) for twill.)

Remember, ideally, the number of wraps per inch that you use is actually the number of wraps in 1 ¼" on a ruler. Whether you use the wraps in 1 inch or 1 ¼ inch will effect the resulting epi, and I recommend using the 1 ¼" number to get an epi which will make a better cloth. An example of epi for plain weave using 5/2 pearl cotton: if there are 32 wraps in 1 ¼", ½ of that gives you 16 epi. If you only wrapped 1"-worth (25 wraps) and divided that by 2, your epi would be 12 rather than 16—not enough for a more stable cloth.

To review: For plain weave divide the number of wraps per inch by 2. For twill (as explained above,) multiply by 2/3 or by .67. The sidebar explains how the epi for twill is determined as well as for other weave structures.

> ***Sett for Plain weave*** = *diameters, or wraps per inch, divided by 2*
>
> ***Sett for Twill weave*** = *diameters, or wraps per inch, times 2/3 (.67)*

What if you don't take 1/2 or 2/3?

What if you didn't know about the intersections of the weft and just used the number of diameters for your sett for a plain weave fabric? See Figure 501a. It shows the warps close together with no space left for the wefts—this fabric is called a warp-faced fabric (a fabric where the warp is predominant). Notice that the wefts are far apart. This has to occur in order for the warps to remain straight and not splayed out due to the presence of the wefts.

In Figure 501b, you can see that there are spaces for the wefts to go between the warps. The weave is called balanced plain weave because there is the same number of warps per inch (epi) as wefts per inch (ppi).

Figure 501c shows what would happen if you spread out the warps further than the space the weft takes. Then the cloth will be weft-faced (weft predominates), and the wefts will pack down close together during weaving because the warps are so far apart.

The photos on the opposite page show three weavings—all using the same size yarns for warps and weft. However, they have three different setts—one balanced where warp and weft show equally (a), one warp-faced with the warps close together and predominating (b), and a third, weft-faced, with the warps spread apart more and the wefts predominating (c).

Fig. 501

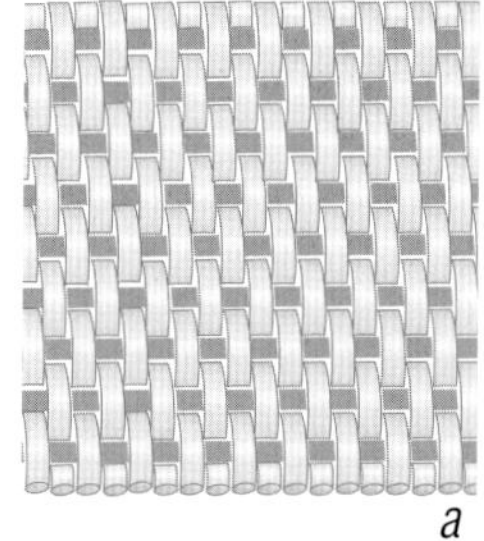

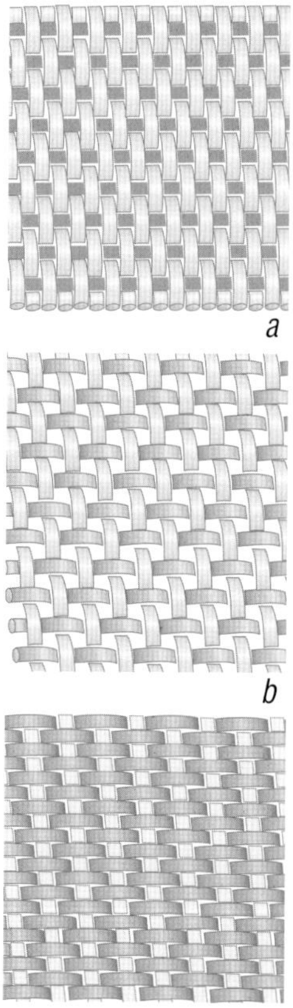

a

b

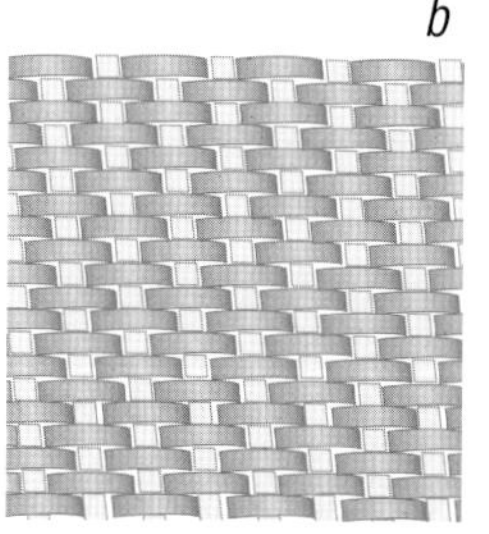

c

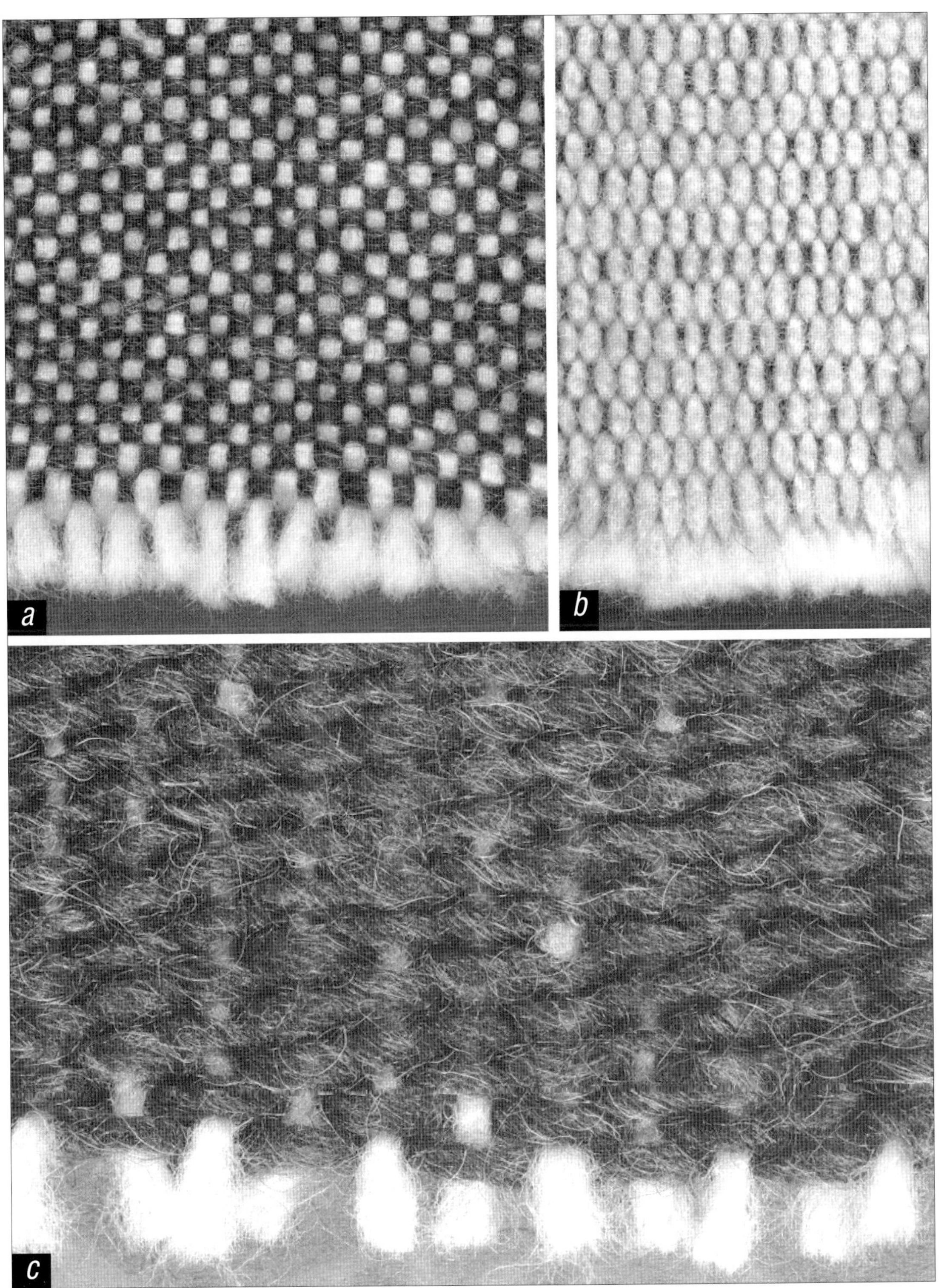
a
b
c

Weaves Other Than Plain Weave

Twill

What if you want to weave a 4-shaft twill fabric (woven on 4 shafts) where the warps and wefts intersect over two, under two? See Figure 500 (repeated here). The sett will not necessarily be the same as for plain weave. It wouldn't be the same even if all the other factors (yarns, purpose, etc.) were the same.

Now, look at Figure 502. See the weft interlacing (or intersecting) with the warp, over 2, under 2? Within the repeat there are 2 weft intersections—2 places where the weft crosses over from the "right side" of the cloth to the "wrong side." See the diameters (circles) of the yarns above the drawing? Notice that there are 4-warps and 2 weft intersections (spaces) in a repeat of this 4-shaft twill. The circles indicating the spaces for the wefts crossing the cloth are marked with asterisks. Space for 2 wefts needs to be made for every 4 warps (one for where the weft goes under the warps and one for where it goes over them) in one repeat. A way to represent this, so a calculation can be made, is to say: There are 6 diameters of yarn in one repeat of the 4-shaft twill. Two are wefts (or spaces for the wefts) and four are warps. I clearly see 4-warps and 2 weft intersections totaling 6-diameters of yarn. (4 warps and two spaces) To find how many warps per inch for your sett, make a fraction, putting the number of warps above the line (4) and the total number of diameters (warps plus spaces = 6) below the line. That would be 4/6. It is a fraction that can be reduced to 2/3.

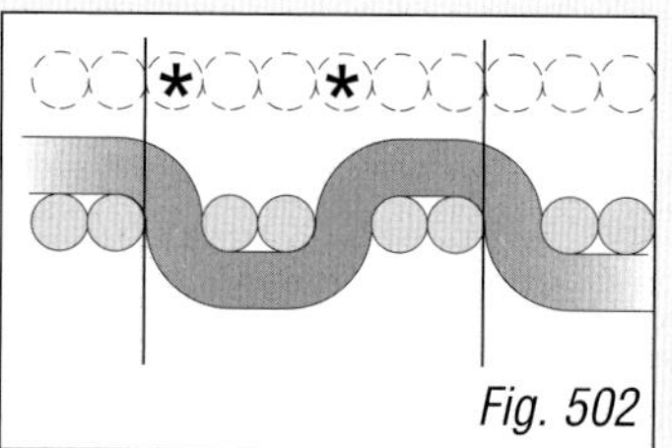

Fig. 502

So, to determine the maximum sett for 4-shaft twill take 2/3 of the wraps per-inch. That is, maximum sett = diameters per inch x 2/3. Since calculators don't have "2/3," you need to make 2/3 into a decimal number. (To do that, take the top number and divide it by the bottom one. 2 divided by 3 = .67).

For the example of a yarn with 20 diameters in an inch, the sett for twill would be .67 times 20 (2/3 of 20). That equals 13 epi (ends per inch). If you wanted plain weave for that yarn, you would have taken 1/2 of 20 and gotten 10. See that the sett for twill is denser than that for plain weave? The reason is that the weft doesn't interlace with every warp: it interlaces after every two warps. Another way to think of it is that the weft will beat down tighter when two warps are together without a weft in between them.

So, if you are wrapping, you will wrap 1 ¼" for a realistic wpi. Then, take 2/3 of that number for the epi for twill.

If you don't have a calculator handy here's an easy way to take 2/3 of a number. First, divide the number by 3—that's 1/3. Multiply the result by 2 to get 2/3.

Weaves other than plain weave and twill

For other weaves, you use the same principle as described above. Draw the diameters of the structure for one repeat. Let's take the example of a 5-shaft satin. In the repeat of the satin structure, the weft goes under one and over 4. I first like to draw more diameters (circles) than there are in the repeat. Then, I put in the weft's path. Next, I put a vertical line at the beginning and end of one repeat. See Figure 503. Then, I begin counting. The number of warps in the repeat is 5. The number of weft intersections (or weft crossings from the front of the cloth to the back) is 2 (5 warps plus two spaces for the weft = one repeat of the structure). The total number of diameters in the repeat (total of all the warps and wefts) is 7, and 5 out of the 7 are warps, so my fraction becomes 5/7. To make it into a decimal, divide 5 by 7 to get .7. Lastly, multiply .7 by the wraps per inch (let's say 20), and the sett would be 14 epi.

More about other weaves in my first book, ***Winding a Warp & Using a Paddle***, beginning on page 97.

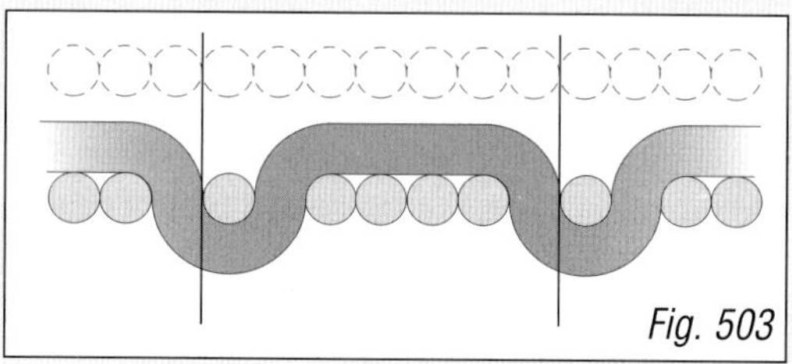
Fig. 503

Allowing for the purpose

There is another issue to consider: the purpose. Do you want a firm, an open, or a medium weight cloth? Figures 504 a, b, and c show the same yarns, all used in a balanced plain weave (warps and wefts show equally). What it means is that there's not one perfect sett for a given yarn and weave.

Calculations using Ashenhurst's rule are given on page 270 and in the sett charts in the Appendix on page 381.

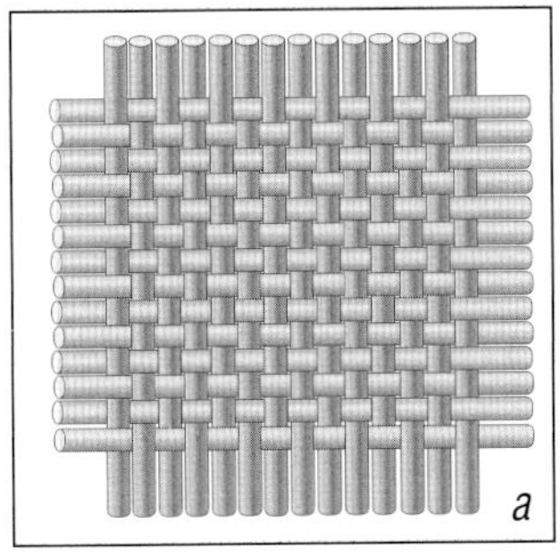

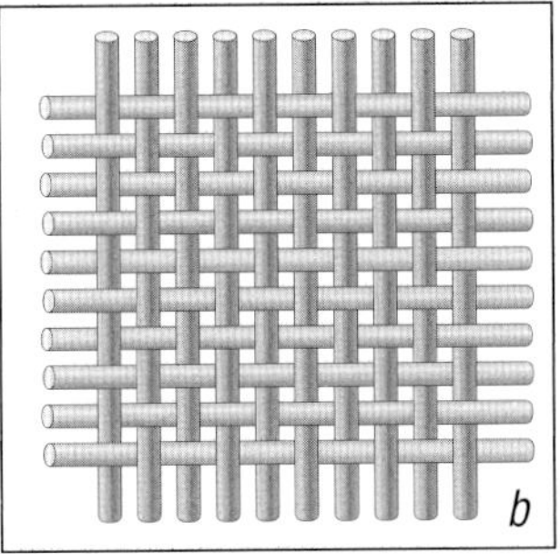

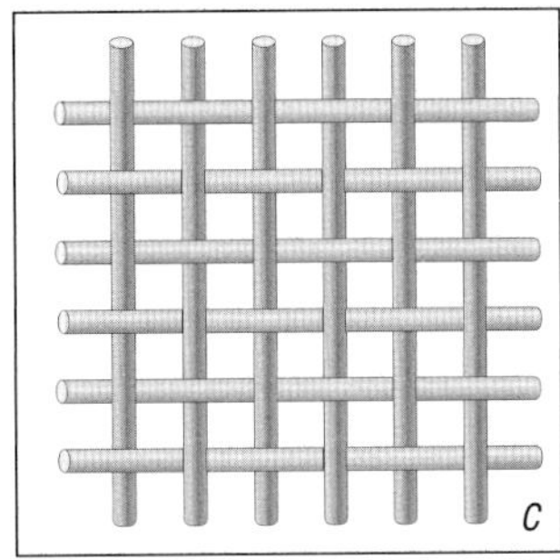

Fig. 504

How to select the sett for a purpose

You've seen that there can be a variety of setts for balanced plain weave.

Find the ***maximum*** sett for your weave structure. (1/2 the diameters or 2/3, depending upon whether you are going to weave plain weave or twill.) Remember, for the diameters use either the calculated Ashenhurst diameters or the 1¼" worth of wraps on the ruler. The numbers will be slightly different, but you can check them with the sett charts on page 381 to make your sett decisions.

Take a percentage of the maximum sett to suit your needs. Say, a yarn is to be used for upholstery in a firm weave. If the maximum sett for your weave with that yarn is 30, then 90% of that number would be the ballpark figure to try for upholstery fabric (90% times 30 = 27 epi). Then, say you wanted the same yarn for pillows (not such a firm fabric), you might use 80% of the maximum sett number for your pillow sett (80% times 30 = 24 epi). What if you wanted a shawl—loosely woven--to throw over the chair? Then take 50%-60% of the maximum sett (50% times 30=15 epi).

Can you see how helpful his formula becomes? When you calculate the diameters and then the maximum sett for the weave structure and yarn, you can take percentages of that number to allow for what you want to weave.

Another example is for woolen fabric. Woolen fabric is woven loosely with the intention that it will shrink in the finishing process and end up a firmer fabric. 65% is a good number to start with when determining the sett for this type of yarn and fabric.

Percentages for different purposes

Here are the ***percentages of the maximum sett*** for some types of cloth. You can go higher or lower as you determine what your yarn or purpose requires.

90% for upholstery

80% for "production" weaving—see below

60-70% for clothing

65% for woolens

50-60% for delicate fabrics, e.g., shawls

Warp or weft predominant fabrics

The numbers given above are generally used for balanced setts, where the warp and weft show equally. Open up the sett (so that the wefts can pack down more between the widely spaced warps) for more weft predominance, and make the sett closer (more warps per inch) for more warp predominance. See Figures 501 a,b,c on page 276.

Make your weaving easier: Use the 80% number

In industry, a balanced looking fabric is actually a bit more warp predominant than precisely balanced. It looks balanced at a glance, but upon inspection, you will see that there are more warps per inch than wefts per inch. We handweavers can use this principle, too. I almost always do when I want a generally balanced weave. The way to achieve this look is to take 80% of the maximum sett using the Ashenhurst calculation. (See the percentages above.)

Note: *The epi using 80% of the maximum sett is a bit denser or closer than many weavers learned to use to give the look of a balanced weave. Read how this percentage makes weaving easier, with good selvedges, less breakage of warp threads, and more efficient weaving.*

Why it's so wonderful to weave with a slightly closer warp sett:

1. The edges of the cloth (selvedges) don't draw in as much, so the selvedges don't break. The extra warps instead of 50-50 hold out the warp width.
2. You don't have to make sure the weft is put in very loosely. The natural diagonal the shuttle makes when you throw it through, from the last row of weaving to the beater, is usually enough slack for the weft's pathway. (If the weft is put in without any diagonal, it will pull in the edges of your cloth.)
3. There is less trouble with warp breakage. Fragile warp threads can be used because there are more of them to pull their weight on the job.
4. There are fewer wefts (picks) per inch so the weaving goes faster.

Now, don't those reasons sound enticing?

In general, whenever I'm debating between two numbers for a sett, I'll choose the denser number for the above reasons. That means, if I were debating between 6 and 8-epi, I'd tend to choose the higher number of 8. If I'm weaving an open shawl, however, I want it more open than the 80% number, for sure. Of course, my sample will be the ultimate test. Read on for when not to use the 80% number.

When you don't want to use the 80% number

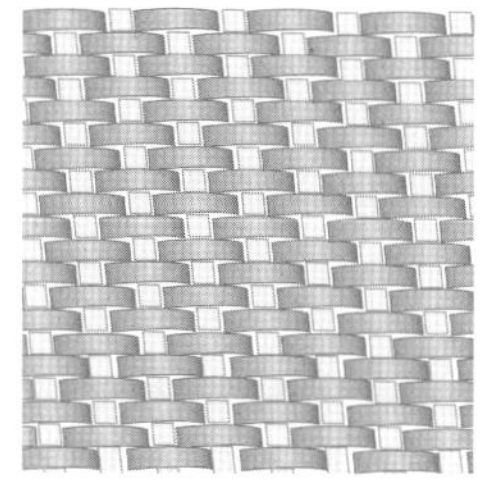

Weft-faced weave

In weft-faced fabrics, the warp is all but covered by the weft. See Figure 501c repeated here. To accomplish this appearance, you have to space the warps far enough apart that the rows of weft will pack down and cover them. There is a method, which can be used as a starting point for experimentation in finding this warp spacing. Use your ruler to wind both the warp and the weft threads together. Alternate the warp and weft threads. Keep them flat. Be careful not to twist or stretch them, but still, push them together until they closely touch. Finally, count only the warp threads in your inch to get the approximate sett. See Figure 505. You probably will use a thicker weft yarn than a warp yarn.

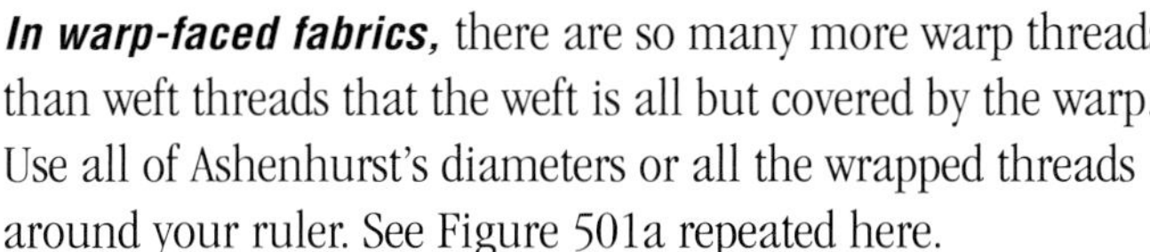

In warp-faced fabrics, there are so many more warp threads than weft threads that the weft is all but covered by the warp. Use all of Ashenhurst's diameters or all the wrapped threads around your ruler. See Figure 501a repeated here.

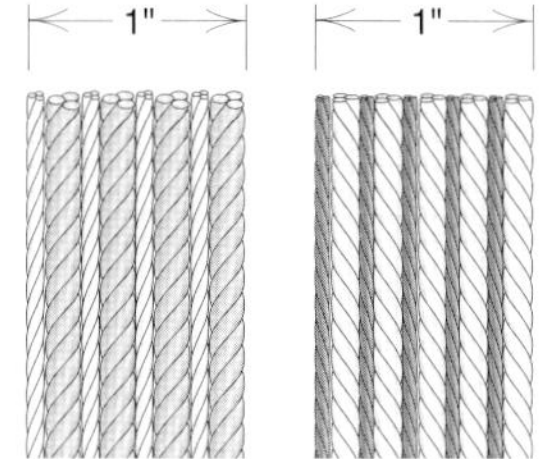

Fig. 505

For thick and thin yarns: If your warp and your weft threads are of greatly different thicknesses, you have to adjust your sett. See my first book, ***Winding a Warp & Using a Paddle***, page 99 for a formula to determine the sett in these cases. For now, you can use the principle shown in Figure 505, above, to get a general idea for a sett to try.

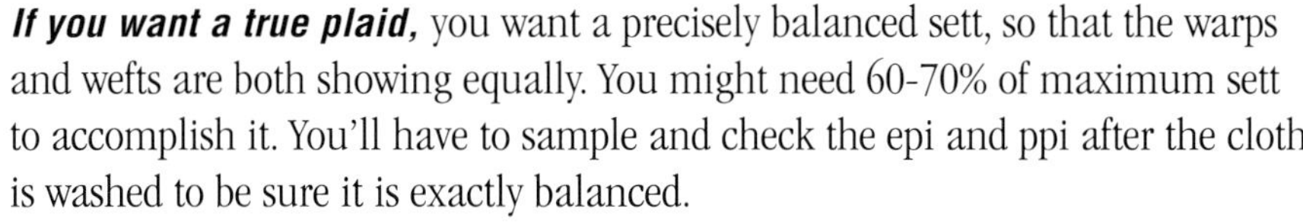

If you want a true plaid, you want a precisely balanced sett, so that the warps and wefts are both showing equally. You might need 60-70% of maximum sett to accomplish it. You'll have to sample and check the epi and ppi after the cloth is washed to be sure it is exactly balanced.

Warp-faced weave

Warning! Read about allowing for width, below.

If a weave has weft emphasis, you can't have the warp threads as dense as 80%. Examples are overshot and summer-and-winter fabrics. Use a plain weave sett here because plain weave is the basis for these two weaves. Then, as a starting point, take 60-70% of their maximum sett, depending on the purpose of your cloth. In other words, don't use the 80% epi in these cases because if you do, the warp threads will be too close together to create the desired effect of these weave structures.

Allowing for width

How dense you set the warp depends on the width of the cloth you are going to weave. A very wide warp will need to be set somewhat more open than a narrow one. With a narrow warp, the beater can beat in the wefts closer than with a wide warp where there is more resistance on the beater from having so many more warp threads. Once, I made a 7" wide sample and then made my project about 36" wide. The wefts didn't beat in the same, and the cloth wasn't balanced with the same number of warps per inch as wefts per inch that were in the sample. It made a significant difference because the project was to be a true plaid where it was important to have exactly the same amount of warp and weft in the cloth to see the color mixing.

Allowing for yarn type

The calculated setts are estimates—where you would start when sampling.

As you've seen, allowance for purpose and weave structure are considerations. The type of yarn needs to be considered as well.

The principle for yarns of various degrees of slipperiness is this. Slippery yarns need to be sett close and beaten closely to be stable enough. If the cloth is too loose, the threads will slide apart making slits in the cloth. Also, the cloth can become too stretchy and not hold its shape.

For fairly slippery yarns, the amount of slipperiness is a factor to consider. The 80% figure is suitable for fairly slippery yarns. It (80% of the maximum sett) is close enough for most fairly slippery silk yarns. Worsted, line linen, mercerized cotton, and Tencel™ can also be considered "fairly slippery."

Very slippery silk or rayon or bamboo might need more ends per inch than the 80% figure. You can try a slightly higher percent—85% of the maximum sett. Use the charts beginning on page 381 for various percentages. You can calculate your own percentages, or choose a sett a "little higher or lower" than the 80% figures given in the charts.

Read on.

For loftier yarns, (fat yarns that are not firm, but are somewhat spongy), you might use a sett of 75% of the maximum. On the charts in the appendix, you can split the difference between the 70% and 80% given. Yarns that expand during finishing, such as unmercerized cotton, might be in this category.

Hairy yarns need to be sett more open than 80% of maximum. If the warp yarns are too close, they cannot pass one another in the headles and reed, and you won't be able to get the sheds to open. Try 65-70% of the maximum sett.

Woolen yarns are meant to shrink, so they should be set more open. Use 65% of the maximum sett so the threads are far enough apart during weaving to allow for them to shrink, making a closely woven cloth after finishing.

In general, I use the 80% of the maximum sett unless for the reasons given above, and for the reasons discussed on page 281, "When you don't want to use the 80% figure."

One final consideration

Early on in this chapter, I said that my final determination of the sett usually was made based on the reed I was going to use. Read about this matter on page 265.

Can you trust your calculations?

Yes, but always make a sample in case you need to make adjustments. See below.

So, this is wonderful news, isn't it? No more worries about sett. You might make adjustments after seeing your samples, but at least you have a good idea where to begin. One word of caution about sampling. I suggest you take a piece of cloth off your warp for a sample. This is important. You might think, I'll make a little sample first, and then I'll know what the sett is, and I won't "waste" my precious warp. You can get good information this way, but remember, if the warp is wider when you make your project, the same sett will not apply that did for a narrow warp on the very same loom. With a narrow warp on a big loom, the beater will tend to pack in the weft more than on a wide warp on that loom. You can expect a wider warp to need to be sett a bit more open than your narrow sample was on the loom. It's the friction of the threads in the reed that prevents the beater from packing down the wefts as much as it would with a narrow warp. You might sample on a small loom, but here, too, there could be a difference with a wider warp on the big loom; so you need to allow for sampling on the actual warp. I usually add 1 yard onto my warps for samples, but 10" or so will probably do.

Weaving a sample

Everyone always says whenever they talk about determining sett, that you must make a sample—that neither calculation nor estimate can be counted on to be exactly what you want. This is true. These calculations give you a good ballpark figure, but you must always allow for making adjustments. How do you make allowances? You plan on making the warp a bit longer than necessary so you can make your sample on the warp itself. Then, you cut off that sample and evaluate it. Does it look how you want? Is it too loose? Too dense? In your sample, you might be trying colors and/or weaves. You must wash or finish your sample in the way it will be done in real life—to determine how much it will shrink or if the colors will run. Some yarns and some weaves shrink more than others do. After finishing, you'll know if you need to weave the cloth longer on the loom so it won't end up too short. You may say, "Cut it off, horrors!! I don't want to waste my precious warp by having to tie it on again." Yes, cut it off, then resume weaving when you know all is O.K. (Perhaps you had to re-sley the reed, or to plan to weave longer for shrinkage).

Cutting off a sample

There are two easy ways to cut off a piece of cloth before the warp is completely woven that use less warp than for tying on again. One method uses the 2-stick heading (described beginning on page 134). Lacing on (see pages 90 and 91) is the other method and uses less yarn.

Needle weaving a sample

You can check different setts by needle weaving to get some idea of what each will look like. See Figure 506. It can be a

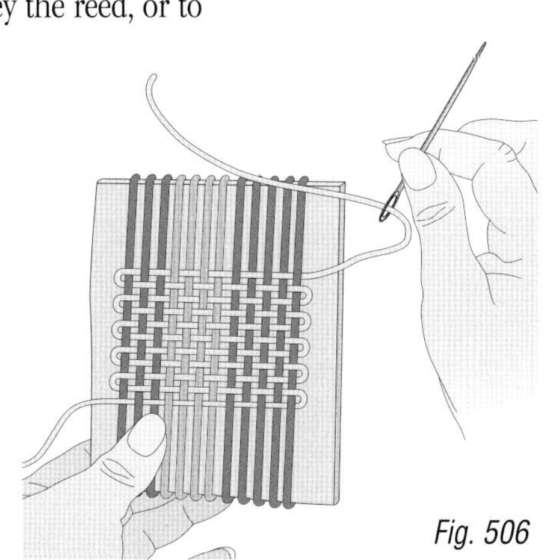

Fig. 506

way to test out color combinations, too. Use a piece of foamcore board or a stiff cardboard, such as the back of a writing tablet and cut it longer and wider than your sample is to be. Wrap the "warp" around the cardboard as shown in the illustration. Tape the beginning and end of the yarn to hold it place on the back. As you wrap, place your "warps" the same distance apart as the epi you are trying out. For example, if you want to try out 10 epi, you should have 10 warps to the inch on your sample. You could mark lines on the cardboard 1 inch apart to make it easier to make your ends per inch accurate. It is efficient to weave the wefts in and out with a tapestry needle in the center area of your cardboard "loom" as shown in the illustration. Trying to get the tapestry needle over and under the threads close to where they are wrapped around the edge of the cardboard is hard to do because there isn't much room to pass the needle in and out.

This kind of sample can only give you an idea of things. The effect of the beater and the width of the cloth will influence how much the wefts will pack in. Remember, that a wider warp will need to have a little more open sett than a narrow one. See page 281.

Summary to find the sett (epi):	
Sett charts	***Plain weave sett chart*** with yards per pound, diameters, maximum sett, and percentages of maximum sett begins on page 381 ***Twill sett chart*** on page 381
To find the **yards per pound of warp yarn**	See the ***sett charts***, page 381
	Use a ***McMorran balance***, page 272
	Calculate from the ***yardage given on the label***, pages 271-274
To find the **diameters of the warp yarn**	***Wrapping method:*** Wrap yarn for 1¼" on a ruler Count the number of threads in that width
	Ashenhurst method: Number of diameters per inch = .9 x the square root of the yards per pound
Decide on the **weave structure**	E.g., plain weave or twill
Find the **maximum sett** for your chosen weave structure	***Ashenhurst method:*** For ***plain weave*** – Ashenhurst diameters x 1/2 (.5) For ***twill*** – Ashenhurst diameters x 2/3 (.67) See pages 269-270.
	Wraps of 1 ¼" on a ruler: For ***plain weave*** – Number of wraps times 1/2 (.5) For ***twill*** – Number of wraps times x 2/3 (.67) See pages 267 and 276
Allow for the purpose	***Take a percentage of maximum sett:*** 90% for upholsery 80% for "production" weaving 60-70% for clothing 65% for woolens 50-60% for delicate fabrics, e.g., shawl
Consider your reed	See page 265
Allow for **special circumstances**	See: "When you don't want to use the 80% figure," page 281 "Allowing for yarn type," page 282 "Can you trust your calculations?" page 283

11 *Planning a Project*

Introduction

In order to plan a project, you need to know certain information besides what you want to make. Suggestions of things to weave are given in the table on page 297. Obviously, you need to know the dimensions of the project, the weave structure, and what yarns you want to use for the warp and the weft. In this chapter, you can learn the other things you need to find out.

See the sidebar on page 297 for suggestions about how to choose the yarns for your warps and wefts.

Before you can measure out your warp threads, you need to have your idea for your project so you can plan how long to make the warp, what color(s), and how many threads you need to measure out. In the chapter on sett, beginning on page 263, you learned how to determine the number of warp threads per inch (epi). In this chapter you'll learn how to determine how long to make the warp, how much warp yarn you'll need, and how much weft yarn.

Using the worksheets on pages 286 and 287, it will be easy to figure out this information without worrying that you'll run short of yarn—surprises you don't want in your weaving life.

The steps for planning projects

1. Dream up an idea for your project.
2. Decide on the project's measurements, colors, yarns, weave structure (plain weave, twill, etc.)
3. Draw a sketch of your warp as shown on the worksheet and described on page 289.
4. Determine how close together the warp threads are to be, ends per inch (epi), as explained in the chapter on sett beginning on page 263.
5. Fill out the worksheets to determine how much yarn you need before you buy it, and how long to make the guide string before you begin measuring the warp. Filling out the worksheets is explained in this chapter. You really can't get started without this information.

The worksheets

I use a worksheet. I make many copies of it and use a new worksheet every time I begin thinking about making a warp. It helps you work out what you need to know, methodically, so you don't miss a calculation, don't have enough yarn, or end up with a too-short cloth. I suggest you photocopy the worksheets provided on the following pages and follow the instructions to fill them out beginning on page 288.

Planning Projects Worksheet

Project(s): ____________________

Date: ____________

Weave structure: ____________ Ends per inch: ______

Source of idea: __________ Reed: ________ Sley: ________

Number of shafts: ________ Ends in each raddle group: ______

Line 1.
Draw sketch of project

Part 1

Previously gathered information

Sett ______epi

Warp yarn ______yards per ☐ pound ☐ ounce* ☐ ball ☐ skein

Weft yarn ______yards per ☐ pound ☐ ounce* ☐ ball ☐ skein

**To get yards per ounce, divide yards per pound by 16*
To change meters to yards multiply meters by 1.09

Part 2

Warp length

	Samples	2.	________inches
+	Heading	3.	________inches
+	Project(s) length	4.	________inches
+	Hems/fringes	5.	________inches
+	Shrinkage (for length) _____%	6.	________inches
=	Woven length	7.	________inches
+	Warp take-up _____%	8.	________inches
+	Front loom waste	9.	________inches
+	Back loom waste	10.	________inches
=	Total warp length (inches)	11.	________inches
÷	Divided by 36		
=	Total warp length (yards) (length of guide string)	12.	________yards

Part 3

Warp width

	Desired width	13.	________inches
+	Shrinkage (for width) _____%	14.	________inches
+	Draw-in	15.	________inches
=	Total warp width	16.	________inches
X	Sett	17.	________epi
=	Total number of warp threads	18.	________ends (threads)

Warp yarns *(attach samples)*

Description	Source	Yd/lb	Color	Cost

Planning Projects Worksheet *(cont.)*

Part 4

Amount of warp yarn needed

Total number of warp threads from line 18 — 19. ________ends (threads

X Total warp length (from above) — 20. ________yards

Total yards for warp — 21. ________yards

÷ Divided by

- ☐ yards per pound
- ☐ yards per ounce*
- ☐ yards per ball
- ☐ yards per skein

22. ________ yards

= Total warp yarn needed (how much to have on hand)

23. ______ pounds ______ ounces* ______ balls ______ skeins

Part 5

Weft Calculations

	Warp width	24.	________inches
+	Take-up _____%	25.	________inches
+	Shrinkage (optional) _____%	26.	________inches
=	Length of each weft	27.	________inches
X	Wefts per inch (ppi)	28.	________ppi
=	Length of weft yarn needed to weave one inch of fabric	29.	________inches
X	Woven length (in inches)	30.	________inches
=	Total length in inches for weft	31.	________inches
÷	Divided by 36		
=	Total yards for weft	32.	________yards
÷	Divided by		

Yards per package of weft yarn

33. ______ pound ______ ounce* ______ ball ______ skein

= Total weft yarn needed (How much yarn to have on hand)

34. ______ pounds ______ ounces* ______ balls ______ skeins

Weft yarns *(attach samples)*

Description	Source	Yd/lb	Color	Cost

Part 6

Yarn totals *(Put the amounts needed on the appropriate lines below)*

Warp yarn

35. ______ pounds ______ ounces* ______ balls ______ skeins

Weft yarn

36. ______ pounds ______ ounces* ______ balls ______ skeins

Total warp and weft yarn

37. ______ pounds ______ ounces* ______ balls ______ skeins

To get yards per ounce, divide yards per pound by 16

The worksheets are divided into six sections, which you'll fill out as you go. Follow along with the text to fill out each section.

Sections

Part 1: Previously gathered information

Part 2: Warp length

Part 3: Warp width

Part 4: Amount of warp yarn needed

Part 5: Weft calculations

Using the worksheets

Part 1: Previously gathered information

In this section, it is assumed that you have already chosen your yarns for your project. Read about choosing yarns in the sidebar on page 297. There is a Catch-22 in a sense. You'll calculate how much yarn to buy on these worksheets, but you need to know what yarns you plan to use in order to do the calculations. You need this information to plan the sett (epi), and so you know how many yards there are in a ounce, pound, ball, or skein. It may mean you go to the yarn shop twice—once to make your selection and to get the information needed and another time to pick up the quantity you need. Instead of another trip, you could have the yarn shipped. Another strategy is to take a few copies of the worksheets and your calculator along with you when you go shopping in the first place.

Of course, if you know the count (see page 272) of the yarn you can get the information from the sett charts on page 381. Just going by the name of a yarn, for example, worsted, or sport yarn isn't enough information to get the yards per pound because there is no standard, and many types of each are available. Most weaving magazines and catalogs give the yarn counts and the yards per pound as well.

Before you can make your calculations, you need to gather the following information and put it on the worksheet for easy reference while you make the calculations.

Sett: the ends per inch (epi). Read about sett beginning on page 263 or refer to the sett charts on page 381.

Warp yarn: yards per pound, per ounce, or per ball or per skein. Read about finding the yards per pound beginning on page 271. Check the label for yardage information.

Weft yarn: yards per pound, per ounce, per ball, or per skein. Read about finding the yards per pound beginning on page 271.

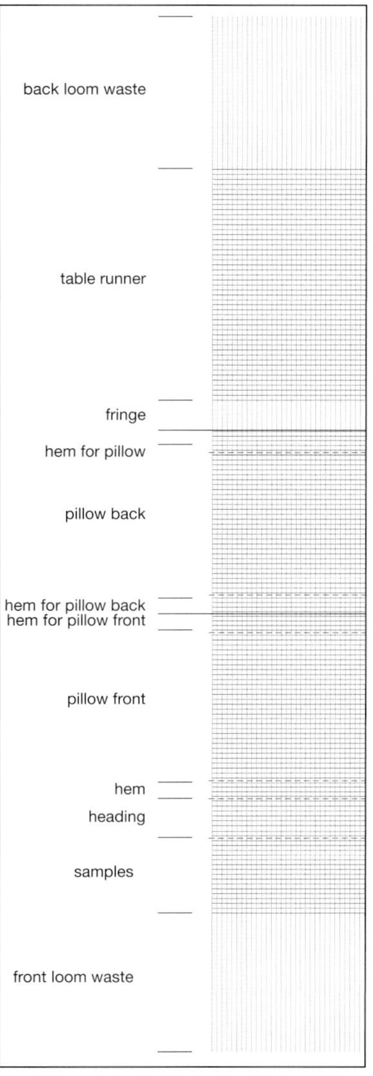

Fig. 507

Part 2: Warp length—Determining the length of the guide string

Line #1: Sketch the plan of the whole warp

To determine how long to make the warp: sketch out the warp and all the things that are to be woven on it. Draw in some loom waste (explained below) at each end. Figure 507 shows a sample sketch for a warp for a pillow and a table runner. Note that I've added extra length for samples, hems, fringes, and loom waste. Draw a sketch for your own project on the worksheet's margin on page 286.

This step has saved me many times. It reminds me to allow for all the extra things that need to be accounted for when determining the length of the warp.

Figure 507 shows how to fill in the sketch. Beginning at the bottom of your sketch, draw in allowances for the front loom waste, samples, and the heading—see below for explanations. Then, draw in a bit for a hem and a space for the pillow front and the hem at the other end of the pillow front. Continue on for the back of the pillow and its two hems. Draw in an allowance for fringe for the table runner and a space for the runner itself. Note that the fringe at the other end will be in the back loom waste (explained below).

Now, begin filling in the blanks on the worksheet

Line #2: Samples

The section at the bottom (the beginning) of the sketch is for samples. It's a good idea to allow some extra warp for trying out your idea and for checking to see how much the cloth might shrink, before you weave your entire project. Read why the sample needs to be on the very warp for your project in the section, "Can you trust your calculations?", in the chapter on sett on page 283. It is also the place where you can try out different yarns and weaves to achieve your goal. I recommend having around 10" for sampling, at least.

Be sure to cut off your sample to see what it looks like off the loom, and to wash it to check for shrinkage. Making and cutting off a sample using the two-stick heading as shown on page 135 is a wise investment.

Line #3: Heading

There are different types of headings you can make. Weaving the heading with weft yarn is described beginning on page 105. Weaving the heading with rags is described on page 180. The two-stick heading is described on page 135. The two-stick heading is a great way to save warp yarn and restore warp tension after you cut off pieces of your cloth. Allow about six inches for the heading.

Lines #4 and #5: Project length, hems/fringes

Finally, you can consider your project itself. How long will it be, how much do you need to weave for hems, or leave unwoven for fringe. Put these measurements on the worksheet on lines 4 and 5 for "project length" and "hems/fringes." In the example sketch (Figure 507 on page 289), areas are shown for both sides of the pillow plus all the hems. Also in the sketch are the spaces for the runner with one of its fringes. (The fringe at the other end of the runner will be included in the back loom waste, described below.)

Line #6: Shrinkage

This is the amount you want to allow for the cloth's shrinkage when it is washed. I usually allow 10% of the length of my cloth for shrinkage unless I have woven that item before and know the actual shrinkage likely to occur. If you suspect your yarn or weave structure will shrink a lot, add more for shrinkage (perhaps 20%)—better safe than sorry. You'll know how much your cloth will shrink after you've woven your sample, but that's too late for determining the length of the warp you need to measure out.

Line #7: Woven length

Now you can total up the woven length for your warp. The lines on the worksheet should be completed up to line #7: "Woven length."

Line #8: Warp take-up

You need to know your woven length first, then, you can add the allowance for warp take-up. Notice in Figure 508b that both the warp and the weft threads bend over and under each other in the woven cloth. Look at Figure 508a and notice that the warps (vertical threads) bend a lot more than in Figure 508b. That bending of the threads needs to be considered or you will run out of warp before you've woven all you need. Different weaves take-up (bend) more than others, so don't forget to add this important allowance into your warp length calculations. Read about this on page 303.

I usually allow 10% for warp take-up unless I'm going to use a weave that takes up more, or I'm using especially heavy yarns that will need more yarn for it to flex and bend over and under the wefts. Figure 508c shows the warp bending so you can see how it "takes up" and gets shorter during weaving.

A warp-face weave such as shown in Figure 508a would require more allowance for take-up—at least 20%.

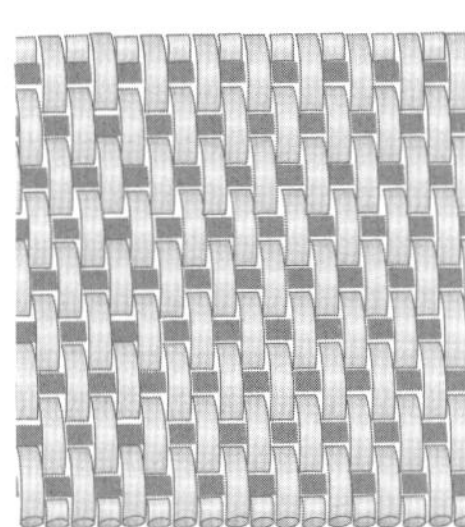
Fig. 508a

Fig. 508b

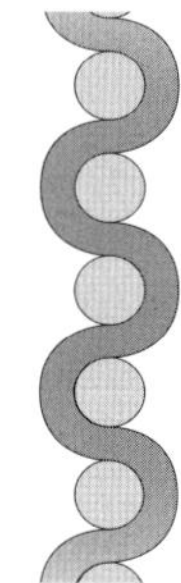
Fig. 508c

Line #9: Front loom waste

A certain amount of your warp cannot be woven into cloth. It's at each end. The front loom waste is at the beginning of the warp. That is the place where some of the warp is used in tying it onto the cloth-beam apron rod (Figure 509a). Front loom waste, might be anywhere from 6-8 inches to 20 inches long, depending on how thrifty or wasteful you are and on what method you use for tying on (surgeon's knots or lacing on). Lacing on, described on page 90, uses the least amount of warp. See Figure 218 on page 90 and repeated here.

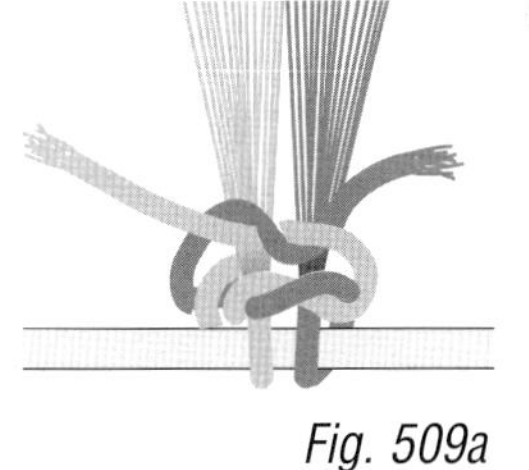

Fig. 509a

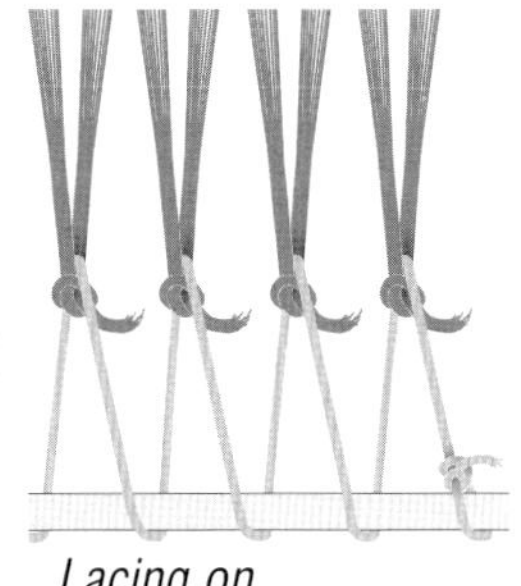

Lacing on

Line #10: Back loom waste

The loom waste at the back of the loom can be seen in Figure 509b. It is the amount that cannot be woven because of the warp's being threaded in the heddles on the shafts. Large looms have more distance between the beater and the back shaft, so they naturally have more loom waste than a small loom would. To know how much to allow, see the illustration and measure on your loom the distance represented by the arrow. Pull the warp beam's apron rod up to the heddles on the shaft furthest back on the loom. Measure from there to a few inches in front of the beater or about one-half the distance between the beater and the breast beam. Add a few more inches here if you warp front-to-back, for tying the knots on the warp beam's apron rod, say, 4-6 inches more.

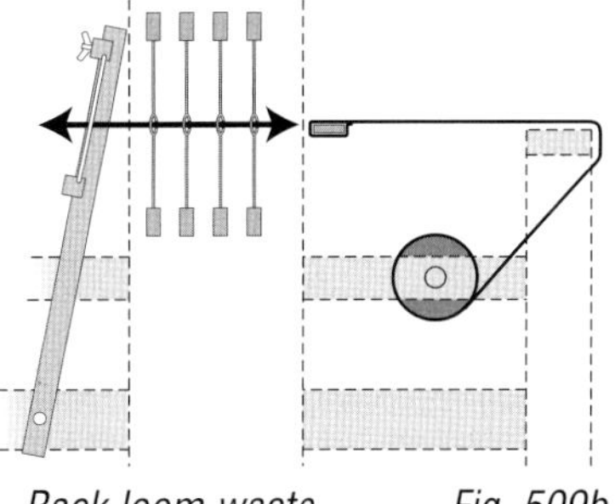

Back loom waste Fig. 509b

Line #11: Total warp length in inches

At last, you can add up the figures and determine the length of your warp in inches. It is the length you want your guide string (described on pages 15 and 157) to be.

Line #12: Total warp length in yards (length of guide string)

Divide line #11 by 36 to get the length in yards. I usually round up any decimal numbers to the next yard. Put that number down at the bottom of the worksheet under "Total warp length," and remember, that's the length the total warp needs to be—the length of your guide string—not the length of your woven project alone.

If your yarn is stretchy, you should make the warp longer than you calculated. To find out how much longer, measure a yard of yarn relaxed and not stretched. Then, stretch it and see how much it expands. That difference will tell you how many inches per yard to add. For example, I have a knitting type of yarn in my studio that measured 36" (1yd.) when relaxed and stretched out to 39" when pulled. In that case, I should add 3" for each yard I calculate for the warp. The yarn will be stretched out on the warping board and on the loom. It will relax when taken off the loom. You need to weave 3" extra for each yard so it will be long enough when off tension. Remember, a very stretchy yarn is not appropriate for a warp yarn because of the stretched and unstretched issue.

Part 3: Warp width

Line #13: Desired width

To know the number of individual warp threads you need to measure out, start with the width you want your project to be: "Desired width." Remember, the width cannot be more than the width of the loom. Measure the width of your loom on the warp beam and make your warp at least 2" narrower. I say, at least—better yet, make it 4" narrower. Troubles can happen if the warp is at the loom's maximum width—the warp threads tend to slip off the edges of the warp beam as it builds up. Then the warp threads will not be all the same length, and thus, the warp tension will not be even. I never make my warps full width since I did it one time and had trouble. However, you can weave wider than the width of your loom by weaving the double width version of double weave. (See page 254.)

Line #14: Shrinkage (for width)

This is an amount to allow for shrinking during washing. I allow about 10% if I'm not sure.

Line #15: Draw-in

During most weaving, the woven cloth will draw in, or end up a bit narrower than the warp was when it was unwoven. This is a natural occurrence that depends upon the weave structure, yarns, and sett (epi). For narrow warps (say 5" wide), I don't add anything for draw-in and consider the 10% for shrinkage to be enough to allow for both shrinkage and draw-in. For wider warps, allowing 1–2" might be a good ballpark number for balanced weaves.

The amount to allow for draw-in isn't a precise quantity. If it really doesn't matter exactly how wide your cloth turns out to be, and you can accept that it is a bit narrower, you might not allow anything, or perhaps just 1" for draw-in.

You might use 1" for 20–36" wide warps and 2" if the warp is more than 36" wide. Note that this might be a little more allowance than will actually occur. If the width is critical, you'll have to weave about a foot or so to see exactly how wide the warp will end up given your project. If it is wider than you want you'll need to drop some warp threads or consider changing your plan and accepting the width.

Draw-in is a normal occurrence, and you need to be aware of it whether you allow any extra width in the warp or not. Too much draw-in is a big problem during weaving and must be remedied or the outside warp threads will continually abrade and break. Read about this issue in the selvedges section beginning on page 302.

Line #16: Total warp width

Add up Lines 13, 14, and 15 for the total warp width.

Line #17: Sett

Once you know the total width the warp is to be and the sett (epi), you can calculate how many ends (warp threads) you'll need. Put the sett (epi) from "Part One: Previously gathered information," on Line #17.

Line #18: Total number of warp threads

Multiply the total width by the warp sett, (Lines 16 and 17) to get the total number of warp threads (ends) to measure out.

It may be necessary to adjust this number to fit your threading draft. For example, if you calculate that you need 470 ends, but your threading has a repeat unit of 8 ends. You will need to decide whether to add 6 ends or subtract 2 ends so your total number will be divisible by 8: either 464 ends or 472, rather than the 470 you calculated.

Part 4: Amount of warp yarn needed

You can now calculate how much warp yarn you need to have on hand.

Line #19: Total number of warp threads

Enter the number from Line 18 here.

Line #20: Total warp length

Enter the number from Line #12 here.

Line #21: Total yards for warp

To find the number of yards needed for the warp, multiply the "total number of warp threads" (Line 19) times the "total warp length" (Line #20).

Line #22: Yards per pound, ounce, ball or skein

Enter this information from Part One: "Previously gathered information." Very often, I need to know the yards in ounces because the project will require several ounces, rather than several pounds. To convert the yards per pound to yards per ounce, divide the yards per pound by 16 (because there are 16 ounces in a pound).

Line #23: Total warp yarn needed

To find out how much yarn you need to have on hand, divide the "total yards for warp" (Line 21) by the "yards per pound, ounce, ball, or skein of warp yarn" (Line 22).

Part 5: Weft calculations

Theoretically, you don't need this information to make your warp, but you will want to have your weft ready as soon as the warp is on the loom. You need to be sure you have enough on hand.

Line #24: Enter the width of the warp from Line 16.

Line #25:Take-up

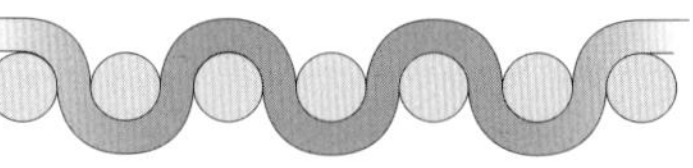

Fig. 510

The wefts will be a bit longer than the width of the warp. Remember that the wefts bend (take up) as well as the warps. (See Figure 510). In Figure 508b, you saw both the warps and the wefts bending. For balanced weaves where the warp and weft show equally, (same number of warps per inch as wefts per inch) as in Figure 508b, the weft take-up (allowance for the weft yarns bending) could be estimated at around 10%. For weft-faced weaves, such as the rep weave in the sampler beginning on page 93 you'll need to add more than 10% because the wefts will do more bending—perhaps as much as 30% or more.

Line #26: Shrinkage (optional)

Actually, allowance for shrinkage has already been considered in warp width. I might add 10% here "for insurance" for the unexpected. I generally like to have on hand a little more yarn that I calculated so I don't worry if I have to take out some weaving, or something else happens that makes me run out of yarn.

Line #27: Length of each weft

Add the three numbers on the lines 24, 25, and 26: to get the length each weft will be. This may need some explaining or repeating. Each weft will be longer than the width of the warp due to take-up and shrinkage. So don't doubt yourself. Instead, check to be sure that the length of each weft is the sum of all three of these figures.

Line #28: Wefts per inch (ppi)

Next, you need to know how many wefts will be woven in an inch of cloth. This number is written as ppi (picks per inch). Wefts can be called "picks" or "shots." Depending upon how hard the wefts are beaten in during weaving and depending on the sett (ends per inch, or epi) of the warp, the number of picks per inch will vary. Again, look at Figures 508a and 508b on page 290, and see that in both, the number of picks (wefts) per inch is different. In balanced fabrics the warps and wefts are about equally spaced. If you're planning a balanced cloth, estimate the ppi (picks per inch) to be the same as the epi (ends per inch). If you're making warp-faced or weft-faced cloth, estimate more or fewer ppi than epi. See page 276.

Line #29: Length of weft yarn needed to weave one inch of fabric

Multiply the numbers from lines 27 and 28.

I think this is the trickiest calculation of all. I always need to visualize what I am calculating. I must note the length of each weft and also the number of wefts per inch. I multiply the two figures together to get how much weft there will be in one inch's worth of weaving. If you follow the directions on the worksheet, you won't go astray.

Line #30: Woven length (in inches)

This calculation is the next trickiest one and has several parts. You need to look back on your worksheet in Part Two to find out the "woven length" (Line 7). Enter it on the worksheet, here, on Line 30. (You are about to calculate how much weft you'll need, and since there won't be any wefts in the front and back loom waste, you will only allow for the length of the warp that will actually be woven.)

Line #31: total length in inches for weft

Multiply the "Length of weft yarn needed to weave one inch of fabric" (Line #29) by the "woven length" (Line #30) to arrive at the "total length in inches for weft." Since the answer on this line will be in inches, it will be a very large number.

Remember, you don't need to consider fringe or loom waste because those areas won't have any weft woven in them.

Line #32: Total yards for weft

Since we usually buy yarn by the yard, you need to divide the number of inches (Line 31) by 36 (Because there are 36-inches in one yard.). Put this figure on Line 32.

Line #33: Yards per pound, ounce, ball, or skein:

You need to know the yards per pound or yards per ounce of your weft yarn, or the number of yards in one ball or one skein. If you're using the same weft as the warp, you have already put the number on the worksheet in the "Previously gathered information" section. More than likely, your weft will be a different yarn. How to find the yards per pound begins on page 271.

You can put the "yards per pound, ounce, ball or skein" for the weft yarn in Part One: "Previously gathered information."

Line #34: Total weft yarn needed (How much yarn to have on hand)

To know how many pounds, ounces, balls, or skeins needed for your project, divide the weft yarn needed in yards (Line 32) by the number of yards in a pound, ounce, ball or skein (Line 33).

Part 6: Yarn Totals

Line #35: Amount of warp yarn needed in pounds, ounces, balls, or skeins

Line #36: Amount of weft yarn needed in pounds, ounces, balls, or skeins

Line #37: Total yarn needed for warp and weft yarns:

If the warp and weft are the same, add the numbers from Lines 35 and 36 for the total amount to buy. If the warp and weft are different, Line 35 tells you how much warp you need and Line 36 tells you how much weft.

And you're finished!! You know how long to make the warp and the guide string, how much warp yarn is needed, and how much weft yarn.

What about stripes in the warp and weft?

You can know how much yarn you need for each color after you've calculated the yarn requirements for the whole project.

Say, you have ***two*** 1" stripes on each border of a dishtowel that is to be a total of 13" wide. You will need 4" worth of yarn for the ***four*** stripes and 9" worth of yarn for the body of the towel. First, look at the epi (Line17) and multiply the epi by the inches you need (4" for the four one-inch stripes). Do the same for the remaining part of the towel. (9 x epi). Now you have the number of warp threads needed for each color. Go to the worksheet and work with one color at a time. On Line 19 put in your inches (say, 4", in this case) then continue on the worksheet, filling in Lines 20, 21, 22, and 23. Now you have determined the amount of yarn needed for the four stripes. Do the same for the remaining 9" of warp, again, beginning with Line 19.

If your stripes are more or less than 1", you can easily calculate how many threads will be in ½", ¼", ¾" and so on. For example, with your ends per inch at 20 epi, there would be 10 ends in ½", 5 ends in ¼", and 15 ends in ¾".

At 20 epi if there were 3½" of a color, you would have 70-ends (warp threads) of that color. [20 epi x 3 = 60 + ½" (10 ends) = 70 warp threads] Put this number on Line 19 and continue on with worksheet through Line 23 to know how much yarn is needed for the 70 ends.

For stripes in the weft, you do the same thing, only you use your ppi (picks per inch, or wefts per inch) instead of the ends per inch (epi). For example, you want a 3" wide band of one color at each end of a piece that was to measure a total of 34" long. You would multiply 3" x the ppi to know how many wefts would be needed to make each 3" band. Double that amount to account for both bands of wefts. Put this amount on Line 30: "Woven length in inches."

Then look at the length of weft yarn needed to weave one inch of fabric (Line 29). Multiply lines 29 and 30 for the number of inches of weft you'll need (Line 31). Continue filling out the worksheet for Lines 32, 33, and 34.

Do the same procedure to find out how much of the other color yarn you need for the body of the piece. The total length is to be 34" Subtract 6" for the two bands, and you will have 28" for the color for the body. Put that number on Line 30: "Woven length in inches." Using the numbers on lines 29 and 30, continue filling out the remaining lines: 31, 32, 33, and 34.

Keeping records

It's a good idea to keep records and photos of your work—before and after weaving. With that in mind, keep all your worksheets for a project and label them version 1, version 2, etc. You never know when you'll want to know this information again.

Always have more yarn on hand for a project than the exact amount you calculated. Consider that you may have to take out some weaving, or you may have to re-sley the reed, making the warp wider and requiring more weft yarn.

Choosing yarns for warps and wefts—what to look for at a yarn shop and online

I wrote this section after going with a student to a yarn shop to buy yarns for her first project. This is the way we navigated the shop with all its bins and shelves of beautiful yarns.

First, walk around, looking at the yarns and asking the clerk to point out yarns that would be appropriate for the project (for example, a scarf, or a table runner) you have in mind. See below for project ideas.

Begin looking for yarns or colors that you love. It might be only that the color is wonderful—or the texture or feel of the yarn. This is a starting point given that there can be so much from which to choose. You are discovering what appeals to you.

Look in the bins with the textures of yarn you like to see if there is a color in that type of yarn, which suits your project. Or, look for the color you like and then try see if that color can be found in a bin with a texture that works.

Start thinking what would make a good warp yarn. There are requirements needed for warp yarns. They must be smooth, strong, neither stretchy nor spongy. Plied yarns are especially good for warp yarns because they are strong. If a yarn is plied, you should clearly see diagonal lines on the yarn. See Figure 511.

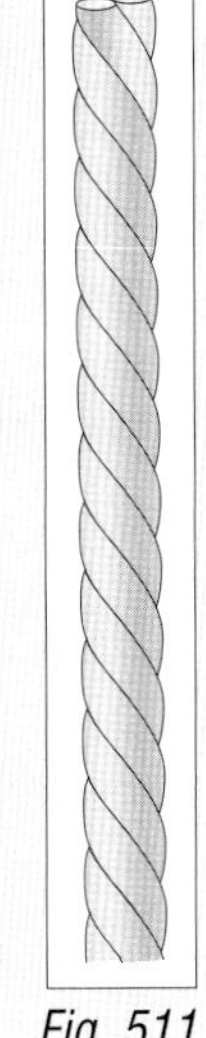

Fig. 511

Ideas for Projects

Check your samplers now and then for ideas

afghan	baby blanket	bag for shuttles, other weaving equipment
belt	blanket	book or journal cover
bookmark	bread basket cloth	cell phone cover
coasters	coin purse	computer case
cosmetic purse	curtains	dish towels
dish cloth	doll things–blanket, rug, scarf	evening purse
eyeglass case	eye pillow	fabric for a vest, clothing
gift wrappers/bags for jam, soap, wine, etc.	guest towels	hot pad
iPod cover	napkins	needle case
pillow	pin cushion	placemat
poncho	pot holders	pouch
purse	rugs, small or runners	sachet bags
sample your ideas	sample new weave structures	sample yarns
scarf	shawl	table runner or mat
throw	tote bag	wall hanging

12 Selvedges

Selvedges are the edges of the cloth where the wefts turn around the outside warp threads. See Figure 512.

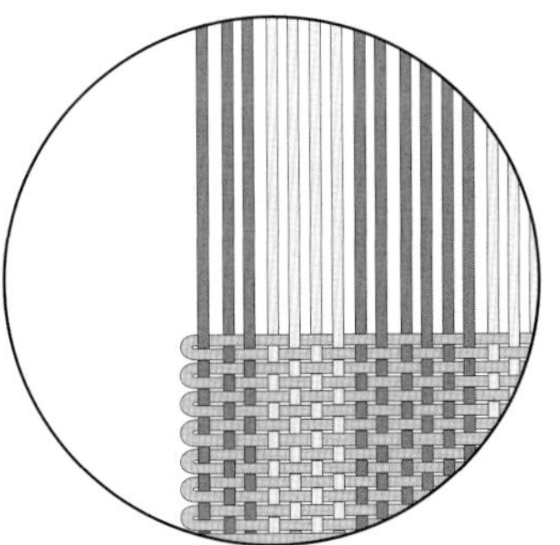

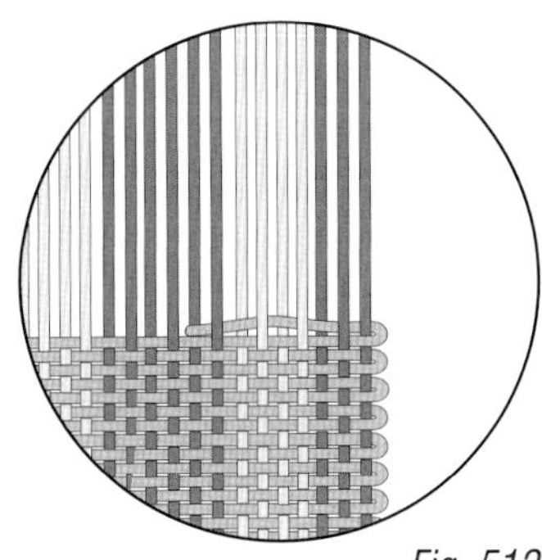

Fig. 512

Hand-woven edges that look nice are even, without notches or loops. Besides being good looking, the threads won't break during weaving—a frustrating waste of good weaving time and energy.

This chapter begins with how to make good selvedges and how to solve a common problem beginning weavers often have (page 302). Following are two ways to make special selvedges.(pages 304 and 306). The remainder of the chapter (beginning on page 313) is devoted to troubleshooting selvedge problems.

A much more comprehensive chapter on selvedges is in my third book, *Weaving & Drafting Your Own Cloth*.

How to make good selvedges

The warp and weft, the loom, yarns, and shuttles work together with your good weaving techniques to make good selvedges.

The warp

The sett (epi) of the warp is a big consideration for making good selvedges. See the sidebar, "How Warps and Wefts Bend," on page 303 about how yarns bend depending upon the sett of the warp.

The wefts

How you insert the wefts into the sheds is very important. Read, "Weaving techniques for selvedges," on the next page.

The loom

The set-up of the loom is involved with making good selvedges in several ways. The beaming of the warp (pages 35 and 172) must be done properly so the tension on the selvedge threads isn't spoiled. Read about selvedge problems on pages 313-316.

Special selvedges can be made to make weaving them easier and to prevent breakage. Read about floating selvedges beginning on page 304, and how to wind separate selvedges on page 306.

There are devices you can use to stretch out the warp to keep the selvedge threads from breaking. Read about temples and stretchers beginning on page 312.

The yarns

The selvedge threads may be different from the rest of the warp yarns. For example, if your regular warp threads abrade and break at the selvedge, you could use a stronger yarn for the selvedges only. See page 315, "Threads too fragile," and, "What threads to use," on page 307.

The shuttles

Read about shuttles that jerk the weft and ways shuttles can cause notches in selvedges on page 94.

The weaving

Following good weaving techniques is important in making good selvedges. These practices include the weaving sequence: how and when to enter the shuttle, to beat, and to change the shed. Read the sections on weaving carefully, beginning on pages 111 and 183. I explain the procedures related to making good selvedges in this chapter.

Weaving techniques for selvedges

Making good selvedges when you are weaving is mainly a matter of how you put the weft into the shed

The diagonal of the weft

Place the weft in the shed on a diagonal as shown in Figure 513. I cannot stress the importance of this procedure enough. The reason for the diagonal is to put some extra slack into the weft, making each weft a bit longer than the actual width of the warp. This extra length is needed because the wefts bend when they pass over and under the warps as seen in Figures 514a. Figure 514b shows in cross section even more dramatically how the wefts bend over and under the warps. Read about this bending in the sidebar on page 303.

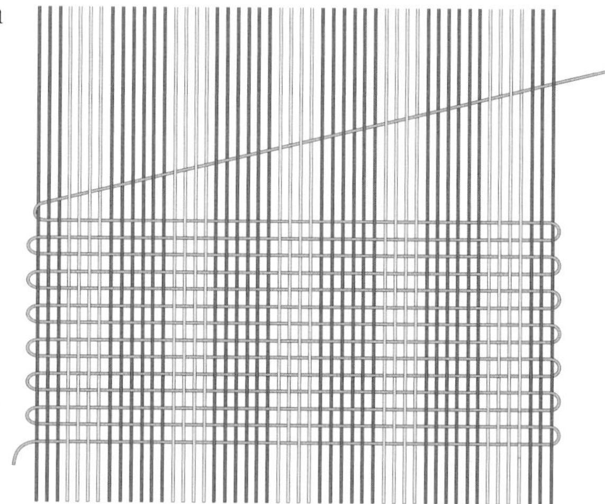

Fig. 513

You can't see this phenomenon while at the loom because the warps are under tension and are straight when the sheds are made. It's not until after the cloth is off the loom that you can see that the wefts are bending (the warps, too). Because the wefts are forced to bend over the warps during weaving, extra slack in the wefts is imperative. In fact, some weave structures require even more slack, see page 128.

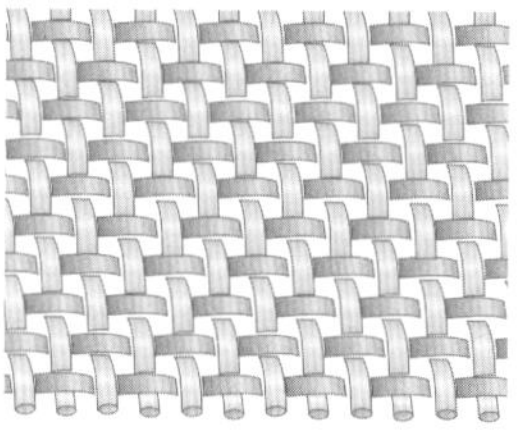

Fig. 514a

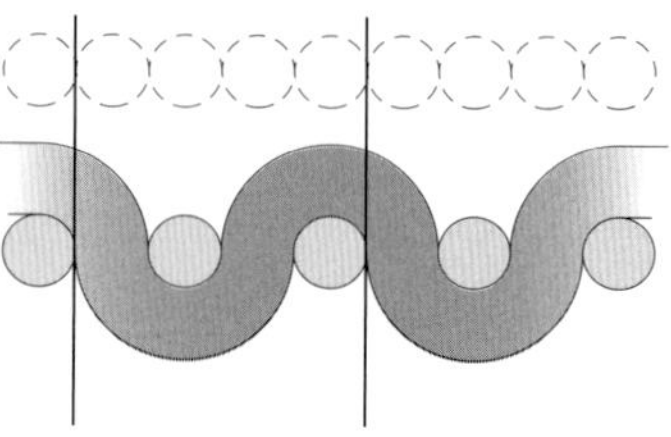

Fig. 514b

A diagonal should form naturally from the edge of the woven cloth (the fell) to the shuttle race. This diagonal can be seen in Figure 515. The shuttle race is the ledge on the beater at the base of the reed where the shuttle rides in the shed. Most, but not all, looms have a shuttle race. Ideally, it is all the diagonal that is needed. Read more about how much diagonal is necessary below.

The natural movement might be to swing the arm back, pulling the weft in an arc down to the fell of the cloth. This shape doesn't allow enough slack in the weft and will cause the cloth to narrow in. See Figure 516.

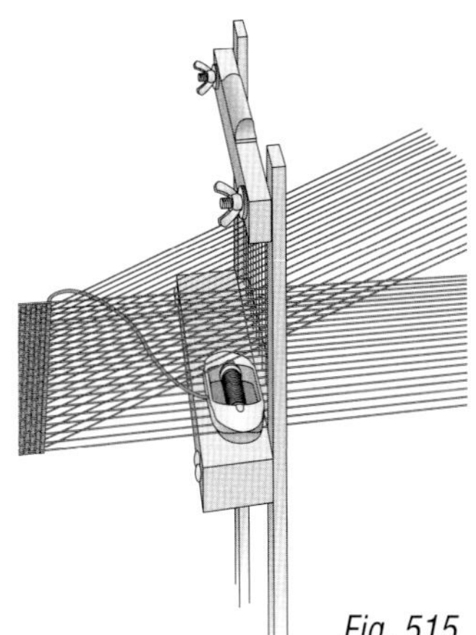

Fig. 515

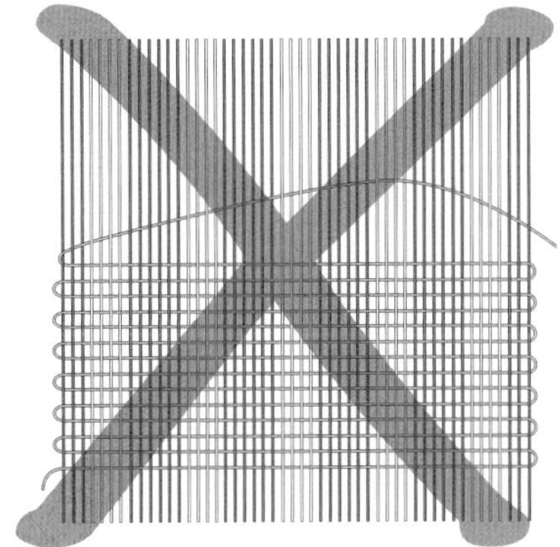

Fig. 516

How much diagonal?

If you don't put in enough slack, the cloth will draw in too much. See Figure 517 on the next page. This is a huge problem (called draw-in) and is to be avoided at all costs. Read about this common problem below and the rules to follow to avoid too much draw-in.

If you put too much diagonal in the weft, little loops will form in the cloth.

The diagonal is just right if the cloth draws in only a tiny bit at each selvedge, say, ¼" or less. Read about natural draw-in below.

Turning the wefts at the selvedges

Snug up the weft against the outside warp thread—neither pulling that selvedge thread in, nor leaving a loop on the outside of it. I like to snug the weft up until it barely moves that outside selvedge thread—just grazes it. The wefts should turn around neatly against the selvedges.

Don't touch the selvedges. You can control the weft at the selvedges with your shuttle. See page 113. Touching the selvedges is a bad habit—it can slow you down and prevent an even rhythm, which is an important aspect of making good looking selvedges.

Draw-In

Draw-in is normal and natural

Woven cloth is typically narrower than the width the warp is in the reed. This narrowing is called draw-in. During the normal weaving of fabrics, even with the best techniques, the cloth will draw in. Acceptable draw-in might be around ¼" or so on each side. However, there are big selvedge problems if the cloth narrows in too much.

A common selvedge problem: Too much draw-in

In my teaching experience, the problem that showed up almost as soon as the weaving began was that the cloth narrowed in too much. If the problem wasn't noticed and dealt with soon, the selvedge threads would begin to break by the abrasion of the reed. Look at the edges of the warp at the fell. Is the reed stretching out the warps way beyond the width of the cloth? If so, can you see why the reed is abrading and breaking the selvedges? Too much draw-in at the selvedges is shown in Figure 517.

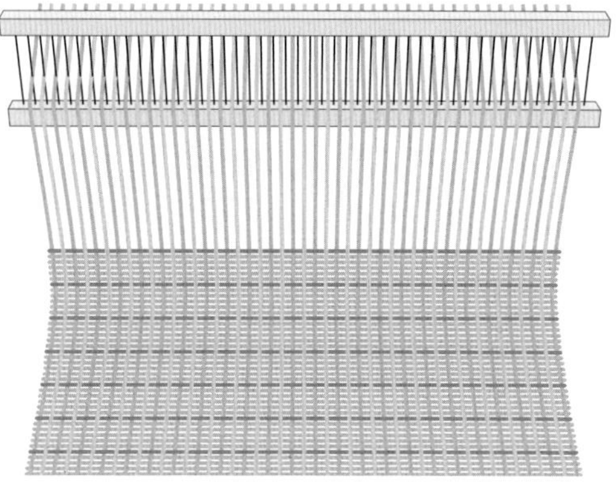

Too much draw-in at selvedges *Fig. 517*

If you have a big draw-in problem, you can use a temple or stretcher cords. See page 312.

To understand more why the cloth draws in and how to control it so the selvedge threads don't break, read the sidebar, "How warps and wefts bend," on the next page.

Three common causes of this problem *(in order of commonness)*

1. The warp tension is too tight.
2. There is not enough slack in the weft. (No diagonal of the weft is put into the shed.) See above.
3. The wefts are pulled too tightly at the selvedges.

Rules to follow to avoid too much draw-in

1. The warp tension should not be tight, certainly not tight like a violin string. Basically, it just needs to be tight enough to get the sheds to open. It should feel firm when you pat it to test the amount of tension, maybe even fairly firm, but definitely not tight. If your selvedges are narrowing in, check the warp tension first.
2. There must be enough slack in the weft that it can bend as it goes over and under the warps. Figure 513 shows the diagonal needed to allow for this slack. You will know you have too much diagonal when loops appear in the weft in the cloth. If the warp only draws in a tiny amount, say ¼" or so on each side, you have put in enough slack. Read about the diagonal, above.
3. Do not pull the weft tight as you put it into the shed. If you do, two things will happen—first, you won't get in the slack you need (see above) and second, the selvedges will draw in too much.

Beginners sometimes try to solve this problem with another problem—putting loops of wefts at the selvedges. This effort does not do anything to widen the warp at the edges. It just leaves unsightly loopy selvedges. The slack in the weft is needed clear across the warp—not just at the edges. Read how the weft should turn at the selvedges, above. Read more about good selvedges on page 113.

Use a temple or stretcher cords when there is too much draw-in. See page 312.

How Warps and Wefts Bend

Here's how the bending works in different sett (epi) situations, and how it affects your cloth's draw-in.

Balanced plain weave is shown in Figure 518a. "Balanced" means there are the same number of warps per inch (epi) as wefts per inch. You can see that both the warps and the wefts bend or curve. The diagonal of the wefts in the sheds provides the slack needed to allow for the wefts to bend. The warps bend after the cloth is taken off the loom when there is no longer any tension on them. Remember, you allowed for this occurrence in planning the length of the warp by adding in an allowance for "take-up." See page 290.

Balanced plain weave

Fig. 518a

In ***weft-faced weaving***, the warps are straight and the wefts do all the bending. See Figure 518b. Notice that the warps are farther apart than for balanced plain weave. Fewer ends per inch (epi) force the wefts to bend so much that there needs to be much more weft in the shed than for balanced weaves. To allow for the yarn to bend over and under the warp threads, more diagonal, or even bubbling of the weft is needed. Read about bubbling on page 128.

Weft-faced plain weave

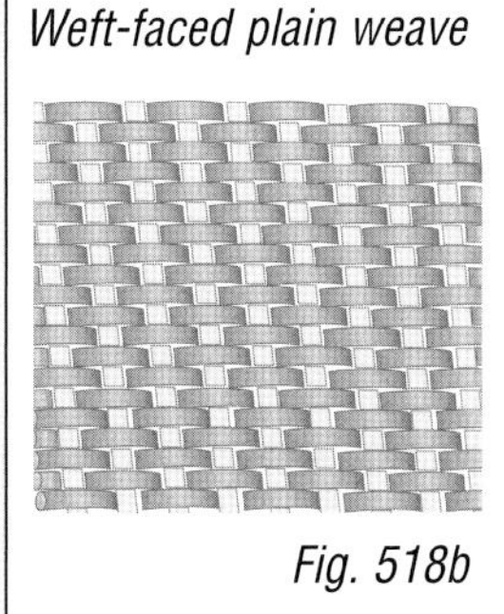

Fig. 518b

In Figure 518c, the warps are very close together (more ends per inch), and they are bending, but the wefts are straight. This is ***warp-faced plain weave***. Warps that close force the wefts to be straight. These warps take up much more than those in balanced weaving do, because they have to curve so much over and under the wefts. Less slack or weft diagonal is needed because the wefts are straight and do not bend.

Warp-faced plain weave

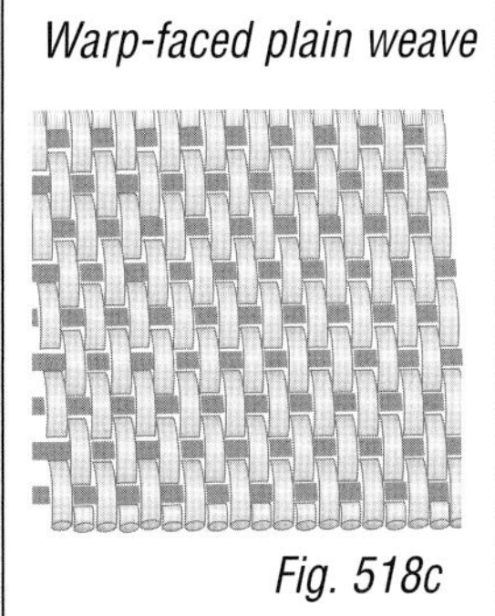

Fig. 518c

Floating selvedges

Floating selvedges are commonly used when the outside warp thread doesn't weave into the cloth, or when it isn't caught often enough because of the structure of the weave. This solution is a great help, and beginners often learn it while weaving their very first project.

There will be one extra thread on each side of the warp for the floating selvedges. I sometimes add these two extra threads, and other times I just use the outside threads on the existing warp. (I make new threads if using the two already in the warp will spoil the design at the edge.)

Here is what to do with the two threads that have been designated as the floating selvedges:

On each edge of the warp, put one thread in the reed in the outside dent, ***but not through a heddle***. See Figures 519 and 521.

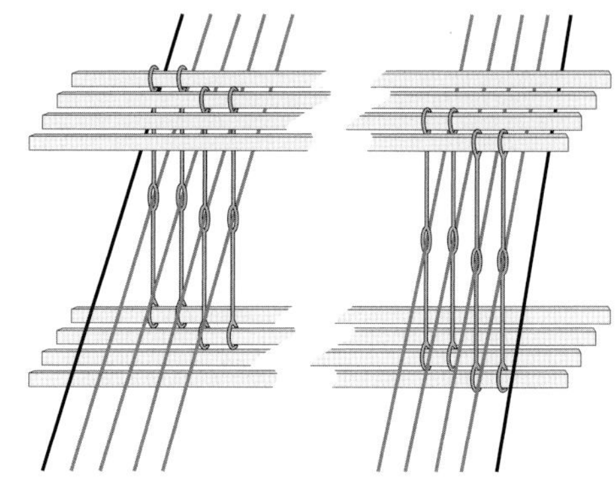

Fig. 519

If you are using threads from your existing warp and the warp has already been threaded, remove the two outside warp threads from their heddles and replace them in the reed. If you are using separately made threads, take them through the castle but not through any heddles and put them in the outside dents of the reed as shown in Figures 521a and b. Tie them on to the cloth apron rod as usual. (How to tension threads made separately follows below.)

Floating selvedges give a warp thread for the weft to go around on every shed, so there is never a thread left dangling out of the cloth at the edge. These floating threads move neither up nor down when the sheds are made, but stay in the middle of the sheds. See Figure 520.

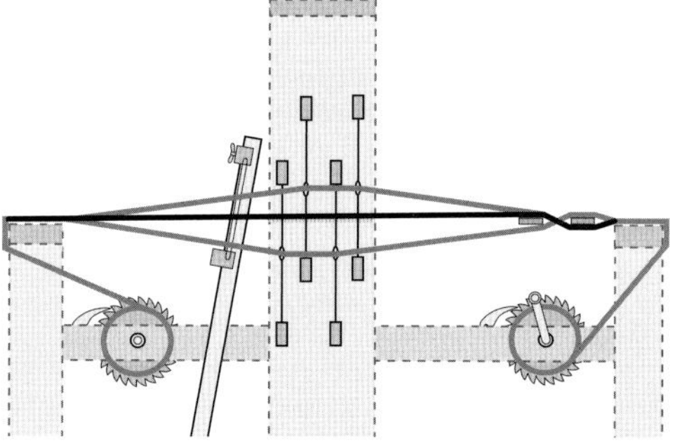

Fig. 520

When to use floating selvedges

I never use floating selvedges unless they are needed because it slows down the weaving a bit.

Twills that only weave in one direction do not need floating selvedges. Read the trick about catching the outside thread for twills on page 119. Only twills that change directions need them, such as herringbone. See page 123.

Use a floating selvedge when two shuttles are used so you don't have to worry about the rotation of the shuttles to catch the outside thread, as shown on page 116.

You can use floating selvedges for basket weave because, in this weave, the shuttle must go into the same shed twice. The floating selvedges prevent the wefts from unweaving on the second throw. Read other ways to catch the outside thread on page 132.

How to enter and exit the sheds

There is a certain way for the shuttle to enter and exit the sheds to make the wefts always catch the outside warp threads. Here is what I do.

Enter the shuttle into the shed over the floating thread and exit the shuttle under it. See Figures 521 a and b. It's easy to push the warp end down with the nose of the shuttle when entering the shed, and the shuttle naturally leaves the shed at the opposite side going under the floating selvedge.

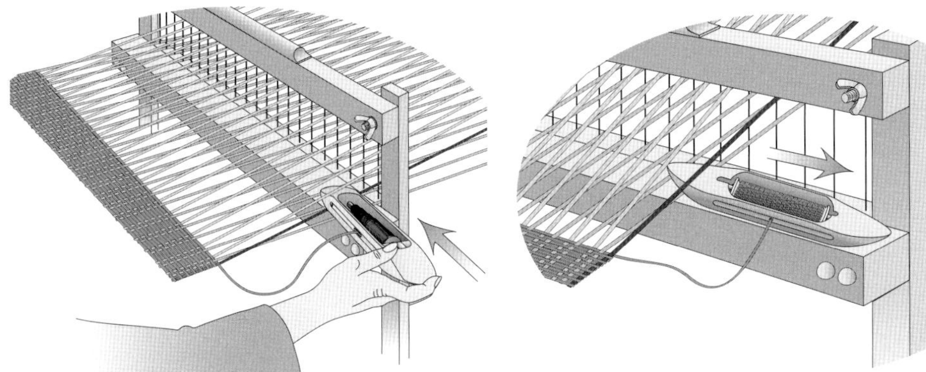

Fig. 521 a and b

With floating selvedges, the weft cannot fail to catch around the selvedge thread at both sides. There are many ways you can enter and exit the sheds to make the floaters do their job; you just need to do it the same way all the time. I prefer the method here because it's easy and works naturally with the way the shuttle enters and exits the sheds.

Enter the shuttle into the shed over the floating thread and exit the shuttle under it. See Figures 521 a and b.

Adjusting floating selvedges

If the floating selvedge isn't high enough in the shed for the shuttle to go under it easily, raise the threads by tying loops of string around them and attaching the loops to the castle of your loom. Raise the loops so the floating selvedge threads float in the middle of the open sheds as seen in Figure 520.

Tension on floating selvedges

Since they don't interlace with the wefts like the main weave, they are likely to get looser as you weave along. You can hook a weight on each one and let it slide along as the warp is advanced. See Figure 522. Because they don't get tighter as a rule, they can be beamed on with the regular warp ends.

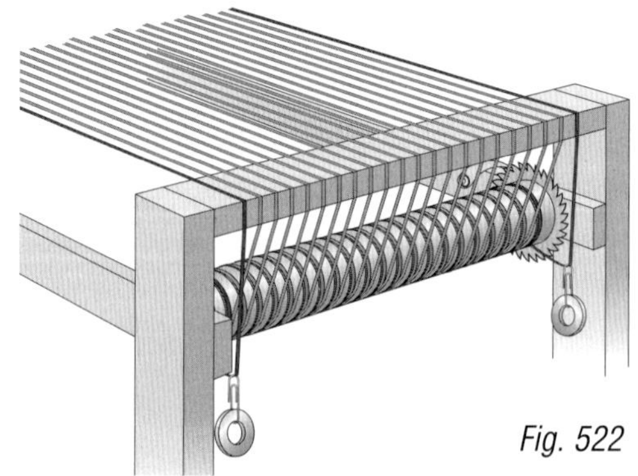

Fig. 522

If you used separate threads for the floating selvedges, they must be anchored at the back of the loom in some way so there is tension on them for weaving. See Figure 523. Read more about weighting selvedges separately on page 308.

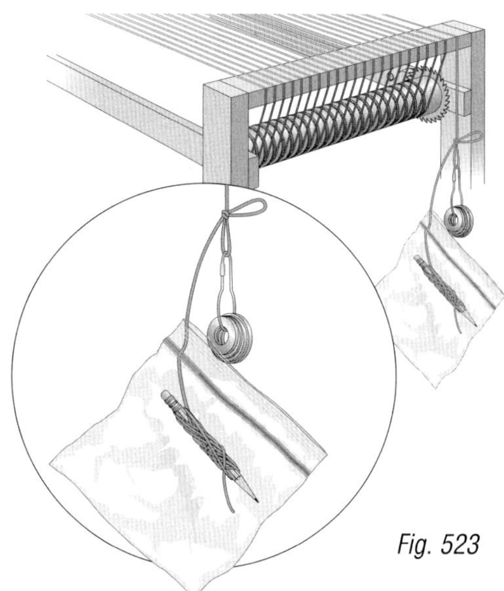

Fig. 523

Winding separate selvedges

Regular selvedge threads often get tight (see page 313). The problem is solved by winding separate selvedge threads. Read this entire section, ending on page 309.

For using separate selvedges, I make 2 tiny warps—one for each selvedge—often, with 4 threads for each. I determine the number of threads to use by the number of shafts in use. That is, if there are 4 shafts, I use 4 threads, if there are 8 shafts, I use 8 threads. For more shafts, see my third book, *Weaving & Drafting Your Own Cloth,* in the chapter on selvedges. They will not be beamed onto the warp beam with the main warp, but will hang over the back beam behind the loom with weights providing the tension on them. See Figure 523. These threads are made separately from the warp threads and sleyed closer in the reed.

More than anything, you want to keep the selvedge warp threads from tightening up. By weighting them separately from the main warp they can weave and take up without getting tight.

When to weight selvedge threads separately

I use separate selvedges for warps that are over 3-5 yards long. I also use them when I begin to weave if I find that the normal warp's selvedge threads aren't supporting the wefts as they turn at the edges. Read about notches in selvedges on page 314.

It isn't hard to do, and it ensures good-looking selvedges that weave without problems. It is more efficient to start with them as separate warps, rather than to find out mid-warp that your selvedge threads are breaking because they are too tight, or that they are becoming so close together that the shed can't open, or that the wefts at the edges are beating down too much as shown in Figure 524.

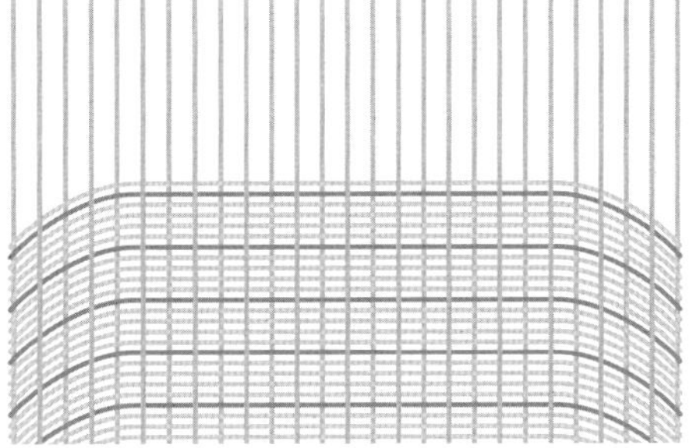

Fig. 524

What threads to use

I double the sett (epi) for the 4 selvedge threads in the outside dents of the reed. However, if the warp threads are too thick to double up, use thinner threads for the selvedge threads. With thinner threads, you can get them closer, and the selvedges look almost machine made. Be sure your threads are plied, (page 297) smooth, and strong.

How many selvedge threads

I use 4 threads for each selvedge when I am using 4 shafts. I may use 8 with 8-shaft weaves—one for each shaft. (Other selvedge solutions are found in my third book, *Weaving & Drafting Your Own Cloth*.)

How to measure the threads

Because they will take up more than the main warp, measure out the selvedge threads longer, say, 10% longer than the regular warp threads.

Measure out 4 threads making only one cross—a thread-by-thread cross at one end. (Read how to measure out warp threads beginning on page 13 and 157.)

Separately, make two of these tiny warps. They need to be completely separate from each other so one can go on each side of the warp. Tie the crosses as usual, and make ties at the beginning and end of the warp and at several places in the middle. It will be hard to make real choke ties because the warps are so tiny.

You can wind your little selvedge threads like a little kitestick on a pencil, bobbin, or small tube, or make a chain. See Figure 523.

Rather than winding up the warps on pencils or making chains, another method is to wind the selvedge warps on pieces of cardboard as shown in Figure 525. There will be two pieces of cardboard—one for each of the two selvedges.

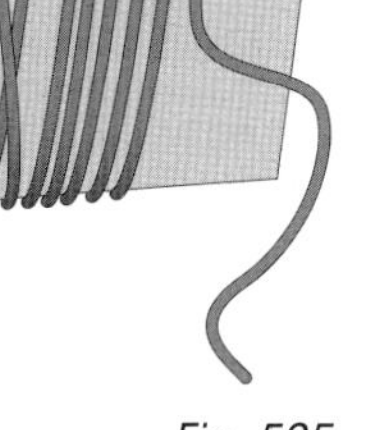

Fig. 525

Put each little selvedge warp in a plastic bag to keep it from twisting and tangling during weaving. See Figure 523.

Threading the selvedges

Thread the selvedge threads one per heddle, one on each shaft: 4,3,2,1.

Putting the selvedges in the reed

You will put in more threads per dent for the selvedge threads. Since the warp will naturally draw in a bit, it is a good idea not to fight it, and to sley the selvedge threads more densely than the body of the warp to keep the threads from breaking.

I double the sett (epi) for the 4 selvedge threads in the outside dents of the reed. However, if the selvedges build up faster than the rest of the fabric, the threads may be too close together. Threads sleyed too closely may keep the weft from packing in. Also, the selvedges may build up faster than the rest of the cloth if they aren't weighted enough. See Figure 526. Read below about how much weight to use.

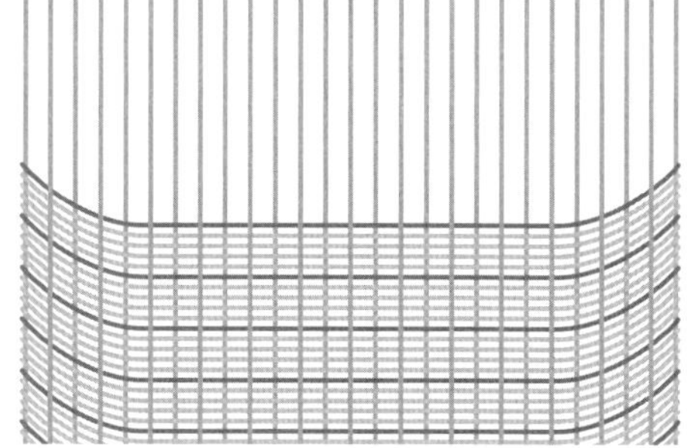

Fig. 526

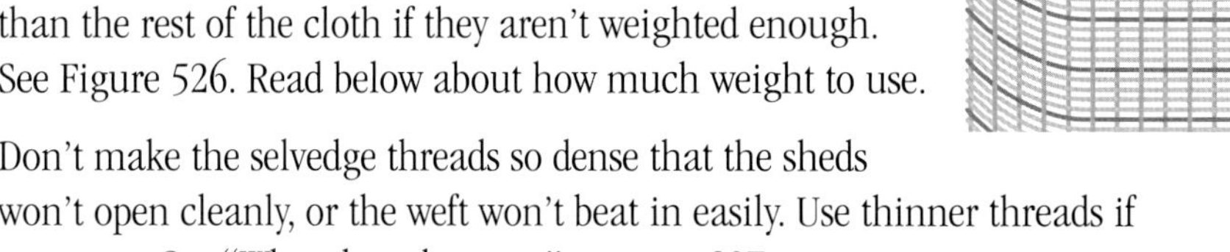

Don't make the selvedge threads so dense that the sheds won't open cleanly, or the weft won't beat in easily. Use thinner threads if necessary. See "What threads to use" on page 307.

How to weight the threads

I have found the "plastic bag and pencil" way to be satisfactory, shown on page 306. Winding up the warps on cardboard works, too (page 307). I use clothes pins to hold the bag and the warp at the knot together, which helps to prevent twisting.

The weights. I like to use nuts, washers or fishing weights for my selvedges. These "weights" are small enough that I can add or subtract them in small increments to adjust the tension. You can also use plastic bottles filled with the amount of water needed for the weight. As the selvedge threads get woven, the weights and their supply of thread rise up. When they reach the back beam, they need to be let down to just above the floor. A small bag of weights is more convenient than a bottle because it doesn't have to be let down so often during weaving since it is smaller.

How much weight? Six to fourteen ounces of weight are needed. I start with 6 ounces and add or subtract, as necessary. The way to know if you need more or less weight is simple. The fell of the cloth will be straight if the weight is correct. See Figure 527. If it curves up at the edges towards the shafts (making a "smile,") it means there isn't enough weight. This is seen in Figure 526. If the cloth curves down at the edges towards the breast beam (making a "frown"), it means there is too much weight as shown in Figure 524. Sometimes, one selvedge takes more weight than the other does. Do whatever is needed so the fell is straight.

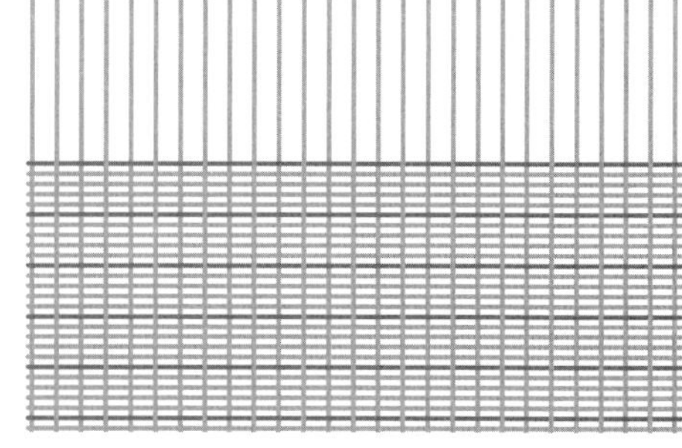

Fig. 527

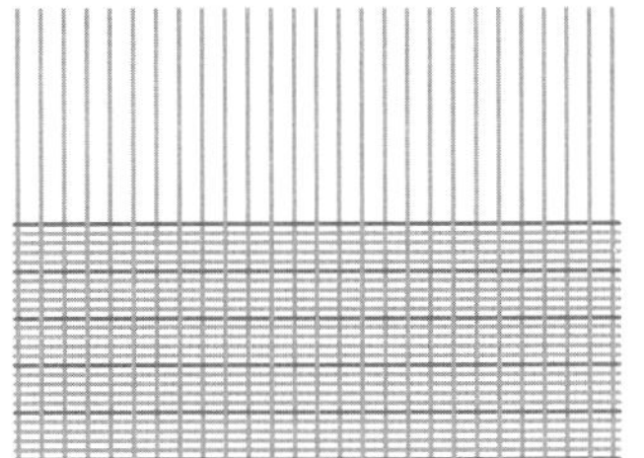

correct weight

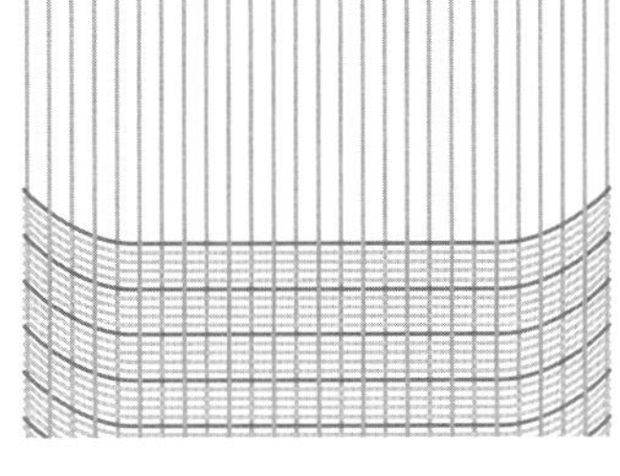

not enough weight

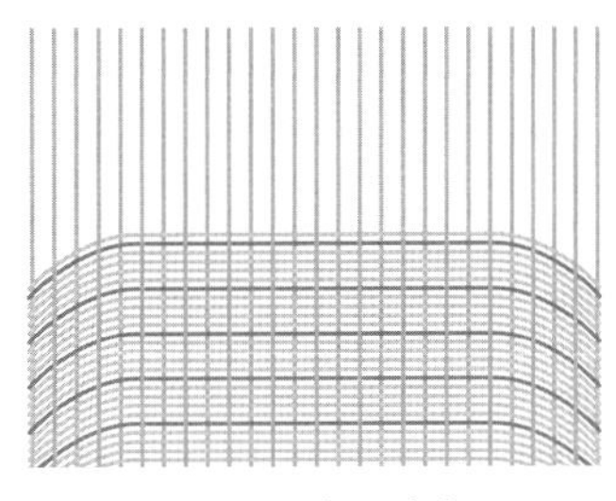

too much weight

It's better to have the selvedge threads a little too loose than too tight. If too tight, the body of the fabric may pucker into the selvedges. It might not be noticeable until the cloth is washed.

When to attach the weights. The weights can be attached after the selvedge strands are threaded in the heddles, sleyed in the reed and tied on to the cloth apron bar.

How to attach the weights. Weights need a loop of some kind so you can attach the selvedge threads. It can be a loop of string or a metal shower curtain hook. See Figures 522 and 523 on page 306.

There is a wonderful knot to tie the weights to the threads. It's easy to undo, which is necessary every time you need to let down the weights for more thread. This is the same knot I tie for weighting supplementary warps, described in my second book, *Warping Your Loom & Tying On New Warps*, on page 156. Here it is again along with the steps to tie it. See Figures 528 a-i. The steps sound more complicated than they are, but if you learn it well, you'll save yourself a lot of time and aggravation in your future weaving life because the knot comes undone quickly.

Knot to Weight Separate Warps

Knot to weight separate warps

Before you begin, be sure the selvedge warps are tied securely onto the front apron rod. The selvedge threads should be hanging off the back beam at the back of the loom.

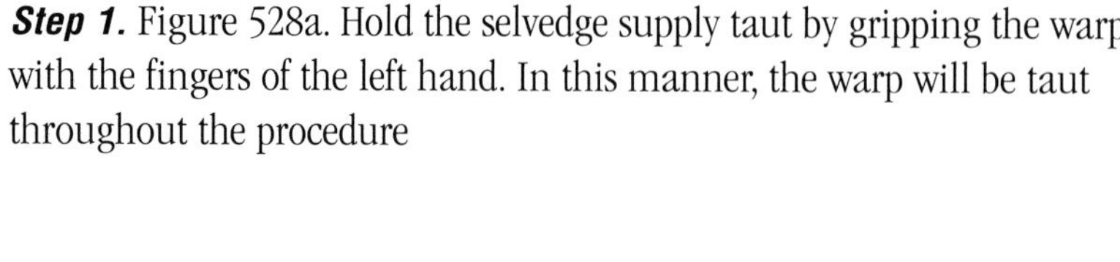

Step 1. Figure 528a. Hold the selvedge supply taut by gripping the warp with the fingers of the left hand. In this manner, the warp will be taut throughout the procedure

Fig. 528

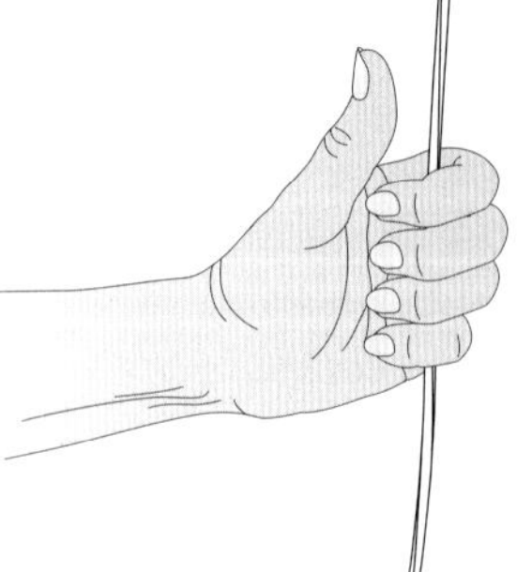

a

Step 2. Figure 528b. With the right hand, pull a big loop of warp through the loop of the weight using your finger and thumb. The left hand continues holding the warp taut, but now just uses the 2 fingers shown in the illustration.

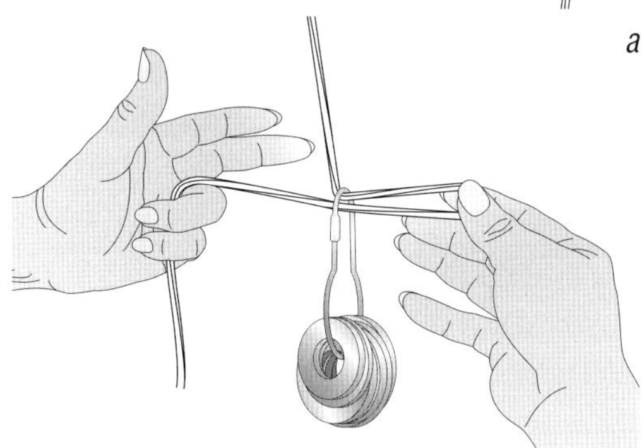

b

Step 3. Figure 528c. With your left hand, adjust your thumb and first two fingers to pinch the warp to the loop of the weight—the right hand still holds the loop of warp.

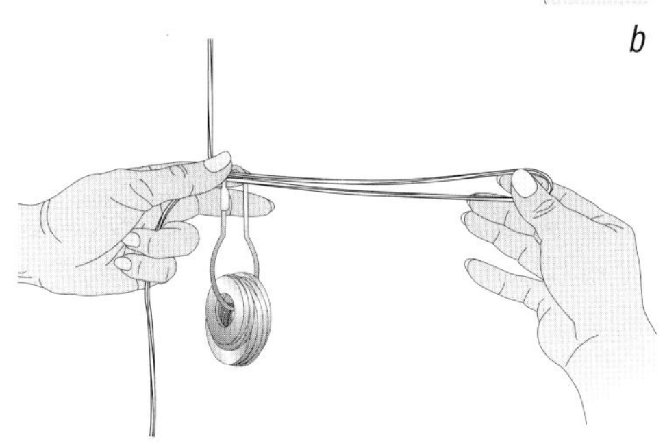

c

Step 4. Figures 528d and 528e. With the right hand, take the loop in front of the left hand's pinch and then behind the selvedge threads.

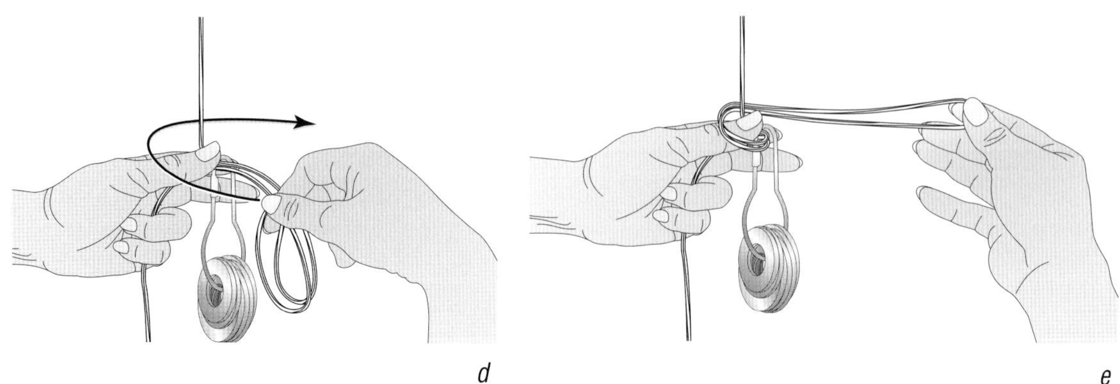

d

e

Step 5. Figure 528f. Readjust your left thumb and index finger so that they will be able to receive some thread (Step 6). (You are letting go of the weight now, but the fingers of the left hand still hold the threads taut.)

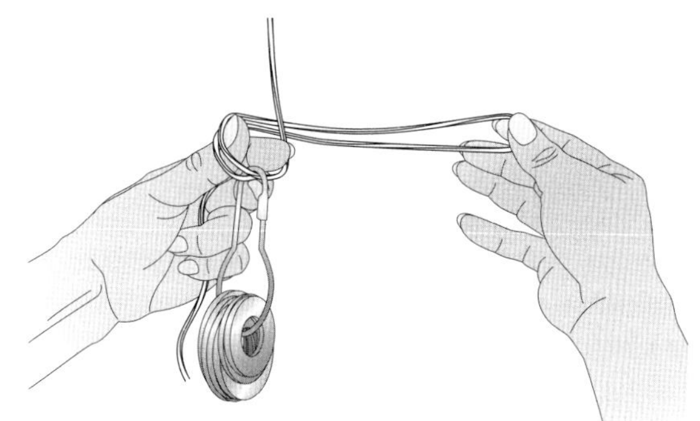

f

Step 6. Figure 528g. Open the pinch in the left hand slightly and accept a small amount from the big loop in the right hand.

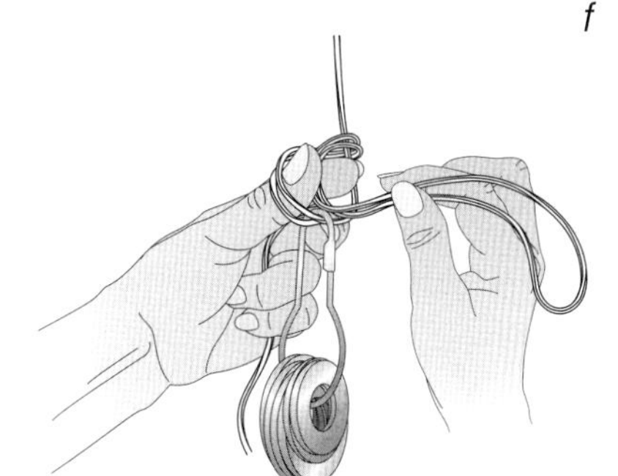

g

Step 7. Figure 528h. Pull on the small loop and enlarge it somewhat. Be sure to hold the loop in the right hand, and do not let it be pulled through by the left hand.

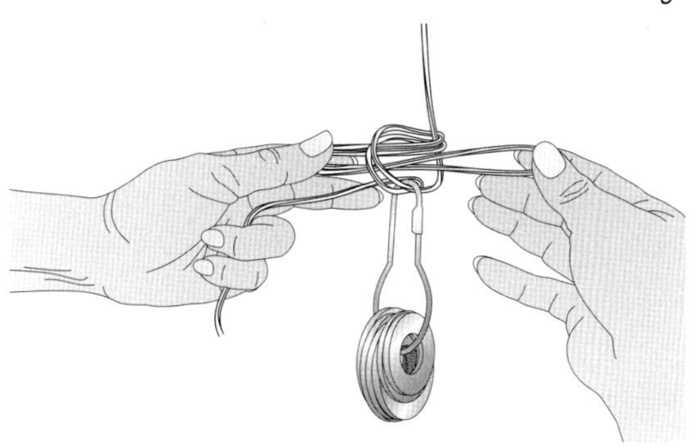

h

Step 8. Figure 528i. With both hands pull down (towards the floor) and cinch the knot tight.

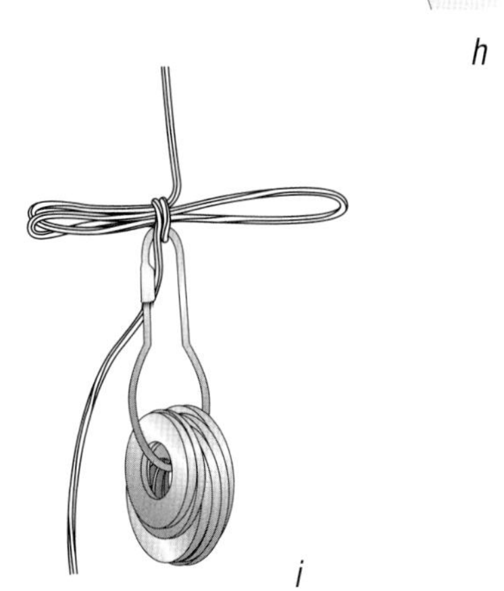

i

To undo the knot, simply pull on the loop that was held in the right hand, drop the weight down, and retie.

Devices that deal with too much draw-in

If everything about your cloth is just as you want it, but the draw-in is causing the selvedges to break. You can stretch out the warp near the reed so the reed can't abrade the threads while weaving.

Temple

A temple is a stretcher that holds the cloth out at the selvedges. See Figure 529. It allows you to snug the wefts up to the selvedges without breaking the threads during weaving. It may be made of wood or metal. Any temple needs to be strong. They are available in many widths for weaving wide rugs or narrow placemats. Read more about temples, below.

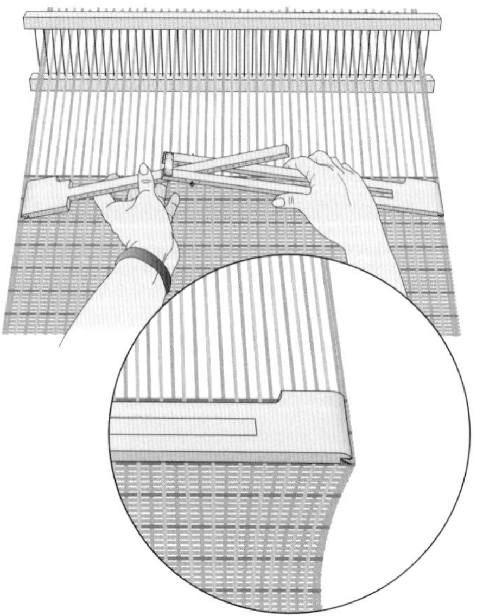

Fig. 529 – Temple

Cord and clip stretchers

This stretcher is a variation of a temple that you can make yourself. See Figure 530. The clips are "Crocodile clips" (also called "croc clips") and are available at hardware stores. They are made to clip tarps and are very inexpensive.

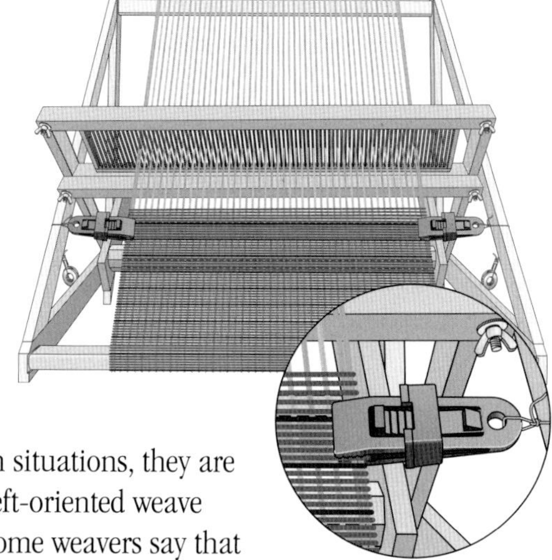

Fig. 530

Using a temple or stretcher

Temples and stretchers can slow you down, but in certain situations, they are necessary. Rug weavers use them. They are helpful for weft-oriented weave structures that tend to draw in more, such as overshot. Some weavers say that if the sett and everything else is right, there is no need for a temple. I encourage you to use one whenever your weaving is drawing in so much that your selvedge threads keep breaking.

Since a temple or stretcher cord needs to be moved frequently, it's a good idea to choose a type that opens and closes easily. The cord stretcher moves very easily. With temples, the method for locking the two bars together should be quick to use, such as a collar that slides back and forth. In the illustration, the collar is the metal part seen next to the left thumb. Some temples are unwieldy, which slows you down and interrupts your rhythm.

The stretchers and temple work more to help with the beater than to preserve the selvedge threads, although they do that, too. They eliminate the drag on the beater and keep the fabric stretched out as the beater hits the fell.

With a stretcher or temple, you can weave your cloth with more draw-in. The draw-in still takes place in the woven cloth itself, but at the fell, the temple holds the warps stretched out, so there is no friction on the reed or abrasion on the selvedge threads. If you like the appearance of the cloth with the wefts drawing in the cloth, use a stretcher or temple. That way, your selvedge threads won't always be breaking from abrasion from the reed.

Positioning the stretcher or temple

Keep the stretcher or temple on the woven cloth as close to the fell as possible, not more than ¼"– ¾" from the fell. Since the fell will be changing as you weave along, you need to move the temple often, perhaps, every ½" in rug weaving, or every 1"– 2" for fabric weaving , or each time you advance the warp.

Stretch out the cloth to the same width as the warp ends are in the reed. The warp threads should be in a straight line from the reed to the fell.

Troubleshooting: Selvedge problems

Selvedges tend to get tight

As the cloth is woven, it becomes somewhat narrower than the warp in the reed. This draw-in is normal, but it's only the selvedge threads that become closer together rather than the threads in the middle of the warp. Because the selvedges threads get closer they tend to take up (see page 290) more than the other warp threads and get tight. Tight selvedge threads can make them break or the cloth to pucker at the selvedges. They may also prevent the shed from opening cleanly at the edges. A good solution is to wind the selvedges separately. See page 306.

Selvedges bow in and out

Advance the warp often. If you notice that the edges bow in and out every few inches, it may be that you waited too long to advance the warp. Remember to advance it often (every 2"–3") to maintain a consistent weft diagonal. When the fell of the cloth is far from the beater, there is more weft in the diagonal from the fell to the shuttle race, which lets the cloth weave wider. If you continue to weave too close to the beater, there will be less weft in the diagonal, and the cloth will draw in more.

It's also important to advance the warp often enough to ensure that the beat is consistent. See page 114.

Mixing plain weave and twill. My beginning students are surprised to see that the twill sections in their samplers are narrower than the plain weave sections. The reason is that plain weave has more intersections of warp and weft than twill does, which makes the cloth wider. Weaving both structures in the same piece could cause problems at the selvedges if some areas draw in a lot more (e.g., the twill).

A solution, if you want to have plain weave and twill sections, is to weave basket weave instead of plain weave. It looks almost like plain weave, yet it draws in just the same as twills do, so the sections won't bow in and out. Read about basket weave on page 118.

Notches in selvedges

If the shuttle is drawn out of the shed too suddenly, the weft will be too tight, and besides causing a pucker across the cloth, it can jerk the selvedge thread and make a dent in the edge.

If a boat shuttle is thrown or caught too fast, it can cause the bobbin thread to tangle and jerk the selvedge. Here is the solution:

Throw the shuttle gently. If the shuttle is thrown harder that necessary, it comes into the receiving hand with the bobbin still spinning: extra yarn is unwound, creating a snarl in the shuttle. The snarl will cause the weft to jerk in at the selvedge. Throw the shuttle with just enough force to carry it across, so the shuttle and its bobbin both slow to a stop as they reach the other side.

The type of bobbin you are using might not be right for the boat shuttle's cavity. Read about this important detail on page 94.

Soft selvedge threads or too much tension on the weft thread can cause the shuttle to pull the outside threads into the shed and notch in the edge. Use separate, weighted selvedges described beginning on page 306.

Edges splay out

See Figure 531. Read how to solve this problem on page 117.

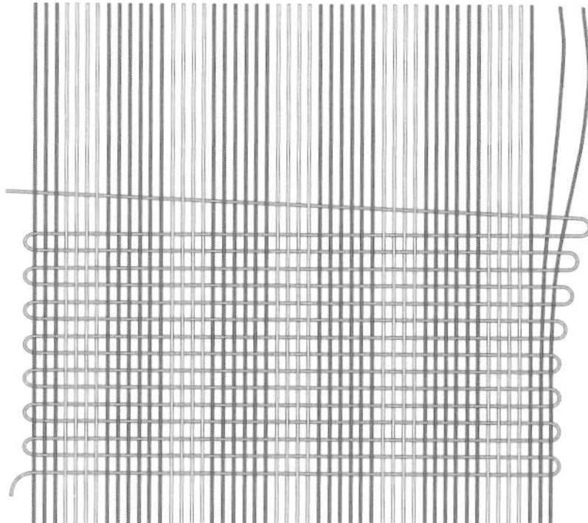

Fig. 531

Selvedge threads break

Too much draw-in. The most common reason for selvedges breaking is too much draw-in, which has been discussed on page 302. If the draw-in isn't too pronounced, try winding and weighting the selvedges separately (see page 306) and sleying them more densely (see page 308). If it is extreme, and you like the appearance of the cloth as it is, use a temple or stretcher. See page 312.

Warp too narrow on warp beam. Beaming the warp on the warp beam narrower than it is in the reed can cause selvedges to break. Just remember, never beam the warp narrower than the width it will be in the reed.

Threads too fragile. Some threads may be just too weak to use for selvedge threads. Use stronger threads for the selvedge and be sure to use plied threads See Figure 532. Plied threads are described on page 297.

A way to try to keep the threads from breaking is by advancing the warp often. That procedure doesn't let the threads stay in one place long enough for the reed (and heddles) to cause serious abrasion. For fragile threads, you might need to do it more often than usual.

Fig. 532

Weaving too close to the shafts.

Weaving too close to the shafts can cause broken selvedge ends because the width of the warp in the reed is greater than the width of the woven cloth, and there isn't enough distance between the shafts and the fell to accommodate this difference.

Excess heddles in the way. It may be that excess heddles riding on the ends of the shafts are abrading the outside threads. See Figure 533. Also see page 61.

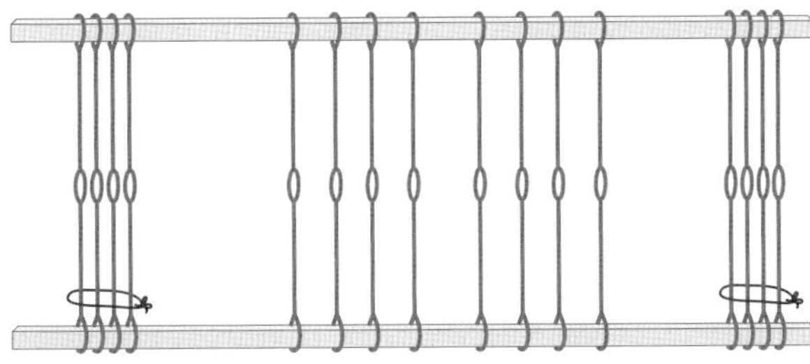

Fig. 533

Fell is concave

The main part of the warp packs in more, causing the fell to curve up like a smile. See Figure 526 on page 308. If you're weighting your selvedges separately, add more weight. If the selvedge threads are beamed onto the warp beam along with the main warp, hang weights on the loose selvedge threads as in Figure 522 on page 306.

Also read about how warps and wefts bend on page 303 and rules to avoid draw-in on page 302.

Make sure your warp tension isn't too tight. See page 302.

Fell is convex

When the fell is lower at the selvedges like a frown, it usually means the selvedges are too tight. Read about it on page 308 "How much weight?"

One side is better

Whatever you do, one selvedge tends to be better than the other. I learned that this phenomenon occurs because one is right or left-handed. Usually, the side opposite your dominant hand turns out better, but it is not always the case. The answer is to observe what you're doing and work toward making both hands work consistently and alike. It may be a small issue, and the selvedges are not actually disfigured, just different from each other. If they don't bother you, let them be slightly different.

Selvedges impede sheds

You might try weaving closer to the shafts where the shed is bigger to force the selvedge threads to open sufficiently for the weft to lie in the shed. However, weaving too close to the shafts can cause problems. See page 315.

Your selvedge threads are too close together if the sheds can't open at the edges. Try skipping a dent in the middle of the selvedge, putting 3 instead of 4 threads in a dent, etc. Try using thinner threads for the selvedges. See page 307.

Uneven warp tension

If the edge threads aren't supported on the warp beam, they will slip off the rolled up warp supply and ruin the warp tension. It could be that you tried to wind a warp that was too wide for your loom. It's never, never a good idea to make warps the full width of the loom. You need at least a couple of inches of empty warp beam on each edge for the outside threads to be supported. It's true whether you're using sticks or paper to pack (support) the warp.

Also, it could be that the warp wasn't beamed on (wound on) the warp beam in precisely flat layers. It is an absolute must for every single warp end to be the same length and therefore, the same tension. You don't want your warp beam to look like a football—thicker in the middle than on the edges. If it does, your edge threads won't be uniformly tensioned. The edges of the warp on the beam should look like cliffs. See Figure 534.

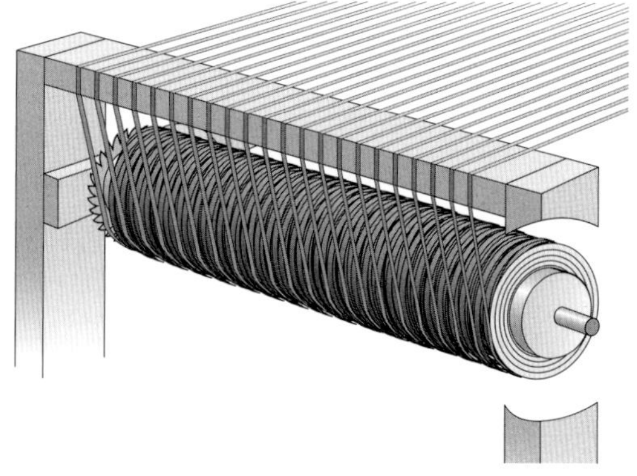

Fig. 534

Read all about beaming properly beginning on pages 35 and 172.

13 *Troubleshooting*

There is a comprehensive section on Troubleshooting in my third book, *Weaving & Drafting Your Own Cloth.*

It's bound to happen sometime—a weaving problem. Practically no problem is unfixable, though, so you don't have to rip up what you've done and start over. In my weaving life, and especially as a teacher of beginning weaving for 12 years, I invented solutions hundreds of times. Maybe, I had to think about it a day or two, but I always felt that something could be done.

I remember when I was a child and a 4-H'er, I would get exasperated and stomp my feet. My mother would tell me to quit for a while. I'd yell back, "I can't stop now!" But, stopping is probably the advice I would give to you if you really feel you are in a bad way. Sleep on it, come back to it, and you'll most probably have an idea or two to try.

In this chapter, I have included the problems that my beginning students often had—and solutions to them. With these solutions and your own ideas, I believe no problem is unsolvable.

To make it easier to find what you need, I've divided the chapter into sections according to where in the weaving process you might encounter the problem, starting with setting up the loom. See the list below.

How to fix broken warp threads (a very important issue) begins on page 322.

A mistake might not disfigure the cloth, and you might choose to live with it. In my work, if it doesn't disfigure, I leave it as it is. How to fix mistakes (if you choose to) is found on page 321. Also shown is how to cut out the warp or to un-weave your mistakes.

Problem	Solution
When Setting up the Loom	
Lost the cross	See page 77. If the raddle is still in place, make a cross by alternating the groups of threads in the divisions of the raddle. See Figure 96, on page 28. Take one lease stick and "weave" it over and under the groups in the raddle. Take a second lease stick and "weave" it in the opposite way to create the second half of the cross. You won't have the precise order of the threads, but it will be better than nothing. If there is no raddle, you'll have to take the threads in order the best you can.
Some threads short when beaming	Mistake at the warping board. See page 53.
End loops not tied	See how to put in the end stick on page 34.
Twists in raddle groups	See page 53. A few twists are normal. If severe, warp yarn is unbalanced.

When Starting to Weave	
Can't get a shed	
Warp not over back and breast beams	See page 104. See Figure 238 for the route the warp must take on the loom. If the warp is not over the breast beam, re-position the apron rod so it goes over the breast beam. If the warp is not over the back beam, if possible, remove the back beam and place it under the warp. If that's not possible, carefully unroll the warp onto the cloth beam at the front of the loom (threads stay in heddles and reed). When the end stick appears behind the heddles, untie the ties holding the end stick to the apron rod—then, put the apron rod over the back beam. Reattach the end stick to the apron rod. Wind the warp onto the warp beam—carefully and tightly as described in Step Seven, beginning on page 43. Page 49 shows how to position the warp correctly after beaming.
Warp wound in the wrong direction	See page 38. If the warp is wound the wrong way on the warp beam, wind the warp forward onto the cloth beam as described in the paragraph above. When the end stick is behind the heddles, carefully re-wind the warp in the proper direction as described in Step Seven, beginning on page 43.
Brakes not engaged	See how brakes work on pages 38, 43, 170, 331.
Not enough room between the breast beam and the beater	Advance the warp, see page 114.
Too much or too little tension on the warp	On many looms, the sheds can't open if the warp tension is too high. If the tension is too little, wind up the cloth beam or the warp beam. If this action doesn't work, see if the beams are wound in the right direction and that the brakes are engaged. See above.

Ties to treadles incorrect length	The ties to the treadles may not be the right length so that when the treadle is pressed, its shaft will not move enough to make a big enough shed for the shuttle to pass through. Read about tying up the treadles beginning on page 95.
Other shed problems	
Thread sags into shed 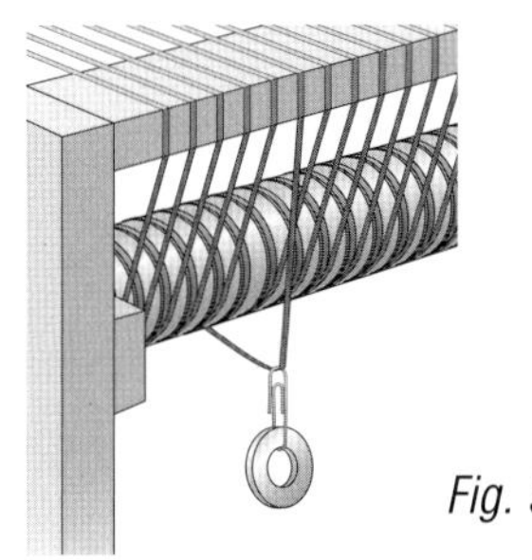 *Fig. 535*	Take up the slack using a pin like a cleat on the cloth. See page 92. Or, tension a thread at the back of the loom. See Figure 535. You can use a learge washer as in the illustration or shower curtain hooks shown in Figure 523, on page 306.
Part of warp goes slack	**If no cloth has been woven:** A warp bundle has loosened on the cloth apron rod. See page 87 and 89. Be sure the last step of surgeon's knots is tied. See page 89. **If some cloth has been woven:** If the knots on the cloth apron rod are secure and the rod is parallel to the breast beam, check the rod attached to the warp beam. You must carefully unroll the warp onto the cloth beam at the front of the loom. Do it in the manner described on page 318, "Warp not over back and breast beams." Check that the apron rod is perfectly parallel to the warp beam. Check if the end loops have slipped on the rod and need adjusting. See page 42. If everything looks O.K. at the warp beam, it's likely that the warp threads weren't under equal tension during beaming—this is essential. Re-wind the warp onto the back beam, similar to on page 318. See page 44, "How to wind the warp tightly." When almost all the warp is wound up, you may see that the threads in the loose area of the warp are saggy and a bit longer than the rest of the threads. In that case, cut off the woven cloth and re-tie the warps to the cloth apron rod. See pages 86-88. ***Warning:*** Cut the warp carefully. See "Cutting off" on page 129, with this important difference: *tie the warp threads with a shoelace knot in front of the reed* as you cut so that they don't come out of the reed or heddles. Also, cut the warp threads far enough from the last weft so you can tie knots to hold the last wefts in place. Instead of cutting off the cloth, you could put weights on bundles of warp threads at the back of the loom. You will have to remove all the warps from the end stick and weight them in bundles and hang them off the back beam. See page 310. I don't recommend this technique for a beginner. More information on weighting warps is in my second book, *Warping Your Loom & Tying On New Warps*, on page 156.
Shafts not the same height	Adjust the shafts to match the height of the others. Looms vary, so look at your own loom to determine how to adjust the height of your shafts. (See page 101.)

Treadle ties uneven	See information about tying up treadles on page 101.
Sheds too small	Try weaving closer to the shafts. Try raising the treadles higher. See page 101.
Loose and tight threads on table looms	Some table looms tension threads unevenly when making the sheds and cause ridges in the cloth. The threads in the bottoms of the sheds are loose and the threads on top are tight. One solution is to build up the back beam by putting a dowel or smooth board under the warp and clamping it to the back beam. This operation makes the warp higher on the back beam and often improves the sheds.

Threading Errors	
A thread stays stationary	A crossed thread. See Figures 249 and 250, on pages 108–109.
Thick or thin vertical lines	A thick line means too many threads were sleyed into a dent. Thin lines are from skipped dents or too few threads in a dent. Un-weave the cloth (page 321) and re-sley the reed (page 81). If the flaw isn't disfiguring, you don't have to fix it. A warp thread might have broken. (See pages 322-323.)
Two or three threads weave together	
Missing thread on a shaft	Make a replacement thread (page 322) and a repair heddle (page 108). Re-sley the reed. (Page 81)
A thread on the wrong shaft	Check the threading in the area and rearrange the threads. Make a repair heddle, if needed (pages 82 & 110). Re-sley the reed (page 81).
An extra warp thread	Remove it, hang it over the back of the loom, and leave it out during weaving. You can leave the empty heddle in place. You may have to re-sley the reed (page 81).

Fixing threading errors

Trace the problem threads back to the heddles. Separate the threads and heddles with your fingers to make the repair and put a hair comb on the separated threads to hold them apart while you work. See Figure 253, page 110 and also here.

How to repair threading errors is found on pages 108–110.

How to make a repair heddle is on pages 82 and 110.

Sometimes, the repair is similar to ***repairing a broken warp thread.*** See pages 322-323.

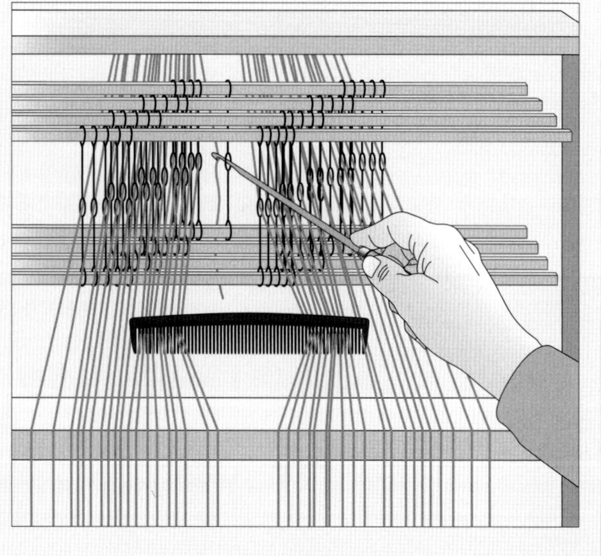

While Weaving Along

Fixing weaving mistakes

Horizontal flaws in the weft direction are weaving mistakes. (A warping mistake will appear throughout the cloth and will be a vertical flaw.)

Repair mistakes either during weaving or after the cloth is off the loom. Unless the mistake is a long way back, it is more efficient to cut out the wefts and fix it as you are weaving. See below.

Repairing mistakes and flaws found in the cloth after it is off the loom is addressed beginning on page 139.

Cut out the wefts instead of un-weaving

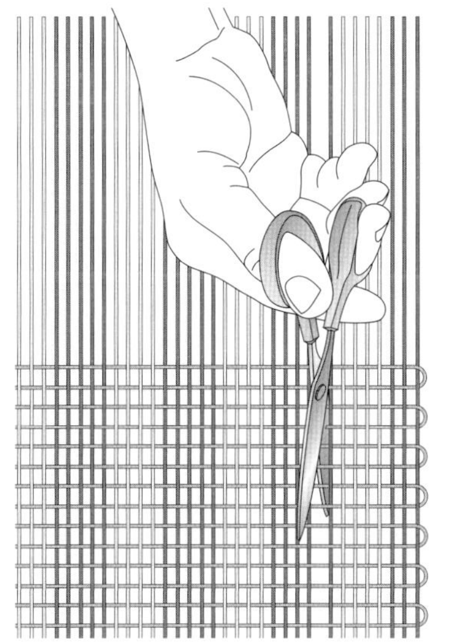

Fig. 536

Cut out the wefts instead of un-weaving, because serious problems can occur that disfigure the cloth if you unweave the cloth weft-by-weft. The reed abrades the warp and when the wefts are dragged out of the sheds, they can fluff up the warp yarns. Bits of yarn can get caught permanently in the sheds, too.

With the shed closed, cut the wefts at each side of the warp, about an inch in from the edge. See Figure 536. Spread the warps apart a bit and snip the weft that's at the fell of the cloth first, and then, succeeding ones, working back into the cloth for about an inch at a time. Continually push the warp threads apart to get the points of the scissors in to cut the wefts, *but not the warps.* Use sharp, pointed scissors and have good light. Be sure to be alert so you don't cut a warp thread by mistake.

After cutting the wefts, pull them out, one-by-one, from the middle of the warp. The wefts still at the selvedges can be removed by plucking at them a bit.

Un-weaving a single weft

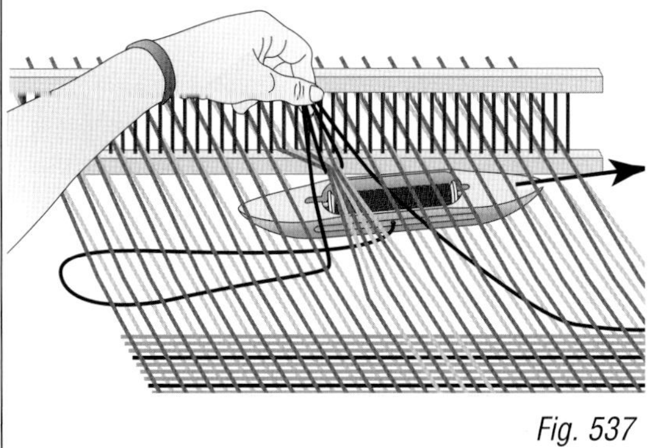

Fig. 537

It's often hard to un-weave a row because the shed won't be clean (on account of the mistake). The thread from the shuttle gets hung up on the problem warp thread and prevents the weft from coming out of the shed.

In that case, with the shed opened, lift up the weft with your fingers where the errant threads are, and make a mini shed, so your shuttle can slide through the problem area. Then, take the shuttle through the remainder of the shed. See Figure 537.

<table>
<tr><td>Broken warp threads</td><td>There are two ways to make repairs: by replacing the warp thread completely (quicker) or by making a splice (the “right” way). See why they break, on the next page.</td></tr>
<tr><td>The replacement method
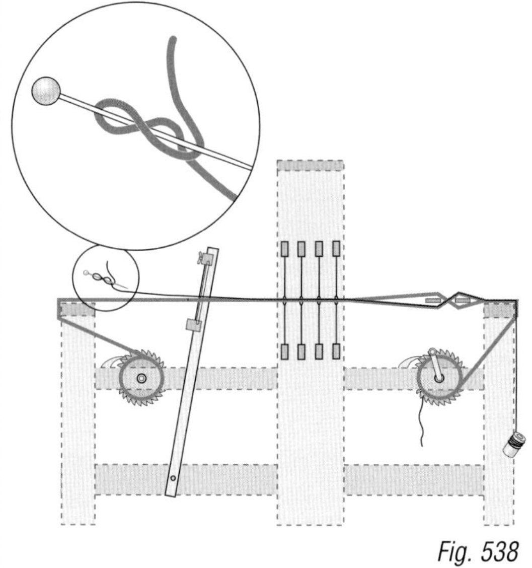
Fig. 538</td><td>Measure out a new warp thread a bit longer than the original warp. Attach one end onto the cloth with a pin like a cleat as seen in Figure 248, on page 108. Take the thread through the reed and heddles, exactly where the broken thread was, and hang it over the back beam with a weight.
See Figure 538 and Figure 255 on page 110.</td></tr>
<tr><td>The splice method
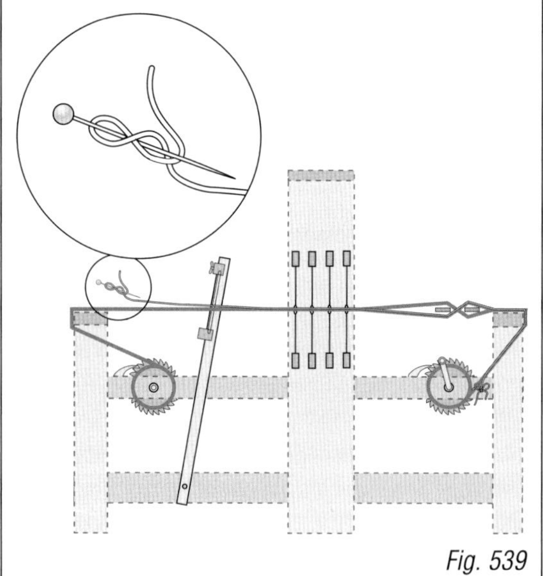
Fig. 539</td><td>Note: Locate the end of the broken warp thread that comes from the warp beam. If you can't find it, use the replacement method.

Measure out a thread a little longer than the length of the distance from the front of the loom to the back beam. Attach one end to the cloth with a pin like a cleat as shown in Figure 248 on page 108. You will attach it now and then re-do the cleat again later to tighten the splice thread. Take the thread through the reed and heddles as far back as possible to the warp beam and tie it to the broken warp thread. Tie them together with a large bow. See Figure 539.

Notice there is some excess thread there—the reason is that the splice is longer than the distance it is spanning. This excess thread is taken up in the big bow. The extra length is needed for reattaching later onto the cloth with a pin like a cleat.

(continued)</td></tr>
</table>

The repair thread must replace the broken thread exactly where the thread belongs in the warp, reed, and heddles. Use a hair comb to hold the warps apart while making the repair. See page 320.

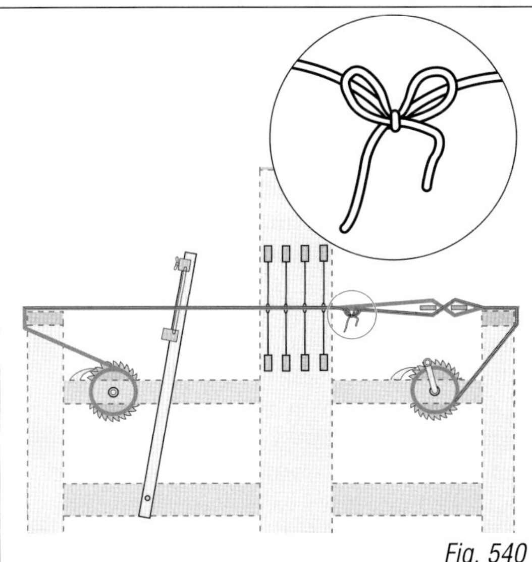 Fig. 540	Now, go to the front of the loom and re-do the thread on the pin so that the warp is under the same tension as the rest of the warp. Continue weaving and advancing the warp until the bow reaches the back shaft. See Figure 540.
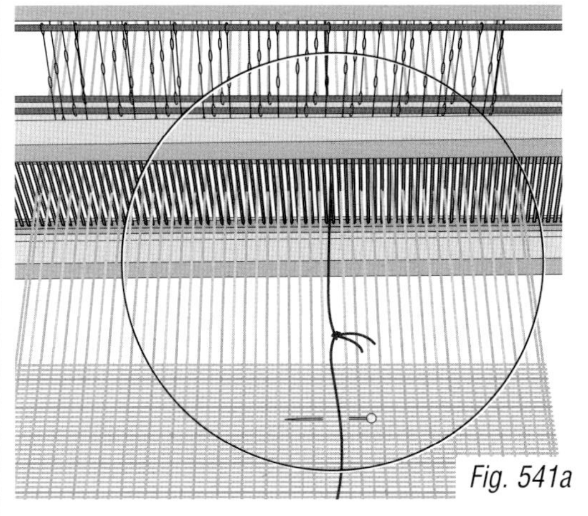 Fig. 541a	When the bow reaches the back shaft, undo the bow and re-tie the ends of the two threads together with an overhand knot and pull the knotted-together threads through the heddle and reed to the cloth. See Figure 541a.
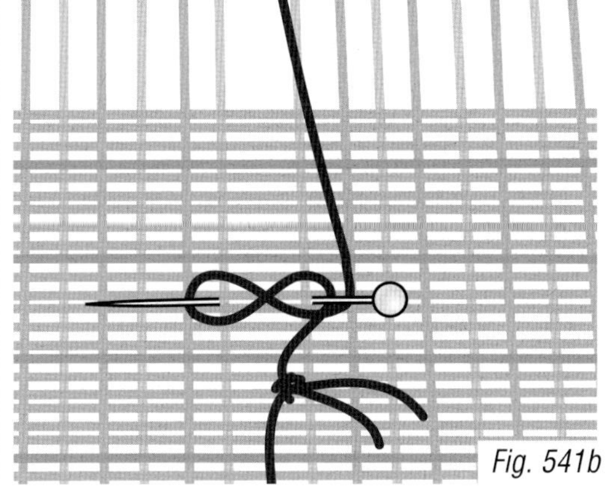 Fig. 541b	Tension the regular warp thread on a pin. See Figure 541b.
Why threads break	The thread isn't suitable for warp. To test if a yarn is strong enough, pull on the ends of a length of yarn 10" to 12" long and try to break it. If it doesn't break easily, it will be a suitable warp yarn.

Other problems while weaving	
Selvedges break	See page 302 and the Selvedges Chapter.
Tangles in boat shuttles	Wind bobbins and load shuttles correctly, page 102. Throw and receive the shuttle properly, see page 314, Notches in Selvedges.
Boat shuttles jerk the weft at the selvedges	Wrong type of bobbin for the shuttle. See page 94. See page 314.
Fell is wavy	If the fell is wavy as seen in Figure 287, on page 123, it may be that bulky straps or cords from the cloth apron rod to the cloth beam are causing lumps and making the wefts wavy. This situation must be corrected or it will get worse and cause warp tension problems. See pages 50, 52, and 123.
Fell is concave or convex	See pages 308 and 309 and 315 and 316.
Warp tension issues	Read "Can't get a shed," on page 318. Shed not clean: – Re-tension any loose warp bundles. See page 89. – Thread sags in shed. See page 319, Fig. 535. – Bulky straps. See "Fell is wavy," above. – Poor beaming. See page 35 or 172.
Warp runs out too soon	Not enough loom waste allowed. See page 291. Not enough allowed for take-up. See page 290.

Problems with the Loom	
Shafts don't move correctly	The lower bar of the shafts is caught on the side of the loom or in among the string heddles. Sometimes, the shafts catch on each other. On a counterbalance loom: cords may have slipped off pulleys at the top of the loom.
Warp rises above the shuttle race	Warp tension is too high. See page 89.
Treadles uneven	Adjust cords tied to treadles. Knots may loosen; use snitch knots (page 96).
Treadle hooks come off	Don't "bang" the treadles or press them hard or suddenly.

For a reference on adjusting looms, see *Warping Your Loom & Tying On New Warps.*

Cloth Isn't Right	
Didn't understand the instructions	The yarns you used were not the same as those in the instructions. Didn't follow the instructions carefully enough. See page 195.
Reed marks—vertical "lines"	Vertical lines or streaks regularly spaced all over the cloth. They are the spaces between the warp threads where the wires of the reed were. Use a reed with two warp ends per dent, if possible. If the dents are really crowded with fine threads, the marks may never come out.
Pattern isn't right	
Pattern on the wrong side of the cloth	The tie-up is reversed. See page 121. How to read tie-up drafts is on page 199.
Tie-up wrong or hooks have fallen off	Tying up the treadles may have been done incorrectly, or some of the treadle hooks may have fallen out. See pages 95-101 and read about tie-up drafts on page 199.
Wrong treadling sequence	Learn to read treadling drafts. See page 199.

Chenille Problems	
Cloth too stiff	Cloth hasn't been washed yet. See page 187.
Snags or worming	Read about this important issue. See page 184.

14 Rigid Heddle Loom

Introduction: Rigid Heddle Loom

By Peggy Osterkamp

I asked Angela Risser to write this chapter because she has taught many people to weave on a rigid heddle loom. Her students learn to weave on the loom by weaving a scarf in a one-day class. It's fun and simple and a great way to start to weave. One can weave on this type of loom forever, or switch to a table or floor loom as described in the other chapters of this book.

There is no end to the amount of experimenting with yarns and colors you can do with these looms. The limit in width is the width of the loom. The length can be from one yard to several yards depending on the loom and the yarn used.

What is weaving?

Weaving is making cloth from two sets of yarns or threads that interlace with each other. See Figures 542 a and b.

A loom makes it easier to "weave" the threads over and under each other. The loom lifts or lowers some threads, and you pass a shuttle filled with yarn under the lifted threads or over the lowered threads. Thus, you don't have to manually manipulate the shuttle to go over and under, over and under the threads.

In this chapter, the simplest weave is described: plain weave (sometimes called tabby). Lots of different variations of this weave can be woven on a rigid heddle loom. In addition to plain weave, you can make the hand-manipulated weaves which are given beginning on page 357.

There are more possibilities that can be woven with more complex rigid heddle looms (for example, looms with 2 heddles), but they are not in the scope of this chapter. (An introduction to using a two-heddle loom begins on page 345.)

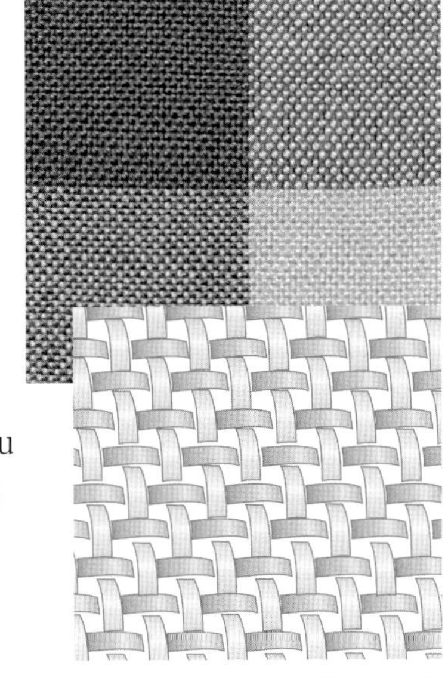

Fig. 542 a and b

What are warps and wefts?

Warps are the threads that are measured out and put on the loom first. Wefts are the threads that cross over and under the warp threads during weaving, See Figure 543.

Fig. 543

What are threads and yarns?

Generally, the two terms are used interchangeably, and that will be the case in this chapter as well as in the rest of the book. Often, one thinks of yarns as being fat and threads a being thin. See Figure 544.

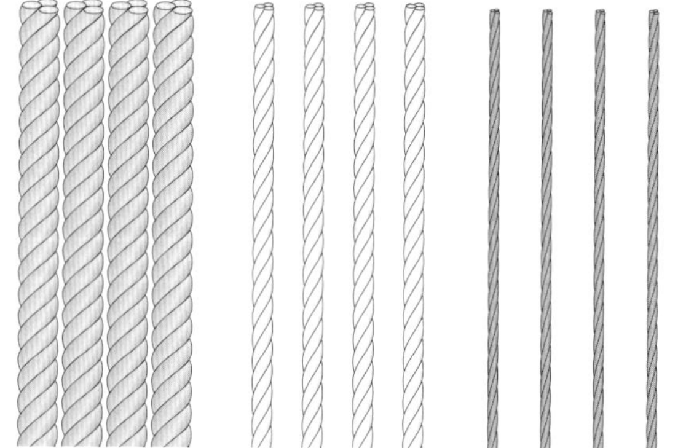

Fig. 544

What is a rigid heddle loom?

See Figure 545. This type of loom uses a "heddle" with slots and holes to lift and lower the warp threads. They are popular because they are small, portable, and not as complex as floor or table looms. The heddle is shown in Figure 546. Sometimes, it's called a rigid heddle reed. The warp threads will be "threaded" into the slots and holes while setting up the loom. This type of loom is also known as a "slot and hole" loom.

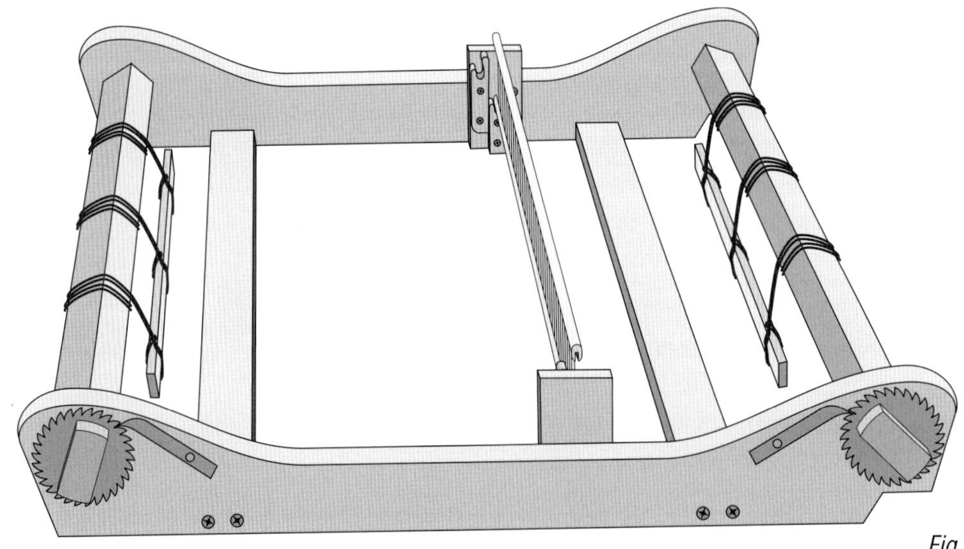

Fig. 545

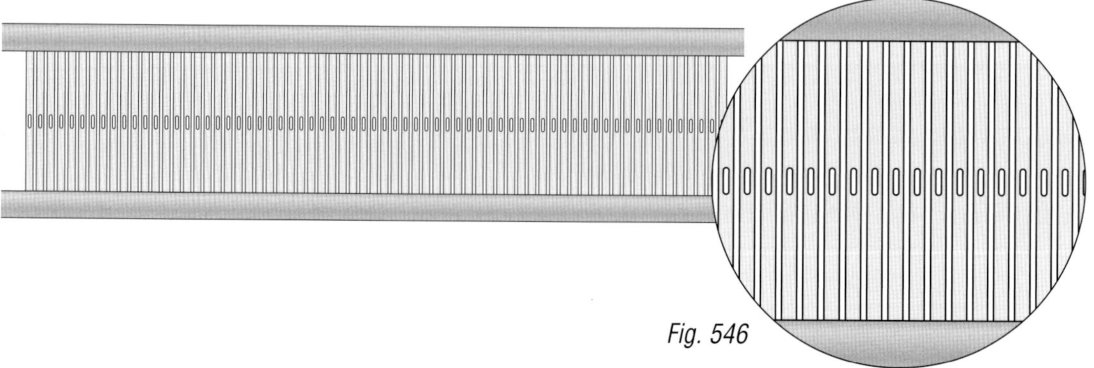

Fig. 546

Rigid Heddle Weaving

By Angela Risser

The rigid heddle loom is a simple loom that allows for quick and easy setting up of the loom, and weaving. You can weave a simple plain weave project or, with experience, a more complex weave or tapestry project. The project explored in this section is a scarf that can be woven in about a day. The techniques you will learn for this project will be transferable to other undertakings such as placemats, dishtowels, scarves, shawls or fabric for clothing. Some of these techniques are also used for floor and table looms, so the rigid heddle loom is a good starting place for those who wish to learn to weave without the investment in larger and more complex looms.

The scarf will be 70" long and 6" wide.

Scarf Requirements

Equipment and Tools

Chair: A chair with a straight back

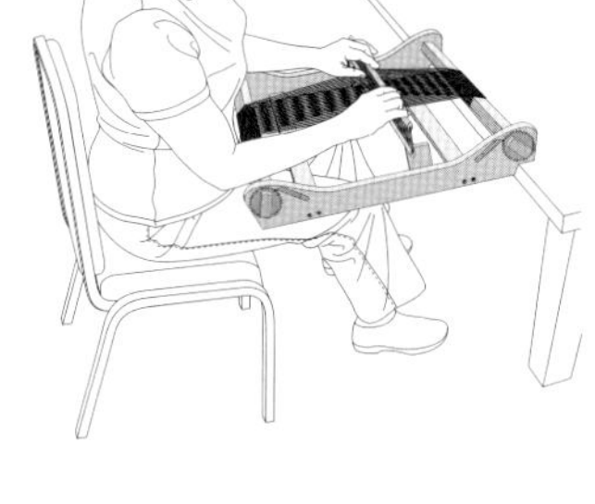

Clamps: Two come with the loom. See Figure 551 on page 332.

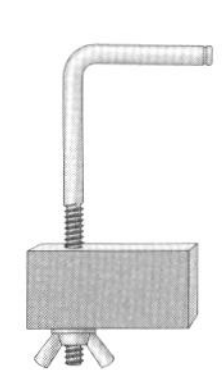

Grocery bag cut into long strips: Cut several pieces 8" wide and as long as the bag for this project. For other projects, I like to have the pieces of paper 2" wider than the width of the project and the pieces as long as you can get from the bags. You'll need enough pieces for a little less than the length the warp will be. For the scarf, the pieces of paper should be 8" wide and enough of them for about 65-70", the length of the warp. You'll use the papers when setting up the loom.

Rigid Heddle Loom: See Figure 545. Figure 547, on page 330, shows the loom with the names of the parts given. Descriptions of the parts of the loom are given in the sidebar on page 331.

Rigid heddle: See Figure 546 on page 328. One comes with the loom. Different sizes are available and can be ordered from the manufacturer. Different size yarns need different size heddles. For this project, use either a size 8 or 10 dent rigid heddle. (These numbers refer to how many slots ***and*** holes are in one inch.) See Sources on page 382. Sometimes, the heddle is called a "rigid heddle reed."

Scissors: These can be fairly inexpensive, but use better ones than those made for kindergarten children.

Stick shuttle: This comes with the loom. You might want a few. You can make one out of very stiff cardboard or foamcore board by cutting out the shape shown in the figure. Make it about as long as your rigid heddle. If cutting out the rounded shapes is difficult, you can cut straight lines instead to make large V-shapes at the ends of the shuttle.

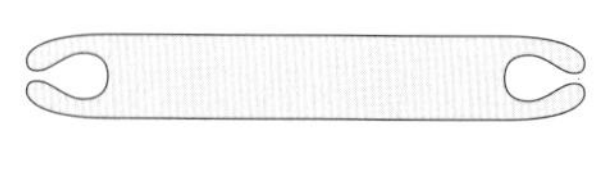

Sticks: For long warps. See page 343.

Lease sticks

End stick

Table: Similar in height to a dining table. A low end-table might also need to be used in addition to a big table.

Warping Peg with Clamp: This comes with the loom.

Tape measure:

Threading hook: This comes with the loom.

Yarn: Worsted weight as shown on page 12 or a yarn that is close to that size but not as fat as the rug wool shown on page 12. You'll need 340 yards for the project. Add 5 more yards if you don't have any scrap yarn available as listed below. Allow enough yarn or whichever is larger: 7 ounces or 340 yards. See page 341 for how to calculate how much yarn is needed for future projects.

Warping board: For longer warps.

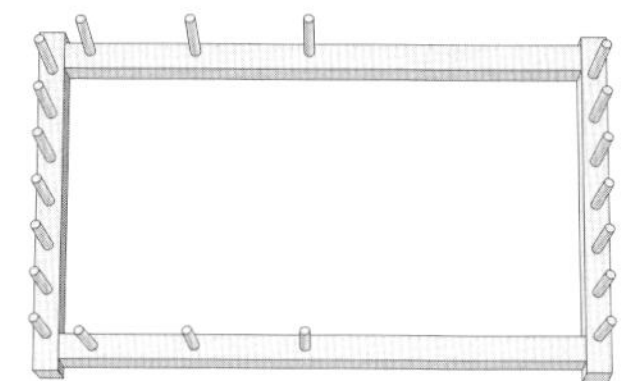

Scrap yarn: You'll need a little bit of odds and ends at the beginning and end of the scarf.

Pick-up stick (optional): Figure 598 on page 370 shows a proper pick-up stick in use. A ruler will do if you do not have a pick-up stick.

Pick-up stick

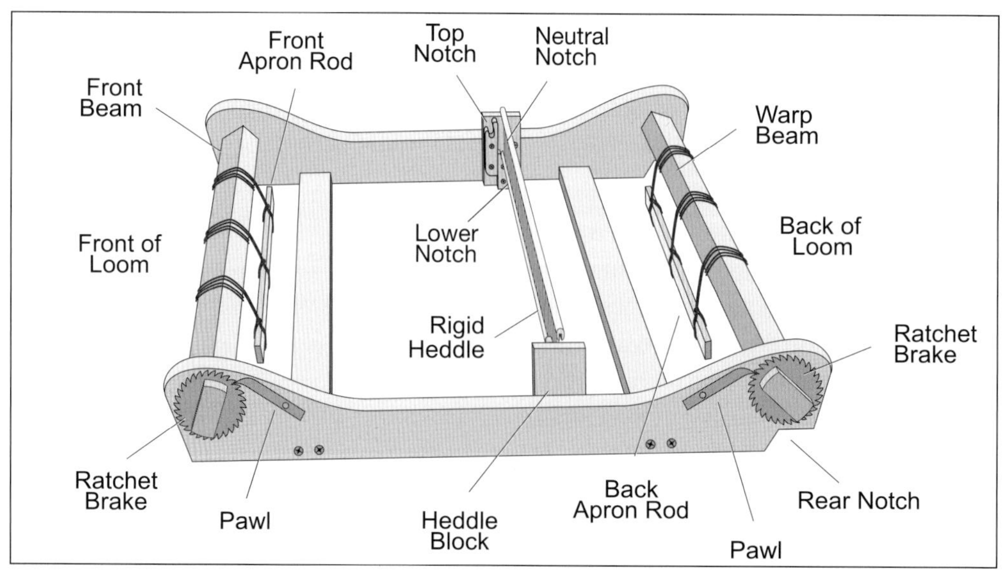

Fig. 547

Parts of the Rigid Heddle Loom

Locate the front and the back of the loom: At the back of the loom, there is a notch or sometimes, a short "leg" on each side of the loom. This is the ***rear notch***. When weaving with the loom in your lap, the notches or legs *at the back of the loom* will rest against a table. The front of the loom will rest in your lap. See Figure 548. Another way to tell the back of the loom is this: the ***heddle block*** is nearer the back of the loom than the front. This makes a larger space at the *front* for the weaver to put the shuttle in and out.

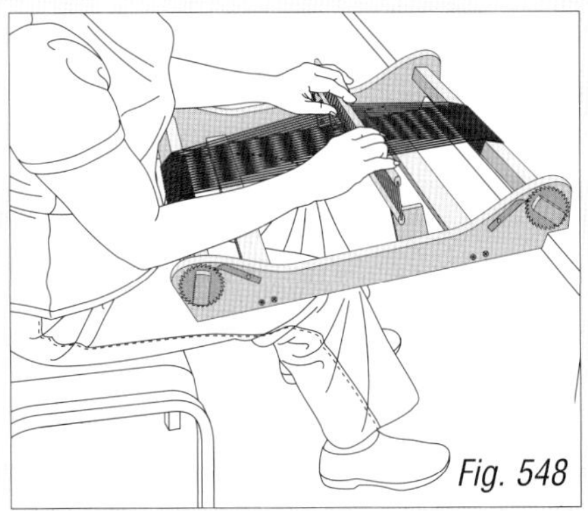

Fig. 548

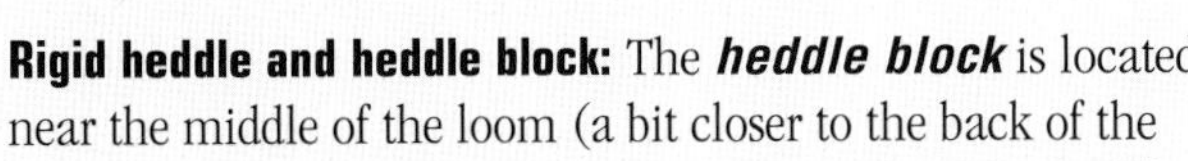

Rigid heddle and heddle block: The ***heddle block*** is located near the middle of the loom (a bit closer to the back of the loom, as mentioned before.) It is the place where the heddle rests during weaving as well as when setting up the loom. The ***heddle*** is shown in Figure 546 on page 328. Notice the holes and the slots in it. How this mechanism works is described on page 336 in the section just before Weaving.

Notice the notches on the heddle block in Figure 547. They will hold the rigid heddle in place during weaving. There are three positions (notches) for the heddle—the ***top notch*** (Figure 549), ***the lower notch*** (Figure 550), and a ***notch for the neutral position***. The neutral position is described on page 332 during setting up the loom. It holds the warp threads level. The ***up*** position (Figure 549) raises every other warp thread during weaving. The ***down*** position (Figure 550) lowers the threads in the holes below those in the slots. The positions are explained in the section on weaving on page 336. Note: The heddle may not stay in position in the notches unless the warp threads are on tension on the loom.

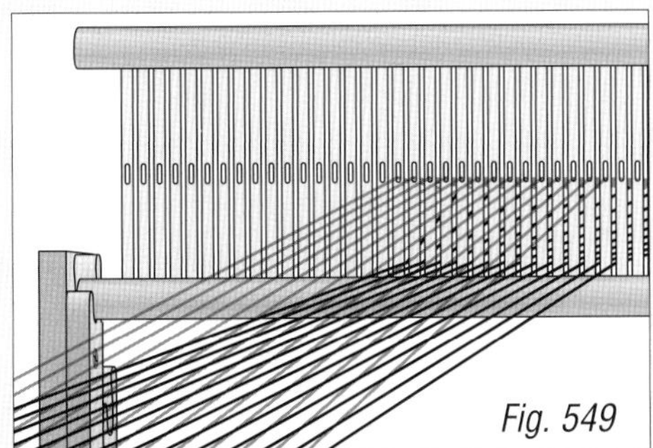

Fig. 549

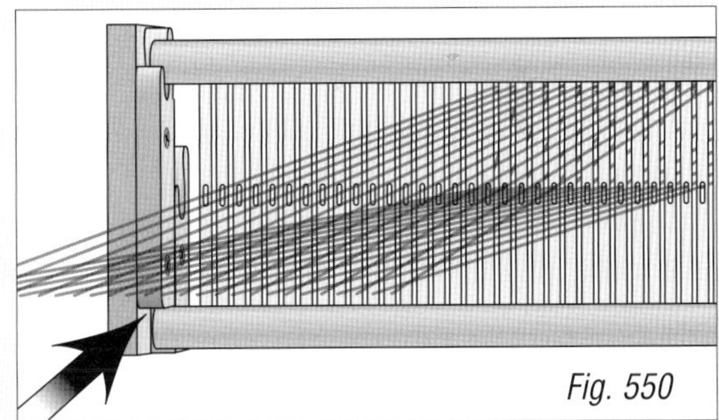

Fig. 550

Beams: There are two beams—one at the front of the loom called the ***front beam***. The cloth will be rolled up on the front beam during weaving. Notice there is a ratchet brake at the end. Brakes are described below. The beam at the *back* of the loom is called the ***warp beam***. The warp threads will be wound up on this beam after they are measured out. Note the ratchet brake at the end.

Ratchet Brakes: The ***ratchets*** are round disks usually made of plastic that have notches or "teeth" all around the edge. Along with the ratchet is a ***pawl***, or lever, and when it is against the ratchet teeth, it acts like a brake and prevents the beam(s) from turning. A ratchet brake is engaged when its pawl is resting between two of the teeth. It is disengaged when the pawl is lifted up away from the teeth.

Apron Rods: There is an ***apron rod*** attached by cords to each of the beams. The ***front apron rod*** is shown at the front of the loom and the ***back apron rod*** is attached to the warp beam at the back of the loom. The warp threads are attached to these rods. Tension can be put on the warp threads for weaving when the beams are wound up and both brakes are engaged. You need tension on the warp in order to weave.

Measure out the warp yarn (called warping)

In this process, you will measure out the warp threads and put them though the heddle in one operation. The threads will be 108" long. There will be enough threads for the width of the scarf, which is to be 6".

For very long warps, see page 343.

1. Clamp the back of the loom to the table using the clamps that came with the loom (Figure 551). There are holes in the frame at the back of the loom for the metal "pins" of the clamps to go in. (The back of the loom should be near the edge of the table.) Be sure you are clamping the ***back*** of the loom and ***not the front*** to the table's edge. One way to distinguish the back from the front is that there is less space between the heddle block (where the heddle will rest) and the back of the loom than there is in the front of the loom. Look at Figure 547 on page 330 and your loom's instructions.

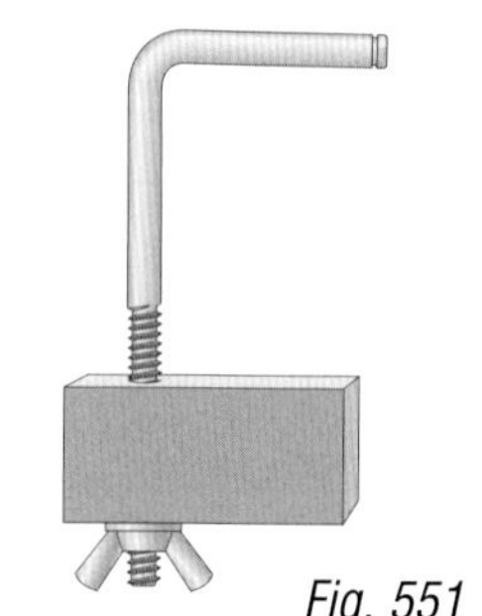

Fig. 551

2. Bring the back apron rod up over the warp beam toward the heddle as shown in the illustration below. Position the rod near the warp beam by rolling the beam with the crank on the beam. Leave enough space between the rod and the beam so you can tie threads to the rod later—2" should do. Engage the ratchet brake on the warp beam so that the beam cannot turn by putting the pawl between two teeth on the brake. (See the sidebar explaining the brakes on page 331).

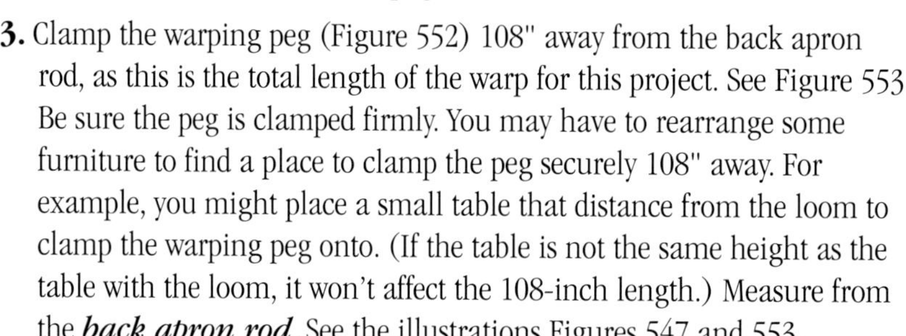

3. Clamp the warping peg (Figure 552) 108" away from the back apron rod, as this is the total length of the warp for this project. See Figure 553. Be sure the peg is clamped firmly. You may have to rearrange some furniture to find a place to clamp the peg securely 108" away. For example, you might place a small table that distance from the loom to clamp the warping peg onto. (If the table is not the same height as the table with the loom, it won't affect the 108-inch length.) Measure from the ***back apron rod***. See the illustrations Figures 547 and 553.

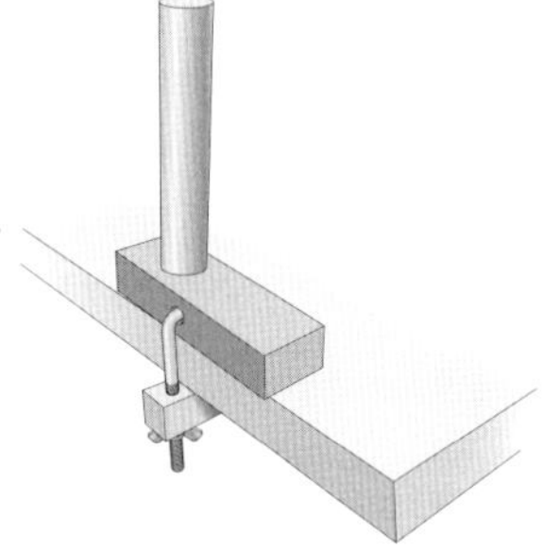

Fig. 552

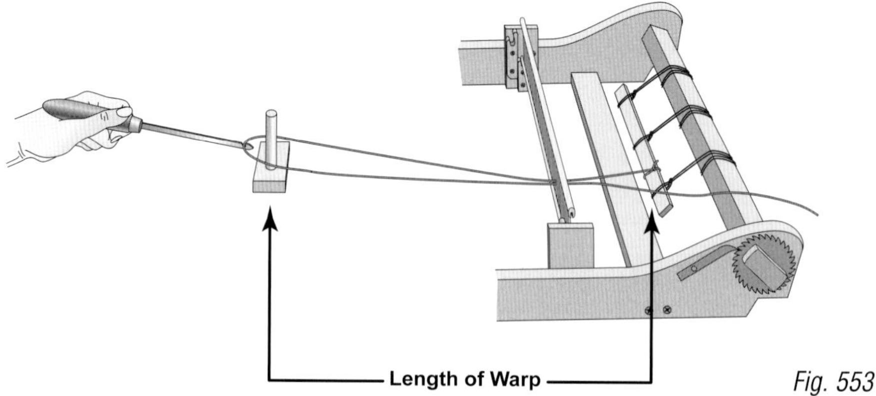

Fig. 553

4. Put the rigid heddle in the heddle block in the neutral position—usually, the notch closest to the back of the loom (or check your loom's instructions). Sometimes, this position is called the "rest" position.

5. Center the warp threads on the loom. Here is how to figure out how to do this job and where to start putting the threads onto the loom as you are measuring. Divide the total width of the project by two, in this example, 3". Measure 3" out on each side of the center on the rigid heddle to determine where the edges of the warp will be. (I usually tie a piece of yarn or string in the slots to mark both outside edges of my projects.) Choose one edge (right or left side) to be the first slot that you will pull the warp through. Tie your warp thread to the ***back apron rod*** so that it lines up with this slot.

   Place your ball or cone of yarn on the floor below the back of your loom. (If the yarn is in a ball or small spool or cone, putting it inside a coffee can or small wastebasket or large kitchen pot will keep it from rolling away from you.)

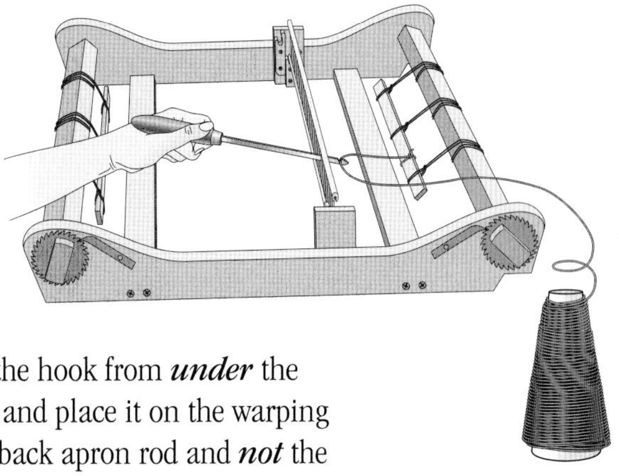

6. Using the threading hook, pull a loop of yarn through your first slot (not a hole) in the heddle, as shown in Figure 554. Then, place the loop of yarn over the warping peg. You now have two warp threads going through a single slot and looping over the peg. See Figure 553.

Fig. 554

7. For the second slot's yarn, grasp the yarn with the hook from ***under*** the back apron rod, pull the loop through the slot and place it on the warping peg. Make sure the yarn only goes around the back apron rod and ***not*** the warp beam. For the third slot, grasp the yarn with the hook over the back apron rod. You will continue pulling loops through the slots in this way, alternating grasping the yarn over and under the rod. (This alternation is needed so that the warp yarns ***catch the back apron rod*** on each pull.) You will soon learn where to grasp the yarn so the yarns go around the back apron rod. Figure 554 shows the thread coming off the cone and attached to the back apron rod. Figure 553 shows the path the warp thread is to take and the rod where it is to go around on the loom.

   Continue pulling loops through each slot and placing each warp loop over the warping peg. Keep the yarns in order on the peg. In other words, try not to cross the yarns over each other on the peg, but lay them row-by-row above each other. There should be just enough tension so that the yarns do not become entangled but not so much that the yarn is strained or stretched.

*Make sure your yarn **goes around the back apron rod** and **not** the warp beam.*

8. You will be done with Step 7 when the project measures 6" across. At this point, cut the yarn from the ball of yarn and tie the end to the back apron rod (opposite the last slot used).

9. Tie a piece of scrap yarn around the warp in a bow about 6" from the warping peg, as shown in Figure 555.

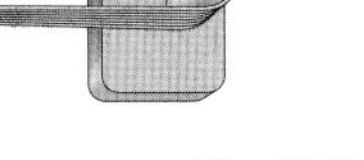

Fig. 555

10. Gently slide the loops off of the warping peg.

11. Take the warp threads as they came from the peg and hold them in one hand. Then begin to wind the warp by turning the crank on the warp beam (the one at the back of the loom). You'll know the right direction to crank when you hear the pawl clicking on the teeth of the ratchet brake. If neither direction "clicks," you'll know that the brake isn't engaged. In that case, engage the brake by resting the brake's pawl on the teeth of the ratchet brake. Read about brakes in the sidebar on page 331.

After the warp is wound around the beam one time, insert heavy paper (grocery bags cut as instructed in the equipment list) between the layers of the warps to keep them separated. Wind the paper along with the warp. See Figure 556. Keep a slight tension on the warp while winding. Then, tug on the warp every so often to tighten the paper and warp on the warp beam. I do this action for every revolution of the warp beam. Tug with just enough pressure to tighten the warps and paper on the warp beam. (Tug gently but firmly—do not tug so hard that the loom comes off the table!)

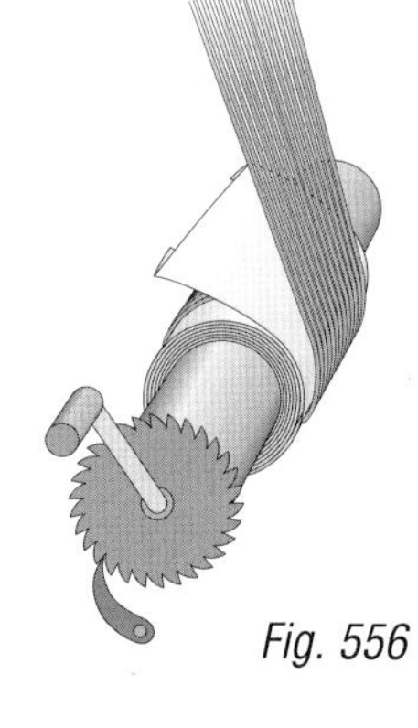

Fig. 556

12. Stop winding the warp when the end loop is about 10" in front of the heddle.

13. Remove the clamps on the loom and turn it to face you so you can work at the front, now. Before, you were working at the side of the loom, when you pulled the loops through the slots, guiding the threads from the back of the loom to the warping peg. Now, you want the loom to sit on the table facing you squarely.

Cut the loops at the end of the warp.

At this point, you have two threads going through each slot. One of these warp threads must be carefully removed from the slot and threaded through the adjacent hole.

Starting from the right or left side of your warp and moving across the warp until all threads are threaded, put the threading hook through the hole adjacent to the slot. With your hook, grab one of the two threads in the slot from behind the hole and pull it through the hole. See Figure 557. Note the cut end of the warp can be seen behind the heddle in the over-all view illustration. Continue with all sets of warp threads. There will be one warp thread in the slot and one in the hole next to it all the way across the warp.

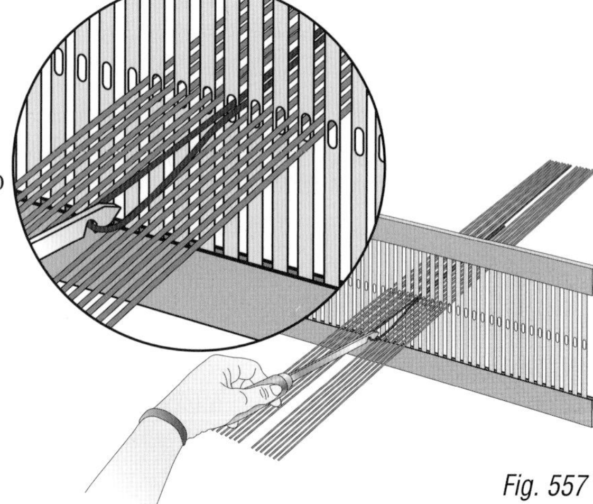

Fig. 557

14. Bring the front apron rod around and over the top of the front beam so that is about 6" from the heddle. Figure 547 on page 330 shows the path the front apron rod should take. Be sure the cords are going ***over*** the front beam.

15. Put the heddle in the "up" position. Then, go to the next step.

16. At this point, the threads are hanging loose in front of the heddle. To tie them onto the front apron rod, divide the threads into 1-inch groups. (Be sure to tie the threads onto the rod only, ***not the beam***.) Starting with the center group and working your way out on both sides (left side, right side, left, right, etc.), tie these groups onto the rod with a surgeon's knot. This knot starts by taking your group of threads over the apron rod, splitting it in half and tying it around the rod as if you are going to tie shoelaces, except, go around twice. See Figures 558 a-c.

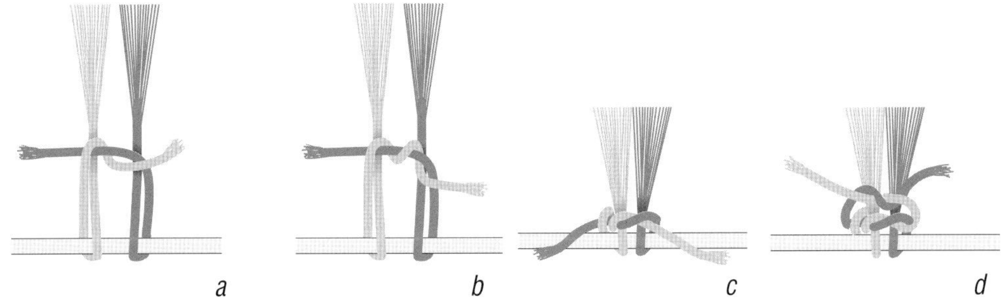

Fig. 558

After all the 1" groups have been tied, work back and forth across the width of the warp tightening all the groups until they are under the same amount of tension. You don't need to untie the knots to tighten the threads because this knot lets you easily adjust the tension by pulling one end to loosen the knot, or both ends to cinch the warps tighter.

You can pat the warp all the way across to tell by feel if all groups are the same. Be sure that the knots are tight when you do this so the threads can't slip and loosen as you go. You'll know if the tension is the same—if threads are neither ***noticeably*** loose or tight. See Figure 559. When the groups are equally tensioned, take the tails of each of the knots and tie them to complete the last part of the surgeon's knot. (See Figure 558d.)

After the warp is secure and the tension equal, you are ready to weave.

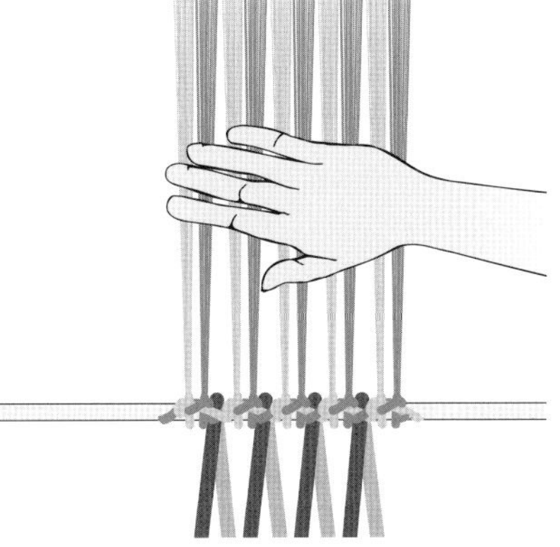
Fig. 559

> ***Note: The amount of tension is important—the warp should feel firm but not tight like a violin string.***

Before you weave

Wind a shuttle

The weft yarn will be wound onto a shuttle. For this project, the weft yarn will be the same as the warp yarn. For other projects, it can be the same color and thickness or different colors and sizes. When more than one type of weft yarn is used, you want one shuttle for each kind of weft yarn in the project.

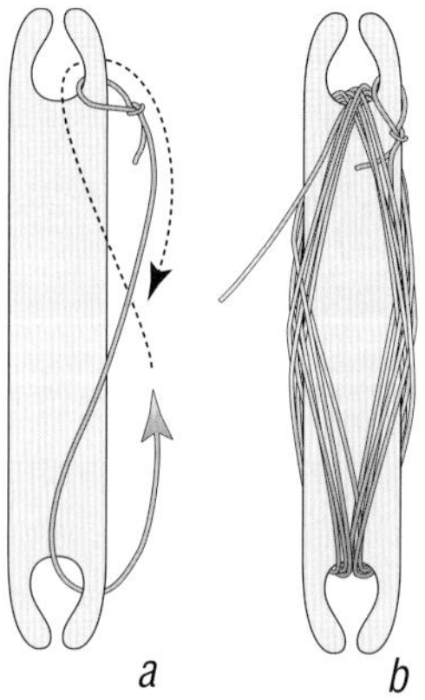

To wind the shuttle, first tie a slip knot (page 350) and hook the loop over one end of the shuttle as shown in Figures 560a and 560b. Wind the yarn according to the illustrations, making figure 8's on the ***edges*** of the shuttle. By winding on the edges, you can get more weft onto the shuttle.

a b

Fig. 560

Understand how the loom works

Before beginning weaving you must first understand the mechanism of the rigid heddle loom. The rigid heddle is alternately raised or lowered to create the space between the warp yarns for the weft yarn to go through. Raising the heddle and resting it in the notch on top of the heddle block makes the first opening for the shuttle to pass through. This opening for the shuttle is called the ***shed***. The raised heddle placement is called the upper shed or the up position. Lowering the heddle and putting it under the heddle block or in the lower notch makes the lower shed (the down position). To weave, you alternately raise and lower the rigid heddle, placing your shuttle through the "up shed" and then, the "down shed." See how to weave on page 337.

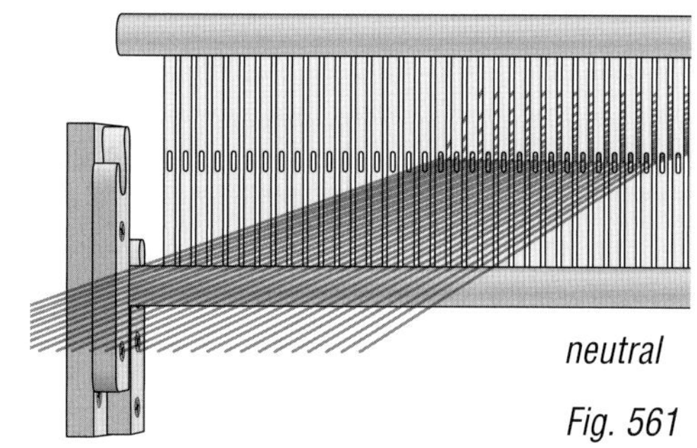

Fig. 561

Looms vary in how the heddle is placed in the up and down positions. There may or may not be actual notches

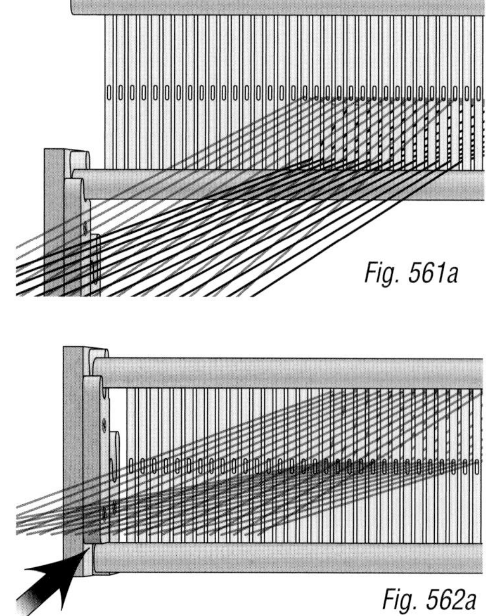
Fig. 561a

Fig. 562a

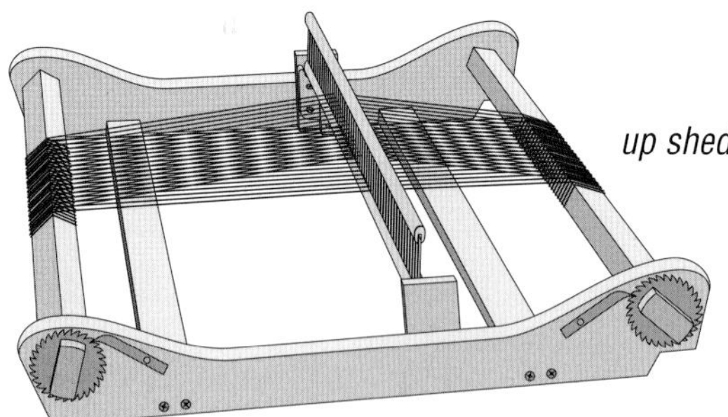

Fig. 561b

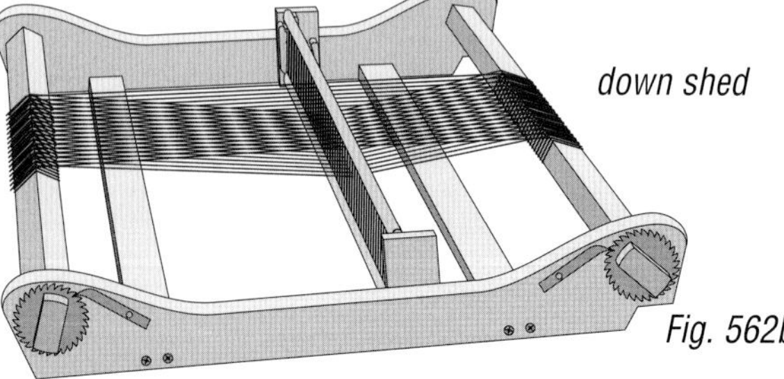

Fig. 562b

for the down shed. In that case, the heddle is just placed under the heddle block itself. However, in all cases, you want to locate the two positions for the up and down sheds. (The heddle was in the neutral position for setting up the loom—neither up nor down.)

Figure 561 on page 336 shows the rigid heddle in the neutral position where the threads are neither up nor down. Figures 561a and 561b show the up shed with the heddle in the upper position—in the top notch. Figures 562a and 562b show the down shed with the heddle in the lower notch. As I said before, sometimes, there isn't a notch, you just place the heddle at the bottom of the heddle block.

Weaving

Position the loom

There are two loom positions you can use while weaving. The most common one is to place the front of the loom on your lap and brace the notch at the back of the loom against the edge of the table. See Figure 548 on page 331. The alternative is to clamp the loom to a table and weave standing up.

Before you begin to weave, I suggest you practice changing the heddle from up to down until you feel comfortable. Figure 563 shows the position of your hands on the heddle while moving it up and down. To make the up shed, lift the heddle with both hands. To make the down shed push the heddle down with both hands. It will take a little effort, but you won't need to yank on the heddle to move it.

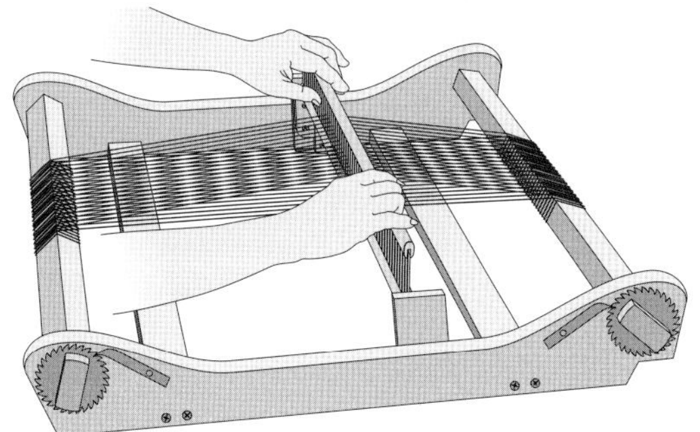

Fig. 563

How to weave

To start, place the front of the loom in your lap with the back of the loom resting on the edge of the table. (Or, stand at the table.)

Note: When you weave the first few rows, you will use your scrap yarn. These first rows spread out the warps so they are no longer in bundles or groups. This part is called the heading. Then, you'll switch to your "good" yarn to weave the actual project. The weaving process for the heading and the project are nearly the same. The only difference will be in the beating stage in Step 3.

Weave the heading

Weave a heading out of scrap yarn to spread out the warp yarns evenly. By using scrap yarn, you will not waste any of your "good" weft yarn. Follow the steps for normal weaving and note what to do differently for the heading in Step 3.

1. Raise or lower the heddle to make a shed (The opening between the raised and lowered warp yarns).
2. Put the shuttle into the shed. For the first weft only, leave a tail to be cut off later, about 1 inch long, hanging out at the side of the warp.

Take the shuttle out so that the weft is in the shed on a diagonal as shown in Figure 564. For all but the first weft with its tail, here is how you'll pull the shuttle out of the shed to make neat edges (selvedges) on the cloth. Hold onto the shuttle as it leaves the shed and tug gently. What you want to do is to pull on the weft so that it turns around the warp on the other edge of the cloth quite closely. I think of the weft as being snugged up to the outside thread just so it touches and barely moves that outside thread. Here, you are concerned with the side where the shuttle ***entered*** the shed. Figure 564 shows that the weft is up against the edge of the warp. The edges of the warp are called the selvedges and to make them look good, the wefts must turn around them in this way.

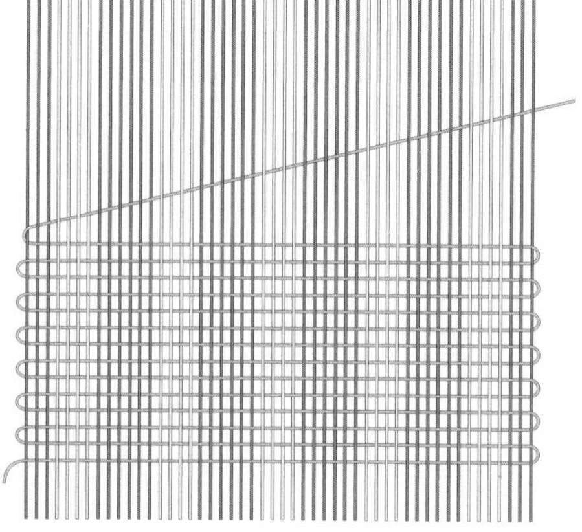

Fig. 564

Note: The diagonal is important; if you don't put the wefts in at a diagonal, the cloth will seriously narrow in (and, if you tug too hard on the wefts). Read more about the diagonal of the weft beginning on page 300.

3. "Beat" in the weft by lifting the heddle out of its position and gently pushing the new weft against the previous weft. You slide the whole heddle forward, and you may tilt it or not, whichever works better to get the weft to be against the previous weft. What ever you do, you want the heddle to be parallel to the edge of the cloth so the new weft is straight. The weft will be on the diagonal when you begin to beat, so you need to keep the heddle parallel to the cloth's edge (called the fell of the cloth).

   You do not want actually to beat it as the name implies. You are simply placing the weft against the one woven before it. How hard you beat depends on the kind of cloth you want. Remember that the cloth will shrink up some when the cloth is washed and become a bit more dense. See page 340.

   For the heading only, you won't "beat" in the weft until three wefts have been entered (3 passes of the shuttle: one pass in each shed). In other words, follow the steps for weaving (2-4), and omit the beating step until 3 wefts have been thrown. Then, beat all three wefts in at once. This action is to spread out the warps so they won't be in distinct groups from the tying on, but will be evenly spaced apart across the width of the warp. If the warp is still in groups, repeat the 3-weft process.

4. Change to the next shed.

5. Repeat steps 2-4.

Note: After the heading, switch to your project weft yarn, wound on its shuttle. Since you will be alternating the up and down sheds, select which shed should be next in the alternating sequence. For information on how to know, see page 115.

Advancing the Warp Forward

After you weave a few inches, the edge of the cloth draws too near to the heddle, and the warp must be moved forward toward the front beam. This process requires that the warp on both beams be released.

1. Disengage the ratchet brake on the front beam by lifting the pawl out of its space between the teeth on the brake. To do it, you'll need to crank the warp a tiny bit tighter so that you can remove the pawl from its space between the teeth of the brake. Flip the pawl out of the way of the teeth so that the brake is disengaged, and the warp is not on tension.
2. Disengage the brake on the warp beam by lifting the pawl from the ratchet's teeth. Now it will be easy to lift the pawl out of the ratchet.
3. Place the pawl back into the teeth at the front beam and crank (wind) the woven cloth up onto the front beam by turning the crank on the beam. You will hear the pawl clicking in the teeth if you are winding the front beam in the right direction. Be careful not to wind up the cloth too much. You want the edge of the cloth to be midway between the front beam and the heddle for when you resume weaving.
4. Engage the brake on the warp beam by putting the pawl on the back ratchet brake between the brake's teeth.
5. Adjust the tension on the warp. Do it by winding up either the front beam or the warp beam so the tension is firm but not tight. You are trying to match the tension you had when previously weaving.

Continue weaving

Using these steps, continue weaving along beginning with Step two—putting the shuttle into the shed. Read on to learn what to do when your yarn runs out on the shuttle, below.

Weave your project

After you weave a few inches, you will have to move the warp forward because the cloth has become too close to the heddle, and there is no longer room for the shuttle to pass. This operation is called "advancing the warp." See the process in the sidebar. With your "good" weft yarn, continue weaving until the scarf is 70" long.

Changing wefts

When your shuttle runs out of yarn, there are several ways to end the thread and start the new one.

The simplest is to leave the yarn in the shed where it ends. Wind more yarn onto your shuttle, insert the shuttle into the same shed, overlapping the new yarn over the end of the old one for about ½" to 1". See Figure 565. However, if this overlap shows too much in the cloth, make the change at the edge of the warp. Read on.

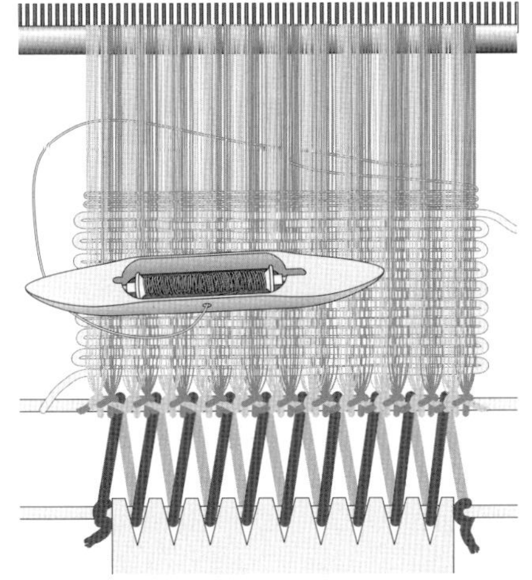

Fig. 565

For some wefts, for example, large wefts or those of a different color, changing in the middle of the shed might show up too much. In that case, you need to make the switch to the new weft at an edge of the cloth. What you'll do, is tuck the end of the old weft into the shed it has just come out of. To do it so the weft does not unweave itself, take the tail around the outside warp thread. Then, put the tail into the shed for an inch or so as seen in Figure 566. If the tail is longer than 1", cut it to about an inch before you tuck it into the shed. Start the new weft in the ***next*** shed and tuck in the tail of the new weft by taking it around the outside warp thread and placing it in the new shed as you did with the tail of the old weft. See the illustration. If the yarn is very thick, start the new weft on the opposite edge of the cloth to avoid making a visible build-up on one edge.

Fig. 566

End your project

Repeat the weaving process until you can't weave any more or your project is the desired length—in this case, 70". At this point, weave two or three rows of scrap yarn; it will help keep the last rows in place while the project is being taken off of the loom.

Remove the project from the loom

Cut the warp off from the back of the loom, at the back apron rod. Do it by cutting the warp loops on the apron rod—that is, cut the threads as far back from the heddle as you can. You can cut all the threads at once. Pull the cut threads out of the heddle. Unwind the fabric from around the front beam and untie or cut off the warp from the front apron rod. If you want fringe, untie the knots rather than cutting the threads.

You will need to take out your scrap yarn and secure the yarns from unraveling with knots, fringe, or stitching. Read how in the section, "Protect the Last Weft," on page 138. How to make fringes begins on page 145.

Wash the cloth

The final step (and to many weavers, the most satisfying) is to wash your project. Usually, I gently wash my projects by hand in lukewarm water with a dishwashing detergent. You can damage the cloth if you use too hot water or squeeze the cloth too hard while it is wet or damp. So, gently swish the cloth in the water and after rinsing, gently roll up the cloth in a bath towel. Again, gently, press on the towel a bit—just to remove the excess water so it isn't sopping wet when you hang it up to dry. Do not squeeze the cloth in any way because unsightly permanent wrinkles can be formed. Hang the cloth to dry over a shower rod. If you feel the cloth will stretch by hanging it over one rod, rig up some system of towel bars or chair backs so you can drape the cloth over more than one rod to support the weight while drying. You may or may not choose to iron the cloth lightly. Read more specifics about washing beginning on page 143.

Cut off the tails of yarns at the side edges flush to the cloth.
Now, you're finished!!

More Information

Future projects

Experiment with yarns and colors

You can experiment with different colors and yarns, and make more scarves. If you use the same size yarns, you can use the information in this chapter, with no other changes. For information about how to plan projects using other sizes of yarns, read about warp and weft calculations below.

Weave a variation of rep weave and log cabin

Since rigid heddle looms have two sheds, you can weave other two-shed techniques. Two examples are found in this book. A Variation of Rep Weave is explained beginning on page 234. Log Cabin instructions begin on page 241. In both of these weaves, you would thread your loom alternating dark and light colors as in the instructions. However, you will weave with two sheds instead of the four shown.

For the variation of rep weave you can weave just one block—using your two sheds for shafts one and two in the drafts. Drafting is explained in the chapter on drafting, beginning on page 195.

Log cabin can be woven with just two sheds instead of the four shown in Figure 479, on page 242. You just thread your rigid heddle loom alternating colors. Figure 480 on page 243 shows how you can change the pattern by how you organize the light and dark threads.

In both weaves, read what to do with the wefts when weaving.

Hand-manipulated weaves are perfect for rigid heddle looms. See page 357.

Project ideas

See page 297 for a list of suggestions for projects to make.

More complex weaves

Read below about 2-heddle weaving. See the suggested reading list on page 348.

Check the Internet for blogs and articles.

Calculations for planning future projects

Note: More detailed information and worksheets are found in the chapter on planning projects, beginning on page 285.

The first step in any weaving project is choosing the yarn and calculating the amount of yarn needed for the project. Below, is a simple way to compute the length of the warp as well as the number of warp threads per inch. Both of these calculations are needed to determine the amount of warp yarn needed for this project. Following that, the amount of yarn needed for the weft can be determined.

1. Determine the length of the warp

First, determine the length and width of the finished scarf you would like to weave. You need to add to the length of the finished piece, loom waste (approximately 24"), take up, and shrinkage (about 10 percent each). See pages 290 and 291.

For example, if you would like to have your finished scarf be 70" long, each warp thread would need to be 108" in length. See calculations at right.

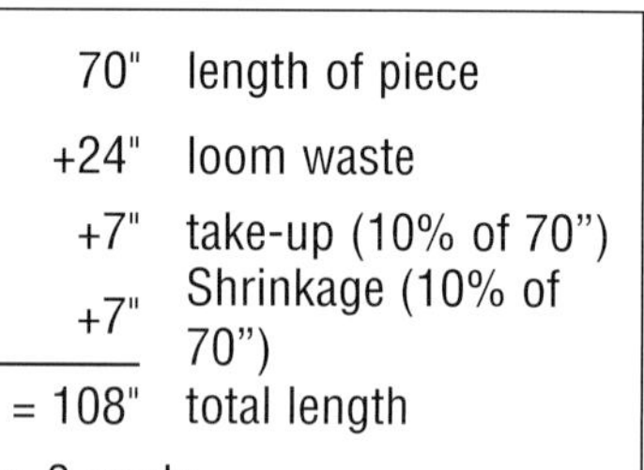

70"	length of piece
+24"	loom waste
+7"	take-up (10% of 70")
+7"	Shrinkage (10% of 70")
= 108"	total length
or 3 yards	

Calculation for warp length

2. Determine the number of warps in an inch (epi)

Next, you need to determine the number of warps per inch (weavers say, "ends per inch or epi"). The simplest way to calculate is to wind the yarn you want to use as warp around a ruler for 1", leaving no spaces between wraps. See Figure 567. Then, count the number of wraps in this 1" and divide by two for the number of threads (ends) per inch. Figure 568 shows why you divide by two. You must space the warps enough apart so that the wefts have room to show in the cloth as well as the warps.

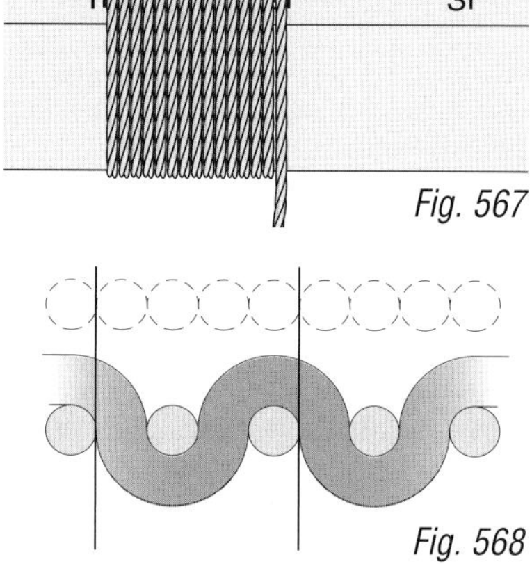

Fig. 567

Fig. 568

Choose the heddle (Figure 546 on page 328 and repeated here) with the number of dents per inch closest to this number. (Dents refers to the number of both slots and holes in one inch on the heddle.) In our example, the warp uses an 8- or 10-dent-per-inch-heddle.

For example, say there are 16 threads wrapped in one inch on the ruler in Figure 567. You would want to use 8 warp threads in an inch. The heddle you would choose would be an 8-dent heddle.

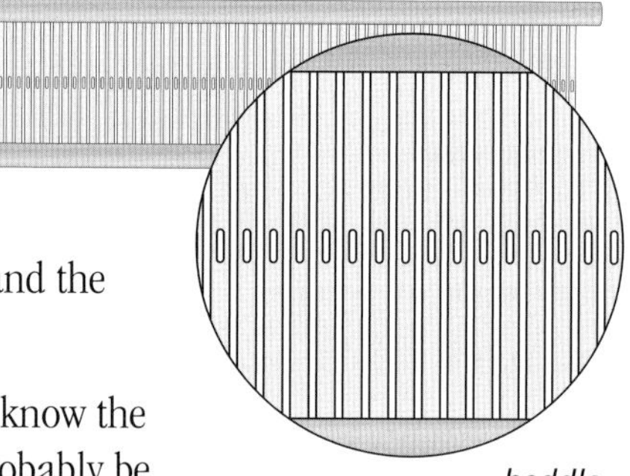

heddle

For a 10-dent heddle, the number of ends per inch would be 10 and the number of wraps on the ruler would be 20.

In our example, I suggest that either size will do because I don't know the exact size your yarn will be—and, in actuality, either size will probably be just fine for your project. Generally, you start out with one size heddle, and you can use a range of sizes of yarns in that heddle. Of course, if the yarn is too fat to slide through the holes and slots without abrasion, you'll need to get another heddle with fewer dents per inch because it will have larger holes and slots with fewer threads per inch.

These sizes are common for use with knitting yarns and with what is considered "worsted weight," as shown on page 12. (Note: Heddles with 12 dents per inch are commonly available for thinner yarns.)

3. Determine how much yarn you need for the warp

Multiply the width of your planned weaving by the epi. to get the total number of warp yarns. In our example: 8 or 10 epi. x 6" weaving width = 48 or 60 total threads of warp yarn.

Finally, to figure how many yards of warp you will need, multiply the total number of warp threads by the length of warp (in yards). Here are two examples of calculations for the scarf project.

In the first example, if your heddle has 8 dents per inch you'll have decided there will be 48 total warp threads. Multiply the 48 threads by 3 (the length of the warp in yards—see the calculation chart on page 342). You'll need a total of 144 yards for the warp.

In the second example, if your heddle has 10 dents per inch, you will have calculated that there are to be 60 warp threads. Multiply the 60 threads by 3 (again, the length of the warp in yards). You will need 180 yards for the warp.

Do you see that you need more yarn for the warp if there are more threads per inch? In our example, I suggest that you can use either an 8 or 10-dent heddle. I allowed enough yarn in the directions so you would have enough regardless of which one you used.

4. Determine how much yarn is needed for the weft

The project described uses a balanced weave where the warp and weft show equally. However, you will need more yarn for the warp than the weft to allow for the loom waste. Loom waste refers to the warp yarn that cannot be woven into cloth. It occurs at the front and also at the back of the loom. In the front of the loom, it is the yarn needed to tie the warps onto the front apron rod. The waste at the back is approximately the distance from the heddle to the back apron rod. This "waste" can, however, become fringe.

The amount of yarn needed for the weft is the same as for the warp, minus the loom waste. For our example, using 60 warp threads for 3 yards on a 10 dent heddle, it comes to 156 yards for the weft (180 – 24=156). For ease of purchasing yarn, some weavers recommend buying the same amount of yarn for both the warp and weft. It will allow extra yarn for repairs, waste and uneven packing of the weft.

Detailed information for other weaves and yarns is in the chapter, *Sett,* beginning on page 263.

Longer warps

For longer warps you can use the warping peg method. Directions for this method begin on page 332. You can also measure out the threads on a warping board. For this method, follow the directions below.

Measuring on a warping board

1. Follow the directions for measuring the warp on a warping board on pages 157 and 158.
2. Make the ties described on pages 159 and 160.

3. ***Do not cut the end of the warp as seen on page 161.*** Chain the warp as shown on page 162.
4. Put lease sticks (page 330) into the crosses as shown here in Figures 569a and 569b.
5. Tie the lease sticks together 1" apart through the holes at their ends, as in Figure 570a.

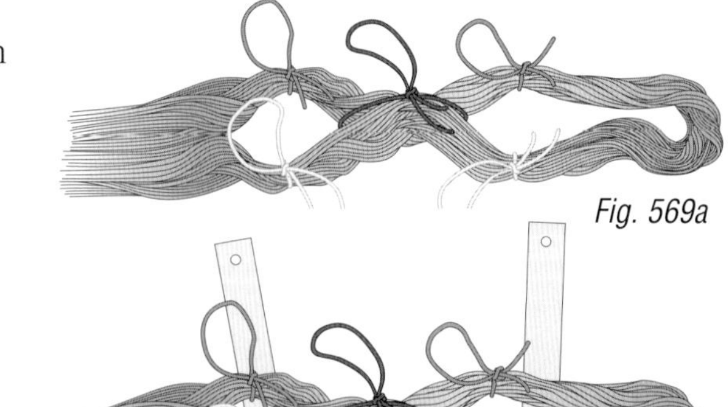

Fig. 569a

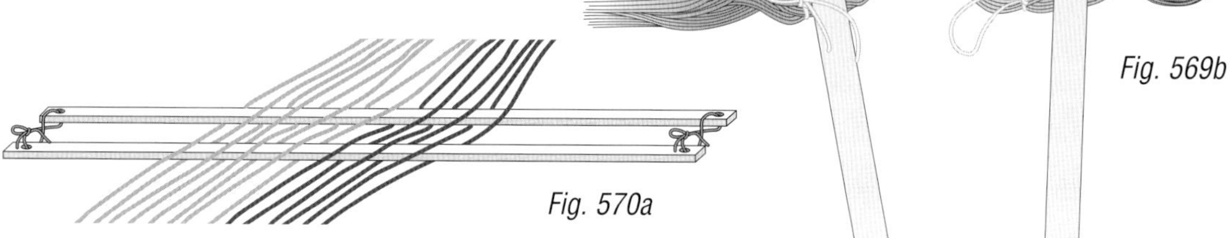

Fig. 569b

Fig. 570a

Thread the heddle

1. Sit at the back of the loom with the warp chain at the front of the loom.
2. Put the heddle in the neutral position.
3. Untie the ties at the cross and spread the warp out on the lease sticks.

Fig. 570b

4. Now, you'll work with the loops at the end of the warp. See Figure 570b.
5. Thread the slots in the heddle by pulling each warp loop from the chain through each slot in the heddle. It means there will be two threads in each slot. Center the warp in the heddle as usual as described on page 333.

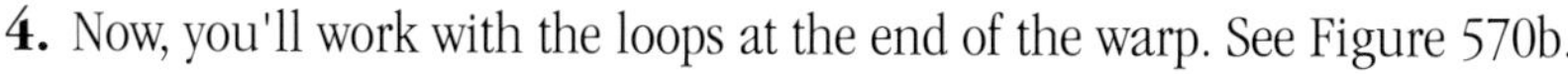

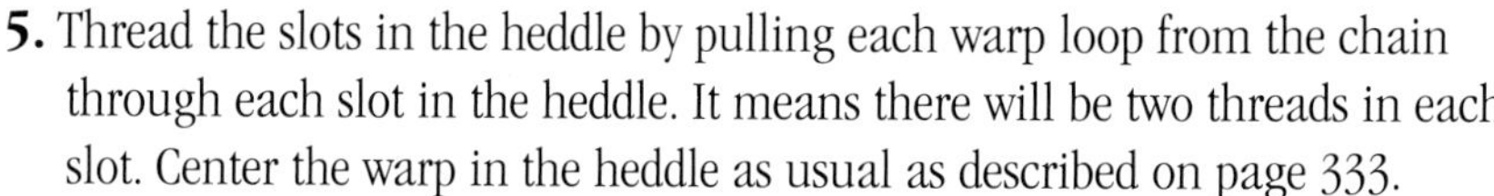

Wind the warp on the warp beam

1. Put an end stick (page 330) in all the loops you just threaded in the heddle, as seen in Figure 570c. Tie a string to hold the loops on the stick as seen in the illustration.
2. Tie the end stick (holding the warp loops) to the back apron rod as shown in Figure 571.
3. Now, wind up the warp on the warp beam. See Steps 11 and 12 on page 334.

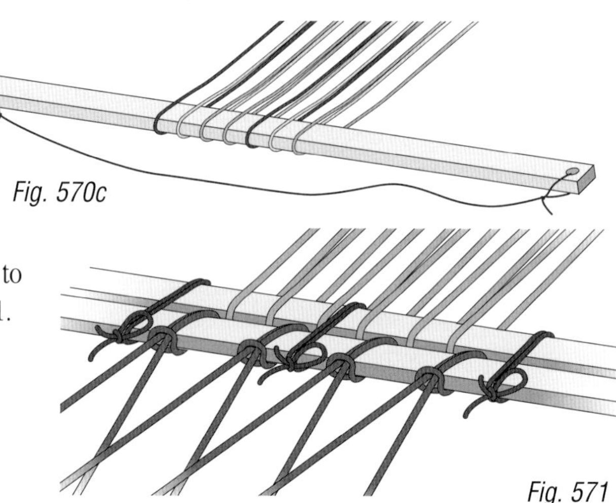

Fig. 570c

Fig. 571

Thread the heddle and tie on the warp

Follow Steps 13 through 16 on pages 334 and 335.

Looms with two heddles

Figures 572a and 572b show a loom with two heddles.

The heddles are to be threaded in a special way. See the sidebar on page 346. Weaving along is like weaving with a single heddle only with two heddles, there are more options for making the sheds, often by manipulating the threads by hand with pick-up sticks. (See page 357.) (For weavers who know about shaft looms, it does not mean you can weave as though there were 4 shafts.)

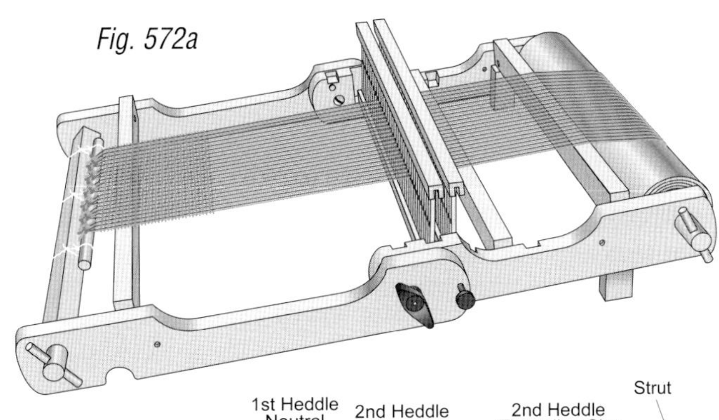

Fig. 572a

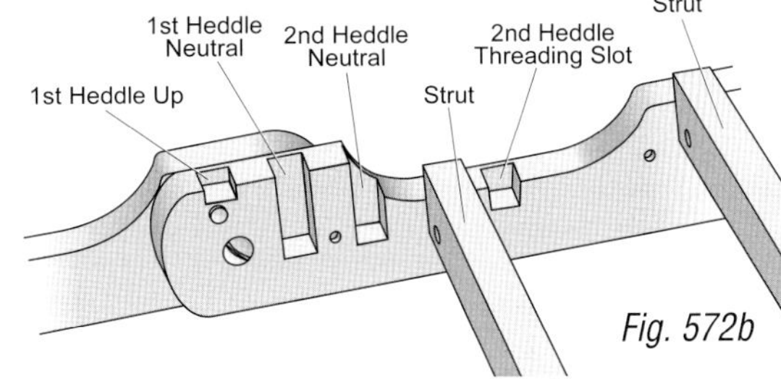

Fig. 572b

For basic plain weave, which interlaces the threads over one, under one, just as for single heddle weaving, the up shed position of the heddles is seen in Figure 573. The down shed is shown in Figure 574a.

Notice that both heddles go up or down together. For the down shed there are no notches in the loom shown here; the heddles slide under the heddle block as seen in Figure 574b. (Notice in the illustration that the heddles are lowered and the bottom of the front heddle can be seen under the curved part of the heddle block itself, rather than being in a specific notch. Figure 572b shows the curved lower part of the heddle block where the heddles are placed for the down shed.)

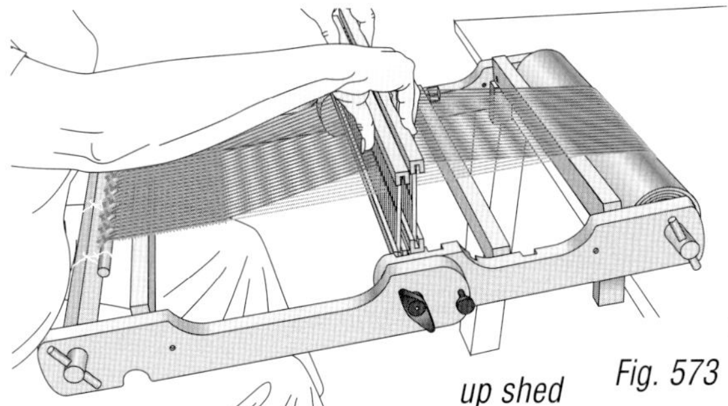

up shed Fig. 573

How to hold the heddles for beating in the wefts is seen in Figure 575. Hold the heddles in that manner when making the sheds as well. Figure 576 shows the heddles in neutral position. Notice that there is no shed.

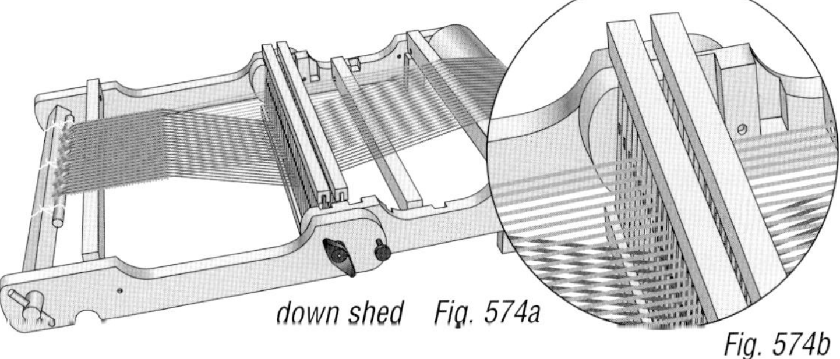

down shed Fig. 574a

Fig. 574b

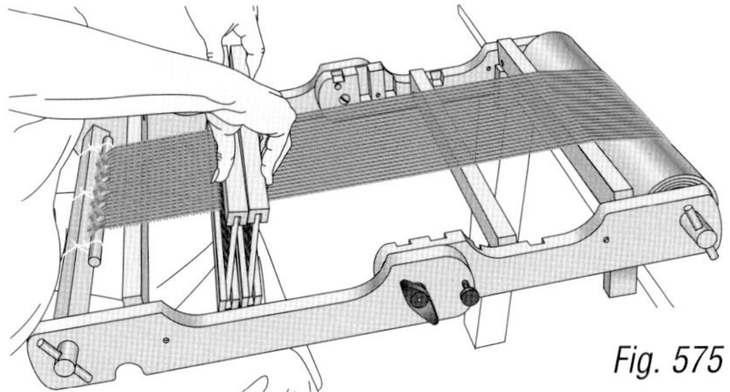

Fig. 575

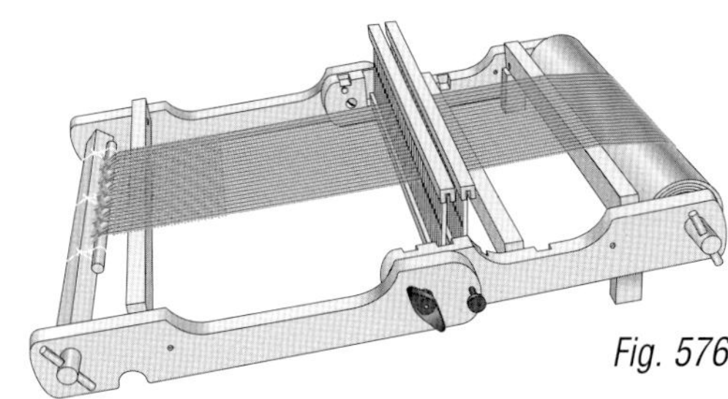

Fig. 576

When to use 2 heddles

You can use thinner warp threads and get more threads per inch in the warp with two heddles. In other words, with two 10-dent heddles you can get 20 threads in an inch (20 epi).

More textures and patterns are possible. Especially, read articles and blogs on the Internet and see the suggested reading list on page 348.

How to use 2 heddles for plain weave

You weave plain weave just as you do with a single heddle except that you raise and lower both heddles together to create the up and down sheds.
See the illustrations on page 345.

Threading a Two-heddle Loom

There are other ways than the one described below to thread 2 heddles. This one will make plain weave.

Attention!! Each thread will eventually end up going through both heddles!!

Thread the heddles

With the front of the loom facing you, place one heddle in the first heddle's ***neutral*** notch. See Figure 572b on page 345.

Thread the heddles this way:

Step One. With the first heddle in place, thread one thread in a hole and three threads in a slot. Repeat across the warp. See Figure 577a. Take the threads in order from the lease sticks as seen in Figures 184 and 185 on page 70.

Step Two. After the heddle is completely threaded, wind your warp onto the back beam in the regular way (page 334). Stop winding when the cut ends are about 10" from the heddle.

Step Three. Read this step carefully. ***Move the threaded heddle to the second heddle threading slot*** (now to be called heddle #2) and then, place the remaining heddle in the first heddle neutral location. This heddle becomes heddle #1. See Figure 572b on page 345.

Step Four. Also read this step very carefully.

As you thread the new heddle #1 (now the front heddle), think in terms of 4-thread groupings. You will be distributing the threads you already have threaded in heddle #2 so each thread will ***also*** be threaded into heddle #1. In other words, each thread will be threaded in both heddles.

First, consider the threads from the first hole and slot (4 total) in the back heddle (#2). Do not take the threads ***out*** of the hole and slot, just grasp them together for now.

Find the corresponding hole in heddle #1 and place ***the hole*** thread and one of the slot threads in the slot to the right of the corresponding hole. Now, two of the four threads in the group have been threaded into the front heddle.

Look at the two threads remaining in the slot and thread one of them into the hole in the front heddle. Thread the remaining thread in the slot to the ***left*** of that hole. (Figure 577b) If you look at the illustration, it will be clear.

That takes care of threading the 4 threads in the group. Consider the next group of 4 threads (one in a hole and 3 in the slot next to it). Thread them as above. Figure 577c shows 2 groups threaded in the two heddles.

For clarity, dark and light threads are shown instead of all one color of warp threads.

There will always be one thread in a hole and three in a slot in the back heddle. When completely finished, there will also be three threads in each slot and one in each hole in the front heddle. Check your work as you go. This threading makes sure that you get the two plain weave sheds. If you follow the dark threads in the illustration, you can see that each one goes into a hole and the light ones only go into slots. This insures that when the heddles are moved together they will make the sheds for plain weave.

Step Five. After the front heddle (#1) has been threaded, tie on to the front beam in the regular way. See Step 16 on page 335.

Adapted from instructions from the Schacht Spindle Co. booklet for the "Flip Folding Rigid Heddle Loom." For more information, go to *www.schachtspindle.com* or email: *info@schachtspindle.com*

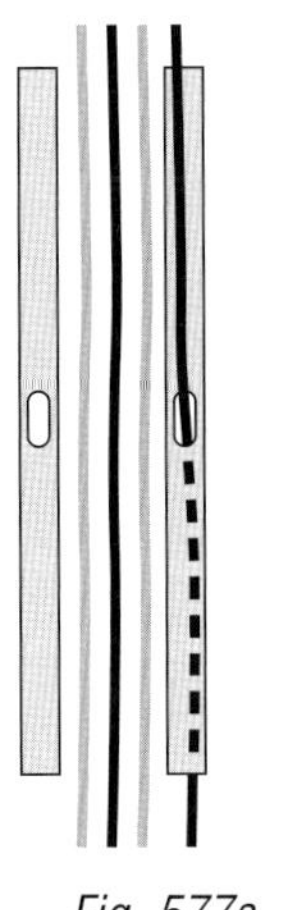

Fig. 577a

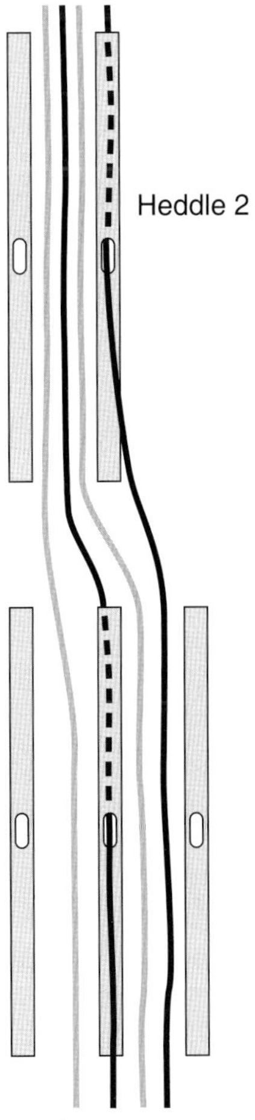

Fig. 577b

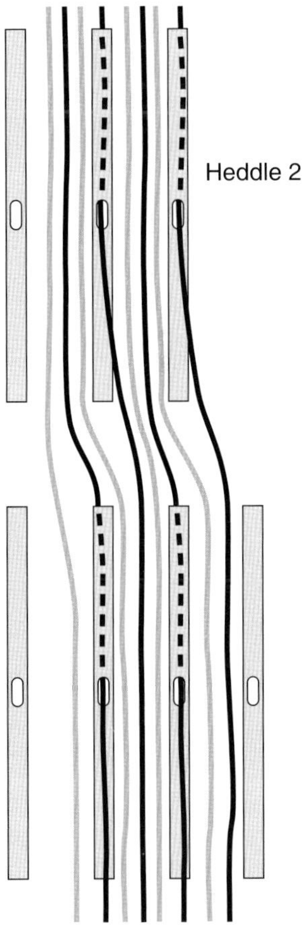

Fig. 577c

Suggested reading for rigid heddle weaving

Davenport, Betty Linn. ***Hands On Rigid Heddle Weaving***. Loveland, Colorado: Interweave Press, 1987.

Davenport, Betty Linn. ***Textures and Patterns for the Rigid Heddle Loom***. Battle Ground, Washington: published by the author, distributed by Fine Fiber Press, 2008, revised edition.

Gibson, Liz. ***Weaving Made Easy***. Loveland, Colorado: Interweave Press, 2008.

Hart, Rowena. ***The Ashford Book of Rigid Heddle Weaving***. Ashburton, New Zealand: Ashford Handicrafts, 2002.

Howard, Sarah and Kendrick, Elisabeth. ***Creative Weaving: Beautiful Fabrics With a Simple Loom***. Ashville, North Carolina: Lark Books, 2008.

Iwamura, Misae. ***Plain Weaving: Try Creating Original Textiles Using Plain Weaving***. Tokyo, Japan: Bunko Publishing, 2002. English translation distributed in the U.S. by Habu Textiles.

Mitchell, Syne. ***WeaveZine***. Warp Thread Media, www.weavezine.com.

Patrick, Jane. ***The Weaver's Idea Book***. Loveland, Colorado: Interweave Press, 2010.

15 Knots

I have a lot of emotions connected with knots—frustration in untying snarls and mistakes, elation of tying a square knot correctly, pride in learning a new knot, and confidence in knowing when a knot is a granny or a square knot. Writing this chapter has elicited all these emotions, but now there's a great feeling of excitement to share my insights for each knot.

In this chapter are the knots I use every day. They are grouped by their similarities, because I think they are easier to learn that way. Learning a few knots that are related helps to reinforce previous information because you use it to make the next new knot. In my second book, *Warping Your Loom & Tying on New Warps*, I show more knots for special occasions.

In weaving, untying a knot is as important as tying it, and the knots that untie easily have a strong advantage. It never fails that the time I tie a knot that can't be undone is the time I've made a mistake, and it must be untied. Then, it's a lot of frustration picking it out or cutting and beginning over again.

Learn to make the knots with two thick cords

I suggest you get two lengths of thick cord and try the knots along with the text and illustrations. I used a flexible rope about ¼" in diameter, but you could also use clothes-line rope. My rope is soft and flexible and not scratchy. I soaked one rope in a pot of strong tea to make it darker and designated it as the "worker" cord whenever one cord seemed to be manipulated more than the other. I hope you have fun!

Which cord is the standing end and which is the tail?

Often, one of the cords is called the standing end, and the other the tail. The standing end is the cord that is very long, which can be attached to something, for example, a spool. That cord's end is not available for making the knot. The tail is simply the part of a cord near the tip, or cut end.

Capsizing, or upsetting, a knot

When a knot capsizes, it loosens or flips inside out. This is sometimes called "upsetting" the knot.

Slip, Overhand, and Half-Bow Knots

These three knots are related and these relationships can help you learn them. A slip knot is an overhand knot with the tail taken ***partially*** through as a loop. An overhand knot is a slip knot with the tail brought all the way through the loop. And a half bow is the beginning part of a shoelace knot with a slip knot on top.

Slip knot Figure 578 on the next page.

A slip knot is a temporary knot that secures a single thread or groups of threads. Its greatest asset is that it can be quickly untied with a jerk with one hand. It's often used to tie groups of warp ends after they have been threaded in the heddles so they won't slip out. Every weaver should know the slip knot because it is used so often—whenever you want to secure something temporarily. It's my favorite knot, and it's the one I almost always automatically tie—just in case I'll need to undo it.

To make a slip knot: To make the first loop, you can use either the tail or the standing end, whichever seems easier to tie in the situation. In this example I'm using the standing end.

1. Make a loop. (I take the standing end over the back of my left hand or over a few fingers and cross the standing end on *top* of the tail of the string.) Hold where the threads cross in a pinch between your thumb and forefinger.
2. Reach through the loop with the right forefinger and thumb and grasp the standing end and pull it through the loop, so that it makes a loop within the first loop. (If you were to begin the knot with the tail making the first loop, and the tail were being drawn through as the second loop, make sure you *pull the tail only part way through,* not completely through. If you pulled the tail through, you wouldn't have the second loop.)
3. Be sure to tighten the knot until you feel it bite. To do that you pull the loop and the tail in opposite directions.

To release the knot: Just jerk on the end you made the loops with, in this case the standing end.

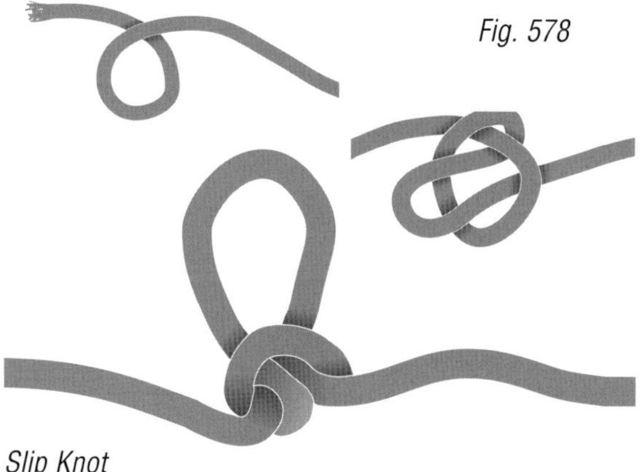

Fig. 578

Slip Knot

Overhand knot Figure 579

To make an overhand knot: Start it the same way you start a slip knot using two tails to make the loop. Make a loop with the tails of the strings. Reach through the loop and pull the tails completely through the loop. To tighten the knot, pull the tails and the standing ends in opposite directions. (Remember, a slip knot can use either the tail or the standing end to start the first loop. With an overhand knot you must begin with the tails.)

This is my next favorite knot. Overhand knots are very secure and permanent because they tighten under tension and are very hard to untie. They are good when tying slippery yarns or two different types of yarns together, or when lacing a warp to the cloth apron rod. They are often used to knot fringe at the end of woven pieces so the last rows of wefts can't come out. It's also used when a lump is needed in a yarn to keep it from pulling out of a hole or slot.

Fig. 579

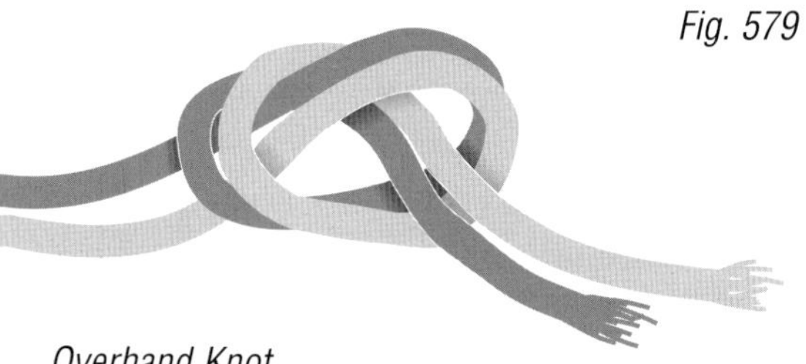

Overhand Knot

Half-bow knot Figure 580 on facing page

A half bow is a bow (shoelace knot) with only one loop. It is very fast to tie, secure, and pulls out with a jerk. You can tie two strings together so they are under tension, just like when you tie a bow around a package. Use a half bow anytime you'd use a bow but want to make it faster and easier to pull out. I use the half bow to tie the crosses when warping and when repairing a broken warp end when weaving. It also can be used on top of a surgeon's knot when tying the warp on to the cloth apron rod.

To make a half bow: I usually tie it with a single string, not with groups of threads.

1. Tie the first part of a shoelace knot. (Figure 589 on page 356.)
2. Make a slip knot on top of that: First make a loop by crossing one of the tails over the other. Then reach through the loop and draw the top tail partially up through the loop making another loop within the first loop. Remember, don't pull the tail completely through but make a loop instead.
3. Tighten the knot by pulling the loop and the other tail in opposite directions.
4. To release the knot, pull on the tail that made the loop (usually the shorter one).

Fig. 580

Half-bow Knot

There is a slower way to make the half bow. You make it like you make a bow except, instead of pulling a loop through for the second half of the bow, pull the string totally through. See bow or shoelace knot on page 356.

Surgeon's, Lark's Head, and Snitch Knots

Most of the knots in this section use the first part of a shoelace knot. The snitch knot uses that plus a lark's head.

Surgeon's knot Figure 581

This is the knot I usually use when tying 1" groups of the warp on to the cloth apron rod. It's fast to make, easy to adjust and has more bite than a half knot (the beginning of a shoelace knot). Usually, the surgeon's knot is enough for the job, but for slippery threads, I tie slip knots on top of the knots (resulting in half bows) after the warps are tensioned evenly.

To make a surgeon's knot:

1. Tie the beginning part of a shoelace knot, but before you tighten it, while the knot is still loose, take the tail you were working with into the loop and out once more. This gives the knot enough bite to hold, yet be adjustable.
2. Tighten the knot by pulling the tails in opposite directions.
3. To adjust the warp tension, pull on one of the tails, and the knot capsizes or loosens. Hold on to the tails and pull the knot away from you to tighten the warp, then pull on the tails to tighten the knot down again.
4. Take the tails and complete the knot as seen in the illustration.

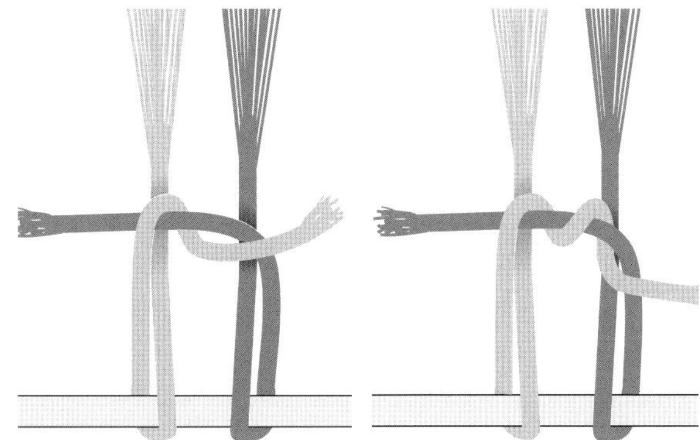

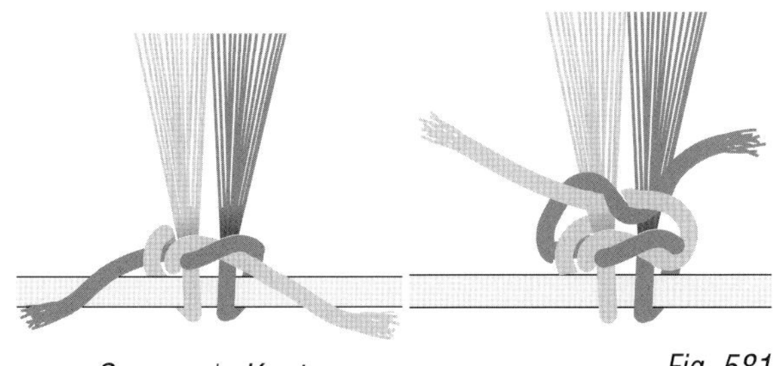

Surgeon's Knot

Fig. 581

Lark's head knot Figure 582

The lark's head is an enormously useful knot and quick to make once you've mastered the thumb and finger pinch action. It's great to use when you have an intact circle with no ends available, such as a rubber band, or

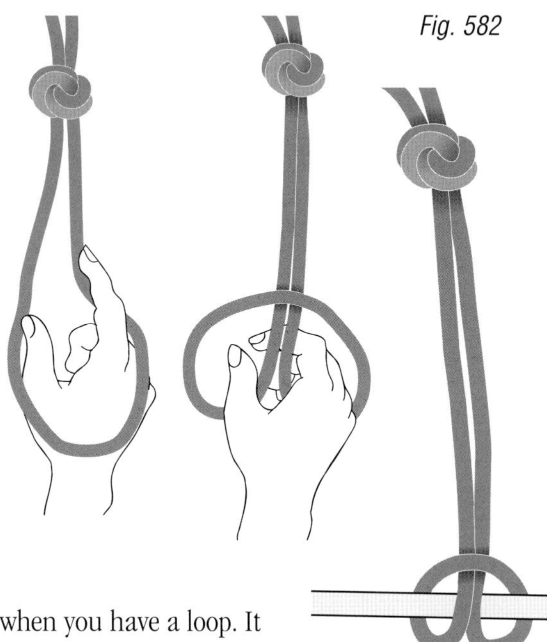

Fig. 582

Lark's Head Knot

when you have a loop. It also can be made with a length of string folded in half (with two tails). It's used to attach things—what is to be attached is encircled and held secure in the knot's loop, which draws up and holds the object tightly. It is extremely secure and can't come undone. In fact, practically whenever a loop is involved, the lark's head is useful. Rather than list all its uses, I'll just urge you to learn to make it.

To make a lark's head knot:

There are two ways to tie this knot, depending on the situation: when you have a loop, or when you have a length of string you can fold in half to make a loop.

Method 1, when you have a length of string.

Fold the string in half and take the tails around a stick, rod, or a ring, and bring the tails through the loop.

Method 2, when you have a loop or a circle.

1. Hold tension on the tails of the loop or the side of the circle with the left hand.
2. Insert your right thumb and forefinger into the loop, spread them wide apart to spread open the loop.
3. Take your finger and thumb around the taut parts of the string until your finger and thumb touch each other.
4. Keeping the finger and thumb together in a pinch, ease the taut strings into and through the original loop as the loop folds over your pinch.
6. Put a stick in where your thumb and forefinger are. The loop can be made large to hold a big stick if needed, such as when you put a warp onto the kitestick.

To release the knot: Simply take out the object that the knot is looped around.

Snitch knot Figure 583.

A snitch knot is very handy and is especially good for tying heavy cords that can be adjusted. A common use is to tie treadles to the loom—the snitch knot saves fingernails

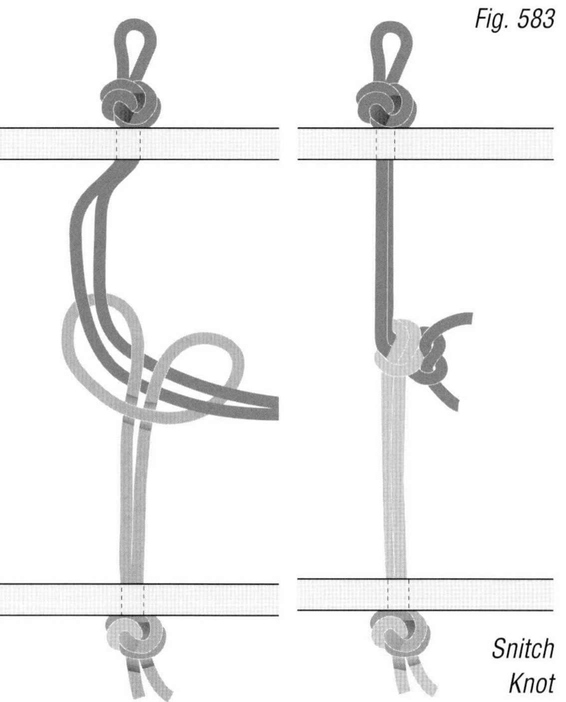

Fig. 583

Snitch Knot

and frustration when adjusting is needed. The knot has a simple concept: it's made in two parts. A loop is made into a lark's head knot, and another cord's two tails are put into the lark's head knot and tied like the first part of a shoelace knot. The shoelace knot can't pull out of the lark's head's grasp when tension is put on the cords. But when tension is slack, the shoelace knot's cords can slide inside the lark's head's grip to adjust the overall length of the cord. It takes time to prepare the cords but they can be used over and over again. A loop is needed for each knot and two tails of another cord.

To make a snitch knot when tying up treadles: Make sure that the cords' anchoring knots in the loom and treadles are big enough so they never pull through the holes in the wood. I prefer to put the tails on the loom and the loops on the treadles. The reason is that if the loops are attached to the loom above, they can cause trouble by "looping" themselves onto unwanted treadles. However, if the tails dangle from the loom, they can't hook onto anything.

1. Make a lark's head in the loop by folding it back on itself. See Figure 582.
2. Pass the tails through the lark's head loop and tie the first part of a shoelace knot with the tails. Don't add the second part of a square or granny knot—it's strong enough if you've tied it with both ends taking the stress of the knot equally.
3. To adjust it, pull on one of the tails of the shoelace knot and the knot is easily undone even if it has been under tension for years. Slide the tails in the lark's head loop to shorten or lengthen the cords. Then, tighten the shoelace knot. It's faster to shorten, so start with the cords too long and shorten as needed.

To untie a snitch knot: Pull on one tail to loosen the shoelace knot. Then undo that knot and slide the tails out of the lark's head.

Half Hitch and Double Half Hitch

These knots both use the half-hitch knot and can be made when you have only one tail for tying.

Half hitch and double half hitch Figure 584.

Fig. 584

Half hitch

The half hitch isn't enough to stand on its own as a knot, but two of them (double half hitch) or even three are very secure. I use a double half hitch to make a loop when putting the first thread on the warping peg. And I use it often when I have only one tail—like to tie one end of a string to something.

To make the half hitch:

1. Using the tail as the worker, bend the end of the string around the object you're tying the string to. Hold the standing end of the string and the tail taut by pulling them against the object.
2. Take the tail and loop it over the standing end of the string. Be sure to go *over* the string and make a loop.
3. Bring the tail around behind the standing end and through your loop.
4. Tighten by pulling the tail and the standing end in opposite directions. You can adjust the size of the loop or you can slide the knot up against the object.

Continue to make a double half hitch:

5. Make another half hitch in the same way (take the tail over and then behind to make another loop and take the tail through the loop). You can make three half hitches for a triple half hitch.

To loosen a double half hitch: Pull on the tail to slightly capsize the knot, which loosens it.

Weaver's Knot

The weaver's knot's characteristics—non-slip and a quick release—are valued not only by weavers but by climbers and sailors, too. The knot can be used whenever two cords are tied together, or to fasten one cord to a loom part. Because it can't be tied under tension, it is a good knot to use when measuring the warp, when you have a slack thread to work with. It can be tied with short ends, but not with very slippery threads, such as silk. It's slower to work than a square knot, but more secure and smaller. So, if a square knot doesn't hold, try a weaver's knot. Even so, some threads aren't compatible enough with each other, or are too slippery to tie either a square or a weaver's knot. An overhand knot can do the job or Jim's fisherman's knot on page 165 in my second book, *Warping Your Loom and Tying on New Warps*..

There are several names associated with the weaver's knot, such as bowline and sheet bend. I found five different methods for tying it, not including the double weaver's knot. The methods looked different, too, because some were shown from one side, and others were seen from the "back." Some resulted in the working thread being a loop and some with the non-working end ending up as a loop.

Two methods are shown here. If you're like me, you best remember the first way you learned. But try to be receptive if someone shows you another way—you may prefer it.

For more methods to tie the weaver's knot as well as other useful knots, see *Warping Your Loom and Tying on New Warps*.

Weaver's knot: the rabbit hole story
Figure 585.

By remembering the following climbers' story, you can always remember this version of the weaver's knot. Imagine a rabbit hole with a tree growing right behind it. Every day the rabbit jumps out of his nest, runs around the tree, and pops back into the hole. Think of the rabbit hole as a length of cord using the short tail end to form a loop. The "tree" (or tail of the cord) ends up behind the "hole" (loop).

Another cord follows the rabbit's daily path. This cord comes up through the loop, runs around the cord tree, and pops back into the loop.

To tighten, pull equally on both standing ends in opposite directions. Release in the same way as for all weaver's knots. (See page 356.)

Fig. 585

Weaver's Knot

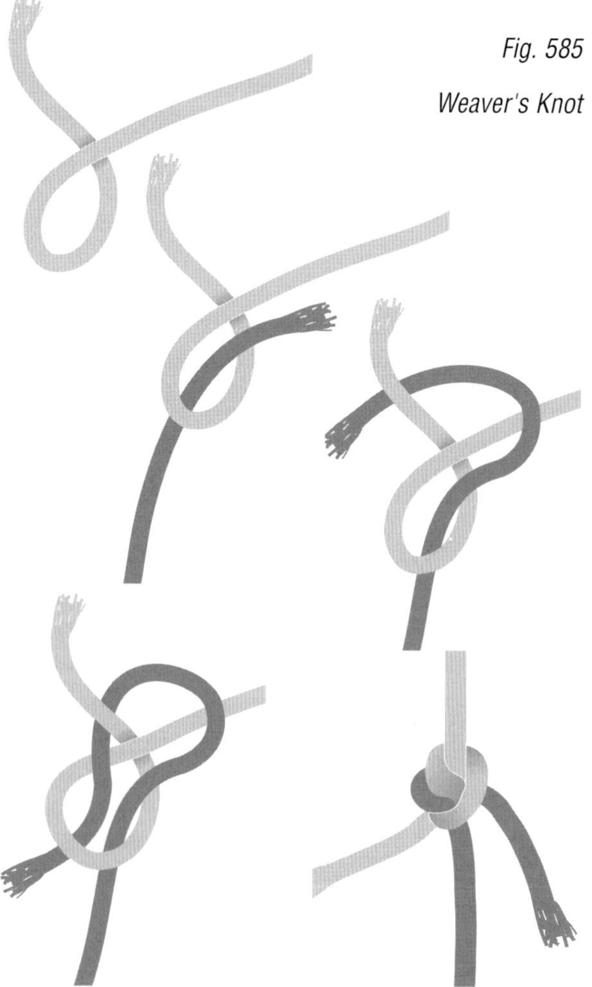

Weaver's knot: made with "ears"
(Figures 586 a-d).

The worker thread should be the longer of the two. In repairing a broken warp, the new thread (being longer) would be the worker, and the existing end would be the non-worker.

1. Cross the two tails, left over right, and hold the crossing part between the thumb and first finger of the left hand. The "ears" are the ends of the tails that should stand up straight (a).
2. The right standing end is the worker thread (the lower right part of the thread in Figure 586a). Take it around over the thumb and pass it behind the left-hand *ear*—just the left one—and bring it to the front between the two ears (b).
3. Drop the worker. Take the right-hand ear, bend it down into the circle, and place it under the thumb so it is pinched by the thumb along with the thread already under the thumb. The bent thread is actually bending on itself and held to itself in the pinch (c).
4. To tighten, continue holding the thread bent on itself in the pinch between the thumb and index finger of the left hand *while* pulling on the remaining standing end with the right hand (d).

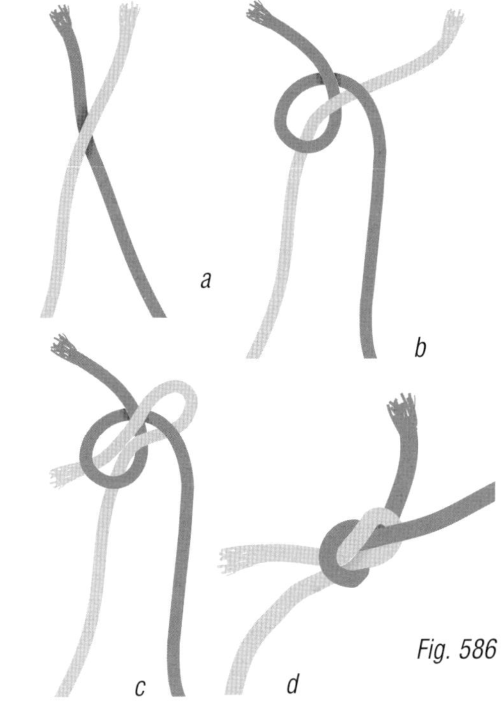

Fig. 586
Weaver's Knot with "ears"

Double Weaver's Knot

Just for fun, I'm including the double weaver's knot. Start with what I call the ***"ears"*** method of tying the weaver's knot (see above). The ***double weaver's knot*** (Figures 587 a-c) is a regular weaver's knot with an additional step. Repeat steps a and b as described in the "ears" method. As soon as you have the thread between the ears (b), take it once around the *right-hand ear as well* (c). Then do the same last steps: take the right-hand ear down under the thumb (d) and tighten by pulling on the right standing end (e).

The double can also be undone like the regular weaver's knots (Figure 588 on the next page).

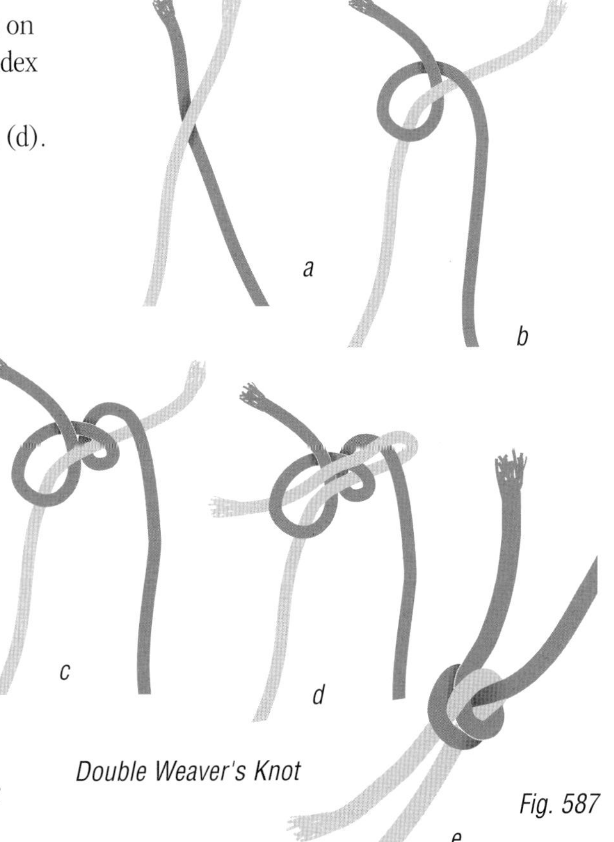

Double Weaver's Knot
Fig. 587

Undo Weaver's Knot and Bow/Shoelace

How to undo any weaver's knot and know if you've tied it correctly

The key to knowing you've tied the weaver's knot correctly is to be able to release or undo it. To undo it, you want to straighten out the thread that makes the "U" in the completed knot. No matter which way you tie it, there is one thread in a U-shape and the other thread winding itself around the first. Pull on both ends of that "U" thread—in opposite directions—to unbend it and straighten it out. The wound-around portion can be slipped right off the straightened thread. You have two fresh threads when you're through. See Figure 588.

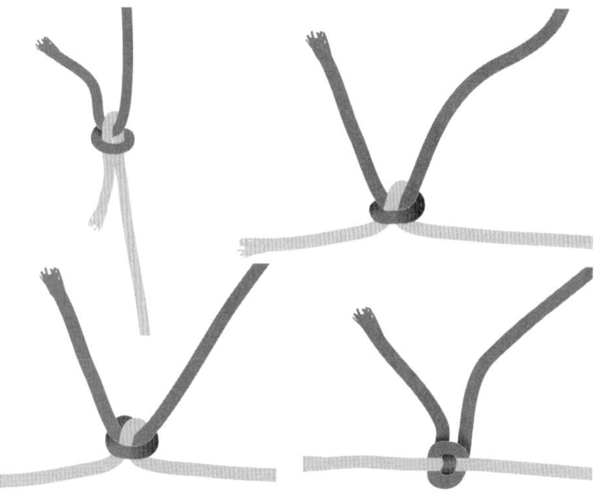

Fig. 588

Bow or shoelace knot Figure 589.

I am surprised at the number of people who have trouble tying the common shoelace knot. It's used whenever you have two tails to tie together securely. It won't pull out, yet it's easy to undo. For example, when you want to tie a string around something, use the two cut ends of the string to make a bow.

There are many ways to tie a bow. Here's the way my babysitter taught me when I was 5 years old.

To make a bow:

1. Tie a half knot, the beginning of a shoelace knot.
2. Form a loop with one of the tails (I usually use the shorter tail for the first loop) and pinch it tightly between your thumb and index finger.
3. Take the other tail across the top of your thumb and behind the first loop.
4. Using your index finger, push the tail through the space where your thumb is, forming a second loop. Remove your thumb as you form the loop.
5. Let go of the pinch and grab one loop in each hand. Tighten the bow by pulling the two loops in opposite directions.

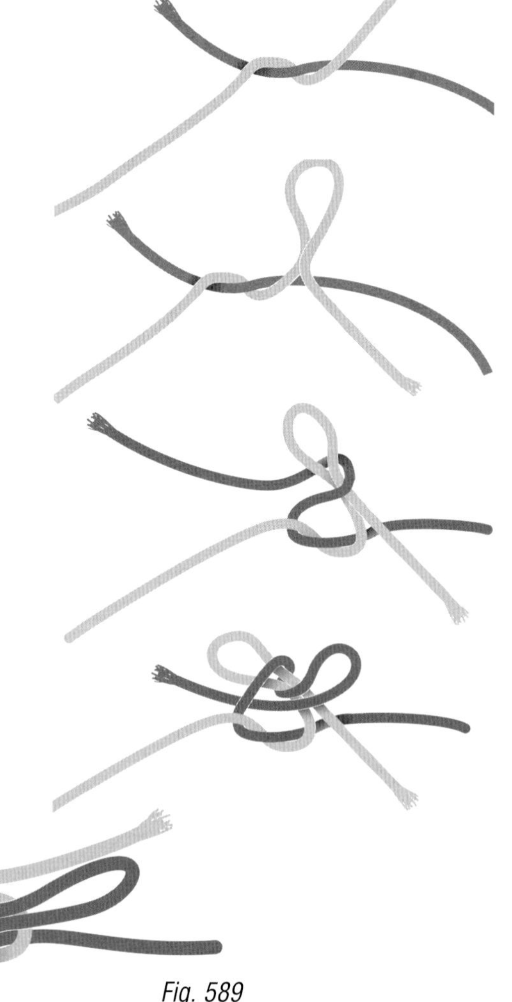

Fig. 589
Bow or Shoelace Knot

Appendix Hand-manipulated Weaves

Manipulating thread by hand

With Tracy Kaestner

Tracy Kaestner weaves, teaches, and sells yarn and supplies. She has been weaving since 1979 and enjoys introducing people to the joys of weaving.
www.lonestarloomroom.com

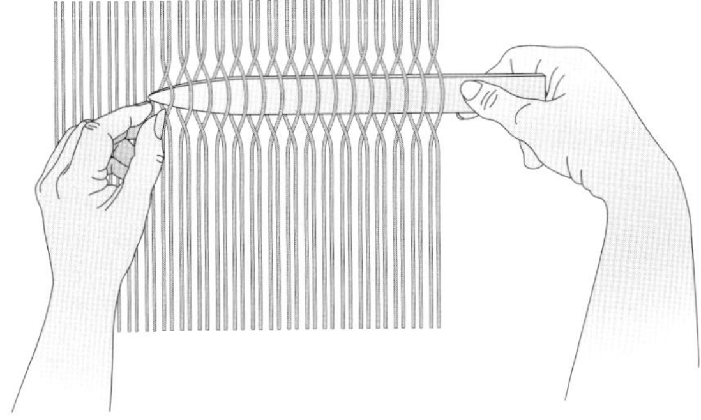

Hand-manipulating using a pick-up stick

Introduction

By Peggy Osterkamp

All the "stitches" or techniques in this section require you to manipulate the warp and/or weft threads by hand. They are slower to weave than "loom controlled" weaves given previously, but they can create interest, texture, and beauty to the cloth. They can be used with rigid heddle looms as well as with floor and table looms.

I put these techniques in the Appendix because they are optional things to try. They aren't really "weaving" techniques but surface embellishments. Some people love to do things like this, and some would rather the loom did everything. You don't need to be proficient at them to be a really "good" (and happy) weaver. I have used the Ghiordes Knot on page 364 quite lot and taught it in classes in appreciating how pile rugs are made.

Only a few years ago I decided to learn to hemstitch after hearing so much praise for it from other weavers. I do like to use it now to protect the last wefts when I cut pieces off the loom. It means I don't have to get out my sewing machine and stitch all the raw edges before finishing the cloth.

This first section is about hemstitching—a good way to begin and end your cloth. It is taken from my third book, ***Weaving & Drafting Your Own Cloth***, beginning on page 160.

All the other manipulations are worked within the cloth itself. I asked Tracy Kaestner to give the directions and drawings for these stitches because she teaches them regularly to her beginning-weaving students. I added what I needed when I tried them out for myself.

Practice these weaves before beginning to work on a project—to see if you like the process and the effect of the "stitches." For now, you can use the end of your sampler to try out some of these techniques. Otherwise, practice them, if they look interesting to you, at the beginning of a new warp (assuming you put on extra warp for sampling).

Note: All instructions are given for right-handers. Left-handers will have to start at the opposite edge.

Hemstitching

By Peggy Osterkamp

Hemstitching is a way to begin and end weaving without having to make fringe or sew hems later. It is a "stitch," done with a needle, that protects the wefts at the edges of the cloth. It can be done when the cloth is off the loom, but it is much faster to do it when the cloth is on the loom and under tension.

The process is only slightly different at the beginning of the fabric from at the end of it. The instructions are given for right-handed people who will always start at the left selvedge and work toward the right. Work from the right toward the left if you are left-handed.

Note: There are many ways to do hemstitching. This is one that I find quick and easy to remember.

At the beginning of the cloth

To hemstitch the beginning of a fabric: When you put in the first weft of the fabric (not the heading), leave a long tail hanging from the left edge of the cloth. The tail should be 2½ to 3 times the width of the warp. It will be threaded into a tapestry needle (page 9) and used to do the stitching after a few more rows of weaving are completed. See Figure 590a.

After weaving an inch or a bit more, thread the weft tail into a tapestry needle. The blunt point on the needle prevents you from pricking your finger and piercing the threads. Some methods prefer to pierce the threads to make the stitching more secure. See Figure 590b.

Begin stitching by holding the weft taut at the selvedge with the left hand. With the needle in the right hand, hover over ¼"–⅜" worth of warp threads, then go straight down between the warps and come out at the selvedge. (Figure 590c.) Tug this stitch so that it wraps around the warps and cinches them up into a bundle.

Point the needle straight up (away from you) along the selvedge for 3 wefts, take the needle down through the cloth there, and come out again through the opening you just made by cinching up the warp bundle. (Figure 590d.)

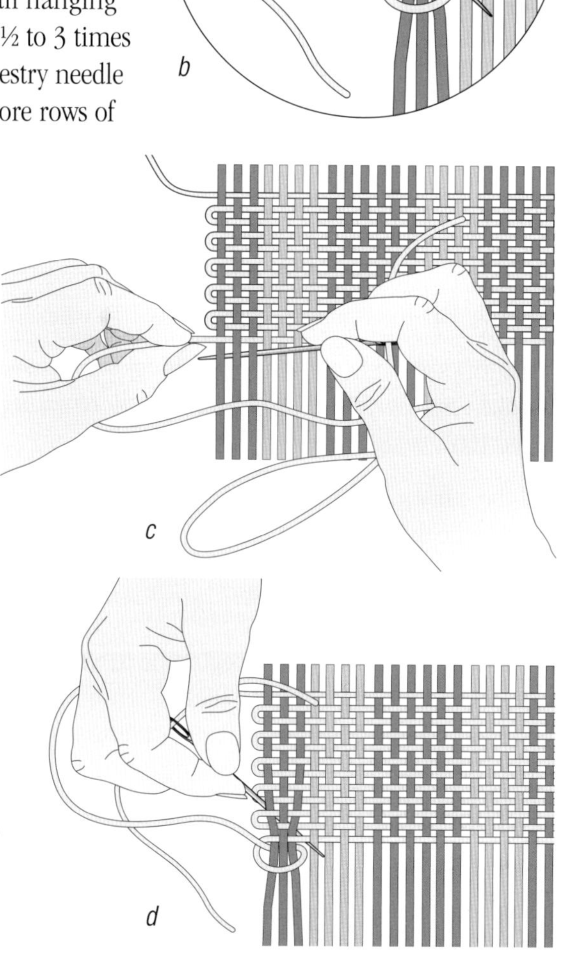

Fig. 590

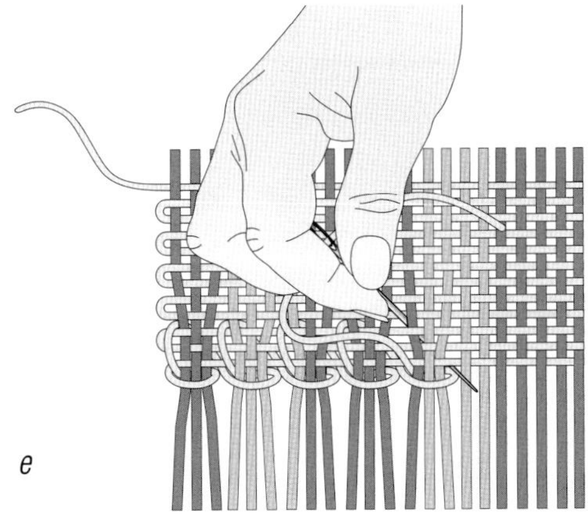
e

Continue on with the next stitch. Hold the weft in the left hand taut and go around the next group of warps (coming out again in the previous opening), tug the stitch to make a bundle, go straight up three wefts, poke the needle down through the cloth, and come out at the opening you just made by cinching up the bundle. Repeat until you reach the right selvedge (Figure 590e). See page 360 for what to do with slippery threads.

Note: My left hand holds the weft taut and does the tugging. It is engaged at all times while the right hand works the needle (Figure 590c).

At the right selvedge, use a tapestry needle to weave the tail into the cloth ½", so it doesn't show, and cut off the remainder of the tail flush with the cloth.

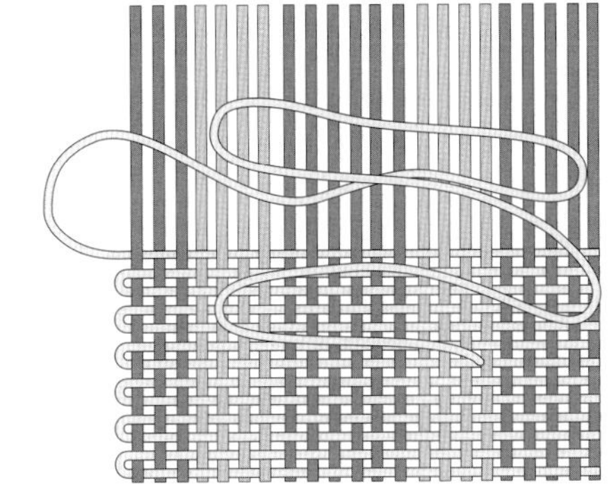
f

At the end of the cloth

At the end of the fabric, make the last weft come out at the left selvedge. Leave a long tail on the last weft (2 ½ to 3 times the width of the warp) and thread it through the tapestry needle. (Figure 590f.)

Begin stitching by holding the weft thread tail taut in the left hand, and with the right hand, go around ¼"-⅜" worth of warps, coming out at the selvedge as you did at the beginning of the fabric.

Point the needle straight toward you, for 3 wefts into the cloth; then poke the needle down through the cloth and come up in the space just made when you cinched up the bundle of warps. Notice that now you'll be poking your needle into cloth, which will be toward you. When you were stitching into the cloth at the beginning of the fabric, the cloth was away from you. See Figures 590 g, h, and i.

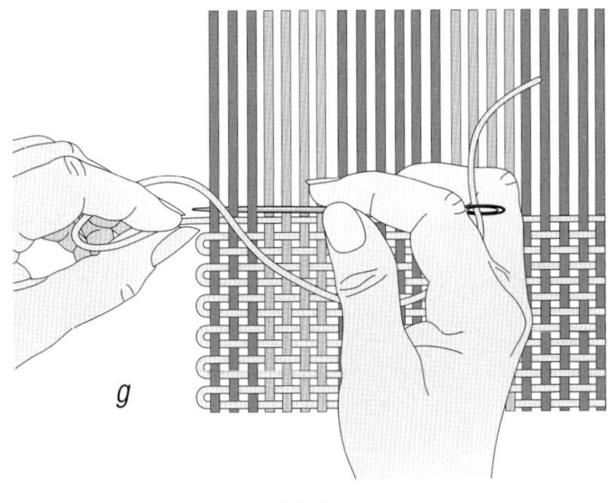
g

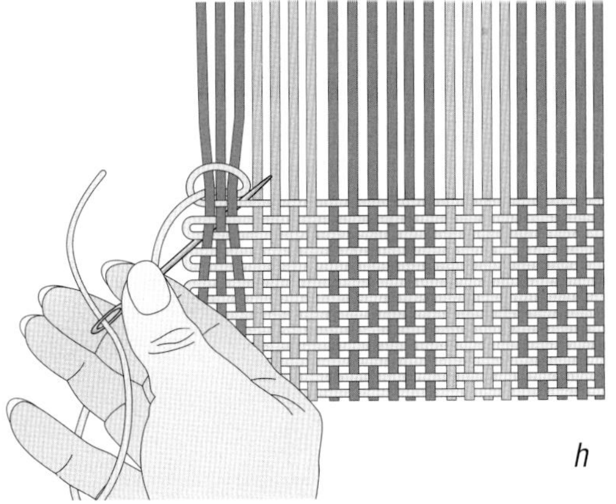
h

i

For slippery threads, stagger where you dig in your needle, to make the stitches more secure. If the needle always goes in after the third weft, the whole hemstitched edge could fall off during finishing. You can dig your needle in alternating between the third and fourth wefts—it looks deliberate, and the stitching doesn't pull out.

Other Techniques

By Tracy Kaestner

Brooks Bouquet

See Figure 592c on the facing page. There are two ways the shuttle moves for this stitch. The first one requires the shuttle to go into an ***open*** shed, counting threads as in the sidebar below. The second way asks you to count ***all*** the warp threads—not just those above the shuttle.

You won't want to close the shed for the second motion of the shuttle because you'll want it open again when you begin the next stitch.

Working with an Open Shed: How to Count the Threads

Some techniques are worked on an open shed and some with the shed closed. Here is how the threads are to be counted when the directions say, "With an open shed, go under a certain number of threads."

See Figure 591 and see that the shed is open and the shuttle is passing part way across the warp before it is taken out of the shed. (Then it will be on the surface of the cloth.) I numbered the threads to show how to count the threads when the directions say go under a certain number of threads. I do it by counting the number of threads that are above the shuttle—that is, the threads the shuttle is passing under. In the illustration, the shuttle is going under 10 threads.

For example: In Brooks Bouquet, the directions say, "with the shuttle in an open shed, go under 2 warp threads." Looking at Figure 591 you would take the shuttle under only threads labeled 1 and 2. Then, you would take the shuttle out of the shed and proceed to the next instruction.

You can use any type of shuttle for these weaves, however, small (6-10" long) stick shuttles are ideal for these hand manipulated weaves. For some, you might not use a shuttle at all, but make small balls of the weft yarn and work with your hands. I have quite a selection of very small stick and boat shuttles that I've collected over time that are perfect.

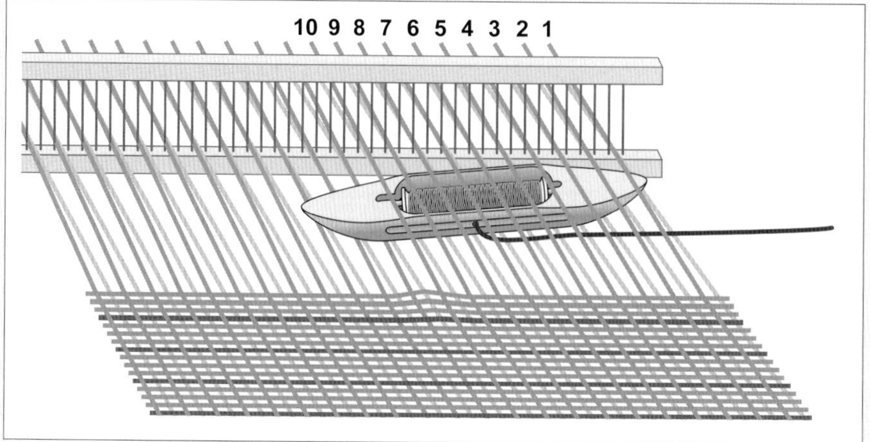

Fig. 591

Begin with some rows of plain weave.
End the plain weave with the shuttle on the right side.
Open the next plain weave shed.

Step 1: With the shuttle in the open shed, go under 2 warp threads and take the shuttle out of the shed up to the top of the cloth. ***That means, go into the shed normally and take the shuttle out of the shed after two threads can be seen on top of your shuttle. You are ignoring the bottom part of the shed completely.*** In Figure 592a, the two threads that the shuttle is to go under are marked "1" and "2."

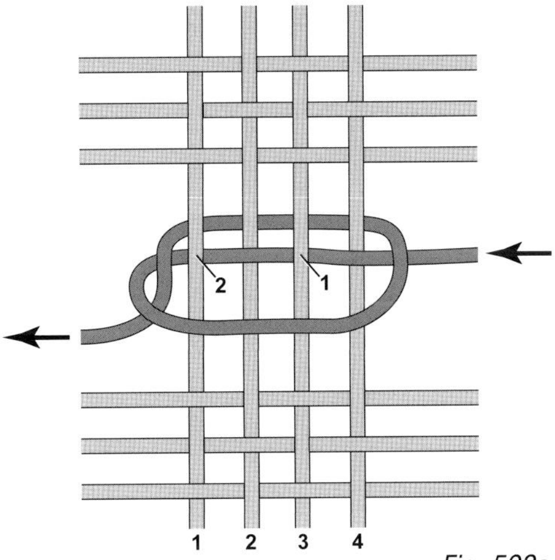

Fig. 592a

Step 2: Next, you move the shuttle back to the right, ***over*** 4 warp threads (here, counting both the top ***and*** the bottom of the shed)—you'll be starting to make a loop. Then, moving again toward the left, take the shuttle ***under*** the same 4 warp threads (Figure 592a).

Step 3: As you bring the shuttle up to the top of the cloth, take it through the loop you have just made around the 4 warp threads (Figure 592a).

Step 4: Tighten the thread around the warps as seen in Figures 592b and c.

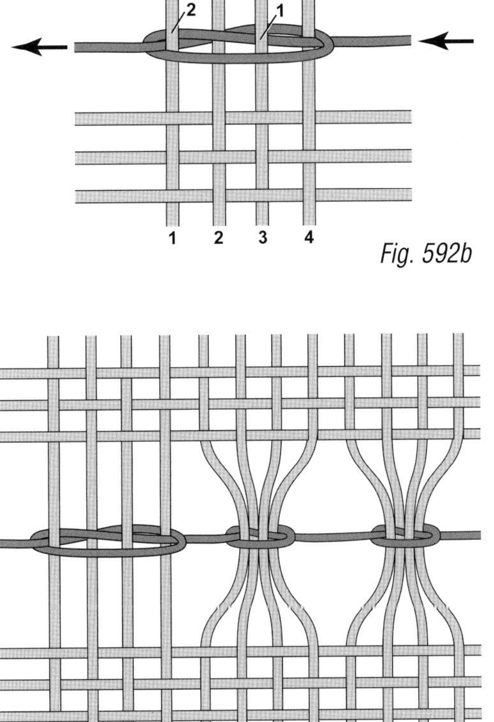

Fig. 592b

Fig. 592c

> **The sequence in shorthand:**
>
> ***Step 1:*** Under 2 ***(shed is open)***
>
> ***Step 2:*** Back ***around*** 4 (over and under 4 warp threads)
>
> ***Step 3:*** Come through the loop
>
> ***Step 4:*** Snug up tight
>
> Keep the shed open as you work across the width of the cloth, making your "bouquets."
>
> Change to the other plain weave shed and weave an ***odd number of rows*** with the shuttle ending on the right again. Begin to make the pattern again.

Notes

The number of threads in the groups depends on the warp thread and the look you want. When you get started, you'll probably think of a lot of variations for this technique.

Be sure to weave an odd number of rows of plain weave between bouquets. It is so that you will always be on the same shed as the first bouquets when making subsequent ones. Then, the counting will always be consistent—you will always go under the same number of threads in each bouquet, and they will be above one another.

Chaining V-shaped stitches

See Figures 593 a, b, and c

This technique makes sideways "V stitches" on the surface of the cloth to create a thick textured row.

You'll use several strands of a contrasting color at once—you might start with 8 strands to see what you prefer. (This stitch will use a lot of thread.) To make the multiple strands, a good idea is to wind the strands between pegs on a warping board. Otherwise, set up something on which to stretch the yarns back and forth, perhaps, between 2 door knobs or around chair legs. When you have measured out the strands, tie the two cut ends of the thread together to complete the loop. You end up with one very long loop or a skinny skein. This "loop" will be the length between your measuring pegs. Note: You will be using both sides of the loop together, so if you want 8 strands to work with, you'll make 4 round trips between your measuring pegs.

The length will need to be quite long since you want enough strands to make the stitches all across the warp without running out. Practice making the stitches for 3-4" or so across, and see how much length is needed for that. Then, you can determine how much length you'll need to go all the way across the warp. For example, if 3" is one-fourth of the way across, you'll need 4 times as much as you've just used to get to the other edge. (Allow for more than you think you'll need.) By the way, you don't have to go all the way across the warp—it's just that you can't start a new set of strands in a row without it showing.

Begin with some rows of plain weave.

Leave the shuttle attached—it can be at either edge of the warp. Here, I've started on the right edge.

Close the shed

Work with the multiple strands.

Step 1: Attach the strands to the first warp thread on the right edge of the warp with a lark's head knot. (See sidebar on the next page.)

Step 2: Manipulate the knot so that the tails of the strands dangle down below the warp between warp threads #1 and #2.

Step 3: Reach with your right thumb and forefinger between warps #1 and #2 and pull up on the dangling threads to make a loop big enough to cover the next 4 threads on top of the warp. (The left hand holds on to the tails below the warp while the right hand pulls up enough of the tail to form the loop.)

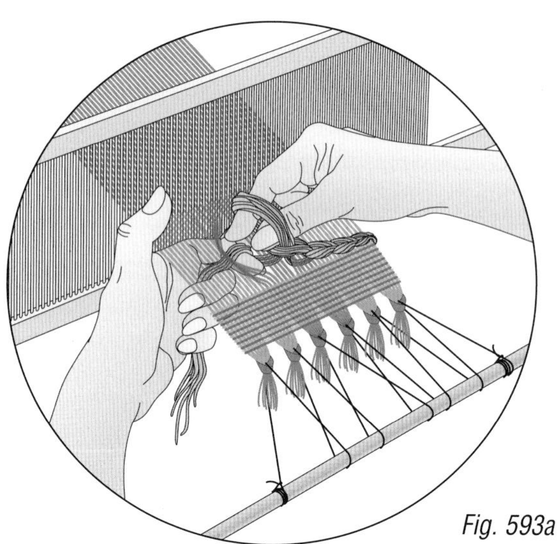

Fig. 593a

Step 4: Put your thumb and forefinger through the loop. Then, poke your finger and thumb between warp threads 5 and 6. Pull a new loop up through the warp and then, through the old loop. (With your left hand, hold on to the tails when you do this.) Pull the new loop up snug, but not so tight as to pull the warps out of alignment. Repeat: loop over 4 warp threads, pull up a new loop between the warp threads #9 and #10 and into the previous loop. Snug up the new loop. One hand will work on top of the cloth and the other will manipulate the tails of the weft from below the cloth. See Figures 593b and 593c. Continue across the cloth.

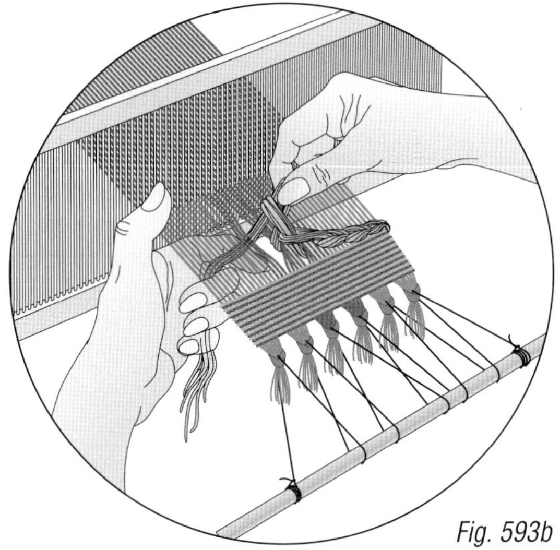

Fig. 593b

Step 5: At the end, pull the tails of the strands through the top loop—weave them back in with a needle. After the row is finished, beat the stitches lightly to snug them up to the fell.

Resume weaving plain weave with the shuttle

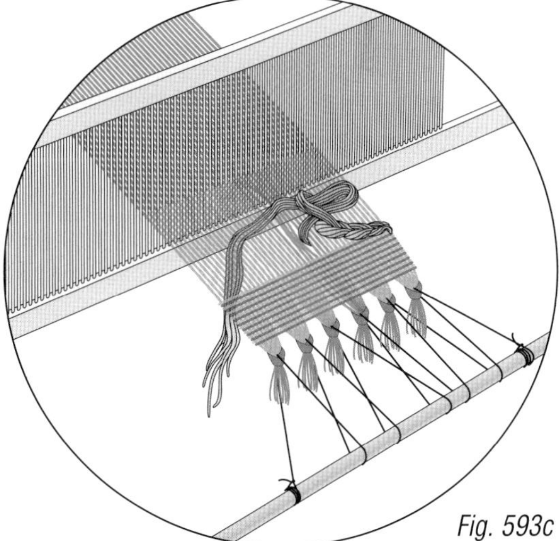

Fig. 593c

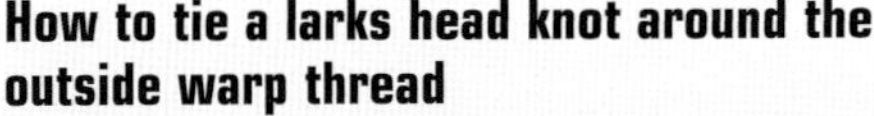

How to tie a larks head knot around the outside warp thread

Note: See page 352 for illustrations of this knot.

1. Hold onto the loop with the left hand, a few inches away from the end of thc loop.
2. With your right hand, take the loop around the outside warp thread—go completely around it.
3. Insert your right thumb and forefinger into the loop, spread them wide apart to spread open the loop.
4. With your thumb and forefinger, grasp the strands held in your left hand and pull them completely through the loop, letting go of the strands with your left hand as you pull them through the loop.

Notes

1. Basically, you are crocheting a chain over the warp threads. Reading how to make a chain on page 162 may help you know what to do.
2. You can go over more or fewer than four warp threads depending upon the look you want.
3. The stitches make sideways V's, or loops within loops.
4. The weft strands are quite thick, but it is easy to push the warps apart with your fingers to make the stitches—even if the warps are fairly close together.

Twining

This technique can be used as an edge finish or in a contrasting color as a decorative stitch. It creates a flat, dashed line on the surface (Figure 594).

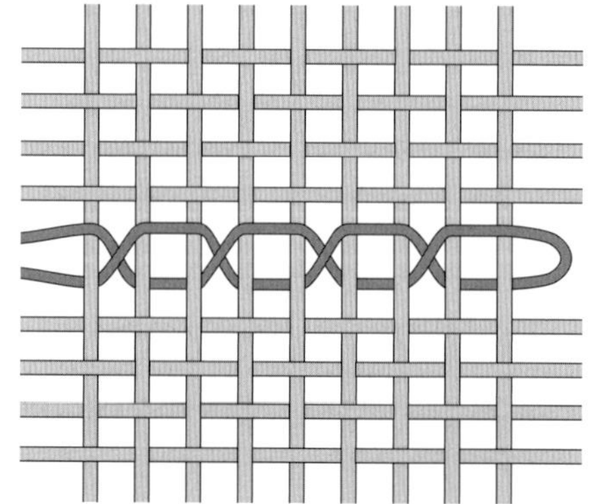

Fig. 594

Weave some plain weave.

Use a separate weft in a matching or contrasting color.

Cut a length of weft as long as 3 times the width of the warp.

The shed is closed.

Start at the right edge of the warp.

Fold the weft in half and center it on the right selvedge thread, one half of the weft goes over 2 warp threads, the other goes under the same 2 warp threads and then they swap places. Repeat across the warp.

Notes

The number of warp threads in the groups can vary according to the look you like. You can experiment with this technique and invent different looks. The main thing is that the top and the bottom "threads" switch places.

Ghiordes Knot

See Figure 595.

This knot is one that is used for making pile rugs. It can also be used for texture and decoration.

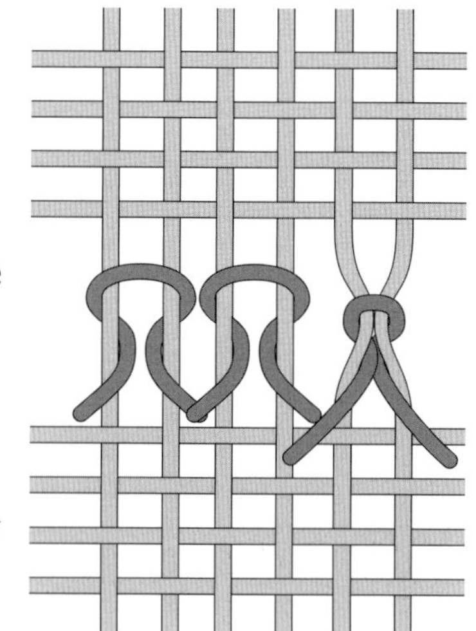

Fig. 595

Usually, a few strands of wool yarn are used together if you want to make pile as in rugs. Yarn or thread of any color or texture can be used if textures are desired. Use single strands or multiples to achieve the look you want.

Start with some rows of plain weave.

The shed is closed.

Cut the yarn in short pieces in your desired color(s)—approximately twice the length you want your pile to be plus a little extra. You want to cut them long enough so it isn't difficult to make the knots. You might cut the pile shorter after it is on the warp and waste some yarn, but it is well worth it so you can make many knots quickly. Experiment with different lengths (and different numbers of strands to use together) to determine what works best for you.

Step 1: Lay a length of one pile yarn (or group of yarns) over 2 warp threads as shown in the illustration.

Step 2: Wrap the ends of the yarn around the 2 threads and bring them back up between the warp threads as shown.

Step 3: Pull on the tails gently to tighten the knot and slide it down snuggly against the previous row of plain weaving.

Step 4: Continue making knots around pairs of warp threads across the warp or where desired.

Don't worry if the pile yarns aren't all equal in length or are too long because you will probably trim them later.

Step 5: Weave two rows of plain weave between rows of knots. This action is important because if you don't, you won't have any cloth, just vertical rows of pile knots that will be separate from each other. It's the plain weave between the rows that integrates the knots into the cloth. The pile usually is long enough so these rows are hidden.

Step 6: Trim the pile to the length desired and for a tidier look.

Notes

This is how many pile carpets are woven. If you look carefully between the rows of pile you can see the plain weave rows. You can also tell where the weaver began and ended a carpet. Because of the way you slide the knots down snuggly in step 3, the pile lies in one direction. Pet the carpet as you would pet a cat. If it's the smooth direction, you are petting the carpet from the end toward the beginning.

If you think you'd like to make a real pile rug, consult books especially written for making rugs.

Also, there are special scissors available for cutting the pile evenly.

Most pile rugs have designs in them made by using different colors for the knots. Geometric designs are easy to make using this technique. For more detailed designs, you would need a very fine scale with thin threads and hundreds of knots per square inch.

Spanish Lace

With this technique, after washing, the fabric looks lacy because the weft curves and shows up more (Figure 596).

You will always work with open sheds. This is an important point. Be sure to read the sidebar: "Working with an Open Shed," on page 360.

You will always be taking your shuttle into open sheds as you normally would—except that you won't go very far into the sheds, and you'll be taking the shuttle back and forth. Say, the shuttle is going left in a shed, then, when it goes to the right it is to be in a new shed. When it goes left again, it will go in a new shed as well. ***Every time you change directions of the shuttle, you will be changing the shed, too.***

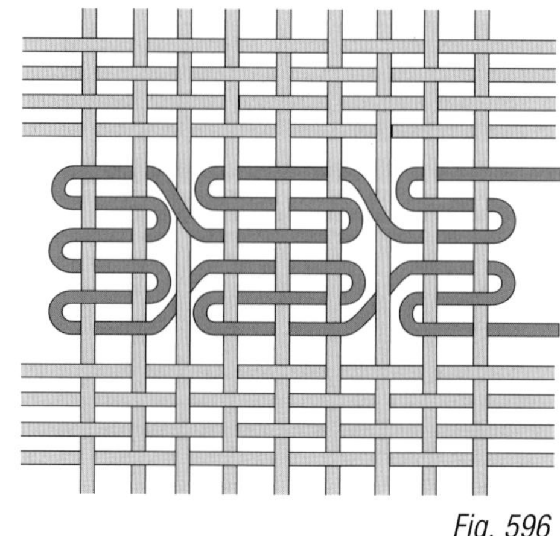

Fig. 596

Basically, this is what you'll do to make Spanish lace: You'll go back and forth with the shuttle (left and right) a bit, then, move on to a new group and go back and forth again and then, on to the next group, and so on, all across the warp.

To get the idea of how to make this stitch, I suggest you read the instructions as you follow along in the illustration. (Remember, when you go under threads, you are counting the upper threads in the shed only. See the sidebar mentioned above for clarification.)

Weave a heading of plain weave, and end with the shuttle on the right edge of the cloth. Divide the width of the warp into groups of threads. You choose how big each unit of lace will be. The illustration shows two sizes of groups: 2 threads and 3 threads. You are the designer and the groups can vary in size. Note there is one thread between each group.

You can weave it just like the illustration, or after you get the idea of how it works, you can start out with experiments. You can try out different sizes of the groups and how many times you want to go back and forth before moving on to a new group.

Follow these instructions to make the pattern in Figure 596, which makes two rows of Spanish lace. (The first row is worked from the right edge to the left edge across the warp. The second row goes across the warp from left to right.)

Open the shed such that the first thread on the right edge is up.

For the first group of threads:

Step 1: Moving to the left, pass the shuttle under one thread (in this case warp #1), and come up out of the shed.

Step 2: Change the shed. Working toward the right, pass the shuttle under one thread, (warp #2) and come out.

Step 3: Change shed. Working to the left, pass the shuttle under 3 threads. You are now going to work on the next group of threads.

For the second group of threads:

Step 1: Change the shed. Moving to the right, pass the shuttle under 2 threads. (In the illustration, notice that you have already made the first row in the group by going under 3 to the left.)

Step 2: Change the shed. Moving to the left, pass the shuttle under 3 threads to complete this group as well as to move on to the next group.

For the third group of threads:

Step 1: Change the shed and pass the shuttle under 1 thread as you move to the right and make the second "row" in the group.

Step 2: Change the shed and pass the shuttle under 1 thread as you move toward the left.

Continue across the warp.

For a second row

A second row of pattern is worked from the left side towards the right side.

To start the second row: You'll follow the same process, but you'll be going from the left edge of the warp toward the right.

Here are the steps:

Step 1: Change the shed and pass the shuttle under one thread, moving to the right. This begins the first group in the second "row" (the one on the left in the illustration).

Step 2: Change the shed and pass the shuttle under 1 thread, moving to the left.

Step 3: Change the shed and pass the shuttle under 3 threads, moving to the right. This completes the first group and starts you on the middle group.

Step 4: Change the shed. Moving to the left, pass the shuttle under 1 thread.

Step 5: Change the shed. Moving to the right, pass the shuttle under 3 threads to finish that group and begin the next.

Step 6: Change the shed, and moving to the left, go under one thread.

Step 7: Change the shed, and moving to the right, go under one thread.

And you're finished with two rows of "lace"!

Note: You will go across the whole warp before beginning the second row of "lace." When you're back where you started, you can weave some tabby. Weave an odd number of rows before beginning to make more "lace" if you want the counting and the placement of the groups to be the same.

Danish Medallion

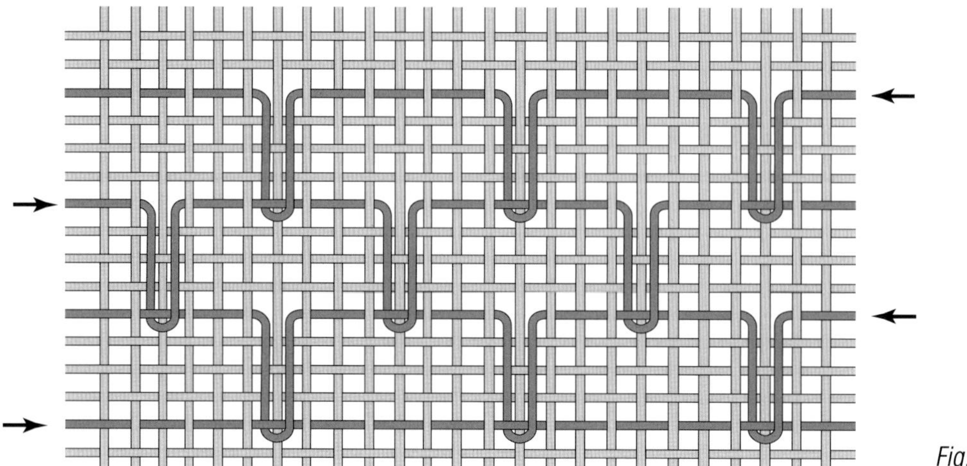

Fig. 597

See Figure 597. This makes a very nice decorative "stitch." All the steps sound confusing, but it is clear what to do when you are at the loom and do as the directions say. You may be quite surprised that your work does look like the illustration. It is a lovely technique.

Wind the "medallion yarn" on a separate shuttle. Often this yarn is a contrasting color. If the same color as the warp is used, it makes a more subtle pattern, which is nice in silk.

You might want a small crochet hook for this technique. A tapestry needle might work for you just as well.

Work on an open shed. See the sidebar, "Working with an Open Shed," on page 360.

Remember always to keep the plain weave order of the wefts.

Weave a plain weave heading and end with the shuttle on the left side such that the outside warp thread on the ***right*** edge of the warp is ***up*** in the completed row, as in the illustration.

Step 1: Open the next plain weave shed. (Now, the right edge thread will be down.) Enter the medallion yarn into the shed and end with the shuttle on the right edge of the cloth.

Step 2: Follow with several rows of plain weave using the same yarn as in the heading. To make the pattern work out, weave an odd number of wefts between pattern rows. In the case of the illustration, three rows of plain weave are woven.

Step 3: Open the next shed. (This is the same as the one for the first medallion shed.) Enter the medallion yarn part way into the shed from the right. You will have carried the medallion yarn up at the selvedge from its first row. ***Note that in the illustration, this row of medallion yarn starts with a partial pattern so the staggered design will work out. In this case, when you begin the row, go under 1 thread as per the sidebar on page 360.***

Step 4: Bring the medallion yarn to the surface.

Step 5: Here is an overview of the next step. In it you will do the preparation necessary to hook the second medallion weft into the first one below it. You will pass the shuttle through a loop you will make in the first medallion weft and then, take the shuttle up to the open shed to continue the stitch. After the shuttle has passed through the loop in the lower medallion weft, the lower weft will be straightened out, which will pull the second weft down, which makes the loop shown in the illustration. (After this step, the initial loop in the first weft will not exist any more.)

Follow these directions. Trace the warp thread next to the one where the shuttle came out of the shed down to the first medallion weft. (It will be a warp from the bottom of the shed.) Using a small crochet hook or tapestry needle, pick up the *first medallion weft yarn* and make a loop on the hook or needle. In other words, where you hook the lower medallion weft should line up with the space where the upper weft came out.

Step 6: Enlarge the loop so that the shuttle can pass through it. In doing this job, you'll be pulling on the bottom weft and distorting things a bit in order to make the loop large enough. Pass the shuttle through the loop.

Even with a cloth where the warp threads are close together, you can easily do this operation. You just push apart the warp threads.

Step 7: Straighten out the bottom row loop. Pull the bottom row straight again so it *pulls the top row down to make its own loop.*

Repeat the steps for more medallions in the row, now passing the yarn under *4 warp threads.* (To make multiple rows of the pattern work out, you need to pass the shuttle under 4 threads from now on as you go across the row, as shown in the illustration.)

Future rows should alternate where the loops are. See the illustration. Remember, to make the design work out, take the shuttle under 4 threads in the open shed and use an odd number of wefts between medallion rows. It is important. You need to have a total of seven warp threads between the medallion loops. It matters because if you don't, the shed sequence won't work out and the staggering of the loops won't be evenly spaced. For clarification on counting threads in an open shed, see the sidebar on page 360.

Leno: a Gauze Weave

by Peggy Osterkamp

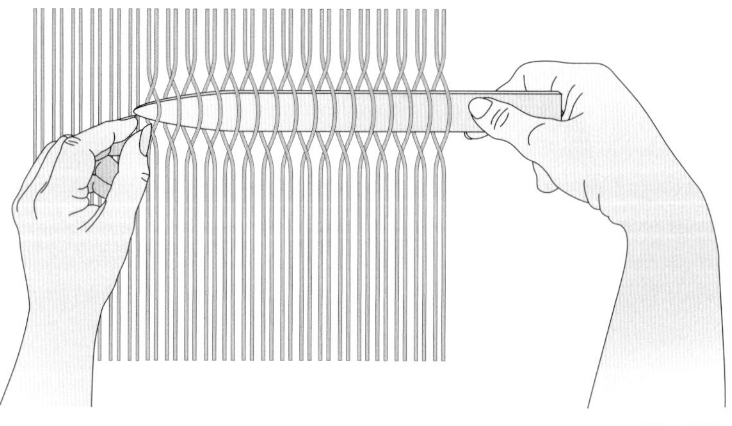

Fig. 598

The warp threads are crossed (not twisted) in pairs or groups on a stick before the weft is inserted. If the cloth is entirely made this way, it is called gauze. (Notice some net bags that oranges come in.) If it is used in combination with plain weave, it is called leno. The pronunciation of the word is "leeno."

You'll need a pick-up stick as seen in the illustration. A ruler can be used if you don't have a pick-up stick. They may come with rigid heddle looms and are available at weaving supply shops. See the Sources section on page 382. The stick should be about an inch wide or a little narrower.

Weave a heading of plain weave. End with the shuttle on the right edge of the cloth.

Have the shed open such that the outside warp thread on the right edge of the warp is up. (Some prefer a closed shed.)

You'll work with pairs of threads on the pick-up stick. The first pair is made up of the first two threads on the right edge of the warp. Pick up the second thread (the lower one in the shed) on the tip of the pickup stick and bring it under and to the right and then, above the first thread. This completes the cross for the first pair of threads, which you will hold on the pickup stick. (The second thread is on top of the stick, and the first thread in under it. Also, the second thread is on the right side of the first thread now.)

Move the stick slightly to the left and repeat: pick up the 4th thread (the ***lower*** one in the shed) and bring it toward the right, under and then above the third thread. Now two pairs of warp threads are crossed and two threads are on top of the stick and two threads are under it. Repeat with the next pairs across the warp. Always pick up the lower thread on the stick and take it under and over on top of its partner to the right.

Continue across the warp. Figure 598 shows how the pickup operation goes along.

When all the lower warp threads are on the pickup stick, turn the stick on its edge, and pass the weft yarn through the shed made with the stick on edge.

Remove the stick carefully.

Change the shed. Enter the weft in the shed in the regular way. This holds the crossed threads in place. The warp threads will now move back to their original positions.

For multiple rows, repeat (after weaving the regular weft row) starting with crossing the threads on the pick-up stick. Single rows of leno can be used.

Soumak

See Figures 599 a and b.

Note: This stitch makes a series of sloped lines, creating a ridge on the surface. The appearance is different if you work all the soumak rows in the same direction (for example, right-to-left) or you make subsequent rows working alternately from right-to-left and left-to-right. Figure 599b shows the alternation of right-to-left, then left-to-right. It's hard to see the difference in a drawing, but it is significant in real life.

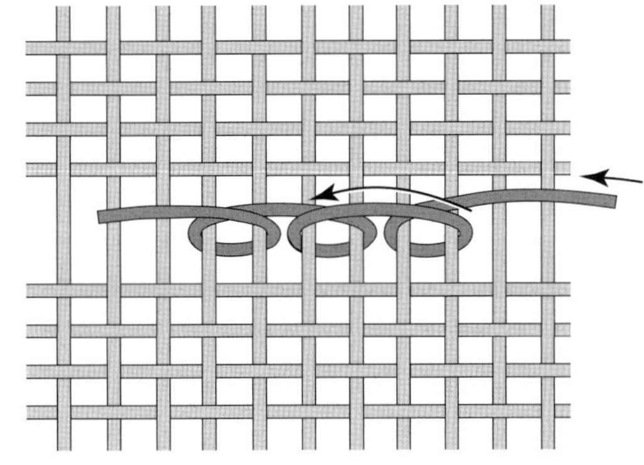

Fig. 599a

Weave some plain weave.

The shed is closed.

The shuttle is on the right side of the loom.

Use the same shuttle that was used for the plain weave, or use a separate shuttle for the soumak thread. See notes below.

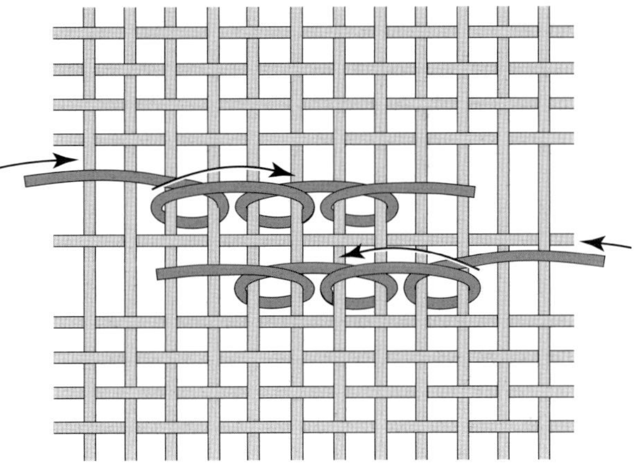

Fig. 599b

Step 1. Go ***over*** 4 threads moving to the left, then, ***under*** 2 threads moving back to the right. Repeat: ***over*** 4 to the left, ***under*** 2 to the right. (I think of it as 4 forward and 2 back.) Continue across the warp.

Step 2. Beat.

Step 3. Resume weaving plain weave.

Several rows of soumak can be done one after the other. More than 3 rows should be separated by at least one row of plain weave. Figure 599b shows how multiple rows would be woven with one row of plain weave separating the soumak rows. If you are making three rows together, in the second row, you will be moving from left to right as seen in the illustration. Otherwise, the row of plain weave will always put your shuttle back to the right. (See note above regarding the different appearances depending upon whether the soumak wefts alternate directions or always go in one direction.)

The same warps are always grouped together in subsequent rows.

The stitches will lie on the surface close together but should not distort the warps. You'll tension them as you go along so they won't be loose and loopy, but sit close to the cloth.

Suggested reading for hand-manipulated weaves

Brown, Rachel. ***The Weaving, Spinning, and Dyeing Book.*** New York: Alfred A. Knopf, 1984.

Collingwood, Peter. ***The Techniques of Rug Weaving.*** New York: Watson-Guptill Publications, 1969.

Davenport, Betty Lin. ***Hands on Rigid Heddle Weaving***. Loveland, CO: Interweave Press, 1987.

Held, Shirley E. ***Weaving***. New York: Holt, Rinehart and Winston, Inc., 1972.

Regensteiner, Else. ***The Art of Weaving.*** New York: Van Nostrand Reinhold Company, 1970.

Appendix Opening a Skein

A skein is a mass of yarn in a large ring (Figure 600). The word is pronounced, "skane."

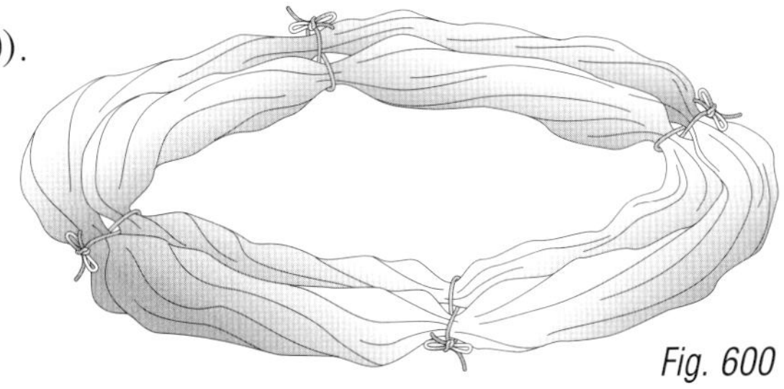

Fig. 600

You must open skeins carefully so the yarn doesn't tangle as it's being wound off the swift (Figure 601). A swift is a device that holds a skein open while you wind it into a ball. Because it also spins around, it is much easier to use than holding the skein on chair legs or someone's hands. If the skein is twisted as in Figure 602, carefully untwist it. Even though it might not look carefully wound, it is. See the ties around the yarn? There usually are two or three ties that encircle the skein, often in a figure-8, as in Figure 603. Another tie or two holds the beginning and the end of the yarn itself. Usually, there is one tie for this purpose with the two ends of yarn tied together and also encircling the skein itself.

It's important that before you untie any of the ties, you make sure your hands are exactly in the center of the ring of yarn. Check your position at each of the ties. Hold your hands in the middle of the ring of yarn and snap them apart a few times. This process untangles any temporary tangles and confirms that your hands are exactly in the center.

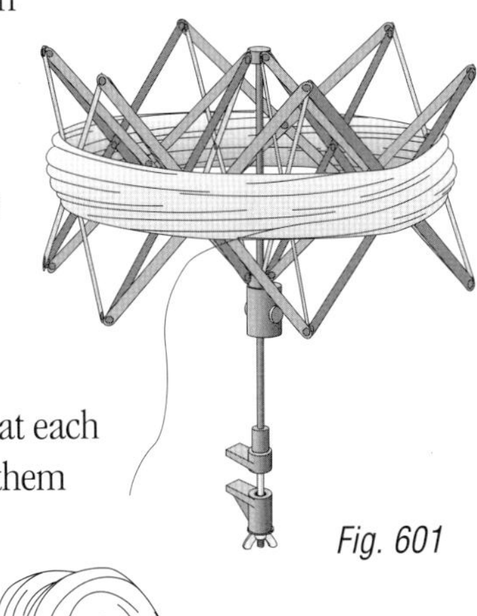

Fig. 601

Before untying anything, put the skein on the swift, a friend's hands, a chair back or whatever you are using to hold the skein open while you wind off the yarn (usually into a ball). Check again that you have found the exact center of the skein. Untie the figure-8 ties first and the ends of the yarns last. Be sure to keep track of the ends! One end will likely be on the outside of the skein and is the one to use to start unwinding. You might have to twist the skein some to get this end on the outside. I tuck the end I don't want to use into the swift, and loosely tie it to a spoke so that it doesn't tangle while I'm unwinding the other end.

Never take the yarn over and under other yarns in the skein—never! Always take the yarn as it comes—that way the skein can unwind smoothly. If you come to a tangle, it's probably just a temporary snag. Snap the skein or strum it, and you'll find that the yarn isn't really tangled and comes off smoothly again. If you feel you must take the yarn over and under another thread because of a real tangle, remember that you'll have to do that over and under process throughout the unwinding. It will be annoying, but may need to be done if you haven't found the exact center of the skein before untying the ties.

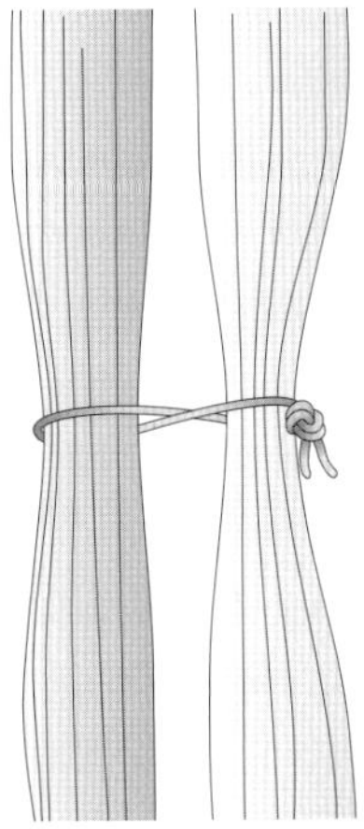

Fig. 602

Fig. 603

Appendix Apron Pattern

Peggy's Weaving Apron

See Figures 604 a and b.

Supplies Needed:

- 1 yard of canvas, awning, or ticking fabric or any sturdy cloth
- Bias tape—one package
- Leather elbow patch—one patch (2 come in a package.)
- D-rings, 4
- Newspaper or grocery bag paper to use for patterns

Refer to Figure 604c on the next page for dimensions. Measurements are approximate.

Please read all of the instructions before you begin.

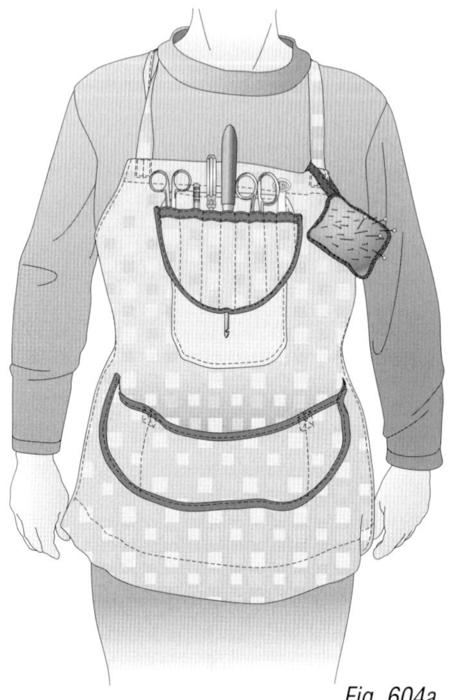

Fig. 604a

Make paper patterns and cut out the fabric

Step 1: Make a one-half-pattern out of newspaper for the main part of the apron. The pattern will be for ½ the apron as though the apron were folded in half, lengthwise. (You'll cut out the apron and the two pockets using ½ patterns in the same way you would cut out a valentine.) Fold your paper in half, lengthwise. Adjust the given measurements to fit you and to leave room on your fabric for the tabs, two pockets, and the ties. On the side opposite the fold, cut out around the outside edges of the paper pattern, following one side of the illustration only. Don't cut the fold edge. When you cut out the cloth, it will open out to full size.

Step 2: Fold the fabric in half lengthwise. Position the long, straight edge of the paper pattern on top of the cloth's fold and pin it in place along the fold.

Step 3: Adjust the pattern, if necessary, to leave room on the fabric for the ties and two pockets shown in Figure 604c on page 375. You might need to make the pattern shorter at the bottom to have room for pocket #2 and to make the pattern narrower on the side to make room for the ties. Make sure there is still enough scrap to cut out pocket #3 and the D-ring tabs.

Step 4: Pin the remaining edges of the pattern to the fabric. On the side opposite the fold, cut out the fabric by cutting around the outside edges of the *adjusted* pattern. ***Do not cut the fold of the fabric***.

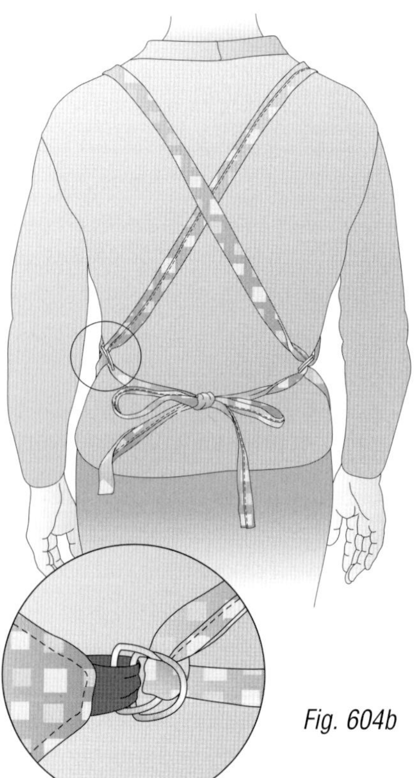

Fig. 604b

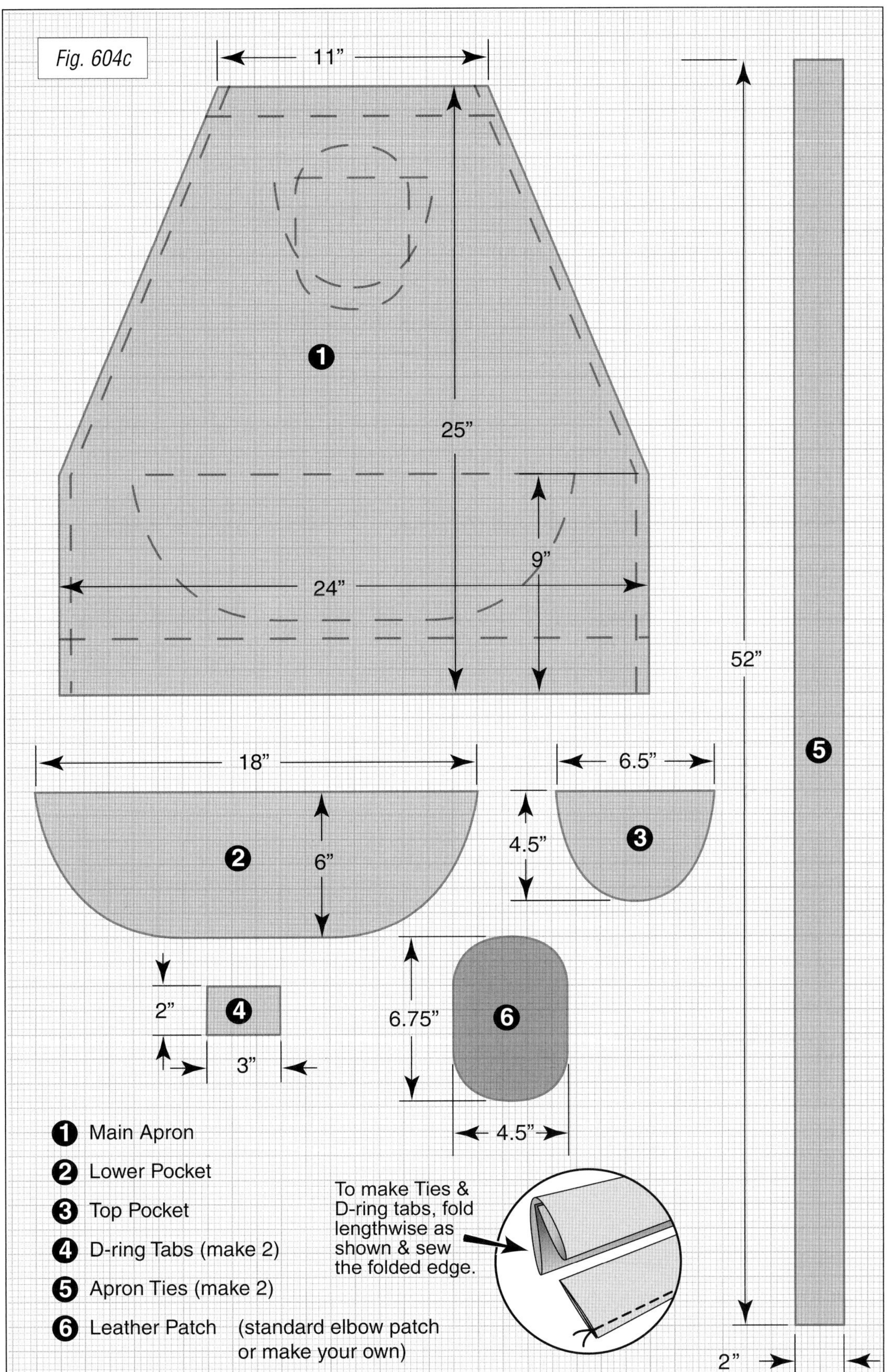
Fig. 604c
11"
25"
9"
24"
52"
18"
6"
6.5"
4.5"
2"
3"
6.75"
4.5"
2"
1 Main Apron
2 Lower Pocket
3 Top Pocket
4 D-ring Tabs (make 2)
5 Apron Ties (make 2)
6 Leather Patch (standard elbow patch or make your own)
To make Ties & D-ring tabs, fold lengthwise as shown & sew the folded edge.

Step 5: Remove the paper pattern and unfold the cloth for the full-size apron.

Step 6: Cut out the fabric for the ties as shown.

Step 7: Make the paper pattern for pocket #2 out of a piece of paper measuring 18" wide and 6" long. Fold the paper in half so it is 9" wide. On the side opposite the fold, cut a rounded shape from one corner of the paper. Whatever you do—don't cut the fold! Draw this shape first to be sure that when you unfold the paper, you will get a nice curve for the whole pattern. Unfold the paper to form the whole pocket pattern.

Step 8: Pin on the opened paper pattern and cut the whole pocket out of the fabric.

Step 9: Make the paper pattern for pocket #3 in the same manner, starting with a piece of paper 4 ½" long and 6 ½" wide. Fold the width of the paper in half so it is now approximately 3 ¼" wide and 4 ½" long.

Step 10: On the side opposite the fold, cut a rounded shape from one corner of the paper. Again, whatever you do—don't cut the fold! Unfold the pattern for a complete, whole pattern for the pocket shown in the illustration.

Step 11: Cut the pocket out of the fabric using the pattern.

Hem the pockets

Step 1: For the lower pocket, #2, stitch bias tape on the curved edge of the pocket to enclose the raw edge. (You'll be attaching the bias tape all along the bottom of the pocket and the curved sides.)

Step 2: Turn the top edge of the pocket under toward the wrong side of the cloth ½", and fold it in again 1" to form a hem. Stitch near the edge of the hem.

The illustration shows bias tape on the top edge; however, I prefer a regular hem as in the text because I think it's sturdier. You could add bias tape as well, for decoration, if you prefer.

Step 3: For the top pocket, #3, Stitch bias tape around the curved edge to enclose the raw edge.

Step 4: On the top of the pocket, stitch bias tape to the raw edge on the inside of the pocket. Fold the bias tape to the outside (enclosing the raw edge) and stitch the bias tape to the cloth to form a hem across the top.

Hem the edges of the apron

Step 1: Hem the sides of the apron by turning the edges in ¼" then, ½" to the inside of the cloth and stitch close to the edges of the hems.

Step 2: Hem the bottom edge. Turn under ¼" then, 2" to form the hem. Stitch close to the edge of the hem.

Step 3: Hem the top edge. Turn under ¼" then, 1" to form the hem and stitch close to the edge of the hem.

Make the ties and D-ring tabs

Step 1: Fold the long edges of the ties and stitch them as shown in Figure 604c. (You'll fold the 2" wide fabric in half and then fold in the edges, too.) You will have very flat and narrow ties. Since the ties are narrow and flat, I think it's better to make them this way rather than folding the fabric in half and sewing the long edge and one short edge, and turning the whole thing right side out so the raw edges are enclosed.

Step 2: Cut out two tabs for the D-rings out of scrap fabric and fold and stitch them according to the illustration for folding the ties.

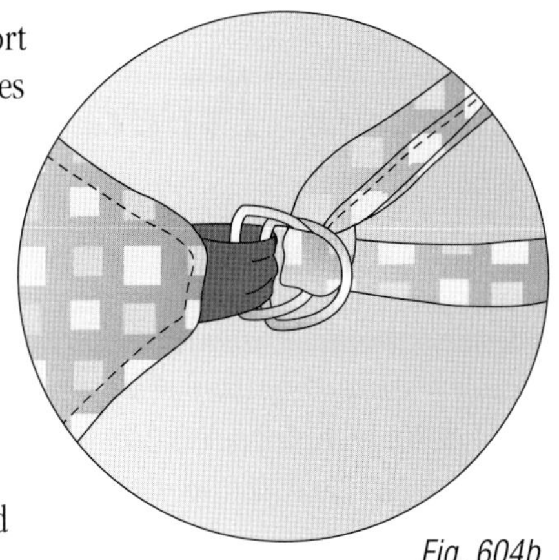
Fig. 604b

Attach D-rings

Attach the D-rings using the tabs as shown in Figure 604b. The tabs holding the D-rings are attached at the sides of the apron at the waistline as in the close-up view. The ties will be threaded through the D-rings as shown the illustration.

Attach the leather patch and pockets

Step 1: Before putting on the patch, cut 2 small squares, approximately ½" x ½", out of the leather patch for reinforcing the lower pocket as seen in the apron's front view. Instead, you could cut them out of the second patch in the package, if you prefer.

Step 2: To find the center of the apron, fold it in half lengthwise. Mark the center so that you can center the pockets on the apron when you sew them on. Determine where you want the top pocket to be. Measure how far down from the top of the apron the top pocket should be. (My top pocket is 2" down from the top.)

Step 3: Pin the leather patch in place as per the illustration so it will extend above and below the pocket itself. Stitch the leather patch on to the apron, close to the edges.

Step 4: Pin the top pocket in place, centering it on the center of the apron and the distance down from the top you planned. Stitch around the sides and bottom of the pocket—except, leave about ½" unsewn at the bottom of the pocket so the threading hook can poke out.

Step 5: Stitch vertical rows of stitches through all the layers (pocket, patch, and apron) on the top pocket to accommodate your tools as in the illustration. (I don't always have two pairs of scissors in the pockets—one slot usually has an emery board in it.) I like the scissors on the right side and my sley hook on the left where the little "pockets" are more shallow. I put my threading hook in the center. Experiment a bit with your stitching. You can always undo the stitches later if you change your mind about where to put them.

Step 6: Stitch the bottom pocket in place. Mine is 4 ½" above the bottom of the apron.

Step 7: I put two vertical rows of stitching on the sides of the pocket to make two small sections—for rubber bands and ChapStick.

Step 8: Stitch the little leather squares on the top edge of the lower pocket, where the stitches for the little pockets are, to reinforce them. See the illustration.

Attach the ties

Step 1: Make small hems in the ends of the ties to cover the raw edges.

Step 2: Stitch the ties to the top corners of the apron, and you're finished. You can see how the stitching is done in a square to secure and reinforce each tie.

Appendix Needle Book

See the pattern, Figure 605.

I made one of these in 4-H when I was 10. It's great for keeping track of your needles—especially, the tapestry needles you need. It's made of a few layers of wool cloth stitched together like a little book. The cover doesn't need to be wool since it won't hold any needles.

Here are the dimensions for the book I use now.

Step 1: For the cover, cut a piece of fabric 6" wide and 3 ½" high. (This piece will make both the front and the back cover.)

Step 2: For the "pages" inside, cut 3 pieces of wool cloth 5 ½" wide and 3" high.

Step 3: Stack the pages so they are centered on the cover fabric.

Step 4: Fold the stack in half.

Step 5: Stitch them together as shown in the illustration.

You can be inventive. Once, I made some needle books in the shape of a circle. They were lovely gifts. For the "pages" inside, I cut different sizes of circles in wool fabric I had woven and crocheted around the raw edges. I crocheted two circles slightly larger than the largest inner circle for the back and front covers. I sewed them all together at the top with a few hand stitches. Then, I put on a little bow to hide the stitches.

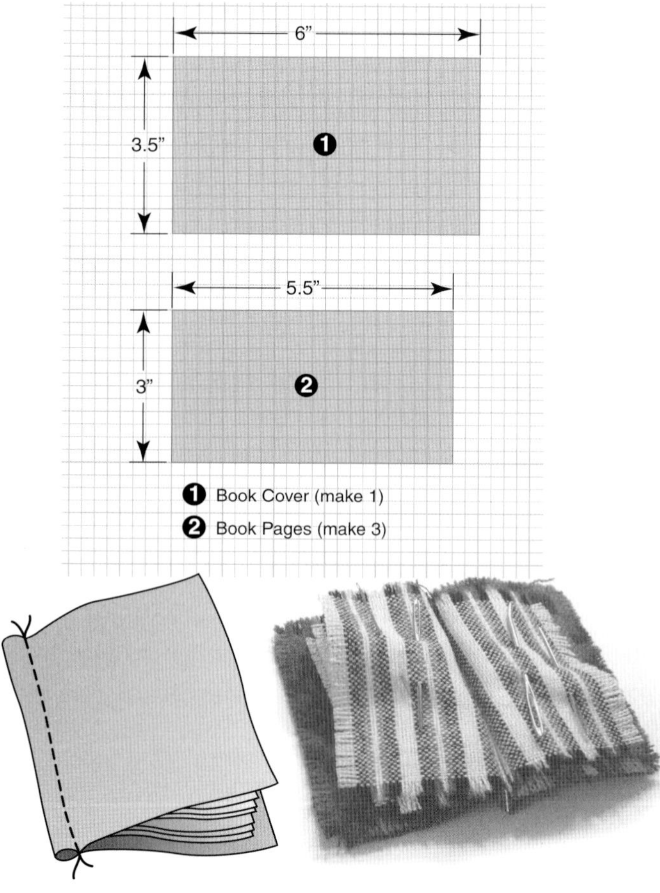

Fig. 605

Appendix Counting String

Besides keeping groups of ends in order for spreading the warp in the raddle, the raddle lease also helps you keep count of the ends as you measure them out.

Using a string to hold together, say, five raddle groups at a time gives you an easy check of how many ends you've measured. If you measure out five round trips on the pegs with a little space between them, they're easy to count. Then push them down firmly to the base of the peg at the raddle lease, so you're always measuring right on the wood of the peg.

The best method I've seen for counting is this special crocheted chain. See Figure 606. Take a long string (about three feet), fold it in half and slip the two tails through the loop at the fold around your first five raddle groups. This makes a lark's head knot over these five groups. See Figure 607. With the tails of the lark's head you will begin to crochet around the bundles as you make them.

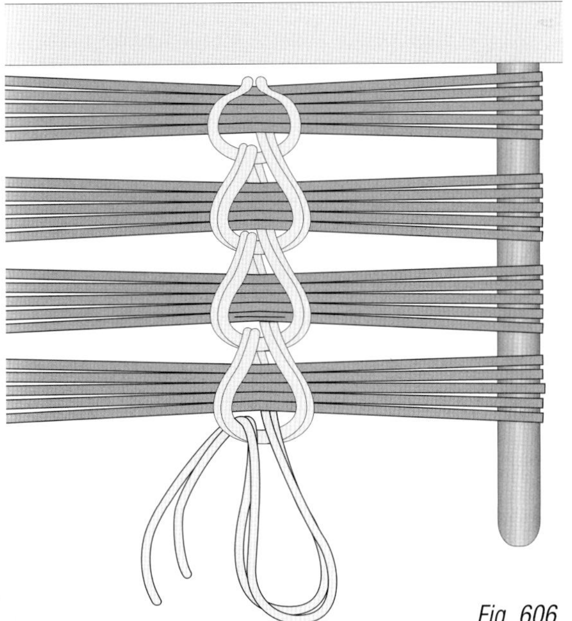

Fig. 606

Measure out your next five groups. Fold the tails between the first bundle and the new one, making a loop. Then put your right thumb and forefinger into the loop, while holding the tails with your left hand.

Encircle the new bundle with a "crochet" by using your finger and thumb to draw up another loop from the tails. Holding onto the tail, pull on the loop to snug it up around the bundle. Leave that loop and the tails dangling (don't pull the tails through the loop, as you'll be tempted to do).

The lark's head knot is the foundation. From now on, you'll crochet-chain using your fingers like this. Measure the next five groups. With thumb and forefinger, reach through the old loop, drawing up a new one from the dangling tails, and tighten to secure the new bundle.

After each crochet, both the loop and the tails should hang freely, ready for the next bundle.

To end the counting string chain, at the last bundle, pull the tails completely through the loop so that only the tails are hanging freely.

Fig. 607

Appendix–Sett Charts

Choosing the epi for the warp (ends per inch)

Read the chapter on Sett (epi) beginning on page 263. These are the charts referred to in that chapter.

How to use the sett charts

1. Know the yards per pound: How to find the yards per pound is given in detail on pages 271-274. There is a convenient worksheet for figuring this amount out on page 273.
2. Know the weave structure: There are two charts—one chart is for plain weave and the second for twill. Both have the same column headings, but notice the numbers below are different. The difference between plain weave and twill setts is explained on page 278. For other weaves, see page 278.
3. Use the appropriate chart—Plain Weave or Twill.
4. Locate the yards per pound for your yarn in the first column in the appropriate chart.
5. Read across that row for some suggested setts that have been calculated by the Ashenhurst formula discussed beginning on page 269.
6. Allow for purpose: The different columns show allowances for the purpose of the cloth—how to adjust the sett for upholstery or delicate shawls, for example. More on allowing for purpose is on page 279.

Lots of leeway for choosing sett

You've read that sett is very important, but please don't agonize over it. There is a lot of leeway in the matter, and one sett might be just as satisfactory as another ***similar*** one. For example, you might be considering 12 epi or 15 epi. In fact, either one might be okay.

Sample first

I always sample at the beginning of a warp to see if I am happy with the results, especially, the sett. Read more about the sample on page 283. Evaluate your sample after it is washed—either you like it or you don't. If you can't decide, probably, it is good enough.

How to determine the actual sett to use.

Check the sett that the chart suggests and then look at the reed substitution chart on this page. If your "number" isn't there, it is quite all right to use another number that is close.

When I decide, I also take into consideration the reed(s) I have. I have 8, 10, 12, and 15 dent reeds. So, I coordinate the calculated epi with what reed I have. Since reeds are expensive, it took me several years to accumulate them. That's the reason most weavers use a Reed Substitution Chart. On page 265, I coordinate reeds and sett. More information about the Reed Substitution Chart is on page 73.

What about mixed warps?

Read what you can do on page 268.

Reed Substitution Chart

When you don't have the ideal reed to sley two warp ends per dent, use this substitution chart.

Sequence in dents = the number of empty spaces in the reed and the number of threads in each space.

Example: 0-1-1 = The sequence to sley the reed, repeated for the width of the warp:
1 empty dent
1 thread in a dent
1 thread in a dent
or "empty-1-1; empty-1-1", etc.

Sequence of warps in the dents	Reed size (Dents per inch)					
	8	10	12	15	18	20
	Warp Ends Per Inch (epi or sett)					
0-1	4	5	6	7½	9	10
0-1-1	5	7	8	10	12	13
0-1-1-1	6	7½	9	11½	13½	15
1	8	10	12	15	18	20
1-1-1-2	10	12½	15	19	22½	25
1-1-2	11	13	16	20	24	27
1-2	12	15	18	22½	27	30
1-2-2	13	17	20	25	30	33
1-2-2-2	14	17½	21	26	31½	35
2	16	20	24	30	36	40

Sett Charts

Directions for how to use the charts are on page 380.

Example: You have a 5/2 pearl cotton that is 2100 yards per pound (ypp). You want to weave a twill, so you would look in the Twill Chart for 2050 yards/pound.

Then, going across that row, look for the purpose of the cloth you want to make.

If you want something very delicate, you would choose the 50% column and see that it is 14 epi.

If, however, you wanted to make a pillow, you might choose the 80% number (22epi). This sett is what I recommend for "regular cloth"—what I use unless I want extra dense or delicate fabrics.

Read about allowing for purpose on page 279.

Your yarn not listed? To make your own calculations, see pages 268-274.

**Ashenhurst's diameters. See Chapter 10, Sett pages 268-274.*

Setts for Plain Weave (tabby) — Listed by Yards Per Pound

Yards/ pound	m/kg	Diameters*	Maximum Plain Weave	90% of max (Upholstery)	80% of max (Production)	70% of max (Clothing)	65% of max (Woolen)	60% of max (Clothing)	50% of max (Delicate)
600	1210	22	11	10	9	8	7	7	6
650	1310	23	12	10	10	8	8	7	6
700	1411	24	12	11	10	8	8	7	6
750	1512	25	13	12	10	9	8	8	7
800	1613	25	13	11	10	9	8	8	6
850	1714	26	13	12	10	9	8	8	7
900	1814	27	14	12	11	9	9	8	7
950	1915	28	14	13	11	10	9	8	7
1000	2016	28	14	13	11	10	9	9	7
1050	2117	29	15	14	12	11	10	9	8
2000	4032	40	20	18	16	14	13	12	10
2050	4133	41	20	18	16	14	14	12	10
3000	6048	49	25	22	20	17	16	15	12
3050	6149	50	25	23	20	18	16	15	13
4000	8064	57	29	26	23	20	19	17	15

Setts for Twill — Listed by Yards Per Pound

Yards/	m/kg	Diameters*	Maximum Twill	90% of max (Uphol-	80% of max (Produc-	70% of max (Clothing)	65% of max (Woolen)	60% of max (Clothing)	50% of max (Delicate)
600	1210	22	11	10	9	8	7	7	6
650	1310	23	15	14	12	11	10	9	8
700	1411	24	16	14	13	11	10	10	8
750	1512	25	17	15	14	12	11	10	9
800	1613	25	17	15	14	12	11	10	9
850	1714	26	17	15	14	12	11	10	9
900	1814	27	18	16	14	13	12	11	9
950	1915	28	19	17	15	13	12	11	10
1000	2016	28	19	17	15	13	12	11	10
1050	2117	29	19	17	15	13	12	11	10
2000	4032	40	27	24	22	19	18	16	13
2050	4133	41	27	24	22	19	18	16	14
3000	6048	49	33	30	26	23	21	20	17
3050	6149	50	34	31	27	24	22	20	17
4000	8064	57	38	34	30	27	25	23	19

Sources

A Weaver's Yarn
1810 Alaska Way
Fairbanks, AK 99709
907-374-1995
www.aweaversyarn.com

AVL Looms
2360 Park Avenue
Chico, CA 95928
1-800-626-9615
www.avlusa.com

Bountiful
Livermore, Colorado
1-877-586-9332
www.bountifulspinweave.com
info@bountifulspinweave.com

Carol Leigh's Hillcreek Fiber Studio
7001 South Hillcreek Road
Columbia, MO 65203
1-800-874-9328
www.hillcreekfiberstudio.com

Carolina Homespun
455 Lisbon Street
San Francisco, CA 94112
1-800-450-SPUN (7786)
www.carolinahomespun.com

Cotton Clouds
5176 South 14th Avenue
Safford, AZ 85546
1-800-322-7888
www.cottonclouds.com

Dharma Trading Co. (Mail Order)
1805 S McDowell Blvd. Ext
Petaluma, CA 94954
1-800-542-5227
www.dharmatrading.com

Dharma Trading Co. (Store)
1604 Fourth Street
San Rafael, CA 94901
415-456-1211
www.dharmatrading.com

Earth Guild
33 Haywood Street
Asheville, NC 28801
1-800-327-8448
www.earthguild.com

Elkhorn Mountains Weaving Studio
50 Hall Lane
Clancy, MT 59634
1-406-442-0354
www.glimakraUSA.com

Española Valley Fiber Arts Center
325 Paseo de Onate St.
Espanola, NM 87532
505-747-3577
www.evfac.org

Gemini Fibres
5062 Mt Albert Road
Mount Albert, Ontario L0G 1M0
Canada
1-800-564-9665
www.geminifibres.com

Glimakra USA Weaving Equipment and Yarns
50 Hall Lane
Clancy, MT 59634
1-866-890-7314
www.glimakraUSA.com

Green Valley Weavers & Knitters, LLC
2115 W. Colorado Avenue
Colorado Springs, CO 80904
1-800-457-8559
www.greenvalleyweavers.com

Halcyon Yarn
12 School Street
Bath, ME 04530
1-800-341-0282
www.halcyonyarn.com

The Handweavers Studio & Gallery
140 Seven Sisters Road
London N7 7NS
England
011-44-020-7272-1891
www.handweavers.co.uk

Harrisville Designs
Box 806
Harrisville, NH 03450
1-800-338-9415
www.harrisville.com

Heritage Spinning & Weaving
47 E Flint
Lake Orion, MI 48362
248-693-3690
www.heritagespinning.com

Hill Country Weavers
1701 So. Congress
Austin, TX 78704
512-707-7396
www.hillcountryweavers.com

John C. Campbell Folk School Craft Shop
1 Folk School Road
Brasstown, NC 28902
1-800-365-5724
www.folkschool.org

Leclerc Looms
1573 Savoie
Plessisville Quebec G6L 2Y6
Canada
819-362-7207
www.leclerclooms.com

Leesburg Looms Inc.
201 North Cherry Street
Van Wert, OH 45891
1-800-329-9254
www.totalrug.com

Lone Star Loom Room
Katy, TX
1-888-562-7012
www. lonestarloomroom.com

Lunatic Fringe Yarns
2291 SW 2nd Avenue
Fruitland, ID 83619
1-800-483-8749
www.LunaticFringeYarns.com

The Mannings Handweaving Studio & Supply Ctr.
1132 Green Ridge Road
PO Box 687
East Berlin, PA 17316
1-800-233-7166
www.the-mannings.com

Schacht Spindle Co., Inc.
6101 Ben Place
Boulder, CO 80301
1-800-228-2553
www.schachtspindle.com

Shuttles Spindles & Skeins
635 South Broadway
Unit E
Boulder, CO 80305
1-800-283-4163
www.shutlesspindlesandskeins.com

Shuttleworks Ltd.
Site 5, Box 9
RR1 DeWinton
Alberta T0L 0X0
Canada
403-938-1099
www.shuttleworks.com

Susan's Fiber Shop
N250 County Road A
Columbus, WI 53925
920-623-4237
www.susansfibershop.com

Unicorn Books and Crafts
1338 Ross St.
Petaluma, CA 94954-6502
1-800-289-9276
www.unicornbooks.com

The Village Spinning and Weaving Shop
425-B Alisal Road
Solvang, CA 93463
1-888-686-1192
www.villagespinweave.com

Weaving Southwest
487 State Road 150
Arroyo Seco, NM 87514
1-575-758-0433
www.WeavingSouthwest.com

The Weaving Works
Seattle, WA 98105
1-888-524-1221
www.weavingworks.com

Sources

WEBS – America's Yarn Store
75 Service Center Road
Northampton, MA 01060
1-800-367-9327
www.yarn.com

Woolery
315 St. Clair Street
Frankfort, KY 40601
1-800-441-9665
info@woolery.com

Yarn Barn
930 Massachusetts Street
Lawrence, KS 66044
1-800-468-0035
www.yarnbarn-ks.com

The Yarn Tree
PO Box 16974
Asheville, NC 28816
718-384-8030
www.theyarntree.com

Index

T

Y